JOSEPH RICHARDSON AND FAMILY

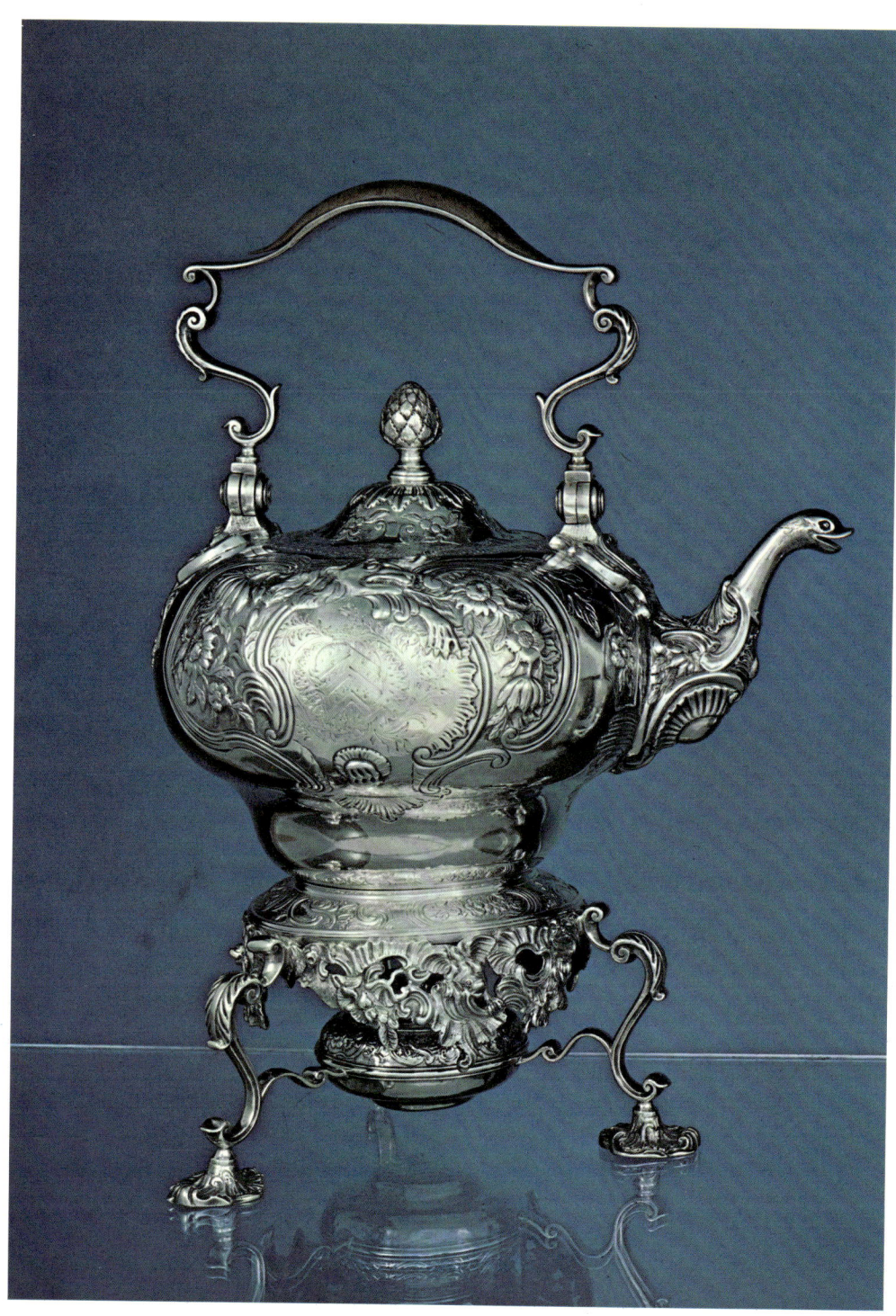

Teakettle-on-stand by Joseph Richardson, *c.* 1755
Courtesy of Yale University Art Gallery, Mabel Brady Garvan Collection.

Contra   2508-47   Cr
                                               11.00
  By 4 tankards 4 poringers 6 Casters 1 tee
              a Sifer Chain   oz dwt Gr
  Pott 1 Salver 5 Can Bodyes & 7 harts wt   233:3:20
  By Makeing the above - - - - - - - - £ 18: 6:
  By fashin of Sundry Small things - - -   1:19: 8
                       d   £
  By 4 2 thimbles 4:4 & Cash 3:0 - - - - -   3: 4: 4
  By a Jack & a Small Stud - - - - - - -   2:10: 9
                     oz dwt   a   d
  By 2 Salvers one wt 9:5 ye other 3:6 &c - 12:11 -
         Quart
  By a tankard weighing - - - - - - 29:11
  By a Quart tankard wt - - - - - - 28:17
  By ye fashin of ye above 2 tan & 2 Sal - - - 5: 0: 2
                                ye
  By a tankard weighing wthout pin - 29:14
                                       £
  By ye fashin of ye above tankard - - - 1:19: 8

  By a Skirt Buckel a od pr Buttons & Chaing a ⎫
  half pistole for Cut Gold - - - - -   ⎬ 0- 2- 6
                                                ⎭
                              oz dwt
  By a quart tankard wt - - - - - - 31:17
  By fashin - - - - - - - - - - - - -   2: 2: 6
  By ye fashin of 3 poringers & milk pott   2: 9 -
                                   a dwt Gr
  By 2 Straight Bodyed Cans wt 14:12:12
                                  o dwt
  By Silver for a pr Buckels - - - 0:19
  By 2 half Pint Cans wt - - - - - 13=18
  By a Milk Pott wt - - - - - -   2=15
  By Cash - - - - - - - - - - - -   0:11 -
                                   a oz
     Salver for widdow hubbert wt 13-1

Joseph Richardson and Family

Philadelphia Silversmiths

by

MARTHA GANDY FALES

Published for The Historical Society of Pennsylvania

by

Wesleyan University Press

MIDDLETOWN, CONNECTICUT

Copyright © 1974 by Martha Gandy Fales

The publisher gratefully acknowledges the support of the publication of this book by The Barra Foundation.

Library of Congress Cataloging in Publication Data

Fales, Martha Gandy
    Joseph Richardson and family, Philadelphia silversmiths

    Bibliography: p.
    1. Richardson family. 2. Silversmiths—Philadelphia. I. Pennsylvania. Historical Society. II. Title.
    TS730.F34   338.4'7'73923722 [B]   74-5911
    ISBN 0-8195-4076-5

The end-papers of this book reproduce pages from the account book of Joseph Richardson concerning dealings with his brother Frank. *Courtesy of The Historical Society of Pennsylvania.*

Manufactured in the United States of America
FIRST EDITION

To

M
C ✲ F

Contents

Acknowledgments	xiii
Introduction	xv

PART ONE: FR

Chapter 1	Francis Richardson, Silversmith (1681–1729)	3
Chapter 2	Francis Richardson, Jr. (1705–1782), Silversmith and Merchant	22

PART TWO: IR

Chapter 3	Joseph Richardson (1711–1784): His Life	33
Chapter 4	Joseph Richardson: His House and Shop	48
Chapter 5	Joseph Richardson: His Silver	75

PART THREE: I·NR

Chapter 6	Joseph Richardson, Jr. (1752–1831), and Nathaniel Richardson (1754–1827): Their Lives	153
Chapter 7	Joseph Richardson, Jr., and Nathaniel Richardson: Their Silver	164

Appendix A	Commonplace Book of Joseph Richardson	199
Appendix B	Settlement of the Hulbeart Estate	202
Appendix C	Scales and Weights Sold by Joseph Richardson	207
Appendix D	Letter Book of Joseph Richardson	210
Appendix E	Inventory of the Shop of Joseph and Nathaniel Richardson	261
	Notes	265
	Bibliography	312
	Index	321

Illustrations

Teakettle-on-stand by Joseph Richardson, c. 1755   *frontispiece*

Figure	Page
1. Maker's mark FR in a heart.	10
2. Maker's mark FR in a shield, with crown above.	10
3. Patch box, FR, 1727.	10
4. Porringer, FR, c. 1720	10
5. Porringer, FR, c. 1725.	11
6. Can, FR, c. 1728.	12
7. Tankard, FR, c. 1725.	14
8. Patch box, FR, c. 1715.	15
9. Pair of buckles, FR, c. 1721.	15
10. Three spoons, FR, c. 1725.	15
11. Gold locket, FR, c. 1720.	16
12. Page from account book of Francis Richardson, 1717-22.	19
13-14. Inventory of Francis Richardson's estate, taken in 1729.	20, 21
15. Maker's mark FR in a rectangle.	24
16. Porringer, FR, c. 1730.	25
17. Pair of porringers, FR, c. 1730.	25
18. Can, FR, c. 1730.	26
19. Face of tall clock.	29
20. Letter from Grace Lloyd to Joseph Richardson.	41
21-22. Inventory of Joseph Richardson's estate, taken in 1784.	49, 50
23. Walnut slant-top desk, c. 1740.	52
24. Entry in invoice book of Samuel Powel of Philadelphia.	55
25. *Plate II* of Cramer's *Elements of the Art of Assaying Metals*, London, 1741.	56
26. *Plate V* of Cramer's *Elements*.	56
27. Face of tall clock made by John Wood, Philadelphia clockmaker.	59
28. Bill for goods bought from Joseph Richardson.	61
29. Page from Joseph Richardson's commonplace book, 1752.	69
30-31. Box of weights and scales of Joseph Richardson.	70, 71
32. Maker's marks	73
33. Coffeepot, IR, c. 1748.	80
34. English coffeepot, John Swift, London, 1753-4.	81
35a. Coffeepot, IR, c. 1754.	82
35b. Cypher for SS as shown in Simpson's *Book of Cyphers*, London, 1726.	82
36. Coffeepot, IR, c. 1765.	83
37. Coffeepot, IR, c. 1770.	83
38. Teapot, IR, c. 1735-40.	83
39. Teapot, IR, c. 1740.	84
40. Teapot, IR, 1740-50.	85
41. Teapot, IR, c. 1755.	85
42. Teapot, IR, c. 1750-60.	86
43. Teapot, IR, c. 1760-65.	87
44. Teakettle-on-stand, IR, c. 1755.	88
45. Milk pot, IR, c. 1746.	90
46. Milk pot, IR, c. 1741.	90
47. Milk pot, IR, c. 1745.	90
48. Milk pot, IR, c. 1755.	90

Figure	Page
49. Milk pot, IR, c. 1765.	92
50. Sugar dish, IR, 1736.	93
51. Entry in Joseph Richardson's account book in 1736.	93
52. Sugar dish, IR, c. 1747.	94
53. Sugar dish, IR, c. 1740–60.	94
54. Sugar dish, IR, c. 1754.	94
55. Sugar dish, IR, c. 1755–60.	94
56. Sugar dish, IR, c. 1765.	95
57. Sugar dish, IR, c. 1765–75.	95
58. Sugar dish, IR, c. 1770–75.	96
59. Bowl, IR, c. 1730–40.	97
60. Bowl, IR, c. 1735–50.	97
61. Bowl, IR, c. 1750.	97
62. Bowl, IR, c. 1750–80.	97
63. Bowl, IR, c. 1760–80.	98
64. One of a pair of tea canisters, IR, c. 1740.	99
65. Teaspoon, IR, c. 1750.	100
66. English painting of man and child drinking tea, c. 1725.	101
67–68. Tea tongs, IR, c. 1750.	102
69. Pair of salvers, IR, 1737.	104
70. Salver, IR, c. 1739.	105
71. Salver, IR, c. 1739–40.	107
72. Salver, IR, c. 1739–40.	107
73. Salver, IR, c. 1746.	107
74. Salver, IR, c. 1760.	108
75. Salver, IR, c. 1740.	109
76. Salver, IR, c. 1740–50.	109
77. Salver, IR, c. 1750–65.	109
78. Salver, IR, c. 1750–65.	109
79. Salver, IR, 1756–61.	110
80. Salver, IR, c. 1760.	110
81. Salver, IR, c. 1770–75.	111
82. Can, IR, c. 1740.	112
83. Can, IR, c. 1740.	113
84. Pair of cans, IR, c. 1737.	114
85. Can, IR, c. 1750–65.	115
86. Can, IR, c. 1750–65.	115
87. Quart tankard, IR, c. 1730–50.	116
88. Tankard, IR, c. 1730–50.	116
89. Tankard, IR, c. 1730–50.	116
90. Tankard, IR, c. 1750.	117
91. Tankard, IR, c. 1750–70.	118
92. Spout cup, IR, c. 1735–40.	118
93. Porringer, IR, 1739.	120
94. Porringer, IR, c. 1738.	120
95. Porringer, IR, c. 1740.	120
96. Porringer, IR, c. 1740–50.	120
97. Porringer, IR, c. 1750.	120
98. Porringer, IR, c. 1750.	120
99. Porringer, IR, c. 1750.	121
100. Porringer, IR, c. 1750.	121
101. Pair of salts, IR, c. 1745.	123
102. Pair of salts, IR, c. 1750.	123
103. One of pair of salts, IR, c. 1750.	124
104. Salt, IR, c. 1755.	124
105. Caster, IR, c. 1740.	125
106. Caster, IR, c. 1750.	125
107. Pair of casters, IR, c. 1750–60.	125
108. Caster, IR, c. 1745.	126
109. Pair of sauceboats, IR, c. 1755–65.	126
110. Pair of sauceboats, IR, c. 1750–60.	127
110a. Pair of sauceboats engraved with the Pemberton crest.	127
111. Soup ladle, IR, c. 1750.	127
112. Soup spoon, IR, c. 1737.	128
113. Tablespoon, IR, c. 1735.	128
114. Group of mid-18th century spoons by Joseph Richardson.	130
115. Three tablespoons, IR, c. 1750.	131
116. Snuff box, IR, c. 1757.	133
117. Snuff box, IR, c. 1760.	134
118. Snuff box, IR, c. 1775.	134
119. Coral and bells, IR, c. 1740.	134
120. Links of buttons or cuff links, hook, and needle case, found among the Richardson family papers.	136
121. Cane ferrule and tip, unmarked, c. 1750.	138
122. Bodkin, IR, c. 1740.	140
123. Skewer, IR, c. 1760.	140
124. Medals cut by Edward Duffield and struck by Joseph Richardson.	141
125. Gorget, IR, c. 1760.	142

Illustrations

Figure	Page
126. Gold locket, IR, c. 1750.	144
127. Gold locket, IR, c. 1750.	145
128. Gold locket, IR, c. 1750.	145
129. Gold buckle, IR, c. 1750.	148
130. Gold buckle, IR, c. 1765.	148
131. Watercolor portrait of Joseph Richardson, Jr.	158
131a. English clock owned by Richardsons.	158
132. Indian wristband, JR, c. 1795.	160
133. Painting by Saint-Memin of an Osage warrior.	160
134. Indian peace medal, attributed to Joseph Richardson, Jr.	161
135. Maker's mark I·NR in rectangle.	167
136. Teaset, I·NR, c. 1780.	168
137. Cream pot, I·NR, c. 1780.	169
138. Cream pot, I·NR, c. 1785–90.	169
139. Coffeepot, I·NR, c. 1780.	169
140. Coffeepot, I·NR, c. 1781.	169
141. Coffeepot, I·NR, c. 1786.	170
142. Teapot, I·NR, c. 1785.	171
143. Teapot, I·NR, c. 1785.	171
144. Teapot, I·NR, c. 1785–90.	172
145. Sugar bowl, I·NR, c. 1785.	173
146. Sugar bowl, I·NR, c. 1785–90.	173
147. Slop bowl, I·NR.	173
148. Tea caddy, I·NR, c. 1785–90.	173
149. Tea caddy, I·NR, c. 1785–90.	174
150. Tray, I·NR, c. 1780.	175
151. Tray, I·NR, c. 1785–90.	176
152. Pair of salts, I·NR, c. 1780.	176
153. Salt, I·NR, c. 1785–90.	177
154. Pair of sauceboats, I·NR, c. 1780.	178
155. Sauceboat, I·NR, c. 1780.	178
156. Covered saucepan, I·NR, c. 1780.	179
157. Can, I·NR, c. 1780.	180
158. Tankard, I·NR, c. 1780.	180
159. Tankard, I·NR, c. 1782.	180
160. Tankard, I·NR, c. 1785–90.	180
161. Chatelaine hooks made by Joseph Richardson, Jr.	181
162. Ladle, I·NR, c. 1785–90.	181
162a. Four tablespoons, I·NR.	182
163. Maker's marks.	183
164. Covered saucepan, JR, c. 1795.	185
165. Saucepan, JR, c. 1800.	185
166. Tea and coffee service, two different JR marks, c. 1795.	187
167. Teapot, JR, c. 1800.	188
168. Cream pot, JR, c. 1801.	189
169. Two tea and coffee services, JR, c. 1800.	190
170. Sugar urn, JR, c. 1794.	190
171. Cream pot and sugar bowl, JR, c. 1800.	190
172. Cream pot, JR, c. 1799.	191
173. Cream pot, J·R, c. 1790.	191
174. Pair of dishes, JR, c. 1795–1800.	192
175. Baking dish, J·R, 1797.	192
176. Ladle, JR, c. 1790.	194
177. Ladle, J·R, c. 1800.	194
178. Tea tongs, JR, c. 1790.	195
179. Gold locket, JR, c. 1790.	196
180. Page of account book kept by Joseph Richardson.	205
181. Page from Joseph Richardson's letter book.	212
182. Bill of exchange, 1759.	215

Acknowledgments

In 1953 John Marshall Phillips suggested the subject of this book to me as suitable for a master's thesis. It proved to be that and much more. Now twenty years later, there are a great many people who have contributed to the story of Joseph Richardson and his family. Foremost were those at Winterthur, particularly Charles F. Montgomery, who encouraged me as a student and later in my efforts to prepare my research for publication. Miss Elinor M. Betts, Miss Helen M. Belknap, Mrs. Elizabeth Ingerman Wood, Charles F. Hummel, Milo M. Naeve, and John A. H. Sweeney were all exceedingly helpful over a long period of time. The acquisition by the Winterthur Library of the Richardson family manuscripts, located during the early days of my research through a lead provided by Bart Anderson of the Chester County Historical Society, made possible a continuous and careful examination of essential materials.

The Historical Society of Pennsylvania, and its late director, Richard N. Williams II, microfilmed vital materials from the Richardson papers in their collection and made them available to me for immediate reference, laborious indexing, and hundreds of readings. They and the Philadelphia Museum of Art permitted close scrutiny of their silver, and Henry P. McIlhenny, Louis C. Madiera, Calvin Hathaway and especially the late Miss Beatrice B. Wolfe, have been unstintingly helpful and patient with my hundreds of requests since they staged the useful and important 1956 exhibition of Philadelphia silver, making available to me the photographic record of it. Miss Josephine

Setze and others on the staff of the Yale University Art Gallery have been most cooperative; and Mrs. Yves H. Buhler of the Museum of Fine Arts, Boston, has cheerily led me to information and objects I might have missed otherwise.

Miss Eleanor Melson, at the Arch Street Meeting House in Philadelphia, guided me through volumes of Quaker records; and descendants of Joseph Richardson, including the late Mrs. Henry B. Wireman, Miss Frances Richardson, and Mrs. Thomas J. Curtin (still a practicing silversmith herself) were invaluable in their assistance. The late Mrs. Alfred Coxe Prime shared bountifully her love of silver and became in these years a dear friend.

The staffs of many local Philadelphia institutions helped me find much needed information, from the Library Company and the Philadelphia Contributionship, to the Pennsylvania Hospital and the Philadelphia County Court House. Arthur J. Pulos of the University of Syracuse, William de Matteo of Colonial Williamsburg and Charles Oman of the Victoria and Albert Museum, supplied the necessary technical assistance. The many present-day owners of Richardson silver, whose names appear with the illustrations in this book or remain anonymous according to their wishes, were indeed generous in allowing publication of their treasures, and patient in awaiting the appearance of the book.

For several years Mrs. Charles G. Watson happily assisted with typing and other necessary detailed work in preparing the manuscript. Miss Francesca Tillona and Mrs. Susan Terdiman gave editorial assistance when it was required. The difficult final typing, particularly of the manuscript material, was meticulously and expertly done by Mrs. James Shields at the risk of permanently destroying her former ability to spell correctly.

Publication at last became a reality with the encouragement of Nicholas B. Wainwright, Director of The Historical Society of Pennsylvania, and Robert L. McNeil, Jr.

Of all the patient people involved with this book, the most patient of all is my husband. For all of our married life he has had to live with the Richardsons! He has advised and discussed with endless fortitude, and has heartened me even at times when I wished that the Richardson family had never come to America.

My hope is that the resulting work will justify in some measure all the efforts and endurance of these people, and that any errors that have crept into the work will be offset by the importance and value of the original manuscript material in the book.

Introduction

WHEN America was first discovered and European governments were encouraging settlement, a chief inducement to emigration was the promise of gold and silver. Among the passengers on board the *Phoenix*, which landed in Virginia in 1608, were two refiners, two goldsmiths, and a jeweler. Although precious metals had been found in abundance in Central and South America, almost two centuries were to pass before a small amount of silver was found and mined in Connecticut. Fifty years more went by before gold was discovered in California.

At this time the artisans who worked these precious metals were called goldsmiths, even though most of their work was in silver; the designations *goldsmith* and *silversmith* were synonymous. Since the twelfth century, the Goldsmiths' Company in London had established standards of purity for both metals and had seen to it that the products of metalworkers were of the required quality.

The goldsmiths and refiners among the first settlers suffered from a dearth both of basic materials and of patronage. The first generation of colonists, who lacked even the essentials of life, accumulated little wealth. Goldsmiths and members of allied crafts were compelled to take up other trades or return to their native lands.

Twenty or thirty years after the first settlers arrived, however, towns began to form in Virginia, Massachusetts, and New York, and a growing prosperity encouraged their inhabitants to look more frequently to the luxuries of life. Because there were no banks, the colonists, as they acquired wealth, continued the Old World practice of turning their unidentifiable silver and gold coins into plate, as solid silverware was then called. This practice provided the owner not only with useful and beautiful objects attesting to his prosperity, but with a means of identification (through marks and engraving) should the silver be lost or stolen. Early American newspapers are filled with advertisements describing lost silver objects, their maker's marks, and any engraving of the owner's initials or arms.

Because the goldsmith's services were sought in urban centers rather than in the countryside, the appearance of goldsmiths in this country closely parallels the rise of cities. New York and Albany soon followed Boston in supporting the art. In the South, where the plantation system prevailed and economic ties with England were especially strong, there was less demand for local goldsmiths. Most of the silver plate and jewelry that found its way there was obtained in London in exchange for shipments of tobacco or rice.

Philadelphia was among the last of the important seaboard cities to be founded (1682), and perhaps because many of the problems of settlement in the New World had already been overcome, it grew rapidly in size and importance. It was about this time that the Richardson family of South Shields, England, made its appearance in the Colonies. Francis Richardson, a mariner by trade and a Quaker by persuasion, arrived in New York with his wife, Rebecca, soon after their marriage in 1680. Richardson prospered as a merchant until his untimely death in 1688. The widowed Rebecca married a Boston merchant, Edward Shippen, also recently bereaved. With Rebecca's two children and Edward's children by his first marriage, the Shippens moved to Philadelphia and became one of the leading families in the city. Rebecca's son, Francis Richardson, Jr., was soon apprenticed to a goldsmith. The growing prosperity of the city increased the desire and demand for silver plate, and goldsmiths commanded a respect and prestige in colonial society similar to that of the professional man today; so young Francis gradually rose to a respected position in the community.

As often happened, Francis Richardson established an occupational tradition for the family: his sons Frank and Joseph were, in their turn, trained to be goldsmiths, and Joseph's sons, Joseph, Jr. and Nathaniel, carried the tradition into the early years of the nineteenth century.

The Richardson family spanned the formative period of our nation's history. The fact that their occupation was important in the growing society means that a study of their lives and work illuminates not only the history of early American silver but also the early history of the nation.

The study of this particular family is especially rewarding because of an uncommon survival of family manuscripts, account books, and letter books, so that more is known of the Richardsons than of any other family of American goldsmiths. So great is the potential usefulness of this source material that much of it has been included in the footnotes and appendices with as little editing as possible. All but the most common abbreviations such as Do. for ditto and mo. for month have been spelled out to eliminate the archaic and difficult raised letters. The common confusing abbreviations such as pr. for both per and pair have been written out. Misspellings remain unless totally misleading, and no attempt has been made to correct the spelling of names since it is impossible to know what many of them actually were. The Roman capital I has been changed to J where intended, and the various eighteenth century abbreviations for et cetera have been changed uniformly to etc. Abbreviated references to money have been converted to £__/__/__ and abbreviated weight references to __oz. __dwt. __gr. Dashes have been eliminated wherever possible, and punctuation and capitalization added only where necessary to insure the full meaning of the original manuscripts.

Of equal importance as source material is the Richardson silver itself. Because of its intrinsic value and because plate was an indication of family wealth, silver has been cherished over the years and passed from generation to generation. Such silver is useful to the historian because much of it is stamped with a maker's mark or engraved with initials, names, arms, dates, or other factual information concerning the lives of individuals who lived during the colonial years. In addition, because important events were frequently acknowledged by gifts of silver, early American silver often documents occurrences of major historical significance.

For the art historian, silver is especially worthy of study. In colonial America, the design of silver followed more closely than that of any other art form, the stylistic development of the arts in Europe. The goldsmith's patrons naturally wanted their silver made in the latest fashion. Styles in silver, unlike those in painting and architecture, could be transmitted quickly from England to America; silver could be ordered and shipped within eight months. It is not presumptuous to conclude that in early America silver ranked as a major art form.

The Richardsons worked from the late baroque and rococo periods into the first period of neoclassical design, thus covering all the important stylistic changes from the end of the seventeenth to the beginning of the nineteenth century. Their silver presents in microcosm the history of the silversmith and his art in this country; it also reflects the progress of the arts in America.

For the social historian, silver provides an insight into life in the early days of the nation. Silver objects served the everyday needs of the people who owned them, and changes in style and form reflect changes in customs from one generation to the next. The Richardsons, themselves, as representatives of the artisans, provide an opportunity to study the group of men who were the backbone of a new society.

PART ONE
FR

. . .this is to acquaint thee, that about ten daies
since here arrived Francis Richardson. . .
                        Letter to William Penn
                        New York, June 25, 1681

Richardson Genealogy

Francis Richardson (?–1688) m. (1680) Rebecca Haward (?–1705)

(Married Edward Shippen (1639–1712) in 1689. Their only child Elizabeth born in 1691, died in infancy.)

Children of Francis Richardson and Rebecca Haward:
- Francis (1681–1729)
- Rebecca (1684–84)
- Rebecca (1685–?) m. (1) Thomas Murray m. (2) (?) Young
- John (1687–88)

Francis (1681–1729) m. (1) Elizabeth Growden (?–1714) (2) Letitia Swift (?–c. 1734)

(Their only child John died in infancy. In 1731 Letitia married Jeremiah Elfreth, whose son by his previous marriage, Jeremiah, served his apprenticeship with her son Joseph Richardson.)

Children of Francis and Elizabeth Growden:
- Frank (1706–82) m. Mary Fitzwater (?–1771)
- John (1708–09)
- Thomas (1709–09)
- Joseph (1711–84) m. (1) Hannah Worrill (c. 1716–47) (2) Mary Allen (1716–87)
- Rebecca (1713–13)
- Benjamin (1714–14)

Children of Frank and Mary Fitzwater:
- Mary (b. 1743)
- Grace (b. 1745)
- Francis (b. 1746)
- George (b. 1747)
- Hannah (b. 1748)
- Elizabeth (b. 1749)
- Thomas (b. 1749)
- John (b. 1752)
- Deborah (b. 1753)

Children of Joseph:
- Elizabeth (1742–1804)
- Grace (1743–44) [by Hannah Worrill]
- Hannah (1748–1817)
- Mary (1749–1835)
- Joseph, Jr. (1752–1831) m. Ruth Hoskins (1756–1829)
- Nathaniel (1754–1827) Unmarried
- Rebecca (1758–1826)

Children of Joseph, Jr. and Ruth Hoskins:
- Mary (1781–1837)
- Joseph (1784–93)
- John (1786–86)
- Sarah (1787–1855)
- Elizabeth (1788–?)
- John (1790–1866)
- Hannah (1791–1866)
- Nathaniel (1793–1872)

CHAPTER 1

Francis Richardson, Silversmith (1681-1729)

On January 27, 1680, a group of London Quakers gathered at Devonshire House outside Bishopsgate to witness the marriage of Rebecca Haward, the daughter of a shoemaker from Uxbridge, and Francis Richardson, a mariner from South Shields in Durham.[1] Soon after their marriage, Francis Richardson and his bride set forth for the New World. In 1681 they settled in New York, which already had a population of more than 3,200, and there Francis Richardson established himself as a merchant, becoming a freeman of the city on October 1, 1683.[2]

Richardson's arrival in New York was important enough to have been called to the attention of William Penn.[3] His increasing affluence is revealed in the accounts of his shipping ventures, which are recorded in several books kept largely by his wife.[4] One of these served as a receipt book and acknowledged payments made by Francis and Rebecca Richardson between 1684 and 1689 for such miscellaneous items as rum, household goods, Negro slaves, land in Pennsylvania, and operating costs on their sloop *Supply*.[5]

The couple's personal life prospered, too. Over the next few years several children were born to Francis and Rebecca Richardson. On November 25, 1681, "was borne my Son Francis Richardson Junior in New York at the house of Governor Lockermans now Jacob Lashners about the first houer in the morning."[6] Two daughters came next: the elder, Rebecca, was born in March 1684, but died a few months later; her name was given to the second daughter, who was born on November 2, 1685.[7] The last child born to them was John, who arrived in 1688 on "the 26th day of the 7th mo. about the 3rd hower in the morning."[8]

On September 30, 1683, William Penn had given by warrant to Francis Richardson, "merchant of New York," a lot in Philadelphia on the southwest corner of Second and Walnut Streets.[9] Although Francis Richardson is not known to have used his lot, there is evidence that he visited Philadelphia in 1687.[10]

Not long thereafter, on July 15, 1688, Francis Richardson died.[11] As requested by his will, written on July 7, 1688, and "Calling to mind the certainty of death," he was buried in the Friends' Burying Place at Flushing, Long Island.[12] To his wife, whom he made executrix, he bequeathed one-third of his estate including a 400-acre lot of land in the township of Crittenham [Cheltenham?], Pennsylvania. To his three children he left the other two-thirds of his real and personal estate, including the lot in Philadelphia granted him by Penn, which they were to receive at the age of twenty-one.[13]

During the next few months, Richardson's widow concerned herself with settling her husband's estate. His death had been followed almost immediately by that of their son John.[14] Even in grief Rebecca was obliged to think of the future, and, since remarriage was the common solution to widowhood, it is not surprising that on September 4, 1689, Quaker friends gathered again, this time at the house of Richardson's old friend, Walter Newberry, in Newport, Rhode Island, to witness Rebecca's marriage to Edward Shippen, a successful Boston merchant.[15]

As a Friend, Shippen had been subjected to maltreatment by Boston Puritans. The seventeenth-century New England diarist, Samuel Sewall, noted that on July 12, 1688, Edward Shippen delivered an open challenge from the Quaker, George Keith, to four Boston ministers to debate the doctrine they preached.[16] Shippen was probably among those Friends persecuted in Boston as a result of such dissension, although it is unlikely that he was ever in danger of being hanged, as a few Quakers were. Perhaps this religious strife was an influential factor in his subsequent decision to bring his family to Philadelphia, the refuge of many Friends.[17] Here Shippen renewed his mercantile enterprises with success and, by 1701, had become mayor of the city. Eventually his wealth was estimated at £10,000 sterling, and he was reputed to have the largest coach and house in the city of Philadelphia.[18] The beauty of the house and gardens on Second Street north of Spruce Street, where young Francis Richardson grew up, was described by Gabriel Thomas in 1698:

> There are very fine and delightful *Gardens* and *Orchards*, in most parts of this Countrey; but *Edward Shippey* [sic] (who lives near the Capital City) has an Orchard and Gardens adjoyning to his Great House that equalizes (if not exceeds) any I have ever seen, having a very famous and pleasant Summer-House erected in the middle of his extraordinary fine and large Garden abounding with *Tulips, Pinks, Carnations, Roses,* (of several sorts) *Lilies,* not to mention those that grow wild in the Fields.[19]

It is likely that sometime between 1695 and 1699 Francis, with one of his stepbrothers, was sent abroad to study,[20] but the apprenticeship records at Goldsmiths' Hall do not reveal that he was trained as a goldsmith in London.[21] If Francis was trained in Philadelphia, the most likely person to have taught him would have been Johannis Nys. Both Nys and Caesar Ghiselin are known to have worked as silversmiths during this period in Philadelphia. However, it is Nys whose name appears in documents concerning Francis Richardson; and it is Nys whose touchmark and work most closely resemble those of Richardson. At any rate, by 1701, when he was twenty, Francis Richardson had begun to practice the art of the goldsmith in Philadelphia, as evidenced by the fact that in that year William Penn recorded in his cash book a payment of £2 to Richardson for making a pair of shoe buckles for his daughter Letitia.[22]

During the summer of 1703 Francis made a trip to Boston to purchase tools needed for his business. On July 15, 1703, he wrote to his mother in Philadelphia:

> Supling my Selfe with what is necessarey for my Trade Though it be such a dule [dull] time with the goldsmith as ever . . . if in case I could prevaile with any of them I question not but they would aske a hundred or a hundred and fifty pounds when I can beter suplie my Selfe with what is most convenant for my trade for a third part of the money in England I see not such grate inCoragement to be in hast to give such an extravegent prises for tueles [tools]. Though could be glad to a geting some on reasonable termes. Seing I cannot I entende for London in the spring if times be any beter then they are. The later end of this month or the begining of the next I entand to sett forward on my journey homewards. . .[23]

A similar letter written to his mother from Boston about the same time, although unsigned and undated, further explains:

> I dont p seave [perceive] I can gett what I entended which is a Stock of tuels with out I give thre times the value as I can have them for In England for and not according to my mind nither So I beleave I shall not have a present ocason of a house so that Benjamin wright may Lett it to home he pleases . . . as to the plate I shall Indever to bring what I can my Brother [a Shippen half-brother] was gon be for I received the Letter or other I should requested him to cary part.[24]

No records have come to light to show that Francis did go to London in the spring. It is rather doubtful that he did, in view of the fact that on September 6, 1704, he again wrote from Boston to his mother, explaining:

> "I have bought . . . one quilt prise £3/10/0 and a Kaine Kouch price £2/10/10 . . . . I have also bought a small parcel of tules and other nessesary belonging to my traid and a pease of drugett for a koate [and] six bottles of canary . . . ."[25]

During the ensuing winter, on February 26, 1705, Francis' mother, Rebecca Haward Richardson Shippen, died and was buried in the Friends' burying ground in Philadelphia.[26]

Just a month before his mother's death Francis Richardson, now twenty-three, and Elizabeth Growden, daughter of Joseph Growden also of Philadelphia, were betrothed.[27] Evidently, Francis had been contemplating matrimony for some time, but, probably because of his mother's death, the marriage did not take place until April 18, 1705.[28] His friend, Walter Newberry, of Newport, had hinted at Francis' intentions in a letter to him dated January 20, 1704: "Am Glad to hear that thou art like to settle & I believe by this, thou knows the Sweetness of keeping bachellours hall, but Cant think that thou wilt long be Satisfyed therewith."[29] On March 10, 1705, Walter Newberry deduced that Elizabeth Growden was the object of Francis' attentions when he wrote him from Boston "thou mentions that J. Growdens daughter is not Likely to live long unmarried: but doth not mention her Spouse: So that I have grounds to think one F. R. is the man . . ."[30]

Francis' bride was born in England. Her father, Joseph, and her grandfather, Lawrence, had migrated from Trevose in Cornwall, to Bucks County, Pennsylvania. By 1684, her father was a member of the Assembly from Philadelphia. Later, he was a member from Bucks County, often being speaker of the house.

In 1706, another marriage took place in Francis' family: his widowed stepfather was married a third time, to Esther James, widow of Philip James and daughter of Barnabus and Sarah Wilcox.[31] The Society of Friends is recorded as having reprimanded Edward Shippen for what one author tactfully refers to as "anticipating the marriage relation."[32] (Shippen was later pardoned and again became a member in good standing.)

After their marriage, Francis and Elizabeth went to live at Letitia Court off Market Street, where he had his shop. There, in time, six children were born to them. Their eldest, Francis, Jr. (usually called Frank), was born February 18, 1706. Two more sons, John and Thomas, were born in 1708 and 1709 respectively, but they died within three days of each other in July 1709. Their next son, Joseph, who was to become the best known, was born on September 17, 1711, and was followed in 1713 by a daughter, Rebecca, who survived only a few months. The last son, Benjamin, was born in 1714, and his birth may have caused the death of Elizabeth Richardson on May 19 of that year, just a week after the boy, himself, died.[33]

Although Francis was left a widower with two sons to raise, it was not until twelve years later on April 30, 1726, that he married Letitia Swift, daughter of John Swift.[34] By February 9, 1729, Francis and Letitia Richardson had moved to Front Street, for it was there that their only child, John, was born. The child was not to survive infancy; he died of smallpox in 1730.

The house on Front Street was only a few blocks from Letitia Court. Francis Richardson was now situated in the heart of the city. His house and shop were on the west side of the first major thoroughfare, at the head of Carpenter's Wharf, and opposite the warehouses lining the busy Philadelphia waterfront. Several other goldsmiths had shops in this area between Walnut Street and Norris' Alley. Most of these buildings were built of brick and stood in a row close to the street. The entrances were at one side with two windows on the left. Two stories high, the houses were usually two rooms deep.[35]

By the beginning of the eighteenth century, Philadelphia was a thriving community of about five thousand whose growing commercial prosperity was spearheaded by Quaker merchants. The West Indies trade, particularly with Barbados, brought in a plentiful supply of silver. The presence of this silver encouraged more and more merchants to commission goldsmiths to turn their surplus Spanish dollars into tankards and spoons as a means of preserving their wealth. Richardson, like other goldsmiths, was well paid for his labor. By 1698, Gabriel Thomas had reported, "And for *Silver-Smiths* [in Pennsylvania], they have between Half a Crown and Three Shillings an Ounce for working their Silver, and for Gold equivalent."[36]

The first goldsmith to practice his art in Philadelphia was probably Cesar Ghiselin who arrived in Chester, Pennsylvania, in 1681. He moved to Annapolis, Maryland, to live and work from about 1717 to 1729, returning to Philadelphia toward the end of his career.[37] Another of Philadelphia's early silversmiths was William Paschall, who died in 1696.[38] When Francis Richardson was admitted as freeman of the city of Philadelphia in 1720, two other goldsmiths, William England and Edward Hunt, were also admitted, but little is known of either.[39]

An early goldsmith more closely associated with Francis Richardson was Johannis Nys, whose shop was on the same street.[40] Nys' workmanship indicates that he might have been trained in New York, although no documentary proof has been discovered to support this. Evidence of an acquaintanceship between Nys and Francis Richardson is recorded in the latter's account book in 1719. These accounts reveal not only that Nys made silver (spoons, porringers, a cup) for Francis and that Francis sold him materials necessary to his trade (a cutting punch, a stamp and pliers, files, argol, and silver and gold), but that on at least one occasion Francis made spoons for Nys.[41]

In addition to his accounts with Nys, Francis Richardson had some business transactions with other Philadelphia silversmiths. One was Philip Syng (1676–1739), who emigrated from Cork, Ireland, to Philadelphia in 1714,[42] but there is no indication that he and Richardson did any work for each other. Another was James Allen. Since only two entries in Francis' account book concern Allen, it does not appear that he was actually apprenticed to Francis at that time, but he did do piecework for him and may have served his time in the years prior to those covered by these accounts.[43]

Francis Richardson's relationship with a hitherto unknown American goldsmith, Robert Keeble, was more complex. The account book indicates that Robert Keeble (also spelled *Cable* and *Keable*) actually worked in Francis' shop.[44] He did piecework as well as work by the day for Francis, and, were it not for the fact that there was a Robert Keeble registered as a goldsmith in London in 1702, one might be tempted to conclude that he was Richardson's apprentice. In fact, he must have worked as a journeyman or even a master in Richardson's shop.

Of the silver Francis Richardson sold in his shop, it is sometimes difficult to tell which pieces he made and which he bought for resale. Fortunately, in many cases he specifies his actual charges for their manufacture. The objects so specified include porringers, tankards, cups, tea tongs and strainers, salvers, pepper boxes, and whistles and bells (children's rattles). Of these, only the porringers, tankards, and whistles are listed with any frequency. Many small objects were recorded as being made by him, including rings, buckles, spoons, scoops, thimbles, buttons, hooks, pincushion hoops, chains ("scissor chain and hart" included), lockets, studs, frames for spectacles, and boxes.[45] These smaller objects formed the bulk of his orders. Some of them—such as rings, buckles, thimbles, buttons, lockets, and spectacle frames—were most frequently made, not of silver, but of gold. One of the few surviving orders for work to be done by Francis Richardson was placed by Samuel Harrison of Herrin Creek on March 22, 1705:

> At the Request of a relation, I desire thee to send me a Gold Ring by the bearer, tis for a woman who desires it may be handsomely made & have this posie—Remember the Giver—I have made the Bills for 7 lbs. If thee will send by the Bearer James Mackland & let me know if there's more due I will satisfie thee to content.[46]

Of the twenty-one different forms recorded as having been made by Francis Richardson between 1717 and 1722, only porringers, a tankard, a mug, spoons, boxes, buckles, and a gold locket are known today. Since Francis worked at his trade for a quarter of a century, and since quantities of work produced earlier by New England goldsmiths survive today, it must be concluded that Francis Richardson probably never made a large number of silver objects. This conclusion is corroborated by his accounts between 1717 and 1722, even though the greater part of his work was probably done after this account book ends. However, those examples of his work that do survive indicate that he was a very capable craftsman.

Two maker's marks are attributed to Francis Richardson. The first and probably his earliest mark is shown in *Figure 1*. A heart-shaped mark such as this was used by other early American goldsmiths—John Hull and Jeremiah Dummer in New England, and Johannis Nys, Cesar Ghiselin, Philip Syng, Sr., and William Vilant in Philadelphia. The other mark attributed to Richardson, the shield and crown mark shown in *Figure 2*, was also popular in New England at that time. Henry Pratt and Philip Syng, who were working in Philadelphia by 1730, used a shield-shaped mark without a crown. These two marks appear on silver forms popular about 1725, another indication that much of Francis' work was done in the latter part of his career.

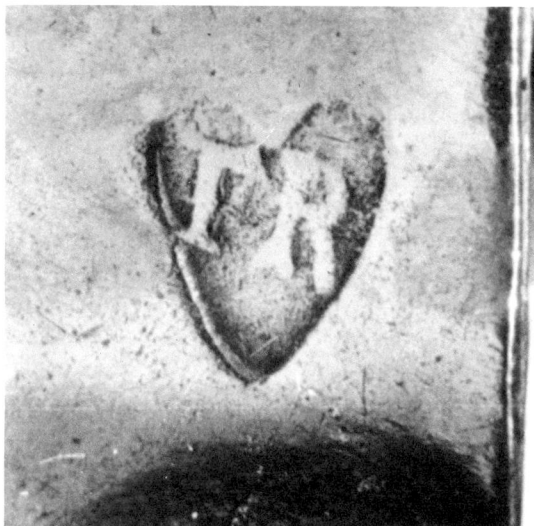
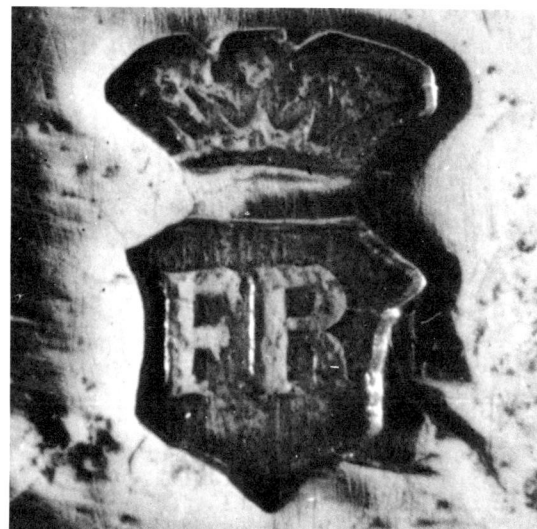

Fig. 1: Maker's mark FR in a heart. The heart-shaped mark was one of the earliest marks used by American goldsmiths and silversmiths in Philadelphia. It was used by Cesar Ghiselin, Philip Syng, Sr., and William Vilant. It appears on buckles (*Fig. 9*) worn by Elizabeth Coates Paschall in 1721. *Courtesy of The Historical Society of Pennsylvania.*

Fig. 2: Maker's mark FR in a shield, with crown above. Another early mark, it was used without the crown by two other Philadelphia goldsmiths, Henry Pratt and Philip Syng. It appears on a porringer (*Fig. 4*) possibly bequeathed by Francis Richardson to his wife. *Courtesy of Mr. and Mrs. Henry W. Breyer, Jr.*

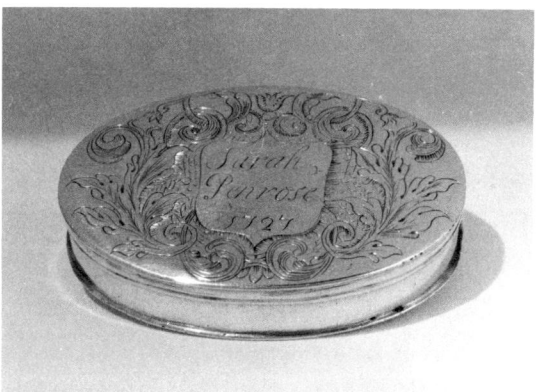
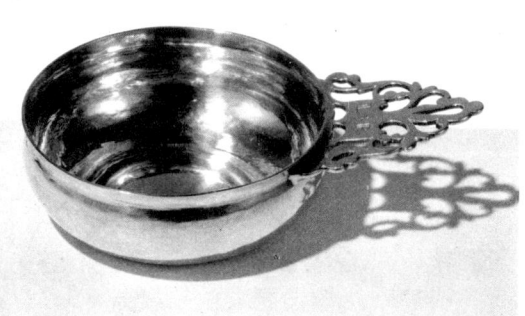

Fig. 3: Patch box, FR in heart, 1727, owned by Sarah Penrose. It is elaborately engraved with boldly curved scrolls and leafage in the baroque style and a light filling of imbrication between the scrolls and the central shield. Length: 2 1/4". *Courtesy of Mrs. Walter M. Jeffords.*

Fig. 4: Porringer, FR in shield, crown above, under handle *c.* 1720. Engraved with initials L°R on handle. Weight: 7 oz. 12 dwt., engraved on base. Possibly one of two porringers bequeathed by Francis Richardson to his widow Letitia in 1729, which together weighed 13 oz. 14 dwt. and were valued at £ 5/0/5 1/2 in the inventory of his estate. Diameter: 5 1/8"; length of handle: 2 5/8". *Courtesy of Mr. and Mrs. Henry W. Breyer, Jr.*

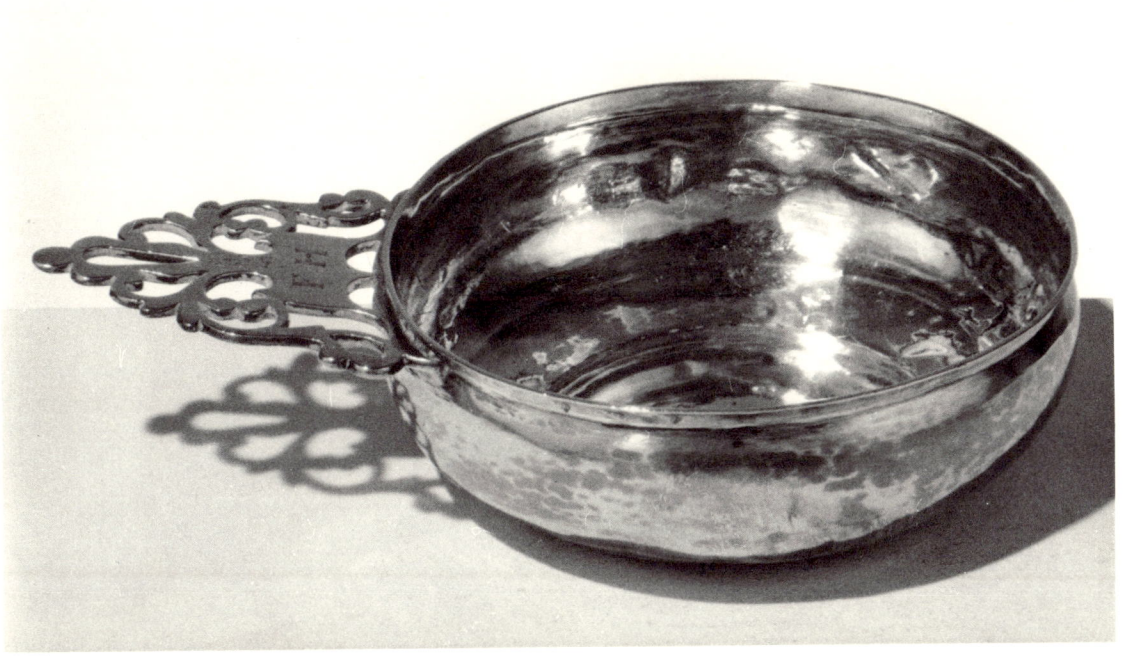

Fig. 5: Porringer, FR in heart thrice on rim right of handle, *c.* 1725. Engraved on handle FH. Diameter: 5 3/16″; length of handle: 2 9/16″. *Courtesy of Mr. and Mrs. David B. Robb.*

The effort to link definitely by documentation any of the FR marks with either Francis Richardson or his son Frank, who also practiced as a goldsmith for a few years, has so far proved unsuccessful. One reason for the failure to locate documented examples of their work is that the period of both men's greatest activity—and that from which most examples survive is not covered by any of the remaining accounts. Most helpful in the attempt to identify the FR marks is the Sarah Penrose box (*Fig. 3*). If the date 1727 on this box is accepted as contemporary, as it certainly appears to be, then the heart-shaped FR mark which it bears may be attributed definitely to the elder Francis, for in that year Frank was only nineteen and had neither come of age nor completed his apprenticeship.

The closest connection with actual documentation is achieved by a silver keyhole porringer (*Fig. 4*) engraved with the initials L✳R and the weight 7 oz. 12 dwt. At his death, Francis, Sr., left his widow, Letitia Richardson, two silver porringers which weighed approximately six or seven ounces each.[47] Since his widow's initials were L. R., it is possible that this porringer is one of the two bequeathed.

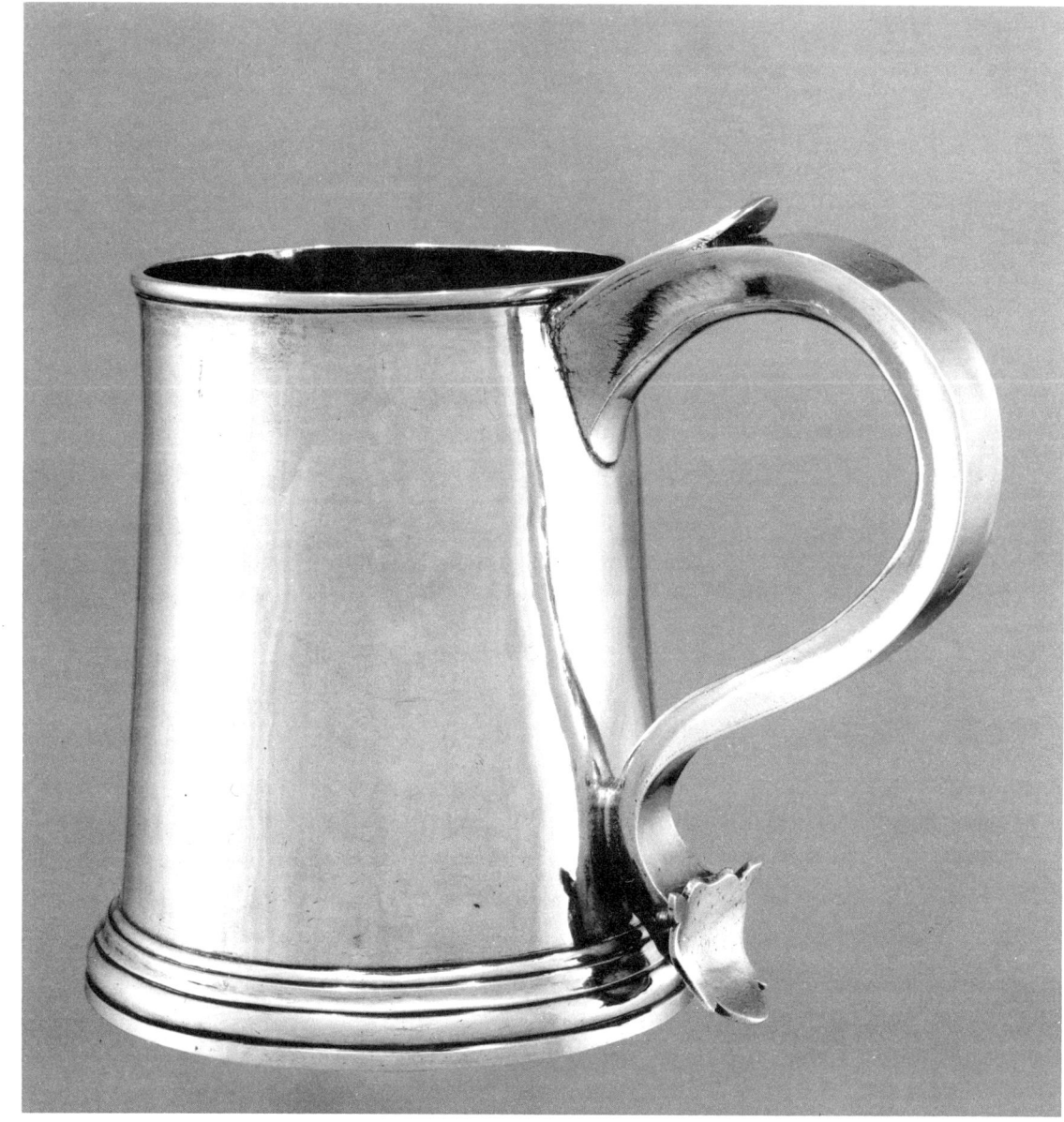

Fig. 6: Can, FR in shield, crown above, on handle *c.* 1728. Engraved on handle PS for Phebe Sharples of Chester County, Pennsylvania, who, according to family tradition, bought the can with money bequeathed to her by her betrothed, Josiah Hibberd, who died in 1727. Phebe married Josiah's brother Benjamin Hibberd in 1732, and the inventory of his estate taken in 1785 listed "a Silver kan & teaspoons, £ 4/17/6." Height: 5 1/8"; diameter of base: 4 1/2"; weight: 17 oz. 13 dwt. 3 gr. *Courtesy of The Henry Francis du Pont Winterthur Museum; photograph by Gilbert Ask.*

Both the porringer and a can, or mug, in the Winterthur Museum bear the mark FR in a shield with a crown above *(Fig. 6)*. On the handle of the can are initials PS, for Phebe Sharples of Chester County, Pennsylvania. According to family tradition, she bought the can with money bequeathed her by her betrothed, Josiah Hibberd, who died in 1727.[48] The design of this can is appropriate to the Quaker aesthetic, for it is characterized by simple lines and plain, smooth surfaces. The bold sweep of the handle and the shield-shaped handle ending are identical with those of a tankard also made by Richardson *(Fig. 7)* with a type of curved thumbpiece characteristic of the Philadelphia school.[49] The mid-band on the body of the tankard and the stepped and domed lid indicate that Francis Richardson and other Philadelphia goldsmiths kept abreast of the London fashions.

Two oval patch boxes also survive. Probably the earlier of these is the one decorated with a slightly embossed Tudor rose *(Fig. 8)*. The rose has a cross-hatched center and two series of petals, each shaped like the spatulate spoon handles of the period. The sharply pointed, ridged leaves between each outer petal are repeated in miniature to form the border of the box.[50] The other box *(Fig. 3)* has no border but has a more elaborately engraved top. In the center of the lid is a large, plain shield (similar to the large, solid shield-shape in the porringer handles) upon which the owner's name is engraved. The shield motif frequently appears in Francis Richardson's work. His use of current baroque design is evident in the boldly curved scrolls and foliage surrounding the shield, with tulip flowers at the top and imbrication in the background.

Buckles and spoons were among the objects most commonly made by Francis Richardson. A pair of buckles in the possession of the Historical Society of Pennsylvania bear the heart-shaped FR mark *(Fig. 9)*.[51] Here Francis achieved grace in the smoothly curved outlines of the buckle and the cusp-shaped void in the center, which accentuate the polished round button on the chape and the pointed tongue.

If anything survives of a silversmith's work, it is usually spoons, and some of Francis Richardson's are known *(Fig. 10)*. One has an engraved $\overset{M}{EM}$ on the back of the spatulate handle and the other two, MH.[52] All three spoons are otherwise very plain, with long rat-tail drops on the backs of the bowls, which narrow sharply on either side of the juncture with the shaft—features characteristic of early spoons.

The same rat-tail drop appears on the top side of the snap plate which fits

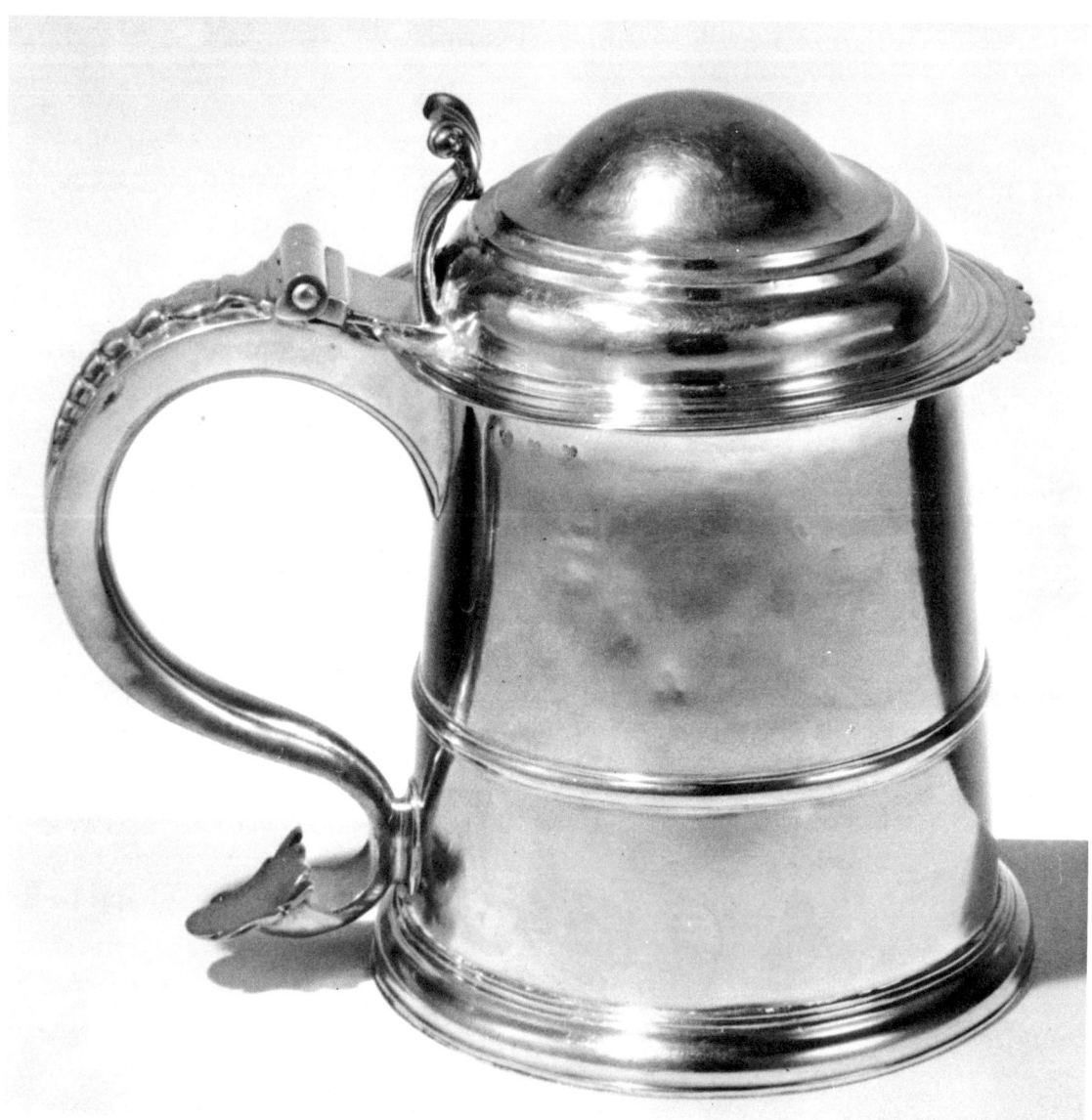

Fig. 7: Tankard, FR in heart thrice right of handle *c.* 1725. Made for William Branson whose initials WB are engraved on the drop of the handle. This type of curved thumbpiece outlined by a horseshoe-shaped ridge is characteristic of Philadelphia tankards of the period,

Courtesy of Estate of S. L. W. Starr; Mrs. Daniel Blain, Trustee.

into the clasp of the only surviving example of Francis' work in gold—a charming locket *(Fig. 11)*, engraved on the back with the original owner's initials SC and with Richardson's FR in a heart stamp.[53] The holes in the back of the locket indicate that originally it held a five-strand necklace, probably of shaped coral beads or hollow gold beads which were popular in the early eighteenth century.[54]

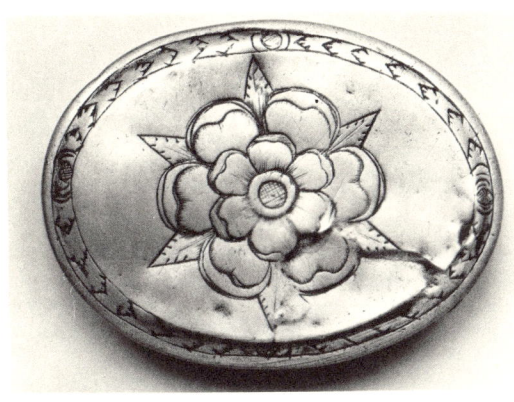

Fig. 8: Patch box, FR in heart twice inside both lid and base, *c. 1715*. Engraved on base EB for the unknown original owner and on lid with Tudor rose design with a cross-hatched center. Length: 2 5/8". *Courtesy of Philadelphia Museum of Art.*

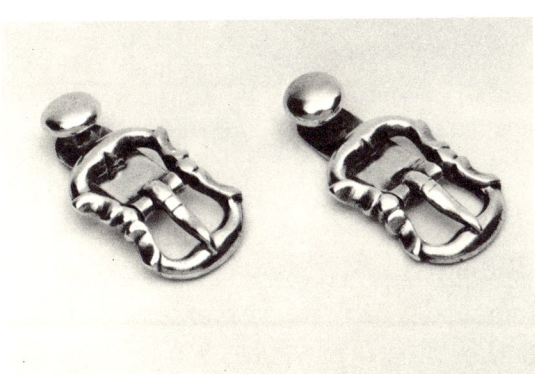 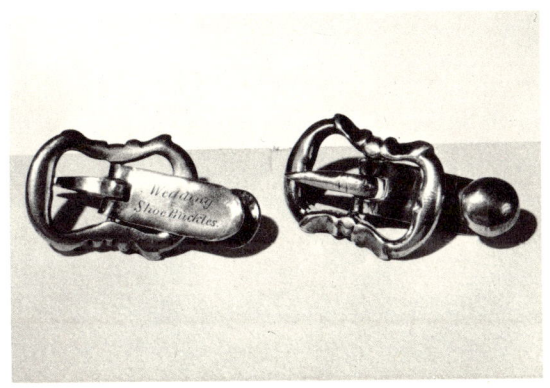

Fig. 9: Pair of buckles, FR in heart on top of each chape, *c. 1721*. Later engraving on back of one *Elizabeth Paschall 11 May 1721* and on other *Wedding Shoe Buckles (Fig. 9a)*. Length: 1 1/4"; weight: 4 dwt. 7 gr. and 4 dwt. 3 gr. *Courtesy of The Historical Society of Pennsylvania.*

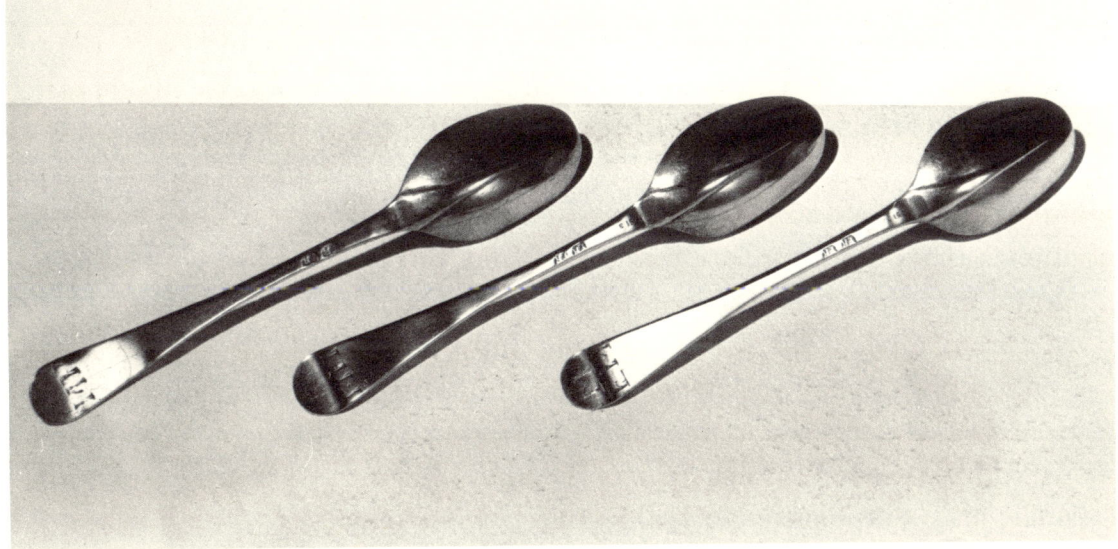

Fig. 10: Three spoons, FR in heart twice on back of each handle, *c. 1725*. Engraved on back of two MH and on other E^{M}M. In 1720 Mary Hill bought a single spoon for which Francis Richardson charged her 3 shillings for making and 4 shillings for silver added. Length: 4 9/16". *Courtesy of Mrs. Edsel Ford.*

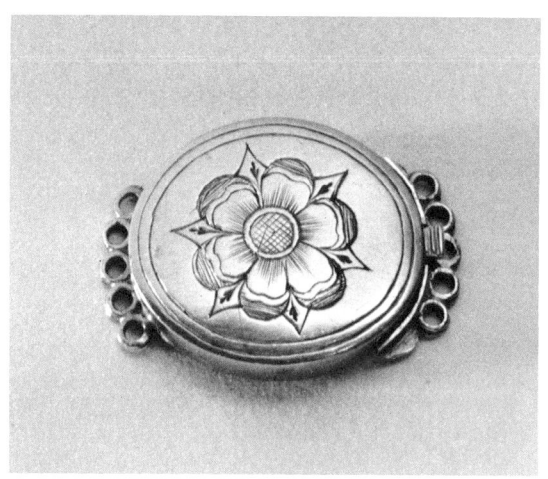 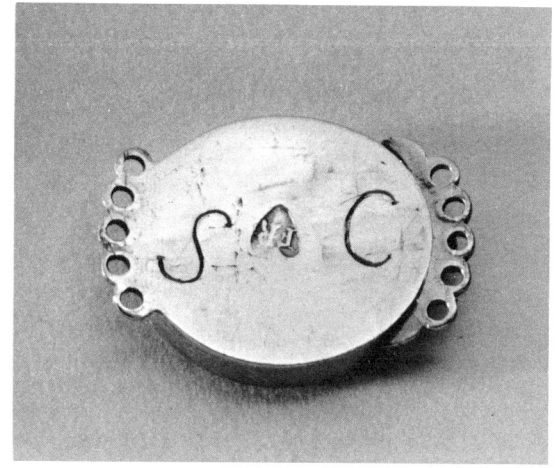

Fig. 11: Gold locket, FR in heart on back, *c.* 1720. Engraved on back with original owner's initials, SC (*Fig 11a*). Once held a five-strand necklace. *Courtesy of The Henry Francis du Pont Winterthur Museum; photograph by Gilbert Ask.*

Among the various objects Francis Richardson is known to have made, there is a noticeable lack of pieces associated with the serving of tea and coffee, beverages then newly popular in the Western world. Except for teaspoons, tea tongs, and strainers, Francis Richardson's only known work of this type was the mending of a teapot in 1720.

He also sold silver and gold objects which he did not specify making. These could have been imported from England or bought from other local craftsmen and tradesmen for resale. Many of these objects are of the same kinds as those he made himself; they include spoons, coral and bells, pepper boxes, snuff boxes, tea tongs, and strainers, as well as smaller objects such as jewelry, spectacles, thimbles, and chains. Others—watchcases, penknives, bodkins, earrings, toothpick cases, bottle tops, and sconces—were not commonly made in America at the time. Hooks and smelling bottles are two types of objects Francis Richardson frequently sold, but it is not known whether he made them or imported them, nor indeed do the accounts indicate whether they were made of gold, silver, or some other metal.

Much of Francis' work seems to have involved repairing, adjusting, and remodeling objects. A common repair job involved putting a new top on a worn thimble. Several times he was asked to "tip with silver a bosom bottle" (a small, flat, glass bottle concealed in a lady's stomacher, to hold water and flowers). He was asked also to mend whips and sconces, to lengthen chains, and to reduce the size of pincushion hoops or ferrules; on occasion he was asked to put new tongues on buckles, to fasten pieces of coral on whistles or put new bells on them, and to put links on buttons. Occasionally Francis engraved initials on silver spoons or pewter plates already owned by his cus-mers.[55]

Cleaning silver was a problem then, as it is today, and customers often brought various objects to be cleaned. Sometimes, in order to restore a layer of pure silver to the surface of an object, it was necessary to pickle the silver by immersing it in a mild solution of acid and then to heat it, a process Francis referred to as "boiling." Another task was to take dents—appropriately called "bruises"—out of hollow ware. The tools and supplies he used for these and other operations are mentioned in his account book.[56]

As his business grew, so did Richardson's need for materials. In 1719, between June 14 and September 6, he made a shopping trip to London. On March 27, 1719, he received a certificate from his meeting to introduce him to friends abroad.[57] Before he left, Francis noted in the back of his account book the items he was to buy and the people he was to see.[58] Evidently, some of the purchases he made in London had to be shipped separately, and occasionally there was some difficulty as when he recorded that he bought sundry goods from John Bell and that "In This parsell their was 1 Doz. of Stockins wanting." Francis sent to John Cadman in Grace Church Street near Lombard Street in London for "sundries" and all sorts of perfumes. From Nicholas Witchell in Burchen Lane he bought dozens of gloves, including twenty-one dozen women's colored kid gloves. The most tantalizing entry of all is: "Bought of Sundry persons Sundryes as Tuells [tools] Silverwair Corrall bosam bottles Divers other things."

Elsewhere, Francis notes his accounts for 1720 and 1721 with John Bell, hosier; Thomas Plumsted, ironmonger; Joseph Tantum, looking-glass maker; and Nicholas Witchell, glover. In return for these goods, Francis shipped tobacco, silver, gold, coins, and silver plate. In at least one instance, Francis ordered from London some goods and equipment for his trade, although it is not known from whom they were purchased.[59]

The resale of English goods to Philadelphia families is duly recorded in Richardson's accounts for the next few years. Imported fabrics, sewing equipment, jewelry, hardware, and glassware all made their way into Philadelphia homes through the shop of Francis Richardson. No less than forty-two looking glasses were recorded as sold by Francis (five of these are specified as "swinging glasses"), as well as English tea tables and tea boards.

For these goods and for his own work, Francis was paid in many ways. Sometimes his payment came in the form of a customer's goods or services.[60]

Many of the food staples required by his family were provided in this manner. Usually, however, Francis was paid in cash, or in old silver and gold objects which, when melted down, would supply him with the necessary raw material to fill the customer's order. In this way, Francis specifies receiving gold chains, an old porringer, a pepper box and grater, silver buttons, spoons, two ounces of plate, and two ounces of broken silver. *(Fig. 12)*

Payments for work on the house and shop also appear in his accounts. In 1717 Francis paid William Rakestraw for 3,250 bricks at various times and for 1,250 "bricks for my front door." He also paid him for "wood and halling [hauling]." Joseph Waite made a forge for Francis' shop in 1719, charging him for a bushel and a half of lime and sixty bricks and for paving the gate. In return, he received from Francis a silver whistle. In 1720 Francis paid William Meed, the paver, cash for work done, and Brother Hasell was credited for mending windows and a padlock and keys. Philip Hiberd, who owed Francis for water and a half-year's rent, paid off part of his debt by carting dirt from Richardson's door.

Even household goods were acquired from customers. In 1722 Francis got a pair of bellows, a shovel and tongs, a brush for the fireplace, a brass pot, a dripping pan, a teapot, and another pair of tongs from Ebenezer Robinson. Clothes for the family also sometimes came from his customers. In 1717 Francis credited his relative Mary Haywood for making shoes for Joseph and himself, and mending a pair for Frank. George House and Iwon Worner [Ivan Warner?] also provided shoes, while Brother Hasell and Daniel Derbory supplied hats. Hannah Emson and Margaret Jones made clothes, and Thomas Broadgate supplied large amounts of clothing for Francis and the boys during 1719 and 1720. Francis also provided clothing for his Negro, Hereford, who got a pair of scarlet stockings on one occasion, and for Robert Keeble, who worked with him and who received caps, gloves, and shoes in partial remuneration.

These accounts also give an indication of where Francis' sons, Frank and Joseph, may have received their early schooling. In 1721 their father gave seven coat buttons and a toothpick, worth £0/10/0 in all, to James Conway, the schoolmaster, for "Schooling," and, in March 1722, a pair of buckles and a pair of gloves for the school master's charge of £0/10/6 for schooling.[61]

The boys had become young men when, three months before his forty-eighth birthday, on August 17, 1729, Francis Richardson died. Frank, twenty-one, had probably just completed his apprenticeship with his father; Joseph,

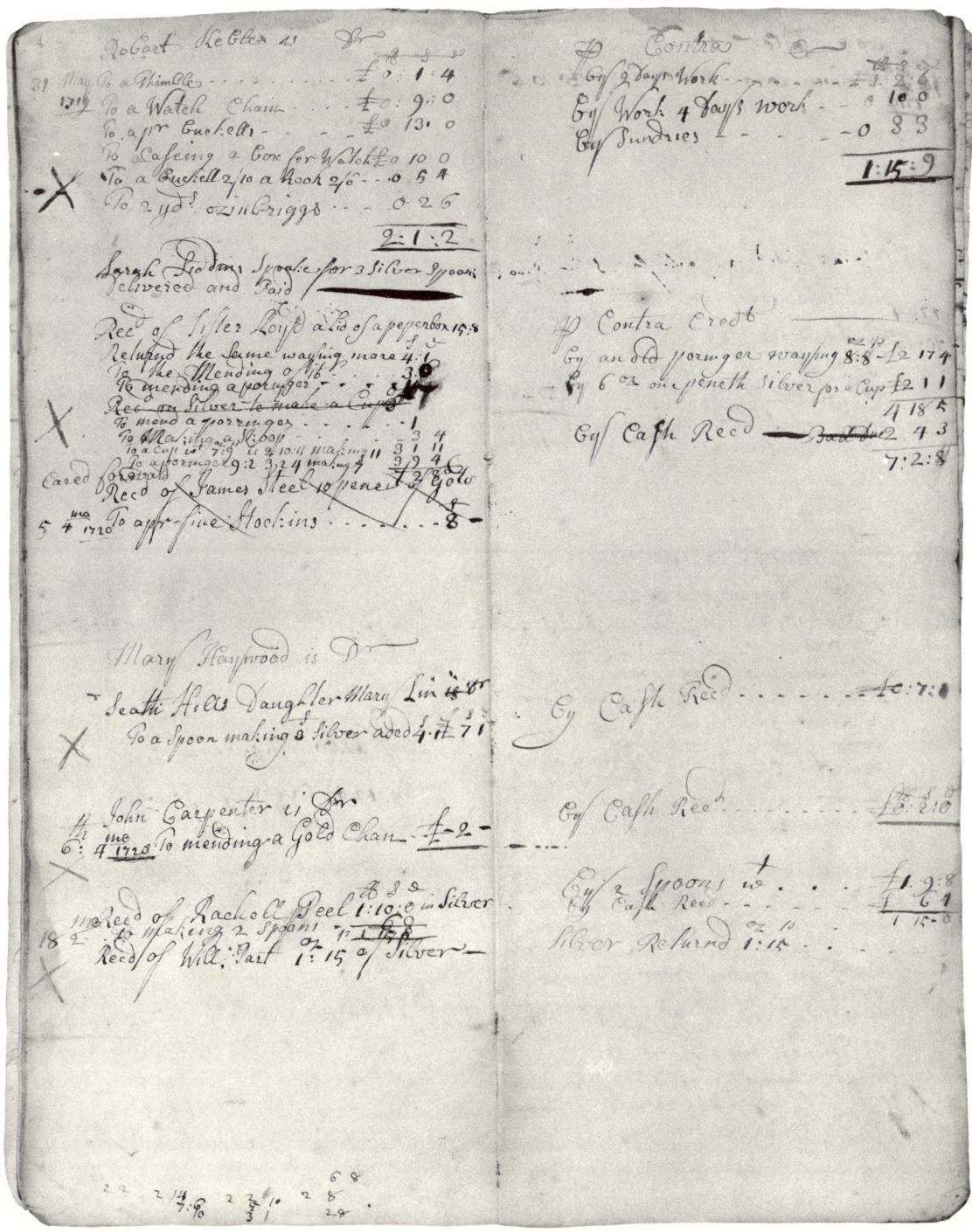

Fig. 12: Page from account book of Francis Richardson, 1717–22. Shows accounts in 1719–20 with shop-worker Robert Keeble, relatives and other customers. *Courtesy of The Henry Francis du Pont Winterthur Museum; photograph by Gilbert Ask.*

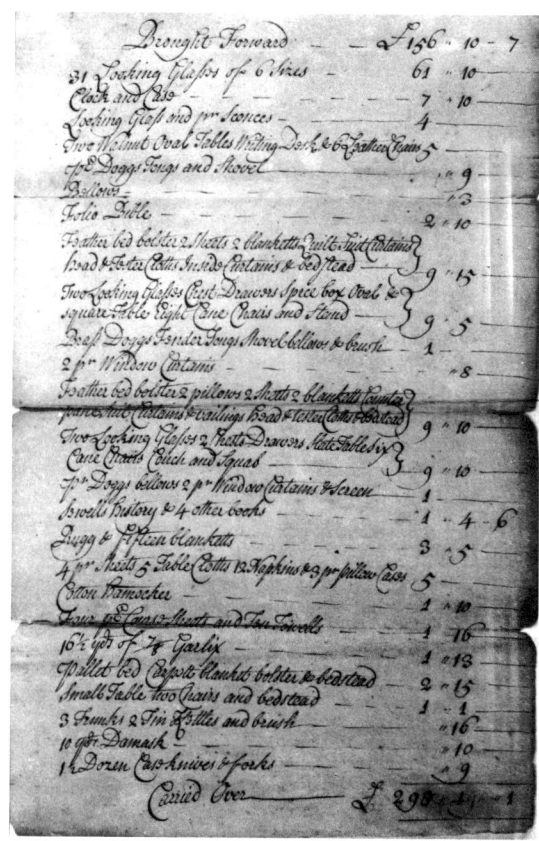

Figs. 13–14: Inventory of Francis Richardson's estate, taken in 1729, listing personal possessions and his goldsmith's tools which his son Joseph inherited. *Courtesy of Philadelphia County Court House.*

only eighteen, had not yet finished his training. Nevertheless, it was to Joseph that Francis left his tools:

> I give ... my eldest son francis Richardson all my part or share of 400 acres of land lying in Kent County on Delaware to hold to him & his heirs forever & the sum of 500 pounds lawful Mony of America in full for his share & portion of my estate.... I give ... my dear & loving wife Latitia my negro girl named homo & the sum of 10 pounds mony ... and also two silver porringers.... I give ... unto my son Joseph my negro boy named Herreford & all my working tools provided he continue & live with his mother in law [stepmother] & carry on my trade for her until he shall attain to his full age of 21 years. I give ... all my messuage or tenement & lot of ground thereto belonging lying on the west side of ... front street in Philadelphia ... wherein I now live & all the rest & residue of my estate both real & personal whatsoever & wheresoever the same may be found unto my said wife Latitia & son Joseph & full power for them to sell & convey the same or any part thereof to such person or persons as shall purchase the same

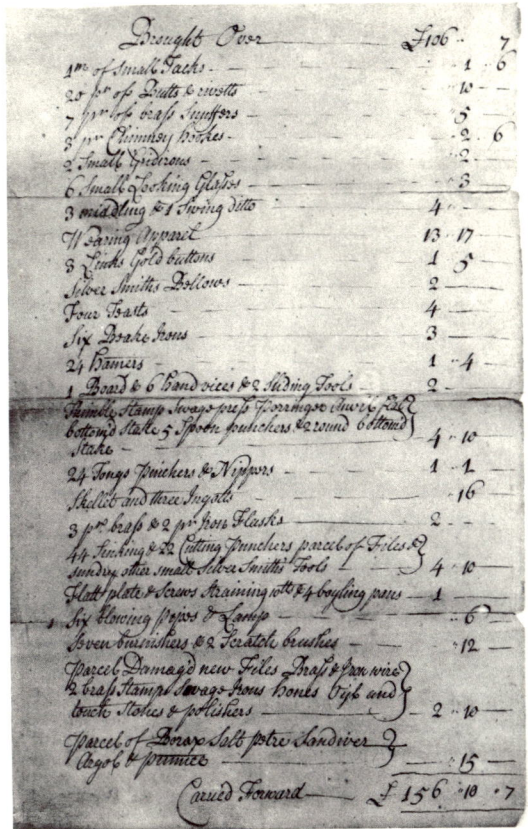
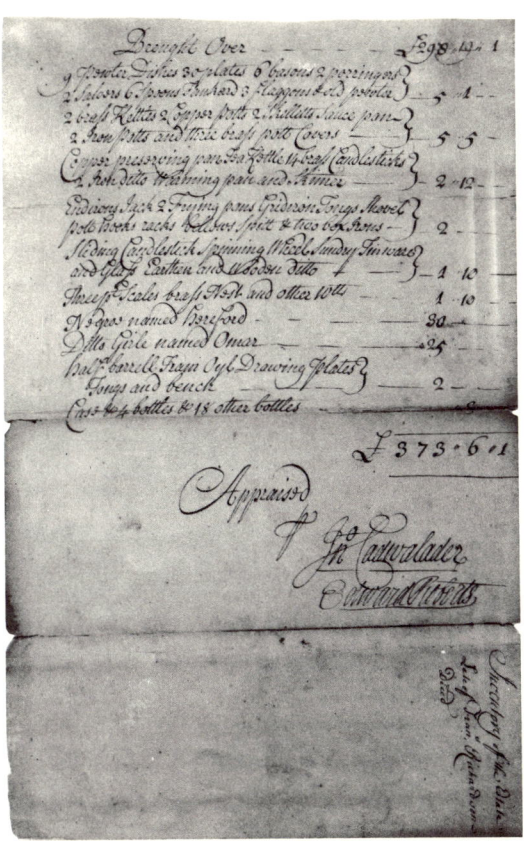

in fee simple or otherwise & the mony arising by such sale to be equally divided between them my said wife & son Joseph share & share alike...[62]

By many standards, Francis Richardson's life had been a successful one. Not only had he provided well for his family,[63] but he had established in Philadelphia a dynasty of goldsmiths who were to carry on his craft and his traditions for a hundred years to come. This legacy passed first to his eldest son, Francis Richardson, Jr.

CHAPTER 2

Francis Richardson, Jr. (1705-1782), Silversmith and Merchant

FRANCIS RICHARDSON, JR., had reached his maturity before his father's death and had decided to pursue a career of merchant as well as goldsmith. His father had combined both activities, and probably had given his son training in both. Because capital was prerequisite for a merchant's career, the £500 and 400 acres of land in Kent County inherited from his father provided Frank with a good beginning.

Soon after his father's death, Frank was importing fabrics from England. In July 1729 he wrote from Kent-on-Delaware to his relative, Edward Shippen, asking him to get some English goods for him, specifically, "duroy, shalloon, ozenbriggs, garlix, and felt hats." He assured Shippen that he would pay promptly and promised that "what I order elsewhere I will allow you commission for . . . ."[1] By February 15, 1738, he was advertising in the *Pennsylvania Gazette* fabrics "Lately Imported, and to be Sold by *Francis Richardson* at the House of *Joseph Richardson*, Gold-Smith in Front Street."

In 1741 Frank was in London buying goods and shipping them to his brother Joseph to be sold in his shop. In a letter from London, dated February 12 of that year, Frank explained to Joseph: "The goods I shall send will be very saleable & a good variety. If thee had not room to expose them to sale let them lye packt up in the chamber till I arive or open & sell what thee conveniently can & let the rest lye. I hear my goods on board Stiles Stevenson are safely arivd & hope thee has sold some & remited me bills."[2]

Francis Richardson, Jr. (1705-1782)

Some weeks later, Frank wrote Joseph to forward bills to J. Mildred for his account, apologizing for the trouble to which he had put Joseph and expressing the hope that Joseph's help was "without prejudice" to his own business. He further explained that if he lived to get home he would probably move to a large store. In this same letter, dated April 3, 1741, he mentioned that he might "bring over another parcel of goods & a Partner with me who has been bred up to merchandize Writes a fine hand a man of a good Character & Can Command a Large credit—Something of this kind has been proposed to me & I dont know but I shel accept...."[3]

The proposed partner was probably named Eversley, for the dry-goods firm of "Richardson & Eversley" appeared in an advertisement in the *Pennsylvania Gazette* on January 3, 1744, requesting customers to pay their debts because Francis Richardson planned to go to London.[4] At the end of the same year, however, the alliance was ended; another advertisement appeared in the *Pennsylvania Gazette* on December 14, 1744, for the payment of debts to Richardson and Eversley, this time because their partnership was being dissolved.

Frank's business activities did not interfere with his personal life; on November 26, 1742, he married Mary Fitzwater. Their courtship must have been somewhat unorthodox, for at the Monthly Meeting of Friends on June 24, 1743, Frank "brought in a paper condemning his and his Wife's unchaste Conduct before Marriage."[5] Their first son was born on May 15, 1746, and was named Francis.[6] Frank and Mary Richardson lived in Chester, Pennsylvania, where Frank acquired several properties and built a large home. Here, Frank's second son, John, and his four daughters were born and grew up, while his business continued to prosper.

Frank called himself a goldsmith until about 1738 and he produced clock work as well as some metal work. On September 9, 1736, he advertised in the *Pennsylvania Gazette* "Very neat clocks & jacks," which he made, sold, cleaned, and mended in his shop on the corner of Letitia Court in Market Street.[7] To this he added the next spring a line of hardware including handles and escutcheons for furniture, tea-table bolts, and desk hinges. A revealing indication of Frank's work in metal was his advertisement in 1734: "Reward for runaway apprentice, Isaac Marceloe, formerly with William Heurtin, Goldsmith of New York."[8]

Most of the information about Frank's career is found in Joseph Richardson's account books.[9] It would appear that as early as 1734, when the accounts

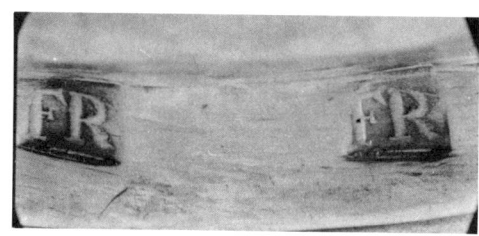

Fig. 15: Maker's mark FR in a rectangle. The rectangular mark was the most common type found in American silver from the second quarter of the 18th century until well into the 19th century. Appears on the porringer *(Fig. 17)* made for John and Ann Richardson, *c.* 1730. *Courtesy of Mrs. Walter S. Franklin.*

begin, Frank was doing work for his brother. From 1734 to 1737, Frank often received from Joseph silver bullion to be made into specific forms—porringers, casters, teapots, cans, tankards, salvers, milk pots, tea tongs, spoons, strainers, buckles, clasps, buttons, chains, hearts, and other small objects. After Frank had finished these pieces, he returned them, along with any remaining silver, to Joseph and was credited with the cost of manufacture.

Of the forms listed in these accounts as made by Frank, only three porringers and a can survive. The porringers are stamped FR in a rectangle *(Fig. 15)*, and are similar in shape to those made by his father (see *Figs. 4, 5*). Young Frank's porringer handles, however, have different piercings, including a smaller opening in the tip of the handle *(Fig. 16)*. Two of the porringers *(Fig. 17)* bear the initials I $\overset{R}{}$ A, of John and Ann Richardson, who were married in 1704 and lived in New Castle County, Delaware.[10] One of John and Ann Richardson's twelve children was Joseph Richardson the merchant, a contemporary of Joseph Richardson the goldsmith. Another son, Robert, became the grandfather of John R. Latimer, prominent shipping merchant in the early nineteenth century.

A can *(Fig. 18)* made by Francis Richardson, Jr., with the same initials I $\overset{R}{}$ A engraved on the handle, was acquired by the Philadelphia Museum of Art in 1959. Before the discovery of this handsome can—also believed to have been owned originally by John and Ann Richardson—porringers were Frank's only known works. There is a strong similarity between his can and the tankard and can made by Frank's father *(see Figs. 6, 7)*. All three vessels have the same sturdy, straight-bodied form, wide base moldings, and the boldly scrolled handles ending in plain, flat shield-cut tips. Both cans have a simple tongue of silver at the top of the handle and are stamped with the maker's mark below the engraved initials on the handle. Frank's can is also marked twice at the

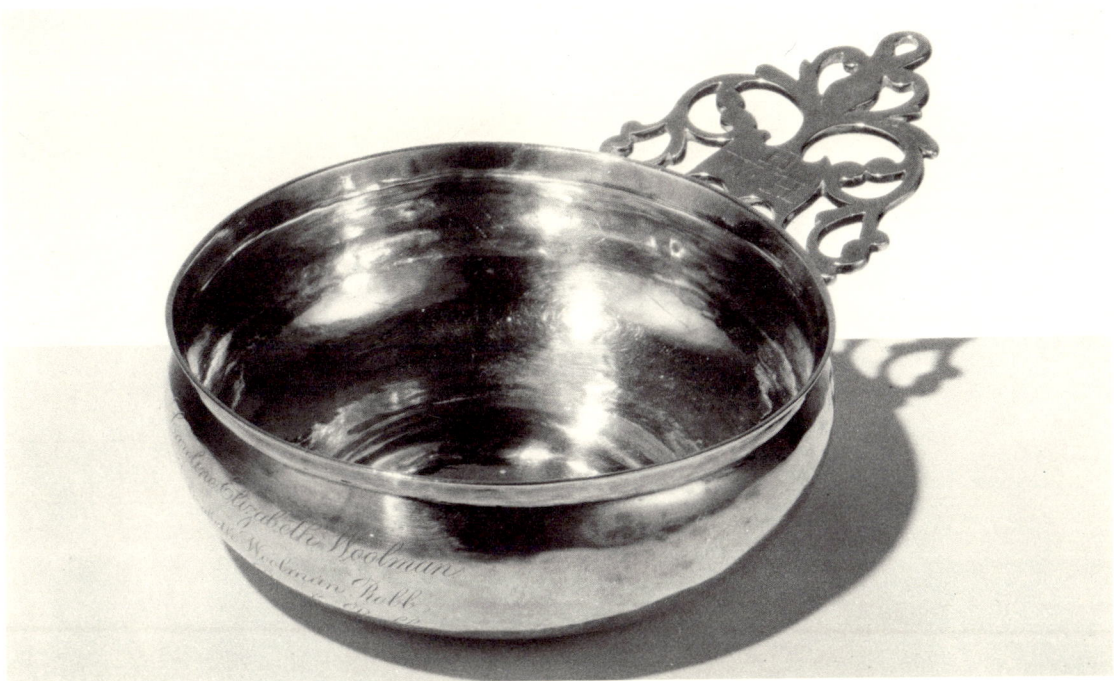

Fig. 16: Porringer, FR in rectangle twice on rim, *c.* 1730. Engraved on handle W^{H}H for original owners, William and Hannah Hudson, who had been customers of the elder Francis Richardson, and on side later with names of subsequent owners *Caroline Elizabeth Woolman / Elizabeth Woolman Robb / David Buzby Robb*. Diameter: 5 3/8"; length of handle: 2 7/8". *Courtesy of Mr. and Mrs. David B. Robb.*

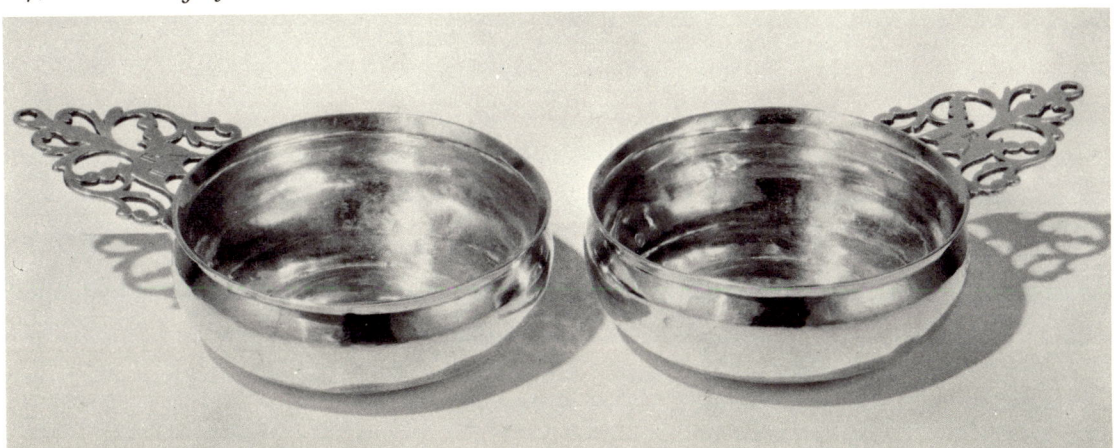

Fig. 17: Pair of porringers, FR in rectangle twice on rim of each, *c.* 1730. Engraved on handles I^{R}A for original owners, John and Ann Richardson of New Castle County, Delaware. Weight: 9 oz. and 9 oz. 6 dwt. Weighed 9 oz. 10 dwt. and 9 oz. 3 dwt. when listed in estate of their grandson Dr. Henry Latimer in Wilmington, Delaware, in 1820. Diameter: 5 1/4"; length of handle: 3". *Courtesy of Mrs. Walter S. Franklin, a descendant of Latimer.*

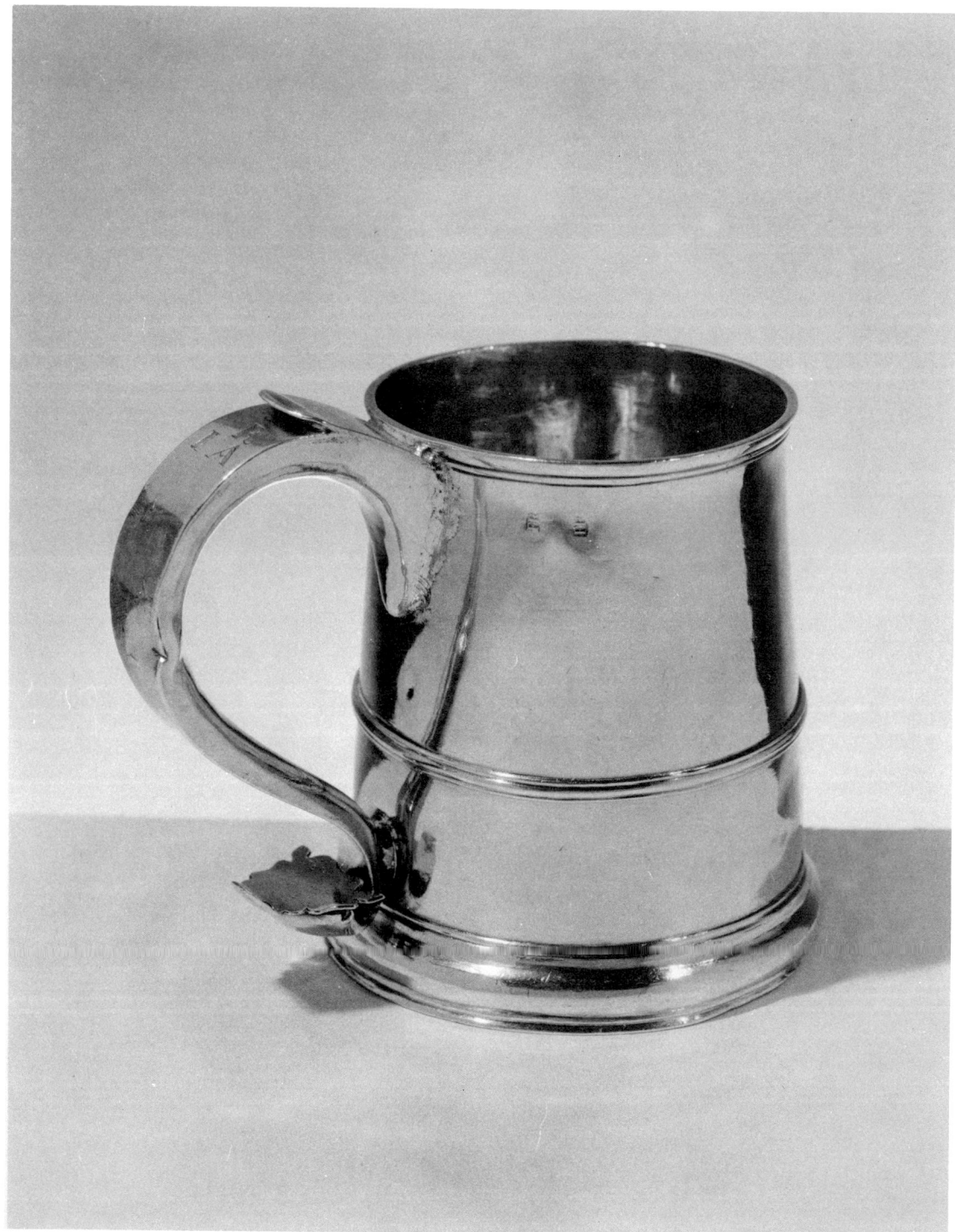

Fig. 18: Can, FR in rectangle twice at right angles to handle, *c*. 1730. Engraved on handle I $\overset{R}{A}$ for original owners, John and Ann Richardson. Weight: 12 oz. 5 dwt. marked on base originally (*Fig. 18a*). A can weighing this amount was listed in the inventory of Dr. Henry Latimer in 1820, along with two others of different weights. Height: 4 1/4″. *Courtesy of Philadelphia Museum of Art.*

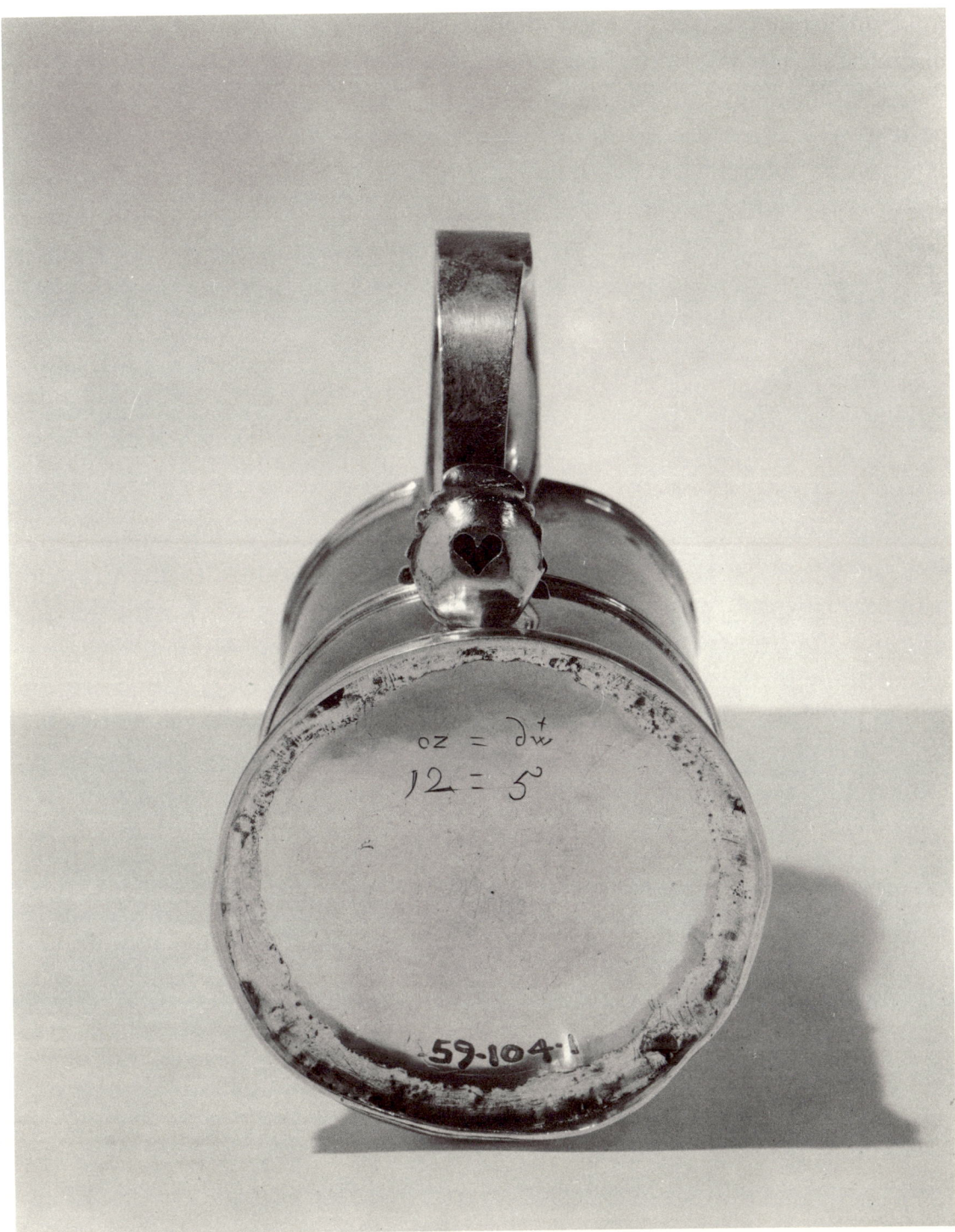

Fig. 18a: The inscribed base of the tankard shown in *Fig. 18*.

right of the handle top, the same place that his father's tankard is stamped three times. The marks on Frank's can, FR in a rectangle, are unusual in that they are placed at right angles, whereas his father's marks on the tankard can be read with the vessel in an upright position. Both the tankard and Frank's can have a molded band just below the middle of the body, double grooving below the rim, and an oval back plate behind the bottom of the handle. One of the differences between this can and the tankard and can made by Francis, Sr., is that the shield-shaped handle ending on Frank's can has an extra cusp in the shape of its sides.

While Frank was making silver objects at Joseph's request, he was also buying pieces that Joseph made, probably for resale.[11] Joseph also did repair and finishing work for Frank, such as mending a pair of large wrought buckles and a gold ring, piercing two strainers and engraving a locket, a pair of gold buttons and studs.

These early accounts refer briefly to the clock and watch business that Frank advertised in 1736 and 1737.[12] His advertisements indicate that he made, sold, cleaned, and repaired clocks and watches. One tall clock with the dial inscribed *Fra Richardson Philad^a. Fecit (Fig. 19)* is known. Although accounts do not show that Joseph engraved the name for his brother, they do record that he provided this service for other Philadelphia clockmakers. A comparison of Joseph's writing of Frank's name with Frank's own signature shows that Joseph's is remarkably similar to the inscription on the dial; therefore it may be assumed that it is Joseph's engraving. Although the dial plate now has no applied ornament in the spandrels, holes in each spandrel indicate where ornaments were once attached. A fleur-de-lis decorates the space between each of the roman numerals marking the hours. In addition to minute and hour hands, in the center area of the clock face are a second hand and dial, and an opening below the maker's name through which the day of the month appears. The clock is housed in a tall walnut case with a glass opening in the door of the case. The top of the case is flat, with a substantial molding characteristic of early eighteenth-century American clock cases.

Perhaps the most significant accounts concerning Frank Richardson are those dated September 1737 through March 1738, the period in which Frank is credited with the making of the last silver objects for Joseph. From the items listed, it is apparent that he was selling out his clock and goldsmith business to his brother. This assumption is further supported by the fact that, during the same month in which Joseph received the clock equipment from

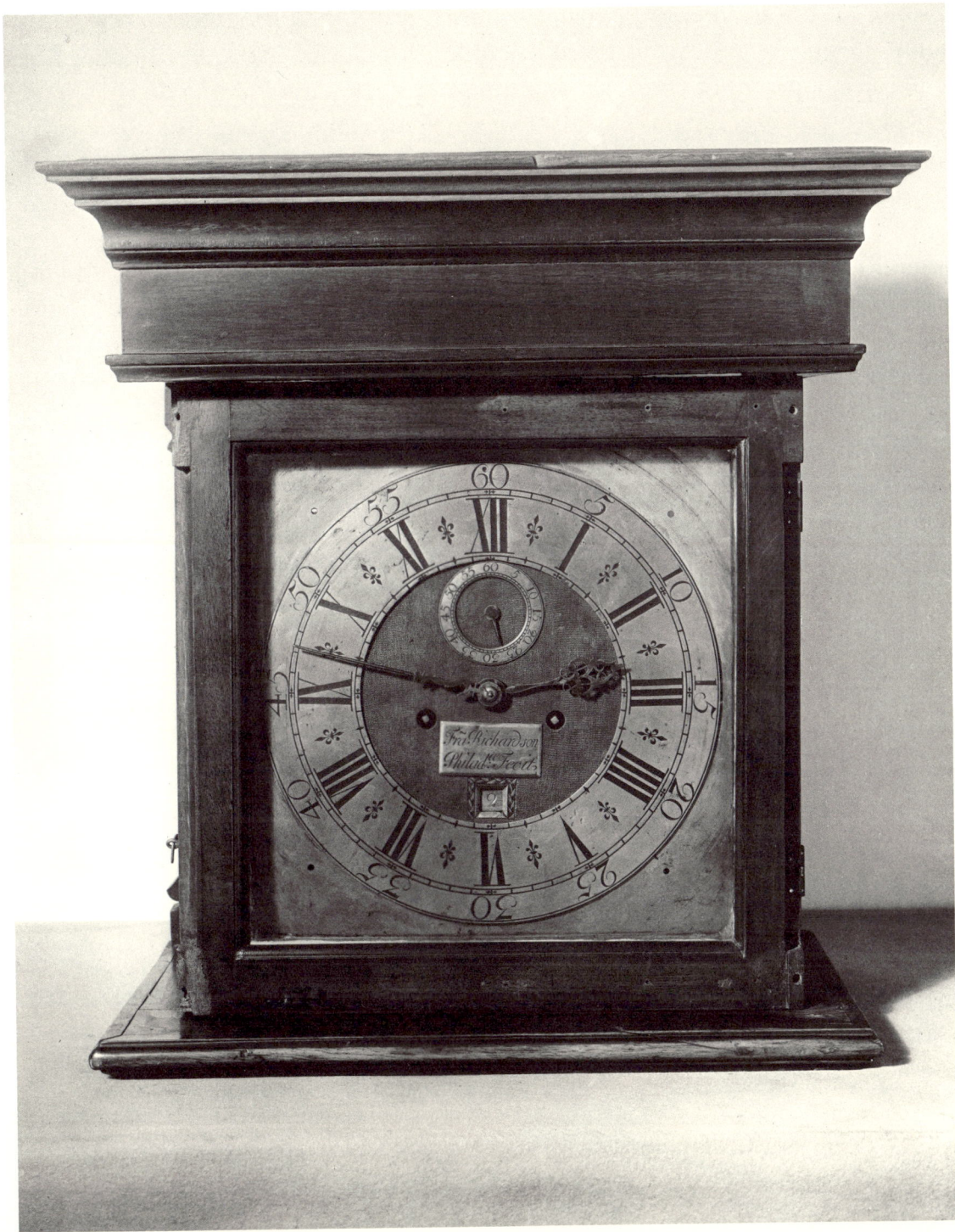

Fig. 19: Face of tall clock. One of the earliest Philadelphia clocks known, it is inscribed *Fra. Richardson / Philad.ª Fecit, c.* 1735. Dial probably engraved by his brother Joseph Richardson. Diameter: 11 3/16". *Courtesy of Philadelphia Museum of Art.*

Frank, he began keeping an account entitled "Clock Business." The equipment Joseph bought from Frank included block tin, brass, bell metal, files, crucibles, a parcel of springs, a molding trough, a parcel of buckle rims, a pair of flat irons, three dozen crystals, two clock movements, and five clock cases.

In the accounts with his brother, Frank is credited with paying cash, gold or silver, or goods (tables, china, bread and flour, and even coconuts), and until 1738, with the making of plate. The accounts show that Joseph looked after Frank's Philadelphia affairs while the latter was out of town. Several times Joseph paid Frank's dues to the Library Company, and he paid freight on shipments Frank made as a merchant. From 1738 to 1740, Joseph often paid out cash on Frank's behalf to others, among whom were Henry Pratt and Philip Syng, Philadelphia goldsmiths. Joseph occasionally purchased goods for Frank, such as skins, cheese, butter, bread, and flour, and received in payment single barrels of some of the supplies. Together, Joseph and Frank shipped two tons of pig iron to Leonard Cousins in Newport in 1740. On another occasion, Joseph charged Frank for two silver cans weighing 24 oz. 10 dwt. which were shipped to Carolina.

Such joint ventures on the part of Frank and Joseph ceased in 1745, for the only accounts between 1745 and 1748 concerning Frank are for his purchase of silver and gold items and silver bullion. Frank either supplied the silver or gold in advance or paid in cash. Between 1745 and the beginning of 1748, he got from Joseph two gold lockets, gold stocking clasps, a silver nipple, and twelve pairs of wrought shoe buckles, further indication that his career as a goldsmith had come to an early end.

Before his death on February 1, 1782, Frank became a shipping merchant of some note. He was a founder of the Pennsylvania Hospital and of the Library Company of Philadelphia and was elected a director of the latter organization for several years.[13] He followed to good advantage the merchant career of his grandfather, leaving to his brother Joseph the continuation of the goldsmith's business through a second generation.

PART TWO
IR

Item I give...unto my son Joseph...all my working tools provided he continue & live with his mother in law & carry on my trade for her until he shall attain to his full age...

                Will of Francis Richardson, 1729

CHAPTER 3

Joseph Richardson (1711-1784): His Life

JOSEPH RICHARDSON was only eighteen years old when his father died in 1729. Although at that time, apprentices did not customarily finish their term before twenty-one, it was Joseph and not his older brother, Frank, who inherited their father's tools. So it was, that Joseph, while still a very young man, took over the business of goldsmith in his father's house and shop on the west side of Front Street, and assumed the support of his stepmother.[1]

Letitia Richardson soon remarried, however; and on July 8, 1731, Jeremiah Elfreth, a Philadelphia blacksmith, became Joseph's stepfather.[2] Within two years Letitia died, leaving Elfreth a widower once again. Joseph and his stepfather had some business dealings during this period; on December 7, 1734, Elfreth was charged for a silver tankard weighing 34 oz. 15 dwt. which cost £ 16/10/1. In January, Joseph noted that his stepfather had owed him for seven months' rent since September 1732, and in the meantime had bought, but had not paid for, several pairs of buttons and a stock buckle.[3]

Joseph Richardson's renting of property to his stepfather is an early indication of an interest in real estate which continued throughout his life. On May 28, 1733, he was sufficiently established financially to buy a lot on Front Street from his uncle, Lawrence Growden, for a sum of £ 260, almost twice his annual gross income.[4] Growden was prominent in Philadelphia affairs. A jurist and a merchant from Bristol, England, he served in the Pennsylvania Assembly from 1734 to 1738. He lived in Bucks County, where he had inherited property from his grandfather, but during the sessions of the Assembly in Philadelphia he lodged with Joseph. This close relationship did not stifle Joseph's business sense, for he carefully kept an account of his charges to his uncle for lodging and meals, stable rent, and even postage due on letters that Lawrence Growden received. When Joseph bought furniture for his uncle's room, he added it to this account.[5] Usually Growden paid his nephew in cash, but in one instance he paid with steel (possibly because he was a principal proprietor of the Durham Iron Works), and occasionally he paid his debts with fabrics such as those he advertised for sale at Joseph's shop in 1738.[6]

His uncle's companionship undoubtedly meant a great deal to Joseph during his bachelor days, and it may have been through Lawrence Growden that Joseph became acquainted with some of Philadelphia's leading merchants, such as Clement Plumsted, who asked him to witness a business transaction in 1737. Because calling upon friends to witness the sale of land or the borrowing of money was a customary business occurrence, Plumsted soon returned this favor in kind to Joseph.[7] In 1741, Joseph bought a house nearby on Front Street from Clement Plumsted, purchasing it in fee instead of buying it outright, which probably would have taken more money than Joseph had available at that time. This meant that he was required to pay Plumsted a ground rent of £6 each year.[8]

The purchase of this property was undoubtedly a result of Joseph's decision to marry for it was here that he and his bride established their home. In the Quaker tradition, their intentions to marry had been declared at a meeting of the Friends on March 28, 1741. As it was customary for two members of the meeting to ascertain that both parties were free to marry, a committee of two Friends appointed to investigate discovered that an unnamed young woman laid claim to Joseph (for unrecorded reasons) and refused to allow him to be married. The committee was soon able "to get the affair accomodated."[9] On August 13, 1741, Joseph Richardson and Hannah Worril, daughter of the late Richard Worril, yeoman of Lower Dublin, were finally married. Thirty of their friends attended the service and signed their marriage certificate. The following year marked the birth of their first child, Elizabeth, known as Betsy. Another daughter, born in 1743, was named Grace (perhaps in honor of Joseph's aunt, Grace Growden Lloyd), but she did not survive infancy.[10]

While acquiring a wife and family, Joseph continued to add to his real estate holdings. In July 1743, he bought in fee from Anthony and Catherine Duché a lot on the east side of Second Street (also called Moyamensing Road). For the use of this land, Joseph paid them £8 a year, and by renting part of this property for £14 a year, Joseph was able to realize a substantial profit.[11]

A considerable portion of Joseph's profits was given to worthy causes. As Frederick B. Tolles has explained: "In the Quaker's mind, the 'Good of Mankind' represented a positive claim upon his material wealth, and no doubt the prospect of being able to help those in need operated as an incentive to further acquisition."[12] Such thinking undoubtedly led Joseph to one of his philanthropic activities, support of the Pennsylvania Hospital. His name appears frequently in the minutes of the Hospital from 1754, when he made his first donation of £5, until the end of his life.[13] He and his family also helped support the Philadelphia Library Company, which was founded in 1731 through efforts of such interested people as Thomas Hopkinson, Benjamin Franklin and James Logan, and which provided many books for the use of the people of Philadelphia.[14] Joseph became a member on March 22, 1743, paying seven pounds for the privilege of owning a share in the Company's books and effects.[15] Although the library was not the exclusive project of Friends, their role in the formation of the Company was great, and, for the first thirty years of its existence, almost half the shareholders were Quakers.[16] Many of the books which the Library Company owned were useful to Joseph in his business, and he spent many hours reading such volumes as Chambers' *Dictionary* and copying pertinent paragraphs into his commonplace book.[17]

Joseph's growing prosperity, however, was soon marred by personal tragedy; in the family Bible, Joseph tersely recorded that "My Dear Wife Hannah Richardson Departed this Life the third Day of the Twelfth Month 1746/7 Between one and two in the morning being about 30 years of age."[18] During the year of his bereavement Joseph hired a housekeeper, Hannah Phips, to carry out the domestic tasks of the household and to care for his daughter Betsy.

One day a young woman named Mary Allen brought a pair of old gold buttons into his shop to be remade. One of Mary's relatives, the widow Hannah Allen, was Betsy Richardson's school mistress.[19] So rapidly did Joseph's friendship with Mary Allen progress that later in 1747 they declared their intention to marry at the Friends' Meeting. Her father, Nathaniel Allen, gave his approval, and this time the Friends appointed to inquire into Joseph's "freedom to marry" met with no difficulty.[20]

Although the marriage was not recorded until February 14, 1748, the merchant John Smith tells of being at the marriage on February 5, 1748: "Abraham Moor—who is lately come to live in town—and Mordecai Yarnal preach'd, & D. Stanton pray'd. Then Joseph Richardson was married to M. Allen. I staid & Signed the Certificate."[21] It is noteworthy that Smith stayed, for elsewhere in his journal he remarked that he left one marriage without signing the certificate because the man being married did not talk loud enough for him to hear.

Soon after he and Mary were married, Joseph was appointed to represent his local meeting at the Quarterly Meeting, and he continued to serve in this capacity from time to time for the rest of his life. He also served in a somewhat paternal role by sitting with the young boys in the gallery at the Friends' Meeting to keep order.[22] At this time Joseph had no sons of his own, but another daughter, Hannah, was born in 1748.[23]

The religious and ethical ideals of the Friends were not confined to the meeting-house; they were put into practice whenever catastrophe befell one of their members. Such was the case when Preserve Brown's brew house burned down in November 1749. John Smith was one of those who went among the Friends to collect money to aid Brown. From Joseph Richardson he received £3, which, for the silversmith's means, was a generous contribution and reflected his staunch adherence to Quaker ideals.[24]

Joseph's contribution might have been even more generous had he not been completing repairs on his house at the time. The shop which he was using was in need of repair, and Joseph decided to pull the building down and begin anew. At the same time, Joseph had the carpenter put some new windows in the house and make minor repairs in the coalhouse in back.[25] Joseph also acquired a summer home, named "Down the Neck," in Germantown; he was following the example of English gentry, as did many Quakers who escaped from Philadelphia in the heat of summer.[26]

The investments Joseph Richardson was making in property in these mid-century years are attributable to the particular importance Quakers attached to property. Because Friends considered property rights absolute, it was natural that much of their wealth should be invested in this inviolable form.[27] To safeguard their investments, many Quakers encouraged the establishment of a fire insurance company. The Philadelphia Contributionship, also called the Hand-in-Hand Company, was Philadelphia's first such insurance company, and Joseph Richardson was an early policy holder.

As soon as the company was functioning, Joseph insured his home and shop—the house for £225, the back buildings for £75, and his workshop in back of the house for £75.[28] It was wise of him to insure his workshop as well as his house, in light of the all-too-frequent newspaper notices of the period concerning conflagrations caused by the fires in goldsmiths' forges. In addition to the £375 policy on his home and workshop, Joseph also insured the property he bought in fee from the Duchés in Moyamensing Township, a three-story building with a wainscoted stair hall and a two-story kitchen.[29] For this property Joseph paid Anthony Duché and his heirs £8 ground rent each year until his death when the total accumulated rent amounted to £328. The property was finally sold by John Duché, Anthony's heir, to Joseph's children jointly for an additional £125 in Pennsylvania currency.

A second daughter, named Mary after her mother, had been born in 1749, and in 1752, after four years of marriage, Mary presented her husband with his first son, who was named Joseph. Two years later their second son was born and named for Mary's father, Nathaniel Allen.[30]

It has been thought that Joseph added to his activities at this time a new role as one of the Managers of the Pennsylvania Hospital.[31] However, although Joseph continued his contributions, and although his brother Frank was chosen to inspect and judge the election of the Managers and Treasurer of the Hospital, it was the other Joseph Richardson, the merchant, who became Manager in 1756.[32] Joseph the goldsmith was aware of the confusion that might arise when two people of the same name lived in the same city, for he wrote to Daniel Mildred in London that "as theire is a merchant in this city of my name I would have the letters directed . . . to Joseph Richardson Goldsmith."[33]

At this time, Joseph was engaged in an important project concerning the Quakers' dealings with the Indians. For a number of years, relations between the colonists and the Indians in the western part of Pennsylvania had been deteriorating. The treaty negotiated by William Penn had preserved their friendship for three generations. It was, as Voltaire said, "the only treaty between these peoples and the Christians which was not sworn to and which has not been broken."[34] But when the newer settlers began to till the fertile lands which belonged to the Indians and which the Proprietors of Pennsylvania had not yet bought, the bond of friendship was severely strained. In 1737, the Delaware Indians, who had ceded all claims to land northwest of the Delaware River "as far as a man could walk in a day and a half," were enraged when the Proprietors enlarged this area by using their fastest runners to "walk it off" (clearing the paths before them to assure more rapid progress). A bribe of £300 persuaded the ruling body of the Six Nations to force the Delawares to leave the newly claimed area; the Delawares left, but not without great animosity. When the Albany Conference of 1754 allowed the Proprietors to purchase more land west of the Susquehanna without even consulting the tribes involved, the mounting tension broke out in violent attacks by the Indians on the unprotected settlers in outlying districts. Those who survived these massacres made frantic appeals to the Pennsylvania Assembly for protection.[35]

These circumstances presented the Quakers with a dilemma which eventually contributed to their loss of political control in the Assembly. Realizing the dangers involved to their people, but at the same time firmly believing that participation in war was evil, Quaker legislators hesitated to send arms to the outposts. They tried to win back the friendship of the Delawares with gifts and concessions, but these once-persuasive techniques were no longer effective. When the aroused populace forced the Assembly to declare a state of war in 1756, the true Quakers, being unalterably opposed to war, followed the dictates of conscience and resigned their government positions. Thus the Quaker majority in the Assembly and their dominance in Philadelphia were forever lost.

Trying to alleviate the situation with the Indians, a large group of Quakers, "from a consideration of the necessity of regaining and preserving the Friendship of the Indians who were the native Inhabitants of this Country," formed The Friendly Association of Regaining and Preserving Peace with the Indians by Pacific Measures.[36] Joseph and several of his relatives were members of this association and signed notes for money lent to the Commissioners for Indian Affairs for the Province of Pennsylvania.

The Friendly Association commissioned Joseph Richardson in 1756 and 1757 to make silver ornaments "for presents for the Indians." Of the thousands of objects which the Commissioners gave to the Indians, Joseph made a total of 2,860 items, including arm bands, wrist bands, hair plates, earbobs, hairbobs, brooches, crosses, gorgets, moons, and rings (see pp. 140–141 and *Figs. 124, 125*). For his labor, Joseph received in 1757 two payments of over £130 each.[37]

The Richardsons' financial situation was further enriched by Mary's inheritance of money, household goods, and property, when her father died in December 1757.[38] Soon after this, on January 29, 1758, Joseph increased his property holdings by buying from his brother and sister-in-law, a lot on the bank of the Delaware River on Water Street for which he paid £900.[39]

The year 1758 also brought the birth of Mary and Joseph's fifth and last child.[40] She was named Rebecca, presumably for Joseph's grandmother.

All this time Joseph's activities as a member of the Society of Friends never ceased. One of the duties of the meeting fell under the title of the "Gospel Order."[41] This basis for discipline was derived from Matthew 18:15-17:

> Moreover if thy brother shall trespass against thee, go and tell him his fault between thee and him alone; if he shall hear thee, thou hast gained thy brother. But if he will not hear thee, then take thee one or two more, that in the mouth of two or three witnesses every word may be established. And if he shall neglect to hear them, tell it unto the church; but if he neglect to hear the church, let him be unto thee as an heathen man and a publican.

From this admonition was developed the Quaker practice of resolving disputes outside the law court and within the meeting. Because of their desire to follow the "Word," and to keep their members from public incrimination, the Quakers provided for personal discussions, hearings, and amicable settlements through the mediation of neutral Friends. Joseph served as an impartial Friend many times. In 1759, when young Hannah Holcomb went off with the army and produced a child, but not a husband, Joseph was appointed to investigate the situation and, if necessary, to prepare testimony against her.[42]

In the 1760's, a reformation movement developed among the Friends, in which the Quaker spokesman John Woolman played a major role, Many Quakers felt that, because of the increasing prosperity of Friends who were unusually successful in their business enterprises, they were straying from their original ideal of the simple life. One logical result was the closer regulation of the members of the Society, illustrated by the more stringent action accorded those who married out of meeting. When James Warner married out of meeting in 1760, and James Coffee, in 1761, Joseph Richardson was one of the members appointed to speak with them in the hope that they would condemn their own actions and, by recanting, be readmitted to the fellowship of the Friends.[43] Not infrequently, Friends were "read out of meeting" for an action which they later renounced, and in some instances they were read out and reinstated more than once. It is to his credit that Joseph never incurred the displeasure of the Society of Friends but remained a member of the meeting through his life.

In the spring of 1760, Joseph's maternal aunt, Grace Lloyd of Chester, died. Her only child, a son, had died at an early age, and she had no immediate heirs. That she was fond of her nephew is evident from an affectionate letter she had written to him several years before *(Fig. 20)*. It is not surprising, therefore, that she provided generously for Joseph and his family, giving his daughters some of her plate and household goods, and Joseph a large property in Chester, as well as £200.[44]

Perhaps because he was the elder nephew, Frank Richardson received an even larger part of her estate. It appears that he received more than he wanted, for he sold a portion of his inheritance to Joseph for a token sum. An indenture was drawn up on August 16, 1760, between Frank and Joseph for two lots willed by Grace Lloyd to Frank, for 5 shillings sterling, "hereby acknowledged as of the brotherly love and affection which he the said Francis now hath and doth bear the said Joseph."[45]

In this same year Joseph Richardson and several other Philadelphia silversmiths joined together in a shipping venture to Guadeloupe. The particulars of this venture are unknown, but those participating included Daniel Dupuy, William Ball, John Leacock, Edmund Milne, and James Satterthwaite. David Harper, a former apprentice of Joseph (see pp. 64, 65) was in charge of the goods which these investors shipped. One of the rich islands of the French West Indies, Guadeloupe had been captured by the British in 1759 and was held by them for four years. It was logical that the colonists should try to take advantage of this trading area. Other Philadelphians had engaged in trade to the French islands when it was illegal during wars with France, and the Society of Friends warned its meeting against being tempted by the great profits which lay in this illicit trade. Only while it was legal did Joseph Richardson sign over to Harper a bond for £120 Pennsylvania currency for the Guadeloupe venture.[46]

The money was signed over on August 7, 1760; in the next few months arrangements were made for shipping flour to this island, and David Harper set out on the voyage. Unfortunately he became ill on the way. On February 4, 1761, he wrote to Philadelphia:

> St. Anns Grantare February the 4th 1761
> Brother Benjamin Harbeson this Voigh [Voyage] is much Longer then Every one concarned Expected, but hope if Will Turne out A Proffit to every one. There is not half the Flower Sold, What is Sold is att a Large Proffit but the Remainder Will fech but little Profit. I have not had one Days Helth Since We Left

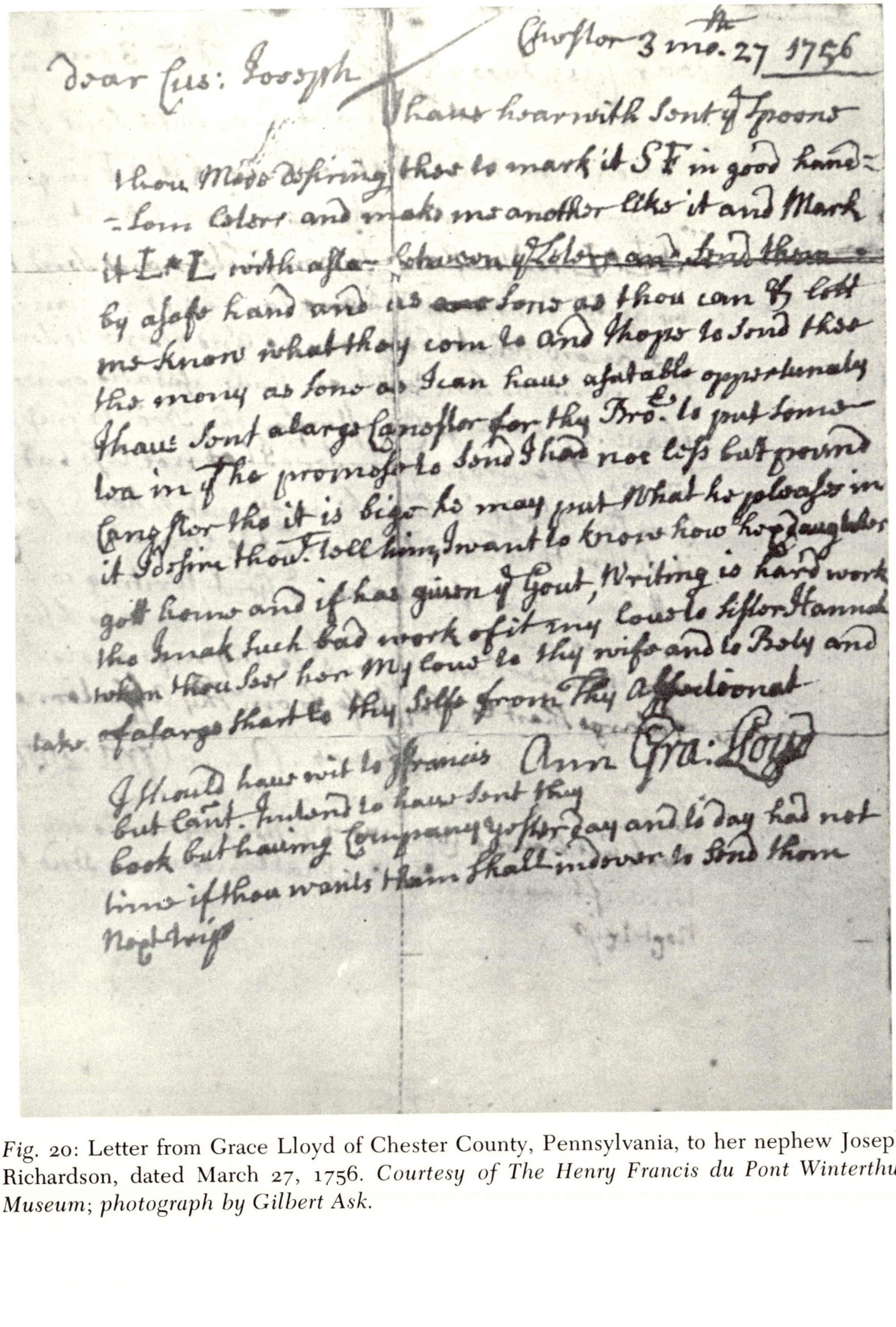

Fig. 20: Letter from Grace Lloyd of Chester County, Pennsylvania, to her nephew Joseph Richardson, dated March 27, 1756. *Courtesy of The Henry Francis du Pont Winterthur Museum; photograph by Gilbert Ask.*

the Capes of Dellower [Delaware]. I got A bad Could Comming Downe the River Which I am Sencible Will be the Death of me. It is fixed on my lungs and I have a Continuel Coffing and Grone A near Skelloton and am Obliged to Live on bread and milk this Month and more.

Your Loving Brother
David Harper.[47]

Harper never returned from this trip, and the investments of the silversmiths had to be returned out of his estate. Joseph Richardson, his former master, was appointed administrator of his estate in April 1761, and that autumn paid back, at least in part, the money which had been invested.[48]

By this time Joseph was a recognized leader among the Friends. Although the organization of the Society was not formal, there were positions of leadership to be filled by members chosen by the group, but no specific training was required for them. Joseph was named overseer of "the Burial Ground" in 1762. On November 26, 1762, he was appointed to a special nineteen-man committee whose purpose was part of the attempt at reformation. The culmination of his service in the Society of Friends came in 1764, with his appointment as an overseer of the meeting, a most esteemed position.[49]

These and other concerns of Friends and Philadelphians were suddenly forgotten in 1765, when the Stamp Act was proclaimed. Previous encroachments upon American liberties had affected only a small part of the population, but this act struck at many groups. The newspapers took the lead in denouncing the measure, and in large part were responsible for stirring the public to more serious action. New York led the protest by agreeing not to import any British goods, and by resolving to increase the production of American goods.[50] On October 25, 1765, Philadelphia framed its own Non-Importation Agreement, and among its many supporters were both Joseph Richardson, goldsmith, and Joseph Richardson, merchant.[51]

The Stamp Act was repealed on March 18, 1766, as announced in a special supplement of the *Pennsylvania Gazette* the next day. From the time he had signed the agreement until the repeal, Joseph stopped his importation of silver goods from England. On June 4, 1766, he wrote to the British firm of Masterman & Archer, with whom he had done a great deal of business:

Trade is & has been at Low ebb among us for some time Past but hope the Repeal of the Stamp act will be a means of Uniting the Colonies in a more close Union with their Brethren in England than Ever which Event I hope will be

> Productive of much Good & Calls for Thankfulness to the Supreem Disposer of all things & Gratitude to the King & Parliment of Great Briton. A Dutyfull Address is Now Prepareing by our Assembly to the King on the Occasion.

Later, when things seemed to be getting worse and the Townshend Acts of 1767 were enacted, he wrote them:

> an Invoice for a Parcell of Goods which I Desire may be Shipt per first Convenient opportunity Provideed the Act of Parliment for Laying a Duty on Glass, Painters Coulers Should be Repeald which it is hoped will be at the Next Setting of Parliment but if these Acts are Not Repealed & a General Exportation of Goods from London to America Doth Not take Place I would Not have thee to Ship any thing to me [52]

Nonimportation was only part of Joseph's participation in the colonists' program. Supporting the encouragement of domestic manufacturing to increase American economic independence from Great Britain, Joseph joined with a group of men in Philadelphia to establish a linen manufactory. As part of his agreement of copartnership, Joseph subscribed £100 toward the joint stock of the company and thus became a shareholder in the manufactory.[53]

Joseph's importation of silver objects from England had increased his retail trade, and the British acts and the nonimportation agreements obviously affected his business adversely. Moreover, because the craft of the silversmith was encouraged by the demands of wealthy merchants with an excess of coins, it was natural that a diminution of their profits eventually resulted in a decrease in Richardson's business. That he was able to withstand such reverses is testimony to his business acumen. He was able to outbid everyone at the sale of a lot in Moyamensing Township on March 10, 1766, paying the substantial sum of £563/12/6.[54]

Joseph continued to share the fruits of his prosperity with those in need. When collections were made by the Society of Friends for the support of the poor, Joseph contributed 2 shillings every month for many years. When the meeting became burdened by debts, Joseph contributed money himself, and his name heads the list of Friends who visited members of their Society to collect funds.[55] In all his activity in the Society of Friends, Joseph Richardson remained true to the precepts of the Quaker rule and practised his beliefs through untiring service. Even when the meeting denounced his nephew for vain and lavish living, he stood fast, and finally brought about a reconciliation.[56]

By 1770, Joseph had both of his sons working in his shop as apprentices. During the apprenticeship which usually lasted five to seven years, he provided their training in his craft and supplied their daily needs. Schooling also was provided, and it is known that Joseph, Jr., was sent to the Friends Public School attended by the sons of many of the wealthy Quaker merchants.[57]

At this time, shipments of silver from England had again been cut off, and according to his letter book, Joseph wrote in October 1770 to John Masterman in London that, since the nonimportation agreement was still in effect, he had "No Expectation of trade being Opened untill the Duty on tea is also taken off." This was Philadelphia's reaction to the act which had caused the Tea Party in Boston. Four months later, however, he wrote again to his friend: "As the Merchants of this City hath Concluded to import any kind of Goods from England except Tea or such other Goods as may hereafter be Charg'd with a Duty Provided they are not Shipt before the 15th of the first Month next, I have therefore herewith sent an Order for a Parcel of Plate."[58]

During this period, the Friends continued their reformation. In 1772, Joseph and Mary Richardson were again affected by this movement when Mary's brother, Nathaniel Allen, was read out of meeting "for using strong Liquors to excess whereby he has been led into unprofitable Company and neglected his business."[59] Evidently Nathaniel never repented his actions, for his name does not appear in subsequent records of the meeting.

Problems of poverty in Philadelphia were increased at this time by the continuous influx of immigrants. Whereas Christopher Sauer had been able to write in 1724, "There are people who have been living here 40 years and have not seen a beggar in Philadelphia," the question of poor relief was now pressing.[60] In 1765 and 1766, new acts were passed by the Assembly to meet the needs of large-scale accommodation of the poor. The managers of the almshouse were authorized to buy a large area of land and to erect a new building which would more adequately care for their people. In order to meet the financial demands of the new program, the Assembly gave the managers the power to sell the old property. Apparently the general financial conditions in Philadelphia in 1767 left no one who could afford to buy the property, and the Assembly again had to carry the burden of the project. Finally, in 1772, Joseph Richardson found himself able to buy some of this property. The four lots that he bought cost £632 and were on the north side of Pine Street near Fourth Street and on the south side of Spruce Street, also near Fourth Street, in a section of town known as City Almshouse Square.[61]

Joseph's expenditures during this year included his continued contribution to the Pennsylvania Hospital and a new investment in the lighthouse at Cape Henlopen. The lighthouse was of great interest to many of the merchants in Philadelphia, for ships carrying goods to and from the city sailed past Cape Henlopen and relied on its beacon. It was probably this business interest that prompted Joseph to give the 6 per cent interest on a £250 certificate for the Henlopen light.[62]

By this time Joseph's sons were coming of age. In 1772, Joseph, Jr., was twenty and Nathaniel was eighteen, and within three years both of them would complete their apprenticeship. Accordingly, Joseph began preparing for their future. He was allowed to assign his share in the Library Company to Nathaniel, and he had the Front Street workshop rebuilt to provide rooms upstairs in which the two young men could live.

It was not, however, an auspicious moment for the boys to be setting up business. The Revolution was gaining momentum in the Colonies, and the first order for silver which the two new silversmiths sent to London remained unfilled.[63] The plight of a Quaker family in Philadelphia at this time was complex. Like Joseph, most of the Quaker merchants had participated in the struggle against oppression from Great Britain by joining in the early nonviolent methods of protest. But when it came to armed opposition, their strong pacifist beliefs took precedence over their affiliation with the Whigs in support of the ideals of liberty and property, and they found it necessary to refuse allegiance to the Revolutionary cause. As frequently happens in wartime, such pacifism was sometimes misinterpreted as disloyalty, and members of the Society of Friends more outspoken than Joseph were accused of being Tories. There was a certain fiscal advantage in the rebels' charging some of the most prosperous Quakers with disloyalty, for it meant that their property could be confiscated and added to the coffers of the Revolutionary cause.

Joseph evidently followed a quiet and unobtrusive course of neutrality, thereby escaping such harsh treatment. Danger was present, however, and early in 1777 one of his friends wrote to offer him a refuge at Maiden Creek: "If thou should think it prudent to remove some part of thy family, if not the whole, as I understand that some friends are not Inclinable to Leave their habitations, but if thou should be of a Different mind please to make free, & look for no further Invitation."[64] But Joseph and his family chose to remain in Philadelphia. They were still there when General Howe and his troops occupied the city. Somehow they had escaped the distrust of the Whigs, who sent some of the Quakers to Winchester, Virginia, when the British army approached the city.

Because of this incarceration of Friends, in December 1776, a committee was formed by the Society to give them aid, and on July 25, 1777, Joseph was appointed to serve on it.[65] Other humanitarian efforts on the part of the Friends continued in spite of the war, and in 1779 they began waging a campaign against the holding of slaves. Joseph Richardson and Jacob Shoemaker were appointed to visit Richard Wistar to convince him that he should not delay the manumissions which he had executed for three Negroes belonging to him.[66] Joseph himself had inherited from his father a slave named Herford.[67] Although it is not known at what time Herford died or was released, it is certain that Joseph did not hold slaves later, for no records show his support of such "property."

During the war period, Joseph, Jr., was married to Ruth Hoskins in Burlington, New Jersey, in 1780, and in 1781 Mary Richardson and Samuel Taylor announced in monthly meeting their intentions of being married. Her mother had been unable to come and so sent her approval to the meeting through Joseph, who also gave consent. The children had been provided with some means by their aunts. Hannah Allen divided her property and silver among them so that each of the children had at least one lot of land. Hannah Growden also gave one half of her estate to the children.[68]

After the treaty of peace was signed between Great Britain and the United States, Joseph, Jr., and Nathaniel renewed their father's correspondence with John Masterman in London which had been terminated at the beginning of the war. In October 1784, it was their unpleasant duty to inform this English friend that "our truly worthy Father whom you have so often kindly noticed quietly departed this life in the 74th year of his age having been gradually wasting ever since the latter part of last winter."[69] On October 4, 1784, Joseph was buried in the Friends Burial Ground in a "walnut riged coffin with tinned handles," made by the well-known Quaker cabinetmaker, William Savery.[70]

Although there were evidently no published obituaries of Joseph Richardson to summarize his career and give a contemporary appraisal of his life, it is possible, from the facts now known about him, to conclude that he was a man of steadfast character and goodness. Although he never held public office of great importance, family anecdotes such as those recorded by Juliana R. Wood reveal him to be a man of "marked excellence and uprightness."[71]

Every aspect of Joseph Richardson's life bespeaks his Quaker heritage.

Strength of character and adherence to principle are distinctive of those who accept the religion of the Society of Friends. Joseph also followed the pattern of the eighteenth-century Quaker in his professional success, becoming one of the outstanding goldsmiths in Philadelphia and all the Colonies. Conforming to the Quaker tradition, he invested his profits in valuable real estate, in trading ventures, and in manufacturing. As was expected of prosperous Friends, he gave unstintingly to worthy causes, to the poor in general, and to needy individuals in particular.

Although he opposed the use of arms, he was a proponent of individual liberties, and supported the Revolutionary cause until it reached the point of war. That he was able to continue to live in Philadelphia during these troublesome times without engendering the wrath of either the American Whigs or the British is evidence of his quiet and uncontroversial nature. His beliefs extended to every aspect of his life and can be seen in relatively inconsequential matters, such as his refraining from making silver vessels for use in the communion service which Quakers denounced, or swords, the use of which he opposed. More than this, though, his actual participation in the Friends' meeting and in their causes is indicative of his being a Friend in action as well as in spirit. Here his career is exemplary, for unlike some of his peers, his personal life was never corrupted by his financial success.

CHAPTER 4

Joseph Richardson: His House and Shop

LIKE many eighteenth-century American goldsmiths, Joseph Richardson conducted his business in his home. Today, a warehouse stands on the site of his Front Street property. No contemporary representations of Joseph Richardson's house and shop are known, but it is possible to visualize the appearance of the property from descriptions of similar houses in Philadelphia as well as from accounts of changes made to the house, the inventory of his estate, *(Fig. 21, 22)* and the insurance survey made of his property in 1752.[1]

Built close to the street, probably sharing a common wall with an identical house next door, and undoubtedly made of local brick, the goldsmith's house followed the common town house plan of a small three-story building, one room wide. In the entrance hall were four fire buckets kept in a convenient place in case of emergency.[2]

The first room one entered was the showroom. Little more than a waiting room, it was sparsely furnished with a coal grate to ward off the chill, a brass coal shovel, a fender, and pokers. Five ordinary chairs placed around the room and two framed maps on the walls relieved the starkness of this receiving area. Being a good Quaker, Joseph did not indulge in ostentation in his home. The maps and a few looking glasses were the only wall decorations. There were no paintings in any of the rooms. The most important objects in the showroom naturally were those for sale; these included a large number of scales and weights, spectacles, and objects wrought of silver and gold. Most

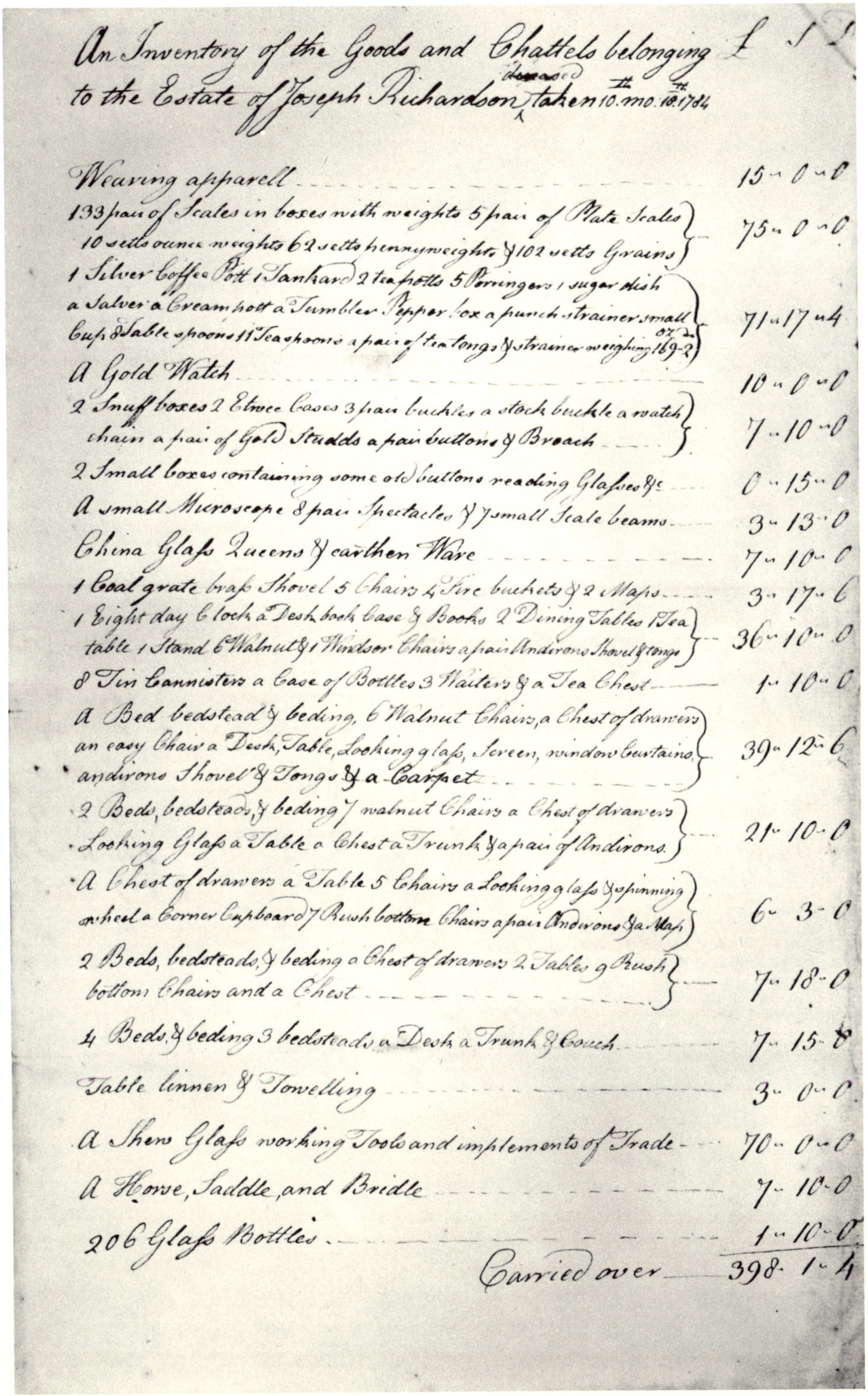

An Inventory of the Goods and Chattels belonging to the Estate of Joseph Richardson deceased taken 10 mo. 10th 1784

	£ s d
Wearing apparell	15 – 0 – 0
133 pair of Scales in boxes with weights 5 pair of Plate Scales 10 setts ounce weights 62 setts pennyweights & 102 setts Grains	75 – 0 – 0
1 Silver Coffee Pott 1 Tankard 2 tea potts 5 Porringers 1 sugar dish a Salver a Cream pott a Tumbler Pepper box a punch strainer small Cup 8 Table spoons 11 Tea spoons a pair of tea tongs & strainer weighing 189 oz	71 – 17 – 4
A Gold Watch	10 – 0 – 0
2 Snuff boxes 2 Etwee Cases 3 pair buckles a stock buckle a watch chain a pair of Gold Studds a pair buttons & Broach	7 – 10 – 0
2 Small boxes containing some old buttons reading Glasses &c	0 – 15 – 0
A small Microscope 8 pair Spectacles & 7 small Scale beams	3 – 13 – 0
China Glass Queens & earthen Ware	7 – 10 – 0
1 Coal grate brass Shovel 5 Chairs 4 Fire buckets & 2 Maps	3 – 17 – 6
1 Eight day Clock a Desk book Case & Books 2 Dining Tables 1 Tea table 1 Stand 6 Walnut & 1 Windsor Chairs a pair Andirons Shovel & tongs	36 – 10 – 0
8 Tin Cannisters a Case of Bottles 3 Waiters & a Tea Chest	1 – 10 – 0
A Bed bedstead & beding, 6 Walnut Chairs, a Chest of drawers an easy Chair a Desk, Table, Looking glass, Screen, window Curtains, andirons Shovel & Tongs & a Carpet	39 – 12 – 6
2 Beds, bedsteads, & beding 7 walnut Chairs a Chest of drawers Looking Glass a Table a Chest a Trunk & pair of Andirons	21 – 10 – 0
A Chest of drawers a Table 5 Chairs a Looking glass & spinning wheel a Corner Cupboard 7 Rush bottom Chairs a pair Andirons & a Map	6 – 3 – 0
2 Beds, bedsteads, & beding a Chest of drawers 2 Tables 9 Rush bottom Chairs and a Chest	7 – 18 – 0
4 Beds & beding 3 bedsteads a Desk a Trunk & Couch	7 – 15 – 0
Table linnen & Towelling	3 – 0 – 0
A Shew Glass working Tools and implements of Trade	70 – 0 – 0
A Horse, Saddle, and Bridle	7 – 10 – 0
206 Glass Bottles	1 – 10 – 0
Carried over	398 – 1 – 4

Figs. 21–22: Inventory of Joseph Richardson's estate, taken in 1784. *Courtesy of The Henry Francis du Pont Winterthur Museum; photograph by Gilbert Ask.*

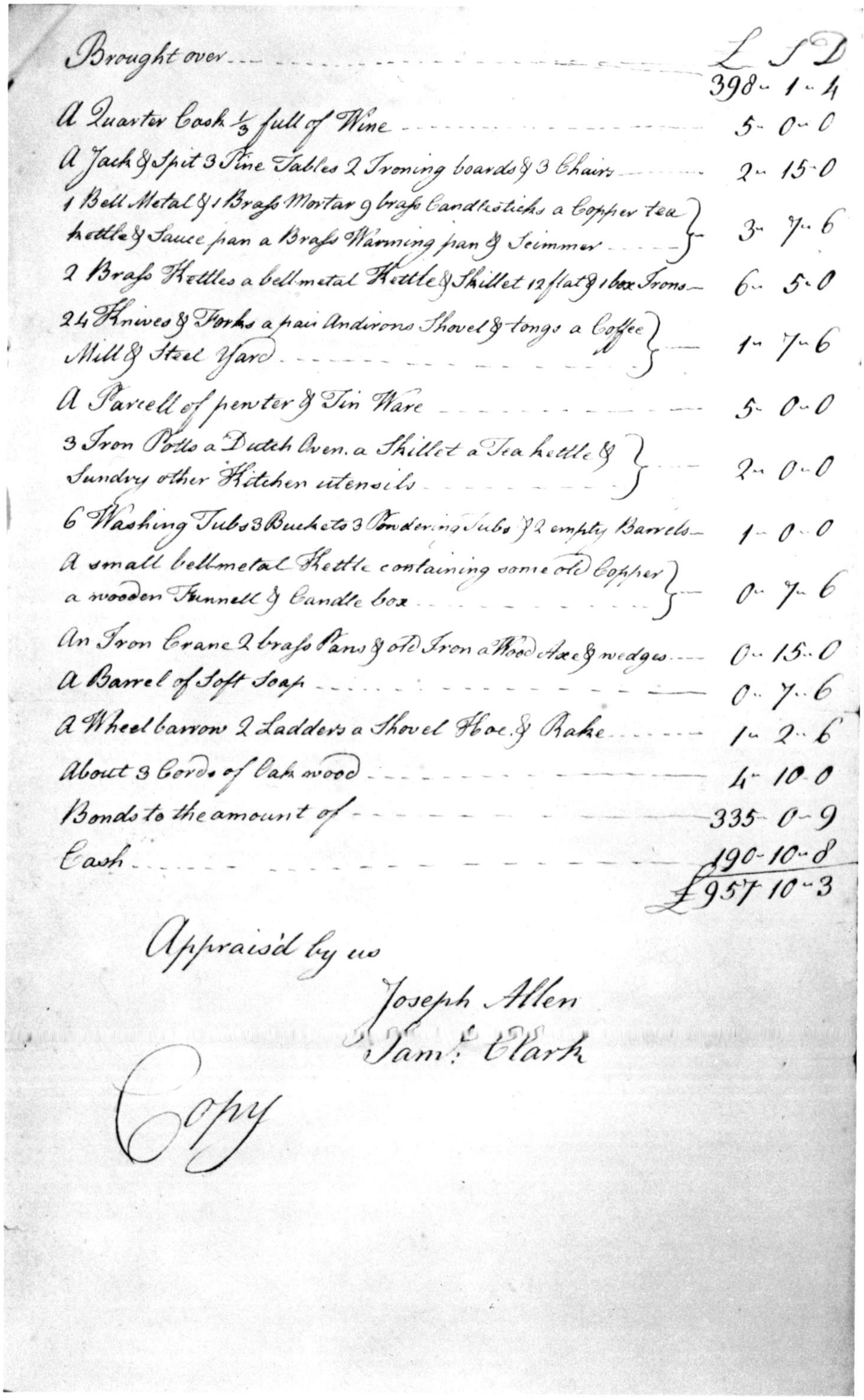

Brought over	£ s d
	398 - 1 - 4
A Quarter Cask ⅔ full of Wine	5 - 0 - 0
A Jack & Spit 3 Pine Tables 2 Ironing boards & 3 Chairs	2 - 15 - 0
1 Bell Metal & 1 Brass Mortar 9 brass Candlesticks a Copper tea kettle & Sauce pan a Brass Warming pan & Scimmer	3 - 7 - 6
2 Brass Kettles a bellmetal Kettle & Skillet 12 flat & 1 box Irons	6 - 5 - 0
24 Knives & Forks a pair Andirons Shovel & tongs a Coffee Mill & Steel Yard	1 - 7 - 6
A Parcell of pewter & Tin Ware	5 - 0 - 0
3 Iron Potts a Dutch Oven a Skillet a Tea kettle & Sundry other Kitchen utensils	2 - 0 - 0
6 Washing Tubs 3 Buckets 3 Pondering Tubs & 2 empty Barrels	1 - 0 - 0
A small bellmetal Kettle containing some old Copper a wooden Funnell & Candle box	0 - 7 - 6
An Iron Crane 2 brass Pans & old Iron a Wood Axe & wedges	0 - 15 - 0
A Barrel of Soft Soap	0 - 7 - 6
A Wheelbarrow 2 Ladders a Shovel Hoe & Rake	1 - 2 - 6
About 3 Cords of oak wood	4 - 10 - 0
Bonds to the amount of	335 - 0 - 9
Cash	190 - 10 - 8
	£957 - 10 - 3

Appraisd by us

   Joseph Allen

   Saml Clark

Copy

Fig. 22.

of the objects were small popular items, such as buttons, buckles, and spoons.

Behind the showroom was a combined living-and-dining room. The family clock in its tall case stood against one wall.[3] Against another was an imposing walnut desk,[4] the closed upper section containing Joseph's books. A plain but elegant piece of furniture, it had a flat, molded cornice above two simply paneled doors and was supported by molded bracket feet; in the lower section were four drawers and a slant-top writing section, where Joseph worked, probably sitting in the Windsor armchair. In the room were two dining tables, as well as a walnut tea table and a little stand. Scattered around the room were six walnut chairs which could be drawn up to the table when dinner was served.

The most impressive room in the house, however, was the second-floor master bedroom, which apparently served as a sitting room. The two windows looking out on Front Street were hung with curtains (the only window curtains in the house), and a large four-poster bed was also hung with curtains and decorated with a wooden cornice at the top. Instead of the usual bare floors, there was a carpet, probably one of the bright Turkey carpets popular at the time, or an English carpet. In front of the fireplace, where the brass knob andirons reflected the fire, was the only easy chair in the house, with a firescreen as protection from the heat of the fire. There was another desk in this room, perhaps the one shown in *Figure 23*, a looking glass, a chest of drawers, a chamber table, and half a dozen side chairs—all of walnut but the looking glass.[5] It seems unusual today for the master bedroom—and not the downstairs parlor—to be the most elegant room in the house, but in Joseph's day this was not uncommon and it is likely that Joseph and Mary Richardson used this room for entertaining guests.

Behind this was another, less elaborate bedroom. The two beds probably had low posts, for there were no bed-curtains. A looking glass hung over the walnut chest of drawers or the walnut chamber table. At the foot of one of the beds was a storage trunk, and at the foot of the other bed, a walnut blanket chest with molded hinged top and two drawers with pierced brass pulls in the base.[6] Seven walnut chairs, one of which was a close stool, were placed around the room.

In back of these bedrooms, probably above the kitchen, was a room which may have served for family dining. More simply furnished than the other rooms, its most prominent feature was the bulky spinning wheel used by Mary Richardson and her daughters. A corner cupboard held the family glass

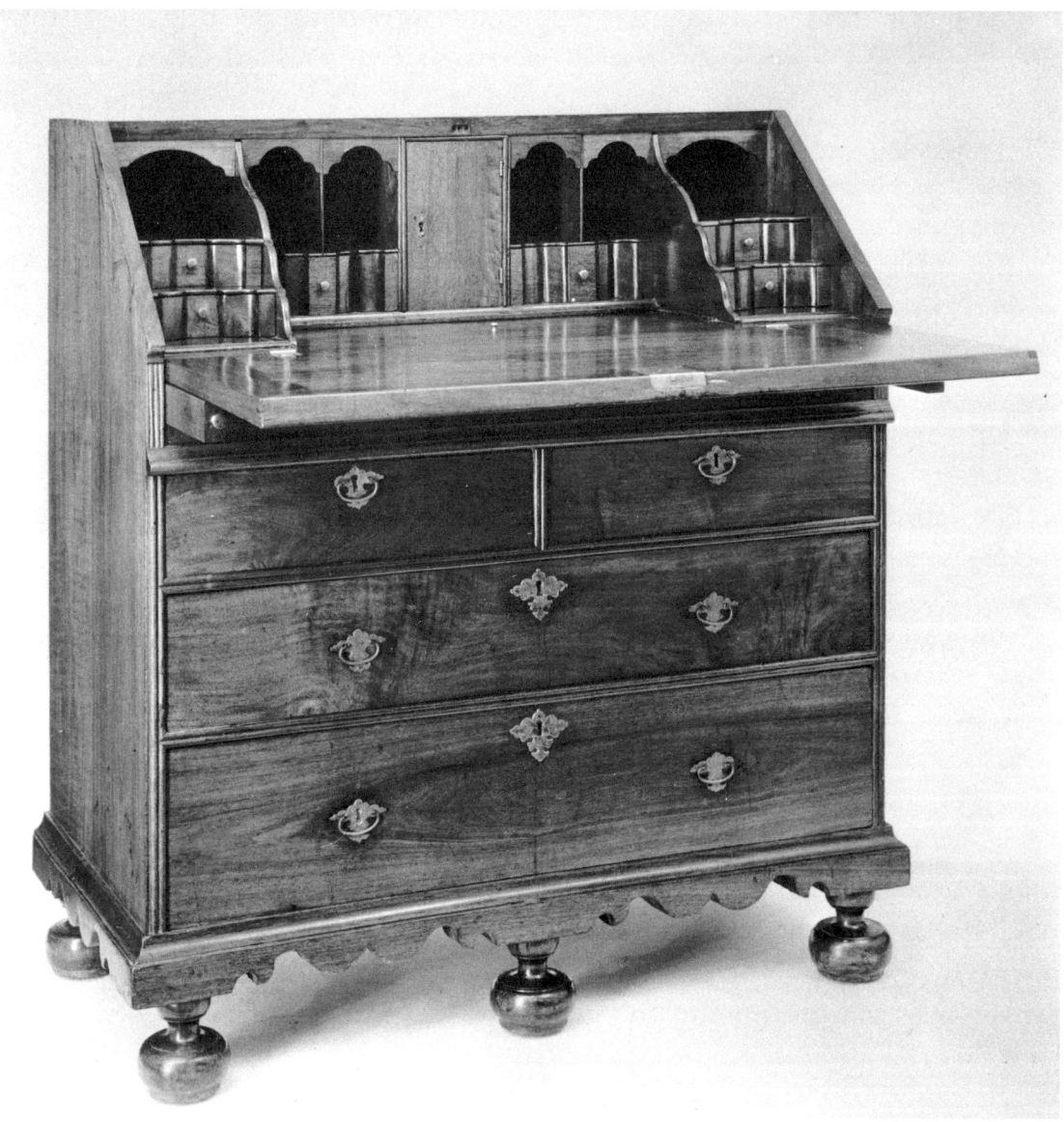

Fig. 23: Walnut slant-top desk, *c.* 1740, believed to have been owned by Joseph Richardson. *Courtesy of The Henry Francis du Pont Winterthur Museum; photograph by Gilbert Ask.*

and china, while the linens were stored in a chest of drawers. There were also a large walnut dining table and a dozen walnut chairs (including seven which were rush-bottomed and one armchair). In addition, the room contained a looking glass and a map.

Over the workshop at the back of the house was a second-floor bedroom occupied by Joseph, Jr., and Nathaniel. Here there were two beds (one a high-post bed with a set of green bed-curtains), two chests, two tables, and nine rush-bottom chairs.

The third floor of the house was furnished with hand-me-down pieces. The old "Kaine Kouch" bought by Joseph's father, Francis, in Boston in 1704 was here, as well as an old oak desk, a large leather trunk, and three bedsteads.

The kitchen was at the back of the house; in fact, in many Philadelphia houses of the day, the kitchen was a separate building connected to the main house by a piazza.[7] Its most imposing feature was a large open fireplace. Meat could be roasted in the Dutch oven or on the spit which was turned by a weight suspended from a clock-like mechanism called a jack. About the room were washing tubs, ironing boards, and powdering tubs. There were three pine tables (one painted), three side chairs, and the usual pots and pans, kettles and skillets, knives and forks, mortars and pestles, a coffee mill, and a steelyard. The family pewter and tinware was kept in this room, as were the warming pans which were carried to the bedrooms at night.

The dishes (including a set of English Queensware, made popular by Wedgwood), bottles and other glassware, three waiters or trays, a tea chest, and tin canisters were stored away in the closets which Joseph had added in the 1750's. Here too, he may have kept his own silver plate (totaling in value £71/17/4), including a coffeepot, two teapots, a sugar dish, a creampot, a salver, a pair of tea tongs, and a strainer, all of which were later listed in Mary Richardson's inventory. Also included was a pint tankard which he later gave to his daughter Elizabeth along with one of his five porringers and two of his eight tablespoons. The rest of his silver consisted of a tumbler, a pepper box, a punch strainer, a small cup, and eleven teaspoons. The total weight of the silver was 169 oz. 2 dwt.; much of it was undoubtedly made by Joseph.

Personal items, such as a gold watch valued £10 which Joseph bequeathed to Nathaniel, and a watch chain, snuffboxes, etui cases, gold studs, buckles, buttons, and a brooch worth a total of £7/10/0 may have included a few items of his own handiwork. He also had a small microscope, and evidently he wore glasses upon occasion, as a pair of reading glasses is also listed among his possessions.

How widely Joseph read is not known, although he was a member of the Library Company of Philadelphia. At his death he owned books and pamphlets valued at £15, but only three of the titles in addition to the family Bible are known. These are preserved among the family papers at Winterthur. All three were works popular among Quakers and were written by Friends: John Foxe's *The Third Volume of the Ecclesiastical Historie* (London, 1631); *The Journal of the Life of Thomas Story* (Newcastle-upon-Tyne, 1747), and *Useful Miscellanies or Serious Reflections, Respecting Mens Duty to God and One Towards Another* (Philadelphia, 1753). From these titles it would appear that Joseph took to heart the advice of William Penn that books, whether religious or civil, should be few, "well chosen, and well read."[8] Much earlier, about 1725, when he was beginning his apprenticeship Joseph had asked his friend Samuel Powel to buy some books for him in England, *(Fig. 24)*.[9] These included "an alphabet Cypher book to Engrave by,"[10] "a book of Drafts to Draw by," and a book "to Ingrave Snuff boxes."

Joseph's shop at the back of the house was valued for insurance purposes at £75.[11] The shop and its garret were finished inside as a house might have been, with baseboards, moldings, paneling around the windows and under the staircase, and nineteen feet of architrave.[12] The dominant feature of the shop was the large brick forge supplied with coals from the coalhouse behind. The open furnace, operated by a huge overhead bellows, provided the heat needed by the goldsmith to anneal the metal as he worked it.[13]

Another prominent feature of the shop was the glass showcase in which Joseph displayed some of his smaller finished objects.[14] Spoons were among the items most frequently kept in the glass cases, as were buckles, buttons, clasps, thimbles, chains, tea tongs, strainers, and whistles and bells. In his commonplace book, under the headings of "account of Silver in the Case" and "Account of Sailes out of the Glass Case," Joseph also listed studs and rings, coral necklaces, seals, and snuffboxes *(Appendix A)*.

Joseph's tools and equipment (which, together with the showcase, were valued at £70 at the time of his death) included everything a goldsmith needed to make a piece of gold or silver into a finished, polished object.

Joseph Richardson's procedure in making a tankard for a customer is illustrative of the way in which he worked. First, it can be conjectured, he took the silver ingots, coins, or discarded pieces of plate the customer had

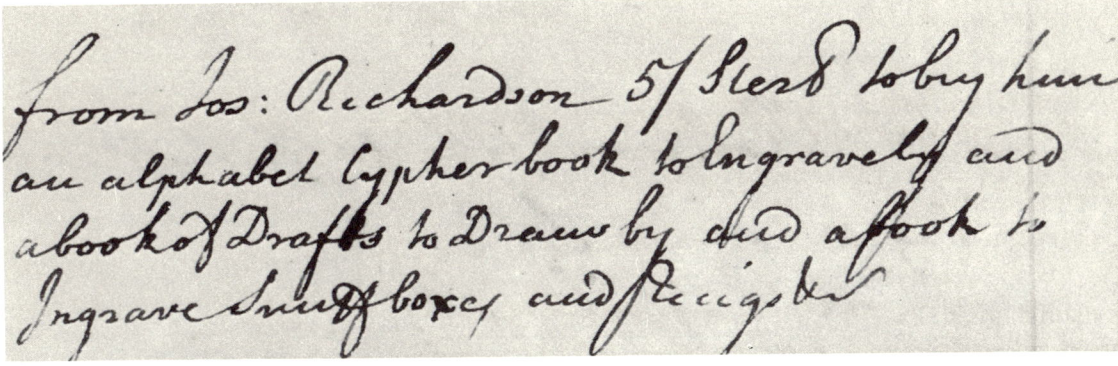

Fig. 24: Entry in invoice book of Samuel Powel of Philadelphia for goods to be purchased in London in 1724-25, noting Joseph Richardson's request for books to engrave and draw by. *Courtesy of The Henry Francis du Pont Winterthur Museum.*

provided him and put them into a pot like one of the "40 black melting pots" he had inherited from his father. When the metal was molten, Joseph added sulphur to refine it and melted it together with steel filings. As the sulphur joined with the iron, the pure metal was left at the bottom of the pot.[15]

Since the pots and crucibles Joseph used in this work were constantly subjected to heat, they had to be replaced regularly. They were bought locally or imported from England.[16] For the next step, assaying the metal *(Fig. 25)*, Joseph used Hessian crucibles, a touchstone and regular scales. Evidently he did not have all the equipment that he would have liked for assaying silver *(Fig. 26)*, for he occasionally sent coarse silver to England to be refined and assayed.[17]

Once the silver was of standard alloy, Joseph poured the molten metal into an ingot mold, where it hardened, and then hammered it into a sheet on a large forging anvil. The anvil was set into a working block, usually a large tree stump which afforded a solid base.[18] It would not move under the heavy blows of a hammer, and the low level at which the anvil was placed eliminated undue strain on the smith's arm. The stump could also be hollowed out in places to provide round depressions into which the silver could be pounded at the beginning of the forging process.

After flattening the silver into a sheet, the smith used his shears to cut out a disc of an appropriate size. For the tankard body he could save time by pouring the molten metal into a round skillet to the thickness and weight desired. The next step was to forge the disc of silver into the body of the tankard. The exact center of this disc was probably marked with a center punch so that, as the piece was hammered up, it could be measured with calipers to ascertain

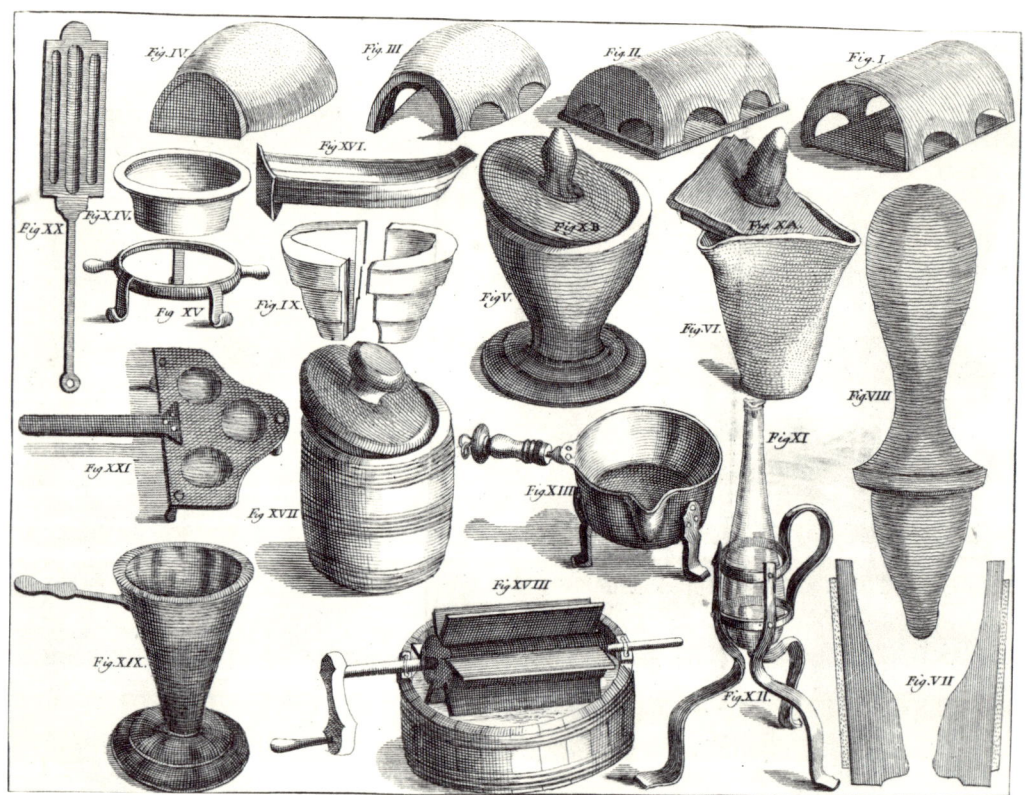

Fig. 25: *Plate II* of Cramer's *Elements of the Art of Assaying Metals*, London, 1741, showing equipment used in preparing metals. *Courtesy of The Henry Francis du Pont Winterthur Museum.*

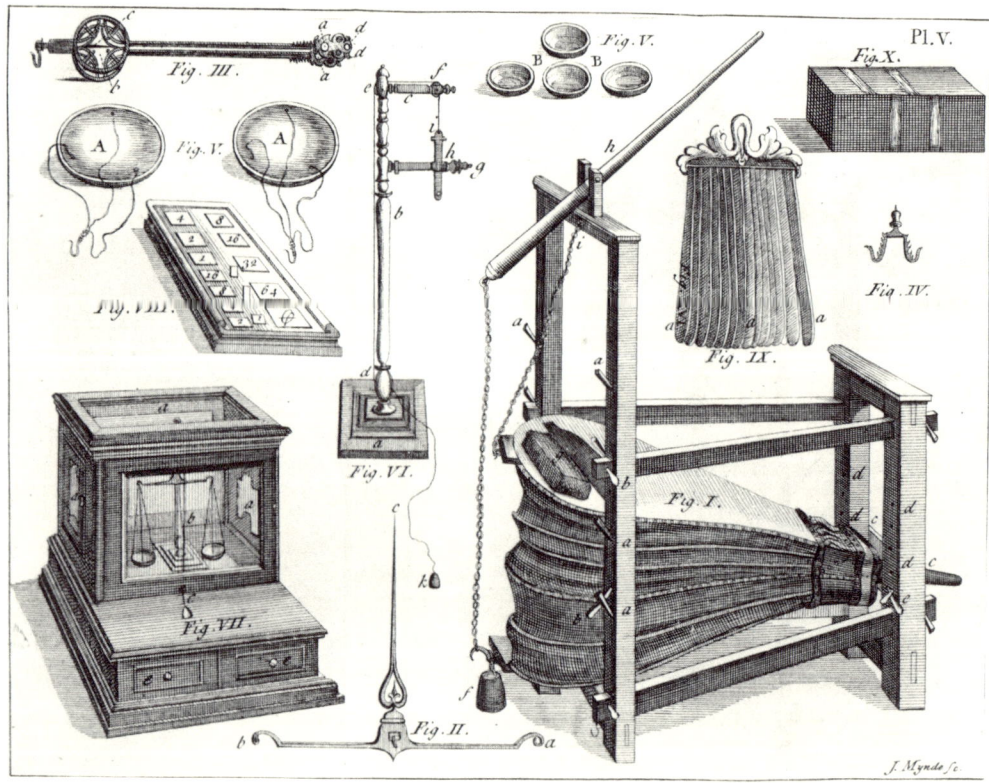

Fig. 26: *Plate V* of Cramer's *Elements* showing weights and scales and touchstone used in testing the purity of metals. *Courtesy of The Henry Francis du Pont Winterthur Museum; photograph by Gilbert Ask.*

that it was being hammered evenly on all sides. Joseph may also have inscribed circles on the disc with his compass to direct the blows of his hammer.

He began by hammering in the center of the disc and working out in a spiraling line to the outer edges. It was essential that he keep the strokes of his hammer even in order to preserve the uniform thickness of the silver. Gradually, the edges of the disc would begin to curve up, and by repeated hammering the smith could deepen the disc into the desired shape. To do this he used stakes of various shapes.[19] Joseph could use the smaller stakes in a vise or in a special fitting at the workbench, a long table probably built into the wall of the shop.[20]

Because hammering made the silver brittle, he had to leave the workbench frequently, taking the piece of silver over to the charcoal forge so that it could be reheated. By pumping the bellows, he increased the heat in the forge until the silver glowed at the proper hue, indicating that the metal had been annealed. In handling the silver, Joseph used his "nealing" tongs. As the metal was heated, oxidation occurred on its surface. To remove the surface impurities, Joseph put the piece into a heated sulphuric acid solution. A layer of fire scale, however, remained below the surface. This gives old silver its deep rich color, but it is sometimes exposed today by overly enthusiastic polishing.

Once he had hammered the body of the tankard to the desired height and shape, Joseph cut more pieces of silver from the sheet and formed them into the lid and the handle. The handle was then attached to the body with silver solder heated by a lamp, fanned by air from a blow-pipe. Moldings for the base of the tankard, the lip, and occasionally a mid-band were made by pulling silver wires through a steel plate on the drawing bench. This long, low bench, which Joseph had inherited from his father, had a pulley arrangement turned by a wheel which made it easier to pull wires through shaped slots in the metal plate at the end.[21]

Some of the smaller parts of the tankard, such as the thumbpiece and the hinge of the lid, Joseph cast in iron flasks filled with a special casting sand in which the pattern had been impressed. He used his files to smooth off the rough edges of the cast parts and to smooth the edges of the moldings that were to be soldered together. A small hand vise held tiny pieces while he filed them.[22]

If he wanted to put repoussé decoration on the body of a piece of silver, the smith used a snarling iron and hammers. The snarling iron was an elongated Z-shaped instrument with a handle that was used to stretch the silver so that it could be hammered and chased. During this chasing process, the body of the piece was filled with pitch, which formed a resilient barrier so that the tools could shape the metal without penetrating it.[23]

After Joseph had fashioned the various pieces of silver, either from molds or with his hammer, he was ready to begin the finishing process, which sometimes required as much time as the actual fashioning. The hammered parts had to be planished with a flat-faced hammer or planishing teast.

When the final hammering was completed, the silver parts were put into the acid bath for the last time and were "boiled up" or "pickled," as the process is called. Once Joseph had assembled all the parts and soldered them together, he could polish the tankard with a scratch brush made of brass wire, a process called *burnishing*. It produced complex patterns of fine lines on the surface of the silver which deflected light in all directions, giving the silver a beautiful and lustrous glow. In his letter book, Joseph made a distinction between burnishing and polishing. It is likely that, to him, *polishing* indicated a more deeply penetrating type of finishing than burnishing, accomplished by turning the piece on a lathe until the sub-surface layer of oxidation was removed.[24]

After the piece was polished, it might be engraved with the owner's initials or coat of arms or with other decorative devices. For this, the object was supported by a sand cushion (a leather bag filled with sand, as seen in Copley's portrait of Paul Revere at the Museum of Fine Arts in Boston), and the design was traced with a graver. For more elaborate designs, the surface could be covered with whiting and the desired decoration traced from a pattern.[25]

Although some goldsmiths, such as Nathaniel Hurd and Paul Revere, developed the engraving process into an art, Joseph Richardson seems to have done comparatively little engraving. In the absence of any signed engraving by him, it is difficult to determine how much of the engraving on silver bearing his mark was actually the product of his own graver.[26] But, because nearly all the porringers made by Richardson are engraved with similar block letters, as are spoons bearing his mark, it is safe to characterize his letters as having pronounced serifs and being shaded, usually with lines slanting down toward the left. The customary arrangement of initials—that of the surname centered above that of the husband's given name on the left and that of the wife's given name on the right—was followed by Richardson, but he usually placed only a single dot in the center of the cluster, rather than a decorative motif. Fre-

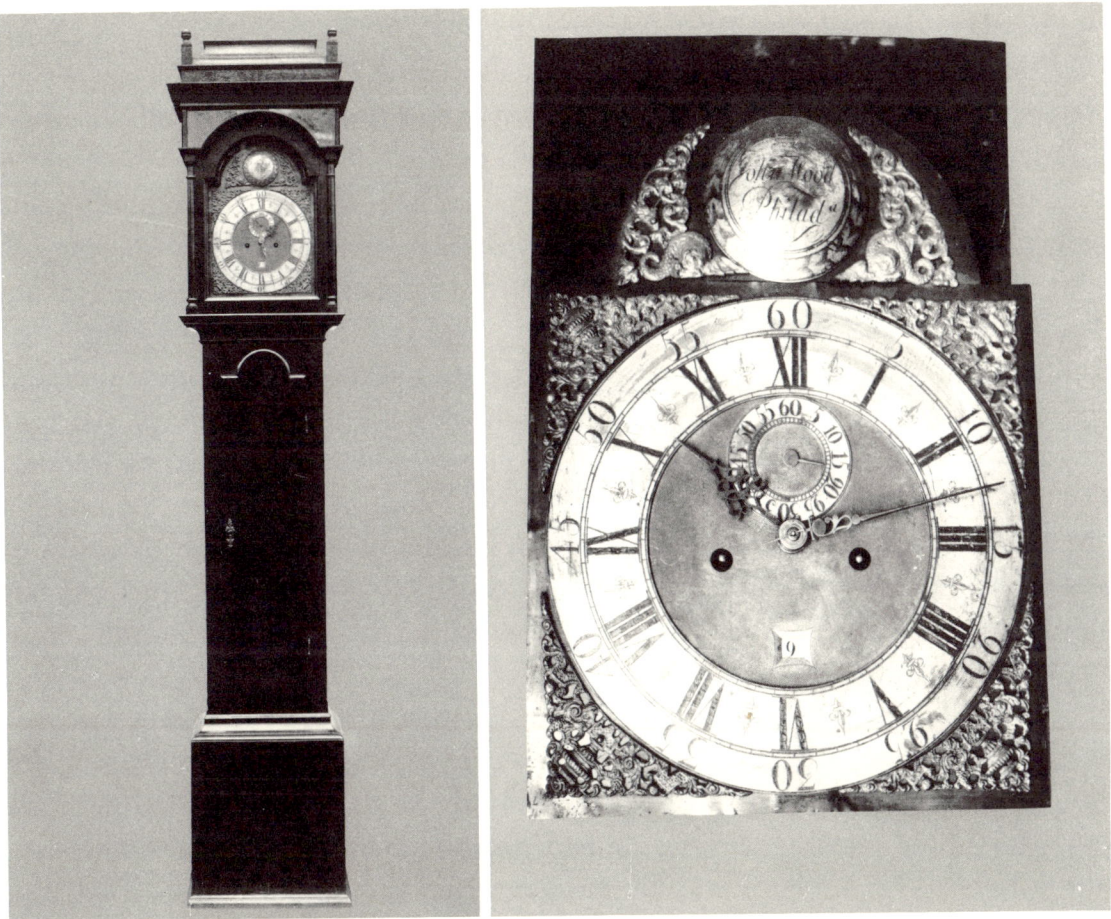

Fig. 27: Face of tall clock made by John Wood, Philadelphia clockmaker, who paid Joseph Richardson in the 1730's for engraving name pieces. Diameter: 12". *Courtesy of Mrs. Addison Savery; photograph by Philadelphia Museum of Art.*

quently Richardson noted in his account book the initials to be engraved on the piece of plate or where there was to be a "posey" on rings or a special inscription.[27]

Joseph is known to have done some engraving on objects which he himself had not made. For his brother as well as for clockmaker John Wood, Joseph engraved brass nameplates which could be affixed to the clock faces to identify their work *(Fig. 27)*. For "Ingraving 6 name pieces at Sundry times," Joseph charged 6 shillings. On one occasion he engraved a gold locket for his brother Frank, and in 1747 he charged Joshua Crosbey for "Engraveing 8 Crests—£0/12/0." In 1738 he charged William Mode for engraving pewter. For the most part, however, Richardson's engraving was fairly ordinary, consisting of simple borders, C-scrolls, diapering, and rosettes. In the case of the script initials in the form of ciphers on some of his tea table silver, the letters are usually attenuated, and the foliation is relatively simple. Only on the pieces made at the height of the rococo style did the engraving on his silver approach a complicated design.

Nowhere in his account books does Richardson record the engraving of a coat of arms on a piece of silver. Relatively few pieces of silver bearing his mark have engraved armorial bearings, and it is possible that this engraving was done by someone else. A pair of cans and a pair of sauceboats bear identical designs: a coat of arms contained in a rather stiff cartouche characterized by rigid blades of grass, leafy tendrils, and flowers *(Figs. 86, 110)*. All four pieces are marked by Richardson and so might have been engraved by him. The few pieces of Richardson silver engraved with figures, birds, or animals reveal a naive and spontaneous charm. The most characteristic example of this engraving is found on a gorget, depicting a Quaker presenting a winged pipe of peace to an Indian *(Fig. 125)*. The design is charming, although somewhat crudely executed.

Another indication of Joseph's lack of interest in engraving is the fact that he made few seals. According to his account books, George Emlen was one of the people for whom he made seals. Evidently Emlen was satisfied with the work, for a little over a year later he had Joseph make another seal for his son. Nevertheless, Richardson was by-passed when the Philadelphia Contributionship needed a seal, and again when the Pennsylvania Hospital arranged for the seal of its organization.[28]

The cutting of dies for coins and the engraving of currency were jobs which goldsmiths were occasionally asked to perform for the government. Because goldsmiths were able to do this sort of work, some of them occasionally supplied their services to unauthorized persons. Counterfeiting occurred early in the history of Philadelphia. The Friends in their Monthly Meeting spoke out against it, and in 1751 several Friends were read out of meeting for "making and uttering Counterfeit Gold Coin."[29] Joseph Richardson evidently never practised this falsification, but another man with the same name did.[30]

Joseph usually charged his customers according to the weight of the metal he was working *(Fig. 28)*. When the object was finished, it was weighed, and its weight (frequently scratched or engraved on the base of the piece) was then used to compute the fee. In 1698 Gabriel Thomas had said, "And for Silver-Smiths, they have between Half a Crown and Three Shillings an Ounce for working their Silver, and for Gold equivalent."[31] In the 1730's and 1740's Joseph, however, normally charged 18 pence per ounce.[32] The rate naturally was dependent upon the economic situation of a given place at a given time.

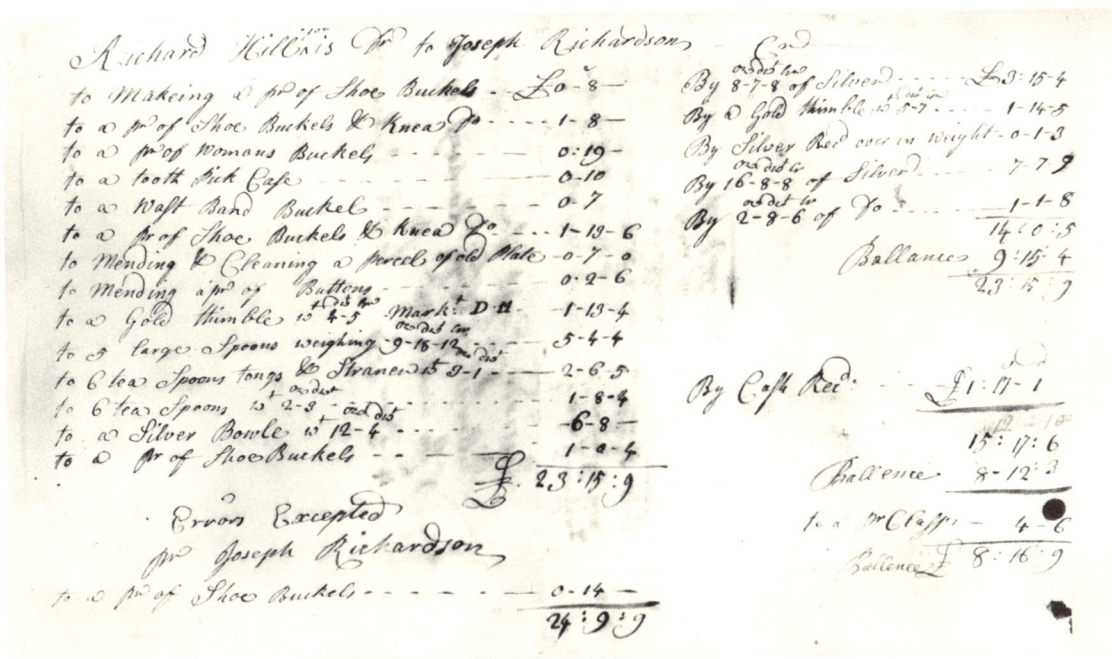

Fig. 28: Bill for goods bought by Richard Hill, Jr., from Joseph Richardson, July 14, 1739. *Courtesy of The Historical Society of Pennsylvania.*

In 1767 Charles Oliver Bruff of New York advertised the same rate Gabriel Thomas had named seventy years earlier—three shillings per ounce for tankards—exactly double the rate Richardson had charged in the 1730's.[33] For small items which required more labor per ounce than large items, Joseph charged more, and often a flat rate. Small work was usually tedious, and it is logical that such items as rings, buttons, or buckles should fall into a higher-priced category.[34]

In estimating his fee, Richardson also had to calculate the cost of the metal which varied as the value of silver fluctuated. In 1738 Richardson valued an ounce of silver at 8 shillings 6 pence but in 1747 it had risen to 9 shillings. The price Joseph paid for old silver in 1765 is indicated in a letter from Samuel Morris to Samuel Powel: "I have sold 4 old battered porringers, a pepper box and 8 Silver buttons amounting to 44 oz. 3 dwt. 12 gr. to J. Richardson @ £0/8/0 per oz.—they were country made & not having the Hall mark would not exceed that price, indeed I had tryed others before him & they would not give more."[35]

This interesting letter also points up the practice of customers bringing old pieces of plate to the goldsmith to be remade. Samuel Powel had himself brought old silver to Richardson to be reworked, as Joseph recorded in his accounts for 1738.[36] Coins, too, were often brought to the goldsmith to be melted down and made into plate. On one occasion, for example, Joseph received 102 pieces of eight from Joshua Crosbey to be made into various objects.[37] If the customer provided the silver, he had to pay only for the cost of Richardson's labor. He sometimes paid in cash, but just as often the accounts were cleared by the barter system or by work done.[38] When Israel Pemberton, Jr., was settling his account in 1736, he gave Richardson gold, a gold thimble, old plate, Spanish silver, regular silver, and cash.

Richardson's annual income can only be estimated, for it is not possible to know whether his accounts were complete, to ascertain the cost of the metal or of his labor in every instance, or to determine his operating costs. However, a rough totaling of his accounts for 1735 comes to about £140, and for 1746, about £155.

As these figures indicate, prices were fairly constant and there was little advance in income, for a single worker could produce only a certain amount of work. However, in order to command a larger trade, a silversmith could take apprentices and journeymen to help him with his work. In 1735, when he was 24 years old, Joseph Richardson already employed two men, in addition to his brother Frank. In Philadelphia, as in England, the apprenticeship system was regulated by law. A legal indenture was drawn up which required the apprentice, who was usually between fourteen and twenty-one, to serve his master faithfully in all things for seven years; in return, the master provided him with a place to live, food, schooling, and instruction in his trade.[39]

Joseph Richardson's apprentices and workers played an important role in his shop, and their activities shed much light on the operation of a goldsmith's business. Joseph's assistants are particularly worthy of study because, with the exception of his sons and two others, very little has been known about them.

The first worker to appear in Richardson's shop, other than his brother Frank, was John S. Hutton, a New Yorker born in 1684/5, who originally had been apprenticed to a sea captain. He was 51 years old when he began to work for Joseph, and he lived to be 109.[40] Through a friend who was a whitesmith, Hutton had learned to work silver, and after 30 years at sea, he began in the silversmith's trade. By 1728 he was referred to as a goldsmith in a petition now in the Rhode Island Governor and Council Records.

Just when Hutton arrived in Philadelphia is not known, but he is first mentioned in Richardson's account book in 1735–36, when he was paid cash for a certain number of days' work, the first of which were "5 Days Work Ending the 17th of the 2nd mo."[41] At this time, John Hutton was paid about £1 for a six-day week. At first, the cost of Hutton's labor and living expenses was shared by Frank Richardson, who, in 1735-36, undertook "an assumption to Pay for John hutton," and provided his food for two weeks. From 1736 to 1740, Hutton was paid for the number of days' work he did: £0/22/6 per week until 1737, and £0/27/6 thereafter. Most of his wages were paid in cash, although Joseph paid Isaac Zane for Hutton's rent in 1739, and Hutton occasionally got such things as food, clothing, fabrics, a desk, teaspoons, and buckles or buttons from Richardson. In July or August, Hutton usually had a week's vacation from his labors, and sometimes he did not work a full week. By the 1740's, Hutton was no longer being paid by the week but by the piece.

Thereafter, Hutton was charged for the materials he received and was credited both for the cost of making the items and for the excess silver returned. It is interesting that he received the same amount for fashioning silver objects that Richardson himself was paid. In 1745 according to Richardson's accounts, Hutton made tumblers, sugar dishes, a teapot, cans, porringers, and a "panican." In the years 1746-48 he also made gold bezeled buttons, tankards, a coffeepot, milk pots, salts, and a butter cup.

Very little silver has yet been ascribed to John Hutton. His mark is listed by Stephen G. C. Ensko as IH or I•H in a rounded rectangle. The Winterthur Museum owns an example of his work, a salver bearing the mark I•H in an oval.[42] The piece was made about 1745-50, and is engraved with the initials
  R
I   S for Joseph Richardson, the merchant, and his wife Sarah. As might be expected, it is similar in every way to Richardson's work.

Hutton's association with Richardson continued into the late 1740's.[43] By 1747, when he was paid "in full of all demands," he was sixty-three years old and ready to begin a retirement that was to last forty-six years. Joseph Richardson had taken a second helper in his shop at about the time Hutton started work. His name was James St. Morris (or St. Maurice), and it may well be that he began as Frank Richardson's apprentice.[44] In return for materials provided him, St. Morris made numerous pairs of buckles and was credited with a clock and case, a watch, and a brass jack. Perhaps after Frank gave up his work as a clock maker and goldsmith, he arranged for his brother to take the full responsibility of St. Morris, for by 1745 Joseph was making payments directly to St. Morris and the latter was making all kinds of buckles and a number of tea tongs for Joseph.

St. Morris was primarily a worker in small plate. Upon occasion he made seals, watch chains, and an odd spur, and mended a sun dial. One of the jobs he performed was washing the sweep from the shop in order to retrieve the filings of the silver. By 1748 he had established himself in business.[45]

Another apprentice in Richardson's shop during this early period was Jeremiah Elfreth, Jr.[46] His father, Jeremiah Elfreth, Sr. had married Richardson's stepmother in 1731. Because young men normally began their apprenticeship when they were about fourteen years old, Jeremiah should have begun his training sometime after 1737. Richardson's account books do not cover the period 1740–45, during which Jeremiah's apprenticeship would have occurred, but in 1744 Richardson recorded in his commonplace book:

8 mo. 8th to Jerey a Salver	£0/ 7/16
to hard Sawder	0/ 5/18
To Silver	0/17/12.

These entries are made along with other charges against apprentices, as are other notations of silver received by "Jerey" in 1743, leaving little doubt that Jerey was Jeremiah Elfreth, Jr., and that he was an apprentice of Joseph Richardson.

It is interesting that the one article of silver mentioned in the account shown above is a salver, because the extant salvers marked by Jeremiah Elfreth, Jr., bear a striking similarity to those made by Joseph Richardson. The cast parts of the salvers are so similar that the same patterns may have been used for their casting. Similarly, some cream pots and porringer handles made by the two men are identical in design. Not many examples of Elfreth's silver survive from his career which lasted from 1745, when he established his own business on North Second Street in Philadelphia, until his death on February 10, 1765.

Another of Richardson's apprentices whose career was even more shortlived was David Harper, the same young man who represented the group of Philadelphia goldsmiths on their ill-fated shipping venture to Guadeloupe (see p. 40). The accounts show that David Harper had begun working in Richardson's shop by 1745 and had already progressed to the point of receiving cash for each piece he made. By 1745 Harper was an accomplished goldsmith; the whistles and bells, casters, and cups he was then making for Richardson required considerable skill. By 1746, Harper had also learned to make salt dishes and tankards and, by 1747, such large objects as teapots, coffeepots, bowls, and sugar dishes.[47] No silver has yet been identified as the work of Harper. For making a teapot, Harper received £1/7/6, the equivalent of a full week's wages in the early days of John Hutton's apprenticeship. Of all Joseph's apprentices, it was Harper who made some of the most interesting small objects. These included "boozes" and buckles for a horse bridle, spectacle frames, nutmeg graters, a cock, spurs, and even a fountain pen.

By 1755, David Harper had finished his work with Richardson and had set himself up in business as a "Gold and Silversmith" in partnership with Charles Dutens, a jeweler who had advertised in 1751 in New York near the Long-Bridge in Broad-Street.[48] Their partnership lasted only a few years, for Harper died in Guadeloupe in 1761. Dutens had gone to live in the West Indies by the end of 1757, according to an advertisement by Edmund Milne in the *Pennsylvania Gazette* on December 29, 1757, explaining that he had taken over Dutens' business. It is possible that Charles Dutens also had worked for a while in Joseph Richardson's shop. Among notations of silver received by apprentices, Joseph listed in his commonplace book in 1743 and 1744 that "Charles" received large numbers of buckles and buttons and a few clasps.

More is known of the next apprentice to appear in Joseph's shop, William Young, a relative of Richardson's.[49] Young was working in Richardson's shop in the 1740's, as is shown by the appearance of his name in Joseph's commonplace book. The first entry is simply to "William a tea Pott." Another entry notes gold, silver, solder, spoons, tea tongs and a gold ring under the name of William.[50]

After Young completed his basic apprenticeship with Richardson, he apparently continued to work in the shop for about nine years. Not until the spring of 1760 did he start his own business. In preparation for this, Joseph Richardson had written to a business acquaintance in London in September 1759: "By this oppertunity, thee will receive a small order from a relation of mine, William young, who served his time with me and is about to set up for himself next spring. If the goods he orders should amount to a few pounds more than what he sends to purchase them, thee may safely credit him."[51]

By the fall of 1761, Young was established in a shop on Second Street three doors above Arch Street, where he offered for sale, "Chased and plain Tea-pots, Sugar-dishes, Cream-pots, Casters and Salts, Silver Handle Knives and Forks, with Cases of Different Sizes," and many other items.[52] Seven years later he completed the time-honored cycle of education in the craft by advertising that "Said Young would take an Apprentice of a reputable Family, and an Ingenious Turn if any should apply within three weeks, to serve not less than five years."[53]

Another person who may have worked in Richardson's shop was Giles Lewis. He and his brother Thomas were the children of the widow Sarah Lewis of Fairfax, Virginia. In 1763, they came to Philadelphia, where Thomas went to Friends' School and Giles became an apprentice of Joseph Richardson.[54] It is not certain whether Lewis was apprenticed as a silversmith or in some other capacity because there is no mention of him in the Richardson papers.

Herford, the Negro whom Joseph inherited from his father in 1729, may also have worked in Joseph's shop. Many goldsmiths, especially in Philadelphia, Maryland, and South Carolina, apparently had trained Negroes working in their shops.[55] It is not known how old Herford was at the time Joseph inherited him, nor is there any known record of the date of his death. It is likely that he was given his freedom before he died.

The last apprentices known to have worked in Joseph's shop were his sons. Joseph, Jr., became fourteen in 1766; his brother, Nathaniel, in 1768. This was the suitable age to begin training. They spent more than the usual seven years in their father's shop, however, waiting until 1777 to start their own business.

A number of goldsmiths did work for Richardson without actually being apprenticed to him or working continuously in his shop. One was Randall Yetton, a little-known goldsmith who was practicing his craft in Philadelphia in 1739.[56] For Joseph he made pap spoons and did other work which was recorded in Richardson's account book. No silver by him is known to survive, but his uncommon initials give hope that his touchmark will someday be identified.

"Randal's work for 4 Days," which was valued at 10 shillings, was charged by Richardson in 1736 against the account of Anthony Bright. Bright, who is listed in the Walpole Society's index of goldsmiths as having worked in Philadelphia in 1740, is virtually unknown today.[57] In the 1730's, however, he and Joseph were exchanging materials needed for working silver, as well as ready-made objects.[58] When he died in 1751, Bright named his wife Jane and "my Trusty Friend Joseph Richardson" as the executors of his will.[59] Joseph Richardson, along with Philip Syng, served as executor for the estate of another little-known Philadelphia goldsmith, Alexander Robertson,[60] and again for the estate of Philip Hulbeart, goldsmith (Appendix B).

Still another relatively unknown silversmith with whom Joseph Richardson was acquainted was Richard Pitts. In 1745 Joseph gave Pitts some gold buttons, solder, and some silver to be made into six pairs of buckles. Only four pairs of buckles are recorded as being returned, at which time Joseph paid Pitts 16 shillings for his labor. Richard Pitts, who was listed by the Walpole Society as working in Philadelphia in 1741, advertised as a silversmith on Front Street in 1744.[61] It is not known whether Pitts was apprenticed to Richardson, for Joseph's accounts for the years just prior to 1745 are missing. However, by 1746, Pitts had moved to Charleston, South Carolina, and little is known of his activities thereafter.[62]

Other goldsmiths with whom Joseph Richardson had business dealings were Peter David and Philip Syng. Peter David's account was a small one: he purchased three sets of silver buttons in 1739, and in exchange he gave Richardson three pairs of small studs and some sleeve buckles. Philip Syng's transactions with Richardson in 1733 show that he made some silver for Joseph, including a shell for a sword hilt, spoons, and buckles; in return, Richardson provided watch chains and a snuffbox for Syng.[63]

Most of Richardson's customers, however, were not goldsmiths, but Quaker merchants or tradesmen. Some were relatives, some were former customers of his father, and many were important residents of Philadelphia. His account books list a few customers who lived outside Philadelphia, such as John Cox of Trenton, John Smith of Jamaica, and the Carolina resident to whom Joseph and his brother shipped a pair of cans in 1737.[64] In the same year Captain William Bell ordered two trays to fulfill a legacy of £10 bequeathed by Samuel Sherlock to Devonshire Parish in Bermuda (see *Fig. 69*).

Most numerous, however, were his local Quaker customers. John Smith and his wife, Hannah Logan, were typical patrons and, when their silver was itemized in 1764, dozens of the pieces listed bore the mark of Joseph Richardson.[65] Their plate amounted to 665 1/2 ounces. It is not surprising that Friend John Woolman protested in 1770 this abuse of Quaker principle:

The Customary use of Silver Vessels about houses hath deeply affected my mind of late years and under a living Concern I have frequently laboured in Families, and Sometimes more publickly to disswade from the Use of these things, in which there is a manifest conformity to Outward show and greatness.[66]

Few Friends heeded his plea, however, and Richardson and his sons continued to supply them with silver for many years.

Evidently the number of customers was such that Joseph Richardson felt little need to advertise during the years he practiced his craft. Some artisans used trade cards or newspaper advertisements to proclaim their skills,[67] but newspaper listings of products (such as those enumerated by Edmund Milne and John David) were spurned by Richardson. Evidently he did not even use a shop sign, since the few advertisements he did place in Philadelphia newspapers make no mention of the name of his shop.[68]

Richardson advertised infrequently, confining his newspaper notices to particular events, such as the sale at his shop of goods owned by others—his brother Frank or his uncle Lawrence Growden—or the recent importation of special articles such as the large bell he had ordered from London for the Court House in York.[69]

On one occasion Joseph placed an advertisement in the local newspaper concerning a piece of stolen silver he had "stopped" from being sold: "Stopped the 10th instant by Joseph Richardson, Goldsmith, a silver lid of a tankard, supposed to be stolen; weighing 6 ounces. The owner by applying to the said Richardson, and paying the cost, may have it again."[70] When a piece of silver was lost or stolen, silversmiths were alerted either by advertisement or by word of mouth. When Joseph heard of a lost or stolen item, he made a note of it in his commonplace book *(Fig. 29)* so that he could watch for it.[71]

Richardson also used newspaper advertising to promote the sale of the large quantities of weights and scales which he imported from London. *(Figs. 30, 31)*. These weights and scales, generally sold in wooden boxes, were used for the accurate weighing of coins in an age when rates of exchange fluctuated and when clipping coins was so widespread that businessmen had to guard constantly against losses. As early as 1744, Joseph advertised in the *Pennsylvania Gazette* on April 19: "Lately imported from London, and to be Sold by *Joseph Richardson*, Goldsmith. A Parcel of Gold Scales and Weights, from one Ounce to half a Grain, in black Shagareen Cases." A quarter of a century later, he was still advertising scales in the local paper. By that time he had also arranged for another kind of advertisement, a printed label which he could affix to the inside of the lid of each box, showing where the scales and weights had been bought, and listing for the convenience of his customers the value and the weight of each of the coins then in circulation. *(Appendix C)*.

The obvious form of advertising for a goldsmith was the touchmark he

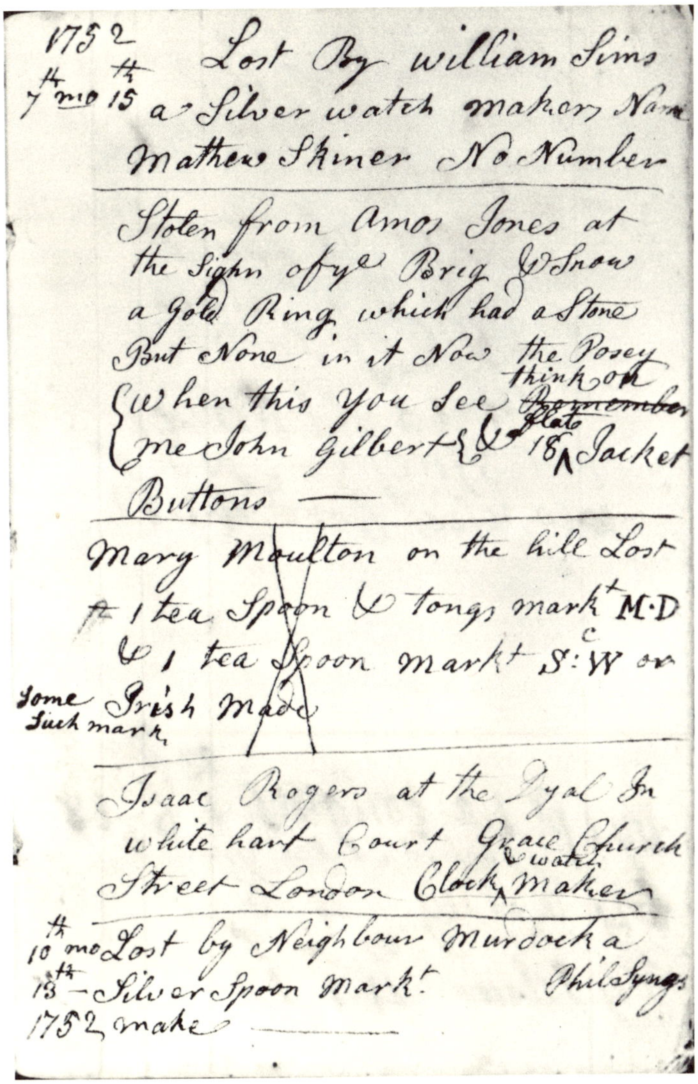

Fig. 29: Page from Joseph Richardson's commonplace book, 1752. *Courtesy of The Henry Francis du Pont Winterthur Museum; photograph by Gilbert Ask.*

stamped on the silver he made. Each goldsmith probably cut his own die for his maker's mark. No eighteenth-century documentation exists showing a goldsmith's payment to another person for the cutting of his maker's mark, nor did any die cutter advertise this service then. Furthermore, there is a relationship between the ability of a particular goldsmith as a seal-cutter and engraver and the skill with which his maker's mark was cut.[72] As might be expected, Joseph Richardson's maker's marks are of good quality, adequately but simply cut.

Like most American silversmiths, Joseph usually stamped only a maker's mark on his silver. In England, the guild hall meticulously required stamping on each piece of plate the assay mark, the date letter, and the town mark, as

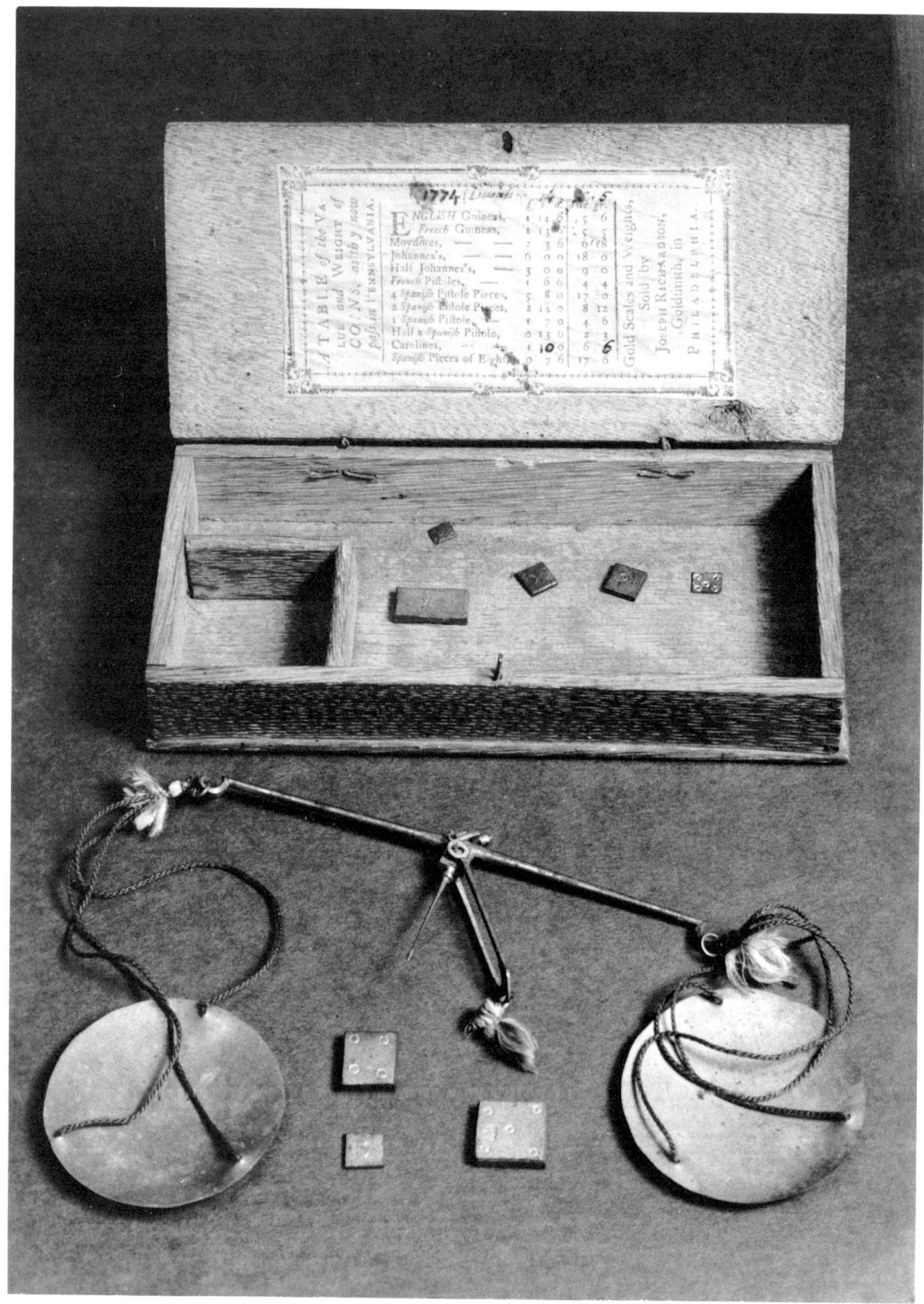

Fig. 30: Box of weights and scales, English, bearing label of Joseph Richardson, 1774. Courtesy of The Henry Francis du Pont Winterthur Museum; *photograph by Gilbert Ask.*

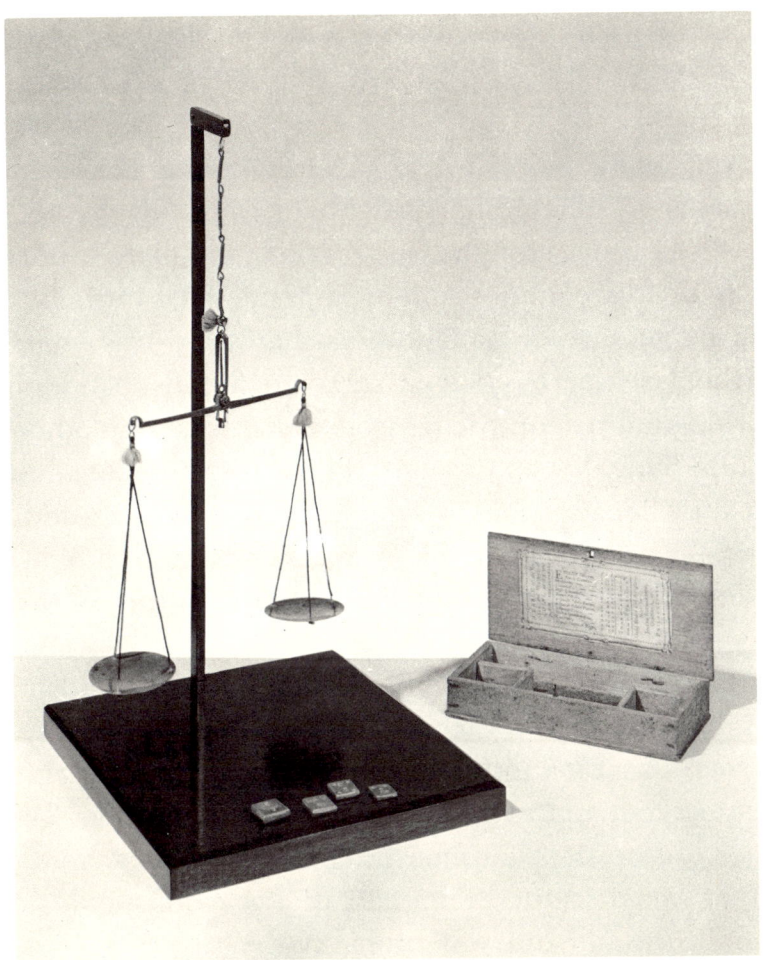

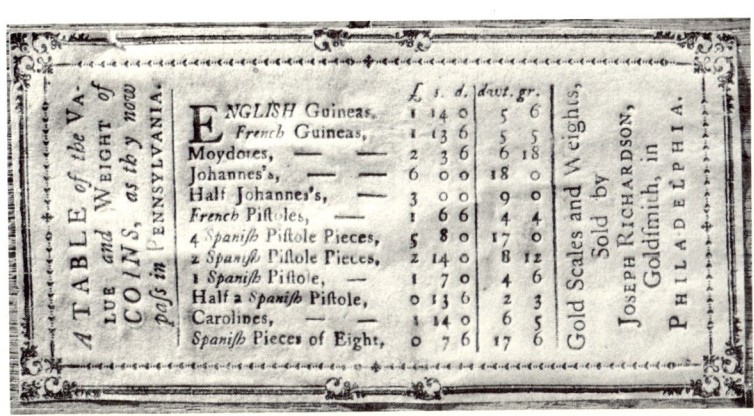

Fig. 31: Box of weights and scales, English, imported and labeled by Joseph Richardson, with weights bearing London hallmark used between 1751–56. *Courtesy of Philadelphia Museum of Art; photograph by A. J. Wyatt.*

well as the maker's mark. As early as 1756, attempts were made in Philadelphia to set up such an assay office. The local silversmiths felt that if the fineness of the gold and silver they wrought was properly regulated, their business in Philadelphia, in nearby colonies, and even in the West Indies would increase. Their petition to the city of Philadelphia, however, was consistently voted down, and further attempts to get it passed were finally abandoned.[73]

At about this time Joseph Richardson and at least one other Philadelphia goldsmith, Philip Syng, began to stamp their silver with an additional mark: a leafy scroll or furl. Because this mark appears on silver made by Richardson only in the 1750–75 period, it is likely that it was a kind of assay mark, the solution of a few Philadelphia silversmiths to the failure of the Assembly to set up an assay office.[74]

Because there were no guild halls in this country, goldsmiths were not regulated in the marking of their work, although most American goldsmiths marked their wares as a matter of custom or pride. Smaller objects were frequently left unmarked, and even in England the regulations on hallmarks do not apply to jewelry, except for mourning rings.[75] When the die for a touchmark cracked, or was discarded for a new die, or when a goldsmith ceased to practice his craft, the old die was probably destroyed.[76] No maker's touchmarks are mentioned in the early inventories of goldsmiths' estates, even when all the other tools of their trade are meticulously listed.

During his career an average goldsmith used several dies to strike his maker's mark on silver. Identifying these various marks with particular makers depends upon documentation. An effort has been made to identify and document the marks used by Joseph Richardson through his account books and the original owners of silver bearing an IR stamp. Because the account books record only the early part of his career, the attribution of his later marks must be based upon other evidence, such as the workmanship and style of the particular piece and its mark.

Richardson used at least four different initial marks and two scroll marks during his career *(Fig. 32)*. Microphotography is helpful in determining the characteristics of the marks and shows the wear which occurs during a die's lifetime. The lighting of the mark for photography, however, can change the appearance of the stamp, and thus great care must be taken in interpreting the photographs. Furthermore, where and how the mark was struck may also affect its appearance in a photograph.

Listed and described below are the marks definitely ascribed to Joseph Richardson:

32a IR in an oval (c. 1730–40). Characterized by slightness of serifs, downward sweep of right foot of R, wedge-shaped left foot giving the appearance of a break in the die. Spoon *(Fig. 113)*.

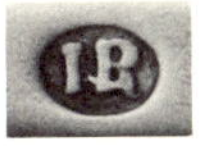

32b IR in an oval (c. 1730–50). Characterized by conjoined foot of I and R, upturned right foot, horseshoe shaped lower half of R, lack of space between base of letters and lower edge of oval. Salver *(Fig. 70)*.

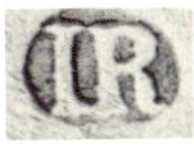

32c IR in a rectangle (c. 1750). Characterized by slightly rounded top right side of square, upturned right foot of R, closeness of serifs on I and R. Sugar bowl *(Fig. 54)*.

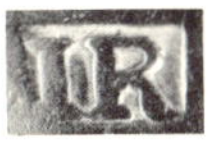

32d IR in a rectangle (c. 1739–75). Characterized by the widely spaced letters, the upturned right foot of the R, the thinness of the horizontal central part of the R, and the closeness of the feet of the R. Beginning in the late 1740's, this mark appears with a notch on the lower right side of the rectangle. This mark appears in conjunction with the scroll marks. Tablespoon *(Fig. 115)*.

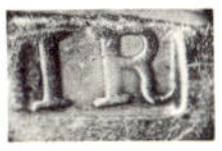

32e Symmetrical scroll mark (c. 1750–70). Intaglio mark with the scroll in the shape of a highly-arched oxbow, scroll on each end and S-shaped mark in center. Used with widely spaced IR in rectangle mark. Sauceboat *(Fig. 110)*.

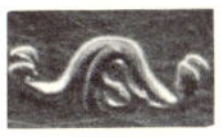

32f Asymmetrical scroll mark (c. 1750–70). Intaglio mark shaped like a seahorse on its side, with a feathery scroll from top center to right. Used with rectangular IR marks. Coffeepot *(Fig. 35a)*.

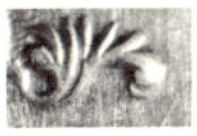

Fig. 32: Maker's marks
  a. IR in an oval. Appears on spoon *(Fig. 113)* probably made for Bartholomew Waide in March 1734/5. *Courtesy of Miss Elizabeth M. Wistar.*
  b. IR in an oval. Appears on tray *(Fig. 72)* made for Hannah Emlen in 1739/40. *Courtesy of The Historical Society of Pennsylvania.*
  c. IR in a rectangle. Appears on Sarah Shoemaker sugar dish, 1754 *(Fig. 54)*. *Courtesy of The Historical Society of Pennsylvania.*
  d. IR in a rectangle. Appears on spoon, *c.* 1750 *(Fig. 115)*. *Privately owned.*
  e. Scroll mark, symmetrical, intaglio. Appears on pair of sauceboats *(Fig. 110)* with Logan arms. *Courtesy of The Metropolitan Museum of Art, New York City.*
  f. Scroll mark, asymmetrical, intaglio. Appears on Sarah Shoemaker coffee pot, 1754 *(Fig. 35a)*. *Courtesy of The Historical Society of Pennsylvania.*

Other marks used by Joseph Richardson may be identified in the future. However, such a large number of spurious marks have been created and attributed to the Richardsons that it may be useful to show one here *(Fig. 32g)*. In 1938 John Marshall Phillips pointed out that Joseph Richardson was among those American goldsmiths whose work has been faked in greatest quantity.[77] Countless examples of spurious silver bearing marks purporting to be those of the Richardsons have been seen, and are still being offered for sale. So great are the problems in detecting forgeries that a study was made of a single group of fraudulent silver attributed to Joseph Richardson, setting forth methods of distinguishing the forged from the authentic.[78] The suspect marks are usually characterized by a lack of skill in the cutting of the die resulting in the letters being crudely cut, uneven, and disproportionate in that the letters are too tall and thin or too short and thick. Stiffness and a lack of sureness in handling the serifs are other traits that suggest a spurious mark.

g. Spurious Richardson mark. *Courtesy of The Historical Society of Pennsylvania.*

Undoubtedly the best preparation for recognizing the work of Joseph Richardson lies in a thorough understanding of the way in which he worked and an analysis of the documented examples he made during his long and capable career.

CHAPTER 5

Joseph Richardson: His Silver

ABOUNDING in eighteenth-century newspapers are such advertisements as: "Just imported from London, a very elegant Assortment of silver Plate and Jewellery, . . . said goldsmith continues to carry on his Business in all Branches; and has now made and ready for Sale a variety of goods in the latest Taste and newest Fashion, viz . . ."

In the preceding century, only a few families could afford to commission a set of silver spoons or, occasionally, a cup and a tankard, and the goldsmith's business was largely confined to making communion vessels for churches or presentation silver for organizations and wealthy individuals. But by the eighteenth century, the members of the burgeoning middle class could well afford to ornament both their houses and their persons with objects of silver and gold. Joseph Richardson, like many of his fellow artisans, found the demand for his handiwork so great that he had to supplement production in his own shop with silver bearing London hallmarks. Importations of silver from England to America rose from a value of £28 of plate in 1697 to £4,700 in 1760.[1]

The total value of yearly shipments of silver from England to America is known through the records at the Public Record Office in London, and the kinds of objects imported are known from local advertisements. Joseph Richardson's letter book, recording his orders for plate from 1758 to 1774, charts the actual course of the plate-importing business. These letters reveal that Joseph ordered silver from London once or twice a year, that it usually took about six months for the goods to arrive in Philadelphia, and that frequently the silver sent was not entirely satisfactory. The letters also reveal that the imported plate not only supplied a demand but served as a model of the latest fashions (*Appendix D*). The purchases abroad were arranged through bills of exchange—a form of money order—or through actual bullion sent by Joseph to the firms with which he dealt. These firms include Thomas Wagstaffe, George Ritherdon, Daniel Mildred, and How & Masterman.[2]

This information, together with the detailed accounts of Joseph Richardson's day books and the large number of surviving objects that bear his mark, provide an unparalleled picture of the wares and activities of a flourishing goldsmith in a mid-eighteenth-century American city. Richardson's records reveal which objects were most commonly made in the goldsmith's shop (spoons, cans, and porringers), and which were more frequently imported from abroad. Joseph apparently did not carry a few items, such as candlesticks, and others, such as fountain pens, cranes, and horse bosses, he sold only rarely. It is evident that such objects as silver cans, tankards, porringers, tea sets, and trays were in great demand, while teakettles, spoon boats, and pannikins were sought only occasionally.

Joseph's records also indicate the relative popularity of similar items, such as a preference for pint cans over half-pint cans as drinking vessels. Here a study of the relative weights of different objects is useful, for we can determine that the average pint can weighed about twelve ounces, while the half-pint can weighed about seven ounces. Such comparative weights are helpful in determining the approximate size of an object when only its weight is known.

The weights given in Richardson's accounts and orders also help to identify objects that survive today. Similar objects were rarely identical in weight, so that a piece which has the original weight scratched on the base can sometimes be linked to a recorded object of the same weight. Even if only the present weight of the object is known, its history can sometimes be traced by allowing for the normal pennyweight loss of silver over the years.

Weights are also useful in determining which pieces recorded in Joseph's accounts were made by his apprentices, and therefore what part they played in the actual making of the silver sold in his shop. Because weight was of primary importance in determining the price of an object—not only because of the cost of the metal used, but also because the goldsmith figured the cost of his labor at so many pennies per ounce of metal—it takes on greater significance to the student of American silver.

It is general knowledge that American silver followed European styles, reflecting the Renaissance tradition in the seventeenth century, the baroque tradition at the turn of the eighteenth century, the rococo characteristics of the mid-eighteenth century, and the neoclassical taste of the late eighteenth century.[3] In fact silver was probably the first art form in the colonies to be affected by stylistic changes, for it was a more widely patronized art than painting or sculpture, and could be imported easily from London so that the American artisan was quickly supplied with models of changing taste.[4] Joseph Richardson actually ordered and received within six months fashionable London silver; he could then copy these designs for his customers, who frequently specified that their plate be made in the newest taste.

The appearance of new elements in American silver has not been precisely dated, because Colonial silver, unlike English silver of the time, does not bear marks indicating the year it was made. However, the records of Joseph Richardson and the objects made by him which can be dated through these records or through the dates engraved on them, provide a detailed picture of the development of various stylistic elements in mid-eighteenth century American silver.

Tea and Coffee Sets

Nowhere is stylistic development more clearly seen than in the coffee and tea sets which became popular in the eighteenth century. Actually, it was not until the beginning of Joseph Richardson's career, around 1730, that silver appurtenances for serving tea and coffee became common in America. At first china vessels were used, and it was not unusual for a family, as it became prosperous, to substitute silver utensils for the china, piece by piece.[5] Paintings of the period show that silver and china vessels were used side by side, and that it was not necessary for all the silver objects to be in the same style *(Fig. 66)*.

Although probably few families in the early eighteenth century had large or complete tea sets of silver, Joseph Richardson's accounts show that as early as 1735 Stephen Armitt purchased a teapot, a milkpot, and a waiter. A few years later, George Emlen purchased a more complete group of silver, including two teapots, two waiters, two sugar dishes, two slop bowls, a milkpot, a spoon boat, a breakfast bowl, and a pair of tea tongs.[6]

Few silver sets ordered at this time included both a teapot and a coffeepot. Samuel Blunston's order in 1737 for a coffeepot, a few months after he had purchased a tea set, was an exception to this rule. One of the first orders for a set that included both a teapot and a coffeepot came in 1747, when James Poolgreen brought 59 oz. 12 dwt. of silver to Richardson "to be made into a Coffe Pott tea Pott Creem Pott & weighter to hold Six Scarcers [Saucers]."

Evidently, coffee was not so popular a beverage as tea. Richardson's accounts prior to 1748 record the making of only three coffeepots. The first pots were small, for tea and coffee were difficult to obtain and therefore were served in small quantities. As the century progressed and these commodities became more common, both teapots and coffeepots became larger. The coffeepot Richardson made for Samuel Blunston in 1739 weighed only 25 oz. 9 dwt., and Joseph charged two shillings for working each ounce. The second coffeepot, which he made in 1746, weighed thirty ounces, and, although it was made by Joseph's shopworker John Hutton, the cost for labor had risen to £0/2/1 per ounce. The third coffeepot was the one made for James Poolgreen in 1747 by another of Joseph's apprentices, David Harper. Like the pot made by Hutton, this one also weighed thirty ounces but Harper's labor was valued at only 15 pence per ounce.

By 1758, when Richardson was ordering silver from London, coffeepots were still not in great demand. In September 1759, however, he ordered from How & Masterman four coffeepots with stands to serve as trays under the pots. Each set was to weigh about forty ounces. The increasing size of the pots, as well as the growing demand for elaborate decoration, is evident from the fact that he specified that all the coffeepots were to hold about three wine pints, and that two were to be neatly chased. The next time he ordered coffeepots from London, he requested that the matching stands also have chased shells on the borders. From 1760 to 1762, the orders for coffeepots increased considerably, and it was during these years that the basic shape of the coffeepot changed.

In 1761 the single-bellied or pear-shaped coffeepot was still in fashion; Joseph ordered three of this form in July of that year. By 1762, however, Joseph was ordering double-bellied coffeepots and creamers in addition to single-bellied coffeepots. Evidently the three-wine-pint size was still most popular, for it was this size that Joseph reordered from How & Masterman in 1762. Richardson did not order coffeepots from London again until 1770, when he reverted to the old-fashioned pear-shaped form in both the three-pint and quart size, but by this time stylish gadrooning around the lid and base was specified.

The earliest known coffeepot bearing Joseph Richardson's mark is an elongated pear-shaped or single-bellied type *(Fig. 33)*. This example can be dated 1748, for it was made by Richardson for his own use at about the time he and Mary Richardson were married, and it was later engraved with their initials and the date.[7] The style popular at the time is represented in the low, domed lid and circular foot. Curved lines are a basic part of the design rather than being superficial ornamentation. The subtley curved spout on one side of the pot is counterbalanced by a carved wooden handle on the other side. Curved ornamentation is applied to the surface in the form of acanthus capping at the top of the spout, strong scrolling, cast-shell appliqué on the lower half of the spout, and a swirled finial.

It is significant that the same basic design elements, with the exception of the finial, are found in an English coffeepot originally owned by the Growden family of Philadelphia, to whom Joseph Richardson was related through his mother, Elizabeth Growden *(Fig. 34)*. It is possible that Richardson ordered this coffeepot from England and sold it to the Growdens, or at least that he saw the coffeepot once it was in their possession.[8]

Similar, but with the increased ornamentation characteristic of the 1750's is the elaborate coffeepot made by Richardson in 1754 at the time of Sarah Shoemaker's marriage to Edward Penington *(Fig. 35a)*. An example of good design in the rococo taste, its double-bellied shape is not so exaggerated as such shapes became toward the end of the rococo period. The elaborate superficial ornament of the rococo style is present in the floral designs on the molded foot; in the repoussé ornament around the base of the spout, the handle sockets, and all around the top; in the curved cast flower finial; and in the engraved cipher on the side. The flat furl of earlier wooden handles is replaced by a highly furled acanthus leaf, and reeding is added to the back of the handle. The chased work on the lobes of the shell ornament at the base of the spout gives textural contrast to the surface of the metal.

The Shoemaker coffeepot is beautifully designed. The acanthus furl at the top of the silver spout is repeated at the top of the wooden handle. Repoussé roses at the top of the body are echoed in the three-dimensional flower finial. The chased C-scrolls in the repoussé ornament and the swirls in the base are more strongly restated in the deep lobing at the base of the spout. This repetition of design in different dimensions creates a pleasing aesthetic

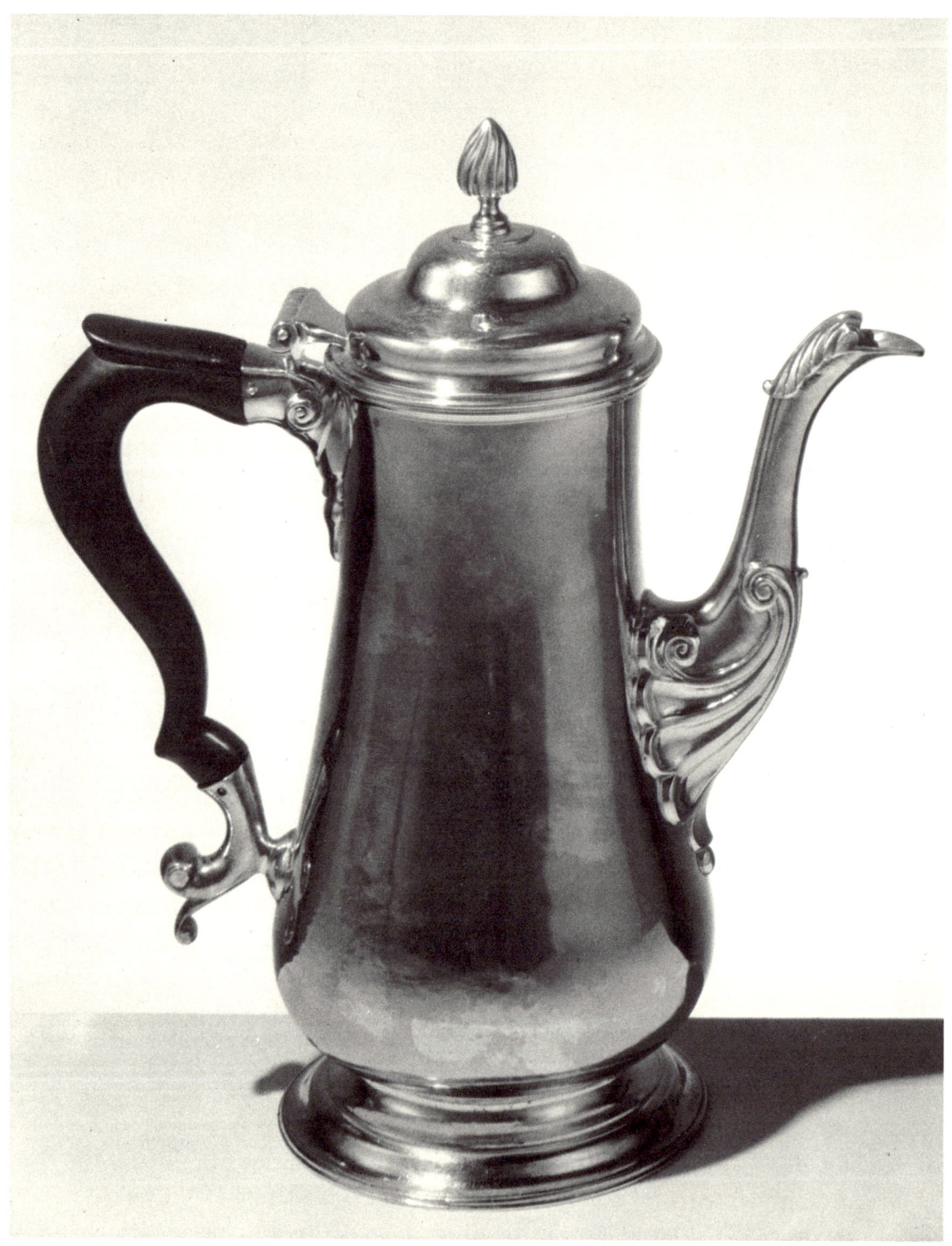

Fig. 33: Coffeepot, IR in rectangle on base, *c.* 1748. Owned by the maker, it is engraved on the base I^{R}M; *Joseph and Mary Richardson 1748* (the year they were married) in later engraving along with the name of *Juliana R. Wood*, a descendant. *Privately owned.*

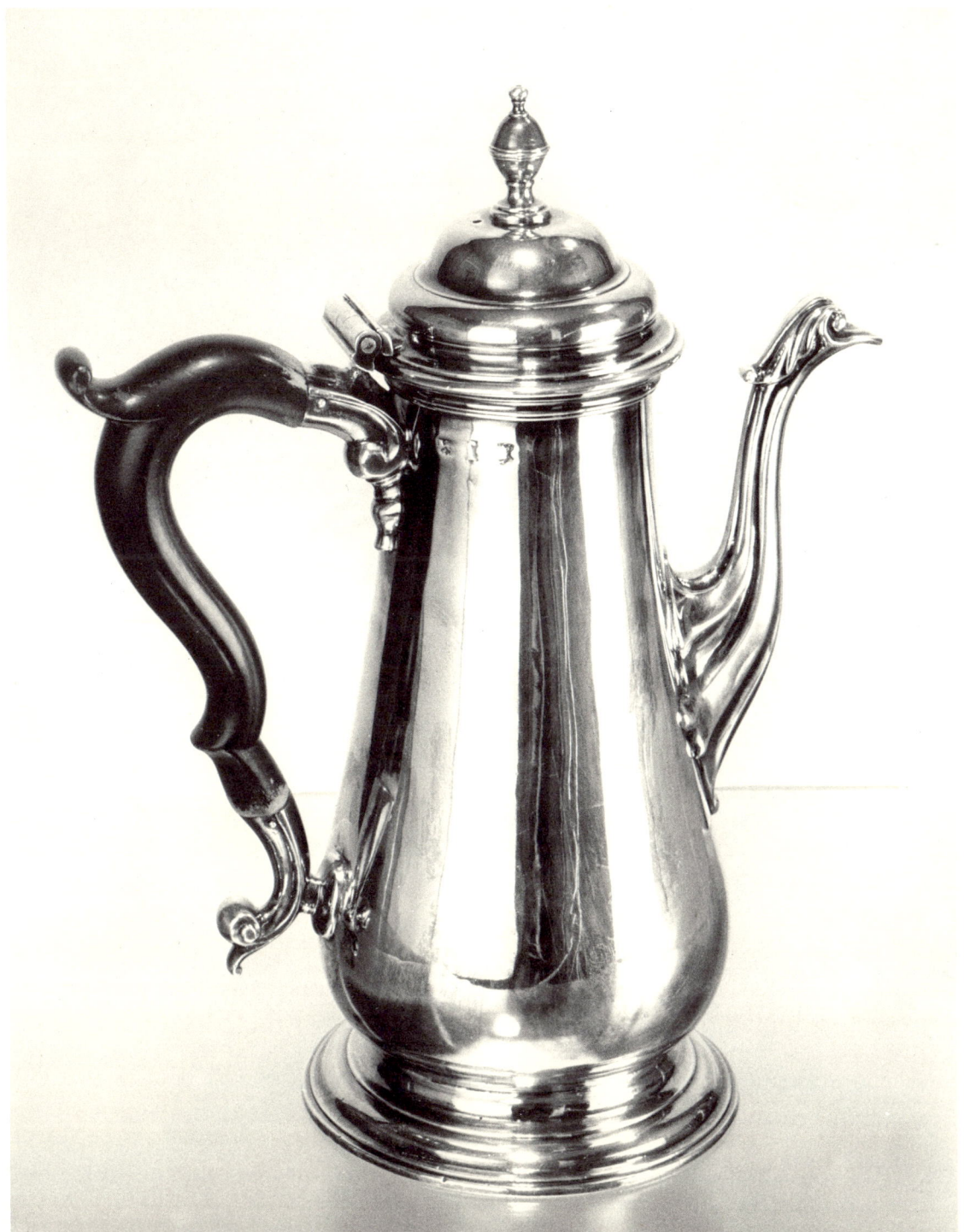

Fig. 34: English coffeepot, John Swift, London, 1753–4. Engraved on base T^GM and originally owned by the Growden family, relatives of Joseph Richardson through his mother, Elizabeth (Growden) Richardson. Later owned by Joseph Richardson, Jr., whose great-great-granddaughter is the present owner. *Courtesy of Mrs. William Shuttlesworth.*

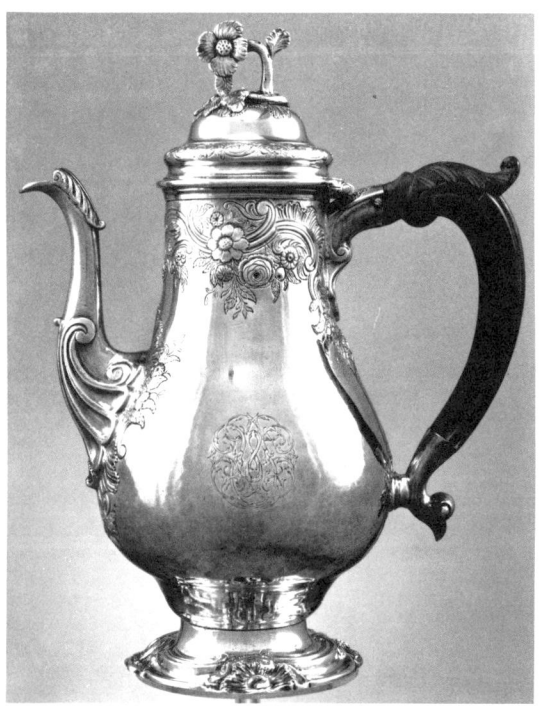 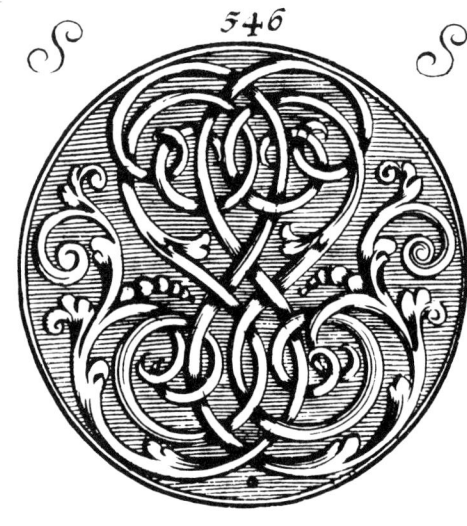

Fig. 35a: Coffeepot, IR in rectangle, furl above, four times on base, *c.* 1754. Cypher of SS engraved on side. Later engraving on opposite side, *Wedding silver of Sarah Shoemaker Married to Edward Penington November 26th 1754*. Height: 11 1/4″; diameter of base: 3 3/4″; weight: 32 oz. 6 dwt. 8 gr. *Courtesy of The Historical Society of Pennsylvania.*

Fig. 35b: Cypher for SS as shown in Simpson's *Book of Cyphers*, London, 1726. *Courtesy of the Henry Francis du Pont Winterthur Museum.*

effect. The spout and the floral finial curve in the same direction, emphasizing the flow of the line and creating the sense of precarious balance characteristic of the rococo style. The transition from the smooth areas of the lid to the cast finial is made by the addition of the cast and chased leaves at the top of the lid, which is surrounded by chased leaves in repoussé. An unusual feature is the placement of the hinge, which, instead of being angled out from the top handle socket to the lid, is placed flat and attached to the lid and directly below at the mouth of the pot.

As this high rococo period came to a close, gadrooning was substituted for repoussé decoration, and the body of the coffeepot became single-bellied again, although much higher-waisted and fuller than the earlier elongated pearshape. A coffeepot by Richardson, characteristic of the 1760's is illustrated in *Figure 36*. The dome of the lid is higher, and the finial, somewhat Chinese in inspiration, is fluted down the upper half. More elaborately cast and chased ornaments are added around the spout and handle joints, and the spout itself is grooved on its upper side.

A similarly grooved spout is found on another Richardson coffeepot,

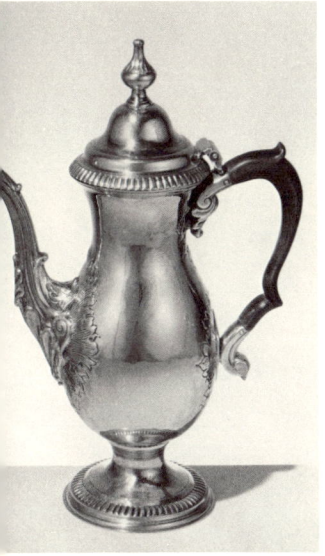 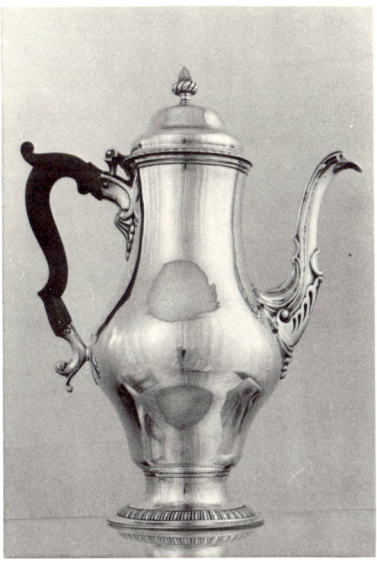 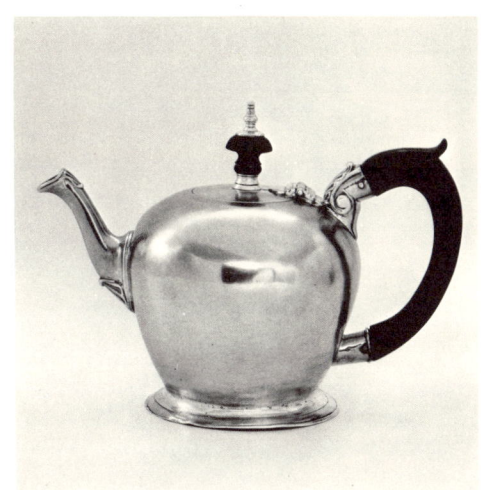

Fig. 36: Coffeepot, IR in rectangle twice on base, *c.* 1765. Height: 14″. *Courtesy of Mr. and Mrs. David B. Robb.*

Fig. 37: Coffeepot, IR in rectangle twice on base, *c.* 1770. IB scratched on base at later date. Height: 12 1/2″; diameter of base: 4 3/8″. *Courtesy of Yale University Art Gallery, Mabel Brady Garvan Collection.*

Fig. 38: Teapot, IR, *c.* 1735–40. Round body, the earliest type known to have been made by Joseph Richardson. Height: 5 3/8″. *Courtesy of The Metropolitan Museum of Art, New York City.*

which has greatly refined gadrooning around its lid and base *(Fig. 37)*. This coffeepot, probably made in the 1770's is noticeably lacking in rococo ornament, although there are heavy cast-shell appliqués on the spout and at the top of the handle. The groovings of these shells and of the gadrooning are repeated in the round in the cast finial, whose entire bell-shaped surface is swirled gadrooning.

Teapots followed the same general development as coffeepots although they were more widely used. In the 1740's, silver teapots were still a distinct luxury, but Richardson's accounts for this period show that he was selling them as early as 1734, and that orders increased steadily.[9] The earliest known Richardson teapot is round with a simple C-scrolled handle and a slightly curved spout which has a flat furl at the top and a symmetrical shell placed upside down at its base *(Fig. 38)*. The flat lid has a rather heavy, exposed hinge and is only slightly decorated around the edge with an engraved border. The wooden knob finial supported by a circular silver plinth is unusual in its design; since many of the Richardson teapots do not have wooden knobs, it is possible that this may be a later addition.

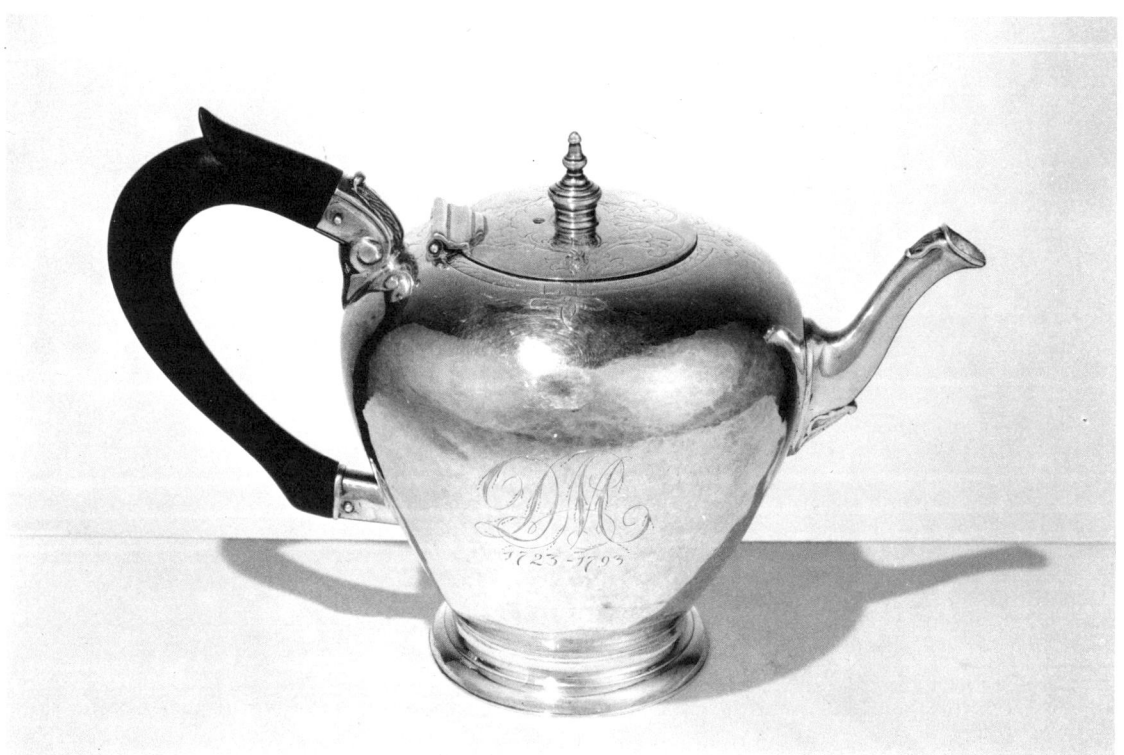

Fig. 39: Teapot, IR in rectangle four times on base, *c.* 1740. Apple-shaped body, engraved DM on base. On side, engraved at end of 18th century, *DM 1723–1793* for Deborah Morris, the original owner. *Courtesy of Chester County Historical Society, West Chester, Pennsylvania.*

In the next decade, Richardson's teapots became more elaborate *(Fig. 39)*. Their lids were more intricately engraved, and the round bodies took on a more pleasing apple shape. In the best teapots, the hinges were hidden and frequently the furl at the top of the spout was more pronounced *(Fig. 40)*. Popular during this early period also was the octagonal shape of the spout. Richardson referred to the octagonal shaping as "eight square," and from 1738 to 1746 he recorded in his accounts the making of teapots with "square" bodies although none with his mark are known today.

The restrained decoration seen in these early teapots of the 1740's was replaced in the 1750's by the engraved, chased, and repoussé ornamentation epitomized by the Richardson teapot shown in *Figure 41* which features an abundance of rococo swirls, C-scrolls, flowers, and ruffles. The abhorrence of a straight line typical of the rococo style is seen in the sudden swelling of the domed lid, surmounted by a large, conelike finial. The teapot's surface ornamentation helps to integrate the varied elements of design, for it flows from the body onto the lid, the base of the spout, and the top socket of the handle.

The next step in the development of this form was the bulging out of the pot at the bottom to balance the domed top, giving the form its inverted pear

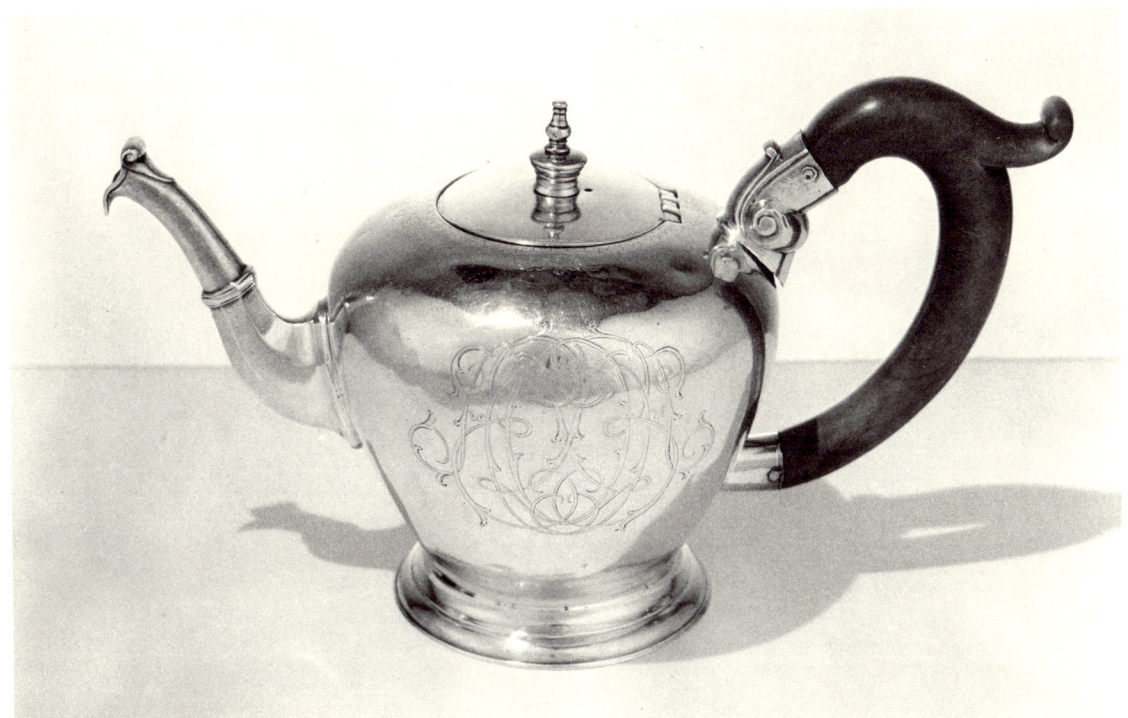

Fig. 40: Teapot, IR in rectangle twice on base, 1740–50. Engraved cypher on side, *HELO*. Original weight marked on base, *18–12*. *Courtesy of Mrs. Walter M. Jeffords.*

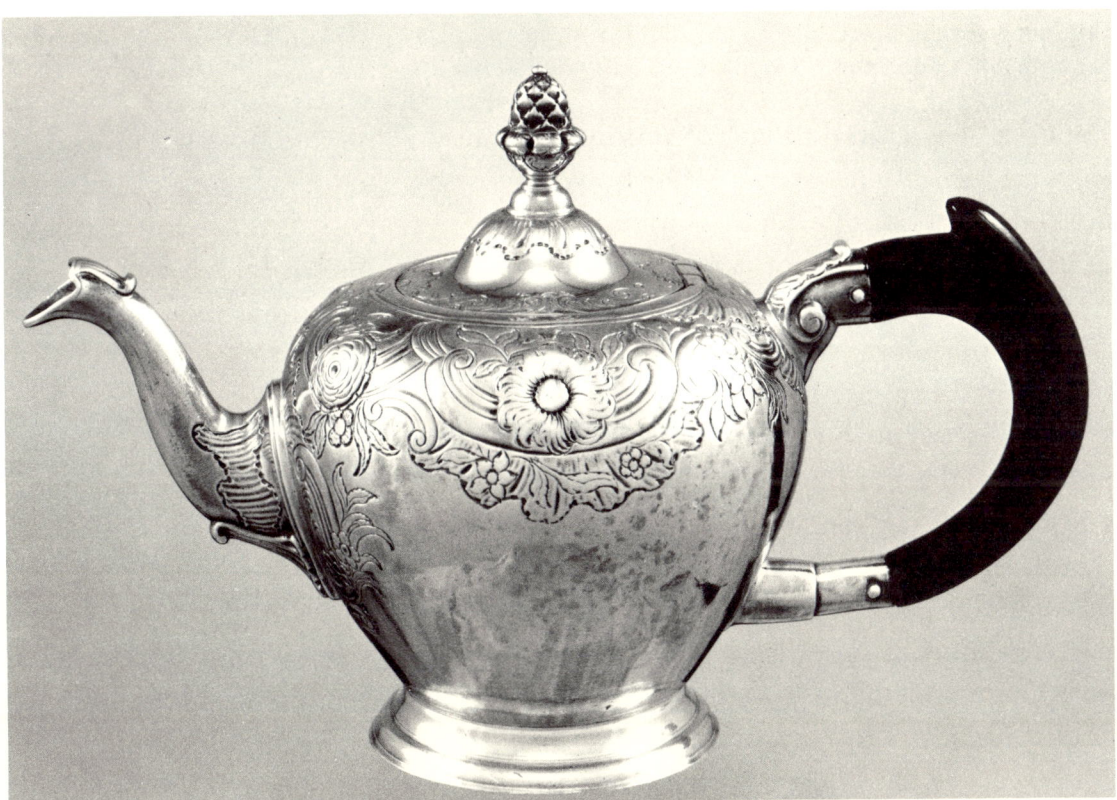

Fig. 41: Teapot, IR in rectangle, scroll above, on base, *c.* 1755. Engraved on base in shaded block letters RC and AR. Height: 5 11/16″; weight: 16 oz. 13 dwt. 19 gr. *Courtesy of The Historical Society of Pennsylvania.*

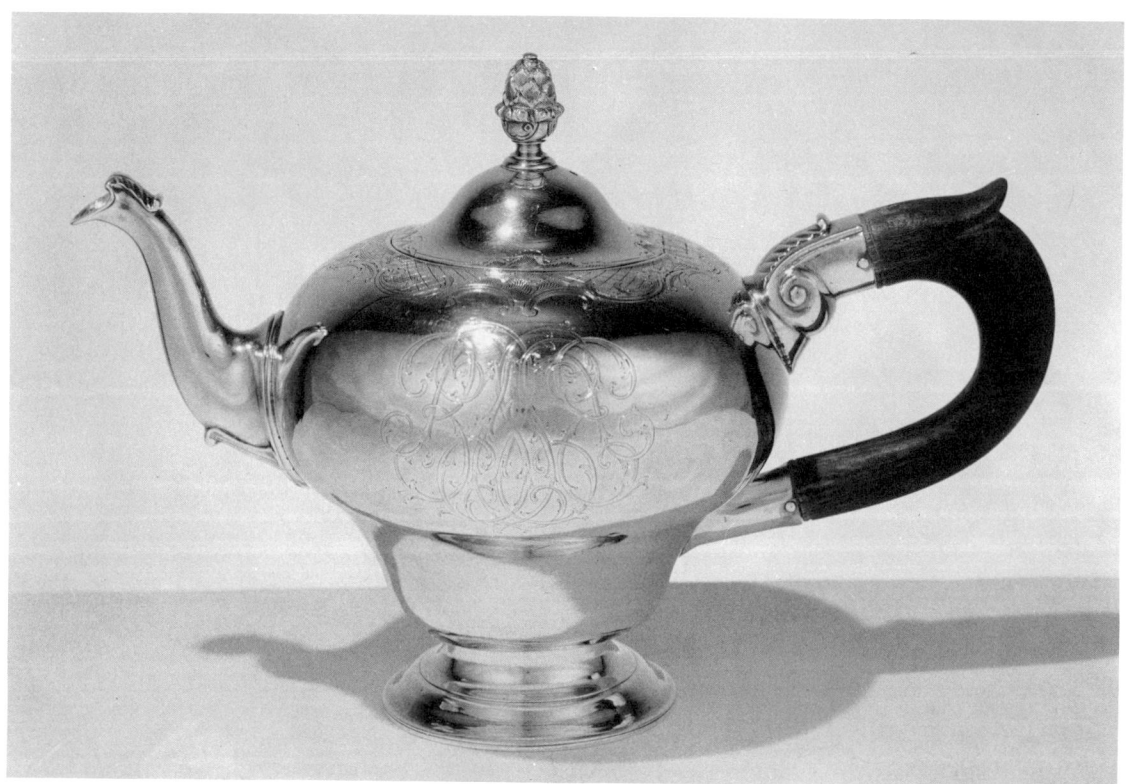

Fig. 42: Teapot, IR in rectangle on base, c. 1750–60. Engraved on side with reverse cypher *ESS*. Owned at one time by Mary Sandwith (née 1732). The teapot was later given to Mary Sandwith Skyrin. Scratched on base with weight: *18 oz. 8 dwt. 12 gr.* Maximum distance between handle and spout: 9 5/16". *Courtesy of Philadelphia Museum of Art.*

shape, as it is called today, or a double-bellied shape, as it was then called *(Figs. 42, 43)*. Richardson's letter book traces this change in form. At first he ordered from London plain teapots and chased teapots, but as early as 1759 he asked specifically for double-bellied teapots, some of which were to be neatly chased while others were to be plain with engraved borders. After 1762 all his orders for teapots were for the double-bellied form, some of which were to have engraved borders.

Of the recorded teapots made in Richardson's shop prior to 1748, the largest weighed 22 oz. 17 dwt.;[10] the smallest, charged to John Fisher in 1745, weighed only 15 oz. 10 dwt. and cost £2/10/0 to make with an additional charge of 5 shillings for its handle. Like Paul Revere, Joseph Richardson occasionally noted in his accounts a charge for the handle of a silver teapot or coffeepot, but he did not indicate that he actually made the handles himself. For teapot handles he charged 5 or 6 shillings; for the only coffeepot handle noted in the accounts he charged £0/7/6. Undoubtedly many goldsmiths carved these handles themselves; other aspects of their craft—making patterns, cutting dies, and engraving—required the same skill as carving.

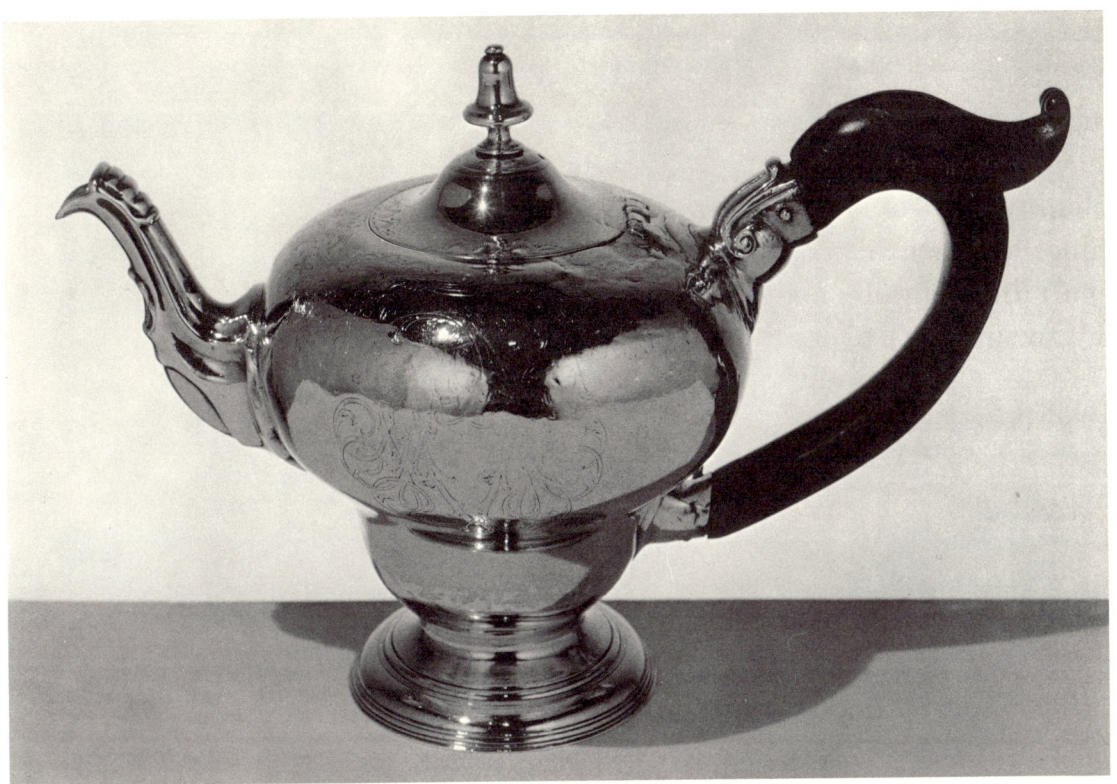

Fig. 43: Teapot, IR in rectangle, scroll above, twice on base, *c*. 1760–65. Owned successively by the Logan, Dickinson, and Norris families and given by Robert R. Logan to the Philadelphia Museum of Art. Engraved cypher too faint to be read. Height: 5 5/8". *Courtesy of Philadelphia Museum of Art.*

Nevertheless, there were people who advertised that they could provide this work for goldsmiths.[11] One item among the Richardson papers provides a clue as to who might have made handles for Richardson's teapots and coffeepots if he did not make them himself: his receipt book records the payment on September 20, 1769, of £6/5/6 to Hercules Courtenay, who lived near Richardson and who had advertised the month before that he was a carver and gilder from London.[12]

A man like Courtenay might have carved the patterns for the elaborate cast ornaments which appear on the teakettle-on-stand bearing the mark of Joseph Richardson (*Fig. 44*). Outstanding not only for its unusual form but because it represents Richardson's most monumental work in metal, this teakettle has an inverted pear-shaped body elaborately worked with rococo scrolls, ruffles, leaves, flowers, and animal heads surrounding the Plumsted family arms. The domed lid has a cone finial framed by the shaped silver handle which stands high above it. The stand on which the kettle rests and in which the burner is housed is made largely of heavy, cast, rococo ornament,

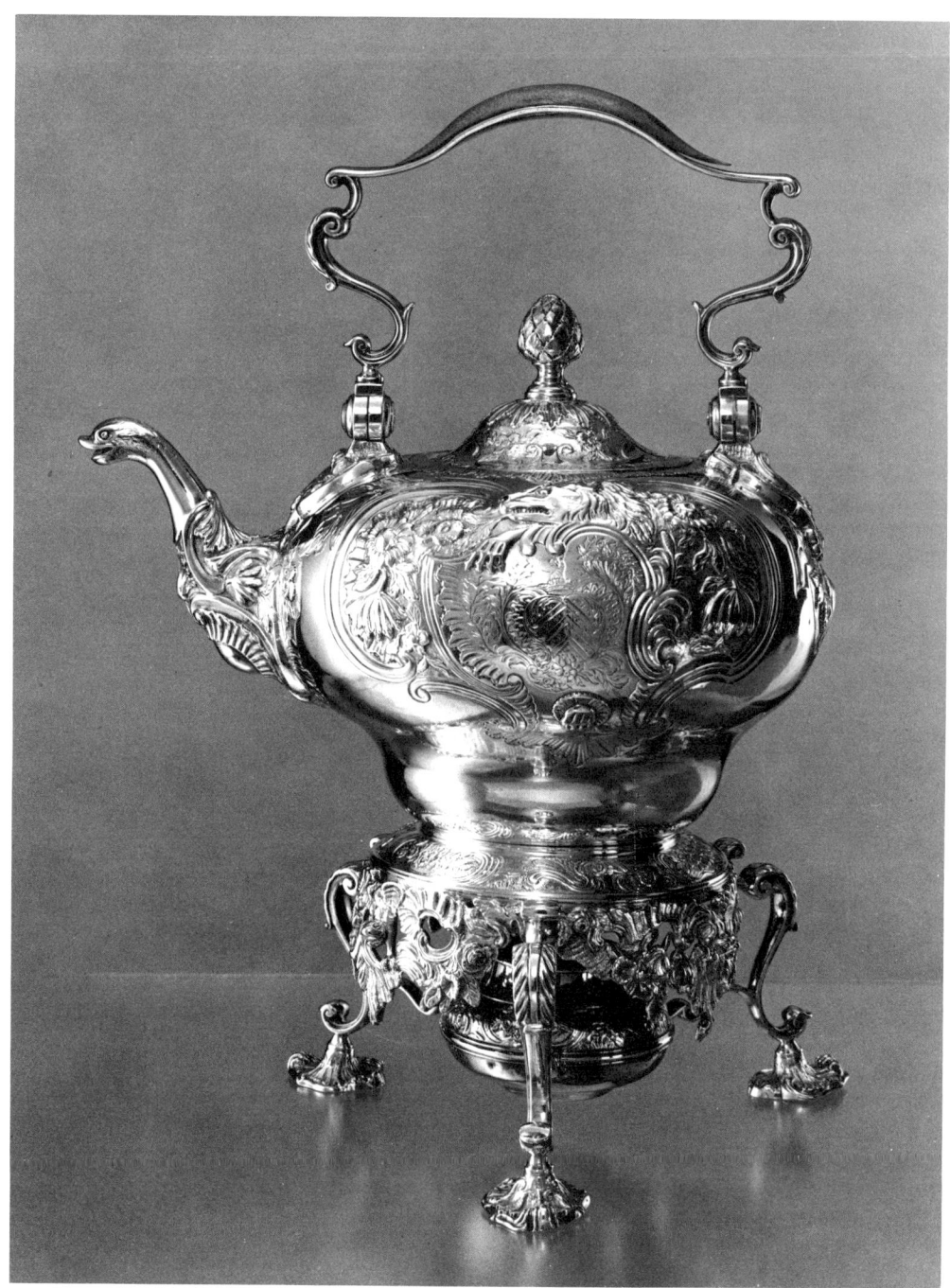

Fig. 44: Teakettle-on-stand, IR in rectangle, scroll above, on base of both kettle and stand, *c.* 1755. Engraved on side with Plumsted arms and crest (*Fig. 44a*). Not mentioned in the 1745 will of Clement Plumsted, the teakettle was left by his wife, Mary, to granddaughter Elizabeth Plumsted. The handle was probably originally wrapped with wicker for protection. Height: 15 5/16″. Weight engraved on base of kettle, *62-14* and on stand, *30-16*, totalling over 93 oz. *Courtesy of Yale University Art Gallery, Mabel Brady Garvan Collection.*

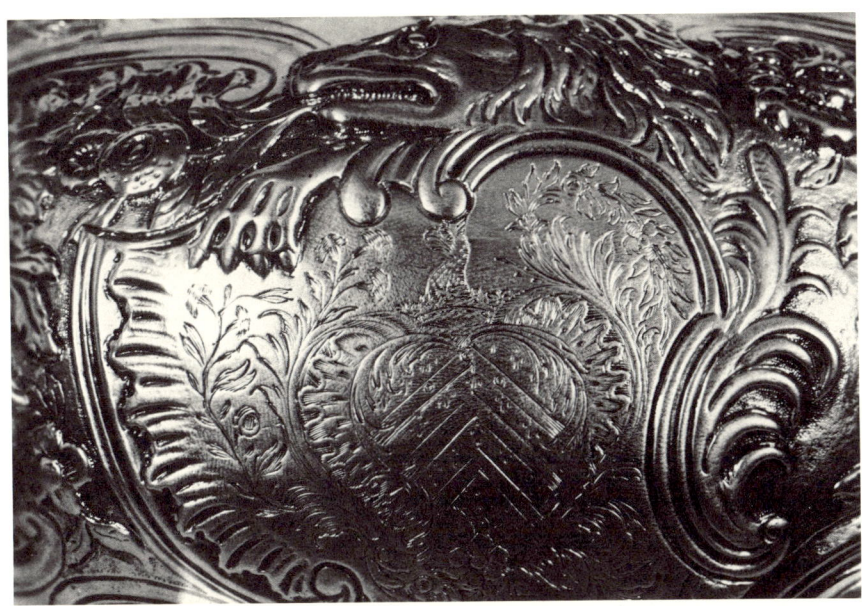

Fig. 44a: Detail of Plumsted arms and crest.

supported by three shell feet and cabriole legs with acanthus leaves at the knees. Even the lamp itself is decorated, a feature not commonly found on similar English forms.

This teakettle, probably made about 1755, was owned originally by the widow of Mayor Clement Plumsted.[13] Several other important Philadelphians owned such kettles. David and Margaret (Evans) Franks who were married at the end of 1743 owned a somewhat similar and very fashionable teakettle-on-stand made by Paul de Lamerie of London in 1744–45.[14]

The Plumsted teakettle-on-stand was probably the only one of its kind fashioned by Joseph Richardson. There are no records of his having imported this form from England, nor is there any indication in his papers that he ever made one for anyone else. Its lavishness, however, attests to his ability to execute even the most demanding patterns.

Accompanying the more important tea and coffee vessels were the articles variously called milk pots, milk ewers, and cream pots.[15] This form was made by Joseph Richardson as early as 1734, when Thomas Leach paid £2/1/8 for the silver in a milk pot weighing 4 oz. 12 dwt. 18 gr. and 18 shillings for its fashioning. By 1738 Joseph was making nearly half-a-dozen milk pots a year. It appears that some people who might not have been able to afford a silver teapot did at least use a silver milk pot with their china teasets.

The earliest known milk pot by Richardson has a circular base, a pear-shaped body with a mid-band; a widely curved, V-shaped spout with a flat top; and a curved, flat handle supporting the right-angled hinge to a domed lid

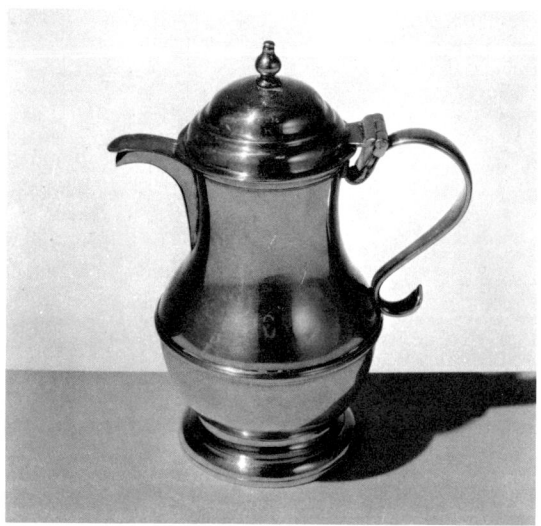 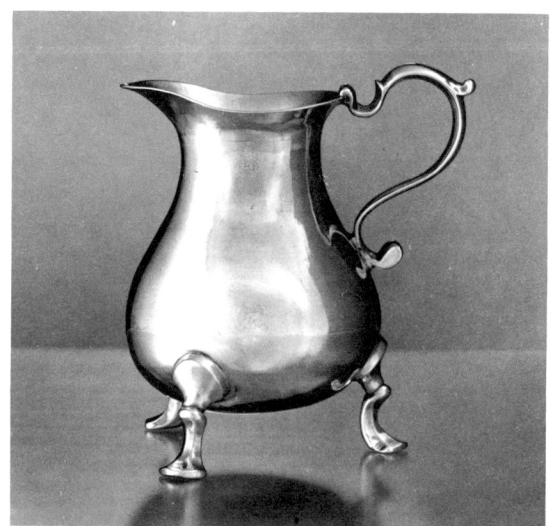

Fig. 45: Milk pot, IR in oval on base, *c.* 1746. Engraved on handle, E·A and marked on base with weight *4-1-12*. Probably the same milk pot for which Samuel Abbot paid £2/4/7 in 1746 since the weights are identical and Abbot married Elizabeth Hastings in that year. Height: *c.* 5″. *Courtesy of Philadelphia Museum of Art.*

Fig. 46: Milk pot, IR in rectangle on base, *c.* 1741. Engraved on base W^{B}R; 1741 added later. Height: 3 7/8″. *Courtesy of Yale University Art Gallery, Mabel Brady Garvan Collection.*

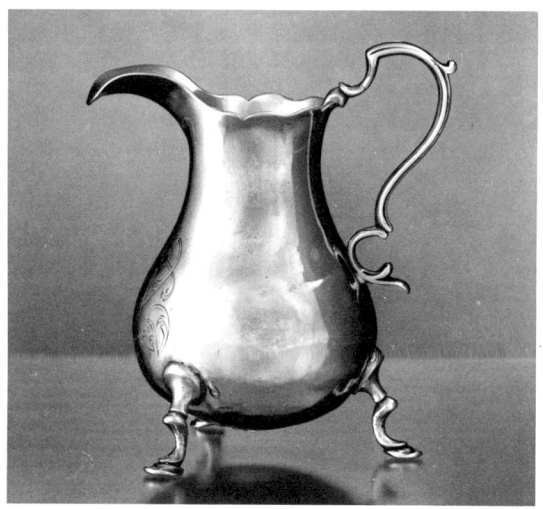 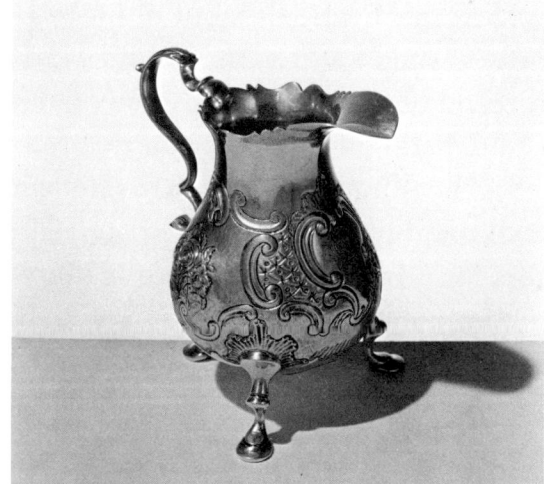

Fig. 47: Milk pot, IR in rectangle on base, *c.* 1745. Engraved on front with cypher SH (*Fig. 78*). Weight: "4 oz. 8 dwt." scratched on base. *Courtesy of Yale University Art Gallery, Mabel Brady Garvan Collection.*

Fig. 48: Milk pot, IR in rectangle twice on base, *c.* 1755. Enclosed in an asymmetrical rococo cartouche on front are script initials *IB*. On the side is a basket of flowers enclosed by C-scrolls and ruffles against a chased and textured background found also on the Shoemaker sugar bowl (*Fig. 54*). Engraved on base W^{B}M. *Courtesy of Mrs. Harry M. Ullman.*

with a cast finial *(Fig. 45)*. Other early milk pots made by Joseph were octagonal, although no examples of this type bearing his mark are known today. His accounts show that he charged Ruth Burden in 1736 for making an "Eight Square Milk Pott £1/15/0" which weighed 18 dwt. These octagonal milk pots probably had domed bases, as did most early examples of this form.

The circular or domed base was soon replaced by three cast pad feet on curved legs which supported a pear-shaped body. One example by Richardson of this type has the same drake feet seen on Philadelphia furniture of the period *(Fig. 46)*. It is typical of the styles of 1741, the date engraved on its base. Its simple scrolled handle and plain lip soon gave way to a double C-scroll handle and a widely scrolled lip *(Fig. 47)*, and its basic form was greatly elaborated in the 1750's with the addition of an acanthus leaf at the top of the handle, an intricately crenellated lip, and chased repoussé ornamentation on the sides of the body *(Fig. 48)*.

The next development in the shape of the milk pot was the double-bellied form Richardson first ordered from England several years after he had ordered double-bellied teapots and sugar dishes. In 1762 he asked How & Masterman to send two double-bellied milk pots along with twenty-four plain, single-bellied ones. The newer type *(Fig. 49)* was characteristically supported by a circular, domed base, rather than tripod legs, and was decorated with widely spaced, whirled gadrooning.

In 1770 the style changed again. In that year, Richardson ordered five of the new-styled cream urns from John Masterman, in addition to fifteen cream pots of the older fashion. The urn as a form has generally been considered a post-Revolutionary design, but Joseph Richardson obviously was familiar with the style several years before the war and may have made milk pots in that shape himself, although none have been definitely attributed to him.

Next in importance to the milk pot was the container for sugar. *(Sugar dish* was evidently the term used in Joseph Richardson's day, for he never speaks of a *sugar bowl*). The earliest known sugar dish by Richardson *(Fig. 50)*, documented by an entry in his accounts *(Fig. 51)* was made in 1736 for Oswald Peel. This dish is particularly important, for the early date establishes its oval mark as the first touchmark used by Joseph Richardson and helps date the appearance of the octagonal form in early rococo silver.[16] The form continued to be made for some time. In 1747 an almost identical sugar dish *(Fig. 52)* was purchased by Samuel Emlen.[17] Although the later dish weighed more, it cost only half as much to make, suggesting that the first fashioning of a new

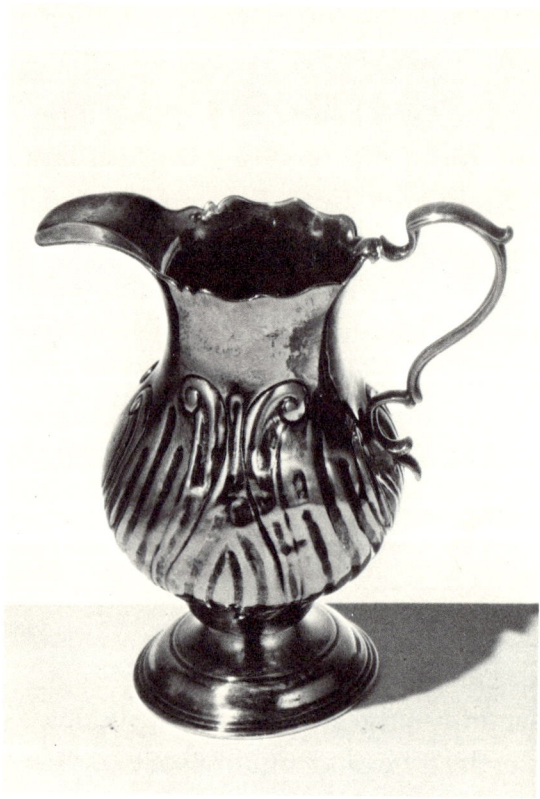

Fig. 49: Milk pot, IR in rectangle on base, *c.* 1765. Height: 4 1/2"; diameter of base 2 1/2"; weight: 4 oz. 19 dwt. 12 gr. *Courtesy of The Historical Society of Pennsylvania.*

design cost more than later ones. After Richardson had made a number of sugar dishes, £1/10/0 became the standard price.[18]

Perhaps the most beautiful of his octagonal sugar dishes was made in the 1750's and is shown in *Figure 53*. Its form is softened by the curved line in the greater flare of the lip at the top of the body, the fluid script cipher of the owner's initials in the front center panel, and the cast finial at the top of the lid.

The curvilinear quality of late rococo silver also manifested itself in double-bellied bodies for sugar dishes. Richardson first ordered this style from England in 1759, specifying that they be "Double Bellied . . . with Covers Neatly Chast to Suit the tea Potts of a Midling Substance." He himself made such a dish in 1754 *(Fig. 54)* to match a coffeepot of the same shape (see *Fig. 35a*). The double-bellied form of its body is repeated in reverse in the double

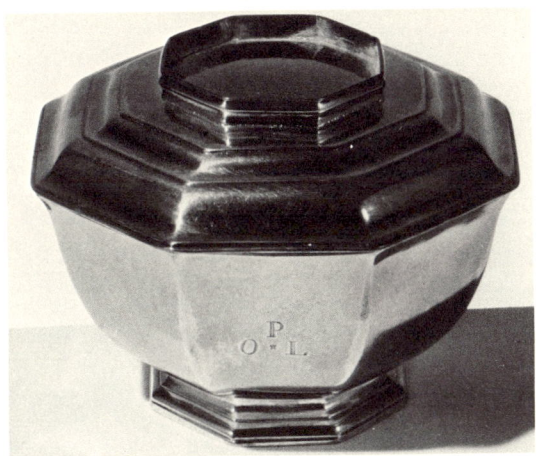

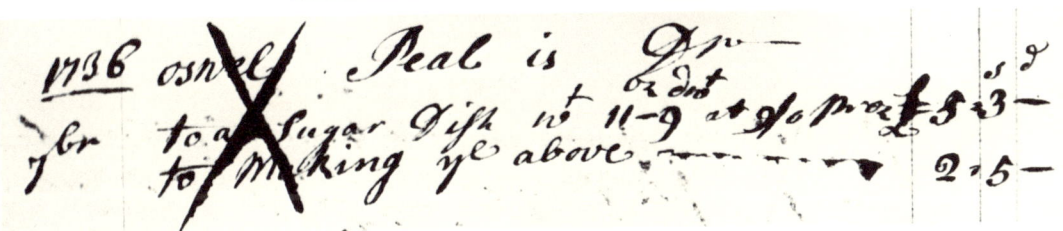

Fig. 50: Sugar dish, IR in oval twice on base, 1736. Engraved on side O$^P_*$L for the original owners, Oswald and Lydia Peel, whose descendants still own the sugar dish. *Courtesy of Mr. and Mrs. William H. Potter.*

Fig. 51: Entry in Joseph Richardson's account book showing purchase by Oswald Peel in 1736 of a sugar dish (*Fig. 50*) weighing 11 oz. 9 dwt. Cross made through the entry indicates the account had been settled. *Courtesy of The Historical Society of Pennsylvania.*

doming of its lid. All the lines are curved, and the curves are accentuated by the scrolls, flowers, and ruffles decorating the body, and by the engraved cipher contained in the central cartouche. This sugar bowl is outstanding because of the rustic cast floral finial placed asymetrically upon the lid and surrounded by chasing simulating the cast leaves. The decoration of the body is further enhanced by the pebbling of the background, which sets off the raised work. Very similar in form and decoration is another sugar dish and its matching apple-shaped teapot, both by Richardson *(Figs. 41, 55).*

Not all sugar dishes of the 1750's were so elaborate. Plain dishes as well as chased double-bellied forms were ordered from London by Richardson in 1759. Examples of this plainer form made in his shop include one owned by Joseph himself *(Fig. 56).* Perhaps its restrained simplicity was more consistent with his Quaker principles. A similar sugar dish *(Fig. 57)* made by him has slightly more ornamentation: a high, full-domed lid with a band of flat engraving of C-scrolls, ruffles, and diapering around a twisted flame finial. This type of finial, also found on Philadelphia furniture of the period, was

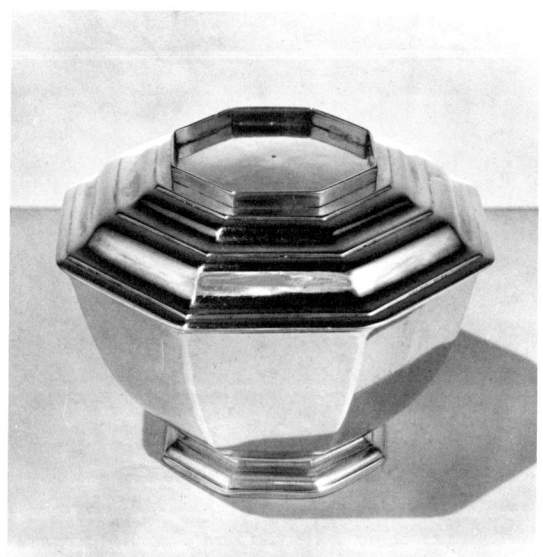 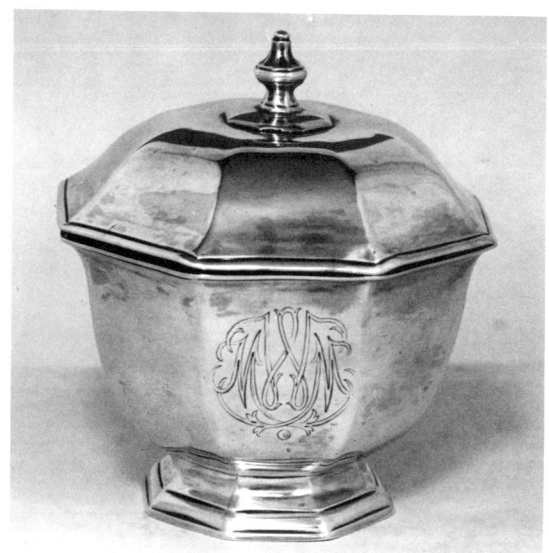

Fig. 52: Sugar dish, IR in oval twice on base, *c. 1747.* Engraved on base E·M for original owner and marked *12·10·12* on base for original weight. Probably the same sugar dish weighing 12 oz. 10 dwt. 12 gr. bought in 1747 by Samuel Emlen for £ 1/10/0. Height: 3 1/2". *Courtesy of Mrs. Walter M. Jeffords.*

Fig. 53: Sugar dish, IR in rectangle, scroll above, on base, *c. 1740–60.* Engraving on base indicates it was originally owned by *Margaret Wistar, 1760.* Engraved MW on front. Mate to bowl *(Fig. 61).* Diameter: 5 3/4". *Courtesy of Mrs. R. Stewardson Taylor.*

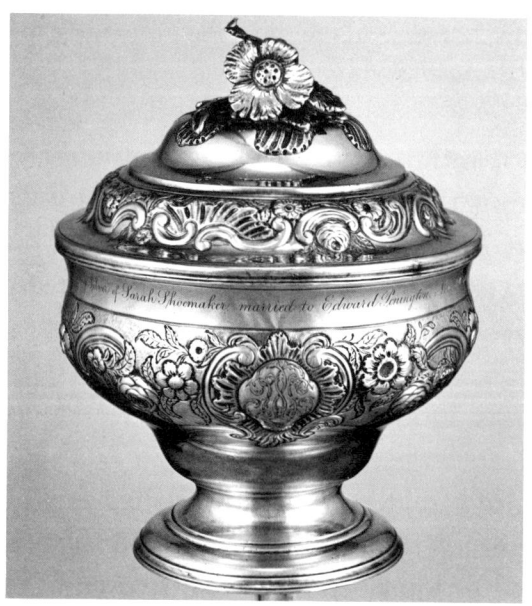 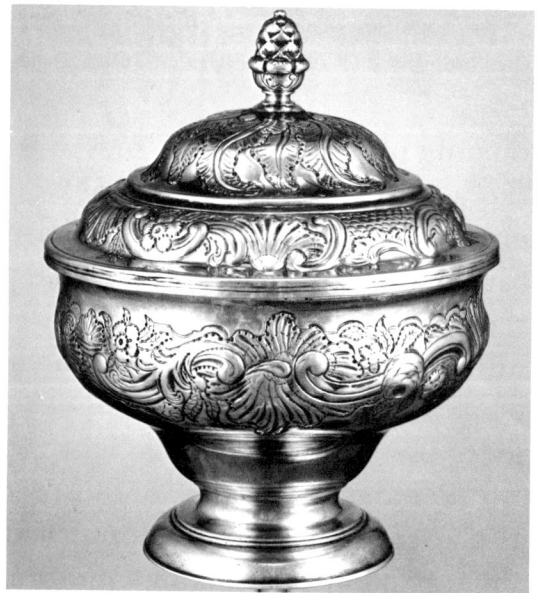

Fig. 54: Sugar dish, IR in rectangle twice on base, *c. 1754.* Engraved in later script around rim, *Wedding silver of Sarah Shoemaker married to Edward Penington, Nov. 26, 1754.* Mate to coffeepot *(Fig. 35a)* with similar inscription. Height: 5 1/2"; weight: 11 oz. 19 dwt. 5 gr. *Courtesy of The Historical Society of Pennsylvania; photograph by Gilbert Ask.*

Fig. 55: Sugar dish, IR in rectangle twice on base, *c. 1755–60.* Engraved on base in shaded block letters R·C and A·R, matching teapot *(Fig. 41).* Height: 5 1/2"; weight: 9 oz. 17 dwt. 14 gr. *Courtesy of The Historical Society of Pennsylvania; photograph by Gilbert Ask.*

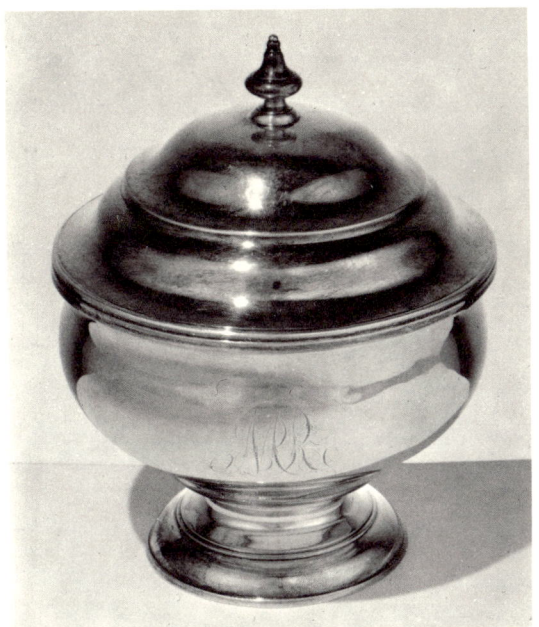 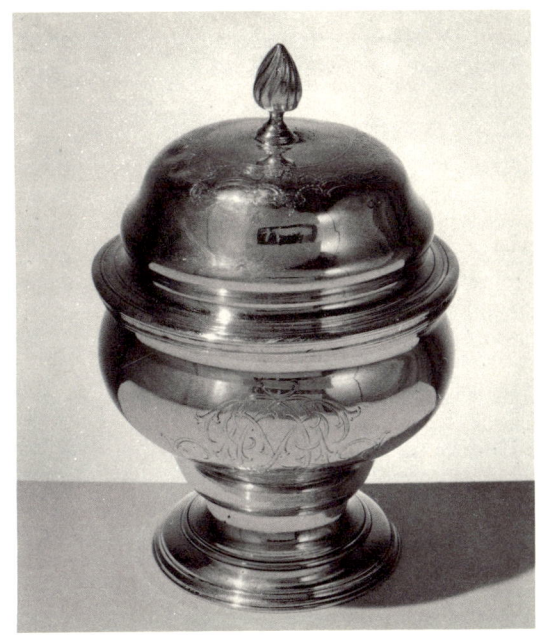

Fig. 56: Sugar dish, IR in rectangle with scroll below, *c.* 1765. Engraved on base I·M with R above for Joseph and Mary Richardson, and on the rim, *Joseph & Mary Richardson / 1748*. Their daughter Rebecca received the dish upon her mother's death in 1788 when the initials RR were added on the base and the script initials *MR* were added on the side. The bowl is gilt inside. *Courtesy of Mrs. Walter M. Jeffords.*

Fig. 57: Sugar dish, IR in rectangle on base, *c.* 1765–75. Florid cypher engraved on side, *LO* and *C* or *I*. *Courtesy of Mrs. Boyd Lee Spahr.*

used on another sugar dish to which Richardson added a border of gadrooning around the rim *(Fig. 58)*. Richardson first ordered sugar dishes with gadrooned borders from London in 1770; thus this dish was probably made shortly after that, near the end of his career.

Tea sets of Joseph's day sometimes included slop bowls into which dregs of cold tea were poured when a cup was refilled.[19] Joseph Richardson made such a bowl as early as 1747, and thereafter all but one of the bowls noted in his accounts were specified as slop bowls or basins. (The term "waste" bowl, used to indicate the same form, evidently came into use later; it does not appear in Joseph's accounts).

Most of the bowls recorded, whether or not called slop bowls, weighed between nine and fourteen ounces, and presumably were about the same size —approximately 1 1/2 pints. Joseph notes that the slop basin Robert Hartshorn bought in 1748 held that amount. But the slop bowl, like other articles in the tea service, became larger as the century progressed. Following the same general design lines as the other vessels, the earliest bowls were "square" in shape and cost £1/10/0 to produce. Oswald Peel was charged £2 for his bowl

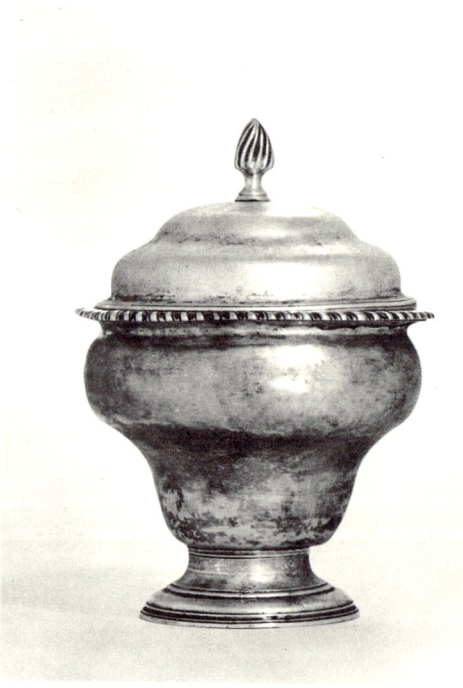

Fig. 58: Sugar dish, IR in rectangle on base, *c.* 1770–75. Engraved inside lid AF. Height: 6 3/16"; weight: 13 1/2 oz. *Courtesy of Yale University Art Gallery, Mabel Brady Garvan Collection.*

in 1747 (it was made by Richardson's apprentice, David Harper, who received £1 for his labors). Richardson and his shopworkers evidently made all the bowls sold in the shop during the period covered by his accounts, and he apparently imported none from England until the 1760's.

The earliest known slop bowl bearing Richardson's mark can be attributed to the first years of his career. It was originally owned by John and Ann Richardson of Delaware, who were married in 1704, and who had been patrons of Joseph's father *(Fig. 59)*. Its wide, round shape is typical of silver design in the early rococo style, as is its lack of superficial ornament. The lines on the circular raised foot, and the lines inscribed around the outside of the mouth of the bowl are the only decoration. At about the same time, Joseph made another bowl—plain, but with an applied molding which emphasizes its purity of line *(Fig. 60)*.[20] The smooth surface accentuates its silvery brightness, and nothing detracts from the reflective powers of the metal itself.

Richardson continued to make both round and octagonal slop basins *(Fig. 61)* until about 1760. However, the upper edges of the later basins flare outward, giving them a more curvilinear (and therefore more rococo) shape than the earlier straight-sided bowls. The curved lip is more graceful, leading the eye outward and around to the foot of the bowl again, rather than stopping abruptly at the top of a straight-sided body. To continue this smooth flowing

Joseph Richardson: His Silver

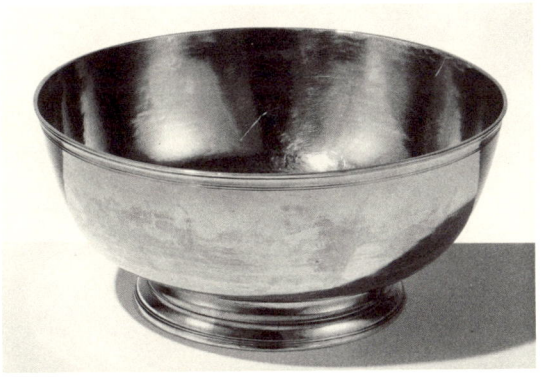
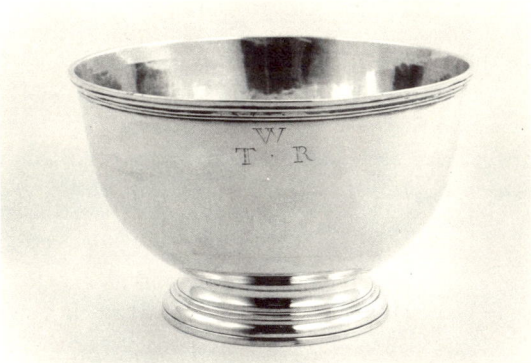

Fig. 59: Bowl, IR in oval twice on base, *c.* 1730–40. Engraved on base in block letters I^{R}A for John and Ann Richardson who were married in 1704. The inventory of their daughter Ann's husband, Dr. Henry Latimer, taken in 1820, calls this a slop bowl and notes its weight as 17 oz. 8 dwt. The original weight scratched on the base was 17 oz. 8 dwt. Diameter: 7 1/4"; height: 3 1/2". *Courtesy of Mrs. Walter S. Franklin, a descendant of the original owners.*

Fig. 60: Bowl, IR in rectangle twice on base, *c.* 1735–50. T^{W}R engraved in shaded roman letters on front side. The bowl has a history of ownership by the Wistar family but no members of this family have been traced having the necessary initials and living about the time the bowl was made. In March 1738, Richardson "Received of Thomas Willard the sum of £ 6/0/0 in cash towards a silver bowle Received of Do. 6 dwt. 18 gr. of silver towards the above." Height: 2 3/4"; diameter: 4 1/2"; weight: 4 oz. *Courtesy of The Henry Francis du Pont Winterthur Museum; photograph by Gilbert Ask.*

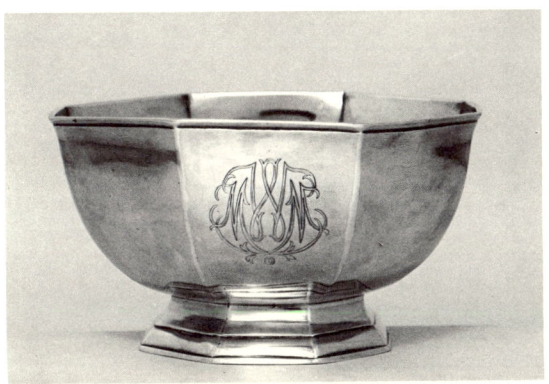
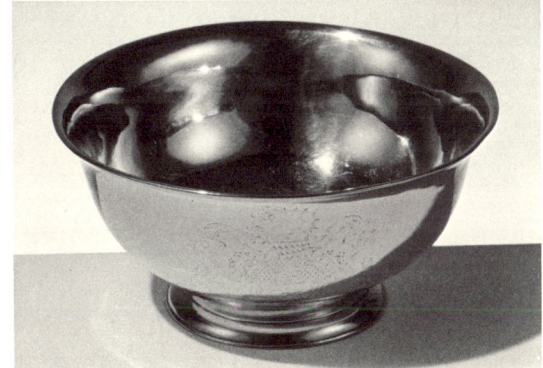

Fig. 61: Bowl, IR in rectangle, furl above, on base, *c.* 1750. Matches sugar dish (*Fig. 53*), originally owned by Margaret Wistar whose cypher is engraved on the side. Engraved on base, *Margaret Wistar, 1760 / Caspar Wistar Haines, 1785 / Reuben Haines, 1812 / Margaret H. Stewardson*. Height: 4 3/4". *Courtesy of Mrs. R. Stewardson Taylor.*

Fig. 62: Bowl, IR in rectangle on base, *c.* 1750–80. Arms engraved on side and initials of original owners I^{F}E in block letters on base, possibly for Jeremiah and Elizabeth (Young) Fisher who were married in 1777. Diameter: *c.* 7". *Privately owned; photograph by Philadelphia Museum of Art.*

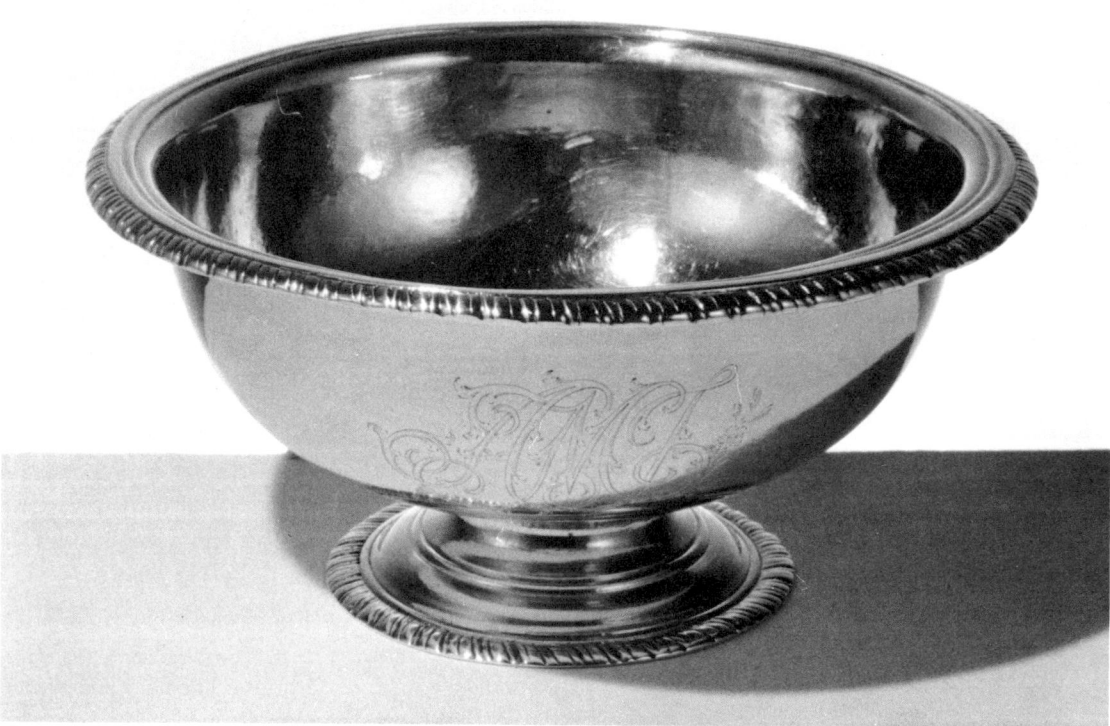

Fig. 63: Bowl, IR in rectangle twice on base, *c.* 1760–80. Flaring lip with gadrooning around edge and around foot indicates it was made toward the end of Richardson's career. Engraved on side in foliate script *AMT*. Height: 3 1/4"; diameter: 6 3/4". *Courtesy of The Henry Ford Museum.*

line, Richardson also replaced the simple block letters he used on earlier silver with an elegant scrolled cipher.

On another bowl *(Fig. 62)* Joseph used an even more rococo design—a beautifully engraved coat of arms. The bowl itself does not have the octagonal panels found on earlier examples; it is simply a rounded bowl with a plain flaring lip. About 1770 a gadrooned edge was added to this basic form *(Fig. 63)*. Richardson's requests for "chased" slop bowls from England were replaced by orders for slop bowls "with gadrooned borders," and these were the kinds of bowls he was making at the end of his career.

Like slop bowls, silver tea caddies or canisters were sometimes added to tea sets in the eighteenth century. Porcelain caddies were much more common, but some English silver caddies were owned by colonial American families, and occasionally this form was made by American silversmiths.[21] One pair of tea canisters *(Fig. 64)* bearing Richardson's mark survive today. Owned originally by Oswald and Lydia Peel, they are mentioned as two "square" canisters in the will of Lydia Peel in 1785 when she bequeathed them to her daughter Grace.[22] Still owned by two different lines of the family,

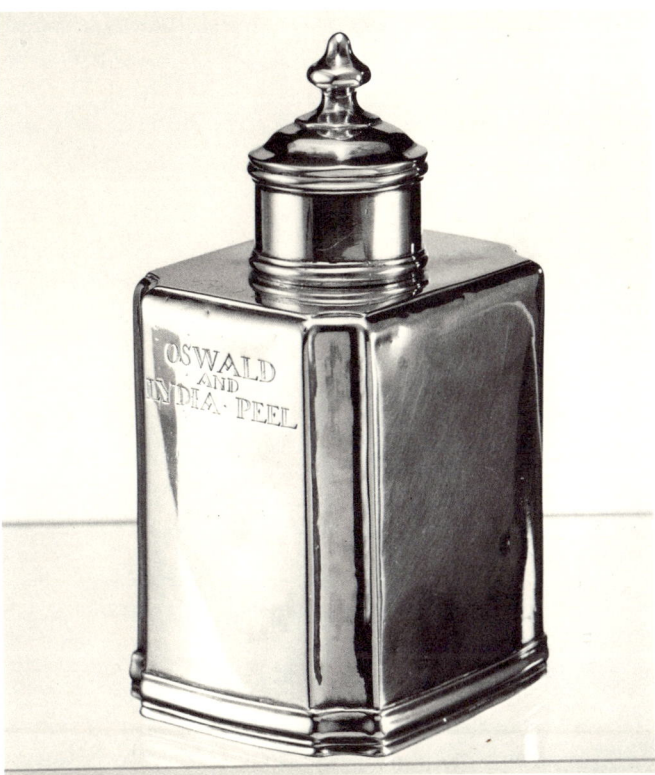

Fig. 64: One of a pair of tea canisters, IR in oval twice on base, *c.* 1740. Engraved in block letters on narrow end *OSWALD / AND / LYDIA PEEL* and on top in script *Green Tea*. Bequeathed by Lydia Peel in 1785 to her daughter Grace along with the matching canister which is also still owned by Lydia's descendants. Scratched on base is the weight 12 oz. 5 dwt. Height: 5 3/4". *Privately owned.*

one is engraved with the names of the various owners. Both are engraved on the top "Green Tea." Although these caddies are not recorded in Richardson's account book, a pair weighing in all 13 oz. 17 dwt. and purchased by George Emlen in 1740 for £2 are noted.

The most common objects used in the serving of tea and coffee were little spoons, and these survive in the greatest number. Frequently bought in sets of six, usually together with strainers and tea tongs, they cost about £1/6/0 per half-dozen, and weighed 2 oz. 1 to 3 dwt. in all. Joseph's charge for making them was generally 9 shillings, although many sets were sold at a flat rate with no specific notation of the cost of fashioning.

By the 1740's, customers were buying teaspoons by the dozen, and in the next twenty years Richardson ordered hundreds of spoons from England to satisfy the demand.[23] These imports ranged from plain teaspoons, weighing about five pennyweight each to heavily decorated teaspoons with flowered heads and heels, weighing between seven and eight pennyweight each. The

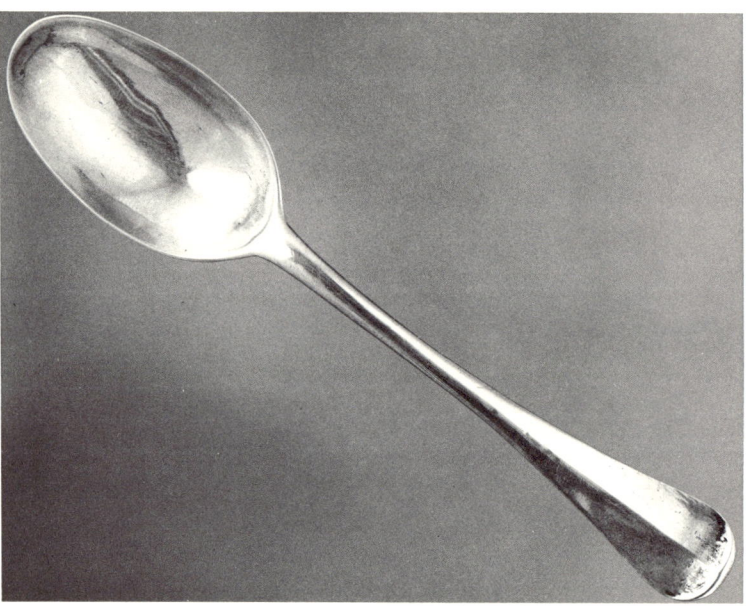

Fig. 65: Teaspoon, IR in rectangle twice on back of handle, *c.* 1750. Midrib handle, shell drop on back of bowl, engraved on handle in block letters S·W and in later script *Wyatt*. Length: 4 31/32". *Courtesy of Colonial Williamsburg*.

stylistic development of the teaspoon followed that of the larger spoons (see pp. 129–130).

Typical of the many surviving examples of teaspoons made by Joseph Richardson is a set of six spoons *(Fig. 65)*, whose handles are engraved with the original owners' initials, as was customary. On a number of occasions Joseph recorded in his account book how the teaspoons were to be marked; for example, in 1745 he noted, "6 tea Spoons to be made for widow Kirkbride markt M•K."

Occasionally a small elongated tray called a "spoon boat" was used to hold the teaspoons *(Fig. 66)*. The spoon boat was made of china or silver, and although no American examples of the latter are known to survive, Joseph Richardson made silver spoon boats for at least three customers between 1737 and 1738.[24]

No tea set was complete without a pair of tongs, and Joseph both made and sold them throughout his career.[25] The tongs were often bought with sets of teaspoons, and together they generally cost between £2 and £3 for the silver and the fashioning. So popular had tongs become by the 1750's that Joseph imported large quantities from London, specifying to How & Masterman on different occasions that the tongs be of the handsomest pattern, "pritty large," neat, double or single jointed, and that they were to weigh 1

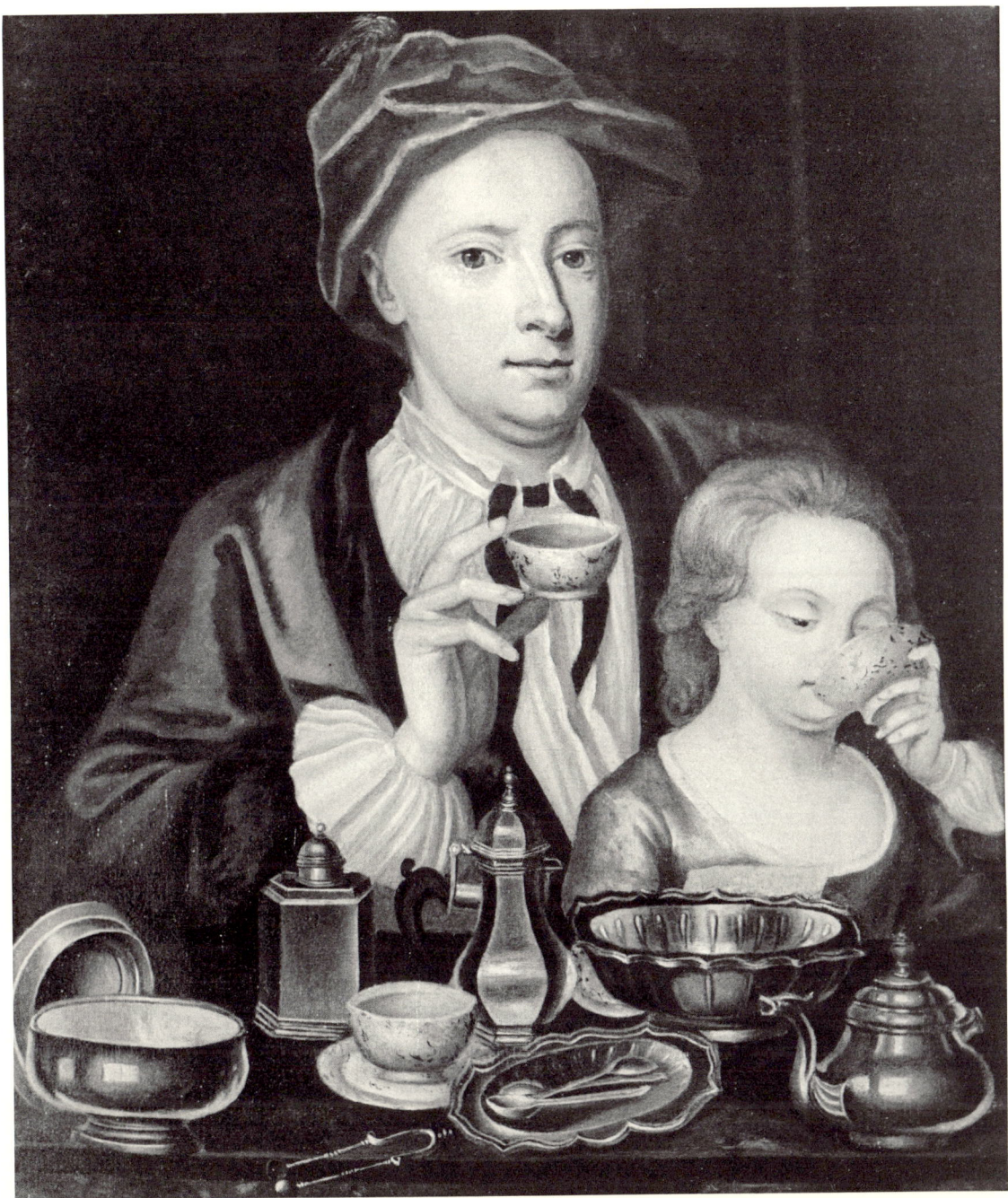

Fig. 66: English painting of man and child drinking tea, *c.* 1725. Illustrates the variety of styles combined in early silver teasets and the forms used: teapot, milk or water pot, sugar bowl, tea caddy, waste bowl, spoon tray, teaspoons, and tea tongs. Joseph Richardson is known to have made all these items. *Courtesy of Colonial Williamsburg.*

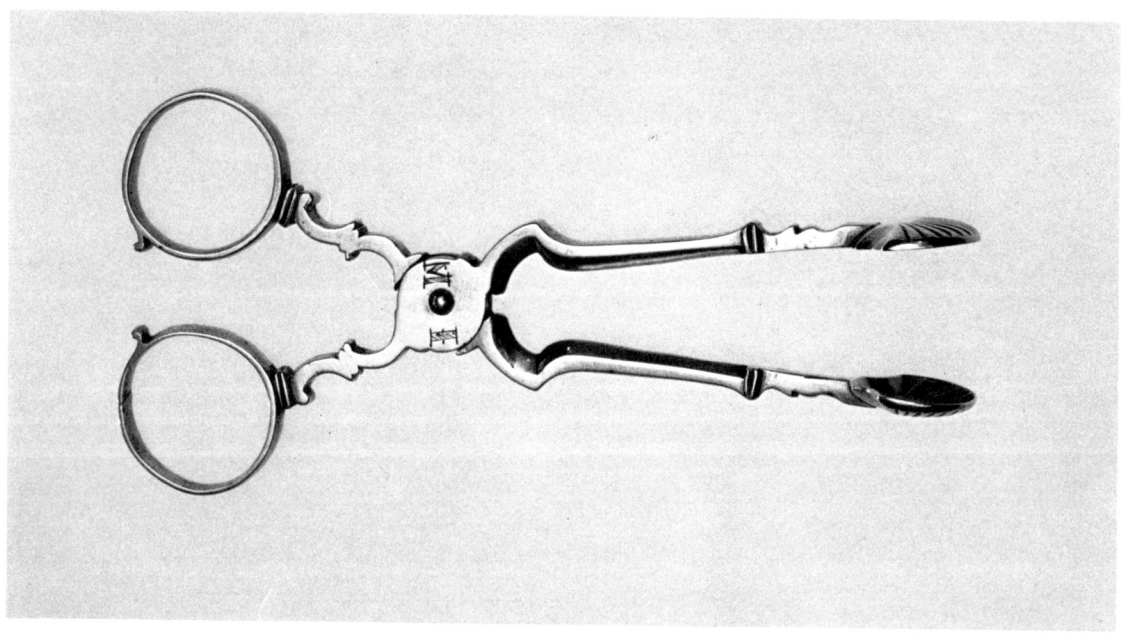

Fig. 67: Tea tongs, IR in rectangle in each of shell grips, *c.* 1750. Hinge engraved MI. Length: 4 1/2"; weight 1 oz. *Courtesy of Mr. Philip H. Hammerslough.*

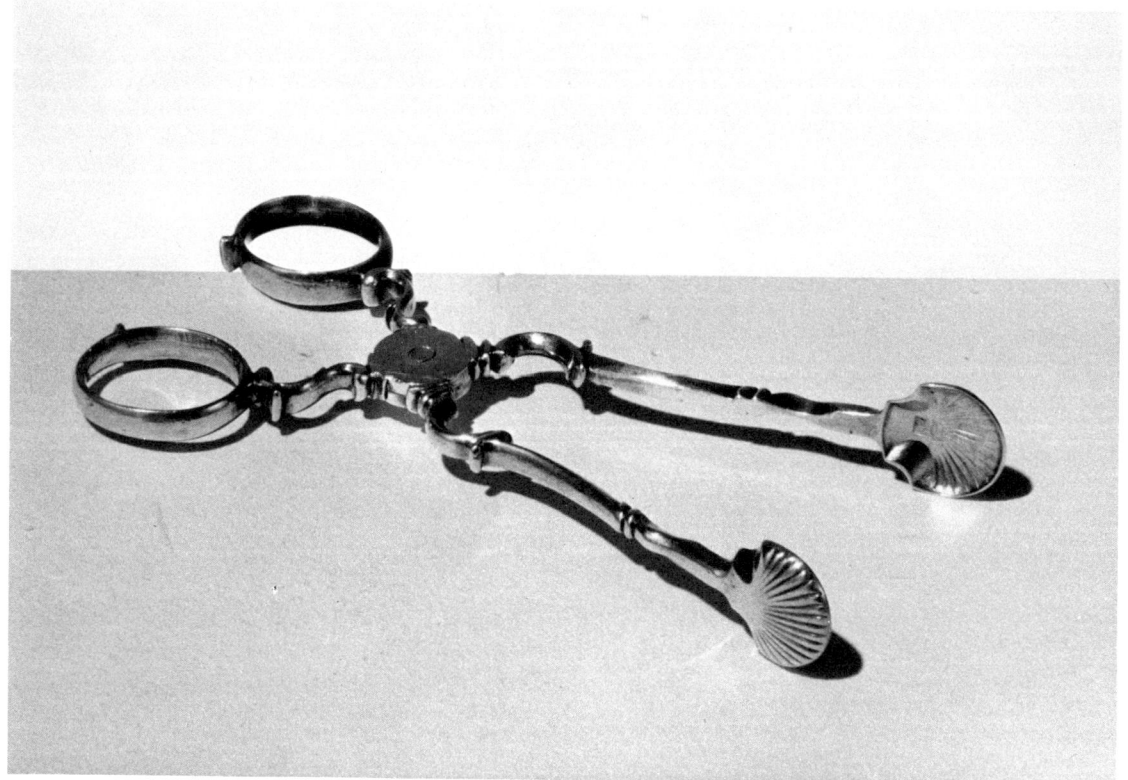

Fig. 68: Tea tongs, IR in rectangle in each of shell grips, *c.* 1750. Length: 14 15/16". *Courtesy of Chester County Historical Society, West Chester, Pennsylvania.*

oz. 5 dwt. Daniel Mildred and George Ritherdon also supplied tongs to Richardson, but he most frequently ordered them from How & Masterman, often along with a half-dozen teaspoons and a strainer in a shagreen case.[26]

Surviving tongs bearing Joseph Richardson's mark are all of the scissor type. The earliest examples *(Fig. 67)* have simple circular finger holds with diminutive spurs on the inner side. The hinge pin is exposed in the center of a circular joint, where the original owners' initials are engraved. At first the arms were plain and rather straight, with scallop-shell grips, but as the rococo style progressed, the arms were composed of C and S-scrolls *(Fig. 68)*. One pair of tea tongs in the fully developed rococo style at the Philadelphia Museum of Art has elaborately scrolled arms and two furls on the ovoid finger holds. By the end of Joseph Richardson's career, the tongs had become bow-shaped. No examples of this type with his mark have been found, but as early as 1763 he ordered "pierced spring" tea tongs from How & Masterman.

In addition to tea tongs, some colonial tea tables boasted a rarer form—the strainer spoon, in modern times called a "mote spoon." These spoons with pierced bowls were used to remove tea leaves from the cup, and their long, thin, pointed handles were used to clean the strainers inside the base of teapot spouts.[27] Few examples bearing American marks have been identified, partly because the handle shaft is so narrow that a full mark could not be struck on it. Richardson's accounts give no indication that he ever made or sold this form, nor is it included in either the list of silver kept in his glass showcase or in the lists of silver ordered from London. Although several such spoons have been attributed to him, none has clearly identifiable marks, and because no other documentation has been found, it is doubtful that he ever carried this item in his shop.

Ordinary strainers, however, were both made and imported by Joseph Richardson. Requests for strainers, especially together with orders for teaspoons and tongs, were frequent in the 1730's. By the 1740's the orders were more often for punch strainers than for tea strainers, and these were purchased separately.[28] Some orders specified that the strainers be marked with the owners' initials, as Joseph noted in 1738 when an unidentified person requested his to be marked A:L. In one instance in 1739 the length of the strainer made for Abraham Skinner is specified as being five inches long (this is the only linear measurement for an object in the entire account book).

Like strainers and bowls, trays were used in tea and coffee services, as well as separately. In the eighteenth century, trays were generally called

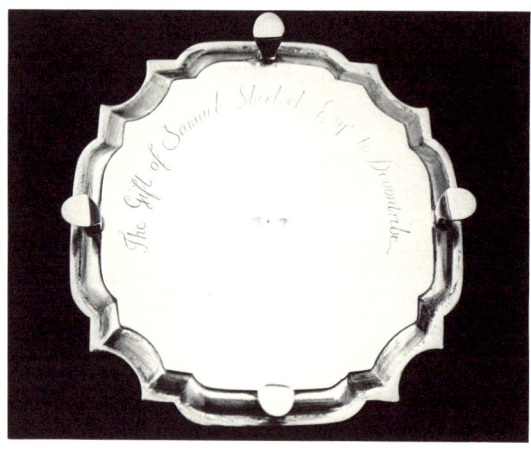 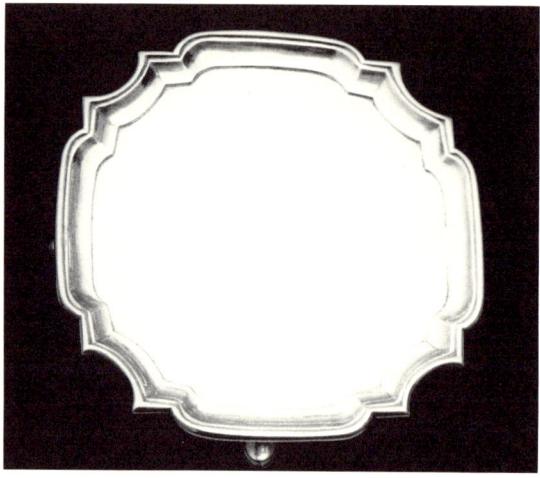

Fig. 69: Pair of salvers, IR in oval twice on base, 1737. Engraved on base, *The Gift of Samuel Sherlock Esq. to Devon tribe.* Samuel Sherlock, Chief Justice in Bermuda, died in 1736. By his will he gave "unto the Church in Devon Tribe [*i. e.*, Parish] aforesaid ten pounds money to be disposed and laid out for that use as my Executor and Executrix thinks fitt." In his account book for 1737 (*Fig. 69a*), Joseph Richardson recorded receiving silver and two gold coins (a moidore and a pistole) from Captain William Bell, valued at almost £ 10 in payment for these two salvers or "weighters." Diameter: 5 1/2". *Courtesy of Christ Church, Devonshire, Bermuda.*

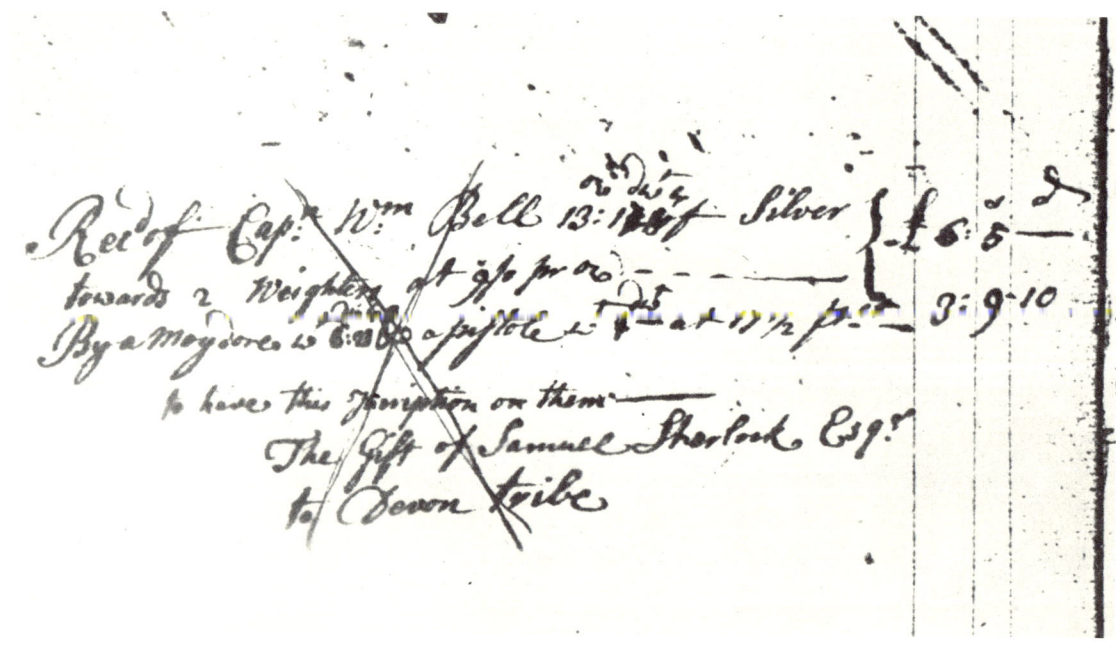

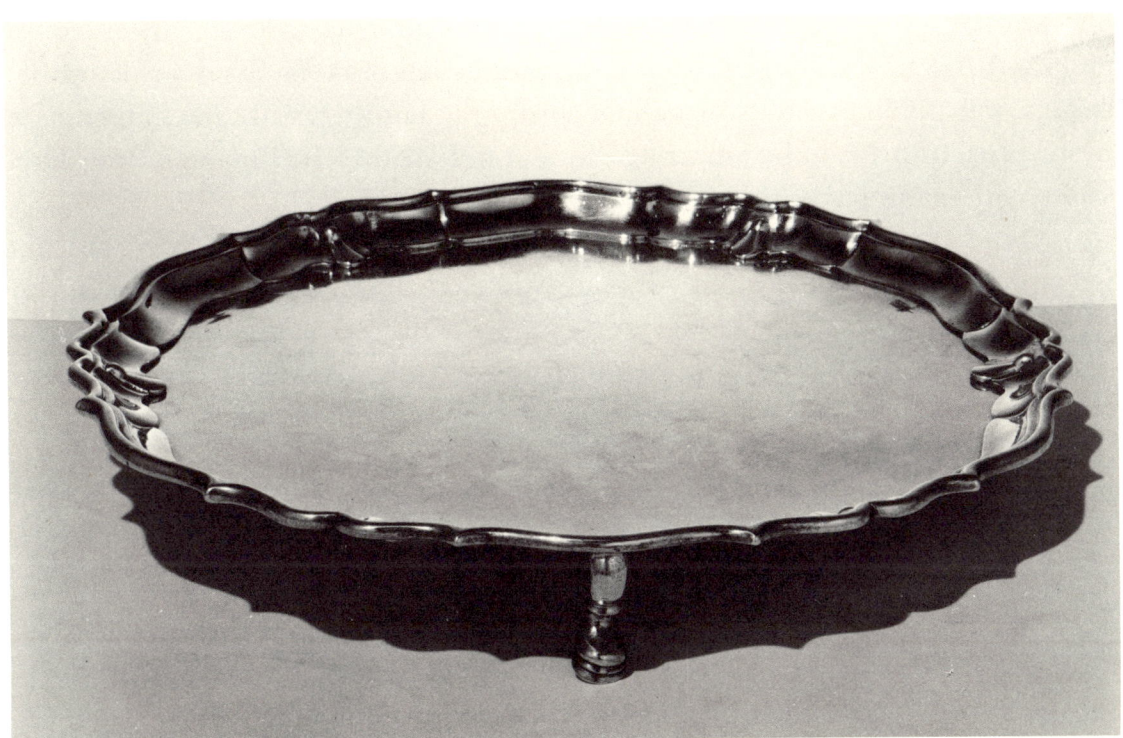

Fig. 70: Salver, IR in rectangle, *c.* 1739. Engraved on base M·E and 22 oz. Probably the same weighter George Emlen was charged £ 2/10/0 for making in additon to the cost of the 22 oz. 12 dwt. of silver in it in 1737. George Emlen married Mary Heath in 1717, just 22 years before he bought this tray. *Courtesy of Mrs. Walter M. Jeffords.*

"salvers" or "waiters." On at least five occasions in his account books, Joseph Richardson used the two terms interchangeably in reference to the same order. These terms also described the stands used under teapots and coffee pots.[29] Most of the salvers in Joseph's earliest accounts were small trays for which he usually charged £1/5/0. For larger trays, he charged twice as much, and in 1746 he charged John Smith £3 for a salver weighing 23 ounces.

The earliest extant salvers by Richardson are the two which were purchased in 1737 as Samuel Sherlock's legacy to Devonshire Parish in Bermuda (*Fig. 69*). More square in shape than circular, they are small, with pad feet and a simple molded edge which is incurved at the corners. Similar but circular in shape were the three salvers bought by George Emlen in 1739 and 1740. One weighed 22 ounces (*Fig. 70*) and was possibly an anniversary present from Emlen to his wife, Mary, whom he had married 22 years before. The other two salvers (*Figs. 71, 72*), have the same cusped border and three C-scroll legs with triple-pad feet, characteristic of trays of the early rococo period.

Similar rim patterns and legs were still being used in 1746, when Joseph recorded the tray shown in *Figure 73*, and as late as 1762 a salver of similar design was given to Sarah Yarnall, according to family tradition, as an engagement present prior to her marriage to Samuel Wetherill *(Fig. 74)*. Both large and small examples of this pattern survive *(Figs. 75, 76)*.

About 1750 a shell-and-scroll border replaced the earlier cusped rim, and examples of this later design by Richardson have been found. They are further distinguished by the lovely engraved ciphers centered on the tops of the trays, and by the double-pad feet supporting them. These salvers first had symmetrical shells, alternately large and small, placed at intervals in the cusped border *(Fig. 77)*; later, symmetrical shells of one size were placed in a border of joined C- and S-scrolls *(Fig. 78)*.

The next change in the style of tray borders was the use of an asymmetrical shell in the C- and S-scroll border. One of this type *(Fig. 79)* was made between 1756 and 1761, at the height of the rococo period. It is Richardson's most beautiful rococo tray design. The curves of furling, tattered shells in the loosely-joined scroll border are repeated in the molded edge and contrast with the smoothness of the tray itself, while the complex reverse cipher of scrolled curves in the center echoes the turbulent design of the border. Several other examples in this style by Richardson are known today *(Fig. 80)*. He not only made this type of tray in his own shop but also imported it from England. In 1760 he ordered from Daniel Mildred some stands for coffeepots which were to have "chased shells on the border," and in 1761 he ordered from Masterman stands which were to have "six shells" on the border.

These orders for English silver document the last change in salver designs sold by Richardson. In 1770, for the first time, he ordered stands with gadrooned borders to match the borders of the coffeepots. This, then, is probably when he first began to make gadrooned salvers himself *(Fig. 81)*. In this last type of salver made by Richardson, there is a cabochon at the juncture of each cusped and gadrooned section in the border, and the tray is supported by cast claw-and-ball feet, indicating once again the similarity between Philadelphia silver and furniture in the Chippendale period.

Other Major Forms

In addition to the newly popular objects associated with the drinking of coffee and tea, eighteenth century goldsmiths continued to make a large group of basically utilitarian objects which had been popular for generations. Fore-

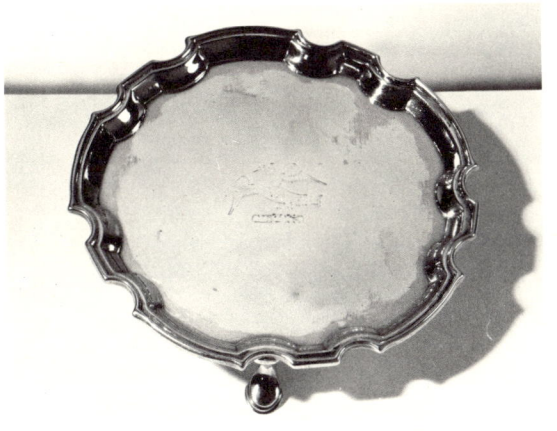 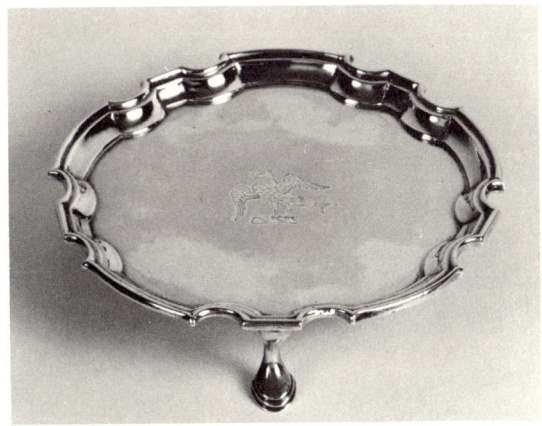

Fig. 71: Salver, IR in oval twice on base, *c.* 1739–40. Engraved on base 4:10 and H✤E for Hannah Emlen whose father paid £ 2/10/0 for making of two weighters weight 9 oz. 2 dwt. 12 gr. in 1739/40, about the time of her marriage to William Logan on the 24th of the 1st month, 1740. Mate of *Fig. 72.* Diameter 4 3/4". *Courtesy of Philadelphia Museum of Art; bequest of Robert R. Logan; photograph by A. J. Wyatt.*

Fig. 72: Salver, IR in oval on base, *c.* 1739–40. Engraved on top with crest of a flapping bird, matching salver in Philadelphia Museum of Art (*Fig. 71*), originally owned by Hannah Emlen. Diameter: 4 3/4"; weight *c.* 5 oz. *Courtesy of The Historical Society of Pennsylvania; gift of Maria Dickinson Logan; photograph by Gilbert Ask.*

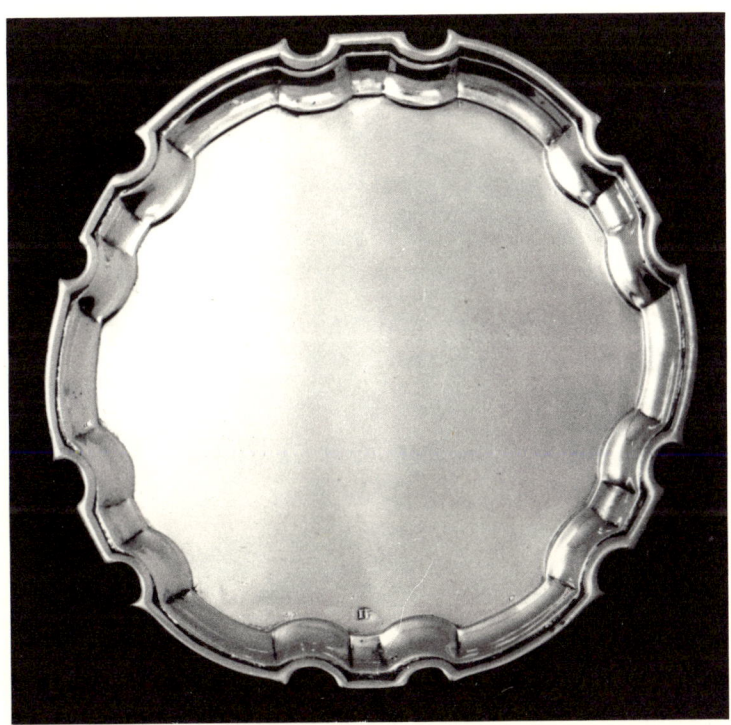

Fig. 73: Salver, IR in rectangle on top, *c.* 1746. Engraved on base *M · Grafton* for Mary Grafton who in 1746 gave Joseph Richardson 5 oz. 1 dwt. of silver towards a salver which was to weigh 8 oz. Diameter: 5 3/4"; weight 7 oz. 12 dwt. *Courtesy of Yale University Art Gallery, Mabel Brady Garvan Collection.*

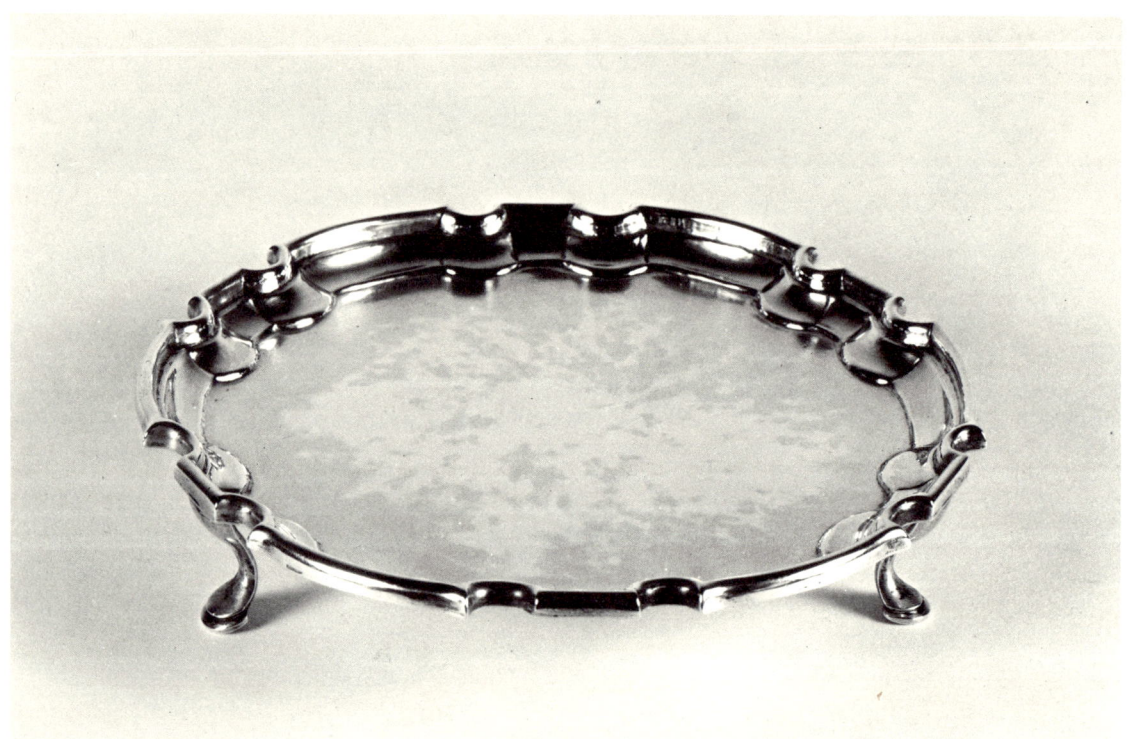

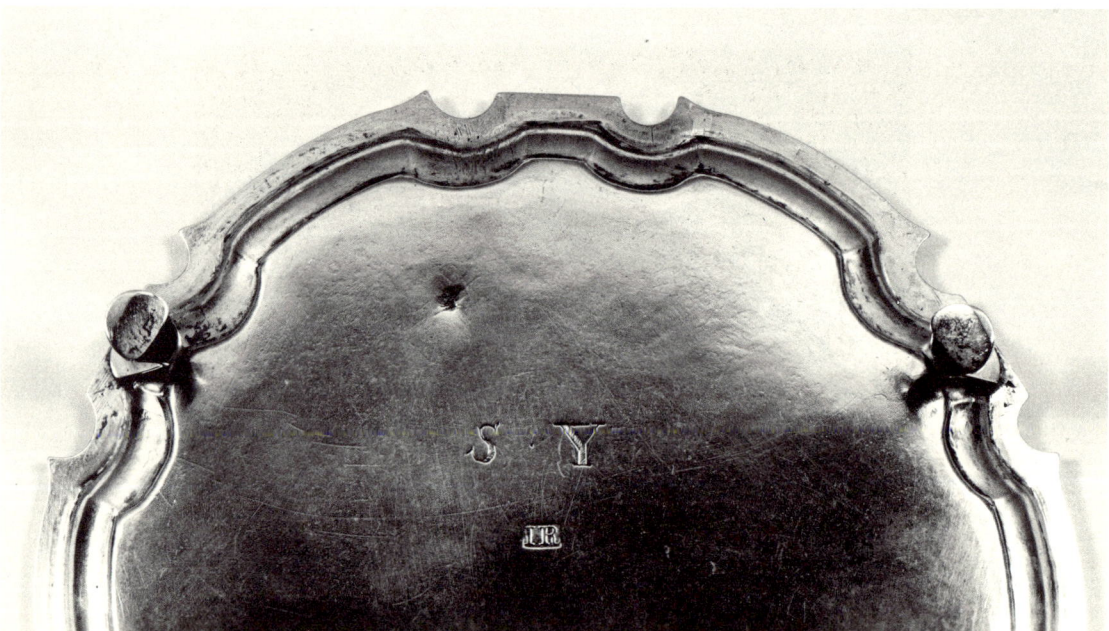

Fig. 74: Salver, IR in rectangle, *c.* 1760. Engraved on base S·Y for Sarah Yarnall (1734–1816), who according to tradition, received it as a gift prior to her marriage to Samuel Wetherill in 1762. It is still owned by a descendant of the Wetherills. Diameter: 5 3/4". *Courtesy of Mr. and Mrs. Paul Tiers.*

Joseph Richardson: His Silver

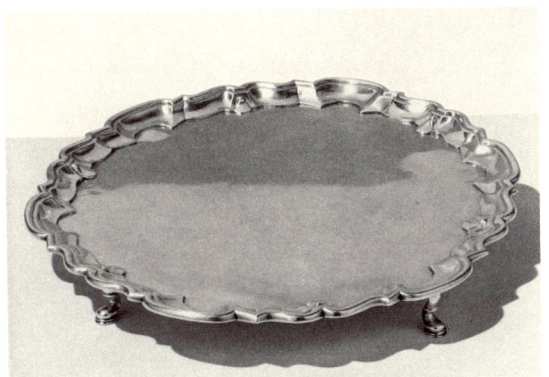
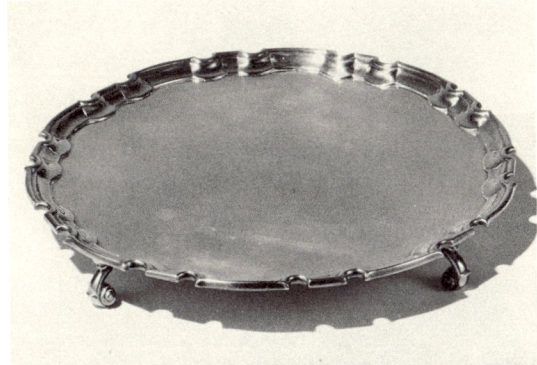

Fig. 75: Salver, IR in oval thrice on base, c. 1740. Engraved on base, *H. Emlen, 1740 / S.L. Fisher / E.F.W.* The large size of this tray makes it of especial interest. Diameter: c. 16". *Courtesy of Mrs. Richard B. Earle, Jr.*

Fig. 76: Salver, IR in rectangle on top, c. 1740–50. Unusual in having scroll feet. Diameter: c. 8". *Courtesy of Chester County Historical Society, West Chester, Pennsylvania.*

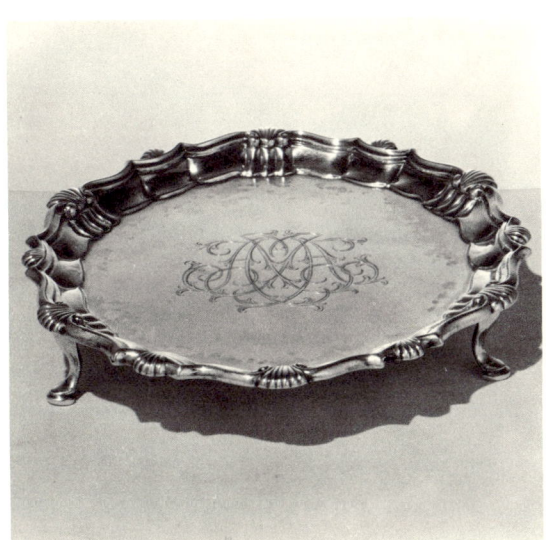
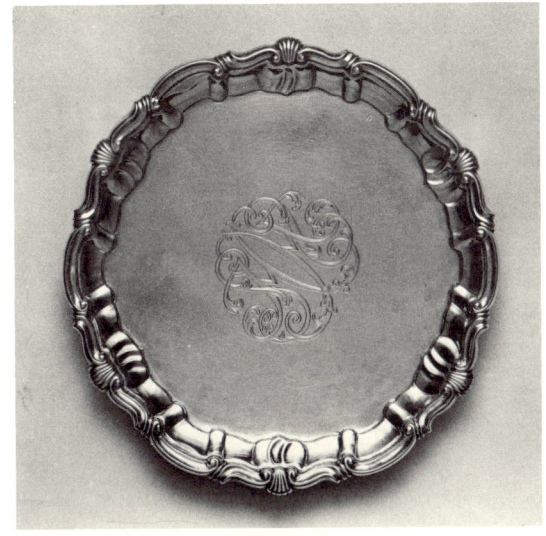

Fig. 77: Salver, IR in rectangle on top, c. 1750–65. Engraved on top with cypher *IA* and on base with names of later owners. It was given by Sally Morris to her daughter Sarah Wistar, who gave it to Sarah Hopkinson. *Courtesy of Mrs. Walter M. Jeffords.*

Fig. 78: Salver, IR in rectangle on top, c. 1750–65. Engraved with cypher *SH* (see Fig. 47). *MSD* later engraved on base. Diameter: 6 7/8"; weight 9 oz. 9 dwt. scratched on base. *Courtesy of Yale University Art Gallery, Mabel Brady Garvan Collection.*

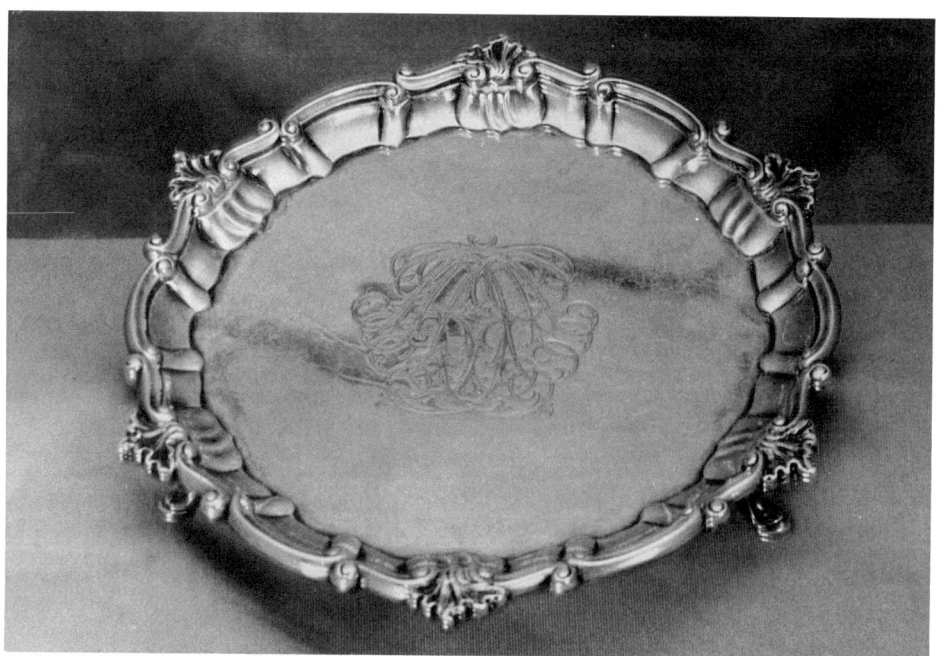

Fig. 79: Salver, IR in rectangle twice on base, 1756–61. Engraved on top with cypher *FRR* for Francis and Rebecca Rawle who were married in 1756. Five years later, in June 1761, Rawle was killed by the accidental discharge of his fowling piece while shooting. Diameter: 8"; weight: 11 oz. *Photograph courtesy of J. Herbert Gebelein.*

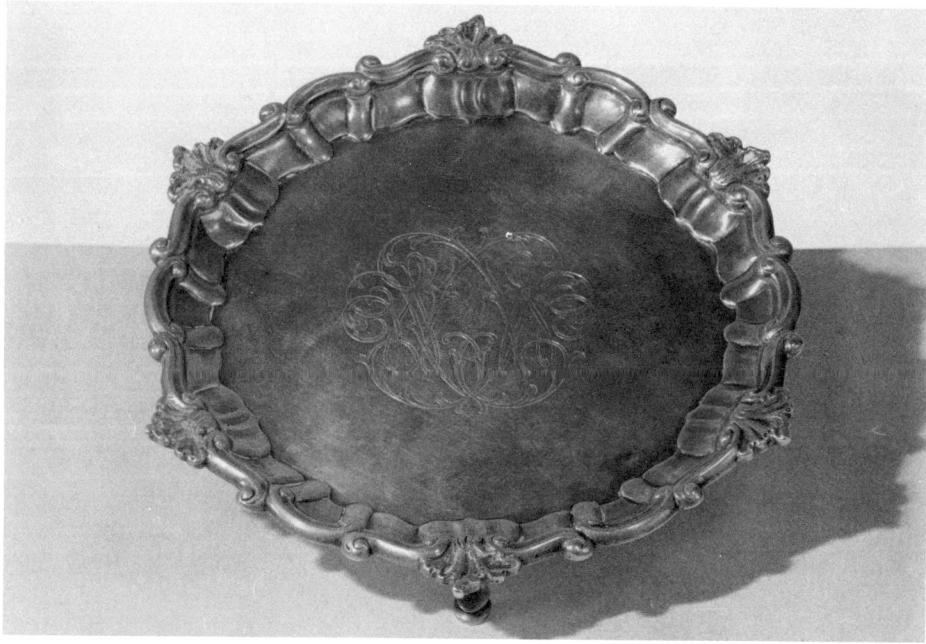

Fig. 80: Salver, IR in rectangle on base, *c.* 1760. Engraved on top with cypher *SW*. This type of tray Richardson also ordered from England. In 1760 he specified from Daniel Mildred, trays with "chased shells on the border," and in 1761 trays which were to have six shells on the border. Diameter (maximum): 6 15/16". *Courtesy of Estate of S. L. W. Starr; Mrs. Daniel Blain, Trustee.*

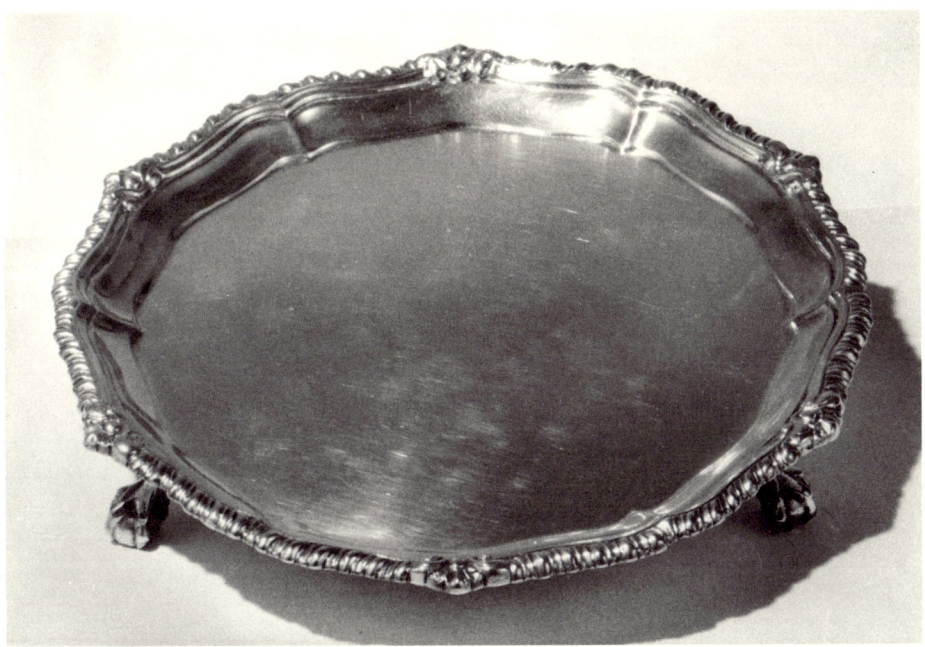

Fig. 81: Salver, IR in rectangle twice on base, *c.* 1770–75. Engraved on base, *Sarah Morris to Samuel Coates 1775*. In this year Sarah Morris died and Samuel Coates was married. Diameter (maximum): 6 3/4". *Courtesy of Miss Elizabeth Gardner Coates.*

most among these were drinking vessels, which can be found in the earliest inventories of estates of settlers in the New World. In the seventeenth century the most popular vessels were standing cups, covered cups, caudle cups, little dram cups, beakers, and tankards. In the eighteenth century the tankard, the can, and the porringer became the most frequently demanded drinking utensils.

Almost one hundred cans (sometimes spelled "cann") were recorded by Richardson as having been sold in his shop from 1735 to 1748. These cans came in pint and half-pint sizes, but almost twice as many of the larger size were sold. Of these, 25 were not specified as to size except by weight and only one was noted in the quart size, weighing 19 oz. 14 dwt., the "Belleyed Can" bought by Abraham Bickly in 1739. That these cans were frequently bought in pairs is indicated by the fact that 4 pairs of half-pint, eight pairs of pint, and 4 pairs of unspecified cans were included in these orders. The usual weight for a pair of pint cans was 24 to 25 ounces; for a pair of half-pint cans, 15 to 17 ounces.

The heaviness of the cans is a result of the cast handles that were applied to one side of the body; casting always requires more silver than does forging

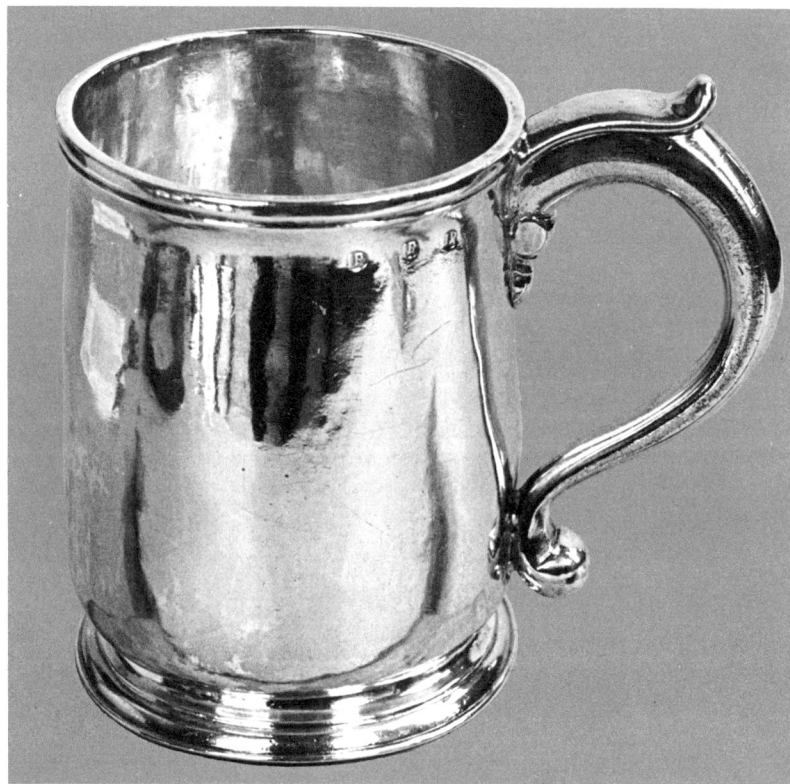

Fig. 82: Can, IR in oval thrice left of handle, *c.* 1740. Family history states that this can was made out of the personal silver effects of Thomas Chalkley, after his death at Tortola in 1741. Engraved on back of handle MC, probably for his widow Martha Chalkley, on front in classical script *MS to IT 1830*, explained by a later inscription on the base, *Martha Smith, grand-daughter of T. C. to her nephew, Jonah Thompson. J.T. to his niece Rebecca Thompson, 1841.* Height: 3 15/16″. *Courtesy of Philadelphia Museum of Art; gift of Miss Lydia Thompson.*

or raising. But, except for the handle, the only additional part was a circular raised foot, so that this form did not require a great deal of fashioning. Consequently, cans were among the forms most often made by apprentices. Both John Hutton and David Harper made cans for Richardson in the 1730's and 1740's, as did his brother Frank. It appears from the accounts that Joseph received about 3 or 4 shillings more for each can than he paid an apprentice for making it.[30]

Perhaps because cans were fairly easy to make, Joseph did not import many from London. One of his few orders to England for this form was placed with How & Masterman in 1760 for "1 Pair Pint Cans Pollished." Not until 1770 did Richardson again order polished pint cans, and since this was his last order for them, one might surmise that he preferred making his own.

The style of cans did not change much in the mid-eighteenth century. The

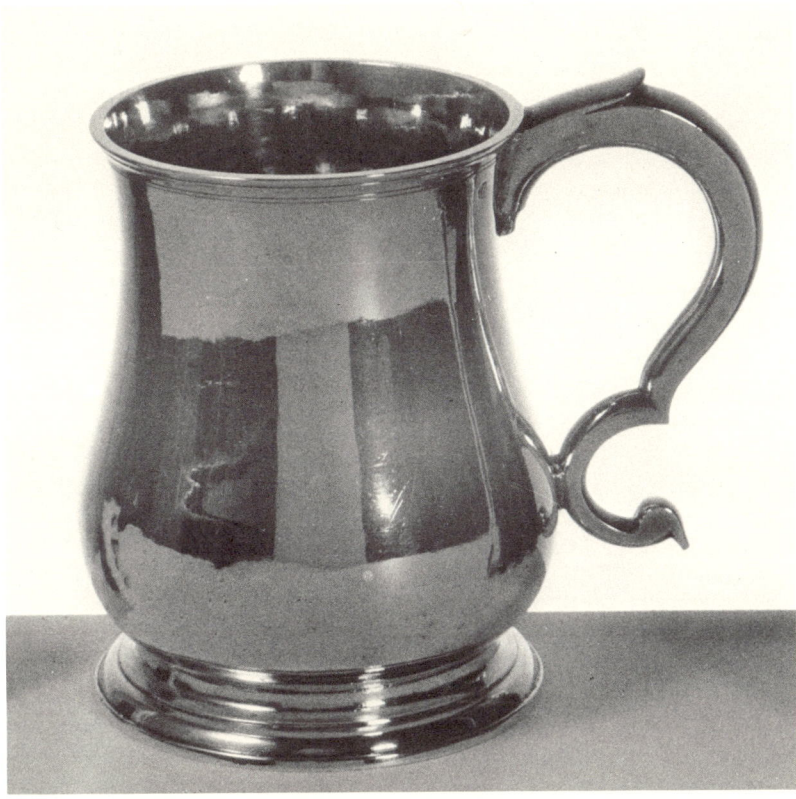

Fig. 83: Can, IR in oval left of handle, *c.* 1740. Weight 12 [*oz.*] .08 scratched on base at a later date. *Courtesy of Philadelphia Museum of Art; bequest of Robert R. Logan.*

only adjectives Richardson used in his accounts to describe their appearance are "Straight Bodyed" (in 1735) and "Belleyed" (in 1739). The straight-bodied can was made for him by his brother Frank and was probably similar to the one shown in *Figure 18*. It is not certain whether Joseph ever made this earlier straight-sided type; none by him are known to survive. The nearest thing to a straight-sided can by Joseph was made about 1741 *(Fig. 82)*. Although its base is slightly rounded, it lacks the more flaring top characteristic of mid-century examples. The flaring, more curvilinear form *(Fig. 83)* usually had a broken C-scroll handle instead of the simple C-scroll seen on the earlier can. As this style developed, the body of the can became more round-bellied, and the ending of the handle more widely scrolled *(Fig. 84)*.

Once developed, the bellied form endured for many years. In the 1750's and 1760's it acquired rococo ornamentation: asymmetrical cartouches containing coats of arms were engraved on the center front, and an acanthus leaf on the top of the handle replaced the earlier flat furl *(Figs. 85, 86)*. This is the

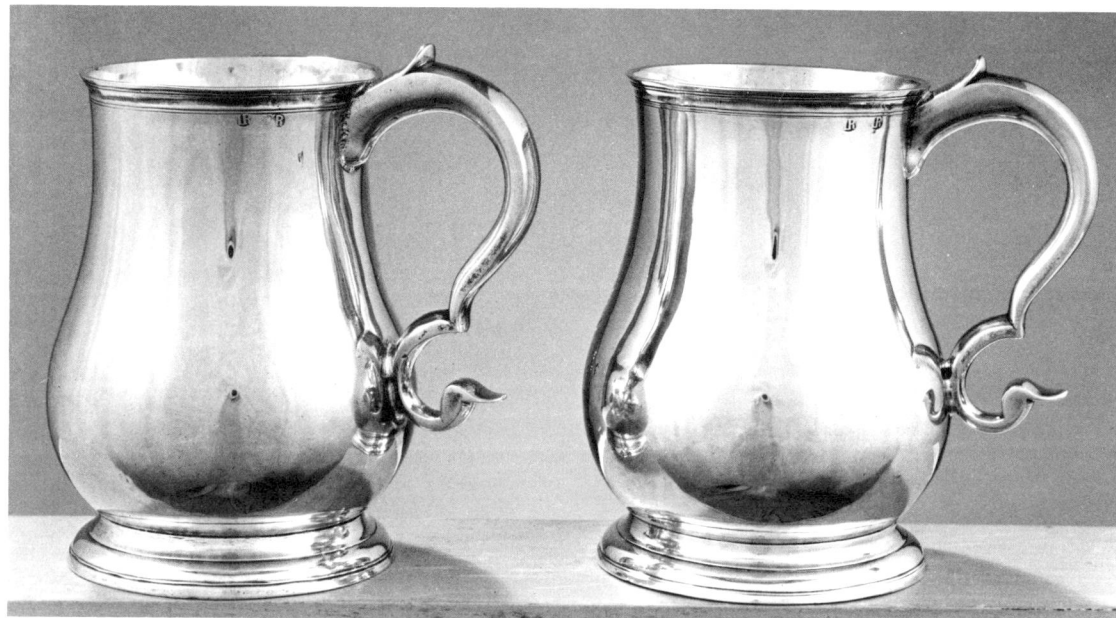

Fig. 84: Pair of cans, IR in oval twice left of each handle, *c.* 1737. Engraved on base H^{R}M and in later script *ER* on front. Original weights: *8 oz. 2 dwt.* and *8 oz. 5 dwt.* on other, engraved on base. Hugh Roberts married Mary Calvert in 1735 and was credited in Richardson's accounts in 1737 for 12 oz. 14 dwt. 12 gr. of silver received for making a pair of half pint cans. Height: 4 3/8"; weights: 7 oz. 14 dwt. 11 gr. and 7 oz. 16 dwt. 21 gr., showing a loss of about 8 dwt. each over the years. *Courtesy of The Historical Society of Pennsylvania; photograph by Gilbert Ask.*

most frequently encountered type of can made by Joseph Richardson, and he continued to make it until he retired.

Another prominent form of drinking vessel, used for several centuries was the tankard. Joseph Richardson made dozens of tankards and apparently never imported any from England. The tankards' chief characteristic is a lid perhaps to keep the beverage warm or to keep out impurities. A thumbpiece, or "purchase," was placed on the lid just in front of the hinge to facilitate its opening. Seventeenth-century American tankards were characterized by a very flat, low lid, but in the eighteenth century the lids became stepped and domed.

By far the most popular size was the quart tankard—almost three quarters of the tankards Richardson sold were of this size. Generally the quart tankard weighed between 29 and 32 ounces, and sometimes as much as 34 ounces. Joseph sold three-pint tankards on at least eight occasions in the period 1735–48, and these weighed from 34 to 42 ounces. The 1 1/2 pint tankards weighed about 24 ounces, and the pint tankards, about 17 ounces. Whatever the size, Richardson charged 18 pence per ounce for making the vessel.[31]

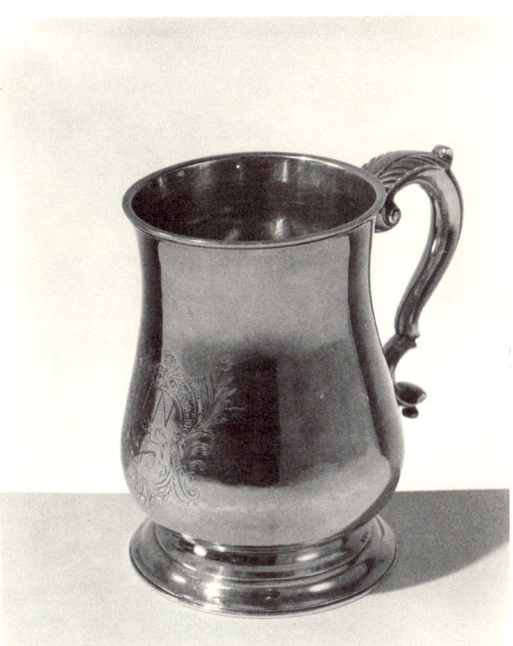

Fig. 85: Can, IR in rectangle with scroll on base, *c.* 1750–65. One of a pair beautifully engraved with Logan arms in rococo cartouche on front of body. Engraved on base SL and SLW, and scratched *to* W. Also scratched on base is the weight, *14 oz. 17 dwt. 12 gr.* Height: 5 1/16″. *Courtesy of Estate of S. L. W. Starr; Mrs. Daniel Blain, Trustee.*

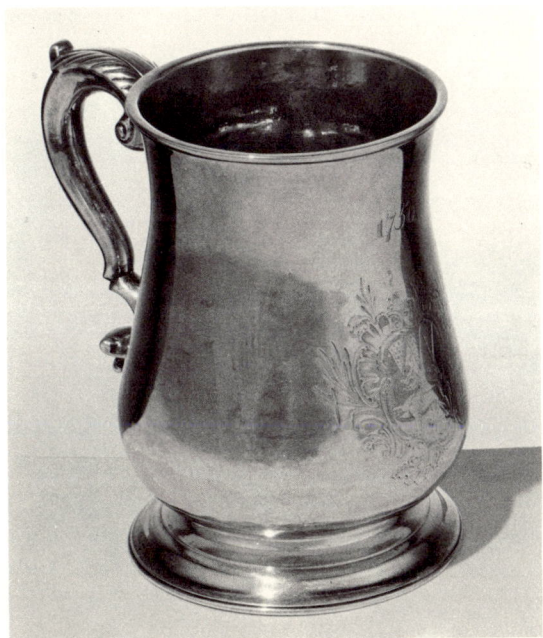

Fig. 86: Can, IR, in rectangle with furl on base, *c.* 1750–65. Mate of *Fig. 85*, engraved on the base with the initials SL, probably for Sarah Logan, and SLW as well as the weight *14 oz. 3 dwt. 18*, indicating it was a pint-sized can. The date 1750 was added above the Logan arms engraved on front. Height: 5 1/16″. *Courtesy of Philadelphia Museum of Art; photograph by A. J. Wyatt.*

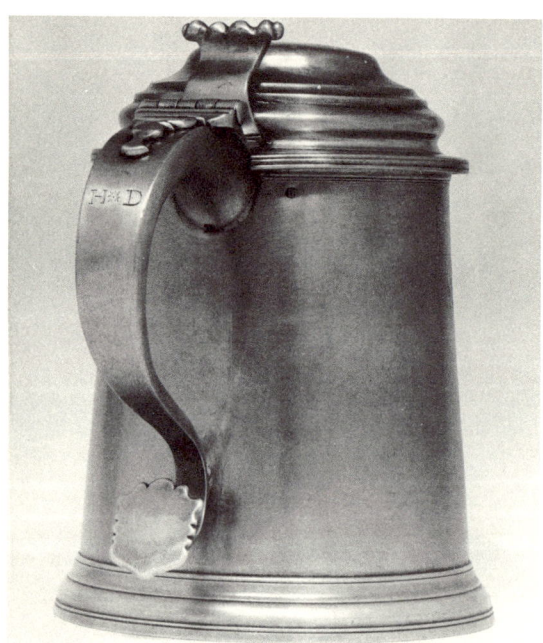

Fig. 87: Quart tankard, IR in oval each side of handle, *c.* 1730–50. Later goldsmith's mark HP in rectangle twice on underside of lip, verifying later repair of lid. Possibly the mark of Henry Peterson who was working in Philadelphia about 1787. H∗D (originally H^{P}D) engraved in block letters on back of handle. On the base is scratched the original weight *29 oz. 16 dwt.* and *29-13 1787* for its weight at the time it was repaired. Height: 7″. A mate to this tankard, without the HP mark, is privately owned. *Courtesy of Yale University Art Gallery, Mabel Brady Garvan Collection.*

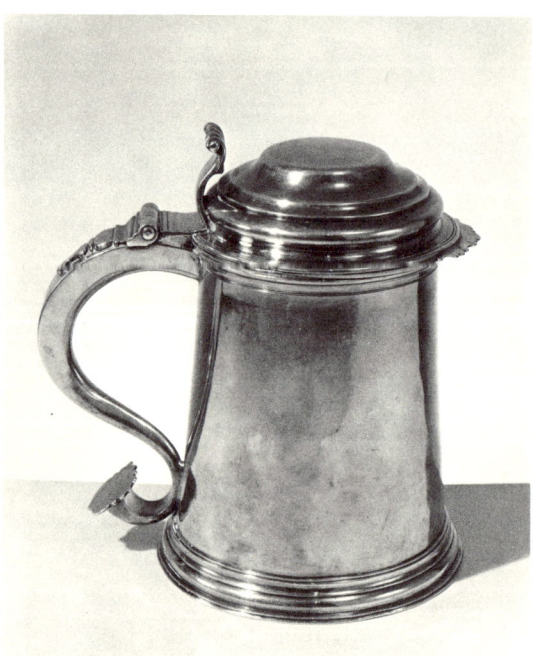 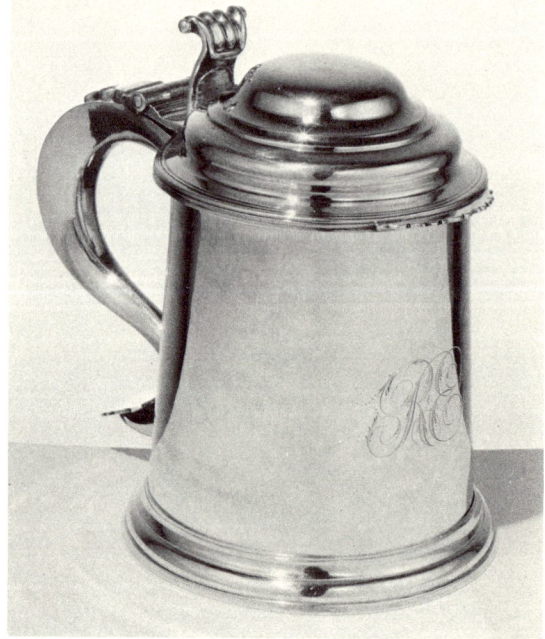

Fig. 88: Tankard, IR in oval, *c.* 1730–50. Height: 7 7/16″. *Courtesy of Estate of S. L. W. Starr; Mrs. Daniel Blain, Trustee.*

Fig. 89: Tankard, IR in rectangle twice on base, *c.* 1730–50. Engraved on front of classical script *RE* for owner about 1800. Engraved on base with weight *33-18. Courtesy of Mrs. Walter M. Jeffords.*

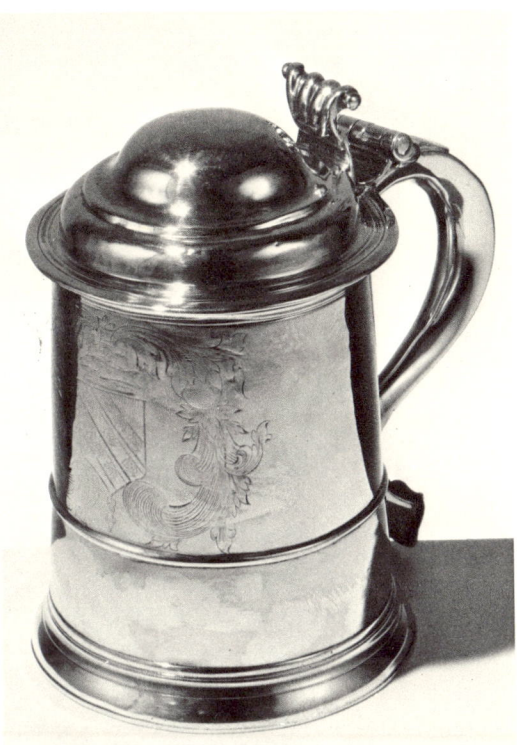

Fig. 90: Tankard, IR in rectangle twice on side, *c.* 1750. Engraved on front are the Penrose arms and on the handle T^{P}S for Thomas Penrose (1709–57), a leading Philadelphia ship builder, and his wife Sarah Coates. Also engraved on handle IP for James Penrose (1737–71), ancestor of the present owner. Overall height: 6 1/8". *Courtesy of Mr. Boies Penrose.*

Frequently Richardson made a note in his account book of the engraving to be put on the handle of the tankard, such as "marked John McCoole" in 1739, but none of his known tankards can be traced to specific account entries. Usually the engraving consisted of initials rather than full names. An example by Richardson *(Fig. 87)* is particularly interesting because it was repaired in 1787 by Henry Peterson, who put his mark on the lid at that time. This is Richardson's earliest known tankard and is typical of the many he made. It has a scrolled thumbpiece with a horseshoe-shaped outline, a widely sweeping S-curved handle, and a plain shield-shaped terminus at the base of the handle *(Figs. 88, 89, 90)*.

A similar tankard (possibly by Richardson, though the mark is sufficiently blurred to cause some doubt) was given to Old Swedes Church in Philadelphia in 1772 by Mrs. Elizabeth Vanderspiegle. This tankard does not have a crenate lip, and it has a high, straight step in the center of the domed lid.[32] In these features, it resembles another handsome Richardson tankard of the period *(Fig. 90)*, which is further decorated with a mid-band, a detail added in the second quarter of the century, and engraved with a large coat of arms.

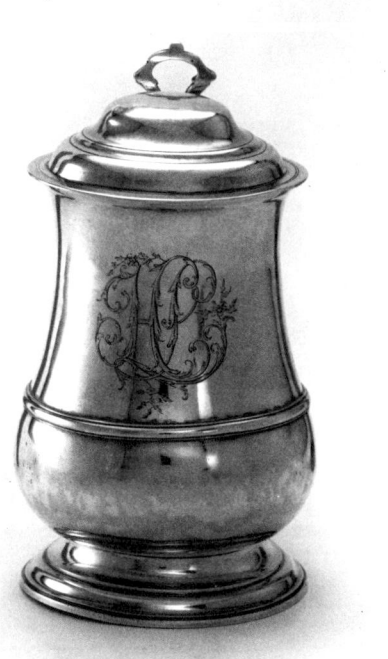 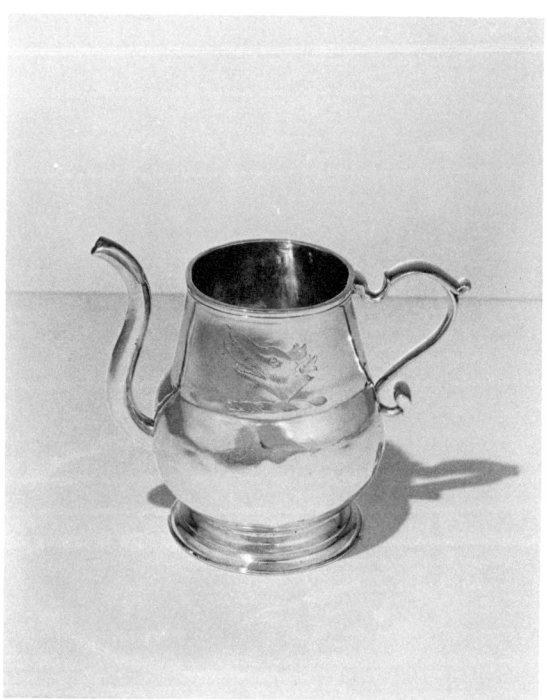

Fig. 91: Tankard, IR in rectangle twice on base, *c.* 1750–70. Engraved on front in florid script *HL* for Hannah Ladd of Haddonfield, New Jersey, and on base, S•M to H •'L. Features not expected in Richardson's tankards are the bellied shape, open thumbpiece, and circular scribings outlining the steps of the domed lid. Height: 7 9/16"; weight: 32 oz. *Courtesy of Mr. Philip H. Hammerslough.*

Fig. 92: Spout cup, IR in oval twice on base, *c.* 1735–40. Engraved on side with Pemberton crest. Unusual in having spout opposite handle rather than at right angle to handle. A late survival of a vessel used in the 17th century for feeding invalids and children, this is the only known Philadelphia spout cup. Height: 3 1/2". *Courtesy of Philadelphia Museum of Art.*

Another tankard with a mid-band, attributed to Richardson but quite different from his other known tankards, has the pear-shaped or bellied body supported by a circular domed foot characteristic of cans of this period (*Fig. 91*). The majority of tankards made by Joseph Richardson have straight sides, and this style remained constant throughout his career. The open thumbpiece and circular scribings outlining the steps of this tankard's domed lid are also not unexpected of Richardson.

Although cans and tankards were the most popular drinking vessels in the eighteenth century, cups and tumblers were also used. The *Oxford Universal Dictionary* defines a tumbler as a "drinking cup, originally having a rounded or pointed bottom, so that it could not be set down until emptied; often of silver or gold; now, a tapering cylindrical or barrel-shaped glass cup without a handle or foot, having a heavy flat bottom." This definition contradicts the only reference to this form in Joseph Richardson's account books which specifically describes tumblers as having both handles and feet. These were the three tumblers that shopworker John Hutton made for Joshua Fisher and which were engraved with the names of his children, Esther, Lydia, and Thomas. It is possible that Richardson sold other examples of this form but recorded them as cups or cans in his accounts.

Many kinds of cups were sold in Joseph's shop. In 1734 John Knowles bought a pint cup weighing a little over nine ounces and costing £0/14/5 for fashioning; in 1745–46 Edward Catherell ordered a half-pint cup. Also mentioned in the accounts was the rarer cordial cup that apprentice David Harper made for Richardson to sell to John Clifton in 1747–48. Still another unusual cup made by Joseph Richardson is the spout cup *(Fig. 92)*. This form used for feeding invalids and children was frequently found in New England in the seventeenth century. By the early part of the eighteenth century it had gone out of fashion, so that it is surprising that Richardson was making this type of cup as late as the 1730's.[33]

Porringers, with shallow bowls and flat handles, were widely used in this country and were among the items most frequently manufactured by American silversmiths. Less common in England, porringers were rarely imported, and Joseph Richardson apparently never ordered any from London. But he sold hundreds of porringers made by himself or by his brother and his helpers.[34] So popular were these porringers that they were generally bought in sets; one of the largest sets, which included six porringers, was bought by Oswald Peel in 1747 for £24/07/10 1/2. The cost for making a porringer was 10 or 12 shillings. Occasionally the charge was figured at 18 pence per ounce of silver worked, but because the porringers normally weighed seven to nine ounces, the cost for working the silver was the same in either case.[35]

Joseph Paschall and Caspar Wistar bought two of Richardson's earliest surviving porringers *(Figs. 93, 94)*. These have the handle design characteristic of Richardson's early porringers—a keyhole piercing at the apex of the handle and a solid, shield-shaped area at the handle's base on which the owner's initials were engraved. Numerous examples of this type bearing Richardson's mark have survived *(Figs. 95, 96, 97)*.

A slightly later variation of this basic form omitted the two half-round openings at the base of the handle. An example of this type, made in the late 1740's, is seen in *Figure 98*, and two others are shown in *Figures 99, 100*. All but one of these porringers has the owner's initials engraved on the handle, with the square capital letters facing away from the bowl. This pattern met with such favor that Richardson continued to make it throughout his career, as

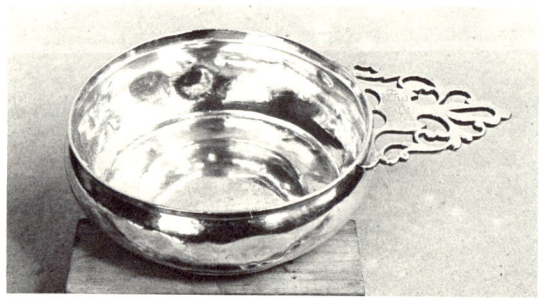 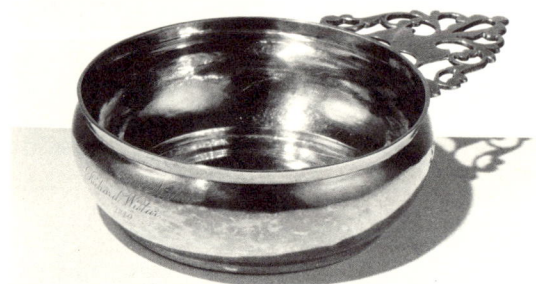

Fig. 93: Porringer, IR in oval twice left of handle, 1739. Engraved on top of handle I^{P}E for Joseph and Elizabeth Paschall whose names appear in later backhand script on the porringer. Two weights appear on the base: *7 oz. 18 dwt.* deeply scribed and *7 oz. 15 dwt.* lightly scratched. Joseph Paschall was charged in Richardson's accounts for 1739 £ 2/8/0 for the fashioning of four porringers weighing 31 oz. 13 dwt. Length: 7 1/2". *Courtesy of Philadelphia Museum of Art; gift of Miss Lydia Thompson.*

Fig. 94: Porringer, IR in oval twice on rim, c. 1738. Engraved on top of handle C^{W}C for Caspar and Catharine (Jansen) Wistar who were married in 1726. In 1738 Caspar Wistar was charged £ 2/8/0 for four porringers weighing 31 oz. 5 dwt., one of which is this one. In 1746 Wistar bought two more porringers weighing together 16 oz. 16 dwt. and costing £ 1/5/0 for their fashioning. Diameter: 5"; length of handle: 2 5/16". *Courtesy of Mrs. Joseph Carson.*

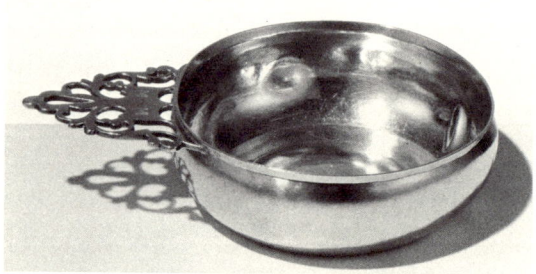 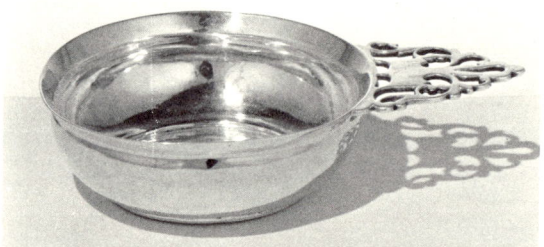

Fig. 95: Porringer, IR in oval twice on rim, c. 1740. Engraved MM on top of handle, *SP·MP / R·B* on bottom of handle, and scratched on the base in crude script *I Jones 1798*. Length: 7 7/8". *Courtesy of Philadelphia Museum of Art.*

Fig. 96: Porringer, IR in rectangle twice on back of handle, c. 1740–50. Engraved on top of handle I^{M}M, possibly for John and Mary Mather, John having been charged by Richardson in 1747 for six porringers. *Courtesy of Mrs. Walter M. Jeffords.*

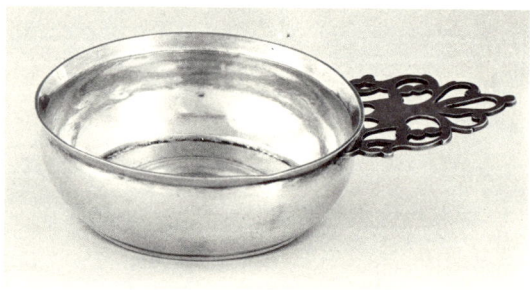 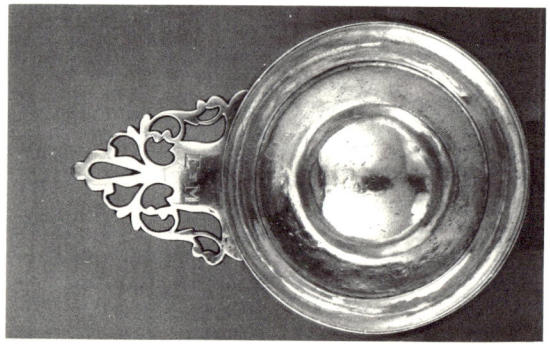

Fig. 97: Porringer, IR in rectangle on back of handle, c. 1750. Length: 6 15/16". *Courtesy of Museum of Fine Arts, Boston; gift in memory of Dr. George Clymer by his wife.*

Fig. 98: Porringer, IR in rectangle, c. 1750. Engraved on top of handle E✸M possibly for Evan Morgan who was charged by Richardson in 1747 £ 1/4/0 for two porringers weighing 15 oz. 1 dwt. Diameter: 5"; length of handle: 2 9/16". *Courtesy of Yale University Art Gallery, Mabel Brady Garvan Collection.*

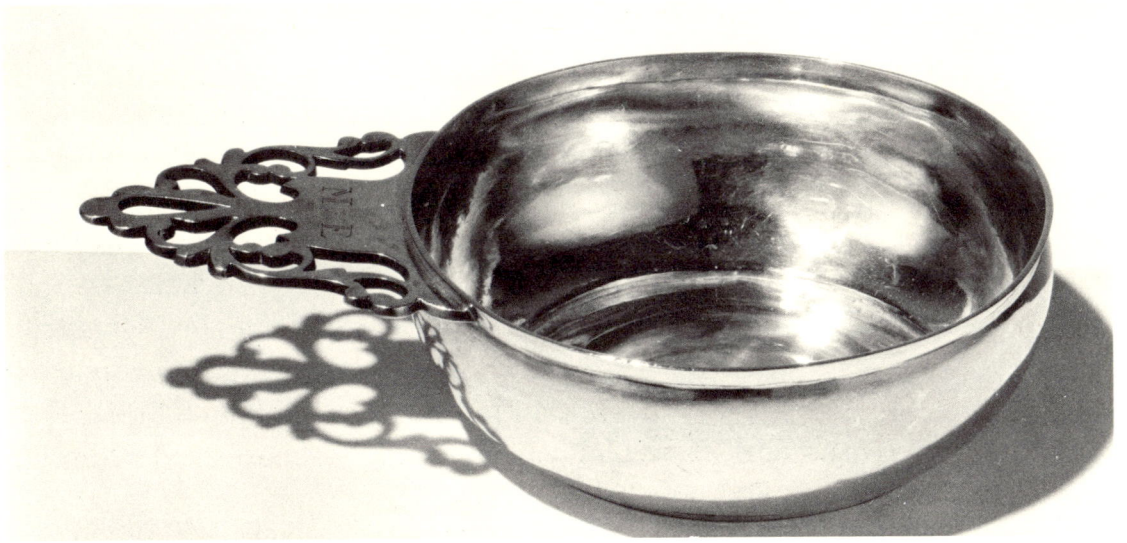

Fig. 99: Porringer, IR in rectangle on back of handle tip, *c.* 1750. Engraved on top of handle M·E. Diameter: 5 1/4"; length of handle: 2 5/8". *Courtesy of Mr. and Mrs. Henry W. Breyer, Jr.*

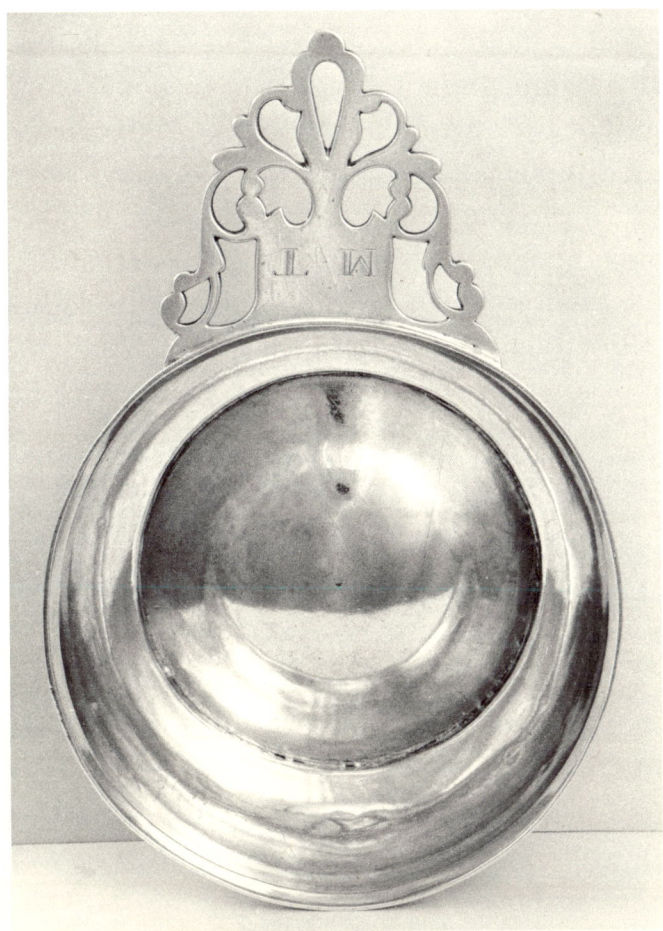

Fig. 100: Porringer, IR in rectangle on back of handle tip, *c.* 1750. Engraved on top of handle MT. Length: 7 13/16"; diameter of bowl: 5 1/4"; weight: 7 oz. 16 dwt. 20 gr. *Courtesy of The Historical Society of Pennsylvania; gift of the Newbold family; photograph by Gilbert Ask.*

did many American goldsmiths until the beginning of the nineteenth century.

Salt dishes were another major form usually bought in sets. Prior to 1748, Richardson recorded selling 28 pairs of salt dishes, five of which his helpers, Hutton and Harper, made in whole or in part. Salt shovels to accompany these dishes were supplied for only four pairs, and half of these were made by Harper. Today, no salt shovels and relatively few pairs of salt dishes by Richardson are known. The earliest salt dishes made by Richardson were probably what he called "Square salts" in 1738, and "of the Newest fashion—8 Square" in 1747 *(Fig. 101)*. These salts had widely shaped octagonal bases and wide oval depressions in the tops of their trencher bodies.

Soon after this, however, the style changed, and salt dishes became rounded and raised on three triple-pad feet *(Fig. 102)*. This new style of salt dish had a delicately chased edge around the top in the form of diagonally placed straight lines, and an enlarged triple-pad design at the tops of the legs joining the three feet to the body *(Fig. 103)*. Occasionally the lines decorating the edge of the dish were straight rather than diagonal *(Fig. 104)*.

It is possible that Richardson made some salt dishes in the rococo style with ornate, chased repoussé decoration on the body, but none by him are known to survive. In the late 1750's and 1760's salt dishes usually had fully developed gadrooned edges at the top, as did those that Richardson ordered from How & Masterman in 1762: "4 pair of plain salts gadrooned edg all of a size so that any two of them may fellow each other."[36] With these he requested salt shovels and glass dishes (including eight spares) which fit inside the silver ones to protect them from the salt. Although few glass liners have survived household use, a pair of English salt dishes with gadrooned edges now at the Museum of Fine Arts in Boston retain their original clear glass liners, which also have gadrooned edges. Glass liners were also ordered with the first of the new oval, pierced salt dishes which Joseph ordered from London in 1769. No examples of this type bearing his mark are known today, but the fact that Richardson ordered a dozen spare glasses at that time might indicate that he planned to use a few to line pierced salt dishes of his own manufacture.

Another form which required a glass lining was the mustard caster, and Richardson also ordered these from London. Mustard casters were surpassed in popularity only by pepper casters, and frequently they were made and sold in pairs. A spoon occasionally accompanied the mustard caster, for Richardson recorded making a pair of casters and a mustard spoon for William Muckelvane [McIlvain] in 1747, and David Harper made two spoons for casters in

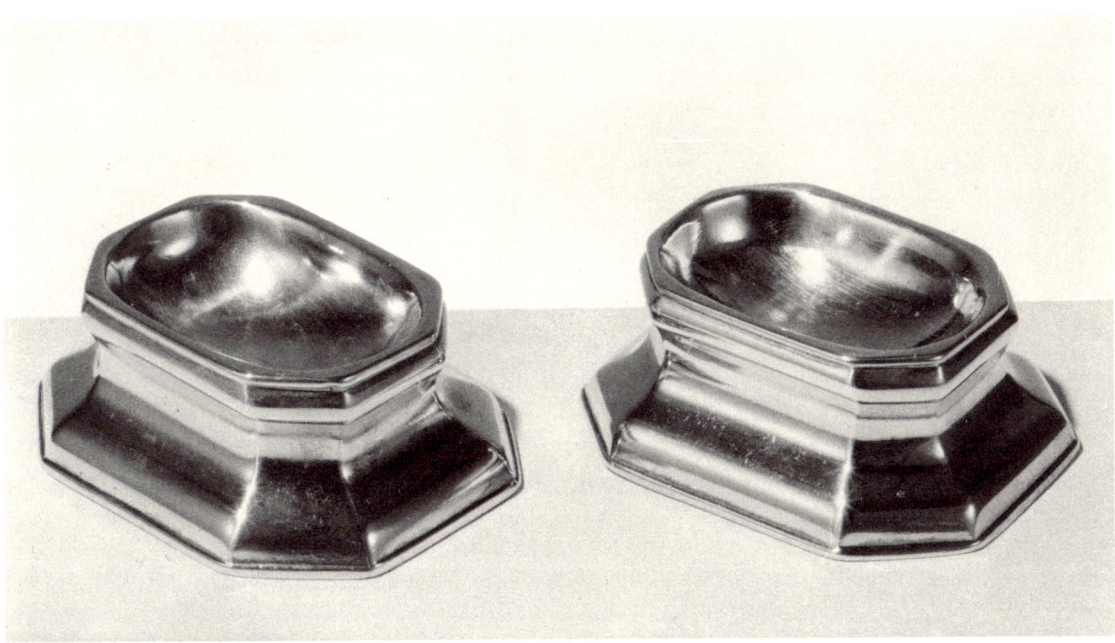

Fig. 101: Pair of salts, IR in oval on base of each, *c.* 1745. Engraved A$^W_*$M. Possibly the salts recorded in Richardson's accounts ordered by Abraham Wincoop in 1745. Length: 2 7/8″. *Courtesy of Mrs. Edsel Ford.*

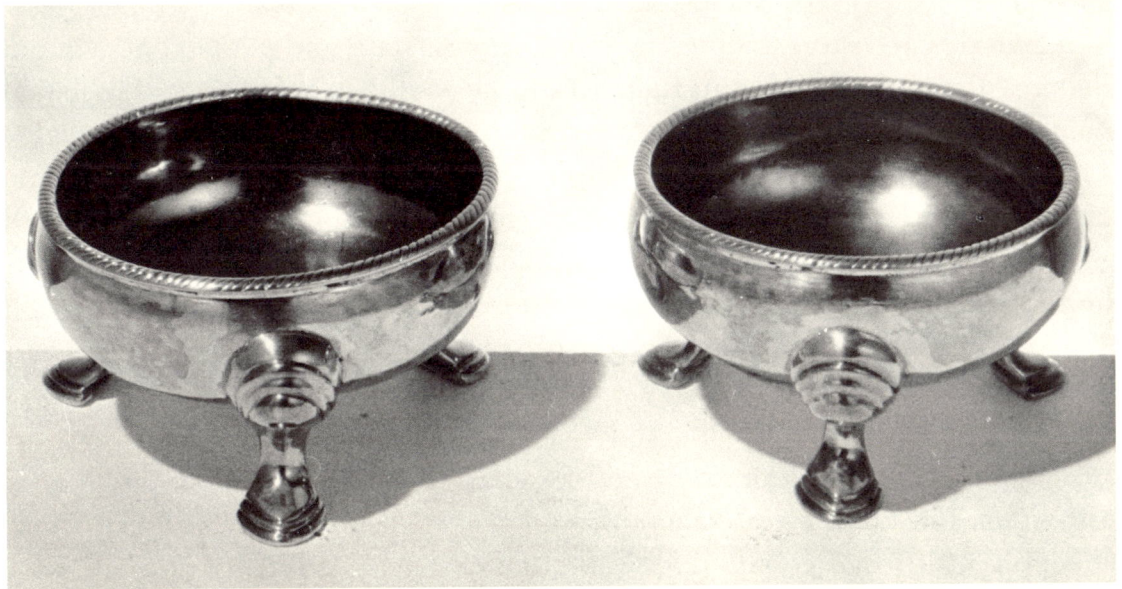

Fig. 102: Pair of salts, IR in oval twice on base of each, *c.* 1750. Engraved on base IP for the original owner. A delicately chased edge around the top is made of diagonally placed straight lines. The interiors of the salts have been sulphurized. Height: 1 1/2″; diameter at rim: 2 1/4″. *Courtesy of Mrs. Walter S. Franklin.*

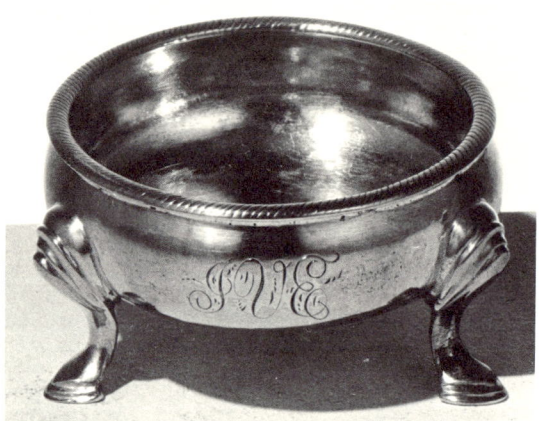 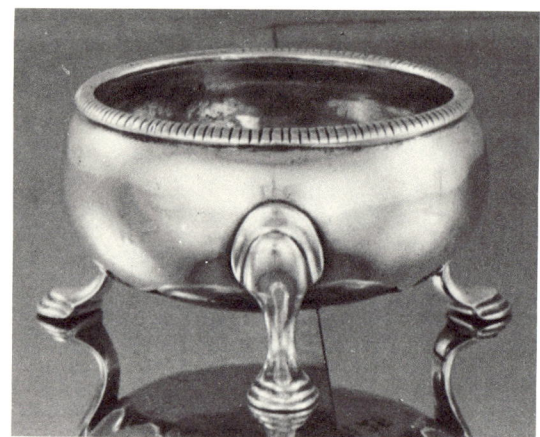

Fig. 103: One of pair of salts, IR in oval twice on base, *c.* 1750. Engraved in later script on front *IUE. Courtesy of Mrs. Harry M. Ullman.*

Fig. 104: Salt, IR in rectangle twice on base, *c.* 1755. Engraved on base R^{I}A. Height: 1 1/2″; diameter of top: 2 7/16″; weight: 2 oz. 6 dwt. The lines decorating the top edge are straight in placement rather than diagonal. *Courtesy of Yale University Art Gallery; Mabel Brady Garvan Collection.*

the same year. According to Richardson's accounts, the normal weight for a pepper or mustard caster was three to four ounces.[37] Joseph usually charged £1 for making a caster and £3 for a set.

Two sets of casters, including shakers for mustard and pepper and a larger sugar caster were recorded in Richardson's accounts in 1736, bought by Israel Pemberton, Jr., and 1738, bought by Samuel Blunston; their total weights were 15 oz. 14 dwt. and 14 oz. 9 dwt. Frank Richardson made two sets of casters for his brother in 1734–35. Silver frames holding sets of casters, with glass cruet bottles, are known to have been made by a few American silversmiths, including John David of Philadelphia, and it is possible that Joseph Richardson made cruet stands although none bearing his mark have been authenticated yet.

Richardson frequently specified "Pierced" casters in his orders to London. Some of these—plain, polished, or chased—were ordered from George Ritherdon, but more were ordered from How & Masterman, who were asked to supply neatly chased and double-bellied casters. Joseph also ordered from How & Masterman a caster frame with a set of neatly chased double-bellied casters and ground glass cruets tipped with silver, and another frame with plain casters.

The earliest type of American silver caster had straight sides and bayonet fastenings to hold the lid to the base. The fastenings were soon eliminated,

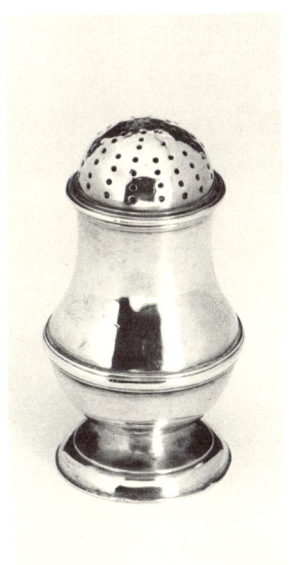 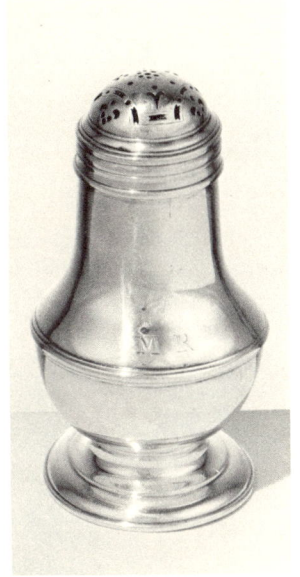 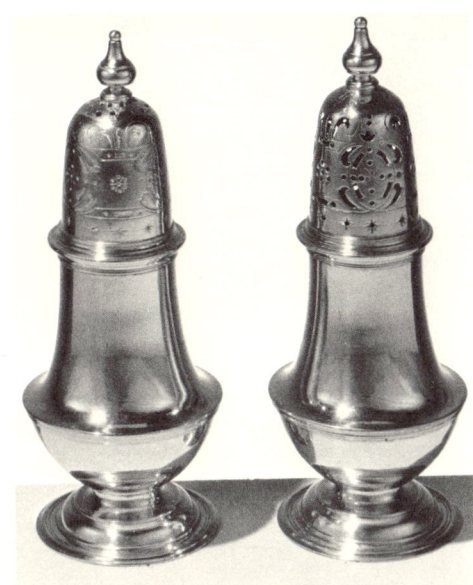

Fig. 105: Caster, IR in oval, twice on base, *c.* 1740. Pear-shaped body and low domed lid indicate date early in Richardson's career. Height: 3 1/8″; weight: 2 oz. *Courtesy of Mr. Philip H. Hammerslough.*

Fig. 106: Caster, IR in rectangle on base, *c.* 1750. MR engraved on side just above midband. *Courtesy of Mrs. Walter M. Jeffords.*

Fig. 107: Pair of casters, IR in oval twice on base, *c.* 1750–60. Engraved I^{B}A, possibly for John Bringhurst and his wife. Marked on base with weight *11 oz. 7 dwt. 12 gr.,* presumably to indicate their combined weight at one time. *Courtesy of Mrs. Harry M. Ullman.*

as was the simple curved handle attached to the body. The earliest extant form by Richardson has a plain, pear-shaped body, no handle, a mid-band, and a round, molded foot *(Fig. 105).* The lids of these early eighteenth-century forms were characterized by low, round domes, flat flanges, and rather simple piercings, although one by Richardson has been found which has a more elaborately pierced lid and no flange *(Fig. 106).* During the next stage in the development of this form *(Fig. 107),* the body of the caster acquired a bulbous urn shape, tapering sharply just above the mid-band. The lids became taller and more elaborately pierced, and a cast finial was added to the top *(Fig. 108).* In the 1740's octagonal bodies were common, but these gave way in the rococo period to the bellied and double-bellied shapes.

Pap boats and pannikins were also used in the serving of food. Neither was commonly made by Joseph Richardson, and there is some confusion in his use of the terms, perhaps indicating his lack of familiarity with the forms. Only once in his accounts, in 1747, did he mention a "Panican" (made by John Hutton), but in the same year he noted that he had received six ounces of silver from Joseph Sims "to be made into a Papcin," so that these two refer-

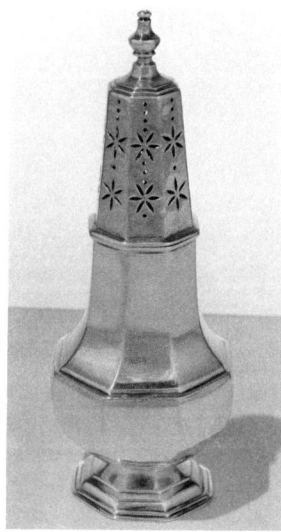 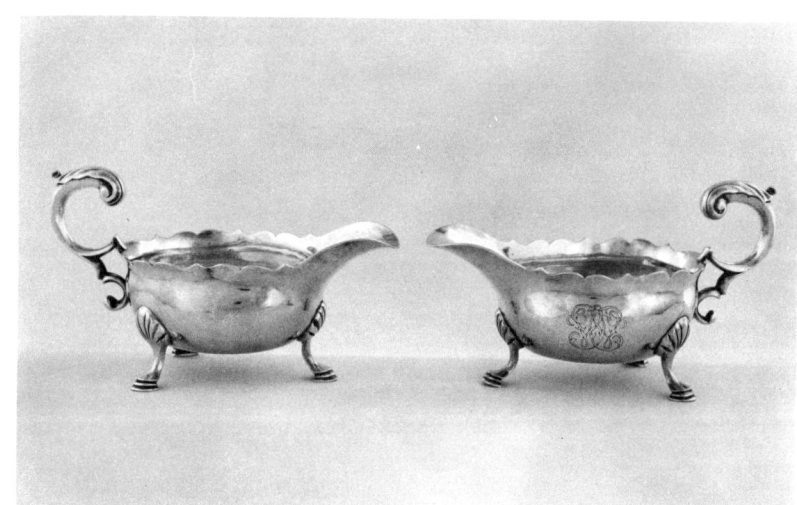

Fig. 108: Caster, IR in oval on base, *c.* 1745. Faceted finial carries the octagonal shaping of the body to the top. *Courtesy of Mrs. Walter M. Jeffords.*

Fig. 109: Pair of sauceboats, IR in rectangle, scroll above, on base of each, *c.* 1755–65. Engraved on side with cypher CW. The conventional convex shell appears here at the top of the curved legs. Length: 7 1/4". *Courtesy of Bortman-Larus American Collection.*

ences might be to the same form. He refers to a papboat only once, in 1738, when Israel Pemberton, Jr., paid him 6 shillings for making one which weighed 2 oz. 12 dwt. 12 gr.

Sauceboats began appearing on American dining tables in the eighteenth century, but Richardson records only two in his accounts prior to 1748.[38] After the middle of the century, however, sauceboats became more popular, and it was customary to buy them in pairs. Three pairs of sauceboats made by Joseph Richardson are typical of the rococo style of the 1750's and 1760's *(Figs. 109, 110).* They have long, low bodies with crenate rims and smooth, widely-shaped pouring lips and are supported on three scrolled legs with triple-pad feet. The free-standing, joined, C-scrolled handles have acanthus furls at the top. The arms or ciphers of the owners were engraved on the side so as to be visible when the handle was at the right and the boat was being used. It would be expected that sauceboats would have shell feet instead of pad feet at the height of the rococo period, but none by Richardson with shell feet has been located. It is also noteworthy that in this period Richardson ordered no sauceboats from England.

Ladles, on the other hand, were frequently ordered from London. These were used in the beginning of the eighteenth century primarily for serving soup. The terms "ladle" and "large soup spoon" were used interchangeably

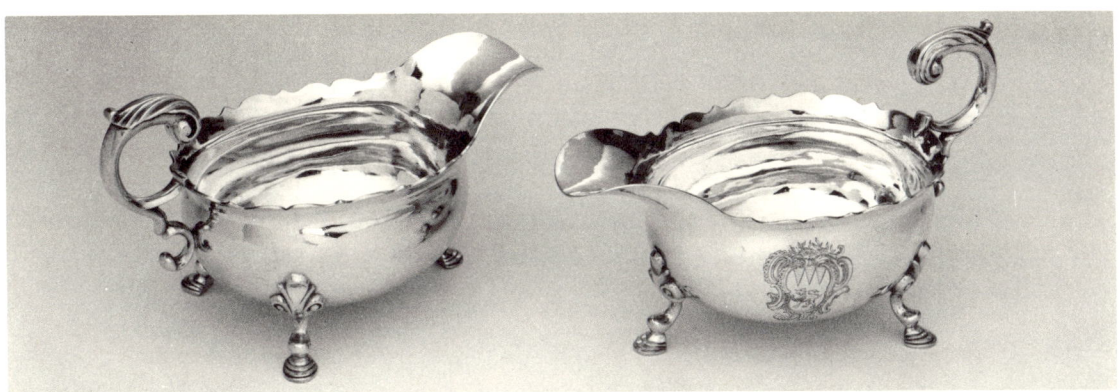

Fig. 110: Pair of sauceboats, IR in rectangle, scroll above, on base of each, *c.* 1750–60. Engraved on side with Logan arms and on base: SL (for Sarah Logan) / HLS (for Hannah Logan Smith) / EFW / SGF. Appliqued cast fleur-de-lis decorate the top of the legs. Length: 8″; weight: 11 oz. 9 dwt. *Courtesy of The Metropolitan Museum of Art, New York City; bequest of Charles Allen Munn, 1924.*

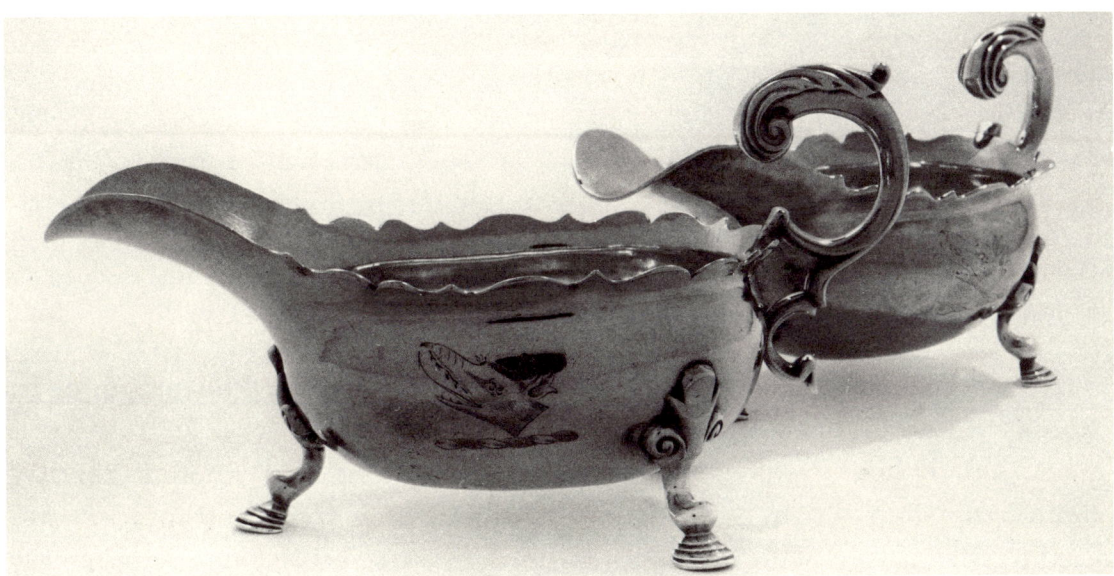

Fig. 110a: Pair of sauceboats engraved with the Pemberton crest, similar in design to the Logan sauceboats, but with an extra furl at base of handle. Length: 8 1/4″. *Courtesy of The Historical Society of Pennsylvania; gift of Henry R. Pemberton*

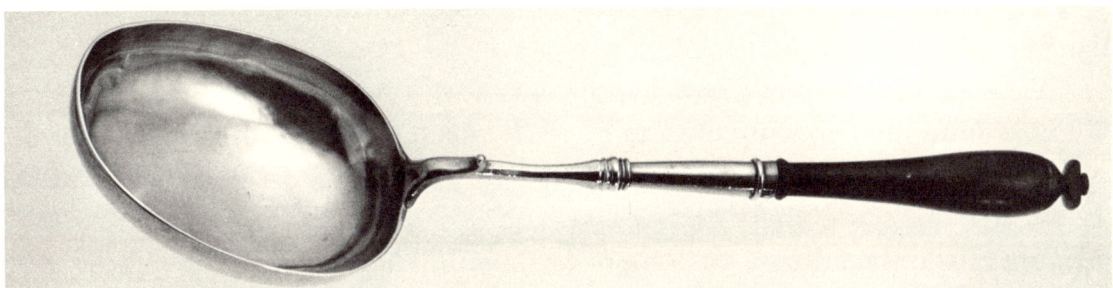

Fig. 111: Soup ladle, IR in rectangle on back of shaft, *c.* 1750. Engraved MH on double drop on back of bowl. *Littell* scratched on bottom of bowl. Turned wooden handle. Length: 15 1/8″; total weight: 7 oz. 15 dwt. including the wooden handle. *Courtesy of Yale University Art Gallery, Mabel Brady Garvan Collection.*

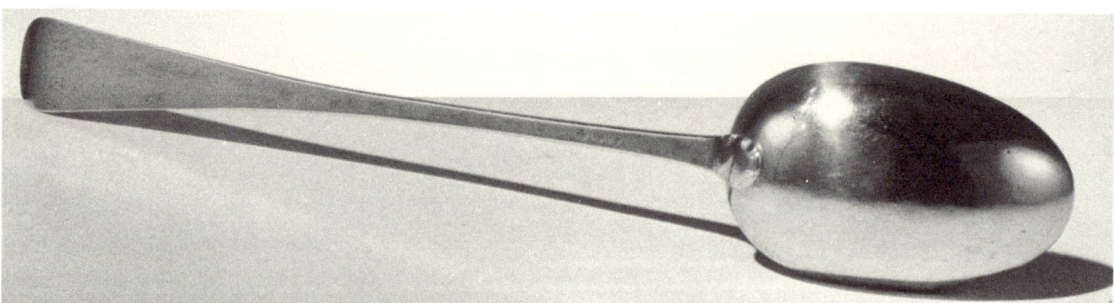

Fig. 112: Soup spoon, IR in oval thrice on back of shaft, *c.* 1737. A soup ladle and two porringers were bought from Richardson in 1737 by Edward Roberts whose initials E·R are engraved on back of the spatulate handle. Length: 15″. *Courtesy of Mr. Robert S. Stuart.*

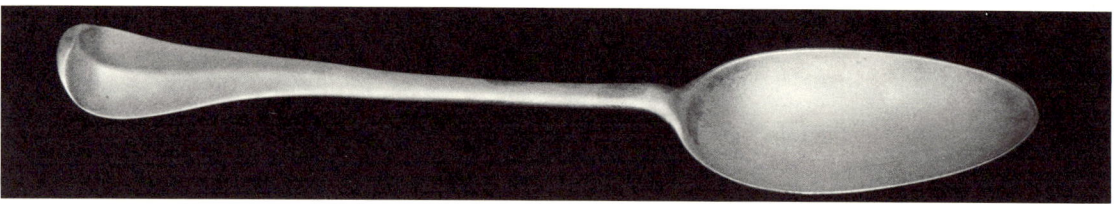

Fig. 113: Tablespoon, IR in oval twice on back of shaft, *c.* 1735. Long rat-tail on back of bowl. Engraved on back of handle B$^W_{\cdot}$E. Possibly one of the items recorded by Richardson in his accounts for March 17, 1734/5 under the name of Betholamy Waide, "6 Large Spoons . . . B$^W_{\cdot}$E on all." *Courtesy of Miss Elizabeth M. Wistar.*

by Joseph Richardson,[39] but when he ordered from How & Masterman he invariably called them "soup ladles."

Although many ladles had silver handles, some had wooden handles, such as the soup spoons with ebony handles which George Ritherdon supplied to Richardson. The bowl of a ladle with a turned wooden handle *(Fig. 111)* made by Richardson is probably similar to the one recorded in his account books in 1740 when he charged Thomas Lloyd for making a soup spoon bowl only. Silver ladle handles *(Fig. 112)* followed the same general style as spoon handles, the earliest type having a spatulate design and a turned-up handle ending.

When both the bowl and handle were of silver, a soup ladle weighed slightly more than six ounces, and the cost was 9 shillings plus the cost of the metal. The largest soup spoon recorded by Richardson was sold to Nathan Levy in 1740; it weighed 7 oz. 4 dwt. and cost £0/10/6 for making. Joseph's accounts list only a dozen customers who bought ladles of any size, indicating that the form was not in great demand in the 1730's and 1740's. By the middle of the century, however, ladles of all kinds were in common use.

Joseph Richardson: His Silver

Punch ladles, only one of which is mentioned in Richardson's accounts, were in more general use toward the end of Joseph's career, and he imported a number of them from Thomas Wagstaffe. There is no documentary evidence to prove that he made punch ladles, but a ladle described as a punch ladle made by Richardson in 1762 and owned by Elizabeth Edwards was shown in the catalogue of the Colonial Dames Exhibition in 1927.

Spoons came in a variety of sizes and were used for many different purposes.[40] In addition to teaspoons and common tablespoons there were several kinds which are not generally known today, including custard spoons, pap spoons, and chocolate spoons. (Evidently pap spoons and chocolate spoons were the same size, for Joseph Richardson spoke of "6 Pap or Chocolate Spoons" in an account with Anthony Morris in 1748.) They were small, as their weights indicate: a pap spoon weighed only slightly over one ounce and cost £0/2/6. Custard spoons may have been the same size, because the five which Israel Pemberton, Jr. bought in 1745–46 weighed a total of 5 oz. 3 dwt.

Spoons of all sorts were most frequently ordered in sets, often of six or twelve. Tablespoons usually weighed slightly less than two ounces each, and Joseph charged 3 shillings for making one. He augmented his supply of spoons by importing some from George Ritherdon and How & Masterman. The English spoons weighed as much as those he made himself and were described variously as being "burnished," "Polished," and "in the newest fashion."

Spoon styles did not change as rapidly as those of other forms in silver. The earliest spoons made in the colonies in the seventeenth century had round or fig-shaped bowls and straight, narrow handles. By the eighteenth century the outline of the bowl had become more rectangular, while the handle ending was flattened, rounded, and curved up slightly at the tip. This pattern was prevalent throughout the Colonies and was the one in which all of Joseph Richardson's identified spoons were made *(Fig. 113)*. Characteristic of his spoons was the flattening of the handle just above the sharply shaped spatulate area.

Richardson used several different patterns for the drop on the back of the bowl of his spoons *(Fig. 114)*. The earliest of these was the rat-tail drop, which was an elongated version of the V-shaped design of the preceding century. The backs of the spoons were more highly ornamented than the fronts because in formal table setting the spoons were placed face down. This is also the reason that the owners' initials appear on the backs of the handles.[41] After

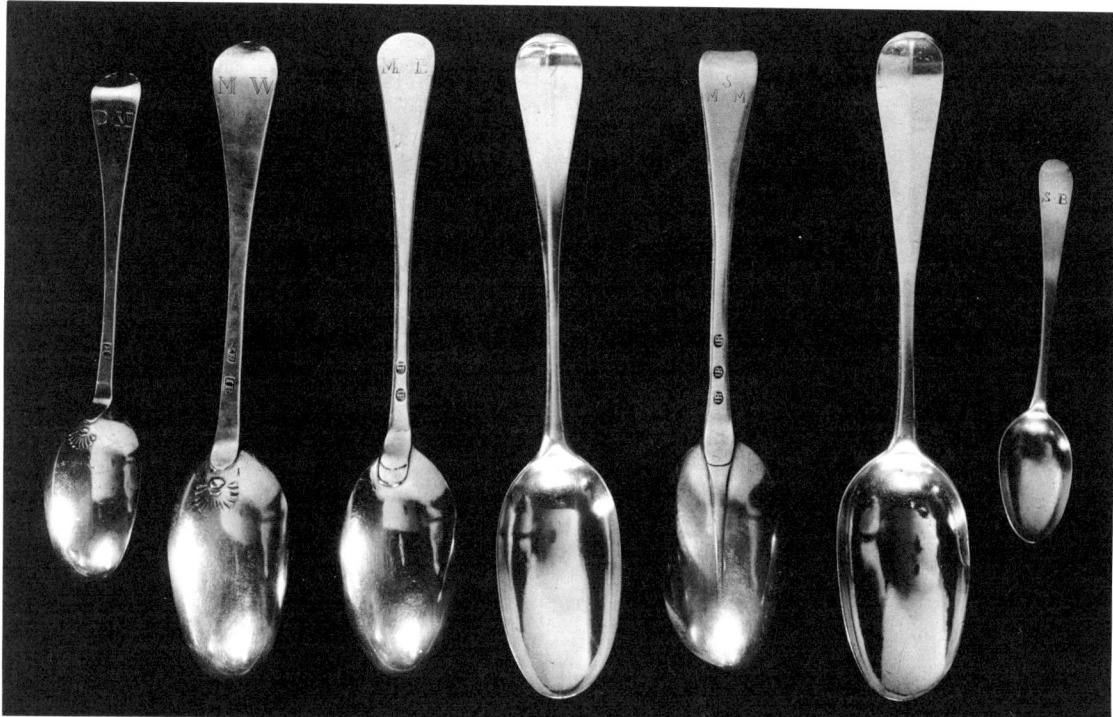

Fig. 114: Group of mid-18th century spoons by Joseph Richardson showing a variety of marks and drops on the back of the bowls. The largest are 8 1/8" long, the smallest is 4 3/4" long. *Courtesy of Mr. Robert S. Stuart.*

the rattail drop began to disappear about 1735, there appeared a type of double drop—a miniature spatulate design above a rounded drop *(Fig. 115)*. This pattern was popular during the middle of the century, but was soon replaced by the more typically rococo shell design *(Fig. 115)*. Although shell drops were used in all the Colonies as well as abroad, Richardson's spoons followed a pattern peculiar to the Philadelphia area: above and separate from a rounded drop were fourteen separated lobes, beneath which was a horizontally placed, arc-shaped drop over a small, oval boss. By the late eighteenth century, the drops on the backs of bowls had become simple ovals, and they were given up almost entirely by the nineteenth century. Richardson is not known to have made these later types, nor did he make spoons with the turned-back handle endings which were introduced about the time of the Revolution.[42]

Minor Forms

In the past, students of American silver have concerned themselves primarily with the major silver forms, and indeed, these objects are the most

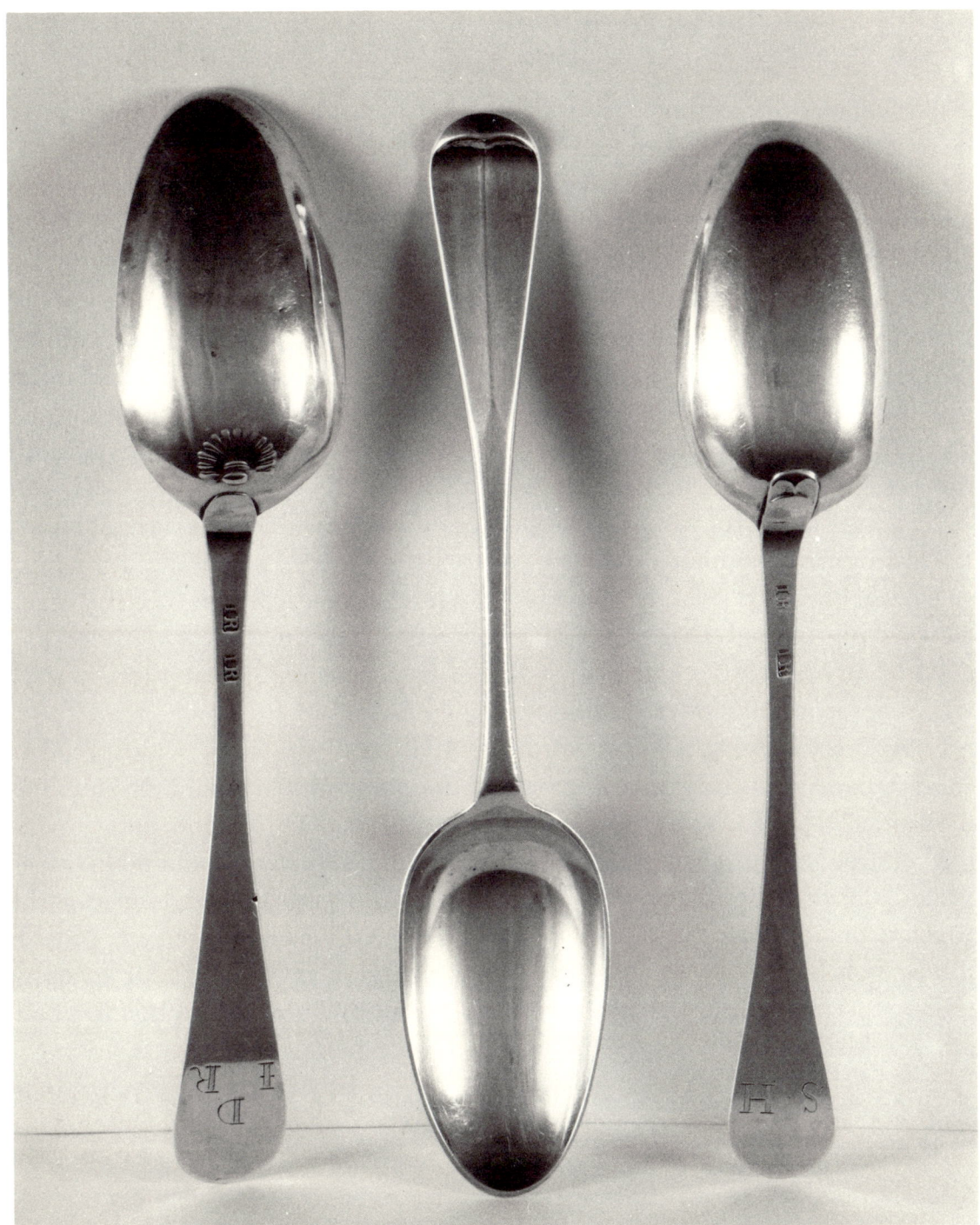

Fig. 115: Three tablespoons, IR in rectangle twice on back of shaft, *c.* 1750, shows shell drop and spatulate drop. Engraved on back of handle, left to right, I^{D}R, MR, and SH. Lengths, left to right: 8 3/8"; 8 1/4", 8 3/16". *Privately owned; photograph by Gilbert Ask.*

important and interesting. It was the smaller items, however, that constituted the artisan's daily trade. These objects, often too small or of too little value to be marked, are frequently difficult to identify today, but Joseph's accounts and his surviving work shed some light on this aspect of his craft. These miscellaneous little silver objects are as accurate a reflection of changing styles as the larger forms. Furthermore, they are a unique index of changing social customs—from the seventeenth century, when only the wealthiest could indulge in silver and gold frivolities, to the eighteenth century, when the rising middle class demanded everything from shoe buckles to stay hooks in precious metals. Most important, these small objects provide glimpses of daily life in the Colonial era which otherwise would be forgotten.

Sponge boxes represent a long-forgotten custom: since the days of Henry VIII, English gentlemen carried these little boxes, which held sponges soaked in herb and spice-laden vinegar, whose aromatic fumes were believed to ward off disease. Later called "vinaigrettes," these objects were seldom used in America, and of all Joseph Richardson's customers, only John Armitt was ever recorded as buying "a Silver Spung Box."

The custom of taking snuff from a silver box was more widespread in America, and a few Colonial women had their portraits painted with snuff box in hand. These flattened boxes, shaped to fit neatly into the palm or the pocket, frequently became darkly tarnished unless they were gilded inside to protect the silver from contact with the treated tobacco. A dozen entries in the Richardson accounts refer to such boxes. The first was bought in 1733 by his fellow goldsmith, Philip Syng, who was charged 12 shillings for Joseph's labor. It is interesting that the next year Joseph bought a snuff box from another goldsmith, Anthony Bright, and paid only half as much for it.

Some of these snuff boxes were made by Richardson's helpers; John Hutton made one for the Dutch Minister in 1739. Evidently the Dutch were heavy snuff users; in that same year "the Dutchman" was charged £2/7/5 for three boxes that cost 24 shillings each to make. Snuff boxes were even made up ahead and kept on hand, and in 1744 Joseph displayed three of them in his glass showcase.

Several snuff boxes bearing Richardson's mark and made in the 1750's and 1760's have survived. One, presented to a young Philadelphia woman by the Governor of Virginia about 1757 *(Fig. 116)*, has all the elements of the highest rococo style that the more impressive teapots and kettles display. Shaped like a rococo cartouche, it is handsomely decorated with a florid re-

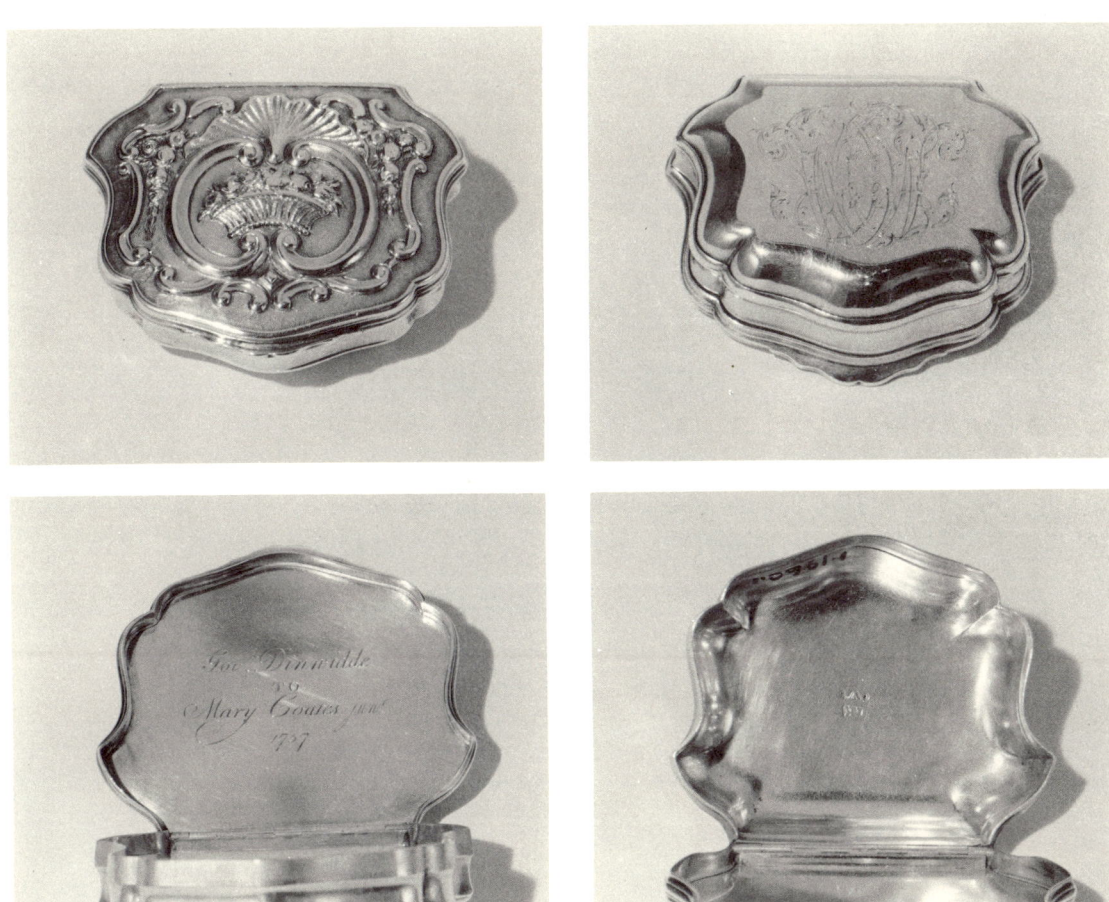

Fig. 116: Snuff box, IR in rectangle, scroll below, inside base, *c*. 1757. Engraved on inside lid, *Govr. Dinwidde to Mary Coates Juʳ, 1757*. Florid cypher *MC* engraved on base. Apparently a gift to the young daughter of Samuel and Mary Coates, with whom Governor Dinwiddie of Virginia stayed while attending a conference in 1757. Length: 3″. *Courtesy of Philadelphia Museum of Art.*

verse cipher on the base and elaborate repoussé work on top.

The same lavish repoussé decoration on the snuff boxes *(Fig. 117)* appeared in the form of carving on fireplace walls and furniture used in Philadelphia homes during the Chippendale period, and it is possible that Richardson might have obtained the pattern for this decoration from Hercules Courtenay, who carved both chairs and interior woodwork in that city.[43] It is also possible that Richardson took these designs from English snuff boxes, such as those which he imported from Daniel Mildred in 1759: "3 Chast Silver Snuf Boxes Gilt Inside with Gold." He ordered plated snuff boxes with chased or stamped lids from How & Masterman in 1760, but he soon stopped importing these boxes and presumably sold only those he made himself.

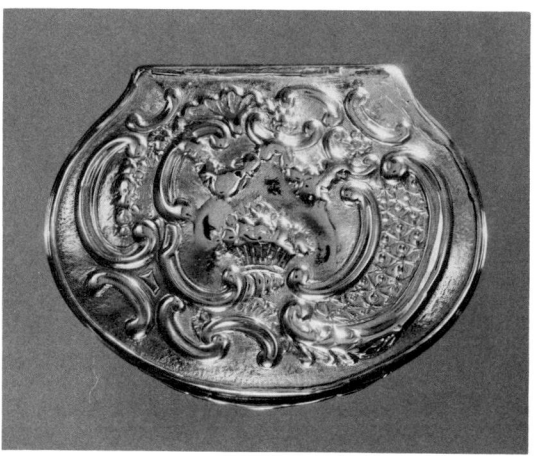 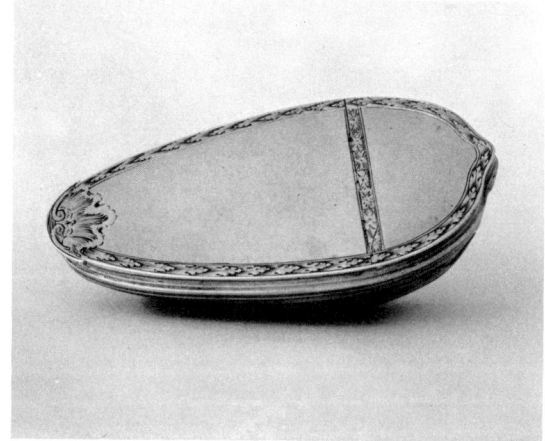

Fig. 117: Snuff box, IR in rectangle, scroll below, inside base, *c.* 1760. Length: 3 1/16". *Courtesy of Yale University Art Gallery; Mabel Brady Garvan Collection.*

Fig. 118: Snuff box, IR in rectangle, inside lid, *c.* 1775. Made of cowrie shell. *Courtesy of Mr. Elliot Richardson, Jr.*

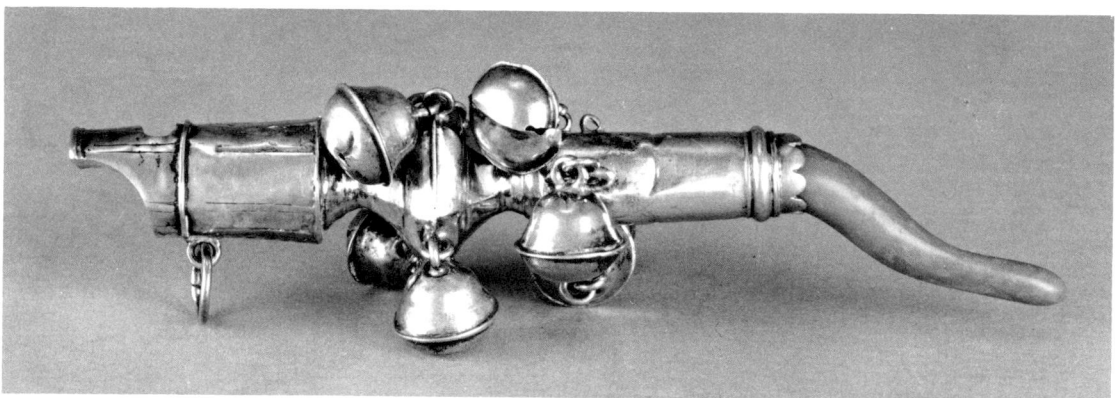

Fig. 119: Coral and bells, IR in rectangle, *c.* 1740. Six bells placed in two rows on octagonal stem. Length. 7 3/4", weight without coral: 1 oz. 8 dwt. 9 gr. *Courtesy of The Henry Francis du Pont Winterthur Museum; photograph by Gilbert Ask.*

At the end of the rococo period, the decoration of snuff boxes was a little more restrained, and engraving, which had always been a favorite means of ornamentation, returned to greater prominence *(Fig. 118)*. The simpler type of snuff box was often made from a cowrie shell, with a silver hinged lid attached to its flat base. Because they fit comfortably into the hand, shell boxes (which are mentioned nowhere in Joseph's accounts of the early eighteenth century) became popular at the end of the century.

Another object that served a specialized purpose was the silver or gold baby's rattle which had a stem of smoothed coral on which the baby could teethe and a whistle in the other end of the silver socket adorned with rings or bells. These rattles were described by Alexander Pope in *The Rape of the Lock:*

> Her infant grand-dame's whistle next it grew,
> The bells she jingled, and the whistle blew.[44]

These luxury items were called "coral and bells," "socket and bells," or "whistle and bells," and cost about 16 shillings to make.[45] The piece of polished coral was often charged separately and ranged in price from £0/7/6 in 1739 to £0/12/6 in 1748. According to his accounts, Joseph made these objects throughout his career. In 1739 James Crison bought a socket and bells weighing 1 oz. 14 dwt. 6 gr. and then had it "changed for an other" which weighed 1 dwt. 17 gr. more. Another customer, Elizabeth Roberts, had the coral and bells she bought in 1736 engraved with the initials of its recipient.

Very few coral and bells made by American goldsmiths have survived, but one attributed to Joseph Richardson is known today *(Fig. 119)*.[46] Its simple design and its octagonal stem indicate that it was made about 1740, at the beginning of Richardson's career. Most of his rattles had six bells and, being rather delicate toys, they were frequently in need of repair. In 1748 John Stamper brought one to his shop which needed a new piece of coral, "mending of the socket," and six new bells. In addition, Joseph imported corals with eight bells from Daniel Mildred. Made of silver gilt, these were undoubtedly in the more elaborate rococo style, which required more time to make and therefore could be produced more cheaply in the large workshops of London.

Although coral and bells have become a rarity, the fountain pen is commonplace today. Fountain pens have been used since the seventeenth century, when Samuel Pepys wrote that he owned a silver pen given to him by Mr. Coventry "to carry inke in."[47] No American-made fountain pens prior to the nineteenth century are known today, but in 1747 Joseph Richardson sold a fountain pen case to Israel Pemberton, Jr., for 10 shillings.[48]

Other rare items in Joseph's accounts that have not been found include a snuff mill, cocks, cranes, and nutmeg graters.[49] Many of these unusual items

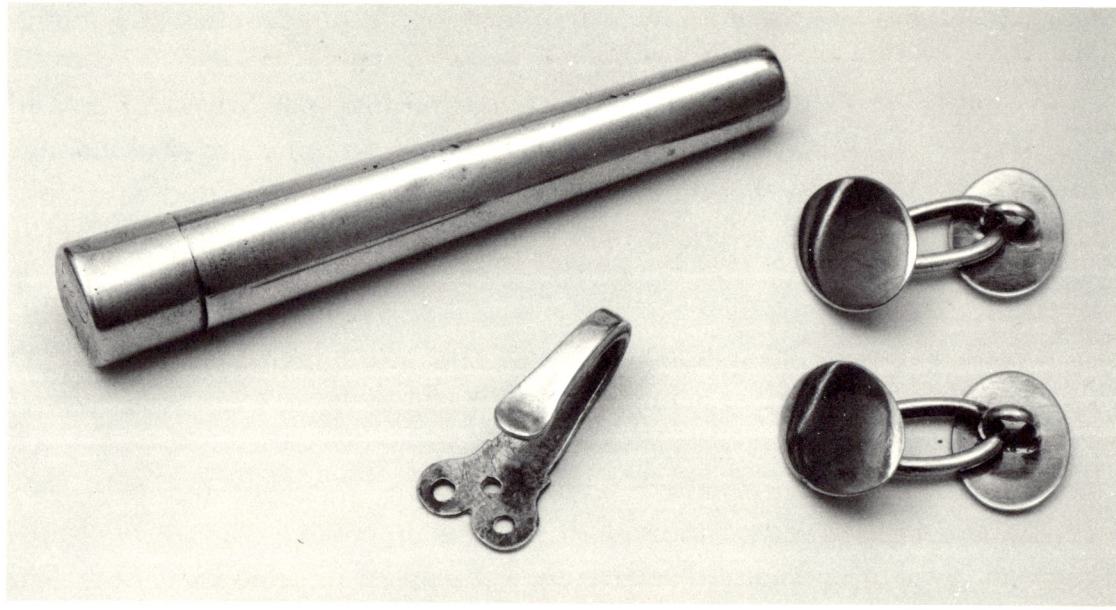

Fig. 120: Links of buttons or cuff links, hook, and needle case, all unmarked but found among the Richardson family papers, mid-18th century. Needle case engraved on top RR probably for Rebecca Richardson, 2 5/8" long. The only reference to this form in Richardson's accounts is to silver brought in by Bezaliel Hughs in 1747 "to be made into a Needle Case." Heart-shaped hook engraved on back of shaft RR, 7/8" long. Links weigh 26 1/2 and 26 3/4 gr. and are 5/8" long and 3/8" wide. *Courtesy of The Henry Francis du Pont Winterthur Museum; photograph by Gilbert Ask.*

were made by David Harper while he was working in Richardson's shop. He also made bosses and buckles for horse bridles, and little eyes for cane heads. Silver lace, nipples for babies' bottles, and even an umbrella are some of the other unusual objects sold in Richardson's shop in the 1730's and 1740's.

Small, but of more general use, was the chatelaine hook which the lady of a household wore in her waistband to hold her scissors, keys, and other necessary equipment. A few marked eighteenth-century American examples have survived, and one made by Joseph Richardson for a member of his family is engraved with a charming mid-century motif—a basket of flowers and C-scrolls *(see Fig. 161)*. Chatelaine hooks were once called "harts" (because of their heart shape) and are listed that way in the accounts of Joseph and his father.

The well-equipped lady might also have purchased knitting needles from a goldsmith, and even little silver needle cases like the one found among the Richardson family mementos *(Fig. 120)*.[50] All sorts of small cases could be bought from the goldsmith, who imported those he could obtain more cheaply from London than make in his own workshop. For example, Richardson ordered sliding pencil cases, with pencils to fit inside them. Ivory memorandum cases or "books," as they were then called, were also imported from London. These flat cases of metal or tortoise shell contained several thin sheets of ivory to write on and had a slot for a pencil on the side. Tweezer and étui (from which the word "tweezer" derives) cases were also imported, as were chased instrument cases.[51]

On the other hand, toothpick cases, which enjoyed some popularity at the end of the seventeenth century, were made by some American goldsmiths, including Francis Richardson, in their own shops; even Joseph recorded making two of them at the beginning of his career.[52] Joseph made watch cases in his own shop in addition to those he imported from Thomas Wagstaffe and George Ritherdon. One watch case of his own manufacture was bought in 1737 by the Philadelphia clockmaker John Wood.[53] Richardson also sold keys, chains, pendants, crystals, and watch straps.

Another type of case which the goldsmith sold was the spectacle case. Richardson ordered green fishskin cases mounted with silver from How & Masterman when he wrote for spectacles set in silver frames, and spare glasses for them. Occasionally he made spectacle frames himself; these cost from 3 to 4 shillings in the 1730's,[54] although in 1746 he paid David Harper 5 shillings for making a pair of temple spectacle frames for him. Rarely were such frames marked by American goldsmiths until the end of the eighteenth century, and none bearing Joseph's mark are known today, though at least nine pairs were recorded in his account books.

Similarly, spurs are known to have been made and imported by Joseph Richardson for sale in his shop. How & Masterman sent both silver and plated spurs to him, and he and Harper made a number of the solid type in the shop. The silver spurs weighed four to five ounces and cost about 18 shillings to make. However, a pair of spurs bought in 1746 by William Cox weighed less and cost more for making, indicating that it was not weight alone but possibly the design which determined the price.

Ferrules and heads for canes and whips were also made by Richardson and Harper. Such small and simply made items were probably not imported. Because they were relatively insignificant, their makers are almost never known, but the ferrules on a cane used by one of his close relatives can be identified through family history as the work of Joseph Richardson (*Fig. 121*). For cane ferrules, Joseph usually charged 4 or 5 shillings, plus the cost of

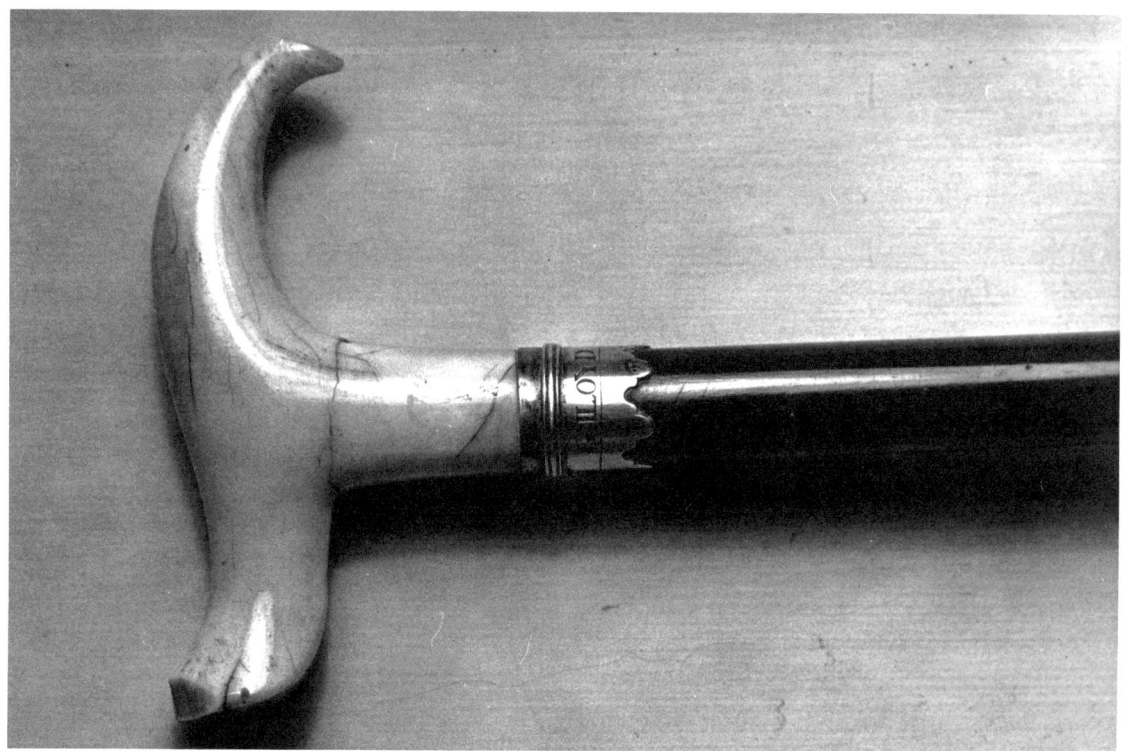

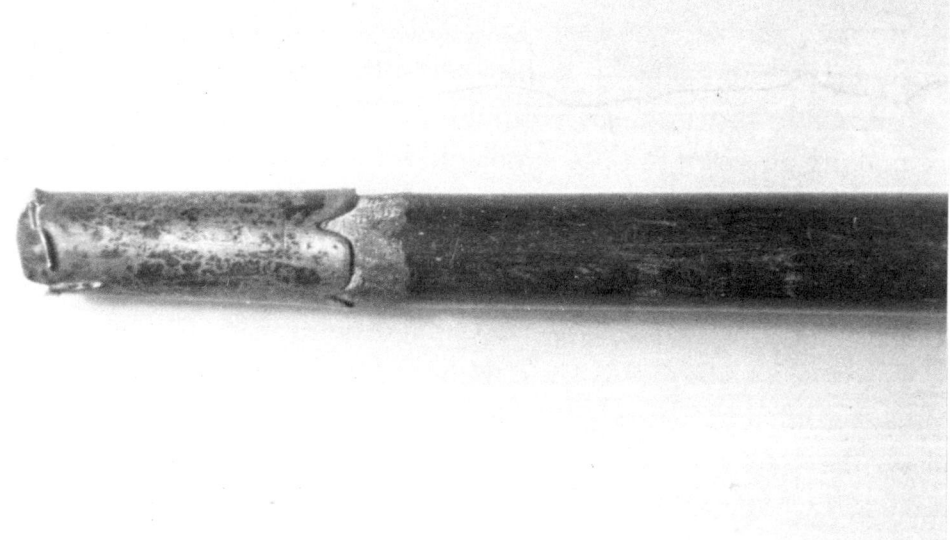

Fig. 121: Cane ferrule and tip, unmarked, *c.* 1750. Originally owned by Joseph Richardson's aunt Grace Lloyd whose name is engraved around ferrule. Grace Lloyd died in 1760, and it is likely the cane was made to support her during the latter years of her life. Traditionally believed by the family to have mounts made by Joseph Richardson. Scalloping of edge of ferrule at end of cane is similar to that on the Richardson coral and bells (*Fig. 119*). *Courtesy of William Penn Memorial Museum, Harrisburg, Pennsylvania.*

approximately four pennyweight of silver which they weighed. Whip ferrules cost only 2 shillings to make, although they weighed no less, while whip heads cost anywhere from 5 to 10 shillings and weighed about ten pennyweight.

Just as the well-dressed eighteenth-century gentleman carried silver or gold-headed canes and whips, his lady often carried a silver-banded pincushion suspended on a chain from her chatelaine hook. Richardson made a number of these pincushion bands for Philadelphia ladies.[55] He also made and had as many as nine on hand in his showcase at one time (Appendix A). Interestingly enough, most of the thimbles Richardson made were of gold rather than silver; they weighed about four pennyweight and cost approximately 6 shillings to make.[56]

Because gold and silver could be penetrated by steel needles, one of Joseph's most common repair jobs was the "topping" of thimbles, and many of the silver thimbles he imported from England had steel tops or were of steel lined with silver. Wagstaffe, Ritherdon, and Mildred all supplied thimbles to Richardson, and dozens came to him from the Masterman firm. These were of different sizes, and Joseph requested repeatedly that they not be very deep. His sons Joseph and Nathaniel Richardson, found themselves compelled to write to Masterman at the end of 1783 to say, "The thimbles you sent us tho good in their quallity are so very deep that common people cannot wear them wish the next may be in moderation."[57]

Another item used in needlework was the bodkin, a long narrow instrument with a large eye and blunt end used to draw tape or cord through hems. Although usually made of steel, the bodkin was sometimes silver. Richardson sold a number of these; one made early in his career (Fig. 122) is engraved around the slots in each end, with the owner's initials in the center.[58]

Two other now outdated items in the eighteenth-century goldsmith's shop were the skewer (Fig. 123), used to hold meat while it was being prepared or served, and the marrow scoop, whose long, narrow bowls of different sizes were used to remove bone marrow, a great delicacy at the time. Both of these forms were rare in American silver and were made by Joseph Richardson only occasionally.[59] Equally rare in American silver are sconces and candlesticks. It is unlikely that Joseph Richardson either imported or made these himself, although on one occasion he charged David Harper 10 shillings for the silver Harper used to make sconces.

Richardson did not often make seals, the specialty of certain American goldsmiths, although one was on hand in his glass case in 1744. Of the several

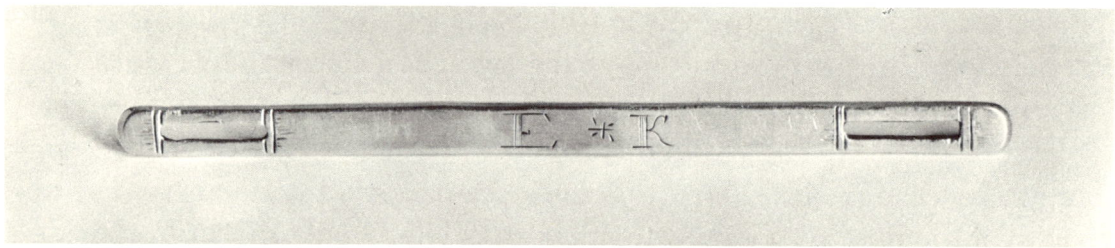

Fig. 122: Bodkin, IR in oval on back of shaft, *c.* 1740. Owner's initials E∘K on side. Length: 3 5/8"; width: 3/8"; weight: 1/2 oz. *Courtesy of Mr. Philip H. Hammerslough.*

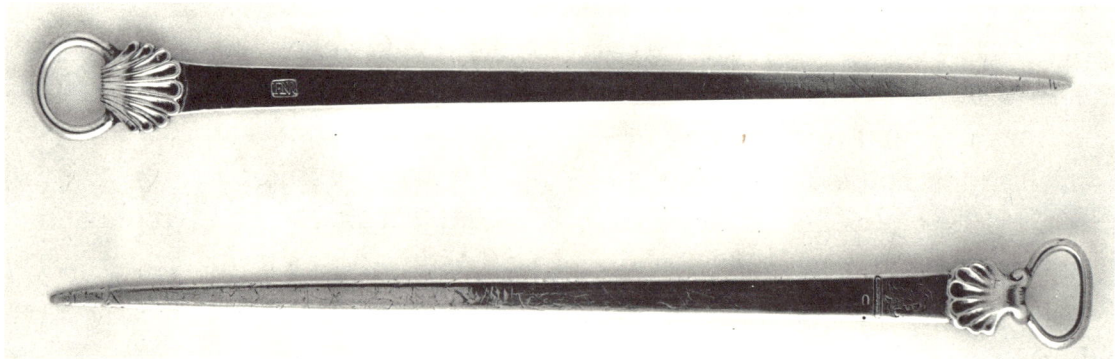

Fig. 123: Skewer, IR in rectangle, *c.* 1760. Engraved with eagle-head crest. Length: 9 7/8"; weight: 2 oz. Skewer, I·NR in rectangle, *c.* 1785. Length: 9 3/4". *Courtesy of Mr. Philip H. Hammerslough.*

gentlemen who bought seals from him, George Emlen was so satisfied with his that two years later he bought one for his son, George. George Emlen, Jr.'s seal was accompanied by a watch chain, as was one bought by Anthony Noble, for gentlemen often wore their seals on such a chain. The usual cost for seal and chain was 13 to 15 shillings; for seal without chain, 4 or 5 shillings.

Similar to the cutting of seals was the cutting of dies, and although Richardson is not known to have cut the dies for medals, on at least two occasions he struck medals from dies cut by Edward Duffield, the Philadelphia clockmaker. One of these was the Kitanning medal of 1756 *(Fig. 124 right)*, one of the first medals presented in the Colonies for war services. The other was the first Indian Peace Medal in the Colonies *(Fig. 124 left).*[60]

Joseph Richardson was a member of the standing committee of the Friendly Association of Regaining and Preserving Peace with the Indians by Pacific Measures. A lender of money to the cause, he also made thousands of silver objects for presentation to the Indians.[61] Because many of these bands, earbobs, rings, and other items were buried with the Indians when they died, few examples of Indian silver marked by American goldsmiths are known to-

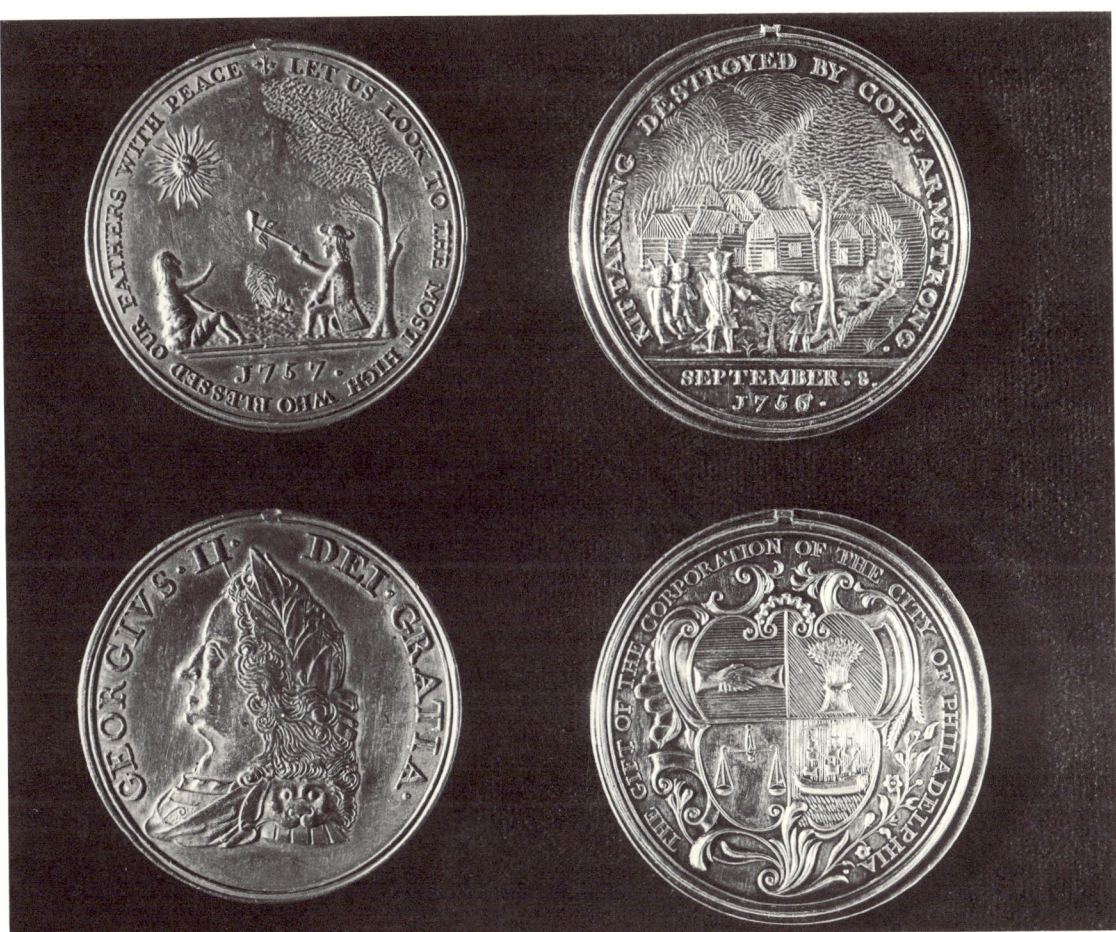

Fig. 124: Medals cut by Edward Duffield and struck by Joseph Richardson. Left, obverse and reverse of Indian peace medal, 1757, given by The Friendly Association of Regaining and Preserving Peace with the Indians by Pacific Measures. Right, obverse and reverse of medal presented by The City of Philadelphia to Col. John Armstrong of Carlisle who was wounded while leading a party which destroyed the Delaware Indians' village at Kitanning in a surprise attack in 1756. On one side is shown the village being burned and on the other side the corporation arms of the city. Diameter: 1 3/4". *Courtesy of The Historical Society of Pennsylvania.*

day. One fine gorget made by Joseph Richardson does survive *(Fig. 125)*; on it is engraved a scene depicting the Quaker offer of peace, showing clearly the extent to which the Friendly Association went to gain the Indians' friendship and indicating Richardson's role in this effort.

Although over a hundred American goldsmiths are known to have made silver hilts for swords, no members of the peaceful Society of Friends are among them. Joseph Richardson is believed to have made no sword hilts him-

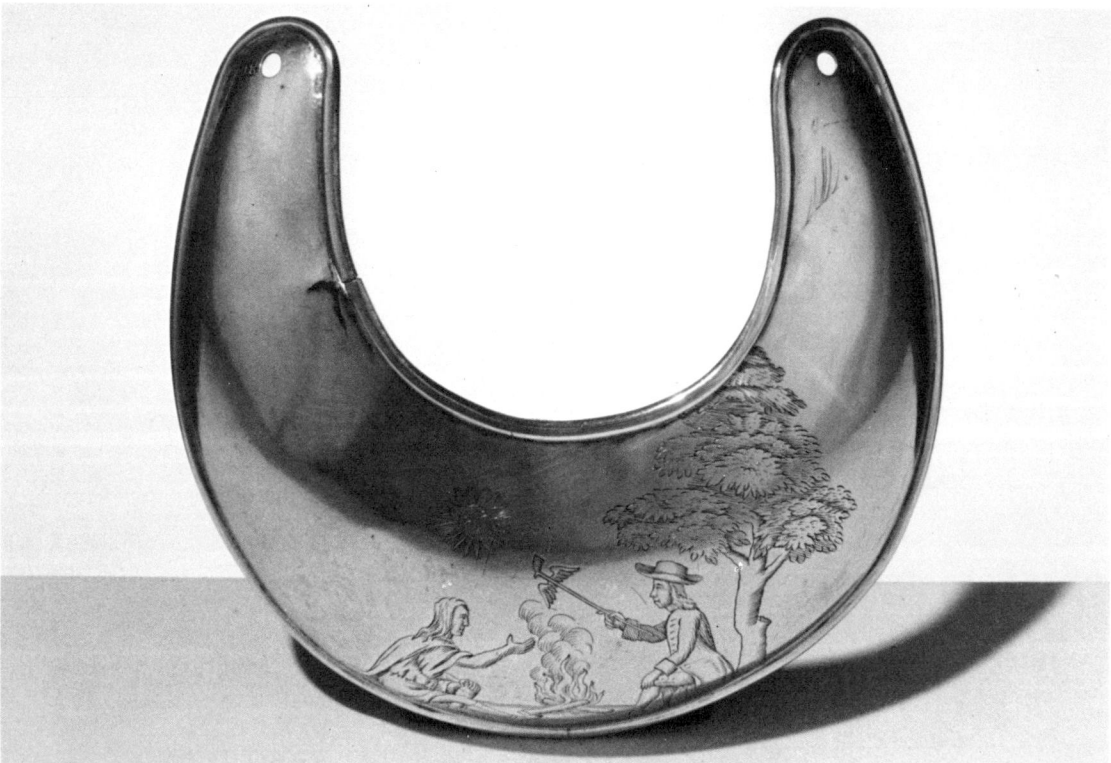

Fig. 125: Gorget, IR in rectangle twice on top at sides of eyelets, *c.* 1760. Presented to the Indians by The Friendly Association. Engraved with a scene of a man, probably William Penn seated beneath a tree offering a peace pipe to another man seated on the ground and looking more like an ordinary mendicant than an Indian. Width: 5 1/4". *Courtesy of The Historical Society of Pennsylvania.*

self although in his accounts he refers to one made by David Harper and to swords repaired by Harper.[62]

Jewelry

From the earliest times, goldsmiths were also jewelers who provided the wealthy with the precious baubles they demanded. By the eighteenth century so many people were able to afford necklaces and fancy shoe buckles that there were, even in America, goldsmiths who specialized in this aspect of their art. Of course, there were certain simple ornaments which any goldsmith could provide, and even those who worked in the country could make rings and buttons. Because these trinkets are so small, and rarely marked by their makers, their significance as an element in the goldsmith's craft has been ignored by students of American silver. For that reason, the information found in Joseph Richardson's account book and the few surviving examples of his work in jewelry assume a greater importance.

The rings which Joseph Richardson made were intended for various purposes. Those designed as tokens of love were suitably inscribed with a "posey."[63] Inside one golden band he was asked in 1745 to engrave "the Posey I Pray Love well & Ever not the Gift but the Giver;" in another, in 1738 "Within this sphere moves all thats dear." Patrick Glassgow bought two rings in 1738 with different posies: one to be marked, "when this u see rem[ember] me from J:T;" the other, "The love is true I bear to you." Unfortunately, none of these rings by Richardson is to be found today, and it is only through the account books that we know of them.

Some of the rings were used by gentlemen as signets to impress their initials or crests in sealing wax. In 1739 Richardson noted that one of these seal rings was to be cut with the initials "E•A," for its purchaser, Edward Anderson. Another type of ring is the mourning or funeral ring. A Renaissance custom which survived into the nineteenth century, mourning rings were mementoes given to the pall bearers and other close friends of the deceased at the time of his funeral and were engraved with his name, age, and date of death. Occasionally symbols of death or even a lock of the dead person's hair were worked into the design. Although this custom was more widespread in New England than in Philadelphia, Joseph Richardson noted in his accounts the sale of a hair ring in 1738, and the sale of a number of mourning rings.[64]

Rings were usually of gold, and their cost, generally over a pound, although the labor for a plain gold ring was only 3 shillings; for a hair ring, 6 shillings; and for a stone or crystal set ring, 8 shillings. The size of the ring varied too, and Joseph often noted the size of a particular ring with alphabetical letters ranging from "F" to "K." Naturally the size of the ring affected the amount of gold required (usually a little over two pennyweight).[65]

In addition to rings, the most frequently requested item of jewelry was the clasp. Functional clasps, usually silver, served as fastenings for shoes, stockings, and cloaks; especially decorative clasps were used as lockets for necklaces. Richardson also made clasps for books and even pocket books, the latter sometimes imported from London. Richardson's failure to make a specific note of the cost of making silver clasps indicates that he may have bought them from someone else for resale or that he sold them at a fixed rate. Both the cost and the weight of the ornamental clasps Richardson sold varied con-

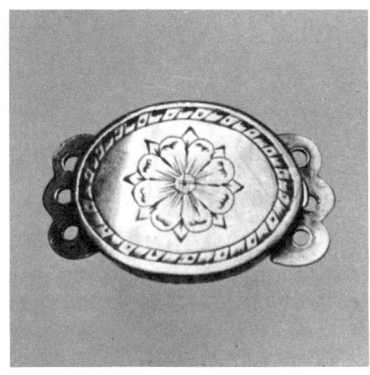

Fig. 126: Gold locket, IR in rectangle, *c.* 1750. M·R possibly for Joseph Richardson's wife, Mary. Length: 7/8″. The central motif is a Tudor rose, and the openings for a three-strand necklace are simply holes cut into the flat piece with no finishing mouldings. *Courtesy of The Metropolitan Museum of Art, New York City; gift of Arthur Sussel, 1948.*

siderably; one of the most expensive was a pair of gold stock clasps which cost £3/4/6 for the metal and 12 shillings for their fashioning.

Clasps used for closing necklaces were generally called "lockets," and were almost always made of gold. Usually weighing from three to four pennyweight with an 8-shilling-charge for labor, their cost was just under two pounds. Joseph Richardson made many of these tiny objects, and several have survived. They were engraved on top with a border, and with either a rosette (*Fig. 126*) similar to that his father had used (see *Fig. 11*), or a more rococo spray of flowers or basket of fruit (*Figs. 127, 128*).

These lockets were meant to hold strands of gold chain or strands of coral or gold beads. Richardson made many such gold beads; they were formed of two hollow hemispheres of gold which had been soldered together.[66] The coral beads Joseph Richardson used were imported and were, of course, less costly than the gold beads: "a Double Necklace of Coral" cost William Hudson, Jr. only 9 shillings; a gold bead necklace could cost as much as 50 shillings. When he ordered the coral beads from London, Richardson paid only four or five pence for a hundred beads. The size of the bead was determined either by its weight (about one grain) or by the number of beads that would measure an inch. Richardson preferred his to be of "midling size," so that nine strung together would measure one inch.

Joseph also used the inch measure in making gold chains, as in 1747, when he charged Joseph Morris for 32 1/2 inches of gold chain, at 10 pence per inch. Although he made chains himself, Richardson imported some from London, specifying that chains to be used for attaching scissors to chatelaines

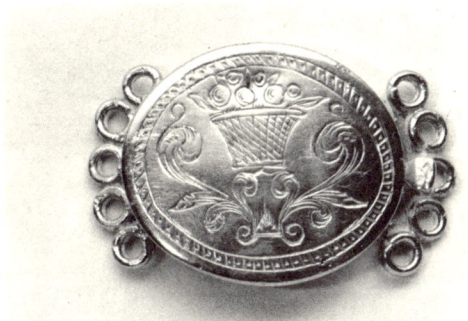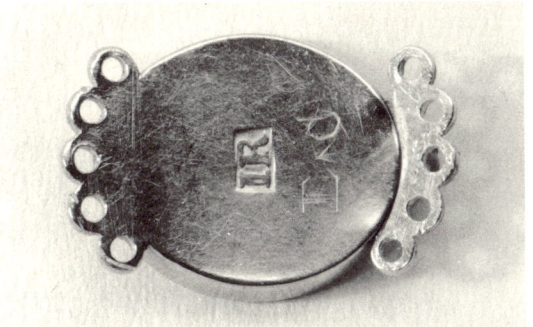

Fig. 127: Gold locket, IR in rectangle, *c*. 1750. Engraved E∘C for Elizabeth Coultas, wife of first city Sheriff of Philadelphia. Five circular shaped openings were cut out from the flat pieces of metal extending on each side of the clasp, and were finished off by the soldering of a wire ring around the top of each hole. *Courtesy of The Henry Francis du Pont Winterthur Museum; photograph by Gilbert Ask.*

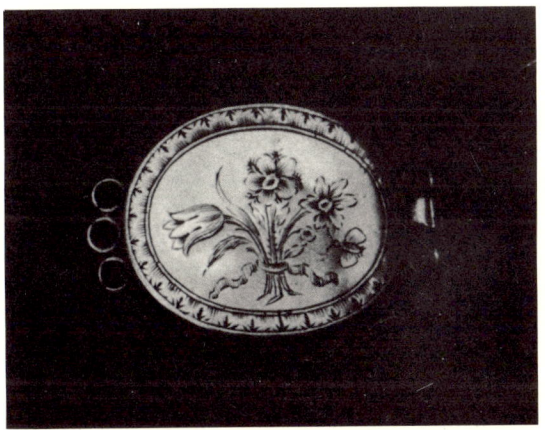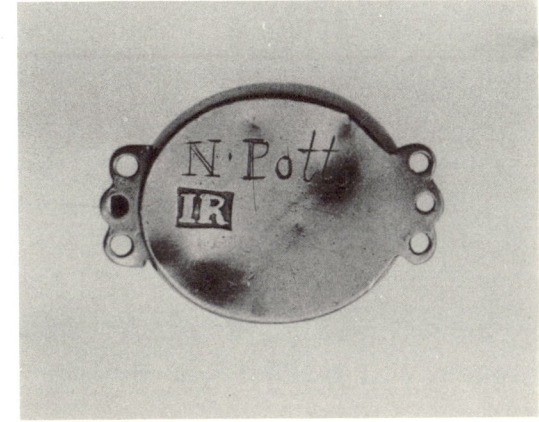

Fig. 128: Gold locket, IR in rectangle, *c*. 1750. Engraved *N. Potts* on back plate. On front, engraved with a spray of flowers, including a daffodil, tied together with a ribbon, and a butterfly or bee fluttering up to them from the lower right side. Length: 1″; width: 11/16″. *Courtesy of Yale University Art Gallery, Mabel Brady Garvan Collection.*

or pincushion hoops be 13 inches long, with hooks. Richardson sold chains for a variety of uses. In addition to scissor and watch chains, Richardson recorded making chains for teapots. In 1739 Lambert Emerson paid £0/1/6 "to fastening a Gold Chain to a tea pott & gold aded." Such chains were used to connect the lid of a china teapot to the top of the handle. Not only did William Fry get a chain and a strainer for his teapot in 1735 but he also got a chain for a milk pot, indicating that a covered milk pot was treated in the same manner.

Both men and women in the eighteenth century had watch chains and these Richardson made and imported, keeping a number of them on hand in his show case. In ordering watch chains from London, he specified that those intended for ladies be plain and neat, while those to be sold to gentlemen were to have two or three strands and could be snake chains. In order to get the kind of chain he desired, Richardson occasionally mentioned impressing the pattern of a chain he liked into some sealing wax at the bottom of his letter.

Earrings were occasionally bought by fashionable ladies, although probably Joseph Richardson was not frequently called upon to supply such ornaments to his predominantly Quaker clientele. Nevertheless, he recorded the making of a few "Gold bobs" and even kept a pair on display in his glass case. The majority of his earrings, however, were made for the Indian trade and were designed to appeal to the American natives.

Another small item which Richardson ordered from London and also made in his own shop was the stock in trade of all American goldsmiths—buttons. Richardson sold buttons for coats or jackets, for sleeves, and for breeches. Some were hollow, others were solid; some were silver, others were gold. They were described on various occasions as "large," "flat," "round," "eight-square," and "bezeled." Those which Joseph imported most frequently from London were set with stones or crystal. On one occasion he ordered "Square table Cut crystol Buttons with cyphers;" on another occasion, three white and three brown crystal buttons to be "strong set." The settings were ordered in both gold and silver, and the sizes varied from "small for children" to "the common size." Whether the buttons were imported from London or made in his own shop, their cost varied considerably, and the price of fashioning was high in proportion to the amount of metal involved.[67] When two buttons were joined together by a simple link to form cuff links, the cost more than doubled. The pair of linked buttons attributed to him through family history *(Fig. 120)* are very simply made and probably typical of those he kept in his showcase.[68]

Richardson apparently ordered neither cuff links or studs from England, probably because they were so small and so easy to make. He noted that he had only one pair of gold studs and one pair of crystal studs in his showcase at different times, because most were ordered to suit personal tastes. The cost of studs varied widely, depending on the design; small silver studs cost approximately 1 shilling each, while gold studs cost about 7 shillings each, regardless of the amount of metal involved.

In 1747–48 James Lord ordered a pair of gold studs which were large enough to be engraved with the initials "B:B," and in the same year Thomas Nixon bought a pair of "flat" studs. Occasionally the studs, like buttons, were set with crystals or stones, as were those made by David Harper for his master in 1747. Joseph Richardson's references to these tiny pieces of jewelry assume particular importance because none have yet been identified as the work of an American goldsmith.

Even smaller than studs were stay hooks, which were purchased almost exclusively by women. Although most stay hooks were made of a baser metal such as steel, two dozen hooks of silver or gold were purchased by Richardson's fashionable customers in the 1730's and 1740's. The price of hooks was high, considering their size, ranging from 9 pence for a silver hook to £0/19/6 for a gold one. Apparently all those Richardson sold were made in his own shop, but because they were so small, they were not stamped with his mark. One small silver hook is included among the Richardson family effects at Winterthur.

Of all small pieces of jewelry made by the eighteenth-century goldsmith, the buckle enjoyed the greatest vogue; consequently, many examples survive today. By 1650, the buckle was so important an article of fashion that the *London Gazette* commented: "Certain foolish young men have begun to fasten their shoes and knee bands with buckles instead of ribbons . . .which surely every man will own were more decent than these new-fangled, unseemly clasps or buckles."[69]

By Joseph Richardson's day, buckles had come into such demand that some goldsmiths specialized in their production. Joseph sold buckles for a variety of uses. The most popular were the buckles used for sleeves, shoes, and stockings, as well as the knee and arm. Occasionally he sold buckles for waistbands, garters, or girdles. The cost of buckles varied greatly, reflecting both the cost of the metal and the complexity of design. Richardson described those he sold in the 1730's and 1740's as "wrought," "cross bar[r]ed," and "threaded."[70]

Many of these, particularly stock buckles, were made of gold. One gold buckle made by Joseph Richardson *(Fig. 129)* is the plain type of buckle used on shoes; it has rounded corners and a cusped cross bar, and is probably simi-

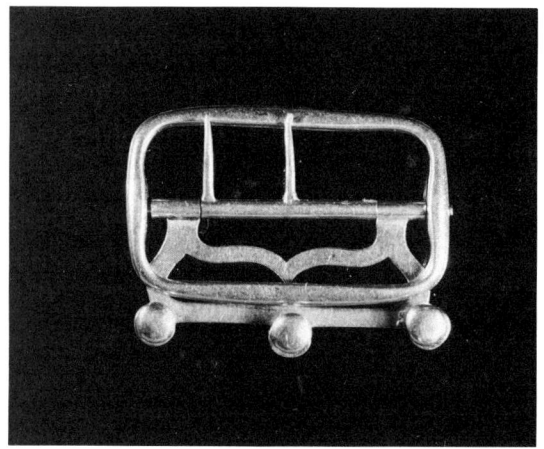 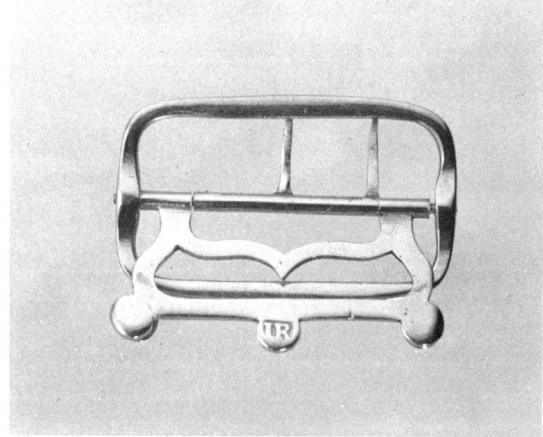

Fig. 129: Gold buckle, IR in rectangle, *c.* 1750. Length: 1 15/16"; width: 11/16". *Courtesy of Yale University Art Gallery, Mabel Brady Garvan Collection.*

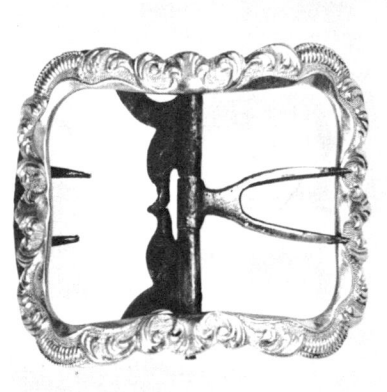 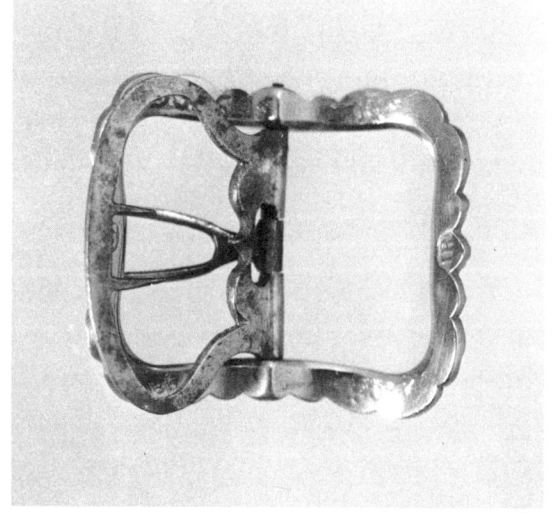

Fig. 130: Gold buckle, IR in rectangle, *c.* 1765. Length: 1 3/4". *Courtesy of Yale University Art Gallery; gift of Walter M. Jeffords.*

lar to the pair of gold shoe buckles for which he had charged Isaac Norris £1/10/0 in 1739. Another *(Fig. 130)* is the much more elaborate stock buckle, whose curvilinear borders decorated with scrolls and leafage reflect all the flamboyance of the rococo influence.

Both types of buckles were imported by Richardson from London, as well as made in his shop. In one order to How & Masterman, Joseph sent patterns of the buckles he desired, although usually he contented himself with merely describing them as "pierced" or "carved," "square" or "rounded," "plain" or "solid." Once he ordered knee buckles to match shoe buckles. The weight of buckles varied from ten to fifteen pennyweight per pair without chapes and tongues to three ounces with silver chapes and tongues.[71]

Buckles were frequently in need of repair, and Joseph Richardson spent a lot of time at this task. In fact, repair work constituted a most important aspect of the goldsmith's business. An inspection of Richardson's accounts indicates that he probably spent half of his working time on repairs, and they therefore represent a considerable proportion of his income. The records also provide evidence of the appearance and characteristics of other forms which Richardson is not known to have made but which he repaired such as fruit plates and chafing dishes.[72]

In all the work of eighteenth-century goldsmiths in general and of Joseph Richardson in particular, the variety was great, and the demand for novelty and fashion seemingly endless. The goldsmith was required by his patrons to keep abreast of the latest fashions, so that his wares necessarily reflect the changes in social customs and artistic taste. Whether imported or made in his own shop, the goods which Richardson sold reveal both his business acumen and his competence as a craftsman.

PART THREE
I·NR

. . . the Shop which my Sons Joseph and Nathaniel now Occupy . . . I will and direct them to have the Use of as heretofore, and . . . I give unto my said two Sons my Show Glass working Tools and Utensils of Trade equally to be divided between them . . .
      Will of Joseph Richardson, 1784

CHAPTER 6

Joseph Richardson, Jr. (1752-1831), and Nathaniel Richardson, (1754-1827): Their Lives

IN 1777, when Joseph Richardson reached the age of retirement, his two sons had completed a long term of apprenticeship with him and were ready to take over the responsibilities of his craft. Thus, Joseph, Jr., now 25, and his 23 year-old brother, Nathaniel, inherited the family business which had been established by their grandfather 75 years earlier and which was now the oldest goldsmith's shop in continuous operation in Philadelphia.

It was a difficult time for the young men to be starting in business. Although Philadelphia was one of the largest cities next to London in the English-speaking world and had a very large group of prosperous citizens who could well afford to patronize the Richardson brothers, the Revolutionary War was under way. Independence had been declared the year before, and in the year that Joseph and Nathaniel began their partnership, British troops under the command of General Howe occupied the city of Philadelphia after bloody victories in the Brandywine area.

Although they were Quakers, Joseph and Nathaniel Richardson are listed in the second battalion of the Philadelphia County militia.[1] Evidently, they were able to pursue their business quietly during this period of turmoil, offending neither the British nor the patriots. Immediately after the British occupied Philadelphia, however, the brothers attempted to renew the trade with England in which their father had engaged. They did so with trepidation, realizing that there was "some doubt wether goods will be permited to be brought hither," and they prudently decided not to send any money in advance.² Their fears were well founded—the goods were not permitted to pass—and they gave up the idea of English trade for the duration of the war.

At this time the brothers were living in the rooms their father provided for them over the goldsmith's shop. Nathaniel Richardson remained a bachelor and made his home with his brother, except for a brief period after Joseph married. Joseph's wedding took place at the Friends' meeting house in Burlington, New Jersey, in 1780, when he was 28. His bride was Ruth Hoskins, the daughter of Joseph Hoskins, whose family had lived originally in Chester, Pennsylvania.³ At the end of 1781, a daughter, Mary, was born. It is not known where the young couple lived before 1788 when they moved into Joseph's parents' house on Front Street.

Immediately after the articles of peace with Great Britain were accepted in 1783, Joseph and Nathaniel wrote to the firm of John Masterman in London, requesting that their order of 1777 be filled and rejoicing "that the communication between us is again open & peace likely to be restored . . . and hope that happy intercourse which has formerly proved so beneficial to both Countrys may still be Cherished."

The goods they had ordered finally arrived at the end of November 1783, but the brothers found that "the high price at which Silver is charged to what it bears in this Country is so great an addition to the price of large articles that it will hardly do to import them." As a result, they confined their next order to small items and asked Masterman to put them in touch with someone who could supply them with orders for scales. Like their father before them, the Richardsons did a lively business in scales and weights, and during the next five years they ordered scores of them from the firm of Sommers & Son.⁴

In the fall of 1784, just as their business was beginning to succeed, their father died, and in 1787, their mother died. According to the terms of the will of Joseph, Sr., the house on Front Street was to pass to Joseph, Jr., and Nathaniel—"As Tenants in Common in Fee"—after their mother's death.⁵ Joseph, Jr., made a note at this time that he had "Removed into Front Street the 23rd of 1st mo. 1788 and began House Keeping next day."⁶ By this time his family had grown considerably. His first son, born just a few months after the death of Joseph, Sr., was named for his grandfather. A second son, John, was born in 1786, but died the same year; a second daughter, Sarah, was born in 1787. After Joseph and his wife moved into the house on Front Street, a third daughter, Elizabeth, was born, followed by another John in 1790, Hannah in 1791, and Nathaniel in 1793.

In addition to the house and shop, Joseph and Nathaniel, as well as their sisters, inherited from their father several lots on Fourth Street, cash, and some of the family silver.[7] All details of settling the estates of both parents were attended to by Joseph and Nathaniel, who kept a receipt book of these matters.[8]

To increase their income, Joseph and Nathaniel invested in shipments of goods to the West Indies, sending grain to the islands in return for sugar, cotton, wool, hides, and money.[9] Rum was sometimes sent from the West Indies, but the Quaker brothers went to great pains to explain to those with whom they dealt that it was "an article we are determined to have nothing to do with." Their agents in the West Indies were Benjamin Gaskin and Maurice Lisle.[10]

Joseph, Jr., and Nathaniel also augmented their business by renewing their orders for English silver and occasionally importing clocks and coral beads as well. Although they were very careful in describing the items they wanted, there were some difficulties in the fulfillment of their requests. These difficulties, together with the import duty, caused the brothers to curtail their foreign orders.[11]

They did, however, commission some work from other goldsmiths in Philadelphia in the 1780's. William Parham, John David, Abraham Carlisle, and Christian Wiltberger all acknowledged receipt of payments from the Richardson brothers.[12] They also made payments to James Trenchard, a well-known Philadelphia engraver who was born in New Jersey but came to Philadelphia where he learned engraving from James Smither. It is possible that Trenchard engraved some of the silver made by the Richardson brothers.[13] Joseph and Nathaniel were also involved with the settlement of goldsmith Philip Syng's estate in 1789. On behalf of Syng's administratrix, the brothers sold a quantity of old silver and turned over the proceeds, £117/2/8, to Philip S. Bunting on July 16, 1789.

Before the next year was over, changes had taken place in the lives of the brothers which altered their partnership. In 1790, Nathaniel decided to give up the goldsmith's craft and become an ironmonger. Together with Isaac Paxton, he established a hardware business. He also worked in wood and often made boxes, workstands, and other presents for his relatives.

His nephew, Nathaniel Richardson, one of the eight children born to

Joseph and Ruth Richardson, eventually became the family genealogist and, in addition to charting a family tree, in 1860 he recorded his memories of various members of the family. Of his uncle, he recalled:

> ... for about the last twenty-five years of his life [he] was retired from business, though having numerous properties to look after and tenants to attend to, his time was moderately occupied.... Naturally of a retiring disposition, which was no doubt increased by a defect of hearing, he went but little into company. He took, however, much interest in the public improvements of the day, and though cautious of his investments often aided them with his money.
>
> Having through life maintained a character of spotless integrity, of meekness and benevolence, he died suddenly of apoplexy ... at the home of his brother Joseph.[14]

When the brothers' partnership was terminated, it was necessary to make a complete inventory of the goods in the shop to determine their value and make an equitable property division. The inventory taken on May 31, 1790, lists the silver objects on hand, as well as the plated wares, and other items which the brothers had made or sold. Some of the items on the list, such as marrow spoons and toast racks, are mentioned nowhere else in the brothers' records. The listing of plated wares is particularly useful because it indicates the currently popular forms, such as candlesticks and egg cups, *(Appendix E)*.

After his brother's departure from the firm, Joseph carried on until about 1801. He again began to place orders with foreign firms. Explaining that the firm of Joseph and Nathaniel Richardson was "being by mutual consent disolved,"[15] he requested Sommers & Son in London to send him boxes of scales and weights. His correspondence with this firm continued for several years, finally terminating in 1796.[16]

Evidently Sommers & Son had heard of the ravages caused in Philadelphia by the outbreak of yellow fever in 1793; Joseph thanked them for the concern they had expressed and, in his letter dated May 9, 1794, mentioned the death of his eldest son, Joseph, who was nine years old.[17] In 1797, another epidemic of fever broke out, and on August 21, Joseph made a note in his account book: "NB The Yellow Fever spreading amongst the Inhabitants of this City I removed with my family to Burlington & my Business was suspended until I returned on the 25th of the 10th mo. 1797."[18]

Joseph may have chosen Burlington because it was his wife's birthplace. At any rate, he bought from Helen Cruon Bauduy of Wilmington, Delaware, a lot costing £825, which was "in Burlington Fronting on the River Delaware & Extending to Pearl Street." It was here in Burlington at Green Bank that he and his family spent the summer months from 1798 to 1805, when he moved from Front Street in Philadelphia and built a house between Ninth and Tenth Streets on Market.[19] His son, Nathaniel, was later to describe the house as being "then quite rural and sufficiently 'out of town' as to render it unnecessary to have any other retreat from the contagion of yellow fever." At this time Nathaniel described his father as a man of "under the medium size, light, active, of quick perception, and prompt decision."[20] *(Fig. 131)*. During the years after the dissolution of the partnership with his brother, Joseph Richardson built up a thriving business, ordering silver from England, acquiring apprentices to help in the shop, and renewing the shipment of provisions to Maurice Lisle in the West Indies until 1792.

Despite the increased pace of business activity, Joseph was able to take a trip to Boston in the summer of 1791. He traveled to New York on the stage with a friend, Jonathan Willis, and stopped in Newport, a city which, like Philadelphia had a Quaker background:

> many Spacious buildings chiefly of Wood [which] appears to have been once in a flourishing condition but now is evidently on the decline many of the buildings going to decay, the Inhabitants its supposed are not more than two thirds the number they were before the War ... appear to be very Civil well behaved People & their appearance so much similar to those of Philadelphia that they seemed quite familiar.[21]

After his return from Boston, where he had visited many Friends, Joseph decided to take as an apprentice in his shop William Needles, a relative who lived in Maryland. After much thought, in 1795, the goldsmith encouraged Needles to come to Philadelphia, but he was careful to make clear what would be expected of him:

> I shall expect thy steady attention to my Business in supplying my place in the Work Shop, by melting for the Hands weighing the Silver out & in and observing that the directions given respecting their work are complied with also to keep thyself employed in such branches of our business as thou art capable of and occasionally to attend the front Shop in case of my absence etc. and in short use thy best endeavours to promote my Interest as tho it were thy own. I think it right also to observe that in case any unforeseen occurrance, such as Sickness

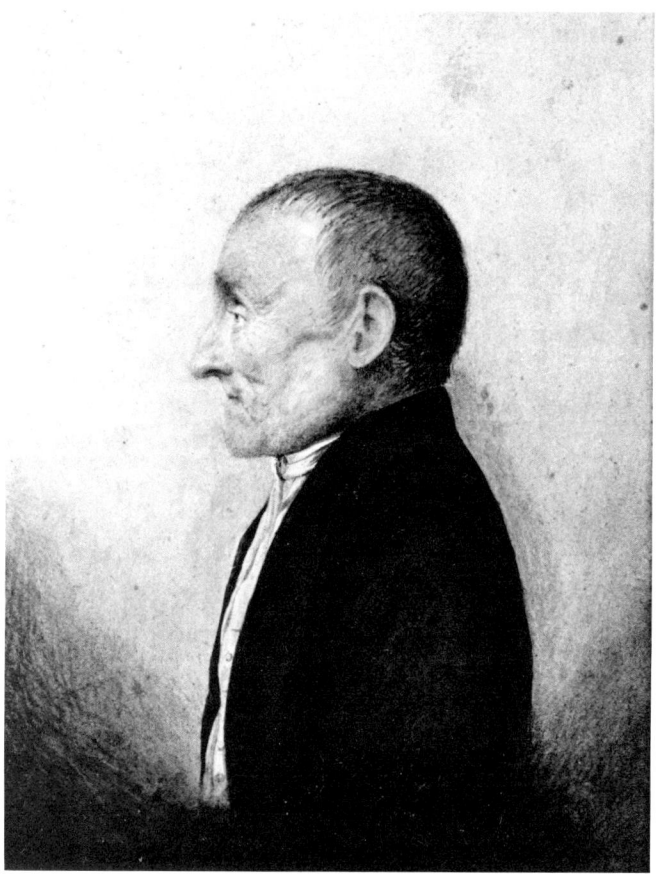

Fig. 131: Watercolor portrait of Joseph Richardson, Jr. *Courtesy of Mrs. Thomas J. Curtin.*

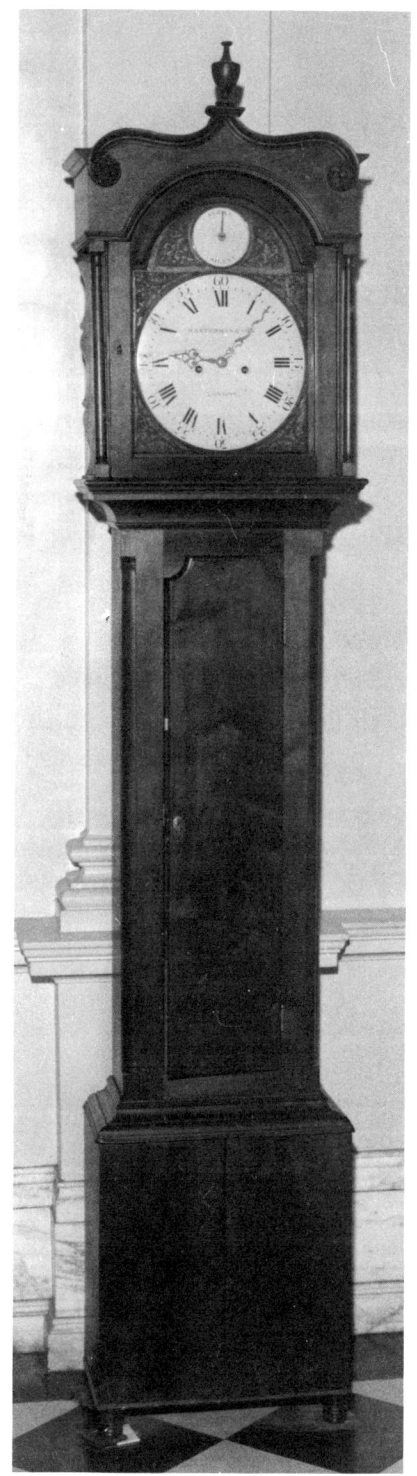

Fig. 131a: One of "2 good 8 day Clocks with plain inameled faces without Cases" ordered by Joseph and Nathaniel Richardson from Masterman and Son in 1783. Six months later they wrote to the London firm, "the Clocks dont quite answer our expectations owing to our not being more particular in describing them, they came very high being twice as much as we had any idea of." Owned by Nathaniel Richardson who gave it to his nephew Nathaniel. Height: 7′ 8″. *Courtesy of The Historical Society of Pennsylvania; Gift of Miss Frances Richardson.*

etc. should render thy absence unavoidable that a deduction should be made for such lost time, in proportion to the Salary.[22]

Joseph had made his offer to Needles in the fall in 1795, but by the end of the year he had become apprehensive over the young man's indecisiveness, and there is some doubt as to whether Needles actually came to Philadelphia.[23] Joseph did take as an apprentice Edward Randolph, Jr., who was bound to him in 1801. In 1809, when Randolph was 24 and had completed his term of service, he married Richardson's niece, Mary Taylor.[24] Nothing, however, is known of his work as a silversmith.

While Randolph was working in the shop, James Howell, a fully trained silversmith, was also "trading under the Firm of Richardson & Co."[25] Apparently Howell moved into the Richardson house at 50 South Front Street in 1805 when Joseph built his house on Market Street and remained there until the end of 1813. During this time Howell also borrowed money from Richardson in a joint bond in the amount of $2,097.61 with two other goldsmiths, Harvey Lewis and Joseph D. Smith. Howell's payments on the bond continued until 1814, and Richardson granted him other notes for $276 and $466.14. The first of these was paid off rather quickly, but the last one was finally terminated by Joseph in November 1814, when he "agreed to give him [Howell] a discharge in consideration of his misfortunes."[26]

Other Philadelphia goldsmiths with whom Joseph Richardson dealt during these years include Samuel Richards, who bought several tea sets from him in 1798 and 1799, and John Myers, who bought spoons with carved handles and engraved ciphers in 1800. Richardson also supplied weights and scales to the goldsmith and importer, Joseph Anthony, and once melted 1,000 ounces of gold dust for him.[27]

From about 1795 to 1802, Joseph employed James Smither, Jr. Perhaps Joseph needed someone to help with the engraving because he, like his father, made numerous pieces of silver for presentation to the Indians. Joseph had been commissioned by the Quaker Society, but Joseph, Jr. received his orders from the United States Government, which had undertaken this method of placating the Indians after the Revolutionary War. Joseph, Jr., made vast numbers of arm bands, wrist bands, gorgets, and other pieces of jewelry, many of which were decorated with the United States emblem (*Figs. 132, 133*). Because hundreds of eagles were engraved on these items, it is little wonder that Richardson was paying Smither between £25 and £50 every few months.[28]

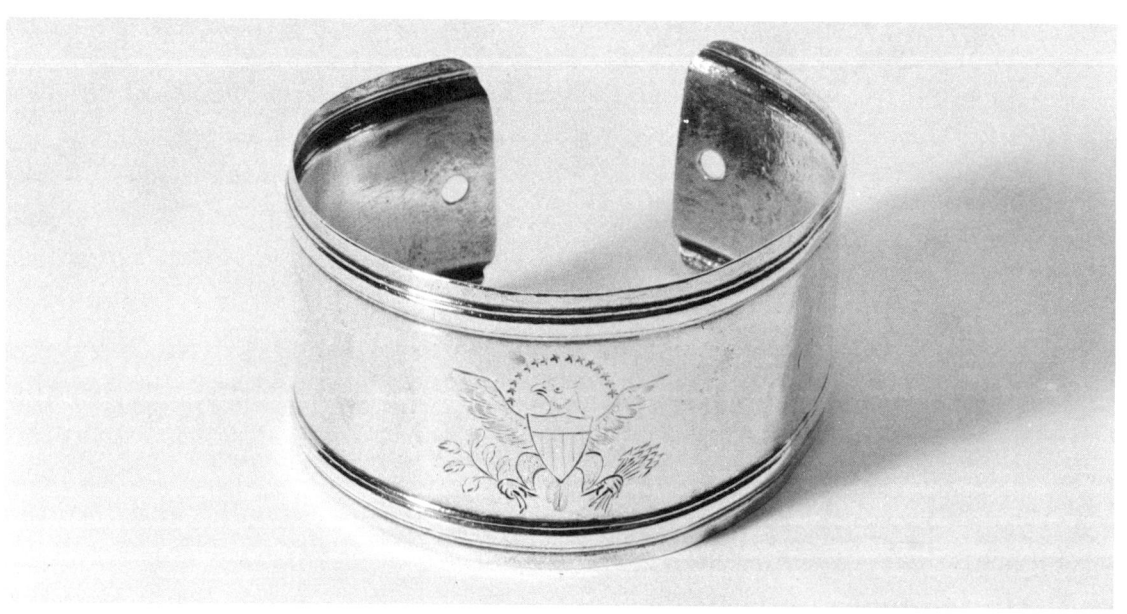

Fig. 132: Indian wristband, JR in rectangle, *c.* 1795. Width: 1 1/2". *Courtesy of The Henry Francis du Pont Winterthur Museum; photograph by Gilbert Ask.*

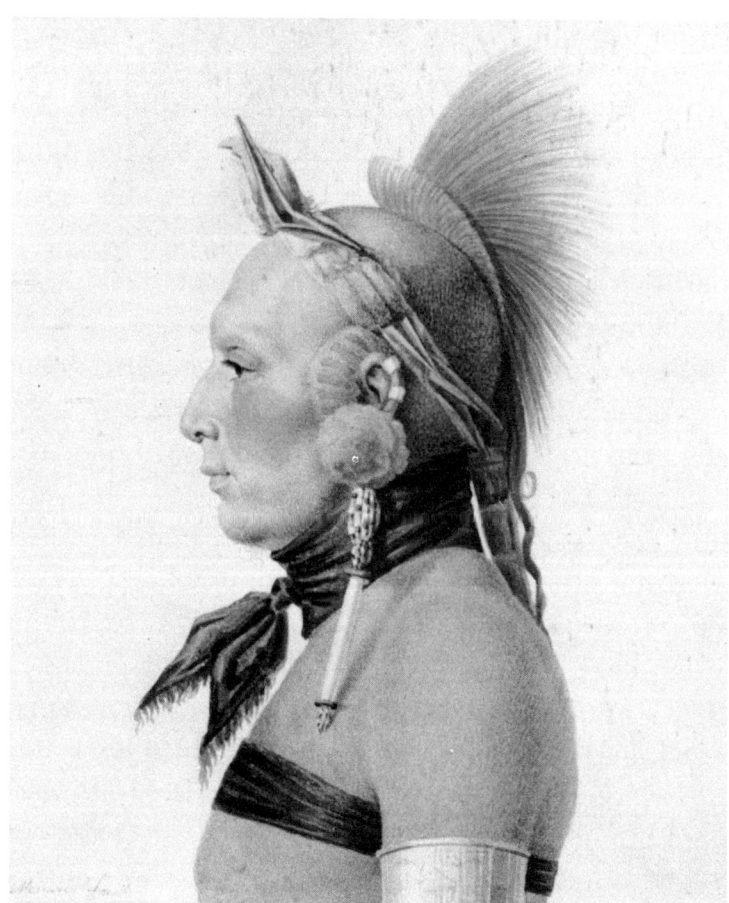

Fig. 133: Painting by Saint-Memin of an Osage warrior wearing a silver armband, *c.* 1800. *Courtesy of The Henry Francis du Pont Winterthur Museum; photograph by Gilbert Ask.*

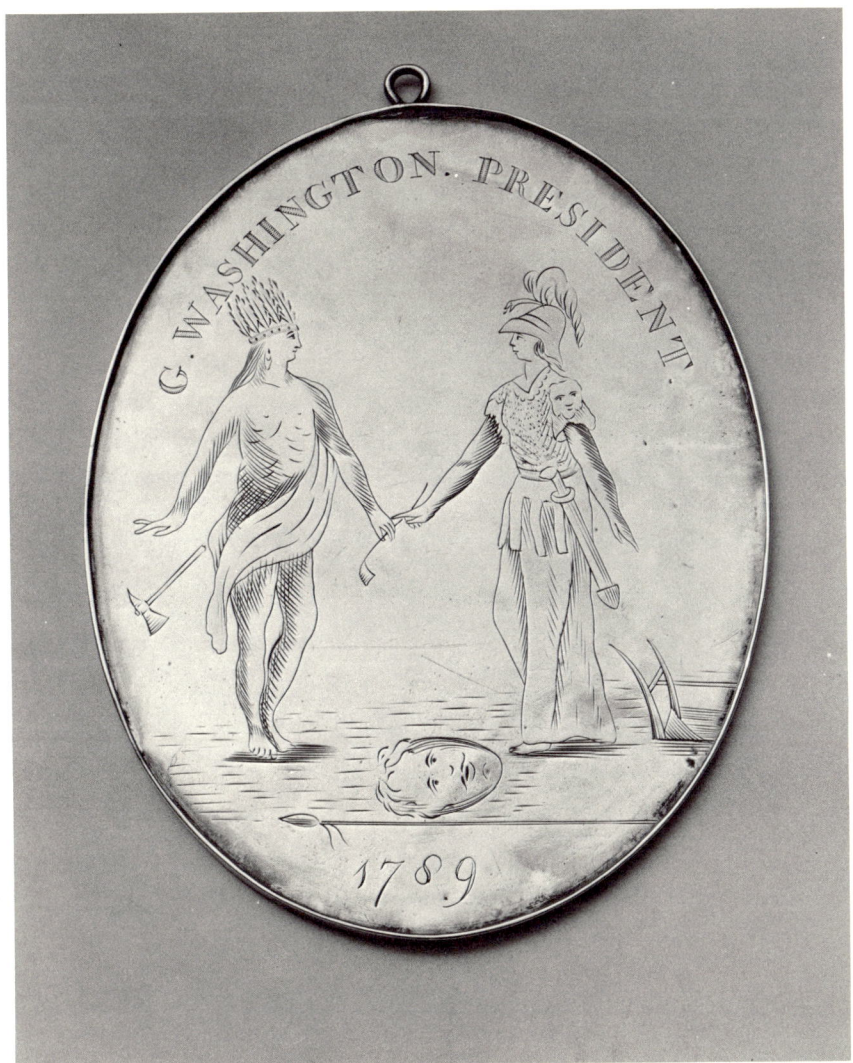

Fig. 134: Indian peace medal, attributed to Joseph Richardson, Jr., *c.* 1789. Length: 5 1/4"; width: 4 1/8". *Courtesy of The Henry Francis du Pont Winterthur Museum; photograph by Gilbert Ask.*

Some of the items were engraved with a portrait of the President or with other symbols of the new nation, and it was to the Southern Indians that the earliest of the presidential medals were presented when a special commission met with them in 1789. One such medal *(Fig. 134)*, similar to those made by Joseph Richardson, Jr., is engraved on one side with the United States seal and on the obverse with figures of Minerva, an Indian dropping a tomahawk, and another Indian holding a peace pipe. Some of these silver ornaments have been found during excavations of the Indians' burial mounds.[29]

George Washington, whose image was shown on some of these medals, was a personal patron of Joseph Richardson, Jr. The goldsmith made over $44 worth of silver as part of the furnishings of the official residence in Philadelphia, as well as a teapot and a slop bowl for Washington's own use, engraved with his family crest.[30] Because of Richardson's connection with the President, the description by the nineteenth-century historian John Watson of Washington's use of silver at the dinner table in Philadelphia is of interest:

> He had a silver pint cup or mug of beer placed by his plate, of which he drank; . . . There were placed upon his table, as ornaments, sundry allabaster mythological figures of about two feet high. The centre of the table contained five or six large silver or plated waiters. The table itself was of an oval shape; at the end were also some silver waiters of an oval form.[31]

So highly did Washington regard Joseph Richardson that in December 1795 he appointed the goldsmith second assayer of the United States Mint in Philadelphia, and from about 1801 Joseph devoted most of his time to this new job. He was to continue in this office for over 35 years, fulfilling his duties, according to an early historian of the United States Mint, "with credit & honor."[32]

Joseph Richardson prospered financially, too. His ledger shows receipt of payments of loans by various members of his family and others, as well as receipts of ground rents for various properties such as his house on German Street, his lots on Pine Street, Fourth Street, and Spruce Street, and from 1808–10, his house and garden in Burlington. From 1796 to 1831, Joseph also received dividends for stocks and shares in various companies. Local corporations included the Schuylkill Navigation Co., the Friends Central School Association, the City of Philadelphia, the Bank of Pennsylvania, the Bank of North America, and the Chesapeake & Delaware Canal Company. He also held some Louisiana stock for a few months at the end of 1816 and the beginning of 1817.

When he died in March 1831, at the age of 79, Joseph Richardson, Jr. bequeathed to his son John his scales and weights and his tools, as well as a small silver cup bearing the crest of George Washington.[33] John was appointed to fill his late father's office as assayer at the Mint, but "Finding the office not congenial with his tastes, and so subjecting him to undue responsibilities, he resigned in April, 1832, holding office only a little over a year."[34]

Joseph's brother, Nathaniel, had died in 1827, and so it was that the uninterrupted family of Richardson silversmiths came to an end after a century of distinguished craftsmanship and unquestioned integrity. The silversmith's art had changed greatly during these years, and its long tradition was disappearing with the advent of mass production and industrialization—a phenomenon which manifested itself even during the lifetime of Joseph, Jr., and Nathaniel. A study of their business and their silver will show the changes that were taking place in the craft, as well as the gradual development of the neoclassic influence which was to dominate the early years of the newly independent nation.

CHAPTER 7

Joseph Richardson, Jr., and Nathaniel Richardson: Their Silver

AFTER the Revolutionary War, American merchant ships were no longer dominated by the British, and goods began to arrive from France and from as far away as China. Greatly increased diversity of products on the market was only one result of this expanded trade. Goldsmiths, however, for the most part simply renewed their trade with England. The reasons for this were enumerated by Lord Sheffield in his 1784 report on the commerce of the country:

> These articles [jewelry, plate, etc.] will be imported [by the American states] from Great Britain. In France, they are either too costly, or too badly designed and finished, to suit the American taste; whilst the British manufacturers of those articles have so far succeeded, in uniting the solid and useful with the showy and elegant, as to have the preference, even in France.[1]

Postwar trade with Britain also brought to the American goldsmiths' shops large quantities of plated silver which, though it had been made since the 1740's in Sheffield, only now came into great demand.[2] Birmingham too, became an increasingly important source of silver for American shops.

At the same time there was a rising sentiment, evident even before the war, that Americans should develop their own industries and support their own craftsmen — that, in fact, it was their patriotic duty to do so. Consequently, artisans of all kinds found much more widespread demand for their products.

The number of goldsmiths working in Philadelphia multiplied rapidly, and shops which had only one or two apprentices were compelled to hire many more. This led quite logically to increased competition, and newspaper advertisements of the day were filled with notices of vast quantities of wares.

By 1788, when the citizens of Philadelphia staged the colorful and extravagant Grand Federal Procession to celebrate the adoption of the Federal Constitution, thirty-five masters, journeymen, and apprentice silversmiths marched, led by William Ball, the senior member of their group, and the standard-bearers, Joseph Gee and John Germon. The white silk banner they carried was decorated on one side with the silversmiths' arms and their motto, "Justitia virtutum regina," and on the other with a figure of the genius of America, holding in her hand a silver urn with the motto, "The purity, brightness, and solidity of this metal is emblematical of that liberty which we expect from the New Constitution."[3]

It is significant that the banner pictured an urn, for this form symbolized the neoclassical trend which had grown rapidly in popularity since Robert Adam introduced the urn and oval motifs into his architectural designs in England in the 1760's. The first documented example of this new style in American silver is a large presentation urn made in 1774 by Richard Humphreys of Philadelphia.[4] These neoclassical elements, emphasizing simplicity of form and preciseness of proportion, as they appeared in American silver included urn and oval shapes, squared handles and bases, French feet, pineapple and urn finials, pierced work, pearling or beading, and uniform and restrained engraving. The actual progress of these various elements in America has never been charted, but because Joseph and Nathaniel Richardson worked in partnership only during the crucial period of this change, from 1777 to 1790, their silver and their letters are an indication of the development of the new Federal style in American silver.

As early as 1770, their father ordered five cream urns (not pots, the old form) from London, so it is not surprising that his sons' first order should include a request for this form. The small cream urn, being relatively inexpensive, was one of the first forms to carry the new style to American tea tables; the only other objects ordered by the Richardsons at that time were small items like buckles, buttons, thimbles, and tea tongs.

Undoubtedly the Revolutionary War delayed the widespread acceptance of the new style, just as it delayed the delivery of the Richardsons' first order from London until 1783. By that time the brothers had added other forms to their request, including a coffeepot, a teapot, and a sugar dish. By the end of the year, they had added casters, sauceboats, cans, and salts.[5] Salts also reflected the new style, because they were to be pierced and provided with blue glass liners. The elder Richardson had ordered oval, pierced salts in 1769, and as early as 1763 he had ordered pierced, spring tea tongs. His sons requested pierced, bow-shaped tongs in 1777, and by 1784 they were asking for pierced edges on trays.

Along with pierced designs and the urn shape, the introduction of pearl work clearly marks the beginning of the new taste for classical ornamentation. The term "pearl work" refers to decoration resembling strings of uniform pearls around the edges of silver objects. These lines of contiguous, large, circular impressions were later called "beading," when they became refined and more delicate, but in all of the brothers' orders they were referred to as pearl work. Both the old double-bellied sugar dish and the new urn-shaped sugar dish that the Richardsons ordered in 1784 were ornamented with pearl work in an effort to satisfy both their conservative and progressive patrons. Similarly, they continued to order coffeepots in the older double-bellied style with cast spouts, while the teapots they requested were in the latest fashion.

Standard patterns to which silversmiths referred contributed to the spread of the neoclassical style. In 1784, the Richardsons ordered four polished cream pots "the size and shape of pattern No. 1 ornamented with pearl work, to weigh about 5 oz. 10 dwt. a piece." At the same time, they ordered four similar cream pots which were to be like "pattern No. 2," and were to weigh only four to five ounces each.[6] When these arrived five months later, Joseph and Nathaniel commented that they were better than any yet received. But they were less satisfied with the cream urns with square feet and pearl work that arrived the following year; the new urns had pearl work only around the top and base, and not between the foot and the body, as they had requested.

Of equal importance to neoclassical silver design was the ellipse, which appeared early in the shape of oval, pierced salt dishes. The Richardsons continued to order these, with blue glass liners, up to their last order of silver from the Masterman firm in June 1789. The oval, of course, is integral to the urn form of the cream pots they ordered, and teapots too had assumed this new shape.

These new English designs were quickly adopted by the American silver-

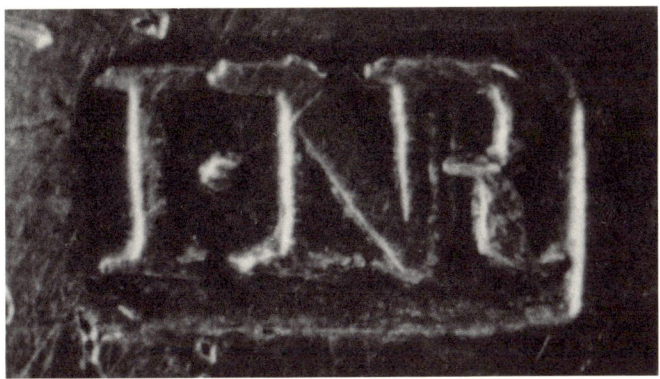

Fig. 135: Maker's mark: I·NR in rectangle. Appears on can *(Fig. 154)*. *Courtesy of Philadelphia Museum of Art.*

smiths. This is evident from the appearance of these elements in the silver bearing the Richardsons' I•NR mark *(Fig. 135)* which belongs to the period between 1777 and 1790. Some of their work can be dated even more specifically, either through engraved inscriptions or from family history. Thus their surviving silver shows the gradual influence of the new style, as the rococo double-scrolled lines, gadrooning, and shells gave way to subtly curved lines, oval and urn shapes, beading, pineapples, and a new symmetry.

An early cream pot *(Fig. 136)* illustrates the style change clearly. Superimposed on a basically rococo double-bellied form with a double-scrolled handle are two lines of large, chased, globular depressions around the lip and foot—an early and somewhat primitive example of pearl work. There are spaces between the pearls, and a certain amount of irregularity results from the fact that each pearl was chased into the silver separately with a circular dapping die. As this pearl work was refined on later pieces, the strings of pearls were made in thin strips of silver, which were then soldered onto the cream pot *(Fig. 137)*. This might more properly be called beading, for there is no space between the regularly placed beads. The cream pot became elongated and had a less pronounced lip and a more highly—and therefore, more attenuated—scrolled handle with a slight furl curving in from the upper section.

The transition was completed when Joseph and Nathaniel made an urn-shaped body for a later cream pot *(Fig. 138)*. In addition to beading at the top and base, it has an extra band of beading in the middle, where the body joins

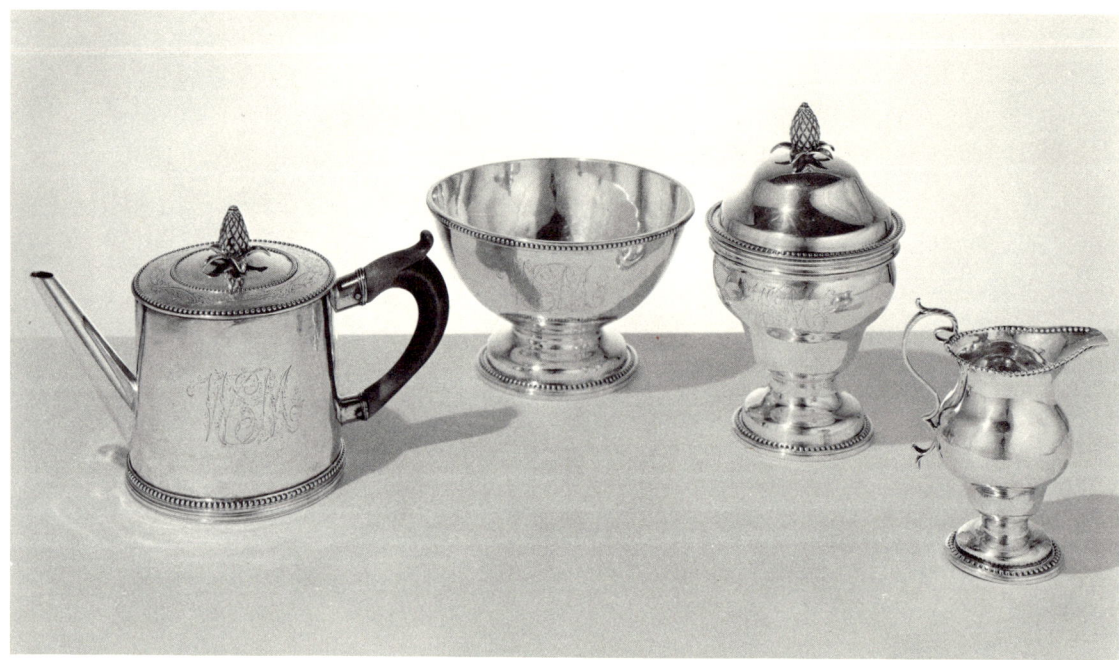

Fig. 136: Teaset, I·NR in rectangle, *c.* 1780. While the teaset in general is in the new classical style, the sugar bowl retains most of its rococo elements, conceding to the new style only in its pearl work and pineapple finial. Engraved on side with foliate initials *WSM*. Height of sugar bowl: 7". *Courtesy of Philadelphia Museum of Art.*

the base, and around the circumference of the ball feet. Another important change effected toward the end of their partnership was the transition from a circular, domed foot to a square base on four ball feet.

A similar transition can be seen in all the other major forms made by Joseph and Nathaniel. One of their earliest coffeepots certainly must have been the one *(Fig. 139)* which is strikingly similar to that made by their father at the end of his career *(see Fig. 37)*. In the 1780's, however, they were also making coffeepots in the double-bellied form *(Fig. 140)*, the only concession to the new style being the addition of a few lines of heavy and wide-spaced pearls and more attenuated and delicate engraving on the sides. Rococo elements—double-scrolled handles, cast spout ornament, bell finials, and shell drops—seemed to have persisted longer in coffeepots than in any other form. Even after pearl work turned to beading, a classical wreath and bowknot encircled the engraved initials, and a pineapple adorned the top, the coffeepot still retained its basic pre-Revolutionary shape *(Fig. 141)*.[7]

Teapots changed more quickly, as is indicated by the noticeable lack of double-bellied teapots made by Joseph and Nathaniel in this period. The teapot almost immediately assumed the new oval shape and straight spout *(Fig. 142)*. The earliest of these had interspaced pearl work but also featured the

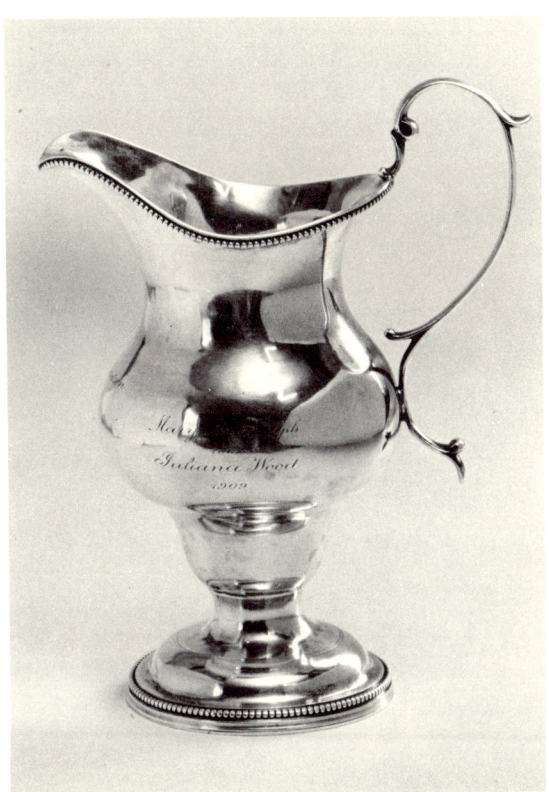 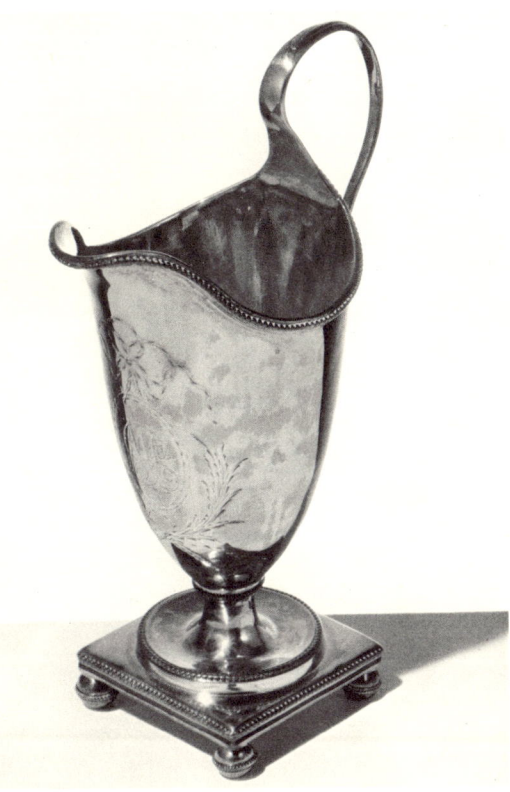

Fig. 137: Cream pot, I·NR in rectangle, *c.* 1780. Engraved in later script with names of subsequent owners but made by Joseph and Nathaniel Richardson for their mother Mary Richardson. Height: 5 15/16″. *Courtesy of Mr. and Mrs. Henry S. McNeil; photograph by Richard Merrill.*

Fig. 138: Cream pot, I·NR in rectangle four times on base, *c.* 1785–90. *Privately owned.*

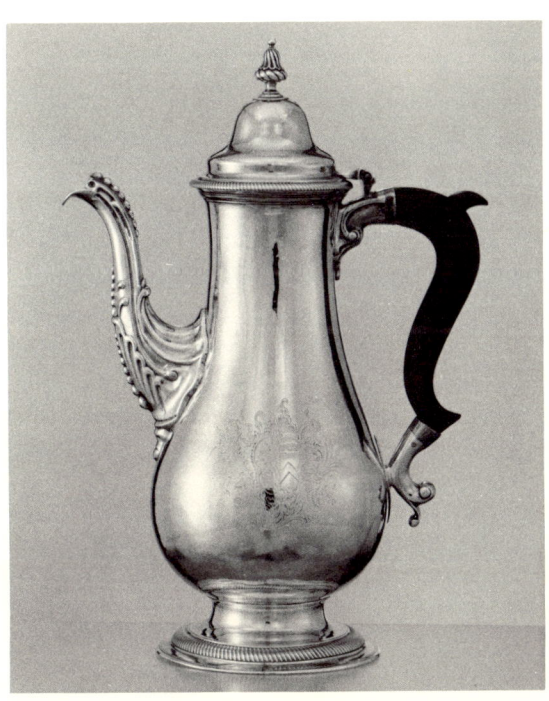 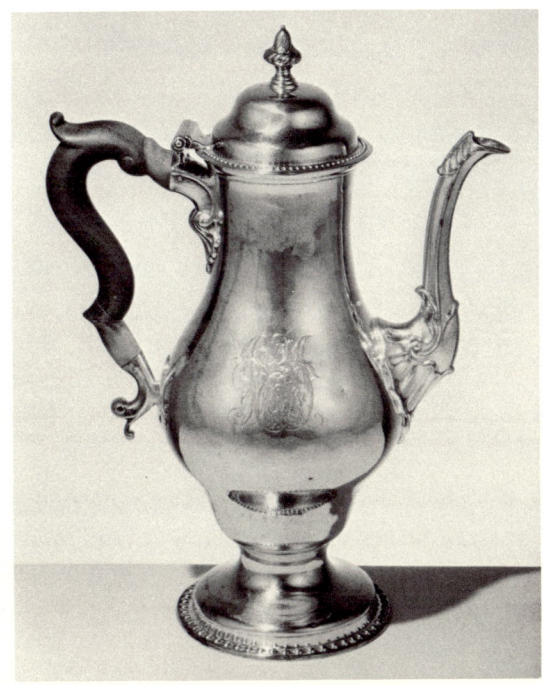

Fig. 139: Coffeepot, I·NR in rectangle, *c.* 1780. Unidentified impaled arms engraved on side. Note similarity of shape and decoration, especially finial, to coffeepot by Joseph Richardson, Sr. (Fig. 37). Height: 11 7/8″. *Courtesy of Yale University Art Gallery; Mabel Brady Garvan Collection.*

Fig. 140: Coffeepot, I·NR in rectangle twice on base, *c.* 1781. Engraved on side with initials of Jared and Elizabeth (Pettit) Ingersoll who were married in 1781. He was a signer of the Constitution. Height: 12 1/2″; weight: 37 oz. 18 dwt. *Courtesy of Mr. C. Jared Ingersoll.*

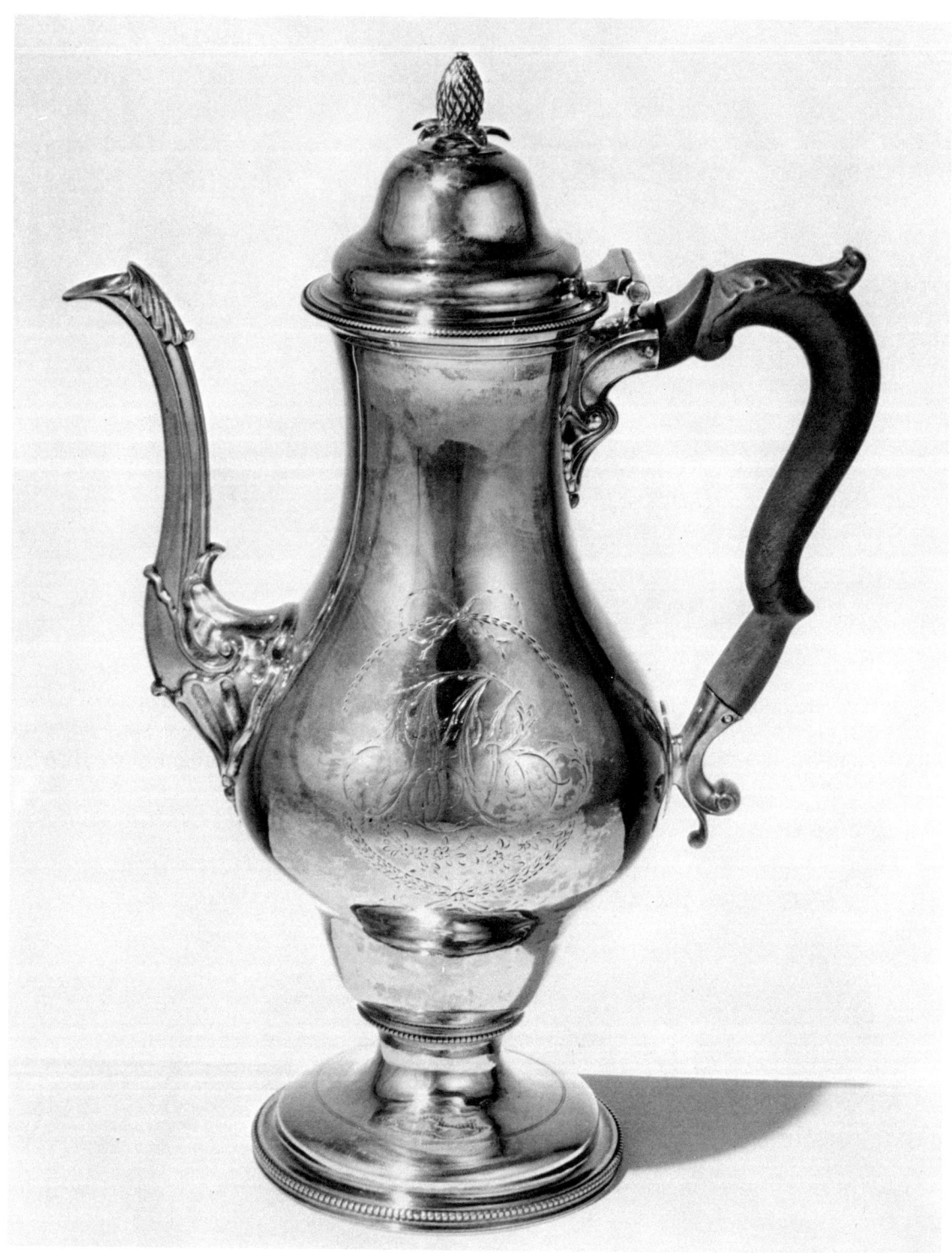

Fig. 141: Coffeepot, I·NR in rectangle twice on base, *c.* 1786. Engraved on side, in a typical classical design of delicate flowers and an ears-of-wheat wreath, with the initials of Margaret Rawle. Part of her wedding silver when she married Isaac Wharton in 1786. Height: 13 1/4"; weight: 38 oz. 13 dwt. *Courtesy of Mr. Wharton Sinkler.*

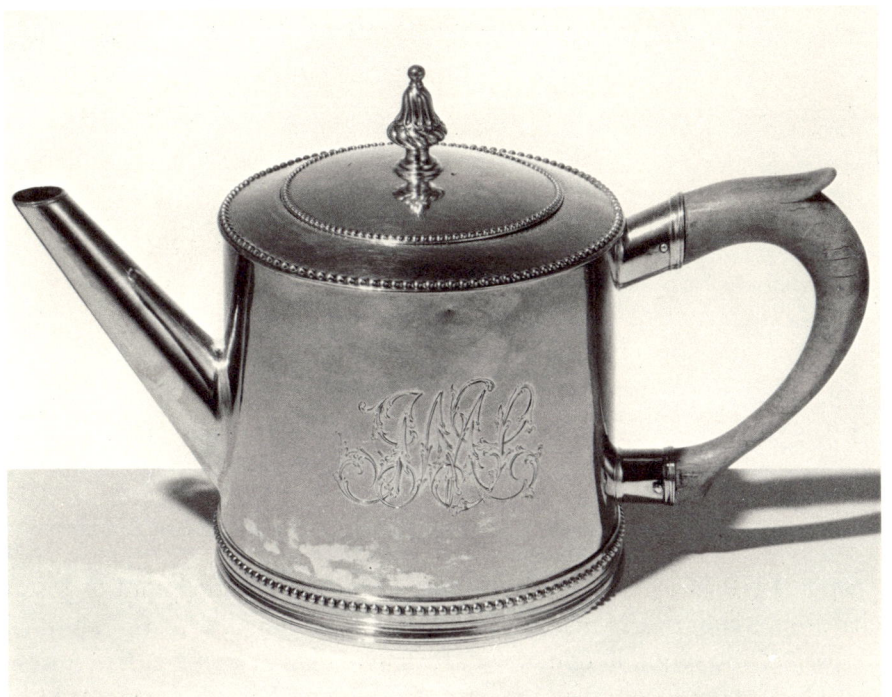

Fig. 142: Teapot, I·NR in rectangle twice on base, *c.* 1785. Engraved on side with initials IMS. Height: 5 3/4". *Privately owned.*

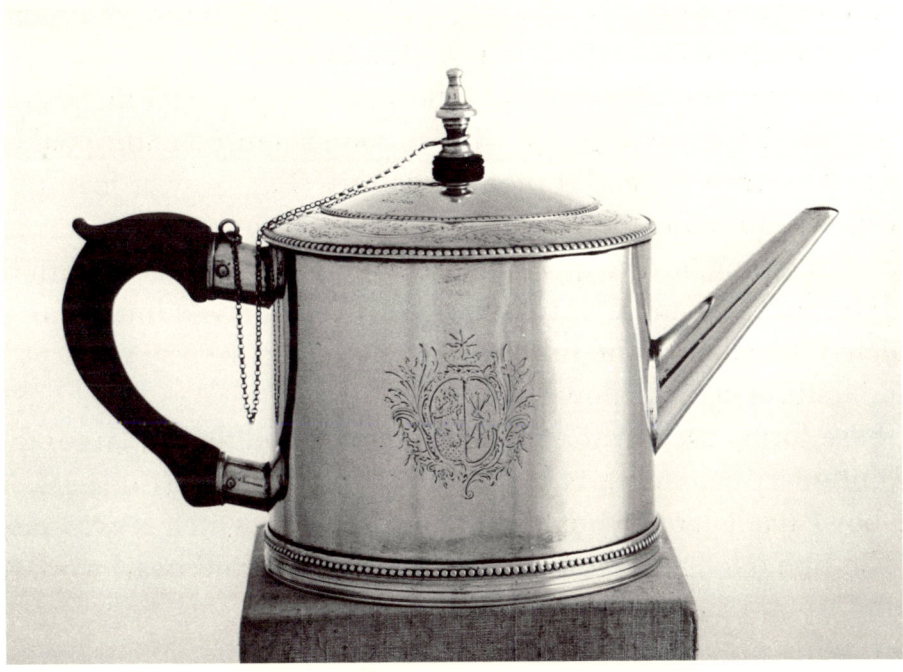

Fig. 143: Teapot, I·NR in rectangle, twice on base, *c.* 1785. Engraved with arms of Powel impaling Willing. Owned by Mayor Samuel and Elizabeth (Willing) Powel. Height: 6 5/8". *Courtesy of Yale University Art Gallery; Mabel Brady Garvan Collection.*

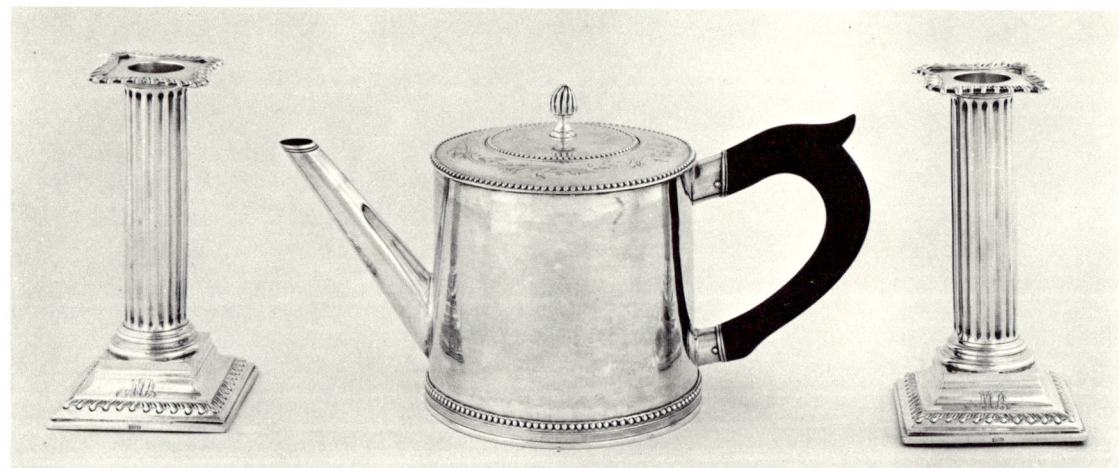

Fig. 144: Teapot, I·NR in rectangle, *c.* 1785–90. Candlesticks attributed to Joseph and Nathaniel Richardson, although the mark differs from the rectangular mark identified as theirs. Engraved on base *MB* in script; height: 5 1/2". Height of teapot: 5 1/8". Gift to Boston Museum in memory of Dr. George Clymer by his wife. Dr. Clymer bore the name of his ancestor, a Philadelphia signer of the Declaration of Independence, who was the son of Frank Richardson's sister-in-law. *Courtesy of Museum of Fine Arts, Boston.*

earlier type of either bell-shaped or flame finials. By 1790, the pearl work on teapots had become more like beading *(Fig. 143)*, the engraved ornament was elongated, and a pineapple finial was added to the top.

Used with the new classic teapot, however, were sugar dishes in the old double-bellied shape *(see Fig. 136)*. These soon acquired additional bands of more refined pearl work and a pierced gallery *(Fig. 145)*, a feature popular only in Philadelphia-inspired American silver. From this, it was a simple transition to the long, urn-shaped sugar bowl on a square base, with beading, galleried rim, and pineapple finial *(Fig. 146)*. The engraved initials on the side also reflected the change: the fuller rococo ciphers gave way to wispy, slanted letters and trails of delicate flowers.

All these forms used in the serving of coffee and tea are larger than their pre-Revolutionary counterparts, particularly the slop bowl *(Fig. 147)*. Not only was the bowl itself larger, but the domed foot on which it was raised was higher. The lip no longer flared so widely at the top, and pearl work replaced gadrooning around the edges *(Fig. 136)*.

During this period, too, the once-rare tea caddy became more common. An exceptionally beautiful example *(Fig. 148)* made by Joseph and Nathaniel has a graceful serpentine shape typical of furniture design of the same period, but in every detail of its delightful decoration it is classical. The pearl work that accentuates its outline is repeated in the engraving of the lid, and the

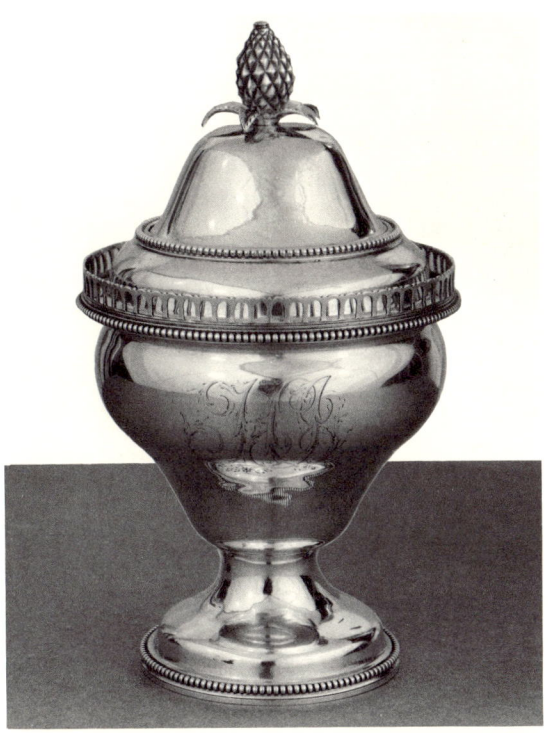
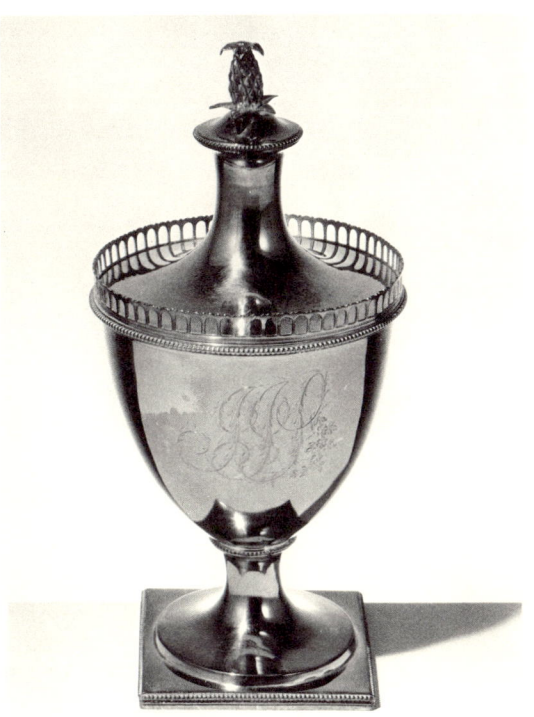

Fig. 145: Sugar bowl, I·NR in rectangle twice on base, *c.* 1785. Engraved on side with foliate HI. Height: 7 3/4"; weight: 11 oz. 9 dwt. *Courtesy of Philadelphia Museum of Art.*

Fig. 146: Sugar bowl, I·NR in rectangle twice on base, *c.* 1785–90. Engraved on side with foliate script IIS. Height: 9". *Privately owned.*

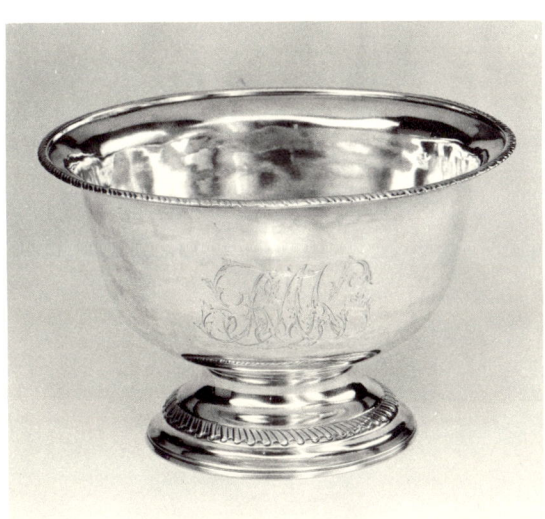
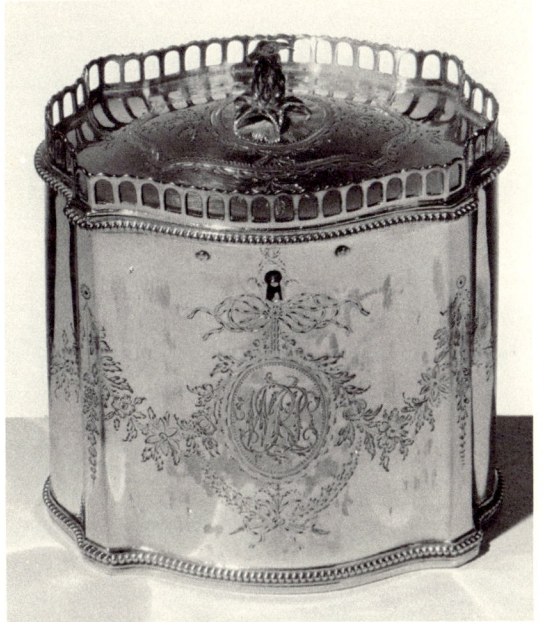

Fig. 147: Slop bowl, I·NR in rectangle twice on base. Engraved in script on side IHW. Diameter: 6 1/2"; weight: 11 oz. *Courtesy of Mr. Philip H. Hammerslough.*

Fig. 148: Tea caddy, I·NR in rectangle twice on base. *c.* 1785–90 Serpentine chest shape, enhanced by engraving on top and sides, with script initials WRL in medallion under lock. A gallery rim and pineapple finial with leafage at both top and bottom add to the full neo-classical effect. Height: 4 13/16". *Courtesy of Mrs. N. Victor Dial.*

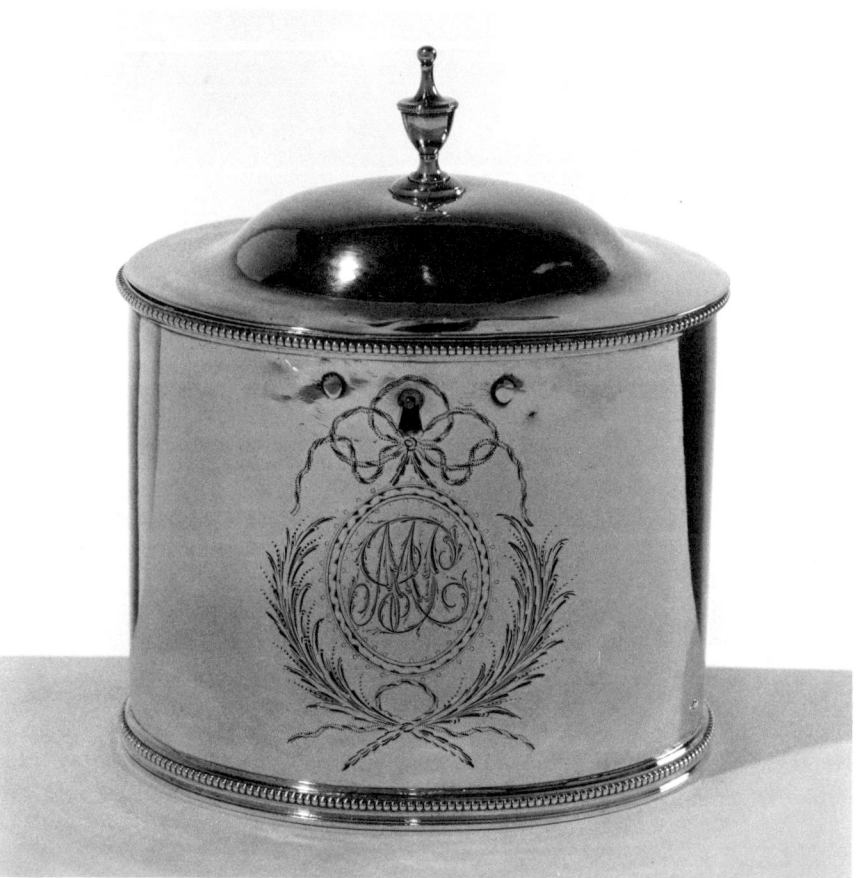

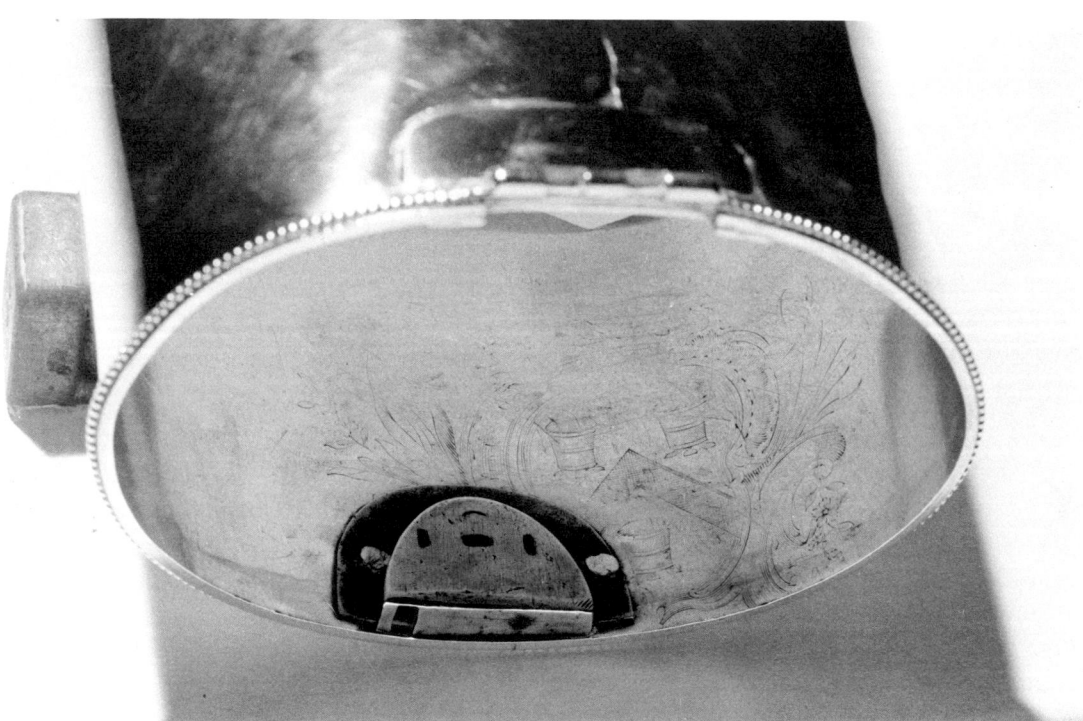

Fig. 149: Tea caddy, I·NR in rectangle twice on base, *c.* 1785–90. Engraved on front under lock, *MP* in medallion, probably for James and Phoebe (Lewis) Morton Pemberton who were married in 1775. Inside reveals remnants of Pemberton arms in rococo cartouche suggesting the caddy was made from an old piece of silver. Height: 5 3/4". *Courtesy of Philadelphia Museum of Art.*

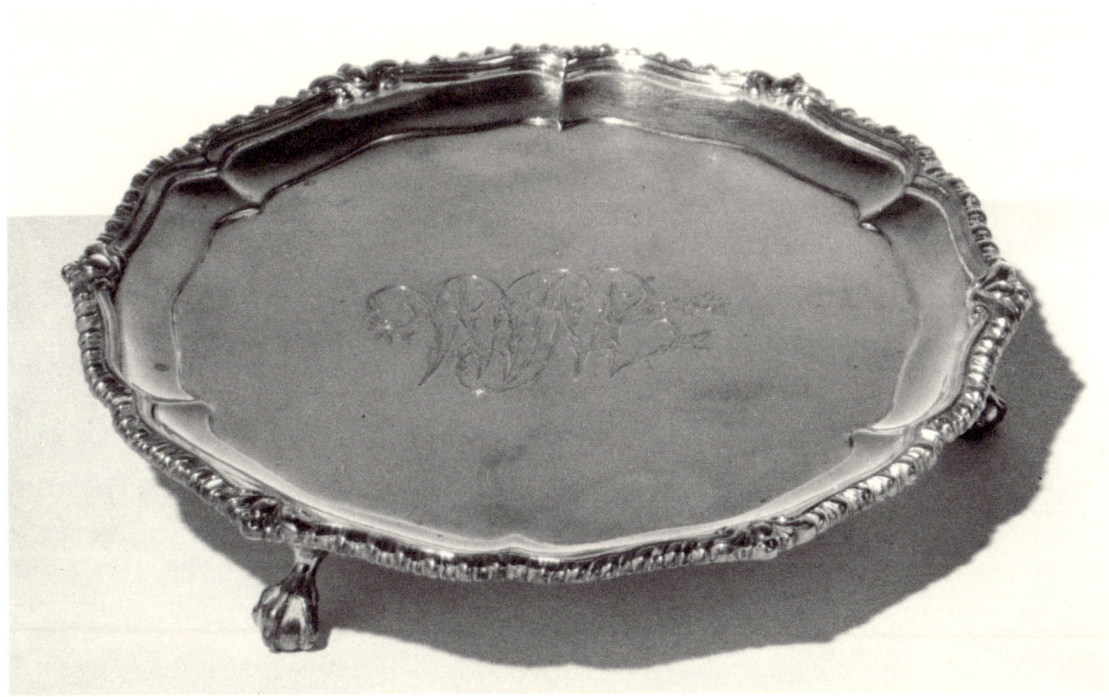

Fig. 150: Tray, I·NR in rectangle twice on base, *c.* 1780. Engraved on top in foliated script WAM. Basically rococo in its design with gadrooned and cusped rim and claw and ball feet. *Privately owned.*

motifs engraved on the side are a veritable encyclopedia of the newly devised modes of ornamentation.

By the end of the Richardsons' partnership, the tea caddy had become totally elliptical. The example shown in *Figure 149* is decorated with beading, and its engraving is restrained in a stylized classical enclosure. It also shows the rare use of an urn finial by the brothers. In general, the urn finial was not commonly used until the last decade of the eighteenth century, and it was the culminating feature of the Federal style.

The post-Revolutionary period also saw an increase in the number and size of trays. Trays now had beaded edges around a pierced border and pierced French feet *(Fig. 151)*, instead of the gadrooned edges made by the elder Richardson as well as by his sons *(Fig. 150)*. The brothers ordered trays in the new style from England as early as 1784, when they specified "pollished Waiters seven Inches in Diameter with pierced borders not over heavy."

Pierced and beaded designs also replaced gadrooning in the salt dishes made during the Richardsons' partnership. The earlier gadrooned version

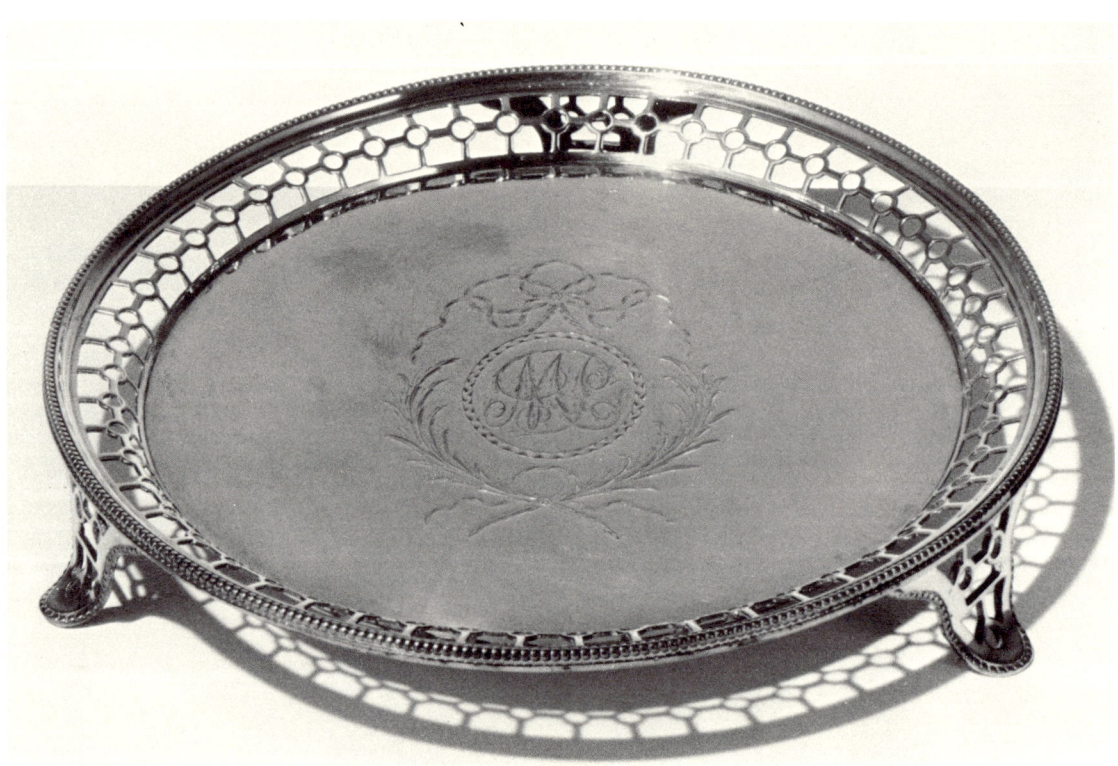

Fig. 151: Tray, I·NR in rectangle thrice on base, *c.* 1785–90. Engraved in medallion on top *MP* for Mary Pemberton. A mate to this tray is also privately owned. *Privately owned.*

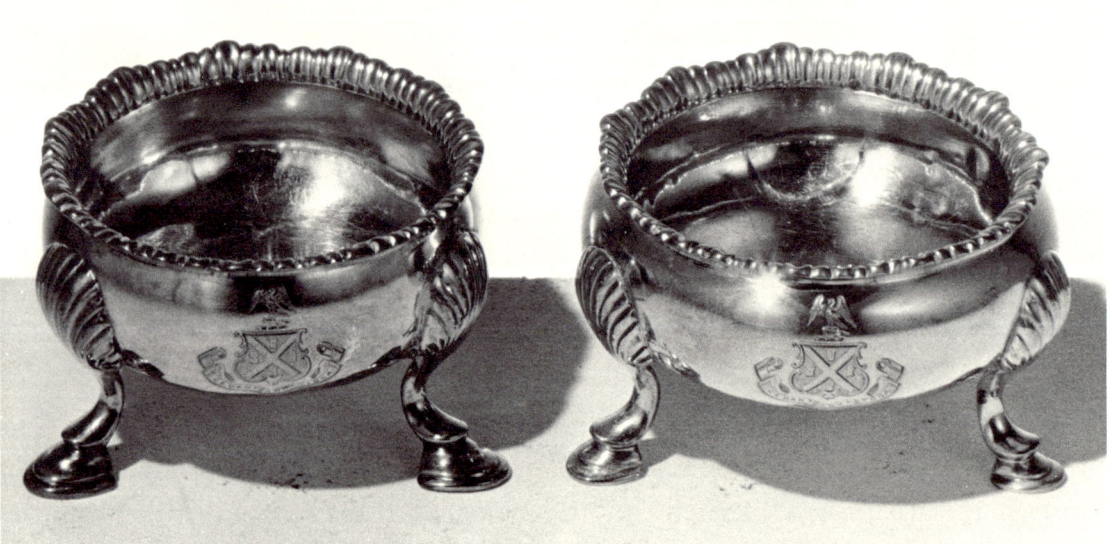

Fig. 152: Pair of salts, I·NR in rectangle twice on base of each, *c.* 1780. Owned by George Read of Delaware, signer of the Declaration of Independence. *Courtesy of Mrs. S. Hallock du Pont.*

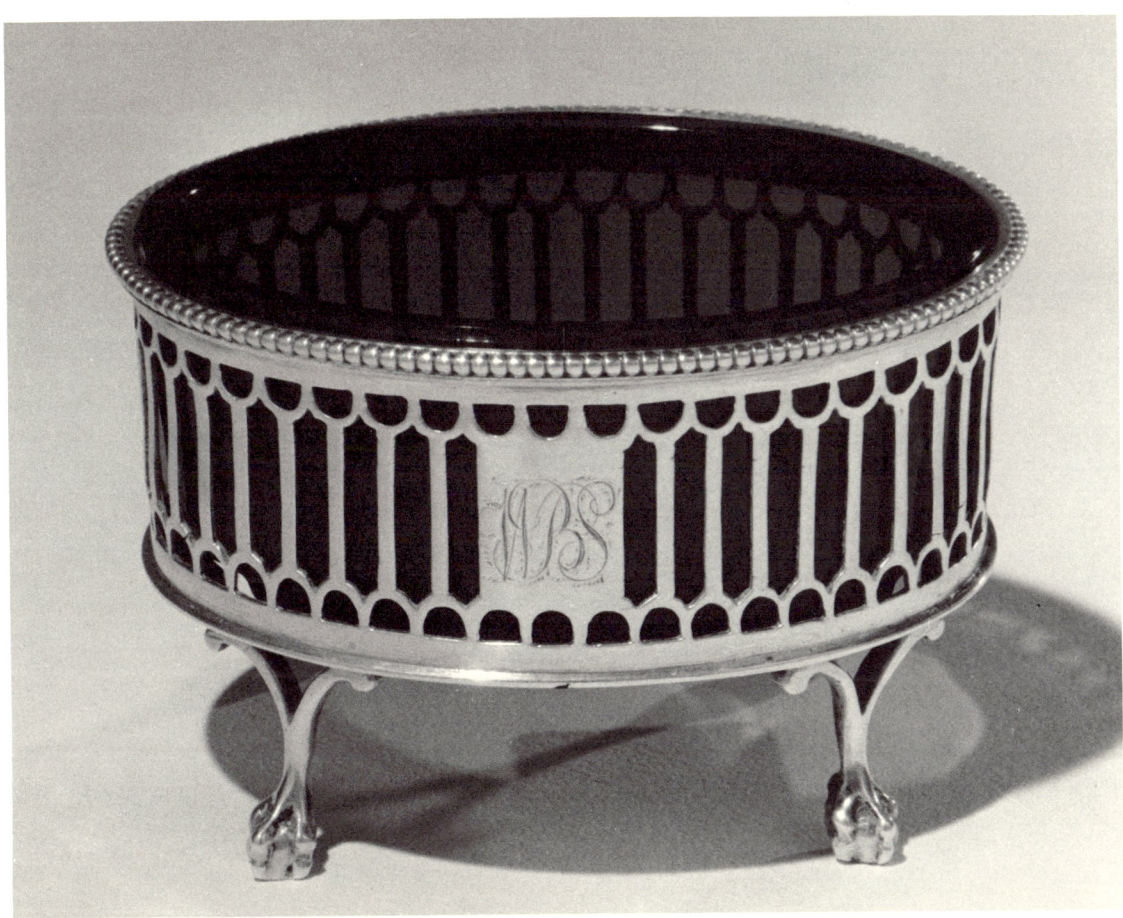

Fig. 153: Salt, I·NR in rectangle twice on base, *c.* 1785–90. Pierced sides and blue glass liner. Engraved on side in script *WBS*. Length: 3 3/8″. *Courtesy of Philadelphia Museum of Art; photograph by A. J. Wyatt.*

(*Fig. 152*) has a round body, curved legs, shells, and a ruffled edge. The later beaded version (*Fig. 153*) has an oval body, pierced sides, and a beaded edge, with only slightly curved legs that end in claw-and-ball feet, a detail remaining from the rococo style.

Joseph and Nathaniel used widely curved legs with shell knees on their early sauceboats (*Fig. 154, 155*). The very coarse pearl work along the edges illustrates the transitional stage during which new ornamental details were superimposed upon a basically rococo design. Saucepans made by the Richardsons (*Fig. 156*) also perpetuate the rococo shaping in a curvilinear body and bell finial.

The cans (*Fig. 157*) made by the Richardson brothers differ from those made a generation earlier by their father only in the style of the ornamental engraving. Perhaps this lack of stylistic change stems from the fact that both the can and the porringer were being used less. Another form losing popular-

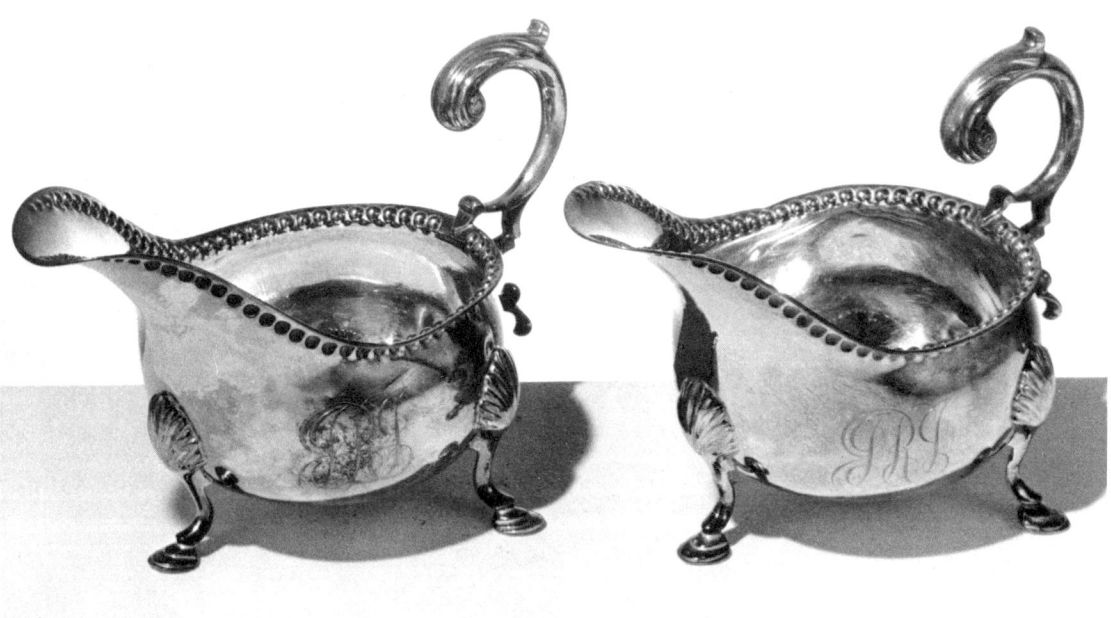

Fig. 154: Pair of sauceboats, I·NR in rectangle twice on base of each, *c.* 1780. Engraved on side *IRI* and originally owned by Jared Ingersoll, an ancestor of the present owner. *Courtesy of Mr. and Mrs. Orville H. Bullitt.*

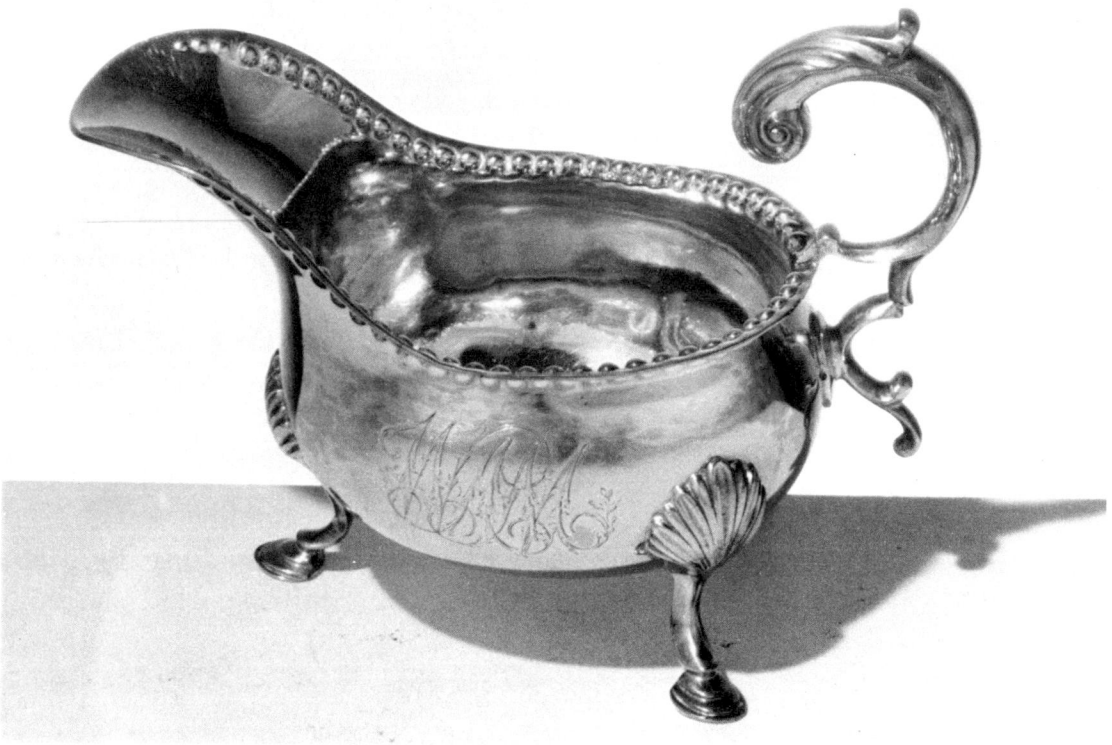

Fig. 155: Sauceboat, I·NR in rectangle twice on base, *c.* 1780. Engraved on side in foliated script *WAM*, as on tray (*Fig. 150*). Length: 6 7/8". *Privately owned.*

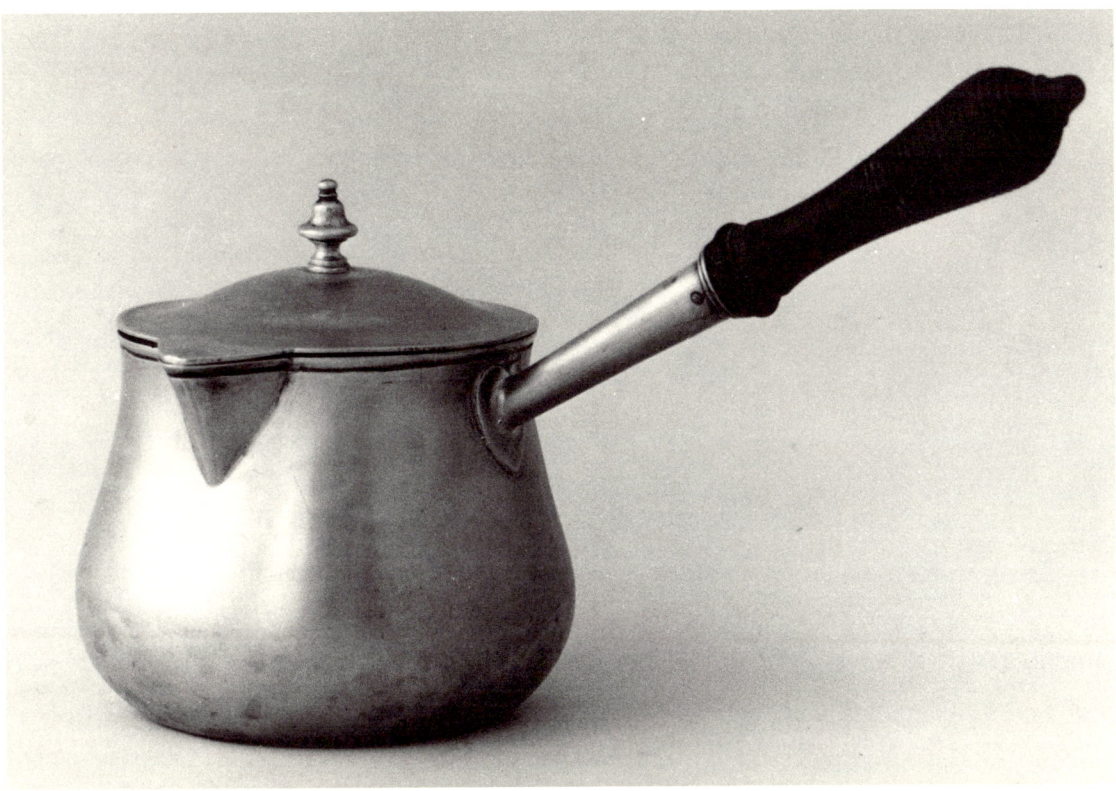

Fig. 156: Covered saucepan, I·NR in rectangle twice on base, c. 1780. Height: 3 3/4". Courtesy of Philadelphia Museum of Art; photograph by A. J. Wyatt.

ity was the tankard, but in its last days it took on a significantly new appearance. The earliest types made by Joseph and Nathaniel *(Figs. 158, 159)* were in perfect keeping with the rococo tradition, but a later example *(Fig. 160)* has the shape of a straight-sided barrel. Called a "hooped" tankard, this type was particularly popular in Philadelphia.[8] The Richardsons' hooped tankard is enhanced by the addition of vertical lines engraved on the body and on the lid to simulate the staves of a barrel. On the lid, a new Greek key pattern encircles a cipher. The squared handle with the flat water leaf on top was also characteristic of the new style.[9]

The hooped tankard is one of the significant forms of the Federal period because it embodies many of the changes that were occurring in the design of silver and the procedures for working it. With the improvement of the flatting mill for rolling sheet metal, it became easier for the silversmith to cut out parts, bend them into shape with a minimum of hammering, and solder them together. Thus he designed a piece of silver such as the straight-sided tankard, with a flat lid and squared handle. Even the thumb-piece could be simply

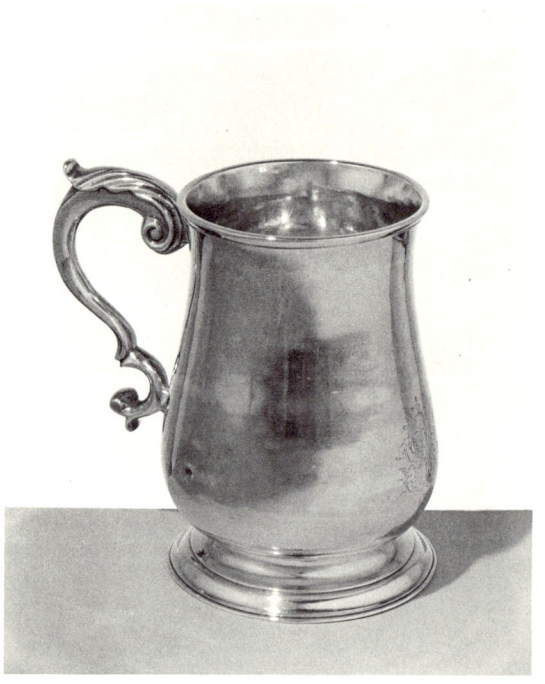
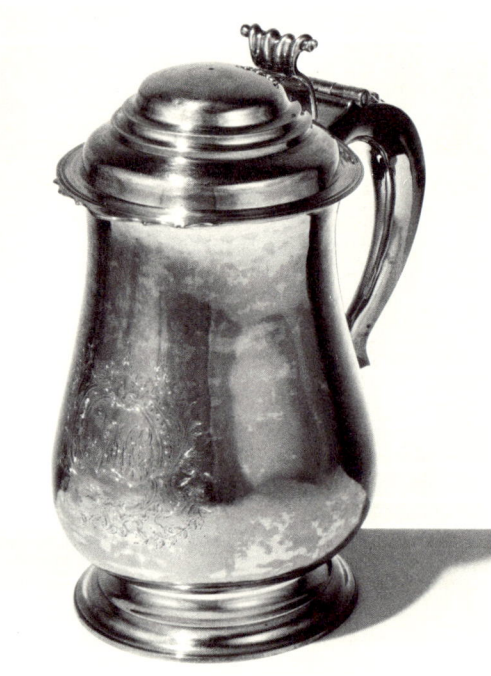

Fig. 157: Can, I·NR in rectangle twice on base, *c*. 1780. Engraved script initials on front. Height: 4 3/16″. *Courtesy of Philadelphia Museum of Art; photograph by A. J. Wyatt.*

Fig. 158: Tankard, I·NR in rectangle twice on base, *c*. 1780. Engraved initials on front in rococo cartouche. *Courtesy of Tiffany & Co.*

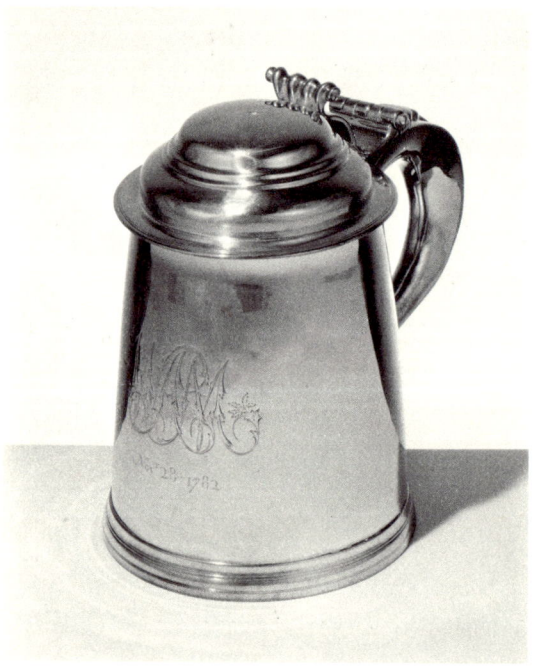
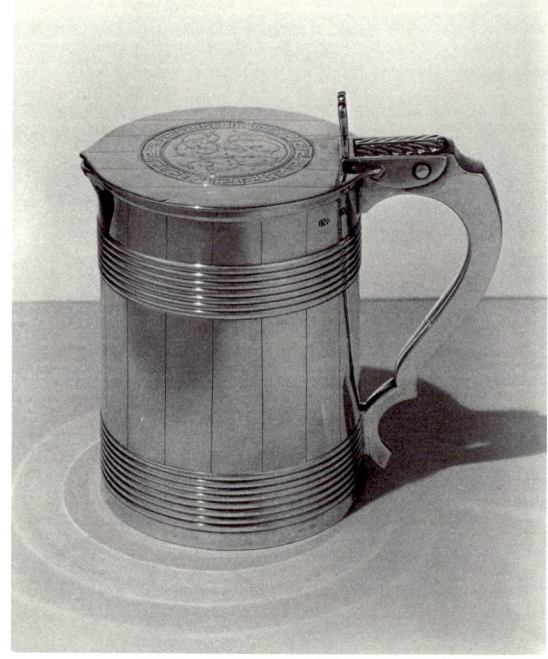

Fig. 159: Tankard, I·NR in rectangle twice on base, *c*. 1782. Engraved on front with initials WAM (*Figs. 150, 155*) and the date *Novr 28 1782*. *Privately owned.*

Fig. 160: Tankard, I·NR in rectangle twice on side, *c*. 1785–90. Hooped design especially popular in Philadelphia in Federal period. *Courtesy of Mrs. Walter M. Jeffords.*

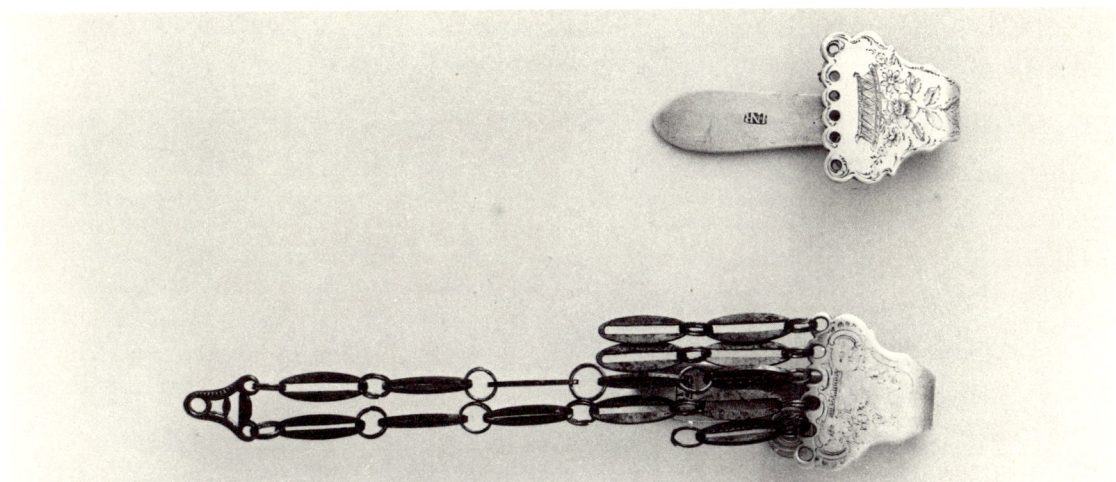

Fig. 161: Chatelaine hooks, (left) I·NR in rectangle, made by Joseph Richardson, Jr., alone, according to family tradition, and engraved *R·Hoskins, 6th mo. 15th, 1780*, for his wife Ruth and the date of their marriage; (right) IR in rectangle, made by Joseph Richardson, Sr., for his wife Mary. It has six points of attachment for chains. Length: (left) 2 5/16″; (right) 5 3/8″. *Courtesy of Philadelphia Museum of Art.*

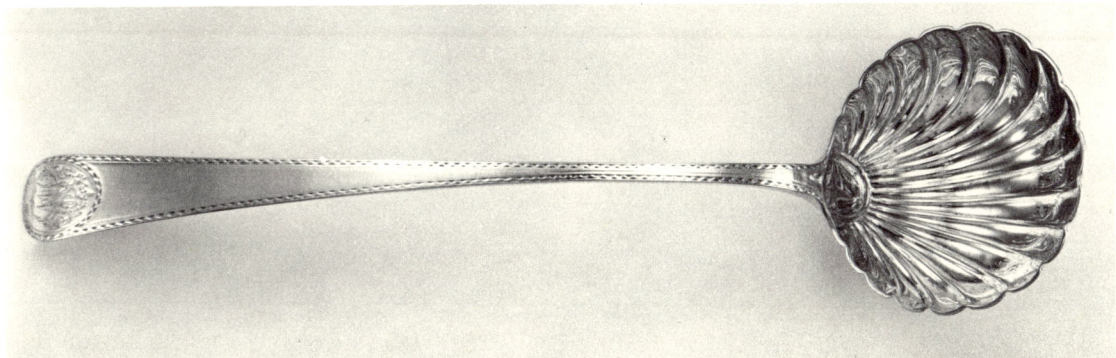

Fig. 162: Ladle, I·NR in rectangle thrice on back of bowl, c. 1785–90. Engraved on handle ending in brightcut oval *MP*. Length: 14 3/16″. *Courtesy of The Henry Francis du Pont Winterthur Museum; photograph by Gilbert Ask.*

a cut-out, pierced piece of flat metal. In the past, the silversmith's equipment had been devised to execute a particular design, but now the machine asserted its authority over design.

Not all forms made by the Richardsons were so significant. In fact, much of their work involved smaller objects, such as the charming chatelaine hook made by Joseph, Jr., for his bride in 1780 *(Fig. 161)*, and many ladles and spoons. The new curved-back handles of the ladles *(Fig. 162)* were decorated with bright-cut borders and attenuated foliate initials inside an oval medallion at the end, and the bowls were made in the shape of scallop shells (undoubtedly the type meant when the two brothers first wrote to England in 1777 for "scollopt Soup ladles"). By 1783 the lobes of the bowl had become nar-

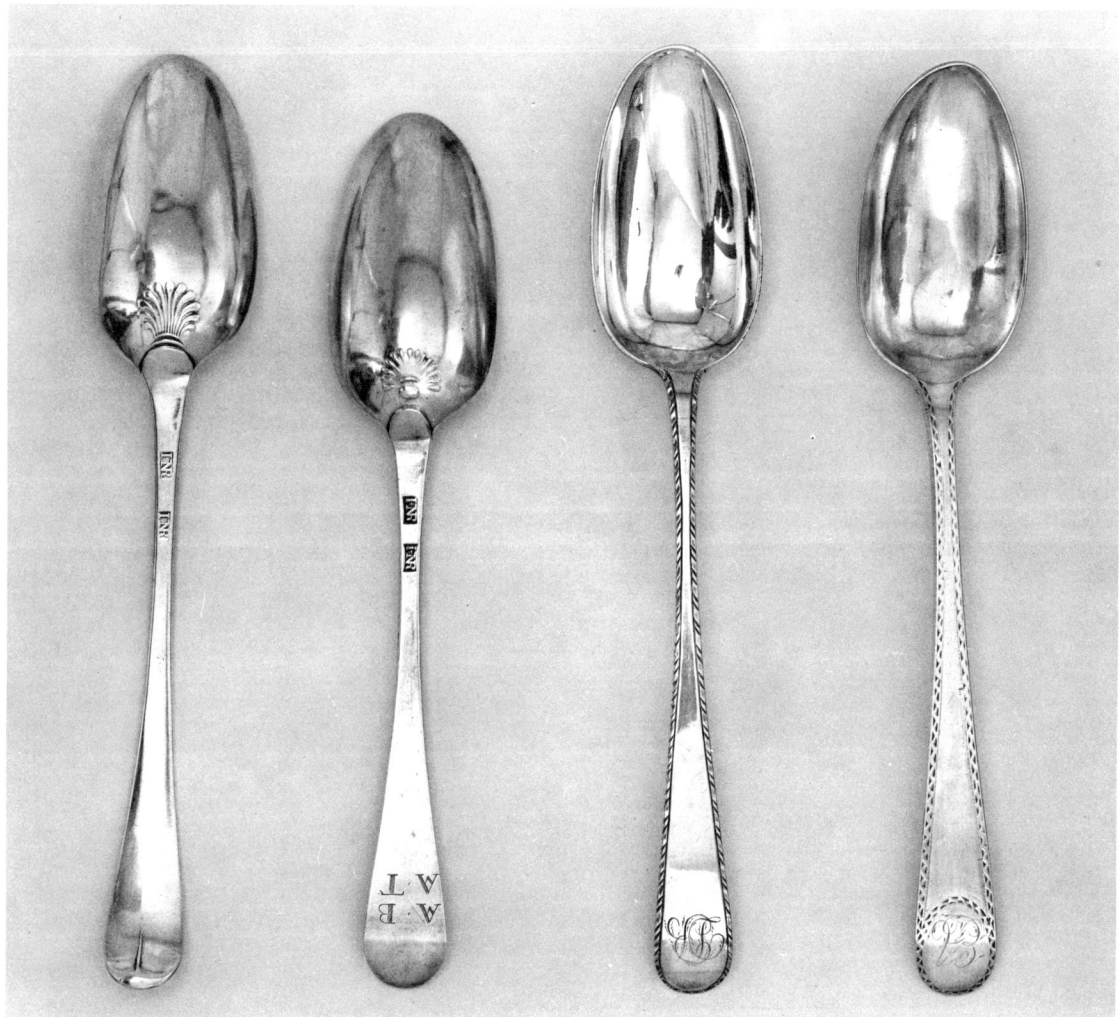

Fig. 162a: Four tablespoons, I·NR in rectangle twice on back of handle. Engraved (left to right) on handle W·M (front); $\overset{F}{A\cdot T}$ (back); $\overset{A\cdot B}{DB}$ (front); EA (front). The two spoons on left show the plumelike shell on back of bowl used by the brothers as well as the earlier shell design from the swage also used by their father. Lengths: 8 13/16"; 8 1/8"; 8 3/4"; 8 5/8". *Courtesy of The Henry Francis du Pont Winterthur Museum; gift of Mr. and Mrs. Alfred Bissell.*

rower and closer together; these ladles were referred to as "Fluted Ladles" in their orders from London.

Spoons had the same kinds of handles found on the ladles, some with bright-cut decoration and some plain with oval ends. On the back of the spoon bowl, the Richardsons continued to use a shell drop as their father had done, but they also had a new swage that he had not used (*Fig. 162a*): their shell design is more plume-shaped and lacks the dot between the drop and the flattened arc-shaped ridge above.

Perhaps the rarest of all the forms attributed to the brothers is a pair of candlesticks (see *Fig. 144*), a form which had not yet become common in

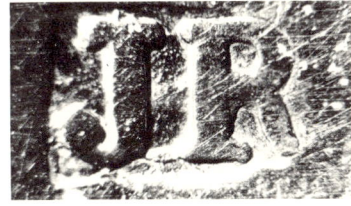 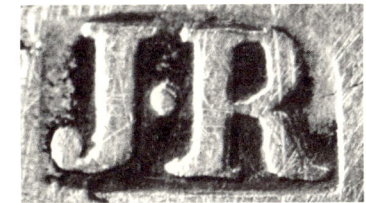 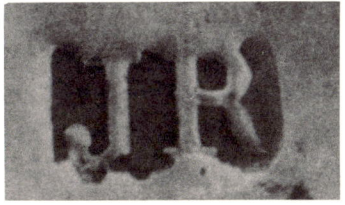

Fig. 163: Maker's marks
     a. JR in rectangle. Appears on wrist band (*Fig. 132*). *Courtesy of The Henry Francis du Pont Winterthur Museum.*
     b. J·R in rectangle. Appears on saucepan (*Fig. 164*). *Courtesy of Philadelphia Museum of Art.*
     c. JR in rectangle. Appears on cream pot and sugar bowl (*Fig. 171*). *Courtesy of Philadelphia Museum of Art.*

American silver. The design derived from a classical fluted column, with a squared flat bobêche and squared base. These may have been modeled after similarly fashioned plated candlesticks then being imported, a number of which were listed in the Richardsons' shop.

The rage for the rococo, then, did not die suddenly; rather, in the words of Thomas Sheraton in the preface to his *Cabinet-Maker and Upholsterer's Drawing Book*, it . . . "caught the decline." As a result, the Richardsons' silver from 1777 to 1790 reflects elements of both styles. As the century ended, the floridness of the older design gave way to the simplicity and restrained grace of the new.

By 1790, when Joseph Richardson, Jr., began working without his brother and stamping his silver with his JR mark (*Fig. 163*), neoclassical taste was well established, and the methods of manufacture were becoming more mechanized. No longer did the goldsmith take his customers' coins to make a piece of silver; instead, he purchased pre-rolled sheet silver from a local supplier.

In 1789 the American Bullion and Refining Office had opened in Philadelphia at Carter's Alley and Second Street. This concern advertised that it would buy old gold, silver, copper, brass, pewter and lead, and that as soon as enough metal had been collected refining would begin. (Philadelphia had long needed a silver refinery; as was pointed out earlier, Joseph Richardson, Sr., occasionally had to send metal to England to be refined.) The American Bullion Office announced that it would soon begin the manufacture of buttons, buckles, and plate and would give liberal encouragement to artists "bred to any of these branches;" furthermore, it would supply artisans with fine gold, silver, and flatted (or rolled) metals.[10]

The establishment of the first Bank of the United States in Philadelphia about this time also had important effects on silversmiths. The money-handling duties carried on by the goldsmith for hundreds of years were taken over by professional bankers. The goldsmiths were now paid for their finished products in cash, in the form of bank notes and United States minted coins.

The changes in procedure are clearly reflected in the records of payment kept by Joseph Richardson, Jr., between 1796 and 1801.[11] Most of the payments now recorded were cash. His father's accounts had constituted a record of an extensive barter system, but only rarely did Joseph, Jr. record payment in kind or even in old silver. The "6 secondhand Table & 6 Tea spoons" brought in by Erick Bollman in 1800 and the ounces of French silver recorded in the same year are exceptions rather than the rule.

Another important development in this period was the proliferation of new forms in silver and of new terms to describe these objects. Although Joseph, Jr., like his father, did not do much advertising, his contemporary, Joseph Anthony, Jr., advertised columns upon columns of different types of silver wares for sale at his shop in Front Street, providing a veritable index to the business of a goldsmith in that year.[12]

The repair work done by Joseph, Jr., reveals much about these new forms and the terms applied to them. Many of the items he repaired—fish knives or trowels, tambour shuttles, wine cocks, tea urns, argyles, and lamps—had not been in general use a decade earlier. He also records repairing a "Save-all," which Samuel Johnson defined as a "small pan inserted into a candlestick to save the ends of candles."

"Boiler" is another term introduced at this time. In 1796 Joseph mentioned repairing the cover of a boiler, and in 1799 he made a silver ferrule turned with beads for a boiler. This new form had a cover with a wooden handle fitting into a socket decorated with beading, and today would be called a covered saucepan *(Fig. 164)*. Joseph made boilers as well as repaired them, and in one case *(Fig. 165)* he added a line of beading around the base molding of the pan in addition to the one around the ferrule.[13]

Much of Joseph's repair work involved plated silver, which indicates how often the new and cheaper ware needed attention. Candlesticks were frequently repaired, along with cream pots, tankards, snuffers, and such new forms as table crosses, coffee urns, goblets, and cake and bread baskets. Although the Richardson brothers did not order plated silver during their partnership, their father had imported plated snuff boxes as early as 1760, and Joseph, Jr., ordered six silver-plated casters and six silver-plated salts with blue linings in 1792. Other forms in plated silver sold by Joseph toward the

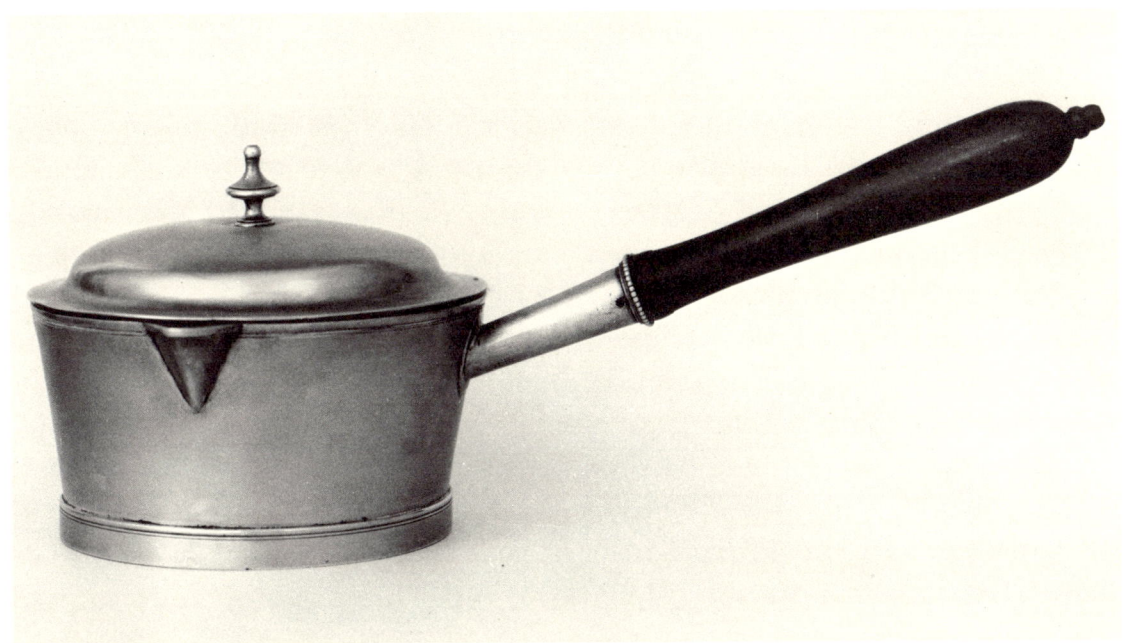

Fig. 164: Covered saucepan, JR in rectangle twice on base, *c.* 1795. Height: 3 9/16". *Courtesy of Philadelphia Museum of Art.*

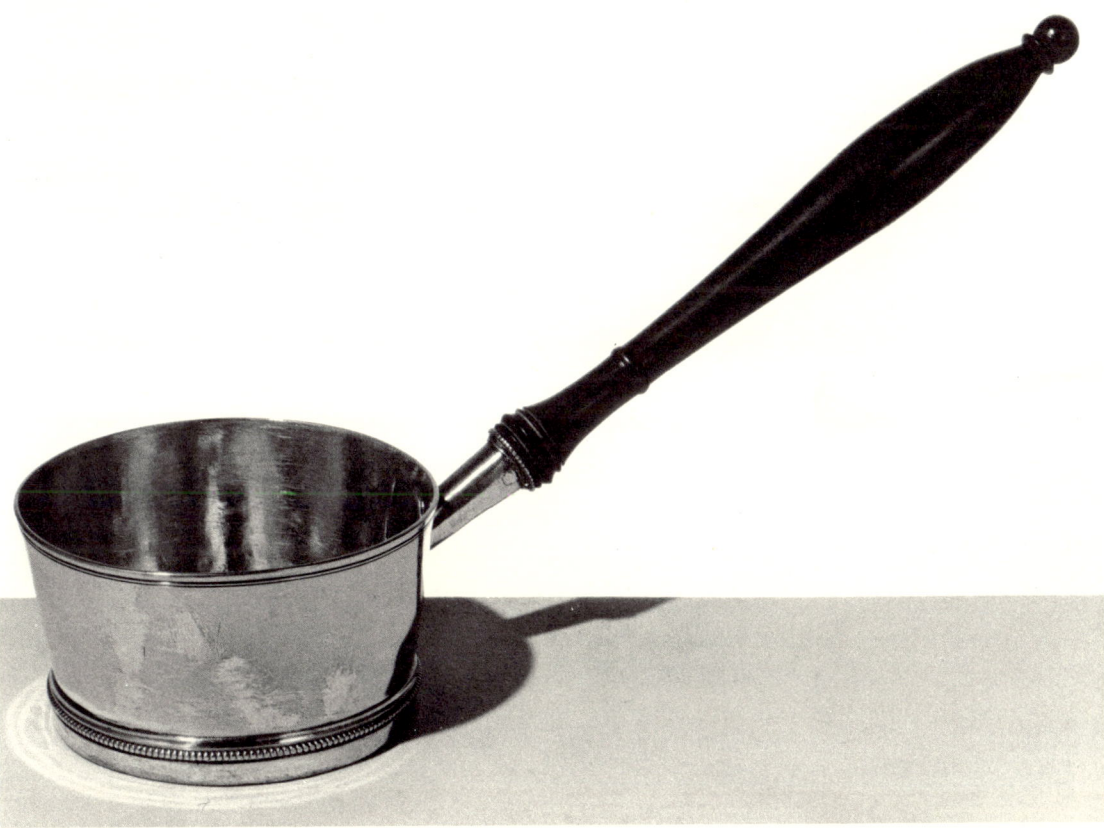

Fig. 165: Saucepan, JR in rectangle twice on base, *c.* 1800. *Courtesy of Mrs. S. Hallock du Pont.*

end of the century included an oval waiter, a label (or bottle ticket), and a chamber candlestick. In addition to plated wares, he also sold some japanned wares, among which were a brown tea urn, "a Blue Japaned Tea Urn full Silvered" on which he had engraved a cipher, and several japanned boilers.

Joseph also ordered from England a parcel of files ("12 Bastard cutt and 12 Smooth cutt Riflen Files") to use in "repairing the mounting of Silver plate work of diffirant shapes," in addition to plated and solid silver.[14] But he soon discovered that various difficulties attended the shipment of silver from England. One shipment of cream pots was so unsatisfactory that he felt compelled to complain: "The burnished work which I had of you last were extreemly ill finished such as I should have been ashamed to turn out of my own Work Shop." He threatened to return any sent in the future unless they were of better quality.[15]

For the most part he continued to order the same sort of goods that he and his brother had requested: salts with spare glasses, sets of six and twelve teaspoons and tongs in cases, single tongs, and whistles and bells of assorted patterns. In 1792, however, he ordered a number of new forms, and in some cases he described the type of decoration they were to have. The cream pots were to be ornamented with "beads," rather than pearl work, and the teapots were to be engraved to match the sugar dishes and tea caddies. The largest objects ordered were the two "light pierced cake baskets," which had become increasingly popular in this period. Extra glass linings for salts, extra glasses for the sets of casters, tablespoons, polished teaspoons, and sugar tongs (engraved and in assorted patterns) were ordered, and in such large quantities as to indicate that Joseph's business was growing rapidly.

In 1793 Joseph received a shipment from Masterman of more than £250 worth of plate, but although he found the work to be very good, the high prices were discouraging. He explained "I fully intended to have remitted to you in full by this opportunity but the State of War Subsisting & some very recent Accounts of failure with you have thrown such a damp upon the drawing of the Bills that few of our Merchants care to venture at present." Joseph, at any rate, closed his account with Masterman in May 1793 and ceased ordering from England.[16]

Thereafter, the wares produced in his shop became Joseph's chief concern, and fortunately there was a great demand for his work. More and more people were able to afford silver, and there were many orders for complete sets of silver. In 1798 Richardson recorded that he made a service for Joseph

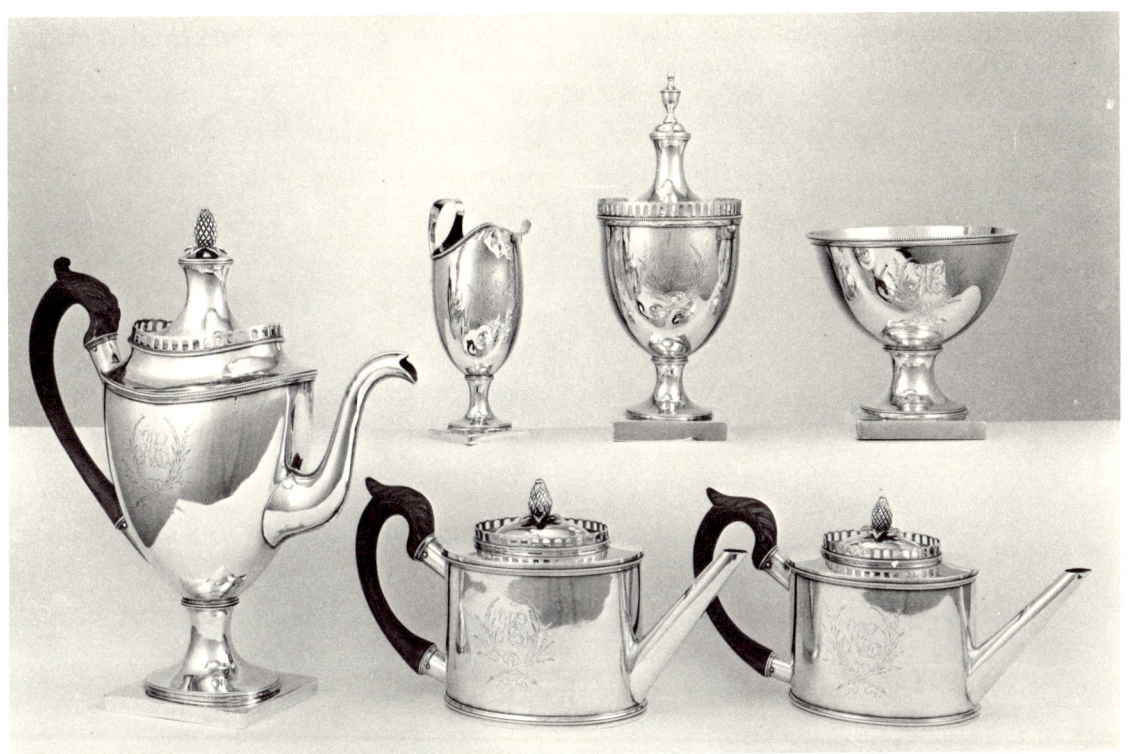

Fig. 166: Tea and coffee service, two different JR in rectangle marks, c. 1795. Nineteen pieces in all including tea tongs and twelve teaspoons. All engraved in script *AE*. Original weights of vessels scratched on base, that of coffeepot being 38 oz., its height: 13". *Courtesy of The Henry Francis du Pont Winterthur Museum; photograph by Gilbert Ask.*

Ball which included a coffeepot, two teapots, a slop bowl, a sugar dish, a cream pot, 25 tablespoons, 18 dessert spoons, 24 teaspoons, sugar tongs, a soup ladle, a punch strainer, a punch ladle, and four salt spoons—the bill for which came to £174/19/5.[17] This was not the only such service Joseph made, but less elaborate sets, without the flatware, usually cost between £90 and £100.[18]

A nineteen-piece tea set *(Fig. 166)* Joseph Richardson made about 1795 reflects the now fully developed Federal style. The teapots are oval, the slop bowl is round and the rest of the forms are urn-shaped. All have beading; all except the teapots are supported on square bases; and all the covered pieces have a gallery rim around the top. The pots have pineapple finials, but the sugar urn has an urn-shaped finial. The coffeepot curves downward slightly along the line of the lid for a more pleasing effect, a feature which became increasingly popular toward the end of the century.

The carved wooden handles were all of similar design, C-shaped with a flat leaf furl at the top. "A neat carved handle" was always added to the cost of teapots and coffeepots when Joseph reckoned his accounts; he usually charged 15 shillings for a coffeepot handle and £0/12/6 for a teapot handle. This sug-

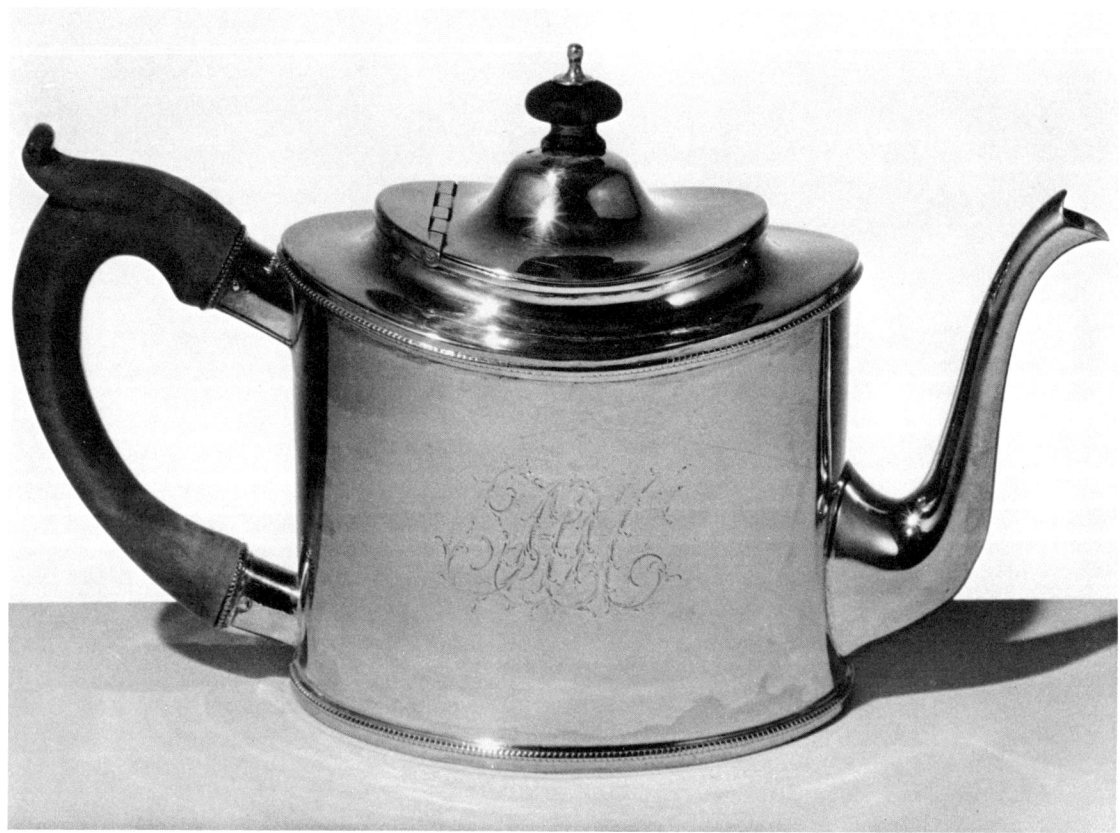

Fig. 167: Teapot, JR in rectangle twice on base, *c.* 1800. Engraved on side in foliated script HH. *Privately owned.*

gests, as do the separate engraving charges he listed, that someone else did the work for him.[19]

Occasionally Joseph's teapots were somewhat plainer *(Fig. 167),* and made without a gallery rim but with a low curve to the lid and a line of beading around the handle ferrule. Some of the teapots had wooden finials similar to the "black button for a Tea pott" for which Joseph charged Joseph Tilghman 2 shillings in 1797. Other types of finials used at the end of the century included pineapples, which were occasionally made of ivory rather than silver (in 1798 he charged Phillip Nicklin £0/11/3 for an ivory pineapple and silver leaf for a teapot, and in 1799 he charged William Sansom 6 shillings for a pineapple for a teapot).

The bases of the vessels were almost always flat, and square or oval. Occasionally before the nineteenth century the bases were raised up on ball feet, as when Joseph charged Christopher Marshall for "adding Balls to feet of a Coffee Pot & Slop Bowl." Most had square bases like the cream pot made by Joseph in 1801 *(Fig. 168)* which represents the peak in the development of this form with its helmet shape, true beading, and high sweeping handle.

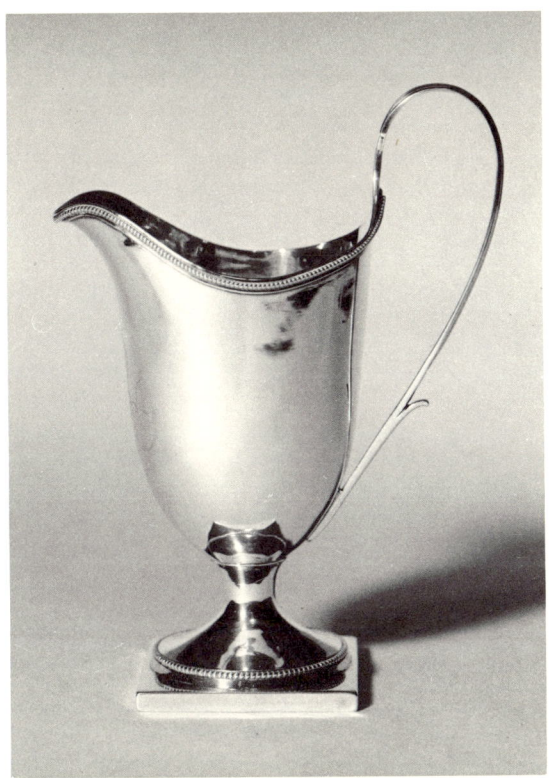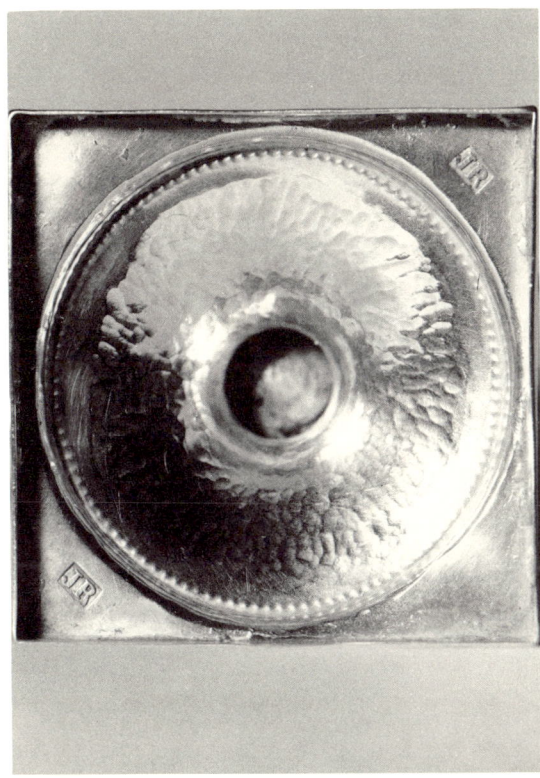

Fig. 168: Cream pot, JR in rectangle twice on base, *c.* 1801. Originally owned by Jane Hill Brinton who married Joseph Trimble in 1801, ancestors of the present owner. *Courtesy of Mr. David M. McFarland.*

One of the few innovations in the shaping of these vessels which occurred during the last few years of the eighteenth century was the appearance of fluting. As early as February 1797, Henry Drinker bought a fluted tea set from Joseph.[20] He also made chocolate pots, another newly popular form, in the fluted style, and in 1800 Richard H. Wilcocks paid £27/13/6 for his "Silver Chocolate Pot flooted." One group of tea-table vessels in this style (actually they are pieces from two different sets) all have fluted sides and bases, and the fluting is repeated in the urn finials *(Fig. 169)*. By 1800, these vessels were rounder and more bulbous than the earlier urn forms. The covers added to the cream pots provide a lovely line which seems to flow directly from the handle into the lip.

In these later pieces the beading so characteristic of Federal silver was gradually eliminated *(Fig. 171)*. The shape of the object itself became all important, and superficial decoration was reduced to a minimum; often a single script initial was the only engraved ornamentation. A cream pot Joseph made in 1799 retained a single line of beading around the lip, but the

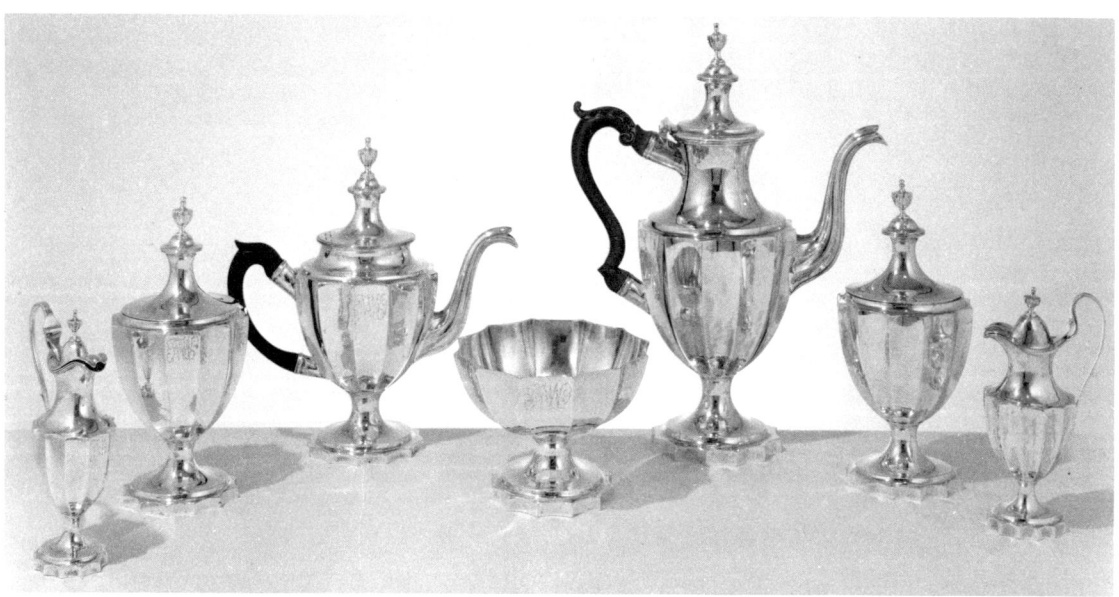

Fig. 169: Two tea and coffee services, JR in rectangle, *c.* 1800. Four pieces on left engraved on front with foliated script *MW*. Height of tallest pot: 14 1/4". *Courtesy of Philadelphia Museum of Art; photograph by A. J. Wyatt.*

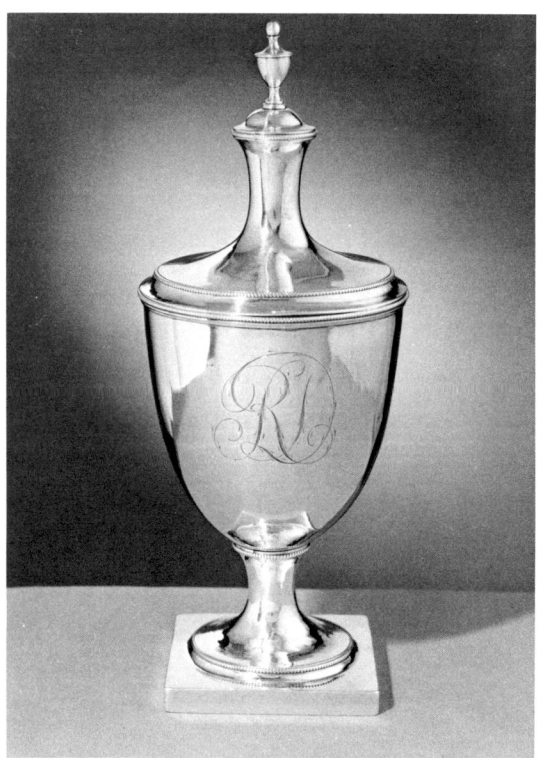

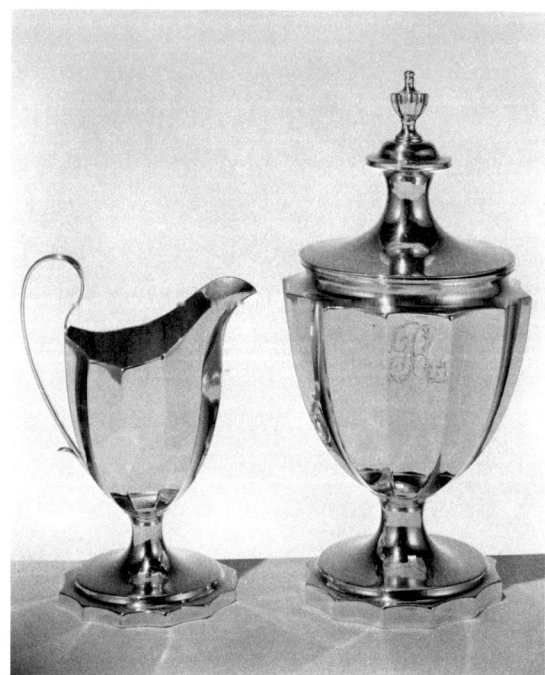

Fig. 170: Sugar urn, JR in rectangle four times on base, *c.* 1794. Engraved on side in script *RD*. Same initials on base with original weight 13 oz. 13 dwt. 12 gr. Height: 9 1/2". *Privately owned.*

Fig. 171: Cream pot and sugar bowl, JR in rectangle, *c.* 1800. Sugar bowl engraved on front in foliated script *R*. Height of sugar bowl: 9 9/16". *Courtesy of Philadelphia Museum of Art; photograph by A. J. Wyatt.*

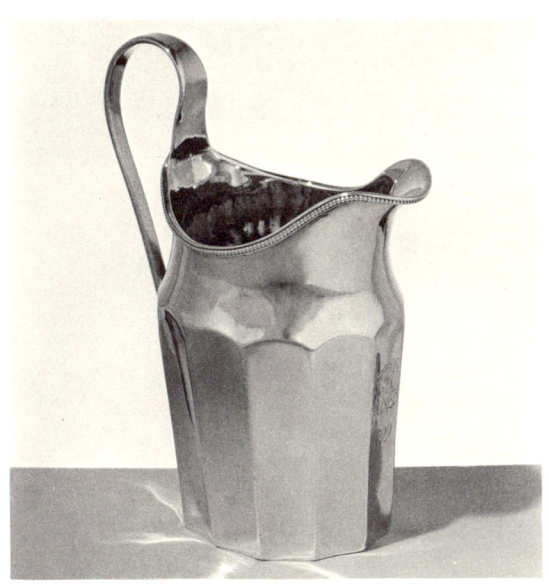 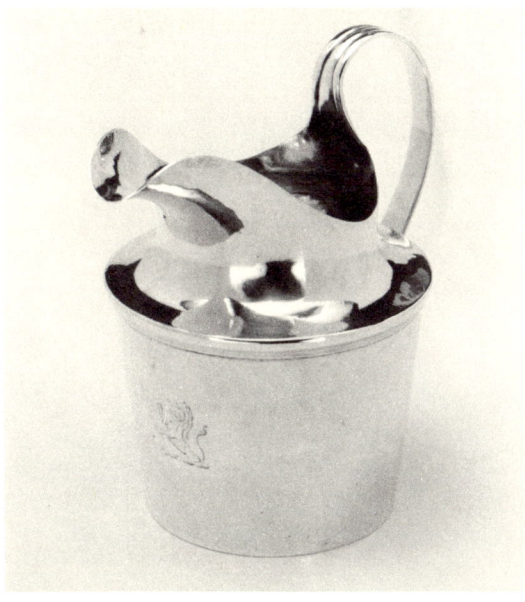

Fig. 172: Cream pot, JR in rectangle, *c.* 1799. Engraved with initials and date 1799. Height: 5 9/16". *Courtesy of Philadelphia Museum of Art.*

Fig. 173: Cream pot, J·R in rectangle on base, *c.* 1790. Engraved on front with demi-lion rampant crest. Height: 4 3/16"; weight 7 oz. *Courtesy of Mr. Philip H. Hammerslough.*

fluting of its sides is so flat that it seems more like paneling *(Fig. 172)*. In some pots *(Fig. 173)*, he created a high-waisted appearance by lengthening the body section and making the upper section shorter. Surface treatment of the metal was limited to the engraved crest on the side and the reeding on the handle.

Reeding was also used on the rims of two fluted dishes *(Fig. 174)* which have been called at various times strawberry dishes or vegetable dishes, and may actually have been baking dishes. Both celery and baking dishes were bought from Richardson by Joseph Higby in 1797. They were large: the fluted celery dish Higby bought weighed over 34 ounces, and the pair of fluted baking dishes together weighed 58 oz. 11 dwt. One of these baking dishes made by Joseph Richardson, Jr., *(Fig. 175)*, can be documented by his account book charge to Joseph Higby since it is engraved with the name "Higbee" and faintly inscribed with its original weight which is, within two pennyweights, half the weight of the pair in the entry.[21]

Fluting also appeared in ladles *(Fig. 176)*, in the form of a shaped bowl and a scrolled handle (called today an Onslow handle) made by a few Philadelphia goldsmiths. Such handles were mentioned in city newspaper advertisements as early as 1763, as "fluted and polished sauce spoons, with scroll heads."[22] In 1797, Joseph charged John Warder £4/17/0 for an oval fluted soup ladle with an engraved cipher. On one occasion he sold a pierced ladle,

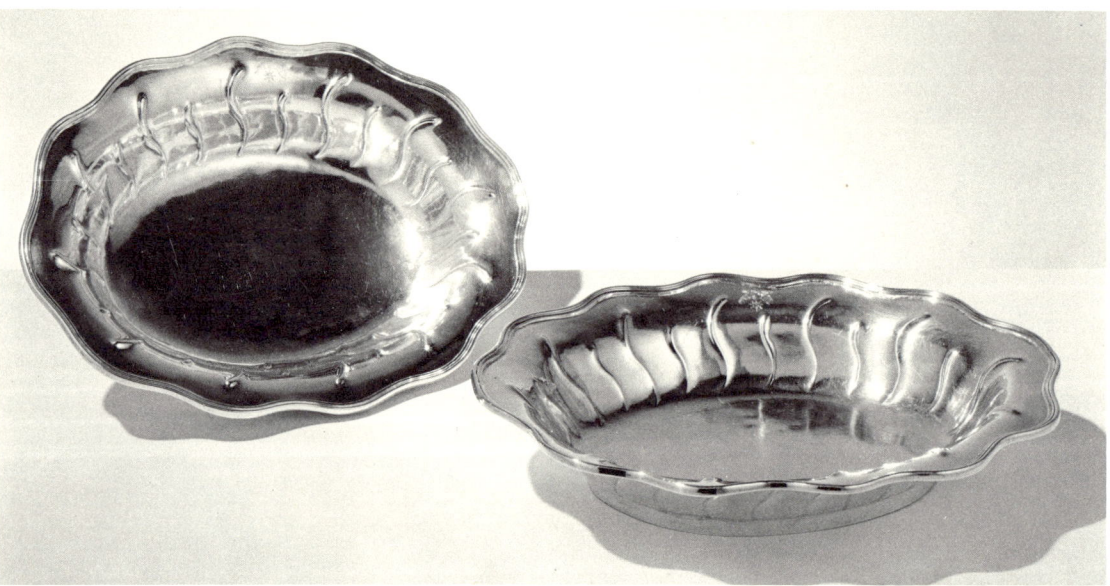

Fig. 174: Pair of dishes, JR in rectangle twice on base of each, *c.* 1795–1800. Formerly owned by Samuel Powel and engraved with his crest. Diameter: 11". *Courtesy of Philadelphia Museum of Art.*

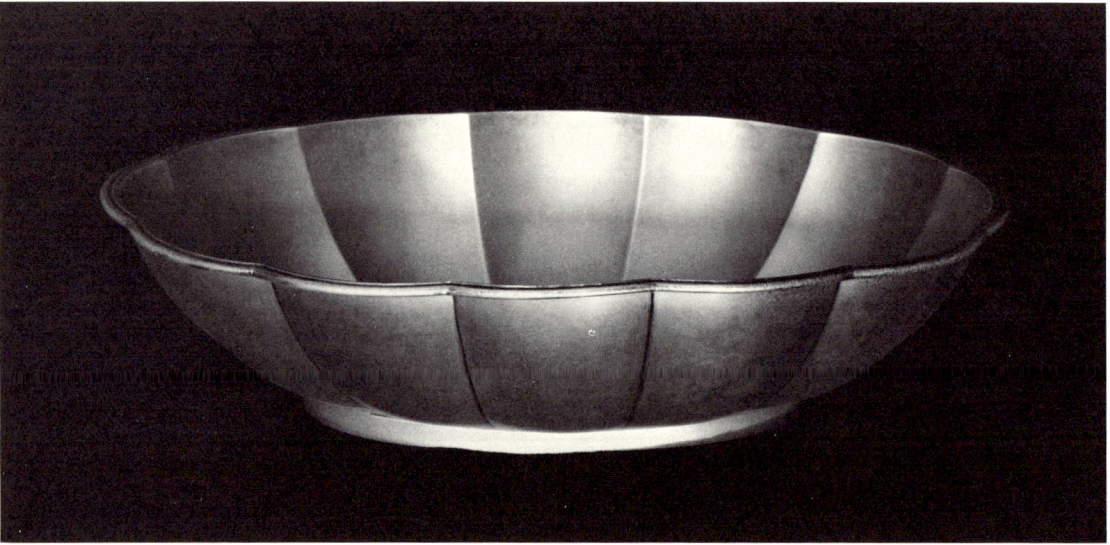

Fig. 175: Baking dish, J·R in rectangle on base, 1797. Engraved in later script on base *Higbee* (*Fig. 175a*). Detail of base shows faint inscription of original weight, *29 oz. 4 dwt.* One of pair bought by Joseph Higby on May 16, 1797, which weighed 58 oz. 11 dwt. and cost £ 52/13/10 (*Fig. 175b*). Length: 12 1/4"; width: 8 5/8"; weight: 29 oz. 2 dwt. *Courtesy of Sterling and Francine Clark Art Institute, Williamstown, Massachusetts.*

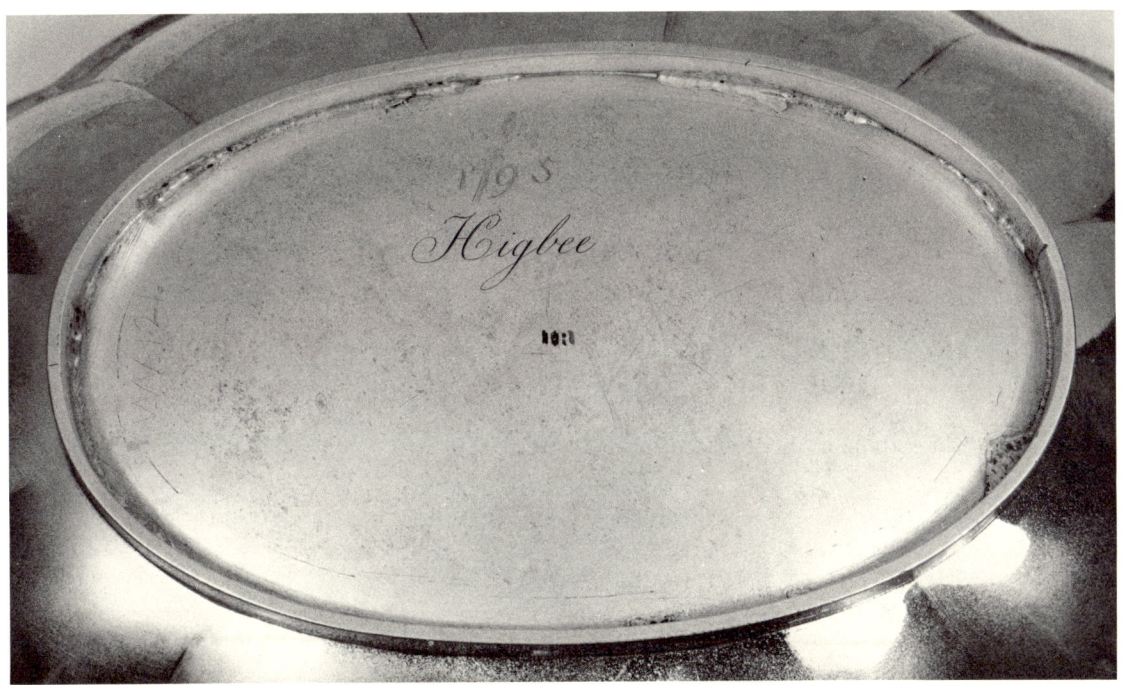

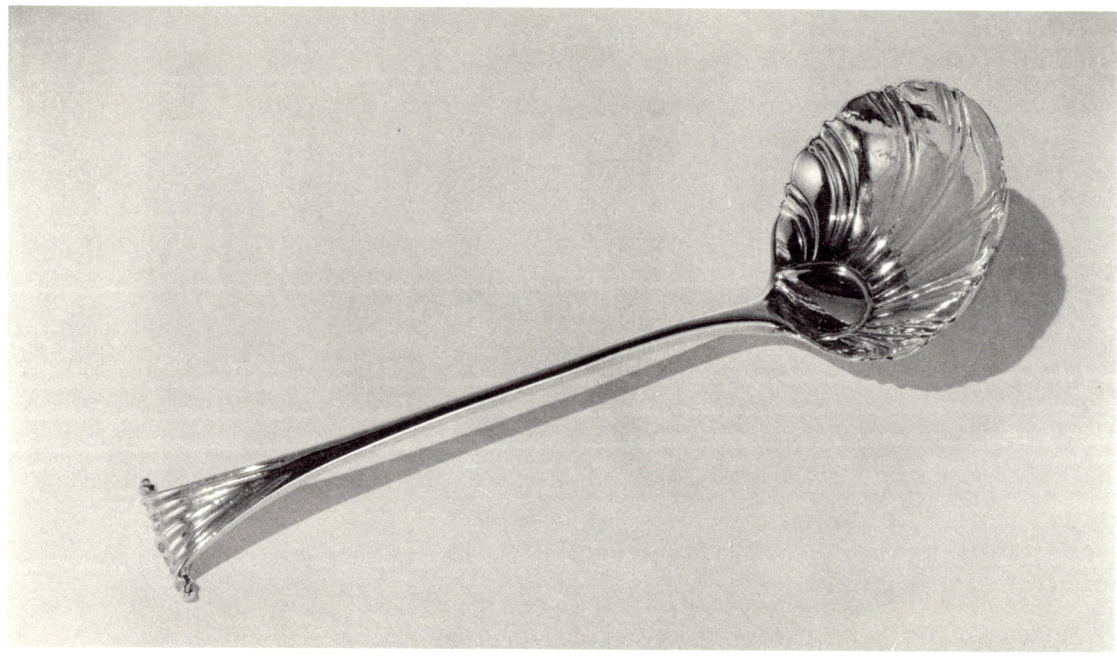

Fig. 176: Ladle, JR in rectangle thrice on back of shaft. *c.* 1790. Onslow type handle and scalloped bowl. Length: 7 7/8". *Courtesy of Philadelphia Museum of Art; photograph by A. J. Wyatt.*

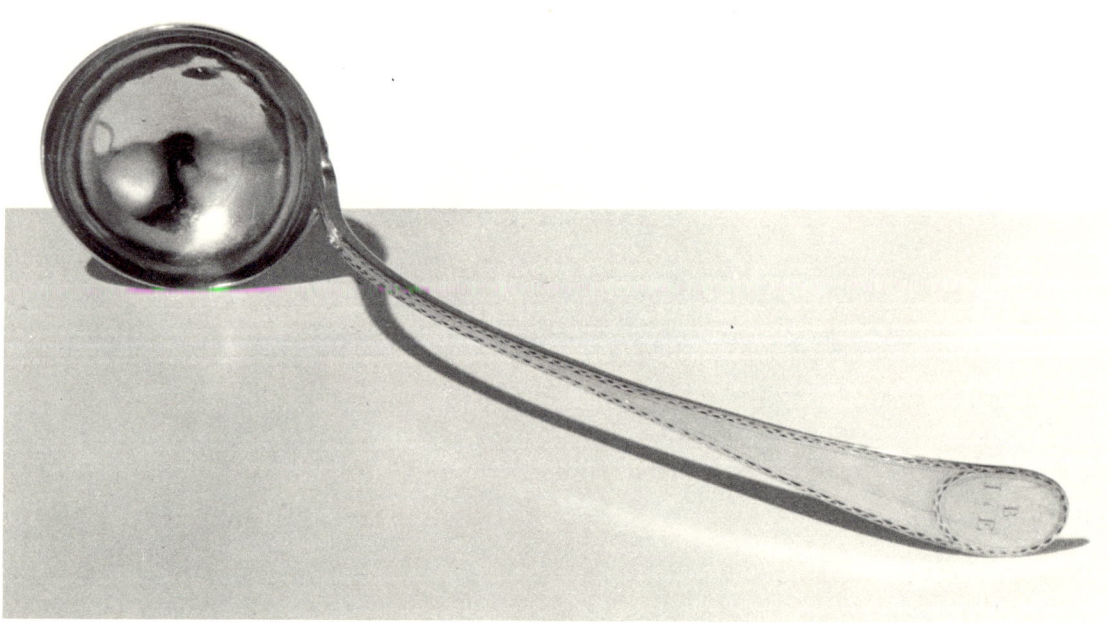

Fig. 177: Ladle, J·R in rectangle thrice on back of shaft, *c.* 1800. Engraved on handle in medallion I^{B}E. Length: 13 3/4". *Courtesy of Mr. Edmund H. Cabeen.*

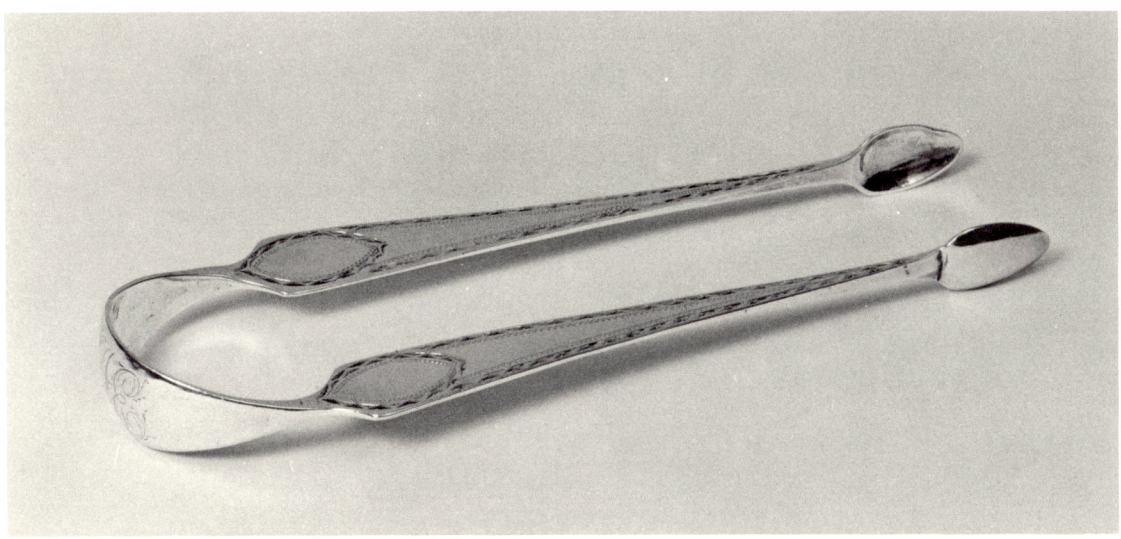

Fig. 178: Tea tongs, JR in rectangle inside bow, *c.* 1790. Engraved *AE* and part of service *(Fig. 166)*. Length: 6 3/16 . *Courtesy of The Henry Francis du Pont Winterthur Museum; photograph by Gilbert Ask.*

but for the most part his ladles, like his spoons, had plain, round bowls and bright-cut decoration on the handles *(Fig. 177)*. This type of sharply cut decoration along the edges of handles was apparently described as "carved" in Joseph's day, because this is the adjective he most frequently applied to soup ladles, cream ladles, gravy spoons, dessert spoons, tablespoons, teaspoons, and tea tongs. The tea tongs he made are characteristic of this "carved" work *(Fig. 178)*, and the shaping of the shaft of the tongs at a right angle to the bow and nippers is an added touch of virtuosity.

Occasionally Joseph made teaspoons or dessert spoons with threaded handles. This is generally thought of as a nineteenth-century pattern in American silver, but as early as 1796 Joseph noted making spoons with threaded handles. In a few instances Joseph recorded that he supplied marrow spoons, or at least "a bowl to a Marrow spoon." He made many other kinds of spoons, including children's teaspoons. Miers Fisher bought six "Childrens Tea Spoons and Tongs" in 1796, and the following year Benjamin W. Morris paid £0/7/6 for "4 small Tea spoons childrens Toys," which weighed less than two pennyweight each.[23] In addition to teaspoons and tongs, other items made particularly for children included "a Silver Mug for Children," coral and bells (which were occasionally gilt), and a gold child's locket and two feet of gold chain, which William Trotter bought in 1800.

Joseph made lockets and chains for adults as well as for children. One

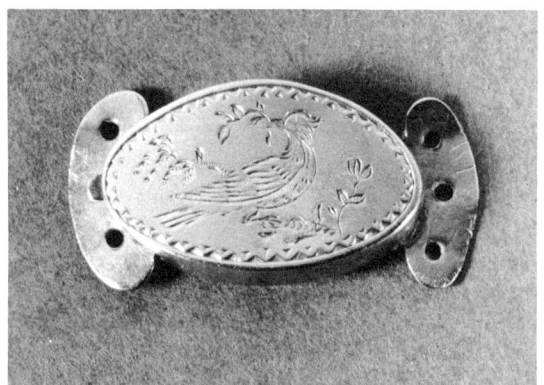 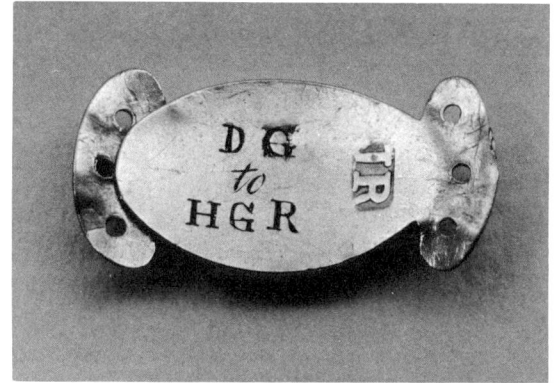

Fig. 179: Gold locket, JR in rectangle on back plate, *c.* 1790. Engraved on back plate at later date *DG to HGR*. *Courtesy of The Henry Francis du Pont Winterthur Museum; photograph by Gilbert Ask.*

lovely carved locket *(Fig. 179)* is engraved with a bird of peace on top, and initials on the back. Other gold items made by Joseph include thimbles engraved with the owners' names, pins, buttons, buckles, glove clasps, a ferrule for a pencil case, beads, and even a bracelet. In 1796, he made a pair of bracelets for William Smith for which he charged £6. He also made earrings, coral necklaces, a diamond ring, and a miniature frame, and repaired a "hair device," a piece of jewelry containing a design made of hair.

All these items are of interest because, together with seals, shoe clasps, spectacle frames, drinking tubes, bodkins, scissor chains and hooks, and pincushion hoops and chains, they reveal the diversity of small objects produced by the goldsmith at the end of the century. On rare occasions, Joseph made an engraved label for a decanter. He also made the "Silver letter S" for Robert Smith. He mentions having made eight silver forks in 1798, although American silver forks were rare before 1800.

Nutmeg graters and snuff boxes were more popular forms, and a grater was bought from him in 1800 by Ruth A. Rutter, with two ciphers engraved on it. The same year, Joseph charged Thomas Norton for "mounting a shell Snuffbox with Silver" and engraving a cipher on it, indicating that he also made snuff-boxes of cowrie shells.

The more common major forms of silver at the end of the eighteenth century still included tankards. They were frequently described now as "hooped and finished inside." "Porter" tankards, with engraved ciphers and ornaments were purchased in 1796 by William Smith. Joseph's records show that he made fewer and fewer porringers, for their popularity was declining, while the number of tumblers he made increased in response to the growing demand.

The term "waiter" had practically replaced the earlier "salver" for trays, and Richardson made a number of these, one of which weighed over thirty ounces and was elaborately engraved. Smaller waiters were often bought in pairs. Another term introduced at this time was "salt cellar," which Joseph first used in 1796. The term "mustard tankard" clearly described the change in form of this container at the end of the eighteenth century, in the same way that the new term "cadee shell" described the shape of the little utensil used to scoop tea from a caddy.

Several of the forms made by Joseph have not survived or have not yet been identified. Among them is a cake basket bought by Elizabeth West in 1799 and a punch bowl bought by Joseph Higby in 1797. The loss of the bowl is particularly unfortunate, for it weighed an impressive 94 oz. 16 dwt. and cost, with its two engraved ciphers and ornaments, £72/12/0. Another form unknown among Joseph's silver today is the sugar basket, one of which was purchased from him in 1796 for £7/10/0 by James Crawford.

The increased variety of the wares which Joseph Richardson, Jr., made, and the specialized names devised to describe them, were indicative of the development of the goldsmith's craft in the eighteenth century. In 1700 the goldsmith in Philadelphia had to depend on occasional patrons whose desires had sometimes to be supplemented by imported goods. By 1800, he was a prosperous craftsman with an ever-increasing number of customers. He continued to import goods, but he turned more and more to specialized American craftsmen to satisfy the demands of his patrons.

All the evidence that survives indicates that Joseph Richardson, Jr., was a capable and clever craftsman, continuing a tradition established a hundred years earlier by his grandfather, passed on to him by his father, and maintained by him until the opening years of the nineteenth century when the effects of mechanization began to cause radical changes in metal work.

It is fortunate that so important a family of goldsmiths as the Richardsons bequeathed to later generations a wealth of silver and documentary evidence through which the history of the art of the goldsmith in America can be re-created and preserved. Joseph Richardson, Jr. himself, summarized the importance these relics might have for us in the future when he described the Indian medal made by his father: "I have no doubt in a future day, it will be considered as interesting . . . as it may serve to show the progress of the arts in our country."[24]

APPENDIX A

Commonplace Book of Joseph Richardson

[A] The small commonplace book *(Fig. 29)* in the Richardson family papers now at Winterthur (DMMC, 53.165.124) was kept by Joseph Richardson from about 1743 to 1752. In it he made miscellaneous notations concerning his apprentices, sales, techniques of refining metal, and lost or stolen silver. Of special interest is the listing of what he kept in his glass show case.

1744 Account of Sailes out of the Glass Case

			Makeing
7th mo.	4th		
		1 Link of Buttons	£0/ 0/ 7
	5th	6 tea Spoons	0/ 9/ 0
		6 Links of Buttons	0/ 3/ 6
		2 Large Spoons	0/ 6/ 0
		8 Jacket Buttons & pair Buckels	0/10/ 8
		6 Do.	0/ 2/ 0
		2 Gold Locketts	0/16/ 0
		1 Pair tea tongs	0/ 7/ 0
		1 Pair of Gold Studs	0/ 7/ 0
	6th	1 Pair Gold Buttons	0/ 8/ 0
		1 Pair of tea tongs	0/10/ 0
	7th	5 Pair of Stock Clasps	0/12/ 6
		1 Sett of Buttons	0/ 1/ 2
		1 Pair tea tongs	0/ 7/ 0
	8th	1 Gold Ring	0/ 3/ 0
		1 Spoon a Stock Buckel	0/ 5/ 6

	1 Pair Knea Buckels	0/ 4/ 0
	1 Pair Shoe Buckels	0/ 4/ 0
	1 Pair Gold Buttons	0/ 8/ 0
	1 Pair Shoe Buckels	0/10/ 0
	1 Pair Shoe & Knea Do.	0/12/ 0
	3 tea Spoons & 4 Link Buttons	0/ 6/10
	1 Corel & Bells EB	0/16/ 0
14th	2 Pair Shoe Buckels	0/10/ 0

Account of Silver in the Case

6 Correls & Bells
9 Watch Chaines
3 Pair tea tongs
19 Pair of Shoe Buckels
12 Girdle Buckels
14 Stock Buckels
1 pair Knea Buckels
18 Links of Buttons
51 Coat & Jackett Buttons
1 Pair Shoe Clasps
5 Silver Locketts
1 Seal
1 Belt Buckel
3 String Corell
9 thimbles
1 Pincushen hoop
3 Snuf Boxes
2 Punch Straners
1 Punch Ladel
6 Large Spoons
20 tea Spoons & 1 Pocket Spoon
2 Straners
1 Pair Crystol Studs
3 Pair of Joynted Clasps for Stocks
11 Pair of Plain Stock Clasps
7 tea Spoons
6 pair Knea Buckels
13 Strings of Corell
2 pair Shoe Buckels
1 pair knea Do.

Drawne
2 Pair Buttons &
6 Pair Silver
3 thimbles

6 Stock Buckels   & 3 Buttons

1744

7th mo. 4th   *Account of Gold in the Glass*
        3 Gold Rings
      73 Links of Gold Buttons
        1 Pair of Gold Sleave Buckels
        1 Pair Gold Bobs
        2 Gold Lockets
        1 Pair Gold Studs
        1 Gold Ring

APPENDIX B

Settlement of the Hulbeart Estate

[B] Among the Richardson papers at The Henry Francis du Pont Winterthur Museum is a small account book kept by Joseph Richardson to record the financial transactions resulting from his appointment (along with Phillip Syng) to settle the estate of Philadelphia goldsmith Philip Hulbeart. While this record book tells only a bit about the life and work of Joseph Richardson, it contains enough material concerning the goldsmith's trade in Philadelphia in the 1760's to warrant an examination here. *(Fig. 180)*.

Entitled "Account of Goods Sold of Phil Hulberts," the notebook begins with an entry dated February 17, 1763, indicating that Philip Hulbeart had died by the beginning of 1763. Probably because of an advertisement of the sale of property of "Philip Hulbeart, goldsmith deceased," in May 1764, his death date was hitherto believed to be 1764.

Of the twenty goldsmiths noted in the accounts in addition to Syng and Richardson, most are familiar to students of American silver, but half a dozen have had none of their work identified. Of those whose work is unknown, George Drewry, Samuel and Thomas Alford, and Michael Brothers are listed by Brix because their notices appeared in local newspapers. George Drewry, who purchased chapes and tongues from Hulbeart's estate in February 1763, had "just opened Shop in Walnut street, four Doors below Second-street" when he advertised in the *Pennsylvania Gazette* of March 17, 1763, that he made and sold "all Manner of Gold and Silver Work."[1]

Samuel Alford, who got old gold from Hulbeart's shop, advertised in 1759 as a jeweller and goldsmith, "late of Barbadoes, new in Lombard Street, near the New Market, Philadelphia."[2] On February 25, 1762 Thomas Alford advertised the same crafts and explains he is "late from Mr. Samuel Alford" and has set up business on Front Street between Chestnut and Market Streets.[3] To compensate for the loss of

Thomas's services, Samuel Alford had advertised a week earlier that he wanted "an apprentice that can be well recommended."[4]

Michael Brothers, who bought a parcel of punches from the estate, also advertised for an apprentice in the *Pennsylvania Packet* of December 7, 1772, explaining at the same time that he had "removed from his late dwelling house at the upper end of Second-street, near the Market and next door to Mr. Benjamin Hooten's hatter, where he continues his business" as a gold and silversmith.[5]

Although no advertisements prove that Benjamin Johnson was a goldsmith, his name appears several times in the estate records with accounts of goldsmiths preceeding and immediately following his. Because of the types of objects purchased by the unknown Samuel Roberts, and the location of his accounts among those of other goldsmiths, it is likely he too was a goldsmith, but again there are no advertisements to substantiate this surmise.

The Hulbeart estate accounts help to fill out our scanty information about these little known mid-eighteenth-century Philadelphia goldsmiths, and it would be useful to find Philadelphia silver bearing maker's marks of GD, SA, TA, MB, BI or BJ, and SR.

The spellings of some of the names in the account book raise a few questions. There are several accounts with John Davey as well as an account with John David. No John Davey is known to have been working as a goldsmith in Philadelphia at this time, and it is quite likely all these entries concern John David.

However, there are accounts with Edmund Mills, Edmond Milns, and Millne which are not so easily explained. In addition to Edmund Milne, who was active in Philadelphia from 1757 to 1813, there was an Edmund Mills listed as a goldsmith in the Philadelphia Directory in 1785. Whether this is another misspelling of the same name or whether there was an Edmund Mills working there from 1763 to 1785 is not yet certain.

In order to notify the public of the sale of Hulbeart's shop goods, Joseph Richardson and Philip Syng paid David Hall, publisher of the *Pennsylvania Gazette*, and William Bradford, publisher of the *Pennsylvania Journal*, a total of £0/12/6 for advertising. The notice dated March 17, 1763, reads as follows:

> TO BE SOLD very cheap by Phillip Syng and Joseph Richardson, at their Houses; the Shop Goods of Phillip Hulbert Junior, viz,
> Silver stone Shoe and Knee Buckles, stock Buckles and broaches, stone gold Rings (one a garnet and diamond,) stone gold ear-rings with cyphers, a neat gilt silver whistle and corel with eight bells, English silver chased and pierced Shoe Buckles, and a neat chased Slop Bowl; sundry's Country made viz. a Sugar Dish, Punch Ladle and Strainers, a Caster, a Pair of Salts, Tea Spoons, Shoe and Knee Buckles plain and chased, a neat chased gold Cane Head, gold Rings, Buttons and Ear Wires jointed, a neat gold stone Locket with corel Beads, Tweezar Cases, steel topt silver Thimbels; variety of stone Sleeve Buttons set in silver, stone Jacket ditto; variety of neat Seals, viz. Piramid Crystel with gold Loops,

Tryangle Crystel Block in silver, French horn Pattern with Cornelians, peirced silver shanked Cornelian; steel with silver stamped Shanks, Cornelian and Glass set in silver and brass, sundry Snuff Boxes, Shells with silver tops, and China with pinchbeck rims, plated Boxes sundry sizes, a neat pair of large chased plated Candlesticks, a pair of ditto, China plated table and tea spoons, Spurrs and Shoe Buckles, Tooth pick Cases, variety of paste Ear-rings and Necklaces, temple Spectacles, steel watch Chains, silk strings, and gilt watch Chains, wig Springs, stay pins, Gun hammers, Key springs, nut crackers, cork Screws and horse Pickers, Pinchback and bath mettel Buckels, Money Scales and weights, large Scales with Troy and Averdupois brass Weights, Watch Glasses, steel Chapes and Tongues, Crucibels binding Wire, Borax, Sandiver, etc.[6]

Many purchases made by goldsmiths were for such basic goods as steel chapes and tongues for buckles, and buttons. In addition, however, John Leacock got a dozen small blue pots, nine pairs of plated shoe buckles, five stock buckles, and one waist buckle. William Young got twenty-four gold rings for which he was given three months to pay. Evidently the rings could not be resold as quickly as he hoped, since six months later Young's account was credited with sixteen gold rings, indicating he had returned that number out of the twenty-four. Stephen Reeves got twenty-seven gold rings and four pairs of gold buttons. Joseph Richardson himself got some dirty burnt lace, one ounce of silver filings, four dozen knee chapes and tongues, and some binding wire.

Of the other commodities sold from the estate, many were necessary to the actual working of silver. Saltpeter, sandiver, rotten stone, binding wire, borax, sliding tongs, ingots of old silver—Stephen Reeves got over fifty-eight ounces of these ingots, scales and weights, black melting pots, nests of large crucibles, scorpers, eight block seals, files, a touchstone, silver solder, iron pots, a blow pipe, a parcel of tools, and a parcel of punches.

A few wrought objects were sold, such as the thirteen cream pots and six watch chains John Bayley bought, and the tea tongs, gold lockets, gold buttons, and six old and six new spoons bought by Daniel Dupuy. A pepper caster, a patch box, silver thimbles, teaspoons, stayhooks, smelling bottles in cases, spoon cases, toothpick cases, spectacles, scissor chains, and silver watches were also sold.

A number of interesting items of jewelry are listed in addition to gold rings and lockets, with descriptive adjectives which suggest their appearance: tortoise shell rings, "Dropt Clustered Gold Ear Rings," jet beads, a pair of stone earrings without drops, and "1 Gilt Broach & a Pair of Enameled Buttons."

There were also, even at this early date, several plated items: shoe buckles, a snuff box and tablespoons, and possibly the "1 pair of french Plate Candlesticks @ £2/15/0 the Candlesticks to be Returned if Not Sold within 3 months . . . the Candlesticks are Returned." Other noteworthy items included in the sale were a pair of enameled candlesticks, gun hammers, nutcrackers, corkscrews, key springs, and "English Carved Shoe Buckels."

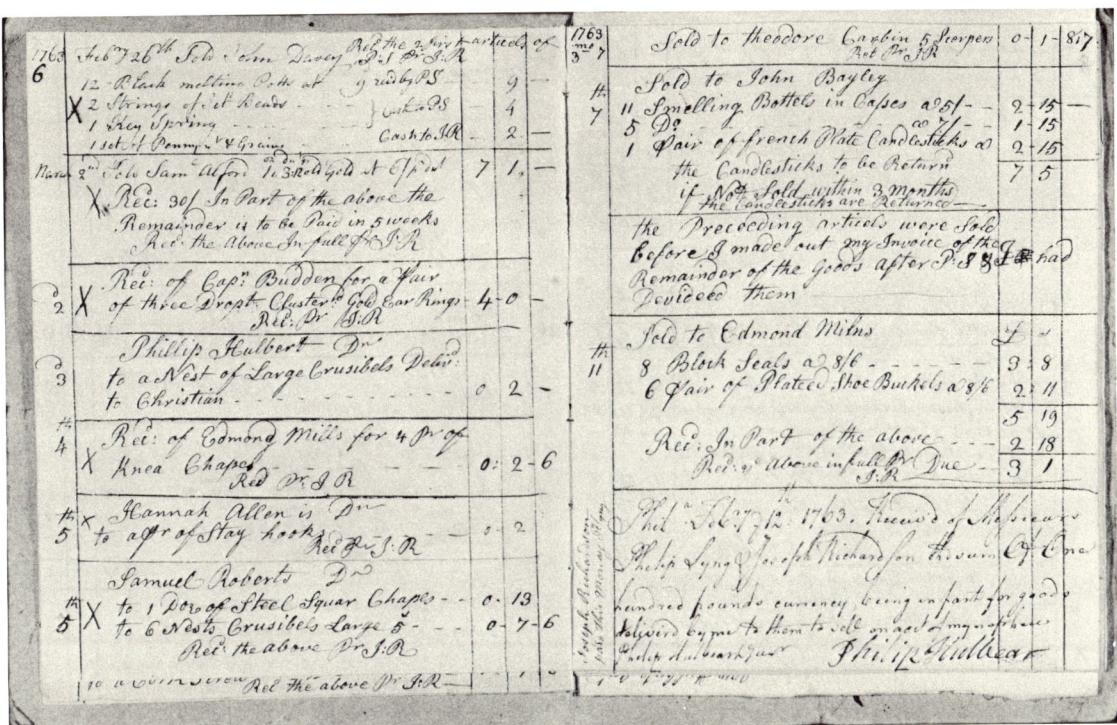

Fig. 180: Page of account book kept by Joseph Richardson, Sr., when settling the estate of Philip Hulbeart, goldsmith, in 1763. *Courtesy of Downs Manuscript and Microfilm Collection, Winterthur Museum; photograph by Gilbert Ask.*

Although the majority of buyers were goldsmiths, some represented allied crafts. John Wood, a well known clockmaker, bought "9 Doz. Brass Watch keys 2 Doz. & 5 Steel Do." "Benjamin Cundee Instrument Maker" got three "Spy Glasses to sell." What is known of Benjamin Condy is found in the advertisement of "Thomas Biggs, Mathematical Instrument Maker, From New York" which appeared in the *Federal Gazette*, September 14, 1792. Biggs explained he had established his business in "the house lately occupied by Mr. Benjamin Condy" who had retired from business, and that he had served his apprenticeship with Condy about fifteen years previously.[7]

Five scorpers were bought by Theodore Carbin, the jeweller working in Philadelphia by 1758, who advertised in 1766 at the "shop lately occupied by Mr. William Ball," and in 1775, as a "well known gold worker, born in Stuttgart, expects to start to Germany in three weeks."[8]

Other purchasers represented all walks of life, and included Richardson's friends like Captain Budden, and relatives like Hannah Lloyd, Hannah Growden, and Hannah Allen. William Hulbeart, brother of the deceased, got a silver seal and numerous buckles, and the goldsmith's uncle, Philip Hulbeart, got "a Nest of Large Crucibels Delivered to Christian."

Many of the objects sold out of the estate are similar to those listed in an advertisement Philip Hulbeart had himself placed in the *Pennsylvania Gazette* on November 5, 1761, as "Just imported from London, and to be sold by Philip Hulbeart, Goldsmith, next door to the "Boatswain and Call, near the Drawbridge." By comparing the list advertised with the items of Joseph's account of the estate, we find the same kinds of buckles and buttons, chapes and tongues, plated tablespoons, etc. In some cases, however, the objects are further described as in the case of "very neat enameled, *Tea* Candlesticks," "*Steel* Nut-cracks," "*French* Paste Necklaces and Earrings," and "*Brass* Blow-pipes."[9]

Additional objects listed in the advertisement but not in the sales of the estate are pumice stone, wig-springs, steel stay-pins, plated spurs, and steel spring spurs. The fact that the items appearing in the advertisement are specified as imported would lead one to assume that the objects which do not appear in the advertisement but which do appear in the estate sales, such as the cream pots, pepper caster, gold lockets, tea tongs, and silver thimbles, might have been of Hulbeart's own manufacture. This assumption is strengthened by the fact that, of the few surviving examples of Philip Hulbeart's work, one is a very ornate cream pot and one is a pair of tea tongs.

The sales from the estate were completed in October 1763, when William Hulbeart put his mark to the following statement:

> Received the 3rd of October 1763 of Joseph Richardson and Philip Syng Two Hundred Forty five Pounds Ten shillings and 8 pence which with Four Hundred Pounds paid my Uncle Philip Hulbert and nineteen Pounds Three Shillings & 5 pence in Goods is in full for Goods put into their Hands to sell by my Uncle Philip Hulbert aforesaid belonging to the Estate of my Brother Philip Hulbert Deceased.

The total of these accounts came to £664/14/1.

The sale of this property was delayed until the spring of 1764, a fact which is explained by Joseph Richardson in his letter to William Hulbeart in England, written on September 10, 1766. He wrote that they had finally finished the sales of the estate and had sent the account and a bill of exchange drawn on Masterman and Archer, London goldsmiths:

> We can assure the that we have done the best we Could for thy Interest but the Scarcity of Money amongst us has been the Reason of its Selling at so Low a Price, we waited in hopes that Leonard Warnts would have Purchased the Ground Rent at Private Sale but found he was not able to Pay for it unless we would sell it much below the Value. Wherefore we thought it best to Sell it at Public Vendue at the Coffee House which we did for £58 as the will find by the account.[10]

APPENDIX C

Scales and Weights Sold by Joseph Richardson

JOSEPH RICHARDSON sold large numbers of scales and weights which he imported from London. On October 18, 1759, he ordered from Daniel Mildred in London "1 Doz. Pair of Gold Scales & weights in Shagreen Cases" (see pp. 68–70).[1] On November 4, 1769, he wrote to John Masterman in London for "6 Doz. Pair Gold Scales & weights 9 dwt. to 1/2 dwt. & a Set of Grains in Shagreen Cases the Penneyweights I would have about 1 grain over weight that I may Regulate them myself. The Scale Beams Should be well Oiled and wrapt in Oil Paper to Prevent there Rusting". His next letter changed this order so that, of the six dozen pair, only two would be in shagreen cases, the others in wooden boxes. This order to Masterman was repeated October 11, 1770 with an additional order for "3 Doz. Do in Shagreen Cases with weights as above – 3 Nests of Troy weights 32 oz in a Nest one of then (sic) Regulated to the Greatest Exactness agreeable to the Standard of England."

Evidently when this order was received, Joseph was not entirely satisfied. He wrote to Masterman again on May 1, 1771 that they had "come safe though not altogether agreable to my mind as the greatest part of the scales are very ordinary . . . ." Perhaps this is why his next letter was to Thomas Wagstaffe asking for more sets of scales and weights:

> I have herein Inclosed a Bill of Lading for a piece of Gold weighing 7 oz. 5 dwt. 8 gr. for which I desire the favour of thee to send me a parcel of money scales one half to be 6 inch & the other half 7 inch Beams & weights from 9 dwt to 1/2 dwt & a set of Grains to each pair of wainscot boxes which I think was the size of the last the shipt me & were Charged @ £ 0/38/0 per doz. I would have them full as good as the last the sent me [no previous order to Wagstaffe for scales and weights is recorded in his Letter Book] & request that they may be well Oiled to prevent their Rusting for want of which many of the former came in a very Rusty

condition whatever the extraordinary Expence may be I shall Chearfully Pay. The pennyweights I would have one Grain over weight I should be pleased to have one Doz. Pair of scales of a better sort & of 2 or 3 Different prises which may serve as a sample for the future please to send them per the first Oppertunity as I much want them & I shall be much Obliged to thee....

His next letter, dated October 14, 1771, excuses John Masterman for the unsatisfactory scales, saying that he did "Suppose thee never saw the scales & weights thee sent me but trusted to the workman as is common in such Cases therefore do not complain of thy conduct therein...."

Wagstaffe's scales suited him much better. On October 16, 1771, Joseph wrote him, "Parcel of Scales & weights which came in good Order & to Satisfaction except the Weights which are most of them too light. I have now sent Some Weights & Desire for the future they may be made Exactly of the same Weight If they are 1/20 of a Grain Lighter they will not Suit." At the same time he ordered additional scales and weights:

20 pair of Scales with Box end Beams
6 Inch & 3/4 Beam in Mahogany Cases
 with a 9 dwt. a 6 dwt. a 5 dwt. a 3 dwt. a 2 dwt. a 1 dwt. & 1/2 dwt.
 & a Sett of Grains to each pair
20 Pair Scales in Black Shagreen Casses
1 Doz. Neat Small Pocket Scales in Shagreen
 Cases the Beam Not to exceed 3 Inches with
 the following weights a 5 dwt. a 4 dwt. a 3 dwt. a 2 dwt. a 1 dwt. & 1/2 & a
 Sett of Grains to each pair.

Not until November 5, 1774 did Joseph acknowledge receipt of the order. He received six dozen pairs of scales and weights instead of the 4 1/3 dozen specified in his letter.

On a small folded sheet found in Joseph's letter book are notations of the sale of scales indicating their price:

Sold 3 pair of Scales & 1 Nest of Crucibles — £1/17/6
Sold 2 pair of Scales — 1/4/0
Sold 3 pair of Scales — 1/16/0
Sold 3 pair of Scales — 1/16/0 (DMMC,53.165.95b).

In the *Pennsylvania Gazette* of September 13, 1770, the following advertisement appeared, "To be SOLD by JOSEPH RICHARDSON, Goldsmith, A Parcel of Money Scales & Weights." Before selling these boxes, Joseph had one of the local printers make up labels to go inside the lid: "A TABLE of the VALUE and WEIGHT of COINS, as they now pass in PENNSYLVANIA." This gives the type of coins generally in use in Philadelphia about 1770.

ENGLISH Guineas	£1/14/0	5 dwt. 6 gr.
French Guineas,	1/13/6	5 5
Moydores,	2/ 3/6	6 18

Johannes's	6/ 0/0	18	0
Half Johannes's	3/ 0/0	9	0
French Pistoles,	1/ 6/6	4	4
4 *Spanish* Pistole Pieces,	5/ 8/0	17	0
2 *Spanish* Pistole Pieces,	2/14/0	8	12
1 *Spanish* Pistole,	1/ 7/0	4	6
Half a *Spanish* Pistole,	0/13/6	2	3
Carolines,	1/14/0	6	5
Spanish Pieces of Eight,	0/ 7/6	17	6.

At the bottom of the label was the advertisement "Gold Scales and Weights, Sold by Joseph Richardson, Goldsmith, in Philadelphia."

A number of boxes with currency tables survive today. Two at the Winterthur Museum are of white oak (called wainscot) with cotter-pin hinged lids and simple hook and eye latches. The boxes are 7 3/16 inches long, 3 1/4 inches wide, and 1 3/8 inch high. Both are dated 1774. One box is without the scales which originally would have been kept in it, and is painted dark green. In the top of the lid are two incised hearts and the brass hook is cut in Germanic scrolls, suggesting that its owner was one of the many Pennsylvania Germans who lived in the area. The other box *(Fig. 30)* has its scales, which are made of steel, with arms 5 1/2 inches in length, and pans 2 1/4 inches in diameter. In the box are a number of pennyweights and grain weights, some of which appear to be original. The label of the latter box is interesting as the value and weights of Carolines had been changed to £ 1/10/0 and 6 dwt. 6 gr. and ducats had been added at a value of fourteen shillings and an illegible weight.

Another labeled box, owned by the Arch Street Historical Society, and now on loan to the Atwater Kent Museum in Philadelphia, is interesting because the name of its original owner, Miers Fisher, is branded on the front side of the box. The name "T. Parry" appears on another box of scales labeled by Richardson now in a private collection. A similarly labeled box is at Old Deerfield, Massachusetts, and is thought to have been owned by John Russell, a goldsmith who served his apprenticeship with Isaac Parker, the first to practice this craft in Deerfield. Another interesting example is at the Philadelphia Museum of Art *(Fig. 31)*. The four brass weights in this set are marked with a lion passant in a shaped cartouche, a mark which was used on London silver from 1751–52 through 1755–56.

Perhaps some of the imported boxes of scales were among the large number of scales Joseph had on hand at the time of his death in 1784. "133 pair of Scales in boxes with weights 5 pair of plate Scales 10 setts ounce weights 62 setts pennyweights & 102 setts grains" were valued at £75. Elsewhere are listed "7 small scale beams." (Will No. 344, Phila. Co. Court House.)

APPENDIX D

Letter Book of Joseph Richardson

In the period before the War of Independence, John David, William Ball, Daniel Dupuy, Philip Hulbeart, John Leacock, and Edmund Milne were among the Philadelphia goldsmiths who advertised silver plate imported from London. Perhaps the longest advertisement of such goods was Edmund Milne's, which appeared in the *Pennsylvania Journal* for December 15, 1763. The enormous listing of goods which he offered for sale gives an excellent picture of the types of wares imported, from coffeepots, teapots, cans, waiters, sauceboats, and flatware to small items such as buckles, chains, all kinds of jewelry, clocks and watches, and sword hilts.[1]

Milne's advertisement also indicates the quantities of plate actually imported. Silver plate exported from England to colonial America gradually increased from £1,500 worth in 1740 to £2,766 in 1746. The years of greatest importation were 1760 and 1761, with just over £4,700 worth of plate imported in each year, and 1764, when £3,996 worth was imported.[2] These statistics are corroborated by Joseph Richardson's Letter Book, which indicates that the years of his greatest importation were between 1759 and 1762. Both sources reveal a noticeable drop in 1766, when only £949 worth of plate was sent from England to the American Colonies. (This drop undoubtedly resulted from the Stamp Act and the subsequent Non-importation Agreement proclaimed by colonial importers.) Within a few years, however, importation had revived, and by 1770 Richardson was again placing large orders in London.

The adjectives Richardson used to describe the types of goods he wanted reflect the changes in styles and in terminology. His Letter Book includes information about tools which sometimes were unavailable in America, some general statements concerning the state of the goldsmith's business in Philadelphia, a few letters dealing with purely personal matters, and even a few references to the political climate on the eve of the Revolution.

Within an 8" x 13" marbleized paper cover are 59 pages of writing, much of it in Joseph Richardson's hand *(Fig. 181)*, and some presumably written by an apprentice or helper. The correspondence, covering the period 1758–74, begins and ends with copies of letters to Thomas Wagstaffe, a Quaker clockmaker working in London from about 1756 to 1793, for a brief time at Carey Lane, and then at 33 Gracechurch Street.[3]

In his first letter to Wagstaffe, Joseph requested the prices of eight-day clocks, but subsequent orders for such clocks do not appear in the Letter Book. Wagstaffe's clocks and watches were imported in the eighteenth century to New England and Maryland, but particularly to Philadelphia, where the Londoner's clock works were often housed in cases made by Philadelphia cabinetmakers, such as the one at the Winterthur Museum labeled by William Connell.[4] In 1764 Wagstaffe sent as a gift a spring dial wall clock to the Pennsylvania Hospital in Philadelphia as a token of "The Regard I bear the Province of Pennsylvania, Respect to the City of Philadelphia in particular and Esteem for its Inhabitants," and as an acknowledgment of "The Distinguishing marks of the Favours I have received from them . . ."[5] The clock still hangs in the library of the Pennsylvania Hospital.

Although Wagstaffe was not a silversmith himself, he supplied colonists with plate.[6] In his first letter to Wagstaffe, Joseph requested him to get the silver ordered from the London goldsmith, George Ritherdon; Richardson sent the same order to Ritherdon, requesting him to deliver the goods to Wagstaffe. Only one other order for plate from Wagstaffe appears in the Richardson letters: a 1760 request for two dozen punch ladles and two dozen lemon strainers. For the most part, Joseph ordered from Wagstaffe watches and tools such as flatting mills, dies, punches, scales, and weights. Detailed descriptions of these tools by Richardson provide a good picture of their actual appearance (see pp. 232, 234, 239–40, 244, 254–59).

The silver watches from Wagstaffe varied from ordinary kinds costing 55 shillings, to £3 watches and "good" watches costing £5 or 5 guineas, some of which had enameled faces. Similar watches were also ordered from George Ritherdon and Daniel Mildred (one of which cost between 6 and 7 guineas). In one order to Wagstaffe, Joseph requested that the watches "be Set to time before they are Shipt."

For a time Richardson asked Wagstaffe to contact George Ritherdon concerning silver orders, but soon he was addressing Ritherdon directly at "two doors without Aldgate." Evidently Ritherdon had made a trip to Philadelphia to sell some of his wares, for Joseph remarked in 1758, "when thee was at this City Some Years ago I Bought Some milk Ewers & other Plate. . . ."

Ritherdon was apprenticed to William Winne in 1743, received his Freedom by Service in March 1750, and was elected to the Livery in April 1758.[7] Sir Ambrose Heal lists "William Winn" as a goldsmith near Aldgate in 1744.[8] However, Ritherdon is not listed in Jackson's book on *English Goldsmiths and Their Marks*, (London, 1921); no mark is given for him, nor is any silver by him known.[9] Britten's *Old Clocks*

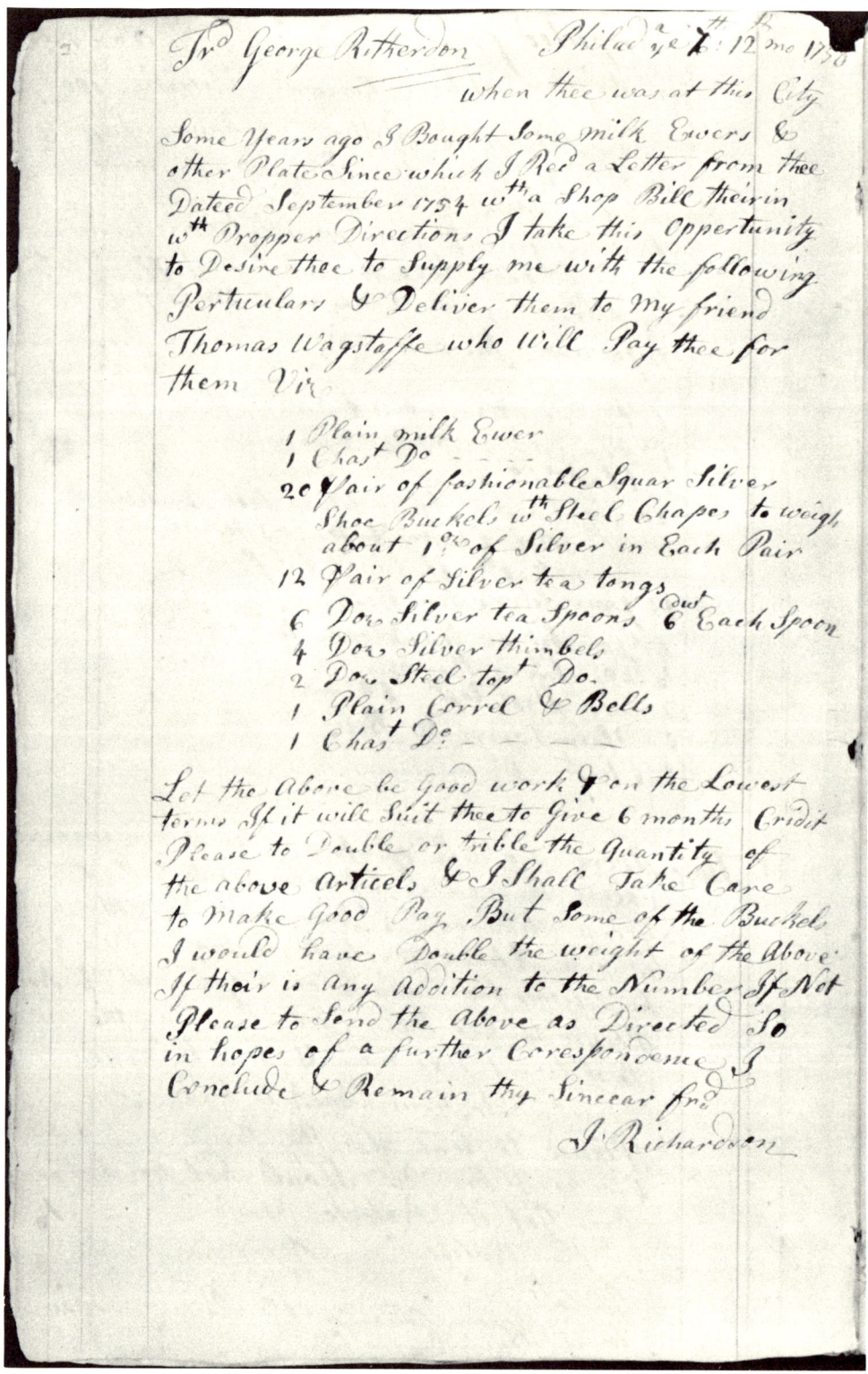

Fig. 181: Page from Joseph Richardson's letter book with first order for silver from George Ritherdon of London, dated the 7th of the 12th month 1758. *Courtesy of Downs Manuscript and Microfilm Collection, Winterthur Museum; photograph by Gilbert Ask.*

and Watches and Their Makers, (New York, 1956), however, lists George Ritherdon at Aldgate between 1753 and 1783.¹⁰

When Ritherdon completed his apprenticeship, he worked at the Sign of the Ship two doors without Aldgate,¹¹ indicating that Ritherdon might have shipped a fair amount of silver. This assumption is supported by the fact that Ritherdon evidently took the initiative in encouraging business dealings with Joseph Richardson, who reminded him that "I Received a Letter from thee Dated September 1754 with a Shop Bill theirin with Propper Directions."

In 1763 Richardson concluded his business with Ritherdon and called for a balancing of their account. During the five years 1758–1763 of their dealings, he had purchased watches and a variety of silver plate including tea services, spoons, salts, casters, corals and bells, thimbles, buckles, chains, pencil cases, and memorandum books.

Between 1759 and 1763 Richardson ordered larger quantities of silver and a greater variety of objects from the firm of Mildred and Roberts. These included pincushion hoops, buttons, chapes and tongues, watch pendants, beads, coral, strainers, snuff boxes, coffeepots, and instrument cases. Joseph had been given the name of the firm of Daniel Mildred by his brother Frank. (Although the first nine letters Joseph wrote are addressed to Daniel Mildred, the remaining four, from July 20, 1761, are addressed to Mildred and Roberts.)

Daniel Mildred's firm was known to many Philadelphians. Unlike Ritherdon, Mildred was not a goldsmith or watchmaker, but a supplier of many different sorts of goods.¹² The goods supplied to Joseph by this firm in greatest quantity were buckles. He ordered both shoe buckles and knee buckles from them, some with chapes and tongues of steel, a very few of silver, and some with no chapes and tongues at all. Some of the buckles were carved, some pierced, some square, and some rounded. At first the shoe buckles were to weigh 15 pennyweight a pair, but two years later the specified weights had risen to 50 or 60 pennyweight a pair. This same firm also supplied large quantities of steel chapes and tongues in various sizes which Joseph Richardson presumably used to replace broken and worn ones and to fashion new buckles.

In ordering plate from England, Joseph tried to find the best bargains. He advised Mildred to get the plate from workmen from whom it could be obtained "at a much Cheaper Rate then from the Sale Shops." On September 28, 1759, when he wrote Mildred that he had received a shipment of plate which he thought high-priced, he also wrote for the first time to How & Masterman whose shop bills he had found in the packages with the plate.¹³ It is likely that, by writing directly to How & Masterman, he hoped to avoid Mildred's mark-up.

Joseph's business dealings with How & Masterman were successful and friendly. He wrote more than twice as many letters (of the 84 letters recorded in his book) to them, as to Thomas Wagstaffe, his next most important correspondent. How & Masterman are the only persons he addressed as "Goldsmith."¹⁴ However, Sir

Charles Jackson does not include them in his large volume on English goldsmiths, nor is there any record of them at Goldsmiths' Hall,[15] and no examples of their work are known today.[16] During the course of Richardson's correspondence with this company, various partners moved in and out of the firm. Joseph addressed Thomas How and John Masterman between 1759 and 1763; How, Masterman, and Archer in 1763; Masterman and Archer in 1765; and Masterman alone between 1769 and 1772.

It is possible that How & Masterman, like Wagstaffe, were Quakers. Frederick Tolles points out that "the merchants in London with whom the Philadelphia Friends had business dealings were almost exclusively Quakers; they included some of the greatest traders in the metropolis. . . ."[17] Mention of the prominent Quaker, John Woolman, in Richardson's correspondence with How & Masterman lends support to this theory.

Richardson's letters to How & Masterman display a unique trust and friendship. He refers several times to gifts they exchanged and to favors they asked of each other. Reflections upon the times or upon political conditions were generally noted in Richardson's letters to Masterman. In 1769, for instance, he spoke of the precarious times, and advised Masterman "to be causious who thee trusts on this Side the water," no doubt declining to say more for fear of being imprudent and giving offense.

During the twelve and a half years that Joseph did business with the Masterman firm, he bought large quantities of silver, some scales and weights, and some crucibles which were to be Holland or German (the English ones, he said, were not as good). Many of the silver forms ordered from Masterman were the same as those ordered from Mildred, Wagstaffe, and Ritherdon, but after 1763 requests for plate went exclusively to Masterman. Richardson did, however, order from both Mildred and Masterman a shagreen case containing six teaspoons, a strainer, and a pair of tea tongs. It is possible that Joseph gave his wife Mary one of these tea sets because in her will she bequeathed to their son Joseph, Jr. "a Silver Tea Pott Six teaspoons a pair tea tongs and Strainer in Shagreen Case . . ."[18]

Joseph's Letter Book indicates that he ordered several kinds of objects exclusively from Masterman. These included spurs (both silver and plated), caster frames with sets of chased or plain double-bellied casters, and ground-glass cruets with silver tops, pocketbook clasps, polished pint cans, slop bowls, and temple spectacles set in silver with green fish-skin cases mounted with silver.

Joseph's correspondence with Masterman ends rather abruptly in 1772, probably because of the increasing difficulty of trade with England immediately before the war. It was not long, however, before his sons renewed the correspondence, and the first letter recorded in their Letter Book was sent to John Masterman on December 17, 1777.[19] On April 15, 1783 they wrote Masterman, "We also take notice of thy Sons connextion with thee in the Business and hope that friendship which has so long subsisted between his Father & ours will be preserved between Us—Father Joins in tenders of Real love with thy Assured Friends INR." Later in the same year

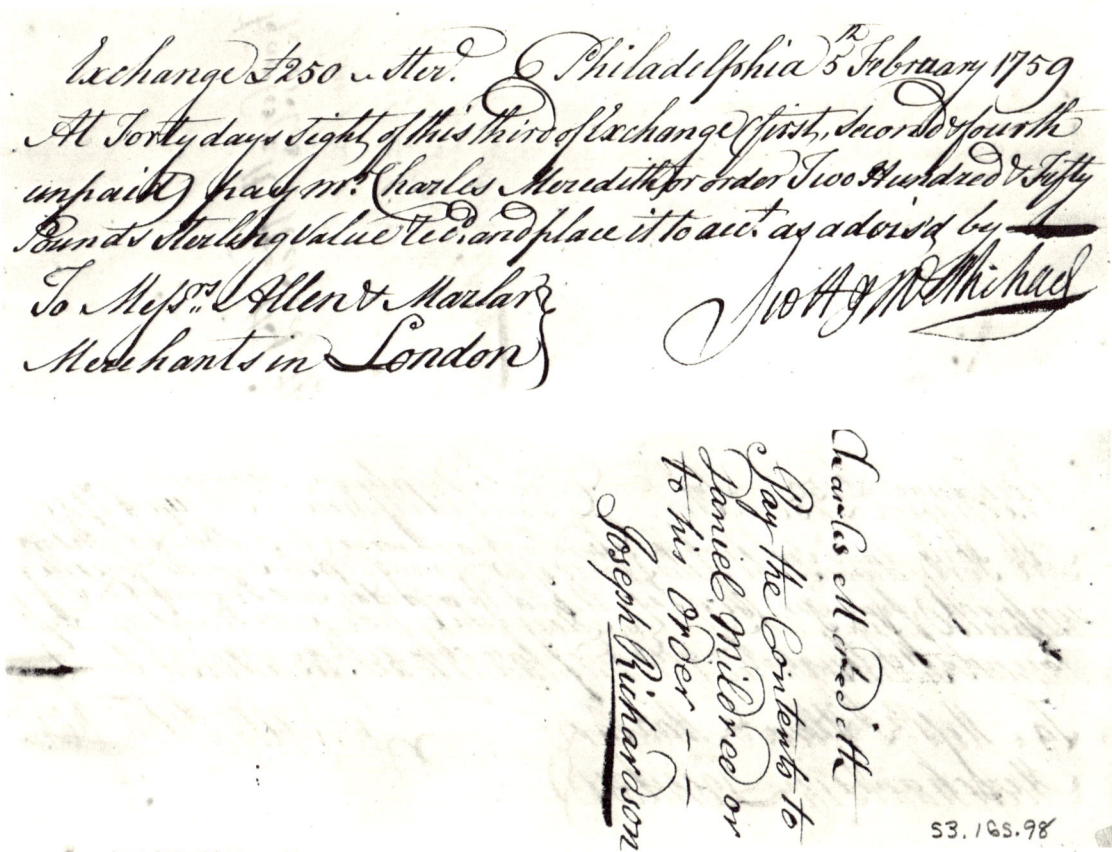

Fig. 182: Bill of exchange, obverse and reverse, for £ 250, dated February 5, 1759, which Joseph Richardson authorized Charles Meredith to pay to Daniel Mildred in London. *Courtesy of Downs Manuscript and Microfilm Collection, Winterthur Museum.*

they said in closing, "Father desires to be kindly remembered to his much valued friend Correspondant."

In addition to supplying plate, these London goldsmiths and clock and watchmakers supplied Joseph Richardson with another very important service; they accepted as payment for their wares, miscellaneous batches of silver, including the sweepings of the shop. These they had assayed and redeemed for Joseph. This service was much needed because there was no assay office or guild hall in America to provide it. Joseph mentioned this problem in a letter to George Ritherdon on November 25, 1761, when he explained that he had "No Convenient apparatus for Refineing."[20]

Both coarse gold and coarse silver, as Joseph called the unrefined metals, were sent abroad to be assayed and went at various times to all the men with whom Joseph dealt. He had to trust them to take all the metal to the assayer, and to give him an accurate account of the findings. The Letter Book indicates that Joseph was somewhat defensive in these matters, and in some instances asked that the assayer's report be sent directly to him. Occasionally Joseph tried to make an assay himself:

"the Gold herewith Sent is but 3/4 of a Carret Grain worse then Standard According to an Assay which I have made off it . . ."

The most revealing letters concerning the assaying of metals are those written in 1763 and 1764. In one letter to How, Masterman & Archer, Richardson agrees with their definition respecting the difference of the fineness of Spanish gold. However, he maintains that the doubloons he sent were not irregular, as they had suggested in their letter to him. Joseph attributes the difference in the evaluations to a possible mistake by the assay master or his employees.

In ordering goods from England, Joseph sometimes included patterns in an effort to clarify what he desired. When ordering steel chapes and tongues for silver buckles from Daniel Mildred in 1759, Joseph asked that they be "Agreable to the Patterns herewith Sent." Unfortunately, however, none of these pattern designs were duplicated in the Letter Book.

Patterns were also sent to Joseph from England to show him what designs were available. In 1759 Joseph wrote both Mildred and Ritherdon requesting numbered and noted buckle patterns made of pewter so that he could choose the designs he might want in the future. The Letter Book does not indicate whether these patterns were ever sent, but it is likely that Mildred substituted printed patterns for the more cumbersome pewter patterns, for, in ordering chapes and tongues in 1762 from Mildred, Joseph indicated the desired sizes by referring to print numbers. Such patterns became more commonplace after large-scale manufacturing got under way at Birmingham and Sheffield, but pattern books or single sheets used in America before the last quarter of the eighteenth century are rarely found today.

Despite the existing records of silver shipped from these London silversmiths, not a single piece bearing their marks has been found either here or in England, and the very good records of silver which have passed through the shop of the J. E. Caldwell Co. in Philadelphia yield no evidence of their work. Since the records at Goldsmiths' Hall indicate that none of these men was ever charged with improperly marking export plate we can only conclude that these men had large establishments, and that their employees might have put their own touchmarks on the silver.

The coffeepot *(Fig. 35a)* owned by Richardson's relatives, the Growdens, was made by John Swift in London in 1753–54. In an exhibition of old silver held in Philadelphia in 1937 under the auspices of the Pennsylvania Society of the Colonial Dames, a number of pieces, bearing London hallmarks and dating from the third quarter of the eighteenth century, had histories of early ownership in Philadelphia. None, however, was the work of any of the men mentioned in Richardson's Letter Book.

In an earlier exhibition of old silver at the Pennsylvania Museum in 1917, a covered bowl was exhibited and described in the catalogue as having a pear-shaped body, a splayed base, and an inscription on the lid, *Hannah Allen to her neice Mary Richardson 1765.* (Hannah Allen was an unmarried sister of Joseph Richardson's wife.) The importance of this piece is explained by the catalogue notation that the piece is English, hallmarked 1759, a year in which Joseph Richardson is known to have been importing silver from England.[21] At that time the sugar bowl was owned by Miss Juliana Wood, a Richardson descendant, and great-aunt of the present owner. When, however, the present owner took her bowl to Stephen G. C. Ensko to have the hallmarks identified, she learned that her bowl is of modern manufacture and possibly a replica of the bowl exhibited in 1917, the present location of which is unknown. Suitable to Quaker tastes, the sugar bowl has a plain round body, is supported by a domed base, and has a domed reel-type lid. It is free of superficial ornamentation other than a few circular scribings around the foot, at the mouth of the bowl, and at the edge of the lid. The inscription on the lid is verified by Hannah Allen's will, posted July 26, 2765, in which she bequeathes to her niece, Mary Richardson, the ground rent of the lot on Spruce Street granted to Robert Lowry, as well as a silver sugar dish.[22]

Another piece of silver which might have had a bearing on the subject of English silver imported by Richardson is a cream pitcher illustrated and described by Bigelow in *Historic Silver of the Colonies*.[23] This pitcher, the location of which is unknown today, was owned by Marsden Perry in 1917 and was described as being helmet-shaped, made by Joseph Richardson, but bearing the London dateletter for 1750–51. The pitcher is so unlike the known work of Joseph Richardson as to discredit the attribution.

An American goldsmith could order and receive English silver within a year. It took from six weeks to two months for a letter written in Philadelphia to reach its destination in London, and several more months before the order was filled and sent to Philadelphia. But frequently there were delays, and occasionally a shipment never arrived. Such was the case in 1760 when Joseph wrote to Daniel Mildred "find thee had Shipt Per Captain House a Parcel of Plate to the Amount of £260/14/0 who is taken by the french." This letter is dated June 6. Several months earlier, on February 28, 1760, the *Pennsylvania Journal* had reported:

> Monday last arrived the Ship Friendship, Captain M'Clelland from London, but brings nothing more than we had by the Packet. The Snow Julian, Captain House for this Port was to Sail soon after him.

Because of such miscarriages, Richardson usually asked the London men to insure the goods they were sending. In ordering the ill-fated goods from Daniel Mildred in 1759, Joseph had specified "whatever thee Ships on My Account I would have thee Make full Insurance theiron." When he learned his shipment was on board the *Julian*, he placed another order with Mildred and said he hoped that "the Money in thy hands when the Insurance made House is Paid will very Near Pay for them." Evidently a shipment from George Ritherdon was also on the *Julian*, for Richardson wrote Ritherdon, "we have a Certain Account that Captain House is taken by a French Priveter & Carried into a french Port in the west Indias Therefore Desire thee to Recover the money Insured on her & Reship the Same Artikels."[24] Joseph Richardson noted a further loss in a later letter to Mildred & Roberts in 1763 concerning the settling of their account:

I have no objection to Your Accounts Except that of Daniel Mildreds in the Year 1760 wherein I am charged with Commissions on Settleing the Loss Per the Julianna However I Shall Submit it to You.

In addition to insurance, there was a duty of sixpence per troy ounce on silver wrought in Great Britain for export. This duty was paid by the maker, who was repaid when the merchandise was exported to foreign countries "provided," Rolt's *Dictionary* (London, 1761) explains, "sufficient security be given to the collector of the port before shipping, that it shall not be relanded in Great Britain." This drawback, which was intended to promote trade, was formalized by a debenture or certificate issued by the proper officer at the Custom House. Rolt explains:

> When a ship is regularly cleared out, and discharged, according to the manner described . . . and actually sailed out of the port on her intended voyage, debentures may be made out from the exporter's entries, in order to obtain the drawbacks, allowances, bounties, or premiums, that are due on the exportation of any goods on board; which debentures for foreign goods are to be paid within one month after demand.

Such particulars about the methods of business transactions in the eighteenth century clarify many passages in Richardson's Letter Book. In his first letter to Daniel Mildred in 1759, Joseph says that since there is a large duty on silverware he hopes Mildred will get the usual drawback on all plate exported. In a letter to Ritherdon in 1760, he said:

> . . . am Informed by him [i.e., the captain of the ship] that You Differed about the Price of the freight that he Required 2 Per Cent on the Value of the Plat which I think an Extraordinary Price & would by No Means Incourage Such a Custom I would Not Run any Risque In Saveing the Expence at the Custom House but would Chuse to Pay it for the future.

There was also a reduction in insurance premiums when ships traveled together, for Joseph continues, "I am Informed that [Captain] Buden Came out with american Convoy & So Expect a Return of Premeum Accordingly." In another letter to Mildred in 1759, he notes specifically the amount of refund in acknowledging the receipt of a bill of lading for "a Parcell of Plate amounting to £239/2/11 after the Deduction of 3 Guineas per cent for American Convoy."

Payments were made by Richardson to the London firms in the form of a bill of exchange. Among the Richardson papers at Winterthur is a packet of bills of exchange dated 1758–60. One of these *(Fig. 182)* was addressed by Joseph Richardson to Charles Meredith with the instruction to "Pay the Contents to Daniel Mildred or to his Order." This bill of exchange was for £250, and was dated the 5th of February 1759. Richardson pointed out to George Ritherdon in December 1760:

> Bills of Exchange are at Present 15 Per cent higher then they were Some time Past Or I Should have Sent A Bill by this Oppertunity but Expect they will be Lower Soon & Intend to Imbrace the first oppertunity to make Remittance to Pay for the following Order.

On a number of occasions Richardson mentions that a bill was protested. (Rolt explained in 1761 that a protest "in commerce, is a summons made by a notary-public to a merchant, banker, or the like, to accept or discharge a bill of exchange drawn on him, after his having refused to accept or pay the same.")

Business dealings with foreign firms were not simple, and the time and patience required are evidenced in Joseph Richardson's Letter Book. He frequently notes that copies of the same letter were sent by another ship so that if one failed to reach London, the other would not be long in arriving. It is fortunate that Richardson's own copies of his letters survive today to provide an unparalleled picture of silver plate importation to the American colonies in the mid-eighteenth century. So important and fascinating are these letters that they are transcribed here in full, with as few editorial notes as possible.

Philadelphia the 7th 12th mo. 1758

Respected friend Thomas Wagstafe

I have herewith Inclosed 100 Pounds Sterling Bill of Exchange Payable to thee which when Received Please to Pay 50 Pounds to Elias Bland Merchent in London whome I shall Desire to Call for it. For the Remainder I would have thee to Send per first oppertunity the following Perticulars & make full Insurance theiron Viz

- 6 Silver watches at 3£ Each
- 1 Plain Silver milk Ewer
- 1 Chast Do.
- 20 Pair Carved Squar Silver Shoe Buckels with Steel chapes & tongues to weigh about 1 oz. of Silver Per pair
- 12 Pair Silver tea tongs
- 6 Doz. Silver tea Spoons to weigh about 6 dwt. Each
- 4 Doz. Silver thimbels
- 2 Doz. Steel topt Do.
- 1 Plain Corell & Bells [rattles]
- 1 Chast Do.

The Above Articels of Silver ware Except the watches I Desire thee to Gett from George Ritherdon 2 Doors without Aldgate whome I have wrote to to Supply them if he follows the Business of a Goldsmith. If Not Please to Get them Elswhare on the Best terms thee Can & Send the Letter Directed to him Back to me Again. Please to Send also the Pricees of 8 Day Clocks. If the Bill Should Not be Duly Paid Get it Protested & Send it Back with the Protest.

from thy friend Joseph Richardson

Direct to me for Joseph Richardson Goldsmith in Philadelphia

Philadelphia the 7th 12th mo. 1758

Friend George Ritherdon

When thee was at this City Some Years ago I bought Some milk Ewers & other Plate Since which I Received a Letter from thee Dateed September 1754 with a Shop Bill theirin with Propper Dircctions. I take this Oppertunity to Desire thee to Supply me with the following Perticulars & Deliver them to my friend Thomas Wagstaffe who Will Pay thee for them Viz

- 1 Plain milk Ewer
- 1 Chast Do.
- 20 Pair of fashionable Squar Silver Shoe Buckels with Steel Chapes to weigh about 1 oz. of Silver in Each Pair
- 12 Pair of Silver tea tongs
- 6 Doz. Silver tea Spoons 6 dwt. Each Spoon
- 4 Doz. Silver thimbels
- 2 Doz. Steel topt Do.
- 1 Plain Correl & Bells
- 1 Chast. Do.

Let the Above be Good work & on the Lowest terms. If it will Suit thee to Give 6 months Cridit Please to Double or trible the Quantity of the above Articels & I Shall take Care to Make Good Pay But Some of the Buckels I would have Double the weight of the Above If their is Any Addition to the Number. If Not Please to Send the Above as Directed. So in hopes of a further Corespondence I Conclude & Remain thy Sincear friend.

Joseph Richardson

Philadelphia the 7th 12th mo. 1758

Friend Elias Bland

I have Desired Thomas Wagstaffe Clock maker at the Ship & Crown the Corner of Nags head Couit In Grace Church street to Pay thee 50 Pounds Sterling on my Account which I Desire thee would Call for in about 40 Days Sight hereof when I Expect he will have Received the Money for the Bills I sent him. If theire is Any More Due to thee Please to Send thy Account & I Shall take Care to Ballence it though I think I have Not been well Used in Severel Perticulars Especily the China for which I sent the Cash Came So high Charged that other People that Bought on Cridit Could Sell theirs at 20 Per Cent more then I Could Gett for mine So that I Expect to be a Looser by them & the Crystol Buttons thee Sent Me one half of them was Glass which I Sold at 1/3 Less then the others wherefore I Expect thee will make an abatement in thy Account And Conclude & Remain thy Sincear friend

Joseph Richardson

Philadelphia the 1st 2nd mo. 1759

Respected friend Daniel Mildred

    Being Recommended to thee by my Brother Francis Richardson who Intends Shortly to Corespond with thee I take the freedom to Send the Incloased Bill of two Hundred & fifty Pounds Sterling with an Invoice for the following Silver ware which I Desire the[e] would take Some Care to Get on the best terms and Good Work and I Shall be willing to Satisfy thee for thy trouble. They May be had of the Workmen at a much Cheaper Rate then from the Sale Shops & as their is a Large Duty theiron I hope thee will Get the Usual Drawback upon all Plate Exported. Please to Ship them per first oppertunity And Make full Insurance theiron. So Not Douting thy Care herein I Conclude & Remain thy Sincear friend

                                          Joseph Richardson

Direct to me for Joseph Richardson Goldsmith at Philadelphia Sent Coppy of this By Bolitho who Sailed the 12th 2nd mo. 1759.

Invoice of Silver Plate etc.

20 Pair of Silver Carved Shoe Buckels the Newest fashion with Steel Chapes & tongues to weigh 15 dwt. of Silver Each Pair
30 Pair of Do. to weigh about 1 ounce of Silver Each Pair
20 Pair of Do. to weigh about 1 oz. 5 dwt. of Silver Each Pair
20 Pair of Do. to weigh about 1 oz. 10 dwt. of Silver Each Pair
20 Pair of Do. with Silver Chapes & tongues to weigh 2 oz. 10 dwt. Each Pair
20 Pair of Small Knea Buckels with Steel Chapes & tongues
 1 Plain Silver tea Pot & Stand about 22 oz. weight
 1 Chast Do. with Stand about 20 oz. weight
12 Plain Cream Pots about 3 oz. 10 dwt. Each
12 Chast Do. to weigh about 3 oz. 10 dwt. Each
12 Pair of Double Joynted Silver tea tongs
12 Pair of Single Joynted Do.
 3 Silver Pepper & 3 Mustard Casters
 1 Pair of Plain Silver Salts with Shovels
 2 Pair of Chast Do. with Glass Linings & Shovels
 6 Doz. of Silver tea Spoons to weigh about 7 dwt. a Peice
 6 Doz. of Do. to weigh about 6 dwt. a Peice
 6 Doz. of Do. to weigh about 5 dwt. a Peice
 6 Doz. of Do. to weigh about 4 dwt. a Peice
 6 Plain Correll & Bells 8 Bell to Each
 6 Chast Do. with 8 Bells to Each
 6 Silver Womans watch Chains Plain & Neat
 1 Doz. of Mens Silver watch Chains with 3 Rows or Strands

1 Doz. of Do. with 2 Strans or Rows
1 Doz. of womans Sciser Chains 13 inches Long the Same Sort of Chain as Pattern
1 Doz. of Pincushen hoops & Chains the Same Sort of Chains
6 Doz. Silver thimbels Sorted Sizes
6 Doz. of Steel topt Do.
6 Cards of Crystol Buttons Set in Silver
6 Cards of Do. with Cyphers
6 Cards of Small Crystol Buttons for Children
50 Doz. of Steel Chapes & tongues for Silver Buckels Agreable to the Patterns herewith Sent 10 Doz. of Each Siz
6 Doz. of Small Knea Do.

Philadelphia the 19th 6th mo. 1759

Daniel Mildred Esteamed friend

Thine Per Captain Patten I have this Day Received & am Pleased to here the Bill I Sent the [e] is Like to be Paid. This Comes to Cover a Bill of Exchange for two Hundred Pounds Sterling which when Paid Please to Place to my Account. If not Paid Please to Send it Back with the Protest Per first Oppertunity Either Directly to this Place or by way of New York as the Advantage by Protested Bills are as much as I Could Expect on any Goods I Should Import. If those Articels I wrote for Answer my Expectation I Purpose to Send Another Invoice for Some of the Same Kind, Interim Remain thy Assured friend

Joseph Richardson

P:S As theire is a Merchant in this City of My Name I would have thy Letters Directed as the former to Joseph Richardson Goldsmith

Joseph Richardson

Per Captain *Nickelson*

Copy Sent By Captain Taylor by way of Cork

Philadelphia 22nd 6th mo. 1759

friend Thomas Wagstaffe

The Incloased I wrote to thee 6 months ago Since which I have Not a Line from thee which makes me Doubt Full wether thee Received it or Not. I have Now Sent a third Bill of Exchange of the Same Tenure & Date and Desire thee would Write me Per first oppertunity and Remain thy Sincear friend Joseph Richardson

Per Captain Nickelson

Philadelphia the 27th 6th mo 1759

Daniel Mildred Esteamed friend

The Above is a Coppy of My Last. I hope My former Order is Shipt & Dayly Expect to here from thee. These Comes with another Invoice for a Parcel of Plate Partly of the Same Kind with the former which I hope thee will forward Per first Oppertunity. I hope the 40 Days Sight before Payment of the Bill or the Non Payment thereof will Not Prevent thy Shiping them as I Shall be willing to Allow thee Interest from the time they are Shipt If Required though I have No Reason to Suspect the Payment theirof. If it would Not be too Troublesome to thee I Should be Pleased thee would Procure a few Puter Paterns from the workman Numbered & Noted by him of Severel Sorts of Shoe & Knea Buckels that I may Chuse My Patterns for the Buckels I may want in future And Whatever thee Ships on My Account I Would have thee Make full Insurence theiron from thy Sincear friend Joseph Richardson

      Philadelphia the 27th 6th mo. 1759

    Invoice of A Parcel of Plate etc.
- 12 Silver Watches at £0/55/0 Per Peice
- 1 Do. at 5 Pounds or 5 Guinies
- 100 Pair of Carveed Silver Shoe Buckels of the Neatest & Newest fashion of Different Patterns to weigh Exclusive of the Chapes & tongues from 15 to 20 Penneweight Per Pair with Steel Chapes & tongues
- 50 Pair of Do. to weigh from 20 to 25 dwt. Per Pair
- 50 Pair of Do. to weigh from 25 to 30 dwt. Per Pair
- 50 Pair of Do. to weigh from 30 to 35 dwt. Per Pair
  All of the above Buckels to weigh as Above Elclusive of the Chapes & tongues & all to have Steel Chapes & tongues
- 20 Pair of Knea Do. with Steel Chapes & tongues to Suit the Largest Buckels
- 3 Chast Silver Snuf Boxes Gilt inside with Gold
- 6 Doz. of Pendents for watches
- 4 Silver Chast Pocket Instrument Casees
- 6 Pair of Cristol Buttons Set in Gold 3 pair of them cyphers
- 6 ounces of Corel Beeds Each Bead to weigh about one Grain
- 12 Peices of Correl to weigh about 5 dwt. Each Peice
- 6 Doz. of Silver tea Spoons with tongs and Straner to Each half Dozen in Shagreen Cases
- 3 Pair of Silver Casters for Pepper & Mustard
- 2 Chast Correls with 8 Bells Gilt with Gold

    a Copy Sent by way of New York the 19th 7th mo. 1759
    a Second Copy by Samuel Sansum 9th 8th mo.

Sent the origanil by way of Cork 19th 7th mo. 1759
Sent a Copy by way of New York the 2nd Copy by Samuel Sansum 9th 8th mo.

Philadelphia the 9th 8th mo. 1759

Friend George Ritherdon

  The Above I Wrote to the 8 months ago with an Invoice for a Small Parcel of Plate as thee May observe by the Date Since which I have Not Received any from thee which makes me Suspect thee Never Received it. I have herewith Sent thee 52 1/2 oz. of Metell Containing Part Silver & Part of other Metels which I Desire thee to Get Essayed & to Sell it for what it will fetch & Creadit me with the Neat Proceeds. If thee art Disposed to Create a Corespondence between us Please to Ship me Per first oppertunity the following Perticulars on the Lowest terms & I Shall take Care to Send the Mony for them Per first oppertunity from these Parts after the Receipt of them & whatever thee Ships on my Account Make full Insurance theiron, If my Cridit is Not Sufficient thee may Send them to John Ralph or any other of thy acquaintance here & I will Pay for them on Sight. So in hopes of a further Corespondence I Conclude thy Sincear

friend Joseph Richardson

P:S Please to Send me a few Puter Patterns Numbered & Noted by thee that I may Chuse the Patterns of the Buckels I may chuse for the future

Joseph Richardson

  Invoice of Sundry Silver ware 9th 8th mo. 1759
  6 Chast milk Potts or Ewers to weigh from 3 to 4 oz.
  6 Plain Do. to weigh as above
  3 Chast Correl & Bells & 3 Plain Do.
  6 Doz. Silver tea Spoons to weigh from 3 to 4 oz. Per Doz.
  1 pair Plain Salts & 1 Pair Chast Do. with Glasses & Shovels
  3 Doz. Silver thimbels & 3 Doz. Steel topt Do.
 100 Pair of Carved Silver Shoe Buckels of the Newest fashions of Different Patterns & Sizes to weigh from 1 ounce to 2 oz. of Silver Per Pair with Steel Chapes & tongues
  20 Pair of Knea Buckels to Suit the Largest Shoe Buckels
  20 Carveed Stock Buckels
  2 Pair of Stone Shoe & Knea Buckels

Sent the origanal Per Captain Hamitt

Philadelphia the 21st 8th mo. 1759

Esteamed friend George Ritherdon

  These may acquaint the that I have Shipt 52 1/2 oz. of Course Mettel Containing Part Silver by Captain Hammitt for which I have Incloased his Receipt & Paid the freight by whome I have Wrote more Largely to which I Refer thee & Remain thy Sincear friend

Joseph Richardson

Direct to me for Jos Richardson Goldsmith at Philadelphia

Letter Book of Joseph Richardson 225

Philadelphia 28th 9th mo. 1759

Esteamed friend Daniel Mildred

Thine of the 23rd of the 6th mo. Last with an Invoice & Bill of Laden for a Parcell of Plate amounting to £239/2/11 after the Deduction of 3 Guineas Per Cent for American Convoy I have Received though at a higher Rate for making then I Expected Mine of the 27th 6th mo. Last with an invoice for a Parcell of Plate etc. I hope thee has Received & Shipt the Goods Accordingly. If Not Shipt I would have the Shoe Buckels to be all of them Square Except Some of them Rounded at the Corners & three fourths of them Peirced & Carved the other fourth Part Carved without being Peirced I am with Much Esteam

Thy Assured friend
Joseph Richardson

[This whole entry above is crossed out.]

Philadelphia 28th 9th mo. 1759

Thomas How & John Masterman

Respected friends, I have lately Received a Parcell of Plate which by a Number of Shop Bills in the Packages I Suppose was Bought at Your House. I think they were very High Charged & hope for an abatement for the future Espechelly in the Spoons & Buckels. I have Notwithstanding Incloased a Bill of 100 £ Sterling made Payable to you with an Invoice for a Parcell of Plate which I Desire may be Shipt Per first Oppertunity on the Lowest terms & if they answer my Expectations it may Create a further Corespondence to our Mutual Advantage. I am with Sincear Respects your assured friend   Joseph Richardson

Direct to I R Goldsmith in Philadelphia

[This whole entry above is also crossed out]

Invoice Sent to Thomas How & John Masterman Goldsmith in London for a Parcell of Plate Viz

28th 9th mo. 1759

- 3 Double Bellied Silver tea Potts with Stands or weighters Neatly Chast Each tea Pot with Stand to weigh from 22 to 24 oz.
- 3 Double Bellied Shugar Dishes with Covers Neatly Chast to Suit the tea Potts of a Midling Substance
- 2 Plain Double Bellyed tea Potts with Stands or weighters to them to weigh from 22 to 24 oz. Ingraved Borders
- 2 Plain Double Bellyed Shugar Dishes of a Midling Substance to Suit the Plain tea Pots
- 12 Doz. of tea Spoons with flowered heads & heals to weigh from 7 to 8 dwt. a Peice
- 12 Doz. of Plain tea Spoons to weigh about 6 pence a Peice
- 3 Pair of Chast Salts with Glass Linings & Ladels
- 3 Pair of Plain Salts with Glass Lingnings & Ladels

3 Pair of Double Bellyed Pepper & mustard Casters Neatly Chast with Glass Linings to the Mustard Casters

3 Pair of Double Bellyed Plain Do. with Glass Linings to the Mustard Casters

2 Silver Coffe Pots with weighters or Stands to hold about 3 wine Pints Neatly Chast to weigh with Stand about 40 oz. a Peice

2 Plain Coffe Potts with Stands to hold about 3 wine Pints to weigh with Stand about 40 oz. a Peice

6 Doz. of table Spoons to weigh about 1 oz. 15 dwt. a Peice Burnished

6 Doz. Do. Pollished to weigh 2 oz. a Peice

1 Doz. of Chast Correll & Bells with 8 Bells

1 Doz. of Plain do.

Philadelphia 28th 9th mo. 1759

Esteamed friend Thomas Wagstaffe

Thine of the 29 & 30th of the 6th mo. Last is Come to hand with the watches & Plate I Wrote for & Expect to write more fully in my Next. By this oppertunity the will Receive a Small order from my ["Kins" is erased] a Relation of mine William Young who Served his time with Me and is about to Set up for himself Next Spring. If the Goods he orders Should Amount to a few Pounds more then what he Sends to Purchase them thee may Safely Cridit him   I am with Due Respects thy Sincear friend

[entry above crossed out]   Joseph Richardson

Philadelphia 28th 9th mo. 1759

Esteamed friends Thomas How & John Masterman

I have lately Received a Parcel of Plate which by a Number of Shop Bills in the Packages I Suppose was bought at your house. I think they were high Charged & hope for an Abatement for the future, Especially in the tea Spoons & Shoe Buckels. I have herewith incloased a Bill of 100 Pounds Sterling made Payable to you with an Invoice for a Parcel of Plate which I Desire may be Shipt per first oppertunity on the lowest terms & if they answer my Expectation it may create a further Corespondence to our mutual advantage. As I have lately Received 240£ Sterlings worth of Plate from London & Sent 200 £ before the Arivel of the first Parcel I cannot Conveniently Spare a larger Sum at Present as I cary on the Business of a gold Smith which Requires a Considerable Stock or otherwise I Should have Sent Cash for a larger order. If it will Suit You to Give 5 or 6 months Cridit from the time they are Shipt Please to Ship the following Perticulars & I Shall think my Self in Honnor Bound to make Spedy Returns for what they amount to more then I have Sent. Let them be Good work and of a Midling Substance & make full Insurance on them. I am with Due Respects Your Sincear friend

Joseph Richardson

P:S Direct to me for Joseph Richardson Goldsmith in Philadelphia. If any Part of my order is left out I would have it to be the Articles last Mentioned in the Invoice.
Joseph Richardson

The Origanal Sent by Captain Budden

Philadelphia the 18th 10th mo. 1759

Esteamed friend Daniel Mildred
    My last of the 27th 6th mo. last with Invoice of the Same Date for a Parcell of Plate I hope thee has Received & Shipt them Accordingly before these Comes to hand I have Now to Acquaint thee of the Receipt of thine Per Captain Duncan with the Goods According to the Invoice therewith Sent & think upon the Whole they are high Charged for the makeing of them — As also of thine per the Pacquet Via New York Adviseing of the Receipt of mine per Captain Nickelson with the 200 £ Bill And am Pleased it is accepted & Like to be Paid these are to Request that thee would Send me Either per Captain Buden or by Captain Bolitho the following Perticulars for which I Purpose to make Remitance to Pay for them befor the Receipt of them & whatever thee Ships on my Account Make Insurance theiron Thy Complyance herewith will Oblige Thy Sincear friend

Joseph Richardson Goldsmith

Invoice of a Parcell of Silver Plate
18th 10th mo. 1759
24 Snake watch Chains with 2 rows
24 Do. with 3 Rows
24 Snake Sciser Chains 13 Inchs with hooks
24 Plain milk Potts or Ewers to weigh from 3 1/2 to 4 oz. a peice
12 Chast Do. to weigh as above of the Comon Siz
24 Pair of Single Joynted tea tongs } of the Hansomest Paterns
24 Pair of Double Joynted Do.
 1 Dozen of Chast Correls & Bells with 8 Bells
 1 Dozen of Plain Do. with 8 Bells
 1 Doz. Pair of Gold Scales & weights in Shagreen Cases
 6 ounces of Corel Beeds to weigh about 4 or 5 Penneyweight Per 100 Beeds
Sent the origanal & a Copy by Via Cork by two Several Vessels who Saild about one time

Philadelphia 24th 10th mo. 1759

Respected friends Thomas How & John Masterman

Mine of the 28th 9th mo. last I hope is Come Safe to hand with a Bill of Exchange for 100 Pounds Sterling & Invoice for a Parcel of Plate If they are Not already Shipt I Desire You would Send me only 4 Doz. of table Spoons instead of 12 Doz. which I wrote for two Doz. of them Burnished & 2 Doz. Pollished & about the Same weight As Per Invoice the Other Parts of the Invoice Desire may be observed I am with Due Respects Your Sincear friend

Joseph Richardson

Direct to me for Joseph Richardson Goldsmith at Philadelphia [written up left margin] Sent the origanal by way of Leverpool by   who Sailed about the 24th 11th mo. 1759

Philadelphia the 14th 12th mo. 1759

Respected friend Daniel Mildred

My Last of the 18th 10th mo. Last by way of Cork with an Invoice for a Parcell of Plate I hope thee has Received a Copy of the Invoice I have here Incloased Least the other Should have Miscaryed I have Per this Conveyance Shipt 25 oz. 2 dwt. 6 gr. of Gold on my own Account which is very Little If anything Worse then Standard Please to Get it Essayed & Dispose of it for the Best Price it will fetch & Creadit my Account with the Neat Proceeds I have also Shipt at the Request of my Brother Francis Richardson 2 oz. 11 dwt. 4 gr. of Course Gold which Please to Cridid his account with the Neat Proceeds theirof Thine Per Captain friend with the Chapes & tongues I Received I am with Due Respects thy Sincear friend

Joseph Richardson

P S Please to Insure whatever thee Ships on my account & Send me the Essay Masters Report of the fineness of the Gold

Joseph Richardson

[written up the left margin] Sent the origanal by Captain friend 14th 12th mo.

Philadelphia the 14th 12th mo. 1759

Respected friend Thomas Wagstaffe

Thine Per Captain Duncan as also thine Per Captain friend with the Goods thee Shipt Per the former I have Received I have Per this Conveyance Shipt 6 oz. 2 dwt. 20 gr. of Gold very little if anything Worse then Standard which I Desire thee would Get Essayed & Dispose of it for the best Price it will fetch And After thee has Ballenced our former Account for what Remains Please to Send Me Per first oppertunity as many Good Silver Watches of about £0/55/0 Price as the mony will Procure & I Desire they may be Set to time before they are Shipt I am with Due Respects thy Sincear friend

Joseph Richardson

P S Please to Insure whatever the Ships on my account & Send me the Essay masters Report of the fineness of the Gold

Philadelphia 21st 12th mo. 1759
Respected friend Daniel Mildred
    These Comes to Cover a Bill of Lading for 27 oz. 13 dwt. 10 gr. of Gold & to acknowledg the Receipt of thine Per Captain Nickelson but to my Great Disapointment find my order of the 27th 6th mo. last are Not Shipt by him as I Sent the origanal of that Order by way of Cork about 8 Days after Nickelson Sailed from Hence I fully Expected my Goods by him Hopeing thee will Ship them As Also my last Order of the 18th 10th mo. Last Per first Oppertunity Conclude thy Sincear frieend
                                                    Joseph Richardson
    Note the Gold above Mentioned is the Same that is Mentioned in my Letter of the 14th 12th month Sent by Captain friend

Philadelphia the 9th 2nd mo. 1760
Respected friends Thomas How & John Masterman
    These Comes to Cover a Bill of Exchange for two Hundred Pounds Sterling with an Invoice for a Parcel of Plate which I Desire may be Shipt Per first oppertunity & that you would make full Insurance theiron   Let them be Good work & of the Newest fashion & on the Lowest terms. I have Not Received any answer from You to mine of the 28th 9th mo. Last But Dayly Expect one & Remain Your Sincear friend
                                                    Joseph Richardson

  1 Silver Caster frame with a Sett of Double Bellyed Casters Neatly Chast with Ground Glass Cruits tipt with Silver
  1 Silver Do. with Plain Double Bellyed Casters etc.
30 Pair of Silver Peirced & Carved Squar Shoe Buckles with Silver Chapes & tongues to weigh from 2 1/2 to 3 oz. a Pair
30 Pair of Silver Knea Buckels to Suit the Shoe Buckels with Silver Chapes & tongues
30 Carved Silver Stock Buckels one half of them Perceed
  1 Dozen of Plateed Snuff Boxes with Chast or Stampt Lids
  3 Pair of Silver Spurs
  3 Pair of Double Bellyed Plain Casters
  3 Pair of Plain Silver Salts with Glass Lineings & Shovels or Ladels
10 Cards of Crystol Buttons Set in Silver
10 Cards of Do. with Cyphers
  6 Cards of Small Do. for Children

12 Dozen of Silver tea Spoons with tongs & Straner to Each half Doz. in Shagreen Cases
6 Doz. of Steel topt thimbels Lineed with Silver

Direct to me for Joseph Richardson Goldsmith at Philadelphia [Written up the left margin] Sent this by a London Vessel & By way of Bristol the 1st Sailed the 10th 2nd mo. The other Soon after

Philadelphia the 16th 4th mo. 1760

Respected friend George Ritherdon
I have Received thy Obligeing Letter of the 26th of November Last the Origanel Per Captain house is Not Yet arived I have here Incloased a Bill of Lading for 40 Ounces of Gold Very little if any thing Inferior to Standard which Please to Get Essayed & Dispose of it for the Best Price & Credit my Account with the Neat Proceeds I have also Incloased an Invoice for a Small Parcel of Plate which I hope thee will Ship Per first oppertunity & make full Insurence theiron   I am with much Esteam thy Sincear friend

Joseph Richardson

Direct to me for Joseph Richardson Goldsmith in Philadelphia

Invoice for a Parcel of Plate 16th 4th mo. 1760
    2 Plain Silver tea Potts with Ingraved Borders with Stands
    2 Shugar Dishes to Suit the tea Potts
    2 Cream Potts or Ewers to Suit the Above
    3 Doz. Silver Slideing Pencel Casees with Pencels to them
    1 Doz. of Iveroy Memorandum Books
    3 Dozen of Table Spoons to weigh from 35 to 40 dwt. a Peice
    3 Dozen of Plain Stock Buckels
    3 Soop Spoons with Ebany Handels
  24 Snake watch Chains with 2 Rows
  24 Do. 3 Rowed
    6 Dozen of tea Spoons to weigh about 6 or 7 dwt. a Peice
  12 Pair of tea tongs
Sent the above by Captain Falconer And by the 3 Brothers who Sailed about the Same time for London 18th. 4th mo. 1760

Respected friends Thomas How & John Masterman
Mine of the 9th of the 2nd mo. Last Covering a Bill of Exchange for £ 200 Sterling with Invoice for a Parcel of Plate I hope is come to hand in which Invoice I wrote for 30 pair of Peirced & Carved Shoe Buckels with Silver Chapes & tongues & knea Buckels to Suit them if they are Not already Provided I would have but 1/3 Part of them Peirced the other 2/3 Sollid & Carved the other Parts of the Invoice

Desir may be observed I am with Sincear Respect Your Real friend Jane Hoskins Desirs her Love to be Remembered to you

                    Joseph Richardson

[written in left margin] 16th 4th mo. 176   Sent this with the above

               Philadelphia 6th 6th mo. 1760

Respected friend Daniel Mildred

  Thine Dateed the 22nd of December last I Received & find thee had Shipt [on the Julian] Per Captain House a Parcel of Plate to the Amount of £260/14/0 who is taken by the french these are therefore to Desire thee to Ship me the following Perticulars Instead of those Shipt Per House I have Contracted this order & hope the Money in thy hands when the Insurance made on House is Paid will very Near Pay for them Desire they may be Sent as Soon as Possible as I much want them Especialy the Buckels in which article I Expect an Abatement Please to make full Insurance on them I am with Sincear Respects thy Assured friend

                    Joseph Richardson

    Invoice for a Parcel of Plate 6th 6th mo. 1760

  2 Chast Silver Coffe Potts to hold 3 wine Pints
  2 Chast Stands or weighters for Do. with Chast Shells on the Border
  2 Plain Coffe Potts to hold 3 wine Pints with Stands
 12 Plain & 12 Chast Cream Potts
 25 Pair of Carved Shoe Buckels with Steel Chapes & tongues to weigh with the Chapes from 20 to 30 dwt. a pair one half of them Peirced
 25 Pair of Do. to weigh from 30 to 40 dwt. Per Pair
 25 Pair of Do. to weigh from 40 to 50 dwt. Per Pair
 25 Pair of Do. to weigh from 50 to 60 dwt. Per Pair
 25 Pair of Knea Buckels to Suit the Largest Shoe Buckels
  6 Pair of Crystol Buttons Set in Gold 3 Pair with Cyphers
  6 Doz. of tea Spoons & 12 Pair of tea tongs
 24 Carved Stock Buckels 1/3 of them Peirced
  6 Doz. Silver thimbels & 6 Doz. Steel topt Do. Lined
  4 Chast Pocket Instrument Casses
  6 ounces of Small Corel Beeds
 12 Cards of Crystol Buttons Set in Silver 1/2 with Cyphers
  3 Pair of Plain Salts with Shovels & Glass Linings
  2 Chast Snuff Boxes Gilt Inside

Sent the origanal by way of New York by Neat & a Copy by Captain Bolitho

                       7th 6th mo. 1760

Respected friend George Ritherdon

  My last of the 16th 4th mo. april last Per Captain falconer with Bill of Lading for 40 oz. of Gold I hope is Come to hand Since which we have a Certain Account

that Captain House is taken by a french Priveter & Carried into a french Port in the west Indies Therefore Desire thee to Recover the money Insured on her & Reship the Same Artikels As Also those Mentioned in the Invoice Sent by falconer (Except the table Spoons which Desire May be omited) As Soon as Possible if Captain falconer Should Miscary Desire the order Sent by him may be Intirely omited And only Reship those Articles that were on board Captain House & whatever thee Ships on my Account make full Insurance theiron the Ballence that may Remain Due Shall take Care to Make Spedy Remittence I am with much Esteam thy Sincear friend
                                                                    Joseph Richardson
Sent the origanal By way of New York by Neat & a Copy by Captain Bolitho

                                                    Philadelphia the 7th mo. 1760
Respected friend Thomas Wagstaffe
   Thine of the 10th of the fourth month Last I Received with the watches & my account Current by which thers a Ballence of £0/16/8 Due to thee out of which when the Deduction for american Convoy is made we shall be very Near upon a Ballence I have herein Incloased a Bill of Exchange for 100 Pounds Sterling made Payable to thee with an Invoice for a Parcel of watches & Some Plate as below. Thy method of abateing in the Price In Proportion to the Pay I much Approve of & Request thee would be as Expeditious as Possible in makeing Returns I have also by the Indian trader Captain Robeson Sent a wooden Pattern & Request thee would gett a Pair of Rowlers for a flating mill [flatting mills were used to roll silver thin] as Near the Siz of the Pattern as Possible. They are for Milling Silver or Gold thin And therefore Should be turned as true as Possible So that if one is Placed on the other we may Not be able to See through them. It is Usual in London as I am informed to make them of Steel throughout or of Sweeds Iron Case Hardened for if they are only Covered with Steel the Steel is apt to Seperate from the Iron as I have Experienced or otherwise to Prove faulty However Shall Depend upon thee to Gett them Done in the Best manner & Conclude with Sincear Respects thy Real friend
                                                                    Joseph Richardson

   Invoice for a Parcell of watches etc. 7th mo. 1760
   one Pair of Rowlers for a flating Mill
   24 Silver Lemon Strainers
   24 Silver Punch Ladels
    2 Silver watches of £5 or 5 Guinies Price Each
   14 Silver watches at £0/55/0 a Peice
P.S. Please to make full Insurance on the above And Direct to me for Joseph Richardson Goldsmith
[written up the left margin] Sent the origanal by Captain Robeson who Sailed about

the 25th 7th mo. 1760 & a Copy by Captain friend & a Second Copy by hamit who Sailed 1st 9th mo. with 2 & 3 Bill of Exchange for £100

Exchange for £100 Sterling at 56 Per Cent

Philadelphia 27 June 1760

At thirty Days Sight of this our third of Exchange first & Second of the Same tenor and Date unpaid Please to Pay Mr. Joseph Richardson or order One Hundred Pounds Sterling for Value Received and Place the Same to Account as Per Advice from Gentleman

Your Most Humble Servants
Francis & Relfe

To Samuel Touchet Esq. & Co. in London
The Above is a true Copy of a Bill Bought of John Relfe all 3 of which I have Sent to Thomas Wagstaffe to London

Joseph Richardson

Philadelphia 20th 10th mo. 1760

Respected friends Thomas How & John Masterman

Yours of the 13th 2nd mo. last by Captain Gibbon & of the 14th 7th mo. by Captain tillit I have Received with the Goods Shipt by them I have herein Incloased Bills of Exchange for 500 Pounds Sterling Made Payable to you with an order for a Parcell of Plate the Last Parcells were Not Altogether Agreable to My Mind & were So ill Packt that Severel of the Coffe Potts were Brused I have Computeed the Value of what I have Wrote for & Suppose the Money will be Sufficient to Discharge the former Account after the Deduction is made for american Convoy for Goods on board Captain Gibbon, & to Pay for what I Now Write for & all Charges If it Should Not You May take Something off from the Invoice & if the Money is More then Sufficient You may add Something to it So as to Ballence our Account I am Obliged to you for the Confidence You have Reposed in Me & Remain Your Sincear friend

Joseph Richardson Goldsmith

P.S. Please to Pay to Elias Bland £7/8/1 it being the Ballence of his Account & make full Insurence on whatever You Ship on My Account

Joseph Richardson

Invoice for a Parcell of Plate 20th 10th mo. 1760
4 Chast Silver Coffe Potts with Stands
2 Plain Silver Coffe Potts with Stands
6 Chast tea Potts with Stands
2 Plain Do. with Stands
6 Chast Shugar Dishes & 2 Plain Do.
 Chast Slop Bowles

    6 Chast & 6 Plain Cream Potts
    6 Pair Plain Casters & 4 Pair Chast Do. with Glass linings
    1 Pair Pint Cans Pollished
    12 Doz. Comon tea Spoons Plain from 3 to 4 oz. Per Doz.
    24 Pair of tea tongs

Sent the origanal By Buden Copy by falconer 2nd Copy By Captain falconer

                                        Philadelphia 20th 10th mo. 1760
Respected friend Daniel Mildred
    These Comes to Cover a Bill of Exchange of 50 Pounds Sterling which when Received Please to Credit my account therewith from thy Sincear friend
                                        Joseph Richardson Goldsmith
Sent the origanal By Buden & By Captain falconer a Copy

                                        Philadelphia 20th 10th mo. 1760
Respected friend Elias Bland
    Thine of the 30th of June Last with thy account I Received & have wrote to How & Masterman Goldsmiths in London to Pay thee the Ballence my trade to London is Chiefly in the Plate way & I apprehend these men Can Serve me at a lower Rate then those that Deale in the Commission Business Hope thee wont Look upon it as out of any Disrespect that I have Dropt our former Corespondence & Remain thy Real friend
                                        Joseph Richardson
[written up the left margin] Sent the origanal by Buden Copy by falconer

                                        20th 10th mo. 1760
Respected friend Thomas Wagstafe
    Mine of the 7th mo. last I hope thee hast Received in which I wrote for a Pair of Rowlers for a flating mill for my own Use etc. Since which I have Directions from one of my Neighbours to write for a Pair for him as also for a Socket Dys & Punches for Stamping Silver or Gold Buttons the Siz & form of the Patterns herein Inclosed which Request thee would Gett made in the Best manner & I Shall be willing to Satisfy thee for thy trouble or if thee has Not Shipt those things I wrote for the [e] may Leve out Part of the watches or Plate in order to Pay thy Selfe from thy Real friend
                                        Joseph Richardson Goldsmith
No. I on the Pattern a Screw Sent the Origanal By Buden Copy by falconer 11th 11th mo. 1760

Philadelphia the 20th 12th mo. December 1760

Respected friend George Ritherdon

Thine of the 20th & 24th of June last by Captain Buden I have Received with the Plate Shipt by him & am Obliged to thee for Shiping them So Expeditiously & Should have Been Pleased to have had my other order by Faulkner but am Informed by him that You Differed about the Price of the freight that he Required 2 Per cent on the Value of the Plat which I think an Extraordinary Price & would by No Means Incourage Such a Custom I would Not Run any Risque In Saveing the Expence at the Custom House but would Chuse to Pay it for the future I am Informed that Buden Came out with american Convey & So Expect a Return of Premeum Accordingly Bills of Exchange are at Present 15 Per cent higher then they were Some time Past Or I should have Sent A Bill by this Oppertunity but Expect they will be Lower Soon & Intend to Imbrace the first oppertunity to make Remittance to Pay for the following Order etc. which Desire may be Shipt as Soon as Possible & make full Insurence theiron

from   thy Assured friend
Joseph Richardson Goldsmith

Invoice for a Parcel of Plate 20th 12th mo. December 1760

    6 Doz. Plain Common tea Spoons to weigh about 5 dwt. a Peice
    6 Doz. Do. to weigh about 6 a Piece
    6 Doz. Do. to weigh about 7 a Piece
    6 Doz. Plain Pollished Do. to weight about 8 a Piece
    6 Pair of Plain Pollished Casters with Glass Linings to the mustard Caster
    2 Pair of Chast Casters with Glass linings to the mustard Casters
    2 Chast tea Potts with Chast Stands to Suit them
    2 Plain Pollished tea Potts with ingraved Borders
    2 Plain Stands Pollished & Not Ingraved to Suit the Plain tea Potts
    24 Pair of Square Carved Shoe Buckels with Silver Chapes & tongues 1/3 of them Peirced to weigh about 3 oz. a Pair
    24 Pair of Knea Buckels to Suit the Shoe Buckels
    12 Large Hansome Double Joynted tea tongs

Sent the origanal by Captain Nathaniel falkner

Philadelphia the 20th 3rd mo. March 1761

Respected friend George Ritherdon

Thine Dateed the 28th of August last I Received with the Goods Shipt by Captain Henry McDugal as Per Invoice my last of the 20th of the 12th mo. Last by Captain falknor with an Invoice for a Parcel of Plate I hope is Come Safe to hand if the Goods are Not allready Provided I would have the Shoe & Knea Buckles Omited I have Herein Incloased a bill of Exchange for two Hundred Pounds Sterling Payable to thee which I wish Safe to hand & Doubt Not it will be Duly Honnoured I have Imbraced the first oppertunity Since my last to Send the Incloased Bill & Should have Sent for a Parcell of watches but bills being Scarce to be had Shall Defer them till an other oppertunity & only Desire thee to Send me Six Doz. of Snake watch Chaines 4 Doz. of them three Rows & 2 Dozen with 2 Rowes with a midle Piece Like the Pattern below I am with Due Respects thy Sincear friend

Joseph Richardson Goldsmith

P.S. Least my last of the 20th 12th mo. Last by Captain Nathaniel faulkner Should Have miscarried I have herewith Sent a Coppy of the Invoice of those Articels I Wrote for by him which with the watch Chaines Above mentioned Desire may be Shipt Per first Oppertunity Except the Shoe & Knea Muckels [sic] & make full Insurence theiron which will Oblige thy Sincear friend

Joseph Richardson

Philadelphia the 22nd 3rd mo. March 1761

[Probably addressed to George Ritherdon]

I have this Day Received thy Account by the [ship] King of Prusia Captain Robeson & have No Exception to it Except that their is No Credit for Return of Premium for American Convony for Goods on Board Captain Buden. I Shall Carefully Indeavour to Render Satisfaction in the Course of our Dealings & Remain thy friend

Joseph Richardson

Sent the origanal by the Indian trader Captain Robeson & a Coppy by way of New York

Philadelphia the 20th 7th mo. 1761

Respected friends How & Masterman

Your Agreeable letter of the 10th 1st mo. last by way of New York Came Safe to hand & must Acknowledg the Improper way of Expresing my meening in Saying the last Parcells when I Should have Said the first Parcell Please to Excuse It. Yours also of the 24th of the 2nd mo. Likewise Came Safe to hand with the Plate Sent by hamitt & am obliged to You for Shiping them So Expiditiously as Success in trade Depends Very much thereon. I have Herein Incloased a Bill for 100 Pounds Sterling Payable to You with an order for a Small Parcell of Plate which Desire May be of the Best work & well finished off there were two of the Chast Coffe Potts which Came last Leekt Near the uper Socket which I Suppose Escaped Your Notice hope as it is Not agreeable to Either of us that there will be No Occation for any more Complaints In future & Remain Your Sincear friend

Joseph Richardson

Invoice for a Parcell of Plate
1 Plain Single Bellyed Coffe Pott to hold a wine Quart about 25 oz.

1 Do. to hold about half a Pint more then the Above
  1 Do. to hold 3 Pints About 32 oz.
  6 Plain Silver tea Potts with Ingraved Borders to weigh about 17 oz.
  6 Stands for Do. about 7 oz. a Piece
  3 Stands for the Coffe Potts to weigh about 10 oz. with 6 Shells on the Border to Suit the Coffe Potts
  1 Doz. Plain Single Bellyed Cream to weigh about 3 oz. a Piece

P: S Please to Gett Insurance made on the above & all other Goods you may Ship me for the future unless I Should Give Perticular Instructions to the Contrary

Joseph Richardson

Sent the above by Captain Buden & a Copy by Hamit

Philadelphia 20th 7th mo. 1761

Respected friends Mildred & Roberts

These Comes to Cover a Bill of Exchange for 100 Pounds Sterling made Payable to You with an Invoice for a Parcell of Steel Chapes & tongues for Silver Shoe Buckels Have Not time to Examin Daniel Mildred's Account but Doubt Not but that it is Right & Expect the Bill herewith Sent will Ballence it & Pay for what I Now Wright for If Not Shall Carefully Remit the Ballence I am Your Sincear friend

Joseph Richardson Goldsmith

Invoice for a Parcell of Steel Chapes & tongues for Silver Shoe & Knea Buckels
  1 Gross of Large Square Steel Chapes & tongues
  1 Gross of Do. a Siz Less
  1 Gross of Do. a Siz Less
  1 Gross of Do. a Siz Less
  1 Gross of Do. a Siz Less
  1 Gross of Do. a Siz Less
  1 Gross of Do. Small
  2 Gross of Small Knea Chapes & tongues
  1 Gross of Large Round tailed Chapes & tongues about the Siz of the Pattern or Rather Larger
  1 Gross of Do. a Siz Less
  1 Gross of Do. a Siz Less
  1 Gross of Do. a Siz Less
  1 Gross of Do. a Siz Less
  1 Gross of Do. a Siz Less
  1 Gross of Do. a Siz Less
  1 Gross of Do. Small

P.S. The Last Parcell of Chapes & tongues that I had from Daniel Mildred Suited Very Well with Respect to the Quality & Request these may be as Good as they were.

I omited in the above to write for Insurance these are to Desire You to Insure whatever You Ship on my Account unless I Should Give Directions to the Contrary 21st 8th mo. 1761

Joseph Richardson

Philadelphia 17th 10th mo. 1761

Respected friend George Ritherdon

    I have this Day Received thy letter with Invoice for a Parcell of Plate on board Captain friend and observe their is a Small Ballence Due to me   If thee Please to Send me a Dozen of Watches at £0/55/0 a piece & 2 at 5 Guinies a Piece   I Shall take Care to Remitt the Ballence Spedily   Peices of 8 will Not Answer to Remitt at Preasent the Insurance being So high if there Should be a Peace they will Naturelly flow from America to London as I apprehend we are many Hundred thousands in Debt to You   from thy Sincear friend

Joseph Richardson Goldsmith

Sent the above by Captain Cundy & a Copy by Captain McClelland

Philadelphia 19th 10th mo. 1761

Respected friends How & Masterman

    These are to Cover a Bill of Exchange for £190/14/4 Sterling Payable to You which when Received Please to Creadit Edmond Milns Account with £154/6/4 theirof & Creadit My Account with the Remainder £36/8/0 as Soon as the Money is Received   I Request that You would Send 3 Protests theirof   If Not Paid by 3 Different Conveyances that I may Recover the Money from the Drawer In behalf of the Creditors

from Your Sincear friend
Joseph Richardson Goldsmith

Sent the above by Captain Cundy & a Copy by Captain McClelland

Philadelphia the 25h 11th mo. November 1761

Respected friend George Ritherdon

    These are to Cover a Bill of Lading for £10/3/0 Sterling & 63 oz. 10 dwt. of Course Silver the Produce of the Sweepings of My Shop as I have No Convenient apparatus for Refineing it have therefore Sent it herewith & Desire that a Gold Essay may be made of it as well as a Silver Essay as it is Probable their may be Some Gold in it

from thy Sincear friend
Joseph Richardson Goldsmith

Sent the Origanel by Captain friend

Philadelphia 31st 3rd mo. 1762

Respected friends How & Masterman

    Yours by Captain Finglass I Received with the Plate according to Invoice in Good order. These are to Cover a Bill of Exchange for 100 £ Sterling with an Invoice for a Parcell of Plate as below there has been no oppertunity Lately Directly from these Parts or I Should have wrote to you Sooner for those articles as I much want them Desire they may be Shipt as Soon as Possible & make full Insurence theron which will oblige your Sincear friend

                                      Joseph Richardson Goldsmith

P.S. I observe there is an Error of £0/2/11 in your last account to your Disadvantage which Please to Rectify & as Captain finglass Came with american Convoy their will be a Deduction of Premium

    Invoice for a Parcell of Plate   31st   3 mo. 1762
- 4 Pair of Plain Salts Gadrooned Edg all of a Siz So that any two of them may fellow Each other with Glasses & Shovels
- 4 Pair of Knurled [pearl] Edg Do. all of a Siz with Glasses & Shovels
- 8 Pair of Spare Glasses for Do.
- 24 Plain Single Belleyed milk Potts to weigh about 3 oz. 10 dwt. a Piece
- 2 Double Belleyed Do.
- 1 Doz. of Double Joynted tea tongs of the hansomest Patterns Pritty Large
- 1 Doz. Pair of Single Joynted Do.
- 1 Doz. Plain Correl & Bells with 8 Bells
- 6 Cards of Brilliant Crystol Buttons Sett in Silver
- 6 Cards of Do. Small for Children
- 6 Cards of Square table Cut Crystol Buttons with Cyphers
- 6 Cards of Do. Small for Children
- 6 Pair of temple Specticels Sett in Silver in Green fish Skin Cases Mounted & with Silver
- 6 Pair of Spare Glasses for Do.
- 3 Silver full Instrument Casees for Women
- 3 Green fish Skin Do. mounted with Silver
- 1 Doz. Ivory Memorandum Books
- 6 Pair of Plain Silver Casters with Glass Linings to the mustard Caster & the mustard Caster Peirced & Lineed
- 10 Ounces of Corell Beeds of a Midling Siz.
- 3 Pair of Silver & 6 Pair of Plateed Do.

Sent the origanal by way of New York   Copy By way of Bristol by Captain Widet

                               Philadelphia the 31st 3rd mo. 1762

Respected friend Thomas Wagstaffe

    Thy Last by Captain Finglass with the Rowlers I have Received in a Rusty Condition   Especielly the Large Pair which are So Bad that the Person for whome I

Sent for them for will Not take them   I have Herein Incloased a Bill of Exchange for 25£ Sterling & Desire thee would Send me a Pair of Button Stamps to Stamp Gold or Silver Buttons Like the Patterns   Except the Ingraveing on the largest Button I would have like the Smallest & I would have the Ingraved Punches Sent in order to Repair the Dies if Occation Should Requir it as also the Plain Punches to Stamp the Buttons with & Desire thee would Send me Six Watches at about £0/55/0 a Piece or as many as the money in thy hands will Produce & Make Insurance on them   thy Spedy Complyance herewith will Oblige thy friend

Joseph Richardson

P.S.   Please to warm the Button Stamps & Rub them over when warm with Bees wax which will Preserve them from Rust

Philadelphia the 2nd   6th mo. 1762

Respected friends Mildred & Roberts

Yours By Captain Buden Received with an Invoice for a Parcell of Chapes & tongues by him which Came to hand in Good order   these are to Desire You would Ship Per first oppertunity 16 Gross of Shoe & 2 Gross of Knea Chapes & tongues for Silver Buckels Rather Better then the Last Parcell   If they Cost Something More & of the Sizes Specifyed below & a Good Silver Watch of about 6 or 7 Guinies Price & Make Insurance on them as Usual

from Your Sincear friend
Joseph Richardson

    Invoice for a Parcell of Chapes & tongues
1 Gross of Large Square Chapes & tongues as Large as Print No. 1
1 Gross of Small Square Do. the Siz of the Print No. 2
6 Gross of Squar Chaps & tongues of 6 Different Sizes between No. 1 & 2
1 Gross of Round Shoe Chapes as Large as the Print No. 3
1 Gross of Small Do. the Siz of the Print No. 4
6 Gross of Round Shoe Chapes of 6 Different Sizes between No. 3 & 4
2 Gross of Knea Chapes & tongues the Siz of the Print

Philadelphia the 30th   11th mo. 1762

Respected friends How & Masterman

The Copy of yours Dateed the 27th of the 7th mo. Last with an Invoice of a Parcell of Plate Shipt on Board the Neptune Captain Shirlock is Come to hand but Shirlock is Not Yet Arived. Herewith is Incloased a Bill of Exchange for 100 Pounds Starling Payable to You with an Invoice for a Parcell of Plate the Pocket Book locks & Clasps I have Sent for as a Sample & Desire to know the lowest Price of them by the Quantity   I Expect the watch Chains at 12 Pence a Piece Makeing one with another & as the Price of Silver is Considerable lowered I hope You will Charge the above at the Lowest terms You Can Afford them the Middle Piece of the watch Chains I would have like the Pattern Imprest below   Please to make Insurance on them & Ship them Per first oppertunity   If Shirlock Should Miscarry Please to Ship the Same articels Except the Specticels as Soon as Possible

from Your Sincear friend
Joseph Richardson

Invoice for a Parcell of Plate 30th   11th mo. 1762

6 Plain Double Belleyed tea Potts with Narrow Ingraved Borders to weigh about 17 oz.
2 Plain Single Belleyed Coffe Potts about 3 wine Pints
6 Plain Pocket Book Locks & Clasps of Different Sorts
6 Pair Plain Pepper & Mustard Casters the mustard Caster Perced & Lineed
6 Pair of Plain Salts
6 Doz. of Snake watch Chains 3 Doz. 3 Rowed & 3 Doz. 2 Rowed

Philadelphia the 25th   4th mo. 1763

Respected friends How & Masterman

I have Lately Received a Parcell of Plate Per the Neptune Captain Shirlock late Master from You in Pritty Good Order Considering they were So long on Board & the Weighter was Delivered as Directed to Charles Stedman   I hope as She Came out with Convoy there will be a Considerable Draw Back from the Premium   I have here Incloased a Bill of Lading for 16 oz. of Gold which is Equal in fineness with the Spanish Coin & hope it will fetch a Price Accordingly when Sold   Please to Ballence our Account & for the Remainder if any Please to Send as Many Silver Double Belleyed Plain tea Potts & Single Belleyed Cream Potts with a few Snake watch Chains as the money will Pay for & Ship them by Captain Buden without Making any Insurance on them   My Desireing a Settlement of our Account will Not in the least lesson our future Corespondence from Your Sincear friend

Joseph Richardson

P.S.   If Buden Should Not be arived before the Receipt of this letter Please to Get 130 Pounds Sterling Insured on him on my Account

Joseph Richardson

Philadelphia the 25th 4th mo. 1763

Esteamed friend George Ritherdon

Thine Dateed the 14th of July last Per Captain Friend with the watches Came Safe to hand & in good order   these are to Cover a Bill of Lading for 300 Spanish Milled Dollors weighing 260 oz. 17 dwt. Consigned to thee which when Disposed off Please to Ballence our Account & for the Remainder Please to Ship me as many watches of 5 £ & 50 shillings a Piece as the [remainder] will Pay for & if Nessasary to Ballence our Account thee may add as many Snake watch Chains as will Ballence it

Please to Send them by Captain Buden without makeing any Insurance on them from thy Sincear friend

Joseph Richardson

Philadelphia the 25th 4th mo. 1763

Esteamed friends Mildred & Roberts

Yours Per Captain Buden Dateed the 23rd of October last I Received with the Chapes & tongues in Good order as to what Remains of my order unshipt you may omit Sending them unless it will be any Disadvantage to You. I have herewith Incloased a Bill of Exchange for 40 Pounds Starling Payable to You which Please to Creadit my Account with when Paid I have No Imediate Occation of anything in Youre way & therefore am Desireous of Ballencing our Account & when Ever a Prospect of Advantage Presents Shall with Pleasure Imbrace the oppertunity of Renewing our Corespondence & Remain Your Obliged friend

Joseph Richardson

Philadelphia the 2nd 6th mo. 1763

Respected friends Mildred & Roberts

Yours of the 17th of Febury last I have Received with a Box of Chapes Per Captain Sparks with your Account Current the Ballence in your favour £49/12/4   Since the Date of which account I have Per Captain Buden Remited to you a bill of Exchange for £40 Starling which I hope is Paid   if So the ballence will be 9 Pounds odd money which I have Requested How & Masterman to Pay   I have no objection to Your Accounts Except that of Daniel Mildreds in the Year 1760 wherein I am Charged with Commissions on Settleing the Loss Per the Julianna   However I Shall Submit it to You & Remain Your Sincear friend

Joseph Richardson

Philadelphia the 2nd 6th mo. 1763

Respected friends How & Masterman

My last of the 25th 4th mo. last by Captain Buden I hope is Come to hand these are to Cover a bill of lading for a Small wedg of Gold Equal in fineness to the Spanish Coin weighing 6 oz. 11 dwt. 13 gr.   Desireing the favour of you to Pay to Mildred & Roberts the Ballence of there Account it being 9 Pounds od money Provideed they Received a bill of Exchange of £40 Starling which I Sent to them by Buden   I hope you will Excuse this trouble & I Shall be Willing to Serve You upon the like or any other occation in these Parts for the Remainder of the money after Paying Mildred & Roberts Please to Send me as many Pair of Shoe & Knea Buckels of the Newest fashion as the money will Pay for Provided they Can be Shipt by Captain Buden   If Not Please to Defer Shiping them till further Directions from Your Sincear friend

Joseph Richardson

P.S.   Please Not to Insure on the above Sent the above by Captain Sparks

Philadelphia the 15th   11th mo. 1763

Respected friends How Masterman & Archer
      Yours by Captain friend with the Goods Shipt by him I have Received as also Yours by Captain Buden & observe the Contents these are to Cover a Bill of Lading for a barrel of Cranberrys which Desire Your Acceptance off & 12 oz. 7 dwt. 18 gr. of Gold & 34 oz. 14 dwt. of Gold lace which when Disposed off Request that you would Pay to Mildred & Roberts the Ballence of there Account which I think is about 50 £ Starling haveing Lately Received a bill of £40 Returned with a Protest from them the Gold herewith Sent is but 3/4 of a Carret Grain worse then Standard According to an Assay which I have made off it & hope it will fetch a Price accordingly
from Your Sincear friend

Joseph Richardson

Philadelphia the 17th   11th mo. 1763

Respected friends How Masterman & Archer
      Since I wrote the Incloased I have Received Yours Per Captain Falconer with Invoice for a Parcel of Plate & Your Account as Captain Friend is Just upon Going I Canot Examin it But Captain Buden is Expected to Sail this fall by Whome I Propose to make Remittance & to write more Perticularly from Your Sincear friend

Joseph Richardson

the above letter of the 15th   11th mo. was Incloased in that Dateed the 17th of the Same mo. & Sent by Captain Friend

Philadelphia the 19th   12th mo. 1763

Respected friends How Masterman & Archer
      Yours of the 7th   9th mo. Last is before Me & I Do agree with Your Definition with Respect to the Defirence of the fineness of Spanish Gold But Cannot Recollect that there was any of the Irregular Dubloons Mentioned in Your letter in the Peice which I Sent but am apprehensive that the Essay Masters or those Imployed by them may Sometimes Make Mistakes & therefore if the Gold I may hereafter Send Dont Nearly Answer the Carrector I may Send with it I would be at the Expence of 2 or 3 Essays Rather then Loose by an imperfect Essay   Am Obliged to You for Your Indeavors towards Settling Mildred & Roberts' Account & have Examened Yours Dateed the 7th 9th mo. September 1763 by which there is a Ballence of £54/6/7 in Your favour but Observe You Have omited Creaditing my Account with Return of Premium for Insurance Per the [ship] Dragon Captain Hamitt & Per Captain Finglass which I apprehend I am Intitled to   I have here Incloased a bill of Lading for

300 Spanish Milled Dollars with an Invoice for a Small Parcell of Plate which Desire may be Shipt by Captain Buden If it Suits Your Conveniency & Remain ["Concludes" is scratched out and erased]   Your Sincear & Obliged friend

Joseph Richardson

  Invoice for a Small Parcell of Plate
 1 Doz. Corels & Bells Plain with 8 Bells
 6 Pair of Peirced Spring tea tongs
 24 Pair Double Joynted tea tongs Large to weigh about 1 oz. 5 dwt. a pair one with an other
 12 Doz. Silver tea Spoons Comon Burnisht to weigh about 6 dwt. a piece
 6 Correll Pieces for Whisels & Bells to weigh about 5 dwt. a Piece

Philadelphia the 2nd   7th mo. 1763

Respected friend Thomas Wagstaffe

 These are to Acknowledg the Receipt of thine of the 7th of the 8th mo. Last with the watches & Button Stamps in Good order & to Desire thee to Procure 3 Sockets with 2 Dies & 2 Plain Punches to Each Socket for Stamping Buttons of the Siz & Pattern of the Incloased Buttons as the Ingraved Punches are with Dificulty obtained & Charged at a very high Price I would have them omitted & only Send 2 Plain Punches & 2 Dies of the Siz & Shape of these Patterns Incloased to Each of the 3 Sockets or Collors   Please to Ship them without Insuring them & I Shall be willing to Satisfy thee for thy trouble theirin & If thee thinks Propper to Send me 6 Good Plain Silver watches with Enameled Dial Plates of 5 Guinies a Piece thee may Depend upon haveing the money for them Per first Conveyance from hence After there Arival from thy Sincear friend

Joseph Richardson

Philadelphia the 15th   3rd mo. 1764

Respected friend Thomas Wagstaffe

 Thy Letter Dateed the 11th mo. 8th Last I Received with the Button Stamps & watches therein mentioned in Good order & have herewith Sent as Per Bill of Lading Incloased 9 oz. 3 dwt. 22 gr. of Gold & 27 oz. 13 dwt. of Metell Containing about 5 oz. 6 dwt. of fine Silver in Every Pound weight with a mixture of about 2 or 3 dwt. of Gold but wether there is a Sufficient Quantity of Gold to Defray the Expence of Seperating I must Leave to thee to Judg off after it is Essayed   I Doubt Not but thee will make the most of that & the Gold & Please to Creadit my Account with the Neat Proceeds   from thy Sincear friend

Joseph Richardson

Philadelphia the 25th   9th mo. 1764

Much Esteamed friends How Masterman & Archer

Your letter by Captain Budden I Received with the Plate by him Sent with my Account whereby there is a Ballence of of [sic] £15/19/3 Due to You which I have No Objection to & have herewith Sent 10 oz. 3 dwt. 18 gr. of Gold to Ballence our Account & for what Remains Please to Send me 12 Cards of Small Childrens Crystol Buttons & 6 Cards of Do. of the Comon Siz & as many Correls & Bells as the money will Purchase   Business at our trade is at Preasent at a very Low Ebb   However if I Should have Occation for any thing in Your way for the future   Shall Prefer your Shop beyond any other & Remain your Sincear friend

Joseph Richardson

Sent the Above by Captain Budden

Philadelphia the 19th   10th mo. 1764

Respected friends How Masterman & Archer
   Captain Budden Left Philadelphia the 25th of Last tho his Ship fell Down the River Some Short time before   If He Should Not be Arived befor this Comes to hand Please to Gett the Value of 10 oz. of Sterling Gold Insured on board his Ship If it Can be Done at what You May think a Resonable Premium & Pl[e]ase to add 4 Doz. of Steel topt Silver thimbles Instead of Some of the Correls I wrote for

from Your Obliged friend
Joseph Richardson

[crossed out below]   As the Publick affairs here the Proprietary Party are at Preasent Pritty Quiet as to any Publick Commotions which I Apprehend is [illegible and discontinued]

[not in Joseph Richardson's hand]

Philadelphia the 18th   5th mo. 1763

Respected friends Masterman & Archer
   Yours by Captain Budden I have Lately Received with Your Kind Preasent for which I am obliged to you.   I find you have Ballenced our Account Agreeable to my Request which I Doubt not is Right.   I have Inclosed a Bill of Lading for 500 Pieces of 8 weighing 432 oz. 4 dwt. & have Drawn upon You for £100 Sterling Payable to William Hulbeart or order, of Bristol, at 30 Days Sight with Hope will be Duly Paid as I have No Imediate Occation of any thing in your way what small Ballence May Remain Please to Creadit Me with. The bearer Hereof Joseph Allen my Brother in Law Being Disposed to make a Voyage to your Parts Partly on Account of trade If any thing Presents Likely to be Advantage I thought Propper to Recommend him to your Notice that if he Should have Occation of any advice or Assistance he may have a friend to Apply to in any Case of Dificulty which he being a Stranger may be Exposed to.   What ever Service you may Extend to him Shall be Acknowledged as if done to my Self from your Sincear friend.

Joseph Richardson

[In Joseph Richardson's hand]   Sent by Captain Budden [up left margin]

Philadelphia the 18th   5th mo. 1765

Respected Friends Masterman & Archer

These are to Cover a Bill of Lading for 500 Pieces of 8 Shipt by Captain Budden who Intends to Sail from this Port this Day if She Should Not be Arived before this Comes to Hand Please to Get the Value of 500 Pieces of 8 Insured on my Account as I have Drawn on You for 100 Pounds Sterling Payable to William Hulbeart of Bristol or Order I would Willingly have the Money Ready to Answer it from Your friend

Joseph Richardson

[written below]   the above Pieces of 8 Stands me in about £187/0/0
[written up left margin]   sent by Captain Ross by way of Cork
[not in Joseph Richardson's hand]

Philadelphia 7th   6th mo. 1766

Friend Rebecca Howell

I Received thy letter a few days ago with a Bill on Benjamin Kendle for £27/14/0 & tenderd it to him the same day to which he made some Objections to the Acceptance thereof Alledging that Some of the the [sic] Shoes where Unsold However he has Promised to make me Satisfaction, & thee may Depend that my Indeavours to Recover the mony for thee shall be the same as if it was my own, & Doubt Not as he is an able man that he will Pay it without given himself or me much Trouble of wich I hope in my next to give the a more Particular Account & Remains thy Friend

Joseph Richardson

[not in Joseph Richardson's hand]

Philadelphia the 6th   mo. 12th 1766

Friend Rebecca Howel

I wrote to thee the 7th of this Instant   Since which I have had some Conference with Benjamin Kendel who Elledges that the goods he had was from thy Son to whome he is to Account for them wherefore I think it would be proper for thee to get the whole Account Debt & Credit Drawn out of such Goods as he had on his own account as also what was upon Commissions which Directions from thee & thy Son to me to Settle with him.   Please to Observe to Credit him with return of Premium If there was any & for what goods he had upon his own Account I think you may very Justly Charge him with Interest after a Reasonable time of Credit he has about 23 pair womans Shoes on hand which I proposed to take in part of Pay & to Dispose of them to the Best advantage in Order to Settle the Account but as I had Not Orders to Settle any Other Account but what thee Directed must Defer it till I here further from the and shall be willing to do the what Service Lays in my Power & am thy Sincear friend

Joseph Richardson

[in Joseph Richardson's hand]
P.S.   I understand that my Brother in Law Joseph Allen wrote to thee for Some Shoes etc. which thee thought Not Proper to Send as he was a Stranger which we

Dont Blame thee for if the Please to Send the Shoes etc. which are mentioned in the Invoice I will be Security for his Makeing thee Good Pay he is Ingauged in Business for the Publick or otherwise he would have wrote to thee himself more at Large from thy friend

Joseph Richardson

[not in Joseph Richardson's hand]

Philadelphia the 4th   6th mo. 1766

Much Esteamed friends Masterman & Archer

    Your of the 16th 3rd mo. last by Captain friend I Received this Day & am Pleased to find my Bill on you in favour of William Hulbeart is Paid & hope you will Excuse my Troubleing you on Such Occations.   The Inquiry Cocerning John Hunt Cooper Shall be made agreeable to your Request & proper Legal Cirteficate I shall Indeavour to Procurre In fase of his Decease of which in my Next I Expect to be more Perticular   I have herewith Inclosed a Bill of Lading for 15 oz. 7 dwt. 6 gr. of Gold which Please to Dispose of to the best Advantage & Credit my account with the Neat Proceeds & Please to Send Per first Convenient Oppertunity one Doz. Plain Correls & 8 Bells & 1 Doz. Chast Do. & 1 Doz. Peices of Correls to weigh about 5 dwt. a Peice one with another & 6 Doz. Steel topt thimbles   Trade is & has been at Low ebb among us for some time Past but hope the Repeal of the Stamp act will be a means of Uniting the Colonies in a more close Union with their Brethen in England than Ever which Event I hope will be Productive of much Good & Calls for Thankfullness to the Supreem Disposer of all things & Gratitude to the King & Parliment of Great Briton   A Dutyful Address is Now Prpareing [sic] by our Assembly to the King on the Occasion. The letter for John Woolman I Delivered to his Brother Uriah Woolman who Promised to Send it by a Careful Hand to him who Lives about 20 miles from this City

[unsigned]

[not in Joseph Richardson's hand]

Philadelphia the 19th   9th mo. September 1766

Respected friends Masterman & Archer

    By Captain Egdon I Shipt 15 oz. 7 dwt. 6 gr. of Gold which I hope is Got to Hand as we have an account of his Arivel & not having any Imediate Occasion for any thing more than what I have wrote for in your way I have Drawn on you for £35/ 7/6 Sterling payable to William Hulbert of Bristol which I desire the favour you would pay on my Account   I have made Inquiry among the Coopers concerning John Hunt Cooper but cannot get any certain Intelegance concerning him as yet & have Since wrote an Advertizement & Published it in the Gazette by which means I am in hopes of Hearing off him of which I hope to be more perticular In my Next & remain Your Sincere friend

Joseph Richardson

[The advertisement Richardson mentioned was carried in the *Pennsylvania Gazette* on September 18, 1766, and is dated September 11th:

> If John Hunt, by trade a cooper, who resided in this city, as I am informed by letters from London, about 15 years past, is living, he is desired to apply to the Subscriber who can inform him of his advantage; or if any person can give any account of him, whether living or not, they are requested to inform me, which shall be gratefully acknowledged by Joseph Richardson, Goldsmith.]

[not in Joseph Richardson's hand]

Philadelphia 14th 11th mo. 1766

Respected friends Masterman & Archer

Yours of 14th 8th mo. last per Captain Marshall Received Since which I have Received Some Inteligence of John Hunt Cooper by a Letter from the Minister of Some Congregation at Carlisle a twon [sic] about 120 miles from this City near which place Said Hunt Resides & is a Member of that Congregation Soon after the Receipt of the said letter the Said Hunt came to this City with whome I have had some conversation Concerning his famaly & place of abode when in England & he informs me that hes [sic] was Born in Stafford Shire & that his Fathers Name was John Hunt, that he had three Brothers Named William, Samuel & George & a Sister Named Margrett that William & Samuel Lived in Woolverhampton in Stafford Shire & where Shoemakers by Trade he appears to me to be about 50 Years of Age. if there is any Estate fallen to him he would be glad to Know & if Not if any Person is Benefited by this Intelligence, I Apprehend some Compensation for his trouble & Expence in taking such a Long Journey would be but Reasonable. I Cannot from your Description Determin wether this is the Man but as he is the only Person that applyed to me of that Name & Trade I thout propper to give as Circomstantial Account of him as I could by which you may be Able to Determin wether he is the person or not. from Your Sincere Friend.

Joseph Richardson

[not in Joseph Richardson's hand]

Philadelphia the 11th 12th mo. 1766

Respected friend Thomas Wagstaffe

By thy Letter of the 22nd 2nd mo. Last I observe thee has Sent the State of our Account & the Ballence Due to thee is £0/21/11 I have now sent a Bill of Exchange for 100 Pounds Sterling Payable to thee which when Received Please to Pay to Rebecca Howell 50 Pounds Sterling when Called for taking a Receipt for it on my Account & for the Remainder after Discharging the old Debt Due to the Please to Send me as many Good five & Six Pound watches as the Money will pay for I hope the will send me such as are good of the Price which will oblige thy Sincere Friend.

Joseph Richardson

P.S   I Doubt not but the Bill will be Accepted & paid but if it should prove otherwise Please to get a proper protest & send it back that I may recover thy Money with Damages from the Drawer.

Joseph Richardson

[not in Joseph Richardson's hand]   Philadelphia 11th of the 12th mo. 1766

Respected Friend Rebecca Howell

   Thy Letter of the 30th 9th mo. Last I have Received with the watch & Shoes according to Invoice the watch dont prove to be So good as might be expexted at the Price   However I shall Endeavour to Dispose of it for the Best Price & Remitt thee the Money My Brother Joseph Allen Complains of there being too many Pumps they not being so Saleable as Shoes I have Now sent to Thomas Wagstaffe a Bill of Exchange for 100 Pounds Sterling [crossed out] Payable after 90 Days Sight which when received I have Desired him to Pay thee 50 Pounds Sterling which Desire thee to call upon him for & Doubt not the Payment thereof when he has Received it   I Should have Chose a Bill of a Shorter time for Payment but could not get it without paying an Extraordinary Price & hope it will not be attended with any Great Disadvantage & am thy Sincere Friend

Joseph Richardson

[not in Joseph Richardson's hand]   Philadelphia the 7th   2nd mo. 1767

Respected Friends Masterman & Archer

   These are   At the   Desire off a   Friend to Request the favour of you to Purchase a Bell of two feet Diameter a Cross the Mouth it is for the Court House at York in the County of York in this Province I would have No wheel gudgens [ie. gudgeons, the pivots on which bells swing] Rope Nor anything Else which may be Nesasary in hanging it but only the Bell with its Clapper I would have a goog [sic] one & whatever the cost may be shall carefully pay I have seen one here which came from London Charged at 14 pence Per Pound which I only mention for your Information without Intending any Restrictions with Respect to the Price   I hope you will excuse my giving you this trouble & shall be glad of an oppertunity to Render you any Acceptable Service that I am Capable off from Your Sincere Friend

Joseph Richardson

P.S.   Please to send it as Soon as Conveniently may be

Joseph Richardson

[not in Joseph Richardson's hand]   Philadelphia the 27th   4 mo. 1767

Respected Friend Rebecca Howell

   These comes to acquaint thee that I have after frequent Applycations Obtained

Benjamin Kendels Accounts Relating to thee & thy Son but as they are Not Satisfactory we have agreed to Submit them to the Detirmination of Owen Jones & John Pemberton two Men of Reputation who I Doubt Not will do the Just part I am sorry I am not able to Send a more agreeable Account of my Proceedings but Benjamin Has Been Indisposed of Late which has Delayed the Settlement I shall do my Endeavor to Get them Settled as Soon a Possible

Joseph Richardson

[not in Joseph Richardson's hand]

Philadelphia 26th   5th mo. 1767

Respected Friend Thomas Wagstaffe

    By My Letter to thee of the 11th 12th mo. last I Desired thee to pay to Rebecca Howell 50 Pounds Sterling I have Now Sent to her 200 Dollars by this Conveyance & therefore Desire thee would Defer the Payment of that Money untill further Orders from thy Friend

Joseph Richardson

[not in Joseph Richardson's hand]

Philadelphia the 15th   10th mo. 1765

Respected friends Masterman & Archer

    Yours by Captain friend I Received with Account of Sales of 500 Dollars Shipt by Captain Buden And am Obliged to you for the Kindness Shewn to my Brother in Law Joseph Allen whom we dayly Expect.   I have Here inclosed a Bill of Lading for 20 oz. 4 dwt. of Gold which Please to Dispose off for the Best Price   I have also Drawn on you for £50 Sterling Payable to William Hulbeart of Bristol or Order which I hope you will Excuse what Ballence may Remain Please to Credit my Account with.

from your Obliged Friend
Joseph Richardson

[not in Joseph Richardson's hand]

Philadelphia the 16th   12th mo. 1765

Respected Friend Thomas Wagstaff

    I have Omited Writing to thee for some time Past I hopes of a Prospect Opening for further Dealings with thee but as that is not Likely to be the Case at Present, as I have Several of those Watches by me which I had of thee Last Therefore Request thee would let me have thy Account Per first Oppertunity & Whatever may be Due Shall be Paid I hope to thy Satisfaction

From thy Friend
Joseph Richardson

[not in Joseph Richardson's hand]

Philadelphia the 10th   9th mo. 1766

Respected Friend William Hulbeart

We have Now to Inform thee that we have finished the Sales of thy Estate here & have Sent the Account herewith & a Bill of Exchange Drawn on Masterman & Archer for the Ballence being £35/17/6 Sterling which Doubt not will be Duly Honored we can assure the that we have done the best we Could for thy Interest but the Scarcity of Money amongst us has been the Reason of its Selling at so Low a Price we waited in hopes that Leonard Warnts would have Purchast the Ground Rent at Private Sale but found he was not able to Pay for it unless we would sell it much below the Value.   Wherefore we thought it best to Sell it at Public Vendue at the Coffee House which we did for £58 as the will find by the Account   Please to write to us Per first oppertunity to Let us know wether the Bills are Paid or not

from thy Friend   Joseph Richardson

[not in Joseph Richardson's hand]

Philadelphia the 1st   6th mo. 1767

Respected Friend Thomas Wagstaff

I have this Day Received thine of the 11th of the 4th mo. Last the Disapointment that must attend the Protesting of the Bill on Godhard Hagan & Co. Both to thee & Rebecca Howell as well as myself Came early under my Consideration & therefore Soon after we had the Account of that Unhappy Affair, I Shipt to the by Captain Sparks 13 oz. 0 dwt. 18 gr. of Gold & to Rebecca Howel by Captain Friend I Shipt 200 Dollars which Gold I hope will Pretty Near Pay for the watches   If thee Should Send the Bill Back Protested I Suppose that it is Recorded at the Notary Publicks office & as the Bill was accepted by Godhard Hagan & Co. thou art Authorized to Recover the money from there & state if it is Sufficient to Pay, or a Dividend with the Rest of there Creditors if there is not Sufficient to Pay the whole. Tench Francis's Estate I Beleave wont Pay 1/4 Part of what he Drew for & it would be with Reluctance that the Merchants here would Look to his Estate for it as it is Properly Godhard Hagan & Company Debt, I Desire thee would Do the best thee can for my Interest & take advice therein if Nessacary & Inform me how matters Stands as Oppertunity & Occation may offer

From thy Friend
Joseph Richardson

[not in Joseph Richardson's hand]

Philadelphia the 29th of the 6th mo. 1767

Respected Friend Rebecca Howell

I have after Frequent Duning Recovered the money from Benjamin Kendall agreeable to the Settlement as Mentioned in mine to thee of the 23rd of Last month which I hope thee has Received which I have now Shipt by Captain Tillet in Milled Spanish Dollars Ninety Seven of which is on thy Account & Sixty Six on Account of Henry Finch which Please to Deliver to him when Arrived & as Insurance is at a low Premium I thought best to get Insurance on them Here which I hope will meet with thy Approbation the Shoes which Benjamin Kendall returned are not yet Disposed off a [sic] many of them are low heals & very Unsaleable thy watch also Remains unsold I shall do the Best I can for thy Interest & am thy Assured Friend

Joseph Richardson

P.S.   I have herein inclosed Benjamin Kendalls Account for thee to Peruse as they are Settled they are of no further use to me & may be some Satisfaction to thee

[not in Joseph Richardson's hand]

Philadelphia 29th   6th mo. 1767

Respected Friend Henry Finch

My Letter to thy mother Rebecca Howel of the 23rd of Last month I hope is come to hand In which I Sent the State of your Accounts with Benjamin Kendall I have after Frequent Duning Recovered the money for which he gave his Notes Payable on Demand which I Received not till the 27th Instant I have now by Captain Tillet Shipt 163 milled Spanish Dollars 66 of which is on thy Account & 97 on thy mothers Account which make up the whole of what Cash I have Received & Some Small matter I have made Insurance on what I have Now Shipt & as the Premium is low I hope it will be approved off thy Channell Pumps Returned by Benjamin Kendall wont Suit our hot wether in the Summer Season therfore dont expect to Dispose of them till fall I Shall do the Best I can for thy Interest & am thy Friend

Joseph Richardson

P.S.   I have herein inclosed Benjamin Kendalls Account for thee to Peruse as they are Settled they are of no further use to me & may be Some satisfaction to thee

[not in Joseph Richardson's hand]

Philadelphia the 11th 5th mo. 1768

Respected Friend Rebecca Howell

I have herein Inclosed thy Account whereby there is a Ballance due to thee of £7/5/4 this Currency and to thy Son in Law Henry Finch £1/13/4 which two Ballences I have in my Letter to Masterman & Archer of the 30th 3rd mo. Last Requested them to Pay to thee which I Hope thee has Received   If any thing More can be Recovered of the outstandind |sic] Debts shall take care to Remitt it & am thy Friend

Joseph Richardson

Philadelphia the 11th   5th mo. 1768

Respected Friend Henry Finch

I have herein Inclosed thy Account whereby there is a Ballance due to thee of £1/13/4 this Currency which I have in my Letter to Masterman & Archer of the 30th

Letter Book of Joseph Richardson 253

3rd mo. Last Requested them to pay to thy Mother in Law together with a Ballance due to her which I hope has been Received   If any thing more can be Recovered of the outstanding Debts I shall take care to Remitt it & am thy Friend

Joseph Richardson

Philadelphia the 11th   mo. 4th 1769

Respected friend John Masterman

Thine of the 7th of 6th mo. last I have Received & Observe the Contents I have herein Incloased a Bill of Lading for 17 oz. 12 dwt. 12 gr. of Gold & an Invoice for a Parcell of Goods which I Desire may be Shipt Per first Conveniant oppertunity Provideed the Act of Parliment for Laying a Duty on Glass Painters Coulors etc. Should be Repealed which it is hoped will be at the Next Setting of the Parliment but if those Acts are Not Repealed & a General Exportation of Goods from London to america Doth Not take Place I would Not have thee to Ship any thing to me   I Expect thee will Send Good work & if they Should amount to Something more then the money Sent I Shall take Care Spedily to Remit the Ballence   Please to make Insureance on those Goods if thee Ships them & thee will oblige thy Loveing friend

Joseph Richardson

  Invoice of Goods for Joseph Richardson
- 4 Silver Double Belleyed tea Pots with Ingraved Borders
- 4 Silver Stands for Do.
- 4 Silver Shugar Dishes 20 Cream Pots to weight about 3 oz. a piece one with another
- 6 Doz. Pair Gold Scales & weights from 9 dwt. to 1/2 dwt. & a Set of Grains in Shagreen Casees the Penneyweights I would have about 1 gr. over weight that I may Regulate them myself
- 6 Cards of Briliant Crystol Buttons Set in Silver
- 2 Dozen Neat Double Joynted tea tongs 1 Doz. Single Do.
- 3 Doz. Plain Silver Stock Buckles & 1 Doz. Carved Do.
- 4 Pair of Pepper & Mustard Casters
- 6 Doz. of Steel topt thimbles Lined Not very Deep
- 12 Pieces of Correll to weigh about 5 dwt. a Piece
- 12 Oz. of Correll Beeds of Such a Size that 9 of them when Strung will measure 1 Inch
- 6 Shagreen Casees with 6 Pollished tea Spoons & tongs in Each Case
- 4 Silver ovel Peirced Salts of the Neatest Pattern with Glasses to them & a Dozen of Spare Glasses of the Same Sort
- 12 Pair of Silver Shoe & 12 Pair of Knea Buckles with Steel Ankers & tongues of the Neatest Patterns
- 6 Pair of Brilliant Crystol Buttons Sett in Gold Not over large   3 of them white the other three Pair Brown Crystol Strong Sett
- 100 Nests of Holland or Germin Crucibles Large fives there are Some that are

made in England but they are Not Near So Good

The Scale Beams Should be well Oiled or wrapt in Oil Paper to Prevent there Rusting

Philadelphia the 27th   11th mo. 1769

Respected Friend John Masterman

The above is a Copy of an Invoice Sent by Captain Falconer I would have but 2 Doz. of the Scales & weights with Shagreen Casees the other 4 Doz. to be in wooden Boxes   I am Senceable Some of the Above Articles are Not in thy way but hope it will Not be attended with much Trouble   Please to add three Scollopt or Shell Soop Ladles to the above   Times are very Precarious with us & therefore think it Nessasary to advise thee to be Causious who thee Trusts on this Side the water   I think it Not Prudent to be more Perticular least I Should Give offence but hope thee will take the hint from thy Friend

Joseph Richardson

Philadelphia the 14th   6th mo. 1770

Respected friend John Masterman

Since my last to thee I have Received thine of the 29th 3rd mo. last & am much Obliged to thee for thy Kind Preasent by Captain Falconer   These Comes by an Acquaintance of mine who has a Piece of Gold weighing 8 oz. 16 dwt. 6 gr. to Dispose off Please to Give him four Pounds Per oz. for it & if after an Assay is made of it it Should Prove of Less Value Please to Charge the Deficiency to my Account the Non Importation Agreement is Still Continued So I have No Expectation of trade being Opened untill the Duty on tea is Also taken off

From thy friend
Joseph Richardson

[not in Joseph Richardson's hand]

Philadelphia the 11th   10th mo. 1770

Respected Friend John Masterman

As the Merchants of this City hath Concluded to import any kind of Goods from England except Tea or such other Goods as may hereafter be Charged with a Duty Provided they are not Shipt before the 15th of the first Month next I have therefore herewith sent an Order for a Parcel of Plate etc. which I desire may be Shipt as soon after the 15th of the month aforesaid as thee Conveniently Can and make Insurance on them   from thy Obliged Friend

Joseph Richardson

Invoice of a Parcel of Plate etc.

One Silver Single Belleyed Coffee Pott to hold 3 wine Pints with Gadround Border Round the lid & foot
One Do. to hold a Quart with stands to them
two Pair of Pollished Pint Cans & 2 pair Silver Spurs
   3 Double Belleyed Silver Tea Potts with Ingraved Borders & Stands for Do.
   3 Silver Sugar Dishes with Gadround Borders
 15 Cream Potts about 3 oz. a piece one with another & 5 Urns
   6 Cards of Brilliant Christol Buttons set in Silver
   2 Cards of Christol Buttons with Cyphers
   2 Doz. Double Jointed Tea tongs & 1 Doz. Single Jointed Do.
   2 Doz. Plain Silver Stock Buckles & 1 Doz. Carved Do.
   4 Pair of Pepper & Mustard Casters with Glasses to the Mustard Caster
   6 Doz. Steel topt Thimbles & 4 Doz. Silver Do. not over Deep
 12 Pieces of Correl to weigh about 5 dwt. a Piece
 12 Ounces of Correll Beads of such a Size that 9 of them Measures 1 Inch
   6 Shagreen Cases with a Doz. of Pollished Tea Spoons & tongs in each Case
   4 Silver Salts with Glasses & Shovels to them
   6 Pair of Shoe Buckles & 6 Pair of Knea Do. Carved but not Peirced with Steel ankers & toungs
   6 pair of Brilliant Crystol Buttons strong sett in gold not over Large 3 of them white & the other 3 of a Light Brown
   1 Doz. of Chased Correls with 8 Bells & 1 Doz. plain Do.
   1 Doz. Pollished Table Spoons of the newest Fashion
   6 Doz. Pair of Gold Scales & weights from 9 dwt. to to [sic] 1/2 dwt. & a set of Grains in Wooden Cases the dwts to be about 1 Grain over weight
   3 Doz. Do. in Shagreen Cases with weights as above
   3 Nests of Troy weights 32 oz. in a Nest one of then [sic] Regulated to the Greatest Exactness agreeable to the Standard of England
   4 Silver Scollapt Soop Ladles in the form of a shell
100 Nests of German or Holland Crucibles Large fives
100 Nests of Do. Small fives

                                        £190

                         Philadelphia the 13th 10th mo. 1770

Respected friend John Masterman
    I omited to add to the above Invoice 3 Silver Slop Bowles with Gadround

Borders which I Now Desire thee would add to the above

from thy Obliged friend
Joseph Richardson

[not in Joseph Richardson's hand]

Philadelphia 5th mo. 1st. 1771

Respected Friend John Masterman
    These are to inform thee that I have Shipt Per Captain Sparks a piece of Gold as Per Bill of Lading if it doth not arive in one week after the Receipt of this Letter I would have 100 Pound Sterling Insured thereon. The Remaining Ballence of thy Account perpose to send towards Fall which I hope will be to thy satisfaction from thy sincere friend

Joseph Richardson

by Captain Falconer

[not in Joseph Richardson's hand]

Philadelphia 5th mo. 1st. 1771

Respected Friend John Masterman
    Thine of the 24th 1st mo. last I have Received with an Invoice of a Parcel of Plate etc. which are come safe though not altogether agreable to my mind as the greatest part of the scales are very Ordinary & the Slop Bowles not agreable to my directions & I thing [sic] high Charged   I have herewith shipt 26 oz. 2 dwt. 6 gr. of Gold by Captain James Sparkes which please to Credit my Account with the neat proceeds   I Purpose to send the Ballence of thy Account towards the Fall which I hope will be to thy satisfaction from thy sincere friend

Joseph Richardson

Per Captain Sparks

[not in Joseph Richardson's hand]

[no date, between letters dated 5th mo. 1st
1771 and 14th 10th mo. 1771]

Respected Friend Thomas Wagstafe
    I have herein Inclosed a Bill of Lading for a piece of Gold weighing 7 oz. 5 dwt. 8 gr. for which I desire the favour of thee to send me a parcel of money scales one half to be 6 Inch & the other half 7 Inch Beams & weights from 9 dwt. to 1/2 dwt. & a set of Grains to each pair in wainscot boxes which I think was the size of the last the shipt me & were Charged @ £0/38/0 per Doz. I would have them full as good as the last the sent me & request that they may be well Oiled to prevent their Rusting for want of which many of the former came in a very Rusty condition whatever the extraordinary Expence may be I shall Chearfully Pay. The Pennyweights I would

have one Grain over weight I should be pleased to have one Doz. Pair of scales of a better sort & of 2 or 3 Different prises which may serve as a sample for the future please to send them per the first Oppertunity as I much want them & I shall be much Obliged to thee from thy sincere Friend

Joseph Richardson

[not in Joseph Richardson's hand]   Philadelphia 14th   10th mo. 1771

Respected Friend John Masterman

Thine of the 3rd 7th mo. last I have received and do suppose thee never saw the scales & weights thee sent me but trusted to the workman as is common in such Cases   therefore do not complain of thy conduct therein but with respect to the Slop Bowles which are charged at £0/8/11 Per oz. when the Coffee Potts are Charged at £0/7/4 is so unequal that I apprehend that thee will make some abatement I have Per this conveyance Shipt 16 oz. 8 dwt. 18 gr. of Gold of equal fineness with spanish Dubloons with which pleas to Ballance my Account & for what remains please to send 6 oz. midling sised Correl Beads & as many fluted Soop Ladles as the money will pay for.   It doth not suit me at this time to send for much plate as a Considerable part of what I had of thee last remains on hand but whenever I shall have occation for any I intend send to my Friend Masterman   from thy Obliged Friend

Joseph Richardson

[not in Joseph Richardson's hand]   Philadelphia the 16th   10th mo. 1771

Respected Friend Thomas Wagstaffe

Thine of the 13th 7th mo. Last I have received with Invoice of a Parcel of Scales & weights which came in good Order & to Satisfaction except the Weights which are most of them too light.   I have now sent Some Weights & Desire for the future they may be made Exactly of the same Weight   If they are 1/20 of a Grain Lighter they will not Suit   I have also Shipt by Captain Sparks 5 oz. 15 dwt. 18 gr. of Gold & £0/19/0 Sterling in Silver And Desire thee would send me the following Scales & weights Viz

    20 pair of Scales with Box end Beams
        6 Inch & 3/4 Beam in Mahogany Cases
        with a 9 dwt. a 6 dwt. a 5 dwt. a 4 dwt. a 3 dwt.
        a 2 dwt. a 1 dwt. & 1/2 & a Sett of Grains to each pair
    20 Pair Scales in Black Shagreen Casses
     1 Doz. Neat Small Pocket Scales in Shagreen Cases the Beam Not to Exceed 3
        Inches with the following weights a 5 dwt. a 4 dwt. a 3 dwt. a 2 dwt.. a 1
        dwt. & 1/2 & a Sett of Grains to each pair
& if it will Suit thee to send a Couple of Watches of about 3 Pound a Piece I Shall

take Care to send Ballance which may Remain Due to thee by one of the first Vessels after their Arrival from thy friend

Joseph Richardson

[not in Joseph Richardson's hand]

Philadelphia the 29th 2nd mo. 1772

Respected Friend John Masterman

Thine of the 2nd of the 12th month last I have Received in which thee Observes the Gold by Captain Sparks dont hold out in the Weight according to my first Letter of the 11th of the 10th mo. last wherein I Said that I should send 22 oz. 4 dwt. 12 gr. wheras it held out no more than 16 oz. 8 dwt. 12 gr. to set that Matter Right I think it nesessary to inform thee that I did ship by Captain Sparks 22 oz. 4 dwt. 12 gr. though thee Received but 16 oz. 8 dwt. 12 gr. for a[s] I wrote to thee to get Insurance on Gold Shipt by Captain Sparks I thought it nesessary to acquaint thee that I had Shipt the Value of the Insurance Intended to be made So it is all right except the 6 gr. which the Piece thee Received weighs Lighter than what I made it which may be occasioned by our weights or Scales not agreeing. I have now by this oppertunity Shipt a Small Piece of gold weighing 15 oz. 7 dwt. 12 gr. for which I Request thee would send me a small Parcel of Plate according to the Invoice below. I am Obliged to thee for thy Kind Intentions to Supply me with Better Scales & weight If I should have occasion but I am at present Supplyed with a Sufficient Quantity

From thy Sincere Friend
Joseph Richardson

  6 oz. of Correll Beads Not Large
36 Carved Stock Buckles
24 Plain Do.
  6 Cream Urns Burnished
  4 Oval Silver Salts with Glasses to them
  6 Plain Correll & Bells with 8 Bells
  6 Chast Do.
  6 Doz. Steel Top Thimbles
  3 Cards of Brilliant Crystol Buttons
  3 Cards of Small Do. for Children
12 Table Spoons Polished of the Newest fashion
12 Pair of Carved Shoe Buckles of the newest fashion with steel ankers & tongues
12 Pair of Knee Do. to Suit the Shoe Buckles with Do.

Philadelphia the 5th 11th mo. 1774

Respected friend Thomas Wagstaffe

Thine of the 27th of the 8th mo. last I have Received Per Captain Waid with

6 Doz. Pair of Scales & Weights And thy Account by which there is a Ballence of £10/19/6 Sterling Due to thee I have Now Shipt Per Captain Nathaniel Falconer 48 & 1/2 Dollors weighing 42 Ounces Consigned to thee in order to Ballence Our Account if it Should Prove Deficient Please to let me know how much the Deficiency is for as I know Not how Silver Sells in London it is Probable it may Not be Exactly the Sum Due to Thee

From thy Friend
Joseph Richardson

[not in Letter Book. Loose Ms. in Richardson Papers. DMMC, 53.165.53.46]
Philadelphia the 26th 10th mo. 1773

Respected friend Thomas Wagstafe

Thine of the 17th 2nd mo. last is before me   And am Sorry thee Should have Changed the workman from a Better to a Worse for I Never had Such flat Beamed Scales from thee before Nor Never Desire any more of them   I have Now Shipt a Piece of Gold weighing 10 oz. 6 dwt. 12 gr. & Desire the favor of thee to Send me as many Pair of Good Scales & Weights for Weighing of Gold as the Money Will Pay for   I would have them Round Beams 7 Inches Long in Wainscot Boxes Or in Mahogany Boxes If the Difference Dont Exceed 3 or 4 Per Doz.   Please to Order them to be well Oiled to Prevent there Rusting & the Penney weights I would have One Grain & No more Over Weight the Weights to Each Pair of Scales as follows

    one 9 dwt.
    one 6
    one 5
    one 4
    one 3
    one 2
    one 1
    one 1/2
    & a Sett of Graines

As I apprehend thee art Capable of Judging between a Good Piece of Work & a bad one I hope thee will take Some Paines to Gett Such as are Good & Well Made which Will Oblige thy friend who would Do as much for thee if it Lay in his Power

Joseph Richardson

P.S.   I have Also to Request thee would Send me an Account how much Below Standard the Gold herewith Sent is & that there May be No Ballence Left unpaid but that our account may be Settled thy Complyance herewith will oblige thy friend

Joseph Richardson

In my Letter By Captain All I Rote for Insurance on the above

[not in Letter Book.   Loose Ms. in Richardson Papers, Ms. DMMC 53.165.53.46]
Philadelphia the 26th 10th mo. 1773

Respected friend John Masterman

Thine of the 6th of the 2nd mo. last is Now before me & Cannot but be Sencably Affected by the Account of those Trying times thee mentions James Best whome the [e] Recommended to me has Lately Arived he Suffered much in his Passage & was Sick for Some time After his Arival he has Now Recovered his health & as I understand has Bound himself for 3 Years to David Rittenhouse the Famos Mathamatition of Ameraca for the Payment of his Passage as I Did Not want a hand

I have herein Incloased a Bill of Lading for 17 oz. 6 dwt. 12 gr. of Gold with an Invoice for a Parcell of Plate Please to Order is So as to Ballence the Account by Leaveing out Some of the Articles if the money wont Pay for all or Ading to them if there is an Overplus I Expect to have Good Work & of the Neatest fashion Hessian Crucibles or None at all for those Made in or Near London wont Stand the fire

From thy Obliged Friend

Joseph Richardson

Invoice for a Parcel of Plate etc.
 3 Cards of Crystol Buttons Set in Silver
 3 Cards of Small Childrens Brilliant Buttons Sett in Silver
 3 Cards of Small Do. with Cyphers Set in Silver
12 Silver Cream Potts to weigh about 3 oz. a Piece
 1 Plain Single Belleyed Coffe Pot to hold 3 wine Pints
 1 Do. Do. to hold One Quart
24 Plain Silver Stock Buckles Not Above 1 Inch & 7/8 in length
24 Carved Do. Do.
 3 Doz. Pollished tea Spoons to weigh about 8 dwt. a Piece & 6 of the Neatest Spring tea tongs in Shagreen Casees
 2 Scolloped Soop Ladles
200 Nests of Hessian Crucibles Large fives
200 Nests of Do. Small fives

P.S. Please to Let me Know the Exact fineness of the Gold here with Sent which will Oblige thy Friend Joseph Richardson in my Letter by Captain All I wrote for Insurance on the Above

APPENDIX E

Inventory of the Shop of Joseph and Nathaniel Richardson

An Inventory of Goods belonging to Joseph & Nathaniel Richardson taken the 31st Day of the 5th Month 1790

	oz.	dwt.	gr.
1 Silver Tankard weighing	31	13	0
3 Do. Tea Potts	57	4	12
3 Do. Sugar Dishes	39	9	0
1 Do. Slop Bason	16	2	0
3 Do. Pint Canns	40	15	0
8 Do. Cream Potts	38	13	0
1 Do. Cadee	14	0	0
2 Do. Salvers	21	9	0
6 Do. Soup Ladles	36	7	0
45 Do. Table spoons	87	17	0
19 Do. Desert spoons	18	18	0
9 1/2 Dozen Do. Teaspoons	45	18	12
38 pair Silver Sugar Tongs	46	10	12
1 Do. Punch Strainer	2	19	0
1 Do. Pepper Box	2	14	0
4 Do. Salts with blue Glasses & Ladles	7	13	0
94 pair Silver Shoe Buckles	157	11	12
23 pair Knea Do.	10	7	0
46 Silver Stock Do.	22	1	0
2 Do. Cocks	4	7	12
5 Do. Watch Chains	2	18	0
1 Do. pair Spurrs	4	8	0
13 Do. Pincushion hoops & Chains	13	1	0
Carried over oz.	722	16	12

	[oz.]	[dwt.]	[gr.]
Brought over	722	16	12
19 Silver Pincushion Chains weighing	8	15	0
4 Do. Scisor Do. with hooks....................	4	6	0
2 Do. Hooks & 4 Hearts for Scisor Chains.................................	1	13	0
10 Do. Knitting Sheaths	2	0	0
1 Do. Do..			
71 1/2 Do. pair Sleeve Buttons & 1 pair Studs.....................................	10	10	0
5 Do. Bodkins		5	12
17 Do. Broaches......................................	1	4	0
10 Do. Hooks & Eyes		13	0
4 Do. Hooks for Knitting bags..................		12	0
1 Do. Marrow spoon & 1 Mustard spoon ...	1	9	0

3 Do. Whistles & Bells with Corals
3 Do. Whistles with Corals
6 Punch Ladles
5 Pocket Nutmeg graters
39 Steel top Thimbles
9 Silver Do.
1 Knitting Reel
1 Silver Snuff Box
11 pair & 5 odd pieces Silver Shoe Clasps
5 Pocket Book locks
2 Silver Salt ladles
15 Pair locket buttons

	oz.	dwt.	gr.
21 Pair Gold Sleeve buttons weighing	3	19	0
19 Gold Lockets	2	6	12

	[oz.]	[dwt.]	[gr.]	[oz.]	[dwt.]	[gr.]
1 Do. Broach & 1 ring		2	15			
1 pair Earrings						
	oz. 6	8	3			
				oz. 754	4	0

6 Pair large Oval Plated Candlesticks
2 Pair Square Do. Do.
4 Pair Chamber Do. Do.
4 Plated Quart Mugs
4 Do.   Pint   Do.
4 Do. Goblets
1 Do. Oil & Vinegar Stand
2 Do. Sauce Boats
3 Do. Cream potts
1 Small Salver
4 Plated Mustard Tankards with blue Glasses
3 Do. Toast Racks
6 Do. Sauce Ladles
25 Do. Egg Cups
30 Do. Labels
50 Do. pair Shoe Buckles
9 Do. pair Knea Do.
2 Horn Tumblers
1 Large pair box beam plate Scales
3 pair Smaller Do.   Do.
12 pair common plate scales
10 pair Smaller Do.
25 pair 7 Inch Money Scales in wainscot boxes
2 pair 6 Inch Do.   Do. in   Do.
6 pair box beam Do.   Do.   in Mahogany boxes
4 pair Do.   Do. with brass stands
15 pair box beam Scales in Shagreen Cases
11 pair pocket Scales in   Do.   Do.
28 pair Do.   Do. in Japan boxes
122 Setts of Apothecary's weights
105 Setts pennyweights and grains Compleat
139 Setts Grain weights
10 Nests of Ounce weights containing 64 oz. each
8 Nests   Do.   Do.   containing 32 oz. each
1 Do.   Do.   Do.

    8 Nests Do. Do. containing 16 oz. each
a Parcel of odd pennyweights as follows
         62   9 dwts.
         53   6 & 5
         75   4
         46   2
         53   1
         78   1/2
a Parcel of odd grain weights
 4 Long and 12 short strings Coral Beads
12 short Strings   Do. inferior kind
30 pieces Coral weighing 7 oz.
26 Shells for snuff boxes
 7 blue Glasses For Salts (DMMC, 53.165.222)

Notes

CHAPTER 1 *Francis Richardson, Silversmith (1681-1729)*

1. The Quaker records are not in agreement as to the former residence of Rebecca Haward (also spelled Howard and Haywood). The Records of Marriages, E-26, 2, at Arch Street Meeting in Philadelphia indicate that she came from Uxbridge in Middlesex, while the Philadelphia Monthly Meeting Records at the Historical Society of Pennsylvania (hereafter HSP) cite Yorkshire.

2. *New-York Historical Society Collections, 1885,* 53.

3. Frederick D. Stone, "A Vindication of William Penn, "*Pennsylvania Magazine of History and Biography,* VI (1882), 175, cites a letter written to William Penn, June 25, 1681, which said, "this is to acquaint thee that about ten daies since here arrived Francis Richardson with thy Deputy."

4. Two account books are preserved at the HSP and another at The Henry Francis du Pont Winterthur Museum; an additional book was sold at auction at the Freeman Gallery in Philadelphia on January 27, 1959.

5. Francis Richardson, "Account Book", Joseph Downs Manuscript and Microfilm Collection at the Winterthur Museum Libraries (hereafter DMMC), MS 53.165.44b.

6. These births are recorded in the family Bible, several pages of which are illustrated in Mary T. Seaman, *Thomas Richardson of South Shields and His Descendants* (New York, 1929), between pp. 34 and 35. The Bible was bequeathed to the Peter Muhlenberg Chapter of the Daughters of the American Revolution in Philadelphia, Pennsylvania by Miss Josephine R. Howell in 1947, according to the *Philadelphia Inquirer,* Oct. 22, 1947. It is now at the National Headquarters of the D.A.R. in Washington, D.C.

7. The entry in the family Bible, which reads 1695 instead of 1685, is an obvious error because it is made between entries dated 1683-84 and 1687.

8. Dates, except in quotations, have been modernized by the editors. Prior to January 1, 1752, when the Gregorian calendar was adopted in England, the first month of the year was March so that this factor has also been taken into consideration when translating the Quaker

method of dating into modern terms. Until the mid-18th century, dates during the months at the end of one year and beginning of the next were often written to indicate both years, i.e. 1681/2. Up to 1700 the difference between the Old Style (Julian) and the New Style (Gregorian) system was ten days since Pope Gregory XIII ordained that ten days be dropped from the calendar in 1582 and that years ending in hundreds be leap years only if divisible by 400. The year 1700 being a leap year in the Julian calendar and a common year in the Gregorian, the difference of the styles during the 18th century was eleven days instead of ten. Hence, a date of the 11th of the 1st month 1681/2 would be modernized to read March 21, 1682 while the 11th of the 1st month 1754 would be January 22, 1754.

9. Seaman, p. 35.

10. On April 27 of that year, "Francis Richardson and Elisabeth Frampton, having laid some matter in Controversy before this meeting" a group of Friends was duly appointed to meet that evening at Elisabeth Frampton's house to do their best to "put an End thereto" (Minutes of the Monthly Meeting, E-1, 34, Arch St. Mtg.). Elisabeth Frampton was the widow of William Frampton, a close friend of Richardson's, who died in 1686 (Josiah Granville Leach, "Colonial Mayors of Philadelphia," *Pa. Mag., XVIII* [1904], 105).

11. Records of Marriages, E-26, 8, Arch St. Mtg.

12. Seaman, pp. 19–20.

13. *Ibid.* p. 35 In September 1688 Abraham de Peyster and Philip Richards made an inventory of Francis Richardson's estate which included a house and ground in sheep pasture valued at £130, a Negro boy, and two Negro women. The total of the estate was £1,860/7/4 (DMMC, PH-405).

According to the inventory, Francis Richardson had on hand at the time of his death, large quantities of fabrics including woolen and silk clothing materials, linen for household uses as well as clothing; chintzes, fustians and other cotton fabrics; stockings, handkerchiefs; and four Millbeak rugs. He also had some spices (nutmegs, mace, cinnamon, cloves), large quantities of nails, fishhooks, scissors, tobacco tongs, chest locks, latches and hinges, tools, playing cards, six sets of curtains and valances, and eighteen olivewood looking glasses.

His house furniture included eighteen chairs, twelve turkey-work chairs, an armchair, four tables, a clock and case, four beds with furniture (hangings), a cane couch, four looking glasses and a glass case, three chests of drawers, two screens, three stands, three pairs of andirons (one of which was brass), a pair of iron dogs, shovels, tongs, and brass fenders, a warming pan, "silver wrought 9 lbs. 6 ounces," a map of Philadelphia (perhaps showing the location of his land in Crittenham (Cheltenham?), two small trunks, one glass case and glasses, one cupboard, earthenware, five candlesticks, a lamp, a parcel of pewter, bellows, a jack and a spit. The final listing is "a Bible in folio & some small bookes £2:10-." This is probably the same Bible in which the Richardson family births were recorded.

14. Seaman, p. 36.

15. Records of Marriages, E-26, 8, Arch St. Mtg. Edward Shippen had had business transactions with Francis Richardson, and was one of those with an outstanding account against Francis' estate at the time of his death. On February 27, 1689, Shippen had acknowledged receipt of £31/6/9 from Rebecca Richardson (DMMC, 53.165.32).

16. Thomas Balch, "Dr. William Shippen, the Elder," *Pa. Mag.*, I (1877), 212–13; *Collections of the Massachusetts Historical Society, 5* (ser. 5, Book I, 1878), 219.

17. Young Francis is quoted as having written that he "was removed to Philadelphia in

1690," although some authorities believe that the Shippen family arrived in Philadelphia in 1694 (Seaman, p. 39; Samuel W. Woodhouse, Jr., "Colonial Craftsmen of Philadelphia," *Art and Archaeology*, (April 1926), 182–86). One child, a daughter named Elizabeth, was born to Edward and Rebecca Shippen in October 1691, but she died in August 1692 (Phila. Mo. Mtg. Rec., p. 49, HSP).

18. Frederick B. Tolles, *Meeting House and Counting House* (Chapel Hill, N.C., 1948), p. 43.

19. Gabriel Thomas, *An Historical and Geographical Account of the Province of Pensilvania and of West-New-Jersey in America* (London, 1698), p. 43.

20. Mrs. Alfred Coxe Prime, *Three Centuries of Historic Silver* (Philadelphia, 1938), p. 76. According to the family genealogist, Mary T. Seaman, "The step-brothers, Francis Richardson and Edward Shippen, were brought up together, and were later sent to Europe for education, and letters of those days state 'They are very hopeful young men, both'" (Seaman, p. 38).

21. The search of the London records was kindly made by Charles C. Oman, Keeper of Metalwork, Victoria and Albert Museum.

22. William Penn, "Cash Book," American Philosophical Society.

23. DMMC, 53.165.57.52.

24. DMMC, 53.165.57.50.

25. DMMC, 53.165.57.57.

26. Phila. Mo. Mtg. Rec., p. 49, HSP.

27. Min. Mo. Mtg., E-1, 202, Arch St. Mtg.

28. This date and information concerning the witnesses of the marriage were found in a photostatic copy of the marriage certificate given the author by Mrs. Alfred Coxe Prime. The original is in the possession of Robert S. Stuart of Philadelphia. (P.G. Seabury, "Early Marriages in Newport, Rhode Island, from Friends' Record," *The New England Historical and Genealogical Register*, XVIII [Albany, 1864], 241). Nathan Stanbury, who saw to Francis' "clearness," was present, as was James Logan. Fellow goldsmith Johannis Nys signed the certificate, as did Peter Stretch, the clockmaker, and John Jones and John Jones, Jr., one of whom may have been the goldsmith listed by Maurice Brix as having died in 1768 *(List of Philadelphia Silversmiths and Allied Artificers from 1682 to 1850* [Philadelphia, 1920], p. 56).

29. DMMC, 53.165.57.54.

30. DMMC, 53.165.57.58.

31. Phila. Mo. Mtg. Rec., p. 49, HSP.

32. William Roy Smith, "Edward Shippen," *Dictionary of American Biography*, ed. Dumas Malone, XVII, 116. Soon after this marriage, Edward Shippen's stepchildren, Francis and Rebecca Richardson, and Rebecca's husband, Thomas Murray, transferred to him the lot of land owned by their father located at the southwest corner of Second and Walnut Streets (Seaman, p. 35). It may be that this transaction had something to do with the difference "long & depending" between Shippen and Murray which the latter reported to the Friends Monthly Meeting on January 30, 1708. The committee appointed to investigate the dispute included some who had been appointed in 1703 to look into differences between Edward Shippen and Francis Richardson. While these matters apparently were settled at the time, in 1711 Edward

Shippen complained to the Monthly Meeting of another difference between them which again was settled through a committee of Friends (Min. Mo. Mtg., *E-1*, 173, 241, 288, Arch St. Mtg.).

33. Seaman, pp. 38, 40.

34. In 1724 Francis and Abigail Golding declared their intentions of marrying but nothing more came of it. When a committee of Friends called upon Francis late in 1725 to find out about the matter, Francis told them the marriage would not take place because Abigail had refused him (Min. Mo. Mtg., *E-3*, 114-15, 130, Arch St. Mtg.) Samuel Powel and John Jones reported, according to custom, that the marriage of Francis and Letitia was carried out in an orderly fashion. Joseph and Frank were perhaps too young to sign the marriage certificate, but Rebecca Young was among the signers. She was probably Francis' sister who, after the death of her husband Thomas Murray, married a Young. Entries in Francis' account book speak of "My sister Rebekah Young" (Min. Mo. Mtg., *E-3*, pp. 134, 135; Arch St. Mtg.; DMMC, 53.165.44).

35. Nicholas B. Wainwright, *A Philadelphia Story* (Philadelphia, 1952).

36. Thomas, *An Account*, p. 31.

37. "Sezor Gisling/John Pearse" are listed as silversmiths who came to Chester, Pennsylvania from England in 1681, on the ship *Bristol Factor* (Edgar P. Richardson, "Remnants, Precious to Antiquaries...," *Antiques, LXXIII* [March 1958], 264). Nothing more is known about John Pearse, but on the 1693 tax list Ghiselin's property is valued at £100 and taxes for £0/8/4. In 1701 William Penn recorded his patronage by payment of "the Goldsmith's note ... Cesar Ghiselin £1-14-0." ("Cash Book," Am. Phil. Soc.). Ghiselin was also among those who in 1708 signed the election certificate of the coroner of Philadelphia, Nicholas Pearse, possibly a relative of John Pearse (Harrold E. Gillingham, "Cesar Ghiselin, Philadelphia's First Gold and Silversmith 1693-1735," *Pa. Mag.*, LVII [July 1933], 244-59). Some of the objects made by Cesar Ghiselin include a silver alms plate and beaker given to Christ Church in Philadelphia by Margaret Tresse, and a remarkable silver folding spoon now at the Philadelphia Museum of Art. That he also worked in gold is suggested by the advertisement in the *Maryland Gazette* for November 16, 1752, "Found a Gold Ring, the Maker's stamp C.G. having a posey on it. The Owner may have it by applying to the finder" (quoted by Gillingham, p. 257). The inventory of Ghiselin's estate taken in Philadelphia on March 7, 1733, following his death in February, lists his tools, including a flatting mill, his folio French Bible, and sundry small French books indicating Huguenot ancestry (*Ibid.*, p. 248).

38. Brix, p. 79. In his will, dated December 16, 1695, Paschall calls himself "silversmith" (William M. Hornor, Jr., "The Richardson Family, Silversmiths of Philadelphia," *Antiquarian*, XIV [May 1930], 42).

39. Alfred Coxe Prime, *The Arts and Crafts in Philadelphia, Maryland and South Carolina*, 1st. ser., 1721-85 (Topsfield, Mass, The Walpole Society, 1929), p. 86; *Minutes of the Common Council of the City of Philadelphia 1704 to 1776* (Philadelphia, 1847), pp. 126, 133. Neither William England nor Edward Hunt is mentioned in the accounts of Francis Richardson in the years immediately after their admission, although there are accounts with a John Hunt and with Englands named Daniel, Joseph, and Mary (DMMC, 53.165.44). An interesting note: in 1720, Edward Hunt was charged with counterfeiting Spanish coins (*American Weekly Mercury*, Oct. 20, 1720, cited by Gillingham, p. 258).

40. Certainly no other goldsmith's name has been spelled so variously by the man him-

self as well as by others. John Marshall Phillips suggests that he might be the Johannis Nys baptised in 1671 and married in 1693 in the Dutch Church at New York ("Johannis Nys." *Bulletin of the Associates in Fine Arts at Yale University,* VI [September 1933], 13). Harold E. Gillingham believed him to have been one of the French Huguenots who went to Holland before coming to Pennsylvania ("A Philadelphia Silver Porringer," *Pa. Mag.,* LV [1931], 170). In Gillingham's article the name is spelled John Nys. Two other variations on the spelling of the name occur in the Isaac Norris, Sr., "Journal," 1709-16: John De Noys, in an entry dated 1712, and in an entry dated 1716, John Neys. Of special interest is the record in James Logan's "Account Book," 1712-19, "pd Jno De Nys for making 6 fforks... £-6" (Samuel W. Woodhouse, Jr., "John DeNys, Philadelphia Silversmith," *Antiques,* XXI [May 1932], 218), indicating positively that some forks were made in America as early as the second decade of the eighteenth century. Nys was also the maker of the rare pair of sucket forks now at the Philadelphia Museum of Art.

41.	9th mo. 24	John Denise [Johannis Nys] is Debtor			
		To 11 Pennyweight Silver	[£] 3	[shillings] 11	[pence]
		To a Small Cutting punch	00 01		6
		To Sundryes as a Stamp and pliers	01 06		6
		To a Shilling Short in the Spoons	00 01		0
		To Silver for a porringer 11 oz. 15 dwt.			
	15th 4 th mo. 1720	To 2 files		2	6
	5th 7th mo. 1720	To a Lookin Glass	2	12	0
		To 3 Spoons wt. 5 oz. 17 dwt. making		7	6
		To Silver Short Returned 17			
	I:D	Left unpaid towards a Ring £0/1/11			
		To a pennyweight Silver Returned Short			
		To Argell 1 oz.			
	15th 3rd mo.	To 1 pennyweight Gold Lent him.			

On the Credit side of the ledger, Nys paid Francis Richardson in the following ways:

	by making 3 Silver Spoons	–	9	–
	by Making 2 Silver Spoons		6	–
4th 4th mo.	by a Spoon making		3	–
	by a poringer weight 9 oz. 1 dwt. Making		10	0
	by a Chape for a buckell 4 dwt.			
	by Silver in a poringer handle 14 dwt.			
	by a cup & poringer making		14	
	by a buchell of Coals	–	–	10
	by making a ferell		1	8
	by a poringer making		11	0

by cash Received her [sic]	3 7	0
by Silver for 3 spoons 6 oz. 15 dwt.		
by 2 bushells Coles		
by making 3 spoons		
by making one Spoon		
by making a porringer		10

(DMMC, 53.165.44).

The similarity noted by Phillips ("Johannis Nys," p. 15) between the early keyhole style of porringer handles used by Nys and Richardson may be explained at least partially by the fact that Nys made four porringers for Richardson as shown in the above accounts. It is also noteworthy that in these accounts Francis used the same "p" abbreviation for pennyweight modernized here to dwt. used by Nys and by several New York silversmiths (*Ibid.*, p. 14). All this supports the theory that Francis may have been apprenticed to Nys.

42. Stephen G. C. Ensko, *American Silversmiths and their Marks III* (New York, 1948), p. 127.

43. In 1719, in return for binding wire, shears, chemical compounds, crucibles, silver, coral, and a pair of roll-up stockings, James Allen was credited:

by 2 doz Silver making	£0	5 [shillings]	0 [pence]
by 5 Silver Spoons	0	11	8
by a Porringer Making	0	9	9
by Cash	0	13	1

In 1720, Francis gave him 18 pennyweight of silver "to work up" and two pieces of coral valued at 2 shillings each. In return, James Allen made him two teaspoons and a spoon to which he added 2 pennyweight of his own silver (DMMC, 53.165.44).

44. The first entry under Keeble's name is in May 1719, when he was charged:

To a Thimble	£0	1 [Shilling]	4 [Pence]
To a Watch Chain	0	9	0
To a pair buckels	0	13	0
To Caseing a box for Watch	0	10	0
To a buckell 2/10 a hook a/6	0	5	4
To 2 yards Ozinbriggs	0	2	6
	2:	1:	2

Keeble paid for this debt		
by 9 Days Work	1	2	6
by Work 4 Days work	0	10	0
by Sundries		3	3

It is interesting that the next and only continuous accounts with Keeble in this particular book do not occur until January of 1721, and run rather regularly through September 1722. In these accounts Keeble is paid in cash for much of his work. The type of work he was doing is not itemized and so does not indicate the type of objects he might have made. He is simply credited with a certain number of days' or weeks' work. On one occasion he is credited

CHAPTER I *Francis Richardson, Silversmith (1681–1729)*   271

"By fatt—£0/1/3 1/2." In 1721 he is charged by Richardson for caps, cash, a pair of buckles, rum, a pair of gloves, a silk handkerchief, a pair of studs, three pounds of shot, and six pounds of nails; in 1722, with a stick worth £0/3/6, cash paid Samuel Wainwright and Jon Merriday upon his account, "1 shilling the box waid," grains of gold, a piece of gold and a shilling, a thimble, a pair of shoes, thread, a stock lock, molasses, a pair of stockings bought from Mr. Flower, and more cash paid Jon Merriday, Bentley Cook, and Richardson's cousin. These are the sorts of accounts ordinarily kept with apprentices, since the master was responsible for their clothing, housing, and education, in return for work done, and it is possible that Bentley Cook, Jonathan Merriday, or Samuel Wainwright was responsible for housing and feeding or instructing Keeble. By the beginning of 1722, Keeble was working for Francis more often (DMMC, 53.165.44). No American examples of Keeble's work are known, raising the question as to whether Keeble put his own mark on his work or whether Francis put his mark on Keeble's work. Investigation by Charles C. Oman in England revealed that Robert Keeble was the son of the pewterer Thomas Keeble, began his apprenticeship with London goldsmith Robert Maunsell on October 11, 1699, and became free on December 11, 1706. Charles J. Jackson, *English Goldsmiths and Their Marks* (London 1921) lists Robert Keeble's mark as being entered in 1702 at Goldsmiths' Hall in London.

45. One other source of information about the objects that Francis actually made is an inventory taken in 1757 of the silver owned by Isaac Norris, Jr. (1701–66), some of which he inherited from his father, Isaac, Sr., and his mother Mary (Lloyd) Norris, as well as from his wife's parents, James and Sarah (Read) Logan. In this listing are the following objects probably made by Francis Richardson or his son Frank:

a Tankard marked AR (Brand FR) Tes [?]	30 oz.	2 dwt.	0 gr.
a Porrenger Stamp FR marked under Handle I N	7	12	0
Ditto with Handle broke—Ditto—on the Handle IN	7	6	0

(David H. Stockwell, "A 1757 Inventory of Silver," *Antiques*, LXIX [January 1956], 58–59).

46. DMMC, 53.165.59.

47. The inventory of his estate lists apart from "90 oz. 14 dwt. wrought & old Silver," "Two Silver Porringers weight 13 oz. 14 dwt." valued at £5/0/5 1/2 (Will No. 127, 1729, Phila. Co. Court House).

48. It is reasonable to assume that this can was made shortly after Josiah Hibberd's estate was settled around 1728, before the death of Francis Richardson and before young Frank came of age. In 1732 Phebe married Josiah's brother, Benjamin Hibberd. The inventory of Benjamin's estate taken in 1785 notes, "To a Silver kan & teaspoons, £4:17:6." The can remained in the possession of the Hibberd family until recent years, having been handed down by Phebe and Benjamin Hibberd's son, Josiah (Gilbert Cope, *Genealogy of the Sharpless Family* [1887], cited by Bart Anderson in a letter to the author, November 26, 1956).

49. The cast and applied knop-and-drop decoration that appears on the back of the handle is seen on other early eighteenth-century Philadelphia tankards. On this drop are the initials WB. The tankard has been published as being made originally for William Branson (Hornor, "Richardson Family," p. 42).

50. This patch box, described as "chased with starred flower," was exhibited at the Boston Museum of Fine Arts in 1956. It is engraved on the base EB (Kathryn C. Buhler, *Colonial Silversmith, Masters and Apprentices* [Museum of Fine Arts, Boston, 1956], p. 94, and No. 308).

51. These simple scrolled buckles are engraved on the back of the chape in later script, "Wedding Shoe Buckles," and are believed to have been worn by Elizabeth Coates Paschall at her wedding in 1721. Although this date falls within the period covered by Francis' account book, the only transaction recorded with a Coates was in 1719 when Elizabeth's mother, Beulah Coates, bought a looking glass and several pairs of kid gloves. Nor are there recorded any Paschall purchases of buckles (DMMC, 53.165.44).

52. In 1720 Mary Hill bought a single spoon, which Francis Richardson charged her 3 shillings to make and 4 shillings for the silver he added (DMMC, 53.165.44).

53. In his accounts for 1717-22, Francis recorded selling gold lockets to Daniel Derbory, John Rutter, and Elizabeth Jackson. The cost was about £1/8/8 for each of these lockets. On July 20, 1720, he debited Daniel Derbory "To a Gold Locket £1/0/8 Making £0/8/0 – £1/8/8 (DMMC, 53.165.44). Included in Francis' inventory in 1729 were "8 dwt. 7 gr. in Coyn'd Gold – £2/9/9 and 2 oz. 14 dwt. 2 gr. wrought Gold – £4/6/0" (Will No. 127, Phila. Co. Court House).

54. The method of forming the holes to receive the strands of the necklace is noteworthy because it changed during the century. The earliest method, illustrated by Francis Richardson's locket, was to cut circular openings into each end of the flat piece of metal forming the back of the locket. The circular openings were then accentuated by soldering a circular gold wire on the top of each so that each opening looks separate and finished. This is in contrast to the later method – both quicker and cruder – of simply drilling holes in the extended sides of the back plate.

55. This and all further information in this chapter about Richardson's accounts is taken from his account book, DMMC, 53.165.44.

56. Sometimes he lent equipment, as in the case of the small flat anvil which he lent to William Mors in 1722. In 1720 Vincent Wagoner got from him files, a vise, and a pair of round pliers. Richardson sold some of the materials used in the working of silver, such as sandever and borax, to goldsmith Philip Syng, saltpeter to Joseph Shippen, and argol to "Abraham the button maker," goldsmith James Allen, and brassfounder Casper Wistar. A dozen scales for weighing coins and ingots of silver were purchased by Richardson from a "Merilander" in 1721.

Bushels of coals, presumably charcoals for the forge, were sold to James Ward, a clock and watchmaker, and were bought from goldsmith Johannis Nys. Among the other accounts, goods of this type include a melting pot, oil stones, pliers, files, and brass wire sold to George Plumley, a brasier; crucibles or "Crusifells" bought from Jobe Goodson; three small crucibles bought by Philip Syng; and "a Nest of Crusifells – £0/2/0" charged to James Allen's account.

Materials common to the craft, also obtained by James Allen from Richardson, included a pound of binding wire, useful in wiring together parts for soldering, a pair of shears, and chemical compounds of borax, sandiver, argol, and saltpeter. A copper boiler was lent to him on one occasion.

Much of the debiting and crediting of tools and equipment involved Richardson's accounts with clock and watchmakers. Peter Stretch in 1721 got two locks from Francis for which he paid £0/4/8 in cash. John Wood in the same year bought an oil stone, three minute clock hands, and three other clock hands, paying for them in cash and old silver. Later in the year Wood was charged "To a Grid Iron to be paid in work £0/3/0." He paid this debt by mending a watch.

While Stretch and Wood are well known as Philadelphia clockmakers, James Ward, another of Francis' customers, is not listed as a clockmaker in the standard books. His accounts with Richardson, however, make it quite evident that he was practicing this craft in Philadelphia in 1719. Over a period of months James Ward bought from Francis some burnt lace and a yard of "stuff," two pairs of stockings, two pairs of gloves, and a looking glass. He also had a pair of buckles made and a chain mended, bought a ring for a watch case, a watch chain, a dozen crystals for watches, a pair of pliers, two small files, two seals, and borrowed a bushel and a half of coals. He paid Francis by mending several watches and a clock, "by 12 Gallons of Beer," and by sundries, a file, and a note for £1/9/6.

In the back of his account book, where he recorded "Memorandum," Francis kept another entry concerning the clock business:

```
3 years   £10/ 2/6 hands for Clocks
        −  2/18/0 Glasses for Clocks
           7/ 4/6 Oyl Stons
        +  1/10/0 pumys Stons
           8/14/6
```

Other related accounts include Robert Keeble's indebtedness "To Caseing a box for Watch £0/10/0," and "Daniel Radley... Debtor... To a Glass for his Clock £0/3/0".

57. It is interesting that another such certificate was obtained by Francis early in 1716, indicating that he had planned to make, and perhaps did make, a trip in that year as well (Min. Mo. Mtg., *E-3*, 16-17, 51, Arch St. Mtg.).

58. Under Memorandum he listed:
>   a pese [piece] of Plush Simment [Cement] Color
>   Corral Necklesses
>   Sundry perfumes Damask powder [a toilet-powder scented with damask roses] and other things
>   Tulipes Ruts
>   a parsell of Holens (Hollands, a type of cloth)
>   Cloth fine
>   Good Colered Sewing Silks
>   Narow Pulesweny
>   To In Quier for Crucked Lain for Cat Gut Strings
>   Make In Querry for Crooked Lain over a gainnst the Dolfin for hones & Calg...
>   Make youse of Colman Next for Cleairing goods his offis at the Coffey house over against the Custam house
>   To make In Querry for John Canbey Brother to Benjamin Canbe being absent two years from his wife.
>   Memorandum to gett a gallon of Bairs Grees

On the same pages Francis made notes of the people he had to see:
>   Eliz Coliston Cross Keais [Keys]
>   Tho Burbin Skiner Street for Silk Handkeche
>   Tho Plumsted Iron Munger In Greacious Street for 4 Nailes & 10 nailes and other Sorts of Wair
>   Mr. Tomson In Lettle Lumber Street Gold Smith Selleth Corrall [James Thompson, goldsmith, is listed by Sir Ambrose Heal, *The London Goldsmiths* (Cambridge, 1935), at the sign of the Golden Key, Lombard Street, London 1709-25].

>   Will   Wesfeld Grape & Camblet Seller Living Near Stocks Marcat near W. Brion
>
>   R. Robart A Habedasery of Small Wair Living over a gainst Herry Colmans In Gorge yard
>
>   Mathew Judkins In Gutter Lain bottle Tipper [Heal lists Matthew Judkins, goldsmith, at Gutter Lane in 1705. It is likely that Francis got silver-tipped bosom bottles from this source.]
>
>   Richard Rigg Linnin Dreaper at the Sign of the Ship in Aldergait Street
>
>   Joseph Holmes at the 3 Nuns Snow hill Linin Dreaper
>
>   John Bell at the 3 foxes in Cloment Lain
>
>   A Clother at Sine of the Shipe in the poltry Stock
>
>   Joseph Robens Coitler [cutler] in Lumber Street
>
>   Cristepher Siphtha a Looking Glass maker at the Sign Looking Glass in Alldermondary. [In *The London Furniture Makers 1660 to 1840.* (London, 1953), Sir Ambrose Heal lists Christopher Sibthorpe, cabinetmaker, at The Japan'd Cabinet, in Aldermanbury, deceased 1730.]
>
>   Will   Roffe a hatter the Signe of the Hosue in Lumber Street Tho Hiam Linin Draper Where W. Newbery Loges (DMMC, 53.165.44).

"W. Newbery" was the son of the Walter Newberry at whose house Francis' mother and Edward Shippen were married, and who had died in 1697 *(Rhode Island Historical Society Collections* XXIV [1931], 75).

59. His orders for these items were placed through other people, viz: "Sent Likewise by Isaac Merrett a Gold Ring wt. 5 dwt. 17 gr. to be Sold and Laid out in Small Correll Neckleses to be sent by Simmins or Captain Combs—Sent by Logick Cristion Spreagele a genea to be Laide out In 50 Nests of Crucifells 30 pounds of Arguell 23rd 5th mo. 1721"

60. In this way Francis received, at various times, fabric and thread; bread and baked goods from Mark Dalmas, the baker; work done by Edward Warner; rum, wood, beer, and molasses; schooling for the children; candles and soap from Samuel Marsey; a case of bottles from Captain Drason; meat, dairy products, chocolate; flour, sugar, and fat; buttons, a whip; and a substitute for his night watch duty.

61. An advertisement concerning this schoolmaster appeared in the *American Weekly Mercury* for November 16–23, 1727: "All Persons Indebted to James Conway of the City of Philadelphia, School-Master, are desired to pay the same with all speed, the better to enable him to pay his, or expell (expect?) Trouble."

62. Will No. 127, Phila. Co. Court House.

63. *Ibid.* The inventory of the house and shop made by John Cadwalader and Edward Roberts on August 13, 1729, with its lists of the types of goods Francis sold in his shop and the furnishings he had bought for his home *(Figs. 13, 14)*, provides an indication of the prosperity he had achieved.

The inventory reveals that he sold silk girdles, papers of pins, wig ribbon, clock cases, coral necklaces, and brass snuffers, in addition to the goods known from his extant account book. Francis still had many looking glasses, perhaps some newly ordered from England, described as "small," "middling," "swing," "of six different sizes," and one "with a pair of sconces." The folio Bible valued at £2/10/0 is probably the one owned by his father in which the Richardson family births were registered.

It is interesting to note that, although Francis Richardson was himself a goldsmith and could have made many silver utensils, the common tableware was for him, as it was for many prosperous people of his day, pewter. Fifty-nine pieces of pewter are listed, in addition to his old pewter, as opposed to two silver porringers and eleven silver spoons.

From the mention of walnut and cane furniture, leather chairs, and a slate table, it would appear that the furnishings of Francis' house were largely in the William and Mary style and were bought between 1695 and 1725. Along with six cane chairs, a "couch and squab" is listed, and it is likely this is the cane couch which Francis bought in Boston in 1704 for £2/10/0.

That the house was well furnished and prosperous in appearance is indicated by such luxury items as looking glasses, a spice box (a form especially popular in Pennsylvania), and window curtains in more than one room. The bedding was plentiful: counterpanes or coverlets, curtains and valances, and head and tester cloths on two of the beds. It is likely that Francis' and Letitia's bedroom was the room in which there were, in addition to the bed, two looking glasses, a chest of drawers, the spice box, an oval table, a square table, eight cane chairs and a stand, fireplace equipment, and two pairs of window curtains. It is likely also that Frank and Joseph shared the room that had, in addition to the bed, two looking glasses, two chests of drawers, the slate table, six cane chairs, the couch and squab, fireplace equipment, two pairs of window curtains, and a screen.

CHAPTER 2. *Francis Richardson, Silversmith and Merchant (1705–1782)*

1. "Three Lower Counties 1655–1805," p. 155, HSP.

2. DMMC, 53.165.53. The next week Frank wrote Joseph, "Thy Camblets, Globes & Invoice from Perkins shall be shipd next week & if Tantum gets them ready the glasses likewise Together with Goods of mine by Captain Wright . . ." (DMMC, 53.165.84). Tantum was undoubtedly the same Joseph Tantum, cabinetmaker in London, from whom their father had bought looking glasses in 1719.

The next month, on March 10, Frank again wrote Joseph from London about some things Joseph wanted Frank to get for him: "pieces of Corral are scarce & dear & therefore have not yet bought them & thy Chapes & tongues are not yet ready but shal bring them with me . . . . The glasses could not be ready by this opportunity but will be shipd next week." (DMMC, 53.165.85). A few weeks later Frank added "I design to bring thee some peices of Corral, & if my money hold out I shal bring the Globes too" (DMMC, 53.165.87).

3. DMMC, 53.165.53.

4. One of Frank's purchases in London was a looking glass for Samuel Morris which he explained "comes high But Joseph Tantum assures me I have it as cheap as any one in London will sell me." Joseph Richardson also was to receive some looking glasses, as Frank went on to say he was enclosing bills of lading and invoices for goods including: "From Joseph Tantum Glasses for thee amount £26/6/6 besides the Charge of Shiping & Insurance. . . . From Mildred £11/11/8 among which is thy chapes & Tongues in Trunk No. 13 No. 7 Contains 2 moon Clocks & a pair of brass Shels for thee amount beside Shiping Charges & box to £9/3/6 The face is designd for my Clock From Dawson & [illegible]." (DMMC, 53.165.87). Jonathan Dawson, clockmaker, is listed as working in London about 1700 in Britten's *Old Clocks and Watches and Their Makers*, 7th ed. (New York, 1956), p. 363.

5. Min. Mo. Mtg., E-3 356, Arch St. Mtg.

6. Of this son, the annalist John F. Watson said: "*Colonel Frank Richardson* was a person of great personal beauty and address, born of Quaker parentage at Chester. As he grew up and mixed with the British officers in Philadelphia, he acquired a passion for their profession, — went to London, got a commission, and became at length a Colonel of the king's life guards. This was about the year 1770." (*Annals of Philadelphia and Pennsylvania, in the Olden Time*, I [Philadelphia, 1868], 560).

7. This advertisement is also cited in George H. Eckhardt's *Pennsylvania Clocks and Clockmakers* (New York, 1955), p. 189, but the author has Frank Richardson confused with the elder Francis Richardson, who, as far as is known, never made clocks.

8. Ensko, p. 110. In a letter from Stephen G. C. Ensko to the author, December 2, 1963, the source of the advertisement is cited as the *American Mercury,* February 18, 1734.

9. Joseph Richardson, "Account Books", H.S.P.

10. C. A. Weslager, *The Richardsons of Delaware* (Wilmington, Delaware, 1957), pp. 38–41. The porringers, which weigh 9 oz. and 9 oz. 6 dwt., are still in the possession of a descendant of John R. Latimer, Mrs. Walter S. Franklin. These are probably the same two porringers listed in the inventory of the estate of Dr. Henry Latimer, father of John R. Latimer, taken on April 26, 1820, as being "In the House No. 123 Market Street Wilmington — *the family residence —*":

1 Porrenger	" [weighing]	—9 oz. 10 dwt.
1 ditto	"	—9 3.

The loss of 3 and 4 pennyweight of silver from 1820 to the present would be the natural result of normal use and polishing.

11. From 1735 to the beginning of 1737, Joseph charged Frank for the making of buckles, double-jointed tea tongs, a whip ferrule, a porringer body and handle, a porringer, six teaspoons, a link of gold buttons, and a teapot.

12. In the spring of 1736 Joseph gave Frank £11 credit for a clock, and 5 shillings for whitening a dial plate. The same summer he credited Frank with £7 for a watch.

13. As early as 1733 he presented books to the Library, one of which was Sir Francis Bacon's *Natural History*. [Seaman, pp. 41–43; Minutes, I, 3, 28, 40, 52, 62, 104, Library Company of Philadelphia; *Catalogue of the Library Company of Philadelphia 1741* (Philadelphia, 1956)].

CHAPTER 3. *Joseph Richardson (1711-1784): His Life*

1. Evidently an apprentice could carry on his deceased master's business even if he had not completed his own full term. Kathryn C. Buhler notes that Paul Revere was allowed to begin work as a goldsmith when his father died, although his term of apprenticeship had not been fulfilled. *Colonial Silversmiths.* p. 47.

2. Seaman, *Thomas Richardson*, p. 38. By a previous wife, Elfreth had a son also named Jeremiah who became a goldsmith and probably served his apprenticeship with Joseph Richardson.   (Records of Marriages, E-26, 118, Arch St. Mtg.).

3. Joseph Richardson, "Account Books," HSP. These three manuscript books are not paginated or dated consecutively so that references must be identified by customer and date of entry. All further reference to Joseph Richardson's charges and payments of account indicate this source.

4. Deed F-6, p. 269, Registry of Deeds, Phila. Co. Court House   The estimate of Rich-

ardson's income is based on his account book entries for 1735 which recorded £139/4/3 as gross income.

5. The furnishings included an "arched moon clock and case," a black walnut table, six chairs bought from William Boyles, a tea table and another table.

6. *Pa. Gaz.*, August 13, 1738. Fabrics included were broad cloths, kerseys, duroys, drugetts, and shalloons. He also had nails and Bristol steel for sale.

7. Logan Papers, II, 46, HSP.

8. DMMC, 53.165.125. The exact location of this land is not known, but it probably was contiguous with Joseph's inherited property, as Plumsted owned land surrounding this lot. In Plumsted's will in 1745 he left to his wife the annuity of £6 "arising from the tenement in the City of Philadelphia where Joseph Richardson now dwells."

9. Min. Mo. Mtg. *E-3*, 328–29, Arch St. Mtg.

10. Seaman, p. 25.

11. Deed H-19, p. 536, Phila. Co. Court House; DMMC 53.165.125.

12. Tolles, p. 55.

13. Minutes, I, 166, Pennsylvania Hospital.

14. George Maurice Abbott, *A Short History of the Library Company of Philadelphia* (Philadelphia, 1913); and the "Minute Book" at the Library.

15. DMMC, 53.165.81.

16. Tolles, p. 155.

17. DMMC, 53.165.124; Albert Cook Myers, *Hannah Logan's Courtship* (Philadelphia, 1904), p. 86.

18. Seaman, between pp. 34–35.

19. Account Book, HSP, *8th mo. 1747*. The widow Allen did work for Joseph in addition to teaching Betsy and for her services she received credit against the purchase of a silver can.

20. Min. Mo. Mtg., *E-4*, 51, Arch St. Mtg.

21. Myers, pp. 156, 171, 199; Records of Marriages, *E-26*, 223, Arch St. Mtg.

22. Min. Mo. Mtg., Nov. 26, 1749, and many other dates until June 29, 1781, Arch St. Mtg.

23. Seaman, p. 25.

24. Myers, p. 269. The same sum given by wealthy Samuel Powel, however, was considered by John Smith to be a paltry donation.

25. Joseph Webb, "Account Book," 1744–54, p. 27, DMMC, 65 X 569.1.

26. Seaman, pp. 25, 44; Tolles, p. 132.

27. Tolles, p. 57.

28. Minutes, July 29, 1752, p. 14, Unfortunately, the survey of this property is one of the few missing records of the Hand-in-Hand Company.

29. Survey No. 76, Phila. Contributionship; DMMC, 53.165.74 and 53.165.125.

30. Seaman, p. 25.

31. Katharine Amend Kellock in her article on Joseph Richardson in *The Dictionary of American Biography*, states, "His civic interest is further evidenced in the part he played in the foundation of the Pennsylvania Hospital, which he served from 1756 to 1770 as a member of the board."

32. Minutes, I, 33, Pa. Hosp. In fact, the minutes for May 6, 1756, specify that it was Joseph Richardson, Merchant, who was chosen manager. (Minutes, I, 208, Pa. Hosp.) The

merchant was a descendant of the Samuel Richardson family of Philadelphia. Further proof that it was he who was elected to the Hospital Board is the fact that the position was left empty by death in 1770, the year in which the merchant, not the goldsmith, died. The entry in the Journal for the week before the election of board members also specified a contribution from "Joseph Richardson (Silversmith) £5." It is interesting that only one other person gave £5, the smallest gift recorded. Benjamin Franklin gave the average sum of £25, and Israel Pemberton was the most generous of all with a contribution of £100 (Minutes, I, 198, Pa. Hosp.).

33. DMMC, 53.165.95.

34. Cited by Marshall Davidson, *Life in America* (Boston, 1951), I, 77.

35. Tolles, pp. 23–28; Thomas Jefferson Wertenbaker, *The Founding of American Civilization, The Middle Colonies* (New York, 1938), pp. 221–22.

36. Gratz Papers, Case 17, Box 17, HSP.

37. Harold E. Gillingham, *Indian Ornaments Made by Philadelphia Silversmiths* (New York, 1936), p. 25; Gratz Papers, HSP.

38. DMMC, 53.165.296. Nathanial Allen's will, posted December 22, 1757, also gave his daughter the silver tankard which had been her grandfather's.

39. Deed H-8, p. 178, Phila. Co. Court House.

40. Seaman, p. 25.

41. Tolles, p. 75.

42. Min. Mo. Mtg., E-6, 144, Arch St. Mtg.

43. *Ibid.*, pp. 305, 378.

44. Will No. 1850, Chester Co. Court House.

45. Deed C-482, Phila. Co. Court House.

46. DMMC, 53.165.133; Min. Mo. Mtg., July 3, 1756, Arch St. Mtg. For further discussion of this trade see Victor L. Johnson, "Fair Traders and Smugglers, 1754–1763, "*Pa. Mag. LXXXIII* (1959), 147.

47. DMMC, 53.165.134.

48. DMMC, 53.165.136.

49. Min. Mo. Mtg., E-7, 34, 87, 271, Arch St. Mtg.

50. Curtis P. Nettels, *Roots of American Civilization* (New York, 1938), pp. 630–32.

51. This document in the Historical Society of Pennsylvania is important because it provides a comparison of the signatures of the two Joseph Richardsons. Other goldsmiths who signed it were Philip Syng, John Bayly, and John Leacock.

52. DMMC, 53.165.95.

53. DMMC, 53.165.80.

54. Deed I-1, p. 415, Phila. Co. Court House.

55. Monthly Meeting of Friends of Philadelphia, 1766–74, Miscellaneous papers, Box 3, HSP.

56. The boy had been charged with irregular conduct, associating with unprofitable company, contracting debts in his minority, and spending time and money in a "vain and lavish" manner. Min. Mo. Mtg., E-9, 101, 418, Arch St. Mtg.

57. Frederick B. Tolles, *George Logan of Philadelphia* (New York, 1953), p. 10. All other references to Tolles indicate his *Meeting House and Counting House*.

58. DMMC, 53.165.95.

59. Min. Mo. Mtg., E-9, Arch St. Mtg.

CHAPTER IV *Joseph Richardson: His House and Shop* 279

60. Carl Bridenbaugh, *Cities in the Wilderness* (New York, 1938), p. 394.

61. William Clinton Heffner, *History of Poor Relief Legislation in Pennsylvania* (Cleona, Pennsylvania, 1913), p. 63; Deed I-11, p. 127, Phila. Co. Court House, Richardson Family Papers (DMMC, 53.165.76). Soon after this transaction Joseph bought another lot on the south side of Spruce Street, west of Fourth Street in the City of Almshouse Square area. A map of the area survives among the Richardson family papers at Winterthur.

62. Charles F. Hoban, ed., *Votes of the Assembly, Pennsylvania.* Archives (Philadelphia, 1935), Series 8, VIII, 7006.

63. DMMC, 53.165.223.

64. DMMC, 53.165.93. See also Tolles, p. 28, and Evarts Boutell Green, *The Revolutionary Generation 1763-1790* (New York, 1953), pp. 217-18.

65. Anna Wharton Morris. "Journal of Samuel Rowland Fisher, 1779-1781." *Pa. Mag.*, 41 (1917), 274-333; Min. Mo. Mtg., E-9, 482, Arch St. Mtg.

66. Min. Mo. Mtg., E-10, 145, Arch St. Mtg.

67. Joseph spelled his name *Herford* while his father spelled it *Herreford*.

68. Min. Mo. Mtg., E-10, 326, Arch St. Mtg.; DMMC, 53.165.298 and DMMC, 53.165.610, 611.

69. DMMC, 53.165.223.

70. Permits for Interment in Friends Burial Ground, Department of Records, Arch St., Mtg.; DMMC, 53.165.113.

71. Juliana R. Wood, *Family Sketches* (Philadelphia, 1870), pp. 16-18.

CHAPTER 4. *Joseph Richardson: His House and Shop*

1. I am indebted to Robert L. Raley, architect of Wilmington, Delaware, for his help with the architectural records in the Richardson papers.

2. The information about the appearance of the house, while conjectural, is based upon Nicholas B. Wainwright's description of the houses in Philadelphia about 1750 in *A Philadelphia Story* (Philadelphia, 1952), and an amalgamation of the information found in the inventory of Joseph Richardson's house at the time of his death in 1784 (Will No. 344, Phila. Co. Court House) and that of his wife at the time of her death four years later (DMMC, 53.165.152)

3. The case of this clock is probably the one purchased by Joseph Richardson from John Spring for £4 in the late 1730's, recorded in his account books.

4. Now in the possession of Robert S. Stuart, and illustrated in Seaman, between pp. 56 and 57.

5. The desk listed here may be the slant-top walnut desk now in the Winterthur Museum (*Fig. 23*). It was sold in 1929 at the Reifsnyder sale, and had been owned by a descendant of Joseph Richardson's daughter, Mary, who inherited possessions of both Joseph Richardson and Captain Edward Fitz Randolph (*Catalogue of the Reifsnyder Collection*, American Art Association, Inc., 1929, No. 686). The style of this desk, with its double-arch moldings and five ball feet, indicates that it was probably made in Philadelphia early in the eighteenth century.

6. Such a chest was also sold in the Reifsnyder auction as Item 616, with the same history as the slant-top desk.

7. It would appear from the records that, at this time, the house was connected to the kitchen. This would explain the order of the sequence of rooms listed in Richardson's inventory and also would be consistent with the mention in his will of a "room over the kitchen."

8. Tolles, p. 144. The three books are now in the Winterthur Collection.

9. Powel Papers, Invoice Book, DMMC, 54.83.19

10. Possibly S. Sympson's *A New Book of Cyphers*, published in London in 1726 and known to have been used as a pattern book for script initials engraved on American silver in the mid-eighteenth century.

11. Minutes, July 29, 1752, p. 14; and Journal, August 4, 1752, p. 16, Phila. Con.

12. Joseph rebuilt his workshop in 1777. Abraham Jones did the work, and he submitted his bill to Joseph for the work. This bill provides the most complete contemporary description of an American goldsmith's shop now known:

> November 17, 1777
> to 50 feet of pine & Cedar Bord at 2d to 1/2 pound Nails
> to hanging Shetter & Nailing up one
> to pulling down Shop
> to Making a fore pannel door & frame at home 2 yeards
> to working Block & fixing anvil
> to 82 feet of Stuf for Bench & Draws
> to puting up Bench with uprights 24 feet at 6d
> to Making Draws & fixing
> two Square & 75 feet of floor in Second Story
> fore Square & 81 feet of Garrot floore
> to 61 feet of plaind pirtison & groved
> to Six yards 5 feet of Doors
> 18 feet of Wash Boards & Six Base
> 39 feet of Gam Casings & ovalow
> 61 feet of Bords under Raftors in Stead of aflins
> 34 feet of Casing garrot Windows
> 28 feet of pin Rails & Shelvs
> 6 feet of Casing under Stairs
> 29 feet of Door frame in Second Story
> 2 paire moldings
> 15 Steps of Staires & platform
> One Square 31 feet of Be of pirtishon
> two Door frames with Mouldings on Both Sides
> 5 Windows Cased hangd
> 5 feet of Casing & molding
> one Ledg Shettor & Stuff
> 19 feet of Arkatrive
> to 1/2 pound Nails
> to 4 feet of Bord for moldings (DMMC, 53.165.107).

13. Because the interiors of goldsmith's shops were rarely described, the main sources of information are contemporary views of English and continental shops such as those in William Budworth, *A New Touchstone for Gold and Silver Wares* (London, 1679), and in

Diderot's *Encyclopédie* (Paris, 1747–72). These engravings, reproduced in many books on silver, show the prominent position of the forge in goldsmith's shops.

14. Little attention has been given to the glass showcase as a common part of a goldsmith's shop. The actual appearance of the case is not known, for no early American goldsmith's cases have been identified positively, but some contemporary trade cards and book illustrations show the glass wallcases or flat countercases used in European shops of the day. One of the few descriptions of an American case is found in the advertisement of John Carnan, also of Philadelphia, in the *Pennsylvania Packet* on July 26, 1773, which mentions the misplacing of a "triangular" silversmith's glass case. That "triangular" might have referred to a shallow slant-top glass case is suggested by an example in the collection of Mrs. Bertram K. Little which may have been used for this purpose. As early as 1709, two glass cases were listed in the inventory of the Boston goldsmith Richard Conyers (John Marshall Phillips, *American Silver* [New York, 1949], pp. 15–16).

On November 16, 1738, the *South Carolina Gazette* noted that "Pennefather's Shop was robb'd of his glass case." George Dowig also advertised in the *Pennsylvania Evening Post*, October 23, 1778, that some new silver teaspoons had been stolen "out of a silversmith's case" and when William Pinchon made plans to leave for Europe he offered for sale, along with goldsmith's tools, "several elegant Glass-Cases." *(Pa. Gaz.*, April 16, 1783).

15. Joseph copied from Chambers' *Dictionary* instructions for refining gold and silver:
When Gold is Refined by antimony it Remaines Brittle & in order to make it tuf melt it again & Cast Some 1/2 the wt. of Salt Peter & Borax in powder into it.
to Refine Silver by Lead or Salt Peter are teadius & Troublesome when Performd on Large Quantityes. This occationed Mr. Homberg to Indeavour to Shorten the opperation which he Effected wth Good Suxesess. he Calcined the Silver with half its weight of Common Sulper & after melting the whole together to Cast a quantity of Steel filings upon it at Several times. upon this the Sulper quitts the Silver & Joyns to the Iron & both is Converted into Scora [scoria which is dross] & the Mettell is found Pure at the Bottom. (DMMC, 53.165.124).

Both of these processes are recommended in *Goldsmith & Silversmiths' Handbook* revised by Staton Abbey (New York, 1952). This book also suggests that sandiver makes a good flux for getting out the iron and steel. These processes explain the presence of borax, saltpeter, and sandever in the inventory of Francis Richardson's equipment inherited by Joseph.

16. Joseph purchased some of these pots and crucibles from his brother Francis and from Anthony Bright. In 1774, "William Hollingshead, Silversmith, . . . Daniel Offley and Thomas Jackson, Potter," offered for sale "A good Assortment of Black Lead Crucibles, made by the said Jackson, In Philadelphia, and found to be much better than any imported" *(Pa. Gaz.*, January 5, 1774). Perhaps this last remark was prompted by importations such as those made by Joseph Richardson, who ordered from John Masterman of London 100 large and 100 small nests of German or Holland crucibles in 1770. (DMMC, 53.165.95). In 1773 he ordered 200 large and 200 small Hessian crucibles from Masterman specifying they must be "Hessian Crucibles or None at all for those Made in or Near London went [won't] Stand the fire" (DMMC, 53.165.95).

17. Joseph Richardson wrote to George Ritherdon in November, 1761:
These are to Cover a Bill of Lading for £10/3 Sterling & 63 oz. 10 dwt. of Course Silver the Produce of the Sweepings of my Shop. As I have No Convenient apparatus

for Refineing it have therefore Sent it herewith & Desire that a Gold Essay may be made of it as well as a Silver Essay as it is Probable their may be Some Gold in it. (DMMC, 53.165.95).

At the time of his death, however, Richardson had in his shop an assay balance which Jacob Duché had put on consignment. This is fully described in a memorandum dated April 30, 1784:

> Left with my neighbour Joseph Richardson to be disposed of 1 good Round Sight hole, Essay Ballance, fitted with Pans & Shifts, a Sett of Silver & Gold weights verry exactly adjusted & fit for Essaying, In a good Glassed Lanthorn with Proper Brass work, a long pair of Corn thongs & a good Pear tree Box to hold them in, cost 7 Guineas — and a paper with Directions concerning the Weights thereto belonging — An Essay Iron plate Furness, properly lined and finished with Muffles, and a Brass Mould to make Coppels with, well worth 20 Dollars And when Sold to pay the Money into the hands of Mr.–Andrew Doz in Philadelphia

18. Such an arrangement appears in one of the few American representations of a goldsmith at work in the advertisement of Daniel You of Charleston, South Carolina, in the South Carolina *Gazette and Country Journal* on August 4, 1767.

19. A variety of anvils and stakes or teasts were needed to make the diverse objects which Joseph produced. (Diderot's *Encyclopédie* shows a number of these.) In addition to the flat anvils placed in the stumps, there were smaller, shaped stakes, such as the four teasts, six beake irons, the porringer anvil, and two round-bottomed stakes which Joseph had inherited from his father (Will No. 127, Phila. Co. Court House).

20. In the late 1730's, Joseph paid John Spring for putting up such a bench (probably an additional bench to be used by Joseph's apprentice), and in 1777 Abraham Jones installed another workbench, probably for Joseph's sons. Jones' bill, noting "Making Draws & fixing," could refer to putting drawers into the workbench, or possibly to the installation of a draw bench (DMMC, 53.165.107).

21. The draw bench, the drawing plates through which the metal was pulled, and the tongs used to pull the metal through were valued in his father's inventory at £2 (Will No. 127, Phila. Co. Court House).

22. On several occasions Joseph recorded in his account books that he bought files from his brother Frank, who had probably bought them in England. Six hand vises were inherited by Joseph from his father, along with a parcel of files.

23. The tools Joseph used came from a variety of sources, as has been noted. Some had been inherited, some were purchased in Boston, and Philadelphia, and some were imported from England. The most interesting imported tools were dies and stamps for making buttons of a particular pattern, and a flatting mill. The latter was used for rolling silver thin, a process previously thought to have been introduced at a later date, but now known to have been used by Joseph and some other goldsmiths before 1760. As early as 1735, a flatting mill was listed in the inventory of Cesar Ghiselin (Gillingham, "Cesar Ghiselin," *Pa. Mag., LVII*, 248).

Chambers' *Dictionary* describes the work of the "*Goldsmith*, or as some chuse to express it, *silver-smith*," in volume II:

> The business of the *goldsmith* formerly required much more labour than it does at present, for they were obliged to hammer the metal from the ingot to the thinness they wanted but there are now invented flatting-mills, which reduce metal to the thinness that is re-

quired, at a very small expence."

Joseph Richardson owned such a mill some years prior to 1760, as he indicated in a letter to Thomas Wagstaffe in July of that year:

> I have also by the Indian trader Captain Robeson Sent a wooden Pattern & Request thee would gett a pair of Rowlers for a flating mill as Near the Siz of the Pattern as Possible they are for Milling Silver or Gold thin And therefore Should be turned as true as Possible So that if one is Placed on the other we may Not be able to See through them. It is Usual in London as I am informed to make them of Steel throughout or of Sweeds Iron Case Hardened for if they are only Covered with Steel the Steel is apt to Seperate from the Iron as I have Experienced or otherwise to Prove faulty (DMMC, 53.165.95).

Swedish iron was considered the very best iron at that time. Case hardening made the instrument more resistant to strain and impact, since it is a process of hardening outer surfaces of steel products so that they are more resistant to wear and abrasion, while leaving the subsurface softer and consequently more resistant to strain.

Several months later Richardson wrote again to Wagstaffe.... "I wrote for a Pair of Rowlers for a flating mill for my own Use & Since which I have Directions from one of my Neighbours to write for a Pair for him..." When the flatting mills were received, Joseph wrote that they were "in a Rusty Condition Especielly the Large Pair which are So Bad that the Person for whome I Sent for them for will Not take them". Another Philadelphia goldsmith, George Dowig advertised "a silversmiths flatting-mill" for sale in 1770, *(Pa. Gaz.,* July 5, 1770), and at the end of the century Charles Gilchrist advertised "Metals containing Gold or Silver purchased by Assay, Silver, & c. flatted." (cited in Prime, *Arts and Crafts* [1721–85], p. 117).

Dies and stamps were also ordered from London. From Wagstaffe in 1762, Richardson ordered:

> a Pair of Button Stamps to Stamp Gold or Silver Buttons Like the Patterns Except the Ingraveing on the largest Button I would have like the Smallest & I would have the Ingraved Punches Sent in order to Repair the Dies if Occation Should Requir it as also the Plain Punches to Stamp the Buttons with." (DMMC, 53.165.95).

The next year Richardson acknowledged receipt of the stamps and ordered further:

> 3 Sockets with 2 Dies & 2 Plain Punches to Each Socket for Stamping Buttons of the Siz & Pattern of the incloased Buttons as the Ingraved Punches are with Dificulty obtained & Charged at a very high Price I would have them omitted & only Send 2 Plain Punches & 2 Dies of the Siz & Shape of these Patterns Incloased to Each of the 3 Sockets or Collors (DMMC, 53.165.95).

Earlier, in 1760, Richardson had ordered from Wagstaffe for one of his neighbors "a Socket Dys & Punches for Stamping Silver or Gold Buttons the Siz & form of the Patterns herein Incloased (DMMC, 53.165.95).

24. "Silver turners," who operated such lathes, advertised as specialized craftsmen in the mid-eighteenth century: "Turns work for Gold-Smiths, viz Tankards, Canns, Casters, Salts." (Isaac Fowls, *Boston Chronicle,* August 1–8, 1768). Samuel Axford, a turner and neighbor of the goldsmith John Fitch, was credited by Fitch on July 22, 1774, with turning a tankard, a "Ewer foot," and a 'Cann foot"—in the latter cases, probably to remove excess solder rather than to polish (Carl M. Williams, *Silversmiths of New Jersey 1700–1825* [Philadelphia, 1949], p. 134).

25. At this stage Joseph probably consulted the pattern books he had ordered through Samuel Powel. Philadelphia goldsmiths are known to have used Sympson's *Book of Cyphers* because of the literal renditions of its patterns on many examples of their silver. Also used by American goldsmiths as a source for coats of arms was John Guillim's *Display of Heraldry*. Copley's portrait of goldsmith Nathaniel Hurd of Boston shows the 1724 edition of Guillim at his side.

26. Both Joseph Leddell and James Smither are known to have engraved silver made by contemporary goldsmiths in Philadelphia.

27. A good example of this occurred in 1737 when he recorded in his account book:
Bespoak by Benjamin Clark   17 Sett of Gold Buttons to be Done the 30th Day of october about 30 shillings price

all E:C	3 Set I:C		1 - B·C
	2 S·C		1 - A·C
			1 : E:L
			1 - N-C
			1 - H-C

28. Philip Syng was selected by the Philadelphia Contributionship to make their seal (Minutes, May 11, 1752, Phila. Con.). The Pennsylvania Hospital in 1751 asked Benjamin Franklin to write to Boston to get a seal for the corporation (Minutes, *I*, 16, Pa. Hosp.), and James Turner was the Boston engraver Franklin arranged to have cut it.

29. Tolles, p. 79.

30. In New Jersey in 1773, the Assembly disclosed:
That Ford had been in the business of money making many years . . . he followed it in New York . . . again entered into it, and made a connection in Philadelphia, with a certain Captain Joseph Richardson, from whom he got a supply of types . . . in 1769 . . . he with Captain Richardson went to Ireland and from thence to London and the manufacturing towns, and Ford applied himself to learn the business of an engraver and type maker. (A. Van Doren Honeyman and William Nelson, eds., *Documents Relating to the Colonial History of the State of New Jersey* [Paterson, 1917], XXIX, Series 1, 16.)

After a four-year chase, Capt. Joseph Richardson of New Jersey was apprehended for his crimes (William Nelson and Frederick W. Ricord, eds., *Documents Relating to the Colonial History of the State of New Jersey* (Newark, 1886), X, 413). Further information about this Joseph Richardson is contained in Kenneth Scott's *Counterfeiting in Colonial America* (New York, 1957), pp. 242–44, 248, 251–52.

31. Thomas, *An Account*, p. 31.

32. According to Richardson's accounts for the 1730's and 1740's, the usual rate was 18 pence per ounce, as this entry indicates:
Mathias Aspdin is Debtor
   to a 3 pint tankard weighing 39 oz. 17 dwt.
   to fashin at 18 pence pr oz – £2/19/9.

33. *The New York Mercury*, April 20, 1767.

34. In 1740 he made a gold ring for Richard Hill, Jr., weighing 2 dwt. 12 gr. and charged him 3 shillings for his work. Joseph had charged Richard Hill 16 shillings for a pair of silver

shoe buckles and a pair of silver knee buckles weighing in all 2 ounces, a rate of 8 shillings per ounce instead of 3. Bruff in New York was also charging 8 shillings for a pair of carved silver buckles. This is the same rate charged by a London goldsmith in 1771 for slop bowls, causing Richardson to protest: "but with respect to the Slop Bowles which are charg'd at £0/8/11 Per oz. when the Coffee Potts are Charg'd at £0/7/4 is so unequal that I apprehend that thee will make some abatement" (DMMC, 53.165.95).

35. "Notes," *Pa. Mag.*, XIX (1895), 531. Samuel Powel had written to his uncle, Samuel Morris, from London the previous December 26, 1764:

> I have just now wrote to my Aunt D. informing her of my intentions of selling my Furniture & Plate in Philadelphia, in Order to purchase new which I design to bring over with me....
>
> As to the Plate, what little of it falls to my Share, it is so old & bruised, that I think it best to supply its Place with new. I imagine old silver will yield as good a Profitt with you as here — if so 'twill be best to dispose of it in Philadelphia. As this is an Article of ready Sale at all Times, I shall be obliged to you to dispose of it & remit me the Money as soon as may be."

cited by Russell Hawes Kettell, ed., *Early American Rooms*, [New York, 1967], p. 117.

36. "Received of Samuel Powel Juner a peper Box mustard pott or Caster & Spoon a Silver Salt a Specticle Case pap Spoon & other small pieces Silver weighing 13 oz. 15 dwt. 12 gr. of Silver to make into a pair of Salts & a peper & mustard Casters."

37. In his account book in 1740 Richardson credited his uncle Lawrence Growden "By a Lewdore & a pistole weight 9 dwt. 11 gr. @ 17 1/2 per cent £3/1/1 By a half Guinea @ £0/17/6 & a Caroline @ £0/34/0 £2/11/6." The "lewdore," or Louis d'or, was a gold coin, as were the pistole and the guinea (the name of the latter indicating the African source of the metal originally used in their minting). Caroline was a name for various coins. Moidores, Johannes, and Spanish doubloons are other gold coins frequently received by early goldsmiths. Silver coins such as the Spanish "real of eight," — which was most often divided into "pieces of eight," — are frequently mentioned in early accounts. In 1745 Richardson credited Esther Beekerdike "By 3 pieces of 8 Received By Henry Graham £1/2/6" to be used in the making of two silver spoons. In 1736 Israel Pemberton, Jr., was credited by 65 oz. 7 dwt. "of Spanish Silver to work up," and in 1737 Mary Mather brought Richardson "2 oz. 4 dwt. 12 gr. of Silver to make into 6 tea Spoons & £0/19/0 Starling in Silver weight 3 oz. 7 dwt. 6 gr. 3 Dollars & 1 oz. 0 dwt. 6 gr. other Silver towards a pint Can Comes to in all £3/14/1".

38. When Thomas Woliston got a pair of salts and a milk pot in 1737 he paid in this manner.

By a pair of blankets	£1/12/ 0
By 2 Silk handcarchefs & a pair of Gloves	12/10
By Silver Received to Make into a pair of Salts 5 oz. 12 dwt. at £0/9/0 per oz.	2/10/5
By 2 quarts of Grass Seed & Bagg	0/4/4 1/2

39. Buhler, *Colonial Silversmiths*, Introduction.

40. Such a remarkable occurrence of old age was appropriately commemorated by placing a wax image of "The venerable John S. Hutton" on exhibition beside figures of Franklin, Hamilton, and Hancock at the Exchange in the New York Museum and Wax Work in 1793, the

year after Hutton's death (Rita Susswein Gottesman, *The Arts and Crafts in New York 1777-1799* [New York, 1954] No. 1280, p. 388). The Philadelphia historian John F. Watson tells us that Charles Willson Peale "was induced to take his [Hutton's] portrait as now seen in the Museum, as he appeared in the last year of his life." Watson writes of Hutton:

> John S. Hutton, aged 109 years.
>
> John S. Hutton, silversmith of Philadelphia, as he related the particulars of his life to the late C. W. Peale, was born in New York, in 1684. He was originally bound apprentice to a sea captain, who put him to school to learn the art of navigation. At that time he became intimate with a boy who worked at the white-smith trade, and he amused himself in acquiring the use of the hammer, by which means he obtained a facility in working at plate-work in the silversmith's business. He followed the seafaring life for thirty years, and then commenced the silversmith's trade. He was long esteemed in Philadelphia, one of the best workmen at hollow work; and there are still pieces of his work in much esteem. He made a tumbler in silver when he was 94 years of age.

(*Annals*, I, 527; II, 578.) The Peale portrait of Hutton has been owned by various members of the Hutton family since the sale of the Peale Museum Gallery in 1854.

Hutton first married Catherine Cheeseman of New York and had eight children by her. He was later married to Ann Vanlear, who bore him seventeen children. When Hutton died in Philadelphia on December 20, 1792, Watson relates "He was borne to his grave by his fellow craftsmen—all silversmiths."

41. The first accounts are for work in February, and then they skip to June, from which point the entries appear with more consistency.

42. Ensko, p. 193. Illustrated in Martha G. Fales, *American Silver in the Henry Francis du Pont Winterthur Museum* (Winterthur, 1958), No. 109. A spoon attributed to John Hutton, exhibited at the Museum of the City of New York in the winter of 1937-38, was listed in the catalogue as being seven inches long and weighing one ounce (V. Isabelle Miller, *Silver by New York Makers* [New York, 1937], No. 158, p. 17). A teapot by Hutton was listed in the 1764 inventory of silver owned by John and Hannah (Logan) Smith: "a teapot makers mark I Hutton 19 1/2 oz." (Smith Papers, VI [1762-65], 103-4, Lib. Co.)

43. Hutton signed Richardson's receipt book on May 2, 1744 for receiving payment "in full of all Demands to this day" (DMMC, 53.165.125). On June 10, 1747, he again noted payment "in full of all accounts to the day of the date hereof" (DMMC, 53.165.125). John Hutton is also noted in an entry in Richardson's commonplace book on the second page, which, although undated, probably was recorded in the 1740's (DMMC, 53.165.124):

to Hutton	16 oz.	11 dwt	
Received	7	14	[crossed out]
Remains	8	17	
to a Scillet	15	17	12 gr.
Returned	6	2	12
	9	15	
for Lid	1	17	14

CHAPTER IV *Joseph Richardson: His House and Shop* 287

To Silver for a Can	14	10	
by Silver Returned	3	15	
to handle for Do.	3	14	18
	18	4	18
	3	15	
	14	9	18

The last record of interest concerning Hutton is an advertisement which appeared in the *Pennsylvania Packet* for July 12, 1783, under the name of Daniel Dupuy, Jr.: "To be Sold or Exchanged for a House in the upper part of the city, a Commodius three story House and Lot in Almond street, now in the tenure of Mr. John Hutton," followed by a description of the house.

44. James St. Morris' name first appears in Richardson's account books in 1735 when Frank was charged for silver given to him, and in 1736 for cash given him. In 1737 an entry shows James' name crossed out and "Clock Business" substituted. The "Clock Business," which was one of Frank's advertised crafts, is charged for clock materials, shoes and clothes for James, and £10 for James' time. Two entries among notes concerning apprentices in Richardson's commonplace book refer to James St. Morris: "James   12 pair Stay hooks & Spoons" and "Morris   1 Doz. pair Buckels" (DMMC, 53.165.124).

45. Brix (*Philadelphia Silversmiths*, p. 90) lists him as a silversmith advertising in 1748 and includes in parenthesis the misleading information, "Servant to Richardson."

46. Carl M. Williams, "An Unrecorded Goldsmith," *Antiques*, LI (January 1947), pp. 40–42.

47. Harper made for Richardson in 1745 the usual small work of buckles, buttons, spoons, and clasps, in addition to sockets and bells, weighters, cans, milk pots, casters, porringers, strainers, and a cup. The following year, 1746, he made salts and a tankard, spectacle frames, punch ladles and salvers; in 1747 a snuff box, teapots, a coffeepot, a watch case, a slop bowl, also nutmeg grater, sword hilts, a fountain pen, and sugar dishes; and in 1748 double jointed tea tongs and a cordial cup.

48. Rita Susswein Gottesman, *The Arts and Crafts in New York 1726-1776* (New York, 1938), pp. 69–70. The advertisement of Harper and Dutens in the *Pa. Gaz.* of February 18, 1755, gave their address as "next door to the Indian King in Market Street," and offered for sale a preponderance of jeweler's work and English coral and bells.

49. The exact relationship between William Young and Joseph Richardson has yet to be determined. Apparently the connection was through Francis Richardson's sister, Rebecca, to whom he once referred as "my sister Rebecca Young." Young's name does not appear in the records of the Society of Friends, but in the records of Christ Church, the marriage of William Young and Grace Price was entered on July 23, 1758. No children of this union are noted, but from 1766 to 1785, a number of children were born to William and Rebecca Young (*Collections of the Genealogical Society of Pennsylvania*, HSP). The Marriage license of William Young and Rebecca Flower was issued on May 5, 1762 (Pennsylvania Marriages Prior to 1790 (Baltimore, Genealogical Publishing Company, 1968) p. 274.

50. Later in the commonplace book this entry occurs:

WY to 1 oz. 5 dwt. 12 gr. of wire
to   2 dwt. 23 gr. Sawder
by thimbles   1 oz. 13 dwt. 9 gr.
to 8 pair buckels 14 oz. 17 dwt.
by 2 pair buckels 1 oz. 15 dwt. 9 gr. (DMMC, 53.165.124).

51. DMMC, 53.165.95.

52. *Pa. Gaz.*, September 24, 1761.

53. *Pa. Gaz.*, June 30, 1768; Ensko, p. 146. Very little silver by William Young is known today. David Stockwell, Wilmington, Delaware, owns a fine tankard by him, and the Museum of Fine Arts, Boston, has a cup with his mark impressed on the base.

54. Min. Mo. Mtg., E-7, 171, Arch St. Mtg. The minutes do not specify which brother was apprenticed to Richardson, but it may be assumed it was Giles, for it was his "intention of marriage" that Joseph was appointed to investigate several years later (Min. Mo. Mtg., E-8, 395, 399, Arch St. Mtg.).

55. John Bailey advertised for sale in Philadelphia in 1763 two Negroes who could work at the goldsmith's trade. George Dowig offered for sale in 1770, along with all of his tools, "a Negroe man, by trade a silversmith." There are frequent advertisements for Negroes who ran away; 36-year-old Tom ran off from William Ball to join the British army in 1778, and John Francis was sought in New York and Philadelphia by goldsmith Benjamin Halsted in 1784.

Perhaps the best description of the Negro trained to the trade of a goldsmith was given in William Faris' advertisement in the *Maryland Journal*, November 9, 1778: "To be sold, a likely young negro fellow by trade a Silversmith, Jeweller and Lapidary; there is very few if any, better workman in America. Any person inclining to purchase the said Negro may know further by applying to the subscriber living in Annapolis". (For further information on this subject see the chapter "Negro Silversmiths-Charleston," in E. Milby Burton, *South Carolina Silversmiths*, (Charleston, South Carolina, 1942), pp. 207-9.

56. Mention of him is made in the advertisement of a Philadelphia schoolteacher which appeared in the *American Weekly Mercury*, December 13-20, 1739. "The Records of Christ Church Philadelphia Baptisms 1709-1768," I, 221, HSP, note the baptism of four-day-old James, son of Randall and Jane Yetton, on January 9, 1738, and the "Burials, 1709-1785," V, notes the burial of Jane, wife of Randall Yetton, on April 2, 1744. Since Randall Yetton's death does not appear in these records, it is possible that he moved to another area.

57. Hollis French, *A List of Early American Silversmiths and Their Marks*, (New York, The Walpole Society, 1917), p.18.

58. Richardson's accounts list charges to Anthony Bright in 1734 of a piece of coral and cash; the credits include a snuff box he made, cash, numerous bushels of coal, and a salver. On other occasions Richardson provided Bright with silver objects, as in the case of a pepper box and a pair of spurs in 1736. In 1738 Bright got linen and cash from Richardson, and in return he provided stay hooks, a stock buckle, and a joint to a box, as well as more cash. It is possible that his mark has been confused with that of Adrian Bancker who was working in New York at the same time.

59. DMMC, 53.165.137. This document also mentions Bright's brother-in-law Henry Surnam, a lapidary in London. Brix erroneously lists Anthony Bright as dying in 1749.

60. In this instance, the executors found it necessary to reimburse William Hinderson

CHAPTER IV *Joseph Richardson: His House and Shop* 289

(possibly William Anderson, goldsmith, New York, c. 1725–46) because Robertson's brother had been bound to him as an apprentice but had run away several times. After compensating Hinderson, the executors finally bound the unruly lad to his brother-in-law, Robert Hoyd, who was a hatter. (DMMC, 53.165.145; 53.165.146).

61. See also Ensko, p. 106.

62. A document dated April 18, 1746, which is filed in the Probate Court Record, states, "I Richard Pitts of Charles Town Goldsmith . . . am . . . Bound and Obliged unto Messieurs Wright and Sarrazin of Charles Town . . . Goldsmiths in the full and just sum of One Hundred and four Pounds . . . ." This document is quoted in Burton's *South Carolina Silversmiths*, (pp. 151–52), where a spoon, owned by the Charleston Museum, and stamped R•P in a rectangle, is described. This serving spoon, 15 1/4 inches long and engraved on the back IFS, was exhibited at the Virginia Museum of Fine Arts in 1960. It was probably made after Pitts had left Philadelphia for Charleston, that is, after 1745.

More recently a tablespoon has been acquired by the Winterthur Museum, also bearing the mark R•P in a rectangle but dated *1739* in what appears to be contemporary engraving beneath the initials $S^S E$. The spoon is particularly interesting in that it is definitely from his Philadelphia period, and also in that it establishes an early date for the spatulate drop on the back of the bowl.

A keyhole porringer in the Clearwater Collection of the Metropolitan Museum of Art bears the mark *Pitts* in script in an oval on the handle, the mark attributed to him by Ensko (p. 224). The handle is also engraved $N^C H$ and engraved on the base, probably at a later date, is *Alice Whipple 1732*. Kathryn C. Buhler suggests that this surname mark is more likely the mark of John Pitts of Boston, c. 1730, to whom a surname mark was given by Francis Hill Bigelow (catalogue, Bigelow sale, Anderson Galleries, New York, 1936, No. 35). Letter to author, August 13, 1972.

While in Philadelphia, Pitts and his wife Mary were members of Christ Church. The listing of baptisms shows that their son Richard was born February 6, 1741, and another son William Welshman was born June 20, 1744. (Collections of the Genealogical Society of Pennsylvania, "Baptisms.").

63. Philip Syng's accounts with Richardson in 1733 read: Philip Syng is Debtor

to fashining of 6 watch Chains		£0/17/8
to a Silver Snuf box	1 oz. 5 dwt. 12 gr.	
to fashing the box		0/12/0
to Silver	1 oz. 6 dwt.	1/ 9/8
	2 oz. 11 dwt. 12 gr.	
Contra is Creditor		
By silver	1 oz. 2 dwt. 12 gr.	
By 2 pair of Shoe Buckels		
By a Shell for a Sword Hilt-weight 1 oz. 9 dwt.		
By fashin		0/5/0
By fashin of Spoons & other things		1/4/8
	2 oz. 11 dwt. 12 gr.	1/9/8.

64. The account entry reads: "Brother Francis Richardson Debtor to a pair of Cans weight 24 oz. 10 dwt. Shipt to Carolina £/10/16/6."

65. The pieces marked by Joseph Richardson in the 1764 inventory of the silver of John and Hannah (Logan) Smith were:
  A salver marked on the bottom HL maker's stamp IR
  2 porringers marked on handle IS maker's stamp IR
  A dozen custard spoons marked HL Makers stamp IR
  2 pint canns marked IS on handle makers stamp IR
  A dozen large spoons marked IS maker's stamp IR
  6 custard spoons maker's stamp IR
  A pair salts maker's stamp IR marked IS
  2 porringers marked HL and 6 custard spoons maker's stamp IR. (Smith papers, VI, 103–04, Lib. Co.).

66. Cited in Tolles, p. 129, fn. 52. Ferdinand M. Bayard, who wrote *Voyage dans l'Interieur des États-Unis* in 1797, remarked, "The Quakers load their tables with silver" (quoted by Charles H. Sherrill, *French Memories of Eighteenth-Century America* [New York, 1915], p. 56).

67. No pre-Revolutionary Philadelphia goldsmith's trade cards are known, although Joseph Anthony, Joseph Lownes, John Gethen, and Simmons & Alexander made use of them in the last quarter of the eighteenth century.

68. At this time a number of American goldsmiths, following English tradition, displayed signs in front of their shops, and it appears that the custom was especially popular in Philadelphia which became well known for its handsome shop signs, some of which were painted by Matthew Pratt, son of goldsmith Henry Pratt. William Dunlap, *The History of the Rise and Progress of the Arts of Design in the United States*, (New York, 1969; reprint of original 1834 edition) I, 102; Ensko, pp. 12–146; Burton, esp. p. xiii; J.H. Pleasants and H. Sill, *Maryland Silversmiths 1715–1830* (Baltimore, 1930). The Golden Cup was one of the most commonly used signs in America, as it was in England. This is not surprising, for the covered cup was part of the arms of the Goldsmiths' Company. In Philadelphia, John Leacock in 1753 worked at the Sign of the Golden Cup. Both William Bartram in 1769 and Thomas Shields in 1771 used the Sign of the Golden Cup and Crown, the latter denoting royal patronage in England. Edmund Milne used the Sign of the Crown and Pearl in 1761, and the Sign of the Crown and Three Pearls in 1763. Pearls were used to signify jeweler's work, as was the Hand, the Ring, or the "Ear Ring." Both Austin Machon in 1759 and Charles Dutens in 1753 advertised as jewelers, Machon at the Sign of the Hand and Earing and Dutens at the Sign of the Ring and Dove. Another favorite sign was a fashionable piece of plate. John Bayley used the Sign of the Teapot in 1763; and Richard Humphreys used the Sign of the Coffeepot (Heal, *London Goldsmiths*, 43; Ensko, pp. 84, 19, 119; Prime, *Three Centuries*, p. 63; Harrold E. Gillingham, "The Cost of Old Silver," *Pa. Mag.*, LIV [1930], 39).

69. Richardson ordered the bell from How, Masterman & Archer on February 7, 1767. Evidently the people responsible in York changed their minds, and Joseph was left with a 437-pound bell which he offered for sale in the *Pa. Gaz.*, November 12, 1767.

70. *Pa. Gaz.*, September 20, 1750.

71. In his commonplace book *(Fig. 29)* Richardson recorded:
7th mo. 15th 1752 Lost by William Sims a Silver watch
          makers Name Mathew Skiner No Number
          Stolen from Amos Jones at the Sighn of the

CHAPTER IV *Joseph Richardson: His House and Shop* 291

	Brig & Snow a Gold Ring which had a Stone but None in it Now the Posey when this you See think on me John Gilbert & 18 flat Jacket Buttons
	Mary Moulton on the hill Lost 1 tea Spoon & tongs markt M•D & 1 tea Spoon markt S$\overset{C}{\ast}$W or Some Such mark Irish made
10th mo.	Lost by Neighbor Murdock a
13th	Silver Spoon markt Phil Syngs
	Stolen from mary Syng 2 tea Spoons Markt T$\overset{I}{}$M & 1 Do. markt M-S (DMMC, 53.165.47).

72. Among the most beautifully cut maker's marks appearing on early American silver are those used by the outstanding Boston engravers and goldsmiths, the Hurds and the Edwards.

73. The *Pennsylvania Archives* record on January 20, 1767: "A petition from the silversmiths of the City of *Philadelphia* was presented to the House and read, setting forth, that there is yearly a considerable quantity of Silver and Gold (wrought in this Province, not only for the Inhabitants, but for several of the neighbouring Provinces, and many Parts of the West-Indies), which would increase and give more general satisfaction, were proper Regulations made, as to the Fineness of the Silver and Gold to be wrought; and therefore praying that the house would take the Premises into consideration, ascertain the Fineness of all Silver and Gold which shall hereafter be wrought, agreeable to the Laws and Customs of *Great Britain*, and appoint a proper Person to assay and stamp all such Manufacturers, made according to the said Regulations, as will admit of it, allowing to such Officer, a reasonable Reward for his Service, and vesting him with such Powers as the House may think useful and necessary."

After much discussion and the recommendations, first of Edward Duffield, and then of Owen Biddle, as a suitable person "for assaying and stamping Gold and Silver Wares," the bill failed to pass and was finally dropped. (*Pennsylvania Archives*, ser. 8, VII, 5964, 5975, 5982–83, 5985–86).

74. Only in Baltimore for a few years between 1814 and 1830 was an assay office established in this country. In the eighteenth century it was not common to indicate on American silver where it was made, although a few New York goldsmiths, such as Daniel Christian Fueter, did use such a marking. Purity markings such as "coin" and "sterling" normally were not employed until the nineteenth century (Ernest M. Currier, *Marks of Early American Silversmiths* [Portland, Maine, 1938]).

75. In 1761, Rolt explained the exceptions to the requirements of hallmarking in London; they applied to those objects which would have been damaged by the mark or were too small to receive marks, and which did not weigh ten pennyweight of gold or silver each (*A New Dictionary of Trade and Commerce* [London, 1761], section on "Goldsmith"). The list specified chains, necklace beads, lockets, buttons, thimbles, coral sockets and bells, pipe lighters, cranes for bottles, very small book clasps and nutmeg graters, jointed clasps, rims of snuff boxes, sliding-pencils, toothpick cases, tweezer cases, pencil cases, needle cases, any filligree work, tippings or swages, mounts, screws, stoppers, seals set with stones, and any gold or

silver vessel "so richly carved or chased, or set with jewels or other stones" that it would have been damaged by the mark.

76. Rolt notes the current London practice in 1761: "their old marks should be broken in the presence of the assayer, on pain of forfeiting 10£ and the further sum of 10£ for using any other mark" (*ibid.*).

77. Phillips, "Faked American Silver," in Ruth Webb Lee, *Antique Fakes and Reproductions* (Framingham Centre, Mass., 1938 and reprinted Northborough, Mass. 1950), pp. 244–52.

78. Martha G. Fales, "Some Forged Richardson Silver," *Antiques*, LXXIX (May 1961), 466–69.

Chapter 5. *Joseph Richardson: His Silver*

1. R. W. Symonds, "The English Export Trade in Furniture to Colonial America," *Antiques*, XXVIII (October 1935), 156.

2. "Letter Book" (DMMC, 53.165.95) See also *Appendix D*. All information concerning Richardson's importation of English silver refers to this source unless otherwise specified. All references to specific purchases of silver from Richardson are to be found in the Richardson "Account Books," HSP, under the customer's name and the date given.

3. Phillips, *American Silver;* Avery, *Early American Silver.* Martha G. Fales, *Early American Silver* (New York, E. P. Dutton & Co. Inc., New York, 1973). The latter two are useful since they also include line-drawings in chart form to show the general dating of various styles according to the shape of the object.

4. Martha G. Fales, "English Design Sources of American Silver, "*Antiques,* LXXXIII (January 1963), 82–85.

5. The development of and social customs relating to the service of tea in this period have been extensively discussed by Rodris Roth, *Tea Drinking in 18th Century America: Its Etiquette and Equipage* (Smithsonian Institution, Washington, D. C., 1961).

6. George Emlen was charged on March 1, 1737; May 20, 1738; and June 28, 1738:

to a Stock Buckel for his Son Joseph	£ 0/ 4/6
to 2 tea Potts 2 Weighters 2 Shugar Dishes	
2 Slop bowls 1 milk pott a Spoon boat &	
a Breakfast Bowl weighing in Silver 113 oz. 5 dwt. 6 gr. @ £0/8/6 pr oz.	48/ 2/8
to Makeing the Above	18/ 6/6
to a pair of tea tongs	0/14/6
to 6 Spoons weight 2 oz. 12 dwt.	1/12/6
	£69/ 0/8.

In 1737 Samuel Blunston placed a large order of silver from Richardson for which he paid £66/18/11. This order included a sugar dish, ladle, a set of casters, a square teapot, a spoon boat, six large spoons, a milk pot, six more large spoons, a sauce boat, two porringers, and a pair of buckles. John Richardson was also charged in 1738 with a silver set consisting of the three most important vessels—a teapot, a milk pot, and a sugar dish. In 1748 Anthony Morris bought what is today considered a full tea set:

to a tea Pott weight 16 oz. 1 dwt. 12 gr. @ £0/8/6	£ 6/16/7 1/2
to fashion	3/ 0/0
to a weighter weight 11 oz. 4 dwt. 6 gr. @ Do.	4/15/3
to fashion	2/ 0/0

to a Shugar Dish weight 10 oz. 2 dwt. 6 gr. @ £0/8/6	4/ 6/0
to fashion	1/10/0
to a Milk Pott weight 4 oz. 5 dwt. 12 oz. @ £0/8/6	1/16/4
to fashion	1/10/0
to a Slop Bowl weight 12 oz. 16 dwt. 18 gr. @ £0/8/6	5/ 8/9 1/2
to fashion	1/ 0/0
to 1/2 dwt. Per oz. Allowance for Wast	0/11/6.

7. This is probably the same coffeepot which Mary T. Seaman refers to as having been made for Joseph Richardson's country home, "Down the Neck," (*Thomas Richardson*, p. 44).

8. Another coffeepot of this type made by Joseph Richardson was listed in the Pennsylvania Museum *Bulletin*, No. 68, 1921, and was then owned by Miss Caroline Sinkler. It weighed 38 oz. 15 dwt., was engraved MR, marked IR in a rectangle, and was 13 inches high.

9. In 1734-35 Frank Richardson made the first teapot recorded in Joseph's accounts. It weighed 16 oz. 12 dwt. and was undoubtedly the same teapot later charged to Stephen Armitt. Frank made another teapot for Joseph in 1737, charging him £2/18/0 for fashioning it. From the accounts. it appears that Joseph began making his own teapots in 1737-38.

10. This teapot was purchased by James Wright in 1748 and cost £6.

11. *Boston Chronicle*, August 1-8, 1768. Isaac Fowls advertised that he "Makes Handles for Coffee Pots Tea Pots, Patterns for Gold-Smiths and Founders." Daniel Trotter, the Philadelphia cabinetmaker, recorded in his account book in 1793 a long list of handles for teapots and coffeepots he carved for goldsmiths, including John David and Joseph Lownes and someone identified only as "R." (DMMC, 67X89.2).

12. *Pennsylvania Chronicle*, August 14, 1769.

13. Richardson paid ground rents to the Plumsteds for the house he lived in which suggests the possibility that the teakettle may have been some kind of partial payment to Plumsted's widow toward Richardson's eventual purchase of the land. (DMMC, 53.165.127).

14. Jessie McNab Dennis "London Silver in a Colonial Household," *Bulletin*, the Metropolitan Museum of Art, December 1967 p. 174-179. Another handsome teakettle, made by George Wickes of London in 1750-51 for presentation by the City of Bristol in England to Philadelphia's mayor, John Clement, was brought to Philadelphia by Clement's daughter shortly after she married William Stocker, the Philadelphia shipbuilder. This teakettle is presently owned by a descendant, Mrs. Richard Swain, and was illustrated in Phoebe P. Prime, *Three Centuries*, p. 173. Still another Philadelphia family, the Cadwaladers, had a teakettle and stand made fifty years later by Edward Lownes in this same rococo style. A teakettle-on-stand by Jacob Hurd, now in the Boston Museum of Fine Arts, represents the only other known eighteenth century example of this rococo form made by an American goldsmith.

15. Richardson made little distinction between the three terms; in 1738 he credited one customer with silver to be made into a "Cream Pott" but charged him for the making of a "milk pott." In the accounts, the term "milk ewer" is used only on a few occasions in 1745, and in one case Elizabeth Sirl was charged for an item called first a "milk youre" and then a "milk pott."

16. Only one unknown sugar dish, made by Frank Richardson late in 1735 and sold in January 1736 to James Macca, precedes the Oswald Peel sugar dish in the account book entries.

17. It also bears an IR in an oval mark, but this mark differs from that on the sugar dish in *Figure 51;* it is more circular in shape and the "I" and the "R" are joined at the base.

18. From 1733 to 1740, six sugar dishes are recorded in the accounts as being made in Richardson's shop; from 1745 to 1748, at least nine were sold, indicating their increased popularity. Although these dishes usually weighed 10 to 12 ounces, Richardson made one in 1745 for Doctor Finney which weighed only 7 oz. 18 dwt.

19. Bowls of this type could have been used for purposes other than the serving of tea. In Richardson's accounts prior to 1747, silver bowls were listed without specification as to use, with the exception of one "breakfast bowl" purchased in 1738 by George Emlen.

20. Even though this bowl is much deeper than the one in *Figure 59,* it is unlikely that it was originally a sugar bowl, for it lacks the markings inside the rim which a sugar bowl acquires as the lid is put on and taken off over the years.

21. A pair of canisters made by Thauvet Besley of New York about 1740, now in the Museum of the City of New York, is engraved with the type of tea each was to contain: *Bohea Tea* and *Green Tea.*

22. Phila. Co. Court House, S-418.

23. In 1760, for example, he ordered from George Ritherdon 24 dozen teaspoons of varying weights, the heaviest of which were "6 Doz Plain Pollished Do. to weigh about 8 [dwt.] a Piece."

24. Richardson charged James Macca one pound for fashioning "a tea Spoon boat weight 3 oz. 4 dwt." on Aug. 20, 1737. On June 19, 1738, he charged Samuel Blunston £5 for a square teapot and a spoon boat, and on May 20, 1738, George Emlen purchased this form with his large order of silver.

25. As early as 1734 he charged his brother 6 shillings for making a pair which weighed 15 dwt., and the following year charged him £0/7/6 for making a pair of double-jointed tongs weighing 19 dwt. 12 gr. One of the heaviest pair of tongs recorded were those bought by Mary Armitt weighing 1 oz. 5 dwt. 6 gr.

26. A set of teaspoons marked by Joseph Richardson in a case—the only one known—was lent to the Pennsylvania Museum Exhibition of silver in 1917 by Dr. Samuel W. Woodhouse but its present location is unknown.

27. Richardson also fixed small strainers inside teapots. In 1736 he charged John Ingliss a shilling for "putting a Straner to a teapot." In 1735 William Fry paid three shillings for a chain and strainer for a teapot.

28. In 1746 John Cox paid 16 shillings for two strainers, and during the following year Caspar Wistar brought into the shop a French crown to be made into a strainer. At that time David Harper was making this form for his master, and the two punch strainers for which he was paid 10 shillings may be the same two Elizabeth Fitzwater bought that year for 11 shillings. Richardson also ordered strainers from London, getting 24 silver lemon strainers from Thomas Wagstaffe in 1760.

29. Apparently neither weight nor size had any bearing on the use of terms, since the accounts show salvers weighing between 3 oz. 6 dwt. and 23 ounces, and waiters from 4 1/2 to 36 ounces. Joseph described them as "small" if they were under 8 ounces and "large" if they were over 18 ounces. The largest waiter recorded, 36 oz. 11 dwt., was bought by Joseph Marks in 1748 for just under £21 including the charge for making (£4/11/3).

30. The pair of cans bought by James Logan in 1746 which weighed 24 oz. 12 dwt. is

undoubtedly the pair of the same weight made at about that time by John Hutton. Hutton was paid £1/10/0 for making them and Logan paid £1/16/0 for labor. Similarly, in 1745 Hutton was paid 15 shillings for making a pint can and Rachel Thomson was charged 18 shillings for its making.

31. This same rate was given Frank Richardson and John Hutton when they made tankards for Joseph, but when apprentice David Harper made a tankard bought at the full price by Joseph Cooper, he was paid at the rate of only 9 pence per ounce.

32. Illustrated in E. Alfred Jones, *The Old Silver of American Churches* (Letchworth, England, 1913), *Plate CX*, it is engraved on the handle A$\overset{R}{\cdot}$M for Andrew and Magdalen Robeson. Andrew died in 1740, and Magdalen in 1769; their daughter Elizabeth, wife of William Vanderspiegle, gave the tankard.

33. It was hoped that this spout cup, which bears the Pemberton crest, might prove to be the "pap boat" charged to Israel Pemberton, Jr., in 1738. However, the weight of the papboat recorded in the accounts, 2 oz. 12 dwt. 12 gr., does not correspond to the present weight of the spout cup. There are no other entries in the accounts of either papboats or spout cups. The Museum of Fine Arts, Boston, has a bill of John Andrew, Salem silversmith, for a spout cup in 1771 made for a known invalid according to Kathryn C. Buhler. Letter to author, August 13, 1972.

34. Between 1733 and 1748 at least 129 porringers are recorded as being sold by Richardson. Both Harper and Hutton helped to supply these, the latter being paid in 1745 £1/10/0 for a set of three which were subsequently sold to John Fisher for £1/16/0. A typical account for this type of shop work is the credit made to Hutton's account in 1748: "By makeing the Bodies of 4 Poringers £1/10/0 By Raising 2 Poringers weight with Silver Returned 17 oz. 16 dwt. £0/15/0."

35. An unusually small porringer was made for Mary Calbert in 1738. It weighed only 4 oz. 9 dwt. 18 gr., but cost her the usual 10 shillings for Richardson's labor. The capacity of porringers varied. In 1737 Pemberton's weighed 5 oz. 9 dwt. and was called a half-pint porringer. The only other capacity specified in the accounts was James Mather's order for two "3 Jell [gill] Poringers" in 1738.

36. In the same order he listed separately and made a distinction between these and the "4 pair of knurled edge do."

37. One caster weighing 5 oz. 8 dwt. was bought by William Plumsted in 1745–46. Its weight might be accounted for either by increased size or by the addition of a cast finial. In 1734 James Bingham also bought a pair of unusually heavy casters—10 oz. 6 dwt. 12 gr. before the addition of another ounce of silver to the feet.

38. Only Samuel Blunston in 1738 and Abraham Taylor in 1746 are recorded as having bought sauceboats from Richardson. Both cost £1/10/0, but Taylor's weighed 13 oz. 2 dwt. while Blunston's, which Joseph also referred to as a saucepan, weighed only 10 oz. 19 dwt. 12 gr. A butter cup weighing 13 oz. 2 dwt., made by Hutton in 1746, may have been the same form. The design of the butter cup is partially indicated by the account: "to Silver for a Butter Cup 9 oz. 6 dwt. to foot for Do. £4/4/12 to handle for Do. £1/15/0."

39. Richardson records a sale to James Macca in two different books, calling the purchase in one place a soup ladle and in the other, a soup spoon, meaning a large serving spoon and not the soup spoon as we know it today. On only one occasion did Richardson note a punch

ladle (which he credited Harper 10 shillings for making in 1746), suggesting that most of the surviving ladles from this period were probably used more often for soup than for punch.

40. In 1740, George Emlen bought a variety of spoons; "to 12 table Spoons 12 Custard & 2 Soop Spoons weighing 49 oz. 14 dwt. at £o/8/8 – £22/10/7 to making 12 table Spoons 12 Custard & 2 Soop Spoons £4/7/0."

41. Most of Richardson's spoons were engraved with owner's initials, and he often noted in his books what initials were to be "marked" on them (contemporary references nearly always spoke of marking rather than engraving, and maker's marks were spoken of as being stamped), as he did in 1734–35 when he noted that Bartholomew Waide's two tankards and six large spoons were to have "B $\overset{W}{:}$ E on all." Possibly a more elaborate type of marking was to be done on Lloyd Zachary's three spoons since Joseph specifically noted a 3 shilling charge "to Ingraveing them."

42. This new handle style can be documented by a negative bit of evidence found in the advertisement of William Haverstick in the *Pennsylvania Packet* on Oct. 18, 1783, which tells that he stopped "Two Silver Table Spoons supposed to be stolen, the handles turned the old fashion way . . . ."

43. Richardson paid Courtenay £6/5/6 in 1769 for an unspecified debt, giving rise to this speculation (DMMC, 53.165.35).

44. Canto V., lines 87–96. Samuel Johnson also mentioned this object in 1750 when he said, "Of all the toys with which children are delighted I valued only my coral." *The Works of Samuel Johnson, LL.D.* (New York: Alexander V. Blake, Publisher, 1844) I, 131. Joseph Addison remembered that, as a child, "I . . . would not make use of my Coral till they had taken away the Bells from it." (*The Spectator*, I, 2.)

45. In one entry Richardson spoke of "a Corel or Socket & Bells," and in another he charged Robert Hopkins for a whistle and bells but credited him with silver received to be made into a coral and bells.

46. It is stamped with a small IR in a rectangle, unlike his other marks, but the details of design and craftsmanship are consistent with Richardson's other work. It is in the Winterthur Museum collections. John Marshall Phillips wrote of this piece: "The rattle is an American one and the mark is that of Joseph Richardson the elder" (Letter to Joe Kindig, Jr., Aug. 28, 1942). Most of the extant examples of this form are silver, but there is a group of mid-eighteenth-century gold rattles made in New York.

47. *Antiques*, IX (June 1926), 384. As early as 1709 Nicholas Bion published in Paris a book illustrating a fountain pen (*Antiques*, IX [January 1926], 33). On May 13, 1824, Thomas Jefferson wrote to Colonel Peyton: "I saw yesterday in the hand of mr Dyer a fountain pen, one of the best I ever saw. he said it was made for him by mr. Cowan, a watchmaker of Richmond and cost him 5 Dollars, the outer tube was of silver, but the two leaves of the pen were gold, and no metal will resist the corrotion of the ink. pray get the favor of mr Cowan to make such an one for me . . ." (Ms. letter, University of Virginia Library).

48. This weighed 19 dwt. and was made for him by David Harper, who received 5 shillings for his work.

49. In 1747 John Smith bought a silver cock from Richardson which weighed 8 oz. 7 dwt. and cost £1 to make, and the following spring he bought a crane which weighed 4 oz. 16 dwt. and cost £1/5/0 to make.

50. The only knitting needles recorded in Richardson's accounts were the five pair bought by William Calendar in 1747 for £0/13/6.

51. As early as 1746 Richardson recorded selling Samuel Griscom a pair of tweezers for £0/2/6. Later he ordered from How & Masterman chased instrument cases as well as "silver full instrument cases for Women" and "Green fish skin [cases] mounted with Silver." In the inventory of Richardson's estate are also listed "2 Etwee Cases" (Will No. 344, Phila. Co. Court House).

52. In 1739 he charged Ann Edwards 5 shillings for making a toothpick case; in the same year he also charged Richard Hill 10 shillings for a toothpick case.

53. In October 1737 he charged clockmaker John Wood £0/8/1 for "Caseing a watch Case silver & making," and the next year charged John Young £1 for making a watch case weighing 1 oz. 14 dwt. Harper also made a watch case for him in 1747 for £0/12/6. His brother Frank was charged £7/3/6 in 1734-35 for a silver watch; in 1736, £7 for "Cash at the Receipt of the Watch," and credited £7 for a watch.

54. The most descriptive of these entries was "a Silver frame to a pair Spective Glasses" which cost William Fry £0/4/6 in 1735-36.

55. In 1737 Martha Cadwalader paid 5 shillings for 2 pincushion hoops. In 1747 Grace Mason paid £1/6/6 for a pincushion hoop and chain weighing 17 dwt. 12 gr. Elizabeth Holton's hoop in 1739 cost her £0/9/6, and in 1747 one was sold for £0/4/9. The flexibility of cost would indicate that the weight and size of these hoops and chains varied considerably.

56. No thimbles bearing his mark survive, but they probably looked like the gold thimble made by Jacob Hurd of Boston about 1740-50, now in the Garvan Collection, Yale University Art Gallery. Hurd's thimble is three quarters of an inch deep, while one in the Museum of Fine Arts, Boston, made about fifty years later, probably by Paul Revere, is one-and-one-quarter inches in depth.

57. November 27, 1783. Joseph, Jr., and Nathaniel Richardson, Letter Book, (DMMC, 53.165.223).

58. Bodkins recorded as sold by Richardson included one bought by Mary Nowland in 1734, one by Anthony Morris, Jr., for £0/2/6 in 1739, and one by Mary Armitt in 1746. Bodkins were not an important item in Joseph's shop. He neither imported them nor kept any on hand in the showcase.

59. No marrow scoops by him are known today although he charged Joseph Hoskins £0/11/6 in 1746 for "a Silver Marrow Scoop Spoon." Whether or not this scoop was actually made by him the records do not reveal.

60. The History of The Indian Peace medal is recorded in the "Register of the Medal Dies of the United States" at the Historical Society of Pennsylvania:

> A Society consisting principally of Friends was formed in Philadelphia in the year 1756 entitled "The Friendly Association of Regaining and Preserving Peace with with the Indians by Pacific Measures." In the year 1757, besides other proofs of its regard for the Indians, and in order that they might be possessed of an object which would frequently remind them of the intentions of their friends, the association had a Medal designed & struck bearing an appropriate devise and motto, which was distributed among them, it has on the Obverse a Bust of George II,

"Georgius II Dei Gratia." Reverse, A man in Quaker dress setting under a tree holding a pipe of peace in his hand over a council fire, an Indian sitting opposite, a sun above them. Legend: "Let us look to the most high who blessed our fathers with peace," in a circle, Exerque "1757."—The die was engraved in Philadelphia by Edward Duffield, and cost the Society £15.—The following letter will authenticate the genuine origin of the die. To Thomas Wistar. Philadelphia, Sixth Month, 12th. 1813. The impressions which I now respectfully offer for thy acceptance, are from dies that have long been in the possession of my predecessor and myself; at the early time they were engraved, coining presses were unknown in this country, they were therefore cut on punches, fixed in a socket, and struck with a sledge hammer. The Indian Medal of 1757, was struck at the expence of the Society (chiefly composed of Friends) formed in Philadelphia, for the express purpose of promoting *peace* with the Indian tribes. The appropriate inscription is truly *characteristic*, and will serve to convey to posterity, a just idea of the men of influence of those days. I remember well the striking of the Indian medal by my father,* it was executed in silver and presented to the Indians by the Society. Although this medal may at present be thought of little value, I have no doubt in a future day, it will be considered as interesting, not only from the occasion for which it was struck, but as it may serve to show the progress of the arts in our country.

Thy Friend,
Joseph Richardson

---

*Joseph Richardson, the elder, was a member of the Friendly Association, and by profession a silversmith.—The author of the above letter [his son, Joseph Richardson, Jr.] was Assayer of the Mint, commissioned December 12, 1795.

61. The Gratz Papers at the HSP include receipts showing that the Friendly Association paid Richardson £132/11/6 on July 14, 1757, and £135/5/0 on Oct. 26, 1757, for his work that year for the society. Over the following years this work included 96 arm bands, 84 wrist bands, 252 hair plates, 216 ear bobs, 48 hair bobs, 1,472 brooches, 374 crosses, 30 gorgets, 48 moons, and 240 rings; an amazing total of 2,860 objects, all made in Richardson's shop. (Harrold E. Gillingham, *Indian Ornaments Made by Philadelphia Silversmiths* [New York, 1936], p. 25.)

62. The only other time swords were mentioned in Richardson's account books, other than as repair work done by David Harper, was in 1733 when Philip Syng was credited "By a Shell for a Sword hilt weight 1 oz. 9 dwt. By fashin £0/5/0." See also Harold L. Peterson, *American Silver Mounted Swords 1700–1815* (Washington, D.C., 1955).

63. Daniel Burnap, a Connecticut clockmaker and silversmith about 1775, defined a "posey" in his notations on prices: "For making of plain gold rings 3 shillings 9 pence, which should weigh about one Dwt. The writing in the inside is called the posy." Penrose R. Hoopes, *Shop Records of Daniel Burnap Clockmaker* (The Connecticut Historical Society, Hartford, 1958), p. 122. Perhaps these were the same as the "Motto Ring" for which Charles Hartly paid Richardson £1/15/0 in 1745.

64. See Martha G. Fales, "The Early American Way of Death," *Essex Institute Historical*

Collections, C (April 1964) 75–84. Thomas Lawrence was charged for six mourning rings in March 1738, and Thomas Hopkinson was charged £2/2/9 in 1739 for one which must have been quite elaborate, since both Richardson and Daniel Burnap normally charged only 3 shillings for making a plain gold ring.

65. Twice there is recorded the receipt of silver to be used toward rings and it is possible that the new rings were to be of silver, although elsewhere in the accounts only gold is specified for use in rings. One of the most unusual rings recorded weighed 2 dwt. 10 gr. but was listed as a *hollow* ring. Abram Wilkbank was charged £1/1/6 for it in 1737.

66. "A Receipt for making Gold Beads," which describes the whole process of making them in the eighteenth century has survived in the memorandum book of Daniel Burnap, Connecticut clockmaker and silversmith, and is reprinted in Hoopes, *Shop Records*, p. 117. The Connecticut Historical Society also has some of the tools Burnap used in making these beads. In 1738 Joseph Richardson noted receiving some gold from James Mickelwain to be made into thirty-four beads, and a little later, more gold from the same customer to be made into one hundred beads.

67. On a single page in Richardson's accounts for 1746, it is noted that Joseph Trotter paid £0/13/4 for the making of 32 coat buttons weighing 3 oz. 15 dwt. 2 gr.; Samuel Griscom paid £0/4/3 for 2 sets of sleeve buttons; and Charles Willin paid £0/9/0 for the making of 18 coat buttons weighing 3 oz. 11 dwt. 18 gr.

68. In the back of one of the account books, Richardson noted 59 links of buttons, or cufflinks as they are called today, weighing a total of only 3 oz. 16 dwt. 18 gr. and costing £1/4/7 to make. This indicates that he probably sold them at a flat rate and did not figure the cost according to individual weight.

69. Cited by G. Bernard Hughes, *Small Antique Silverware* (New York, 1957), p. 176. This book also provides useful background information on many of the lesser forms in silver.

70. The threaded type of buckle was made by Richardson's shop worker, James St. Morris, in 1745 when he was making dozens of buckles for his master.

71. While a few chapes and tongues were noted in the account books as having been made by James St. Morris and Frank Richardson, usually at a rate of 2 shillings per pair, Richardson probably ordered most of the chapes and tongues he sold from London. Daniel Mildred supplied these in various sizes, and described them as being for small knee buckles, "large and round tailed," made of steel for silver buckles, and agreeable to the pattern Richardson sent.

72. In 1738 Richardson charged Thomas Lawrence:
to 3 Silver feet to a fruit Plate   weight 7 oz. 19 dwt. 12 gr.
to workmanship   £10/12/0

This is the only mention in the Richardson accounts of a fruit plate, and since this form is virtually unknown in American silver this entry provides our only knowledge of the appearance of this particular form. It is possible, of course, that the three feet were affixed to a plate made of something other than silver, such as china.

Chafing dishes are representative of another form which Joseph Richardson is not known to have made but which he did repair. Actually this form had reached its peak of popularity prior to Joseph's career and had begun to go out of fashion. As late as 1748, Joseph put a new bottom and handle on a "chafen dish" for Charles Norris, charging 12 shillings for the work. The only other notation in the accounts concerning this form was a charge in March 1738 against Abraim Taylor's account of £0/7/6 for "Mending a Chafen dish & Beating Bruses out etc."

Buttons and buckles were the most frequently repaired items, particularly gold and crystal buttons and links of buttons. In 1748 Richardson charged William Logan 5 shillings for "New Looping 2 Gold Buttons Set with Chrystol." Shoe buckles were the type of buckles most often mended, changed or equipped with new tongues and chapes, although Richardson notes changing at least one shirt buckle.

"Plugging" coins, i.e., filling coins that had had sections cut out of them, was another service Richardson performed. Most of this work appears in the accounts from 1746 to 1748. On one occasion the coins were pistoles, but usually doubloons were specified, as in this case:

Reese Meredith is Debtor
    to Pluging Double Loones   £1/13/0
    to Pluging Do. and gold   1/2/9.

On a number of occasions customers brought their old silver into Richardson's shop to be "boiled" in order to restore a pure layer of silver to the surface. In 1734 George Emlen bought eight new buttons and at the same time had Richardson boil four and one half dozen old buttons. In 1736 Nathaniel Griffitts had old plate boiled, and the following year Joseph Lin brought in thirty-three jacket buttons and an unnamed number of coat buttons to be boiled. Also in 1737 Richardson charged his Aunt Grace Lloyd 5 shillings for "2 Second hand Salvers weighing 17 oz. 7 dwt. 6 gr. to Boyling them & Burnishing them." A year later he burnished an old weighter for Thomas Grime for £0/1/6. Sometimes burnishing and boiling were done in addition to repair work, as in the case of Thomas Leach's tankard in 1734. Joseph charged him 3 shillings for soldering part of a joint on the tankard's handle and "Boyling it & Beating Bruses out of it."

Other objects Richardson mended were cans, sauceboats, bowls, sword hilts, spoons, tongs, salt shovels, rings, watch cases, snuff boxes, sugar boxes, strainers, salvers, porringers, cups, fans, and spurs. In 1746 he put a pin to Andrew Hamilton's teapot for a shilling, in 1748 he provided a handle for John Kinsey's teapot for £0/7/6 and in 1747 he mended Joseph House's china teapot for £ 0/1/6.

In addition to tipping sword scabbards, he tipped pencils, whips and even a deer's foot. David Harper did some repair work for him and in 1747 was credited with mending a pocketbook. In 1738 Abraim Taylor had a pocket case mended. This may have been an étui case similar to one noted in the entry for 1748 against John Wilcox's account "to mending a Silver Case a Rule & a knife handle £0/0/5." Richardson also fixed jacks, cleaned clocks, and pierced strainers.

CHAPTER 6. *Joseph Richardson, Jr.* (1752-1831) *and Nathaniel Richardson* (1754-1827): *Their Lives*

1. Thomas Lynch Montgomery, ed., *Pennsylvania Archives* (Series 6, Harrisburg, 1906), I, 42, 697; (Series 6, Harrisburg, 1907), III, 1014, 1021, 1043.

2. The brothers first made direct contact with their father's old friend John Masterman at the end of 1777, when they sent a bill of exchange for £150, drawn upon James Burn of London, and an order of goods, "which as we are young beginners we hope the [e] will send upon the most reasonable terms and good work." The next letter, sent in the spring of 1778, was an order they feared could not be received (DMMC, 53.165.223); subsequent mention of

CHAPTER VI *Joseph Richardson, Jr., and Nathaniel Richardson: Their Lives* 301

letters written during the partnership of Joseph, Jr., and Nathaniel refer to this book of letters.

3. Seaman, pp. 27–31. Wood, *Family Sketches*, p. 26.

4. In the spring of 1784 a box of scales and weights arrived in a rusty condition, but the brothers "[were] intirely in the dark respecting them." That summer they wrote again that they still had not heard from the person who sent the scales. By September, however, the mystery had been solved: Sommers & Son of London had shipped the goods in question, but their letter of explanation had been addressed to "Jos. & Nicho^s" thus causing the delay in delivery.

This was the beginning of a lengthy correspondence with the firm of Sommers & Son. Joseph, Jr., and Nathaniel had the usual problems of scales and weights arriving in a rusty condition as a result of damp packing paper. Occasionally weights were missing, and in one case there was a difference in terminology: "what we [Joseph & Nathaniel] call 12 inch beam, you call Inch." Some of the sets were to be in mahogany or wainscot boxes, and some in shagreen or japanned cases. They ordered weights for plate scales as well as apothecary weights and "averdupoise" weights. In 1787 Joseph and Nathaniel requested that "as we frequently want Twist for Stringing of Scales we wish you would be so kind as to send us about half a Guinea's worth of green twist the size of the piece inclosed."

In paying for these goods, Joseph and Nathaniel usually sent bars of silver or gold or a bill of Exchange, but once they sent fifty Spanish milled pieces of eight and another time fifty "Spanish Cob Dollars" (according to the *Oxford Universal Dictionary*, "cob" is a name given in Ireland to the Spanish dollar or piece of eight). They requested that, if there were a balance in their favor, goods be added to the order. They also expressed hope that Sommers & Son would send a copy of the bill along with the bill of lading, because it would save them trouble and expense at the Custom House. On May 16, 1787, they explained that since it was very difficult to get goods from New York, they would prefer to have their orders sent directly to Philadelphia. A few weeks later they wrote that the box of scales Sommers & Son had said was on the *Portland Packet* in New York was not. It was a great disappointment to their customers and to themselves that the goods were not sent on one of the spring ships bound for Philadelphia. When at last the order arrived in the fall, they found that the four pairs of tripod scales ordered had not been sent.

Another trying situation arose when Sommers & Son sent Joseph and Nathaniel goods to dispose of on their behalf. The brothers said that while they were willing to do this, Sommers & Son could probably do better themselves. When the consignment arrived in September 1788, the Philadelphia goldsmiths found the scales and weights unsalable because "Goods of that kind are generally imported into this City from Birmingham w[h]ere they are to be had at a much lower rate than from London." Nevertheless, they promised to try to sell them. The following summer the goods were still on hand, and they were awaiting further instructions from London. A year later, they reported that they had at last disposed of the scales and weights, but because they had brought so little, they would not charge for selling them.

5. Will No. 344, Phila. Co. Court House.

6. DMMC, 53.165.221.

7. When Mary Richardson died, she left her sons and daughters several annuities on properties. Joseph, Jr., received a ground rent on a lot on Fourth Street amounting to £3/18/9 a year, and Nathaniel received ground rent of £3/11 a year on a lot on Fourth Street. In addition, she gave Joseph £27/8/0, a silver teapot, six teaspoons, a pair of tea tongs and a strainer

in a shagreen case, a cream pot, and two tablespoons. She gave Nathaniel £42/4/0, two silver porringers, a silver tumbler, and three tablespoons.

Seaman records (p. 26) the existence of a note in Mary Richardson's handwriting, addressed "For my son Nathaniel Richardson, 14th 6 mo. 1766: Dear child, these two pieces of silver were my dear Mother's, I now give them to thee as a token of my love, which I desire thee to receive as such and not to part with unless obliged thereto." Seaman says these were two dollars, one of Charles II, 1662, and the other, William II, 1696.

Her daughters, in addition to ground rents, also received silver. Hannah was given a coffeepot; Mary, a teapot marked I^{R}M, a porringer similarly marked, a pepper box, and six new and five old teaspoons; and Rebecca, a sugar dish, small salver, punch strainer, porringer, and tablespoon (DMMC, 53.165.148).

8. Joseph and Nathaniel Richardson, "Receipt Book," HSP, AM924041.

9. The goods sent from Philadelphia included flour, white and brown bread, crackers, Indian corn, rye meal, and rice.

10. This shipping venture on the part of Joseph and Nathaniel began with a letter on April 29, 1786, sent to Benjamin Gaskin on the recommendation of Hezekiah Williams. They also sent a consignment of goods and a letter to Maurice Lisle on October 24, 1786, for they had been assured by Lisle's father that remittance for the shipment would be made by return of the same vessel for at least the first cost and the freight. On October 20, 1787, the Richardson brothers wrote to Maurice Lisle: "As we follow the Silversmiths business in its various branches we should be glad of any Orders from thee or any of thy friends who may want anything in that way, and we flatter ourselves we can give as good satisfaction therein as any in this City both in respect to quality & workmanship."

This suggestion did not work out as well as they undoubtedly hoped. Less than five months later they again wrote: "We have put a pair of buckles into Captain Hortons hands for thee which we hope will give satisfaction the Chapes & Toungs of those we received from him were much damaged with Rust we did not receive them till a few days ago, shall do the best we can, with them.... Price of Shoe buckles £0/33/0 our Money."

Two months later they noted that the buckles had been returned and that they were sending another pair which they hoped would be satisfactory. Evidently they were, since nothing more is said of them. But neither was any new business forthcoming from this source.

In general, their dealings with Gaskin were more satisfactory, and in the end they had great difficulty with Lisle in freight charges contrary to agreement, mistakes in the charges, and collection of their unpaid remittances. Lisle proved so difficult a person with whom to do business that at the end of 1792, Joseph asked Captain William Brewster to help him collect the balance due him from Lisle, and shortly thereafter he discontinued his correspondence with him altogether.

David Schoepf described this sort of trade in Philadelphia in 1783: "Of this domestic produce, the greater part was formerly sent to the British West Indies, whence was brought back sugar, brandy, cotton, coffee, cacao, mahogany, and silver—part for use in the country and part exported to other colonies and to Europe." (*Travels*, I, 117).

11. In 1783, "2 good 8 day Clocks with plain enameled faces without Cases" were requested along with "20 Oz. small size Corral beads interspersed with longer pieces." Six months later Joseph and Nathaniel wrote that these had arrived, but that the clocks were not suitable, owing "to our not being more particular in describing them," and costing twice as

much as expected. Early in 1785 they wrote that they wanted the coral to be smaller and "mixed with long pieces as they are much better liked here than all round ones." At the end of the same year they declared: "As to the Coral beads . . . the Pipe Coral is so very different from what we desired & so very unsaleable here, that we have taken the liberty of sending them back to you . . . ." At the same time they enclosed a few samples of the type of beads they wanted. Apparently this brought results, for six months later they again ordered some small coral beads.

It was necessary for the Richardsons to be very particular in describing the articles they ordered, but even when they were, they met with unexpected difficulties. "The Soup ladles are also charged high," they wrote in 1784, "the lowest prised ones being £0/3/0 a piece more than our last." At the same time they pointed out that in one letter the bar of gold they sent was credited at £0/76/6 per ounce and in another £0/76/0.

Bars of gold or silver or bills of exchange were the usual form of payment to the London firm, but on one occasion the brothers called attention to the fact that "One of the pieces you may observe is of the old standard therefore we expect it will command a better price." In a few instances, the money was transmitted through a third person. On October 28, 1784, for instance, Joseph and Nathaniel wrote to Masterman & Son: "We called on Daniel Depuy [Philadelphia goldsmith] as you requested and found he was not willing to be at the expence nor run the risque of remitting you the Money neither to give the currant price for a Bill of exchange but would pay us in english Money at Par which considering all circumstances we thought best to accept you will therefore please to charge us with £24/18/2 Sterling which we receiv'd of him." But on another occasion, in 1787, they returned to the London firm a draught on Joseph Wharton, because after making inquiry they found him to be in poor circumstances; "his very household furniture that he at present makes use of is assigned to his Creditors." On October 27, 1785 they wrote: "Our late Assembly have laid a duty of two shillings currancy per Oz. upon all wrought Silver Plate, & 20 shillings per oz. upon all wrought Gold imported into this State, which for the present must put a stop to the importation thereof."

The drawback from the English duty on silver plate also presented problems. In 1786 the brothers noticed that the drawback which the London firm received was "not to the full amount as we understood it was to be received without Fee or Reward." Finally, on May 14, 1788, they wrote the Masterman firm: "Your kind favour of the 14th of 2nd mo. last came to hand and was very acceptable — The decline of business in our line together with the duties laid by our Government upon all wrought Plate imported into this State and duties on your side the water and the advances we are daily making towards perfection in our line of business as well as many other branches of Manufactory opperate strongly against Importation and are the only reasons we can give you why we have not sent you another Order notwithstanding which it will give us much pleasure to hear from you."

12. "Receipt book," HSP, AM924041, William Parham was paid £20/6/3 in February 1780, and £9 in April 1780, "in full of all Accounts." Two more payments were made to this silversmith in July of the same year and in April 1781. Another fellow craftsman, John David, received payments from the brothers: £23/11/0 on June 2, 1787; £54/6/0 "for Gold" on July 19, 1787; £36/3/0 on August 25, 1787; and £77/10/7 on January 2, 1787. These accounts are larger than those paid to other goldsmiths. Abraham Carlisle, who advertised as a goldsmith between 1791 and 1794 at Brooks Court and North Front Street, was paid £24/17/10 in 1787; and another prominent goldsmith, Christian Wiltberger (1766–1851), was paid £2/8/4 in

1787 and in 1788 £7/4/3 1/2 "in full for work done for them."

This receipt book also shows that the brothers paid Williamina Bond £95/6/9 in 1784 for about 23 ounces of old silver. John Galloway received £5/7/11 for "an old Silver Tea pot delivered them in November 1787." In 1789 they paid Emmor Bailey £65/14/0 for a parcel of silver. Patrick Carroll "Receiv'd 5th of the 8th mo.14. 1791 of Joseph & Nathaniel Richardson a pice of Gold which I left with them in pledge the 7th of the 8th mo. 1789." Another interesting payment was made in May 1788 to William Darley [or Darby] of £68/19/8 in cash and their note of hand payable six months after the date in the same amount "for sundry articles of Plated Ware." Also recorded are payments of ground rents and taxes, and payments for work done, such as those made to John Wayne and Thomas Collins in 1790 and to John Wood, Jr., for 36 1/2 days work.

13. Trenchard received from them on July 13, 1786, £16/4/0 in full payment of all accounts up through June 26; and on May 20, 1789, £3/8/6 for all accounts up to March 27 (Receipt book, op. cit.).

14. Seaman, pp. 26–27, 46, 53.

15. DMMC, 53.165.209. Subsequent references to letters written by Joseph, Jr., alone indicate this source.

16. In 1791, Joseph sent an order in his own name requesting that the scales be better adjusted than in the past, and that steps be taken to guard against their rusting. Scales and weights were ordered again, twice in 1792, and in 1794 Joseph ordered "1 Pair 18 Inch box beam Plate Scales as good as can be made for my own particular use in a wainscot box" along with five pairs of twelve-inch box-beam plate scales. However, they turned out to be very inaccurate, and Joseph wrote that if the flat beams he ordered could not be properly adjusted, they should not be sent. Further orders were made in 1795, and after some delay, and being unable to claim the goods for lack of letter or invoice, Joseph wrote that they had arrived and were accurate. The large scales cost more than he had expected, however, and he hoped that the reduction in prices the London firm had mentioned might apply to the last order, too. Moreover, the order had been addressed only to J. Richardson, and someone else had opened it.

At the end of 1795 Joseph called for a statement of the firm's accounts, and ordered more scales and weights. His last recorded letter to Sommer & Son, written on December 2, 1796, informed them that the order had been received and was satisfactory, except for the medicine scales which he had not ordered and which were out of his line. Joseph enclosed a bill of exchange to settle the balance he owed, adding to £0/13/7 to make up for not remitting earlier.

17. The horrors of this epidemic were described on October 1, 1793, by Timothy Pickering: "Nothing is more difficult than to describe the present state of the City. A few days of cold weather seemed to check the disorder & on the return of warm weather, the deaths are again multiplied. Probably, in the whole, full 15,000 have died." Quoted in *The Diary of William Bently, D.D.* (Salem, Mass., The Essex Institute, 1907), II, 64–65, 285 [Oct. 8, 1793].

Pickering went on to describe what Dr. Benjamin Rush and other physicians were doing to cure the fever. For his "disinterested benevolent and important services" during the fever of 1798, Dr. Rush was presented a handsome silver tray made by John Myers of Philadelphia, which is still owned by his descendants.

18. Joseph Richardson, Jr., "Account Book," 1796–1801, p. 43, HSP. A Frenchman visiting Philadelphia that August wrote in his journal, "At that moment yellow fever broke out and filled the Americans with profound terror. Twenty thousand residents of Philadelphia, one third of its population, deserted the city and fled to the country" (*Moreau de St. Mery's Ameri-*

CHAPTER VI *Joseph Richardson, Jr., and Nathaniel Richardson: Their Lives*

can Journey (1793-1798), trans. and ed. by Kenneth and Anna M. Roberts [Garden City, N.Y., 1947], p. 236).

19. DMMC, 53.165.182; Prime, p. 79.

20. Seaman, p. 32. Seaman also illustrates furniture owned by him as well as one of several sundials owned by his descendants and thought to have been made by him.

21. DMMC, 53.165.220. During this trip Joseph hoped to and was able to see Thomas Scattergood while in Boston. His letter book explains that Scattergood was his brother-in-law who, according to the letter sent by Joseph to Sommers & Son in 1794, made a religious visit to England in that year.

22. DMMC, 53.165.209.

23. William Needles' touchmark is recorded by Ensko as WNEEDELS in a rectangle, and his advertisement from Easton, Maryland, on July 28, 1807, in the *Republican Star* is quoted: "Opened a Silver-Smith's Shop near the Market-House." Ensko further states that he was a partner in the firm of Bowdle and Needles and that there is no further record of him after 1818 when Stephen Hussey took over William Needles' shop. Ensko, pp. 98, 249. Pleasant and Sills, *Maryland Silversmiths*, pp. 222–23.

24. Seaman, pp. 47-48.

25. This fact is stated in Randolph's apprenticeship indenture, dated June 2, 1801 (Seaman, pp. 47–48). Several pieces of silver by James Howell were shown in the Colonial Dames Exhibition in Philadelphia in 1938, and a coffeepot by him is illustrated in Phoebe P. Prime, *Three Centuries*, pp. 46–47, 143.

26. Ledger, pp. 271, 257, 259, HSP. The joint bond of Lewis, Howell, and Smith was dated September 18, 1805. By 1807 the principal had been reduced so that Howell paid the interest on $954.10 and Lewis and Smith, on $932.27. The last two men paid off their debt in full in November, 1813. Lewis & Smith are listed in books on American goldsmiths as working in partnership from 1805 to 1811, but these joint payments suggest that they collaborated at least until 1813. This bond also tells us Smith's first name which has not been published before. Phoebe P. Prime, *Three Centuries*, pp. 54, 55, illustration p. 147).

27. The ledger accounts with other goldsmiths are corroborated by entries in Joseph's account book. Samuel Richards, who advertised at 136 South Front Street from 1793 to 1818 (Ensko, p. 110), bought from Joseph in 1798 two teapots, a sugar dish, a slop bowl, and a cream pot; and the next year another tea set, some tablespoons, and some teaspoons, amounting to £99/18/2 worth of plate, for which he paid cash, an iron stove plate, and wharfage of 17,250 bricks (Account Book, p. 90, HSP). In 1800 he purchased six teaspoons with carved handles and engraved ciphers, and about the same time John Myers bought six tablespoons of the same description. Myers, former apprentice to Richard Humphreys, worked in Philadelphia between 1785 and 1804 (Phoebe P. Prime, *Three Centuries*, p. 67). Part of the time he worked on Market Street, where Joseph Anthony had his shop from about 1783 to 1809. In 1796, Joseph Anthony & Son paid Richardson cash for melting 1000 ounces of gold dust for them. Joseph charged £0/7/6 per 100 ounces, so the bill came to £3/15/0.

Earlier in the year, Joseph Anthony & Son had purchased two pairs of money scales and weights—one in a mahogany box with a brass stand, and the other in a wainscot box. Joseph continued to sell these for some time after he stopped ordering them, supplying a pair with silver pans to Caspar Wistar in 1796, two pairs in mahogany cases and two in shagreen cases to Richard H. Wilcocks in 1798, and some to the Bank of the United States in 1800 and to the Bank of Rhode Island in 1801.

28. The name of James Smither, Jr., the engraver, is prominent in both the ledger and the accounts. His father was the James Smither who had made cuts for some issues of Pennsylvania currency before the Revolution, and who had engraved the Humphreys urn which the Continental Congress had presented to Charles Thomson in 1774. He was, however, cited by Thomas Paine in a letter to the Continental Congress in 1788, as a participant in the forging of Continental currency for the British. It seems that when the British abandoned Philadelphia and returned to New York, Smither went with them—he advertised as an engraver and seal cutter there in 1779 in the *Royal Gazette*, (Gottesman, *Arts and Crafts in New York 1777-1799* [New York, 1954], no. 107, p. 44). In 1778, he was charged with treason by the Supreme Executive Council of Pennsylvania (Scott, *Counterfeiting*, p. 256). Nevertheless he returned to Philadelphia by 1786, and died there in 1797.

His son, James Smither, Jr., advertised in 1790 that he conducted an evening drawing school on Walnut Street near Front Street as well as the business of engraving and seal cutting (Prime, *Arts and Crafts, 1786-1800*, p. 73). Because of the frequency and extensiveness of young Smither's accounts with Richardson, it is quite likely that he had a permanent arrangement to do engraving for the goldsmith. The first debit to Smither in the ledger mentioned, "To amount brought from Ledger A page 93 – £610.16.0 1/2," reflecting the enormous amount of business between the two men, and indicating that their relationship predates the surviving ledger and account book, both of which were begun in 1796. The account book is a chronological listing of debits and credits, while the ledger is a summary of accounts under individual names.

From 1797 to 1798, Smither was charged for "Sundries as per Day-book," a thimble, a plain gold locket and coral beads, a sugar dish, a silver seal, six tablespoons, a cream pot, and cash. He was credited "By amount of his Bill," which for a few months' work was between £25 and £50 (Ledger, p. 187). From 1799 to 1802 Smither received, in addition to the sundries recorded in the account book, a number of silver seals (presumably blanks which he could cut himself), tumblers, coffee and tea set items, spoons, a punch strainer, and a silver ferrule for a boiler. During the latter period his bills were lower, amounting usually to only about £25.

In his account book Richardson painstakingly notes the charges for any engraving, recording whether it was for simple initials, ciphers, ornament, or names. This might have served as a check for bills submitted by Smither. Tea sets, tongs, spoons, ladles, cans, and waiters were the objects most commonly engraved, but on various occasions Joseph recorded the engraving of a cipher on a tea chest, ciphers and ornament on a boiler, and "Cyphers & Crests on 2 Rummers & Castor frame." Sometimes he was very specific about what was to be engraved: the lion crest on two teaspoons; a name to be put on Elizabeth Powel's gold glove clasps; "M Pryor" to be engraved on a dessert spoon for Samuel Pleasants; "HP" first on a sugar dish and then on a coffeepot for James Hartley; marking a parcel of spoons "WMB;" and John Guest's teapot "IRG." Some engraving, too, was recorded as being done on plated silver.

It is possible that much of the work Smither did for Richardson involved engraving the arms of the United States on ornaments purchased by the National Government for presentation to the Indians. Enormous quantities were supplied by Richardson through the purveyor, Tench Francis, and after his death, through Israel Wheeler. One entry in the accounts for October 29, 1796 will serve as an example, since it includes all the usual items except for hair pipes and finger rings ordered a little later:

To 30 pair Indian Arm bands weight	185 oz. 2 dwt.	
To 60 pair ditto Wrist bands	98 oz. 3 dwt.	
to 36 ditto Gorgets	59 oz. 15 dwt.	
	343 oz. 0 dwt. @ £0/12/6	£214/ 7/6
To 30 dozen Broaches	16 oz. 13 dwt. 12 gr. @ £0/ 9/0	7/10/0
To making Ditto @ £0/7/6 per dozen		11/ 5/0
To 9 1/2 dozen pair Ear bobs	5 oz. 19 dwt. 0 gr. @ £0/ 9/0	2/13/6
To making ditto @ £0/36/0 per dozen pair		17/12/0
To Chasing 96 Eagles @ £0/2/0		9/12/0
To ditto 120 ditto @ £0/1/3		7/10/0
		£270/ 0/0

The custom of the presentation of Indian silver was described in an advertisement in the Charleston City [South Carolina] *Gazette* on August 12, 1794: "Lost On Thursday night last, by the [Chief] Humming Bird, a broad silver arm band presented him as an ornament by the secretary of war, in Philadelphia; as the band can be of no particular use in its present form, to any person but an Indian, it is hoped whoever may be in possession of it will return it, and receive a handsome reward from Silas Dinsmore." Silas Dinsmore was a graduate of Dartmouth College and a friend of the Cherokee Indians. In 1797 he wrote a letter to Mr. J. Bowditch describing his visits among them which William Bentley quoted in his diary for November 13, 1797: "In opposition to savage prejudices, I have introduced spinning & weaving, & some are now wearing cotton cloth of their own making." (Bentley, *Diary*, II, 245).

29. In recent years, there has been an outbreak in the market of spurious medals which are notorious for their crude, overworked delineation of Washington presenting a peace pipe to an Indian, while a peaceful plowman works in the background. Large oval medals were mentioned, however, on a loose piece of paper in the letter book of Joseph, Jr., in a listing of 50 pairs of arm bands, 42 pairs of wrist bands "For Tench Francis (Purveyor) provided they can be prepared and delivered in the Course of this Week. If not the whole such part as can be finished etc." They listed:

12 Medals 2 Size Engraved as heretofore
 9 do.   3   " the Year 1795.

30. In his account book for June 6, 1796, Joseph recorded, "George Washington is Creditor By Cash. . . . £16/14/2." This entry is explained by Washington's manuscript "Account of Furnishings for the Official Residences of the President in New York and Philadelphia 1789-1796" (DMMC, 65X571). Here under the same date is recorded, "Jos. Richardson—Silver plate per Bill ($) 44.55." The teapot and slop bowl were made by Joseph, presumably before 1796, as they are not noted in his account book. These two pieces, privately owned and not available for illustration, are listed in 1797 in the Household List of Washington's silver, valued at £33/7/6 in Virginia currency. The teapot is unusually heavy, but the slop bowl is scratched on the base with a more common weight of 16 oz. 19 dwt. (Kathryn C. Buhler, *Mount Vernon Silver* [Mount Vernon, 1957], pp. 64-65, *Figure* 32.)

31. Watson, *Annals*, I, 580-81. Moreau de St. Méry also commented on the use of silver at dinners in Philadelphia in the 1790's, "Before dinner and all during dinner, as is the English custom, all the silver one owns is displayed on the sideboard in the dining room" (*American Journey*, p. 266).

32. *Illustrated History of the United States Mint* (Philadelphia, George G. Evans [pub-

lisher], 1888), p. 129. This source also states that "A water color portrait of him dressed in plain Quaker garb, hangs in the assayers' room." The portrait cannot be located there now. An account book for the mint dated 1822 is at Winterthur in the Richardson Family papers. The *Early Proceedings of the American Philosophical Society* note for June 21, 1805, among donations "Specimens of gold from Carbarrus County, North Carolina, with Joseph Richardson's Assay of part of it at the mint, 7 dwts., 7 gr."

33. 1831, No. 68, Will No. 10, p. 42, Phila. Co. Court House

34. *Illustrated History*, p. 129.

CHAPTER 7. *Joseph Richardson, Jr., and Nathaniel Richardson: Their Silver*

1. John Lord Sheffield, *Observations on the Commerce of America* (London, 1784).

2. Although their Letter Book does not indicate that Joseph, Jr., and Nathaniel Richardson ever ordered plated wares from England, the inventory taken at the end of their partnership in 1790 shows that they handled large quantities of it. All subsequent mention of orders for silver by the two brothers refer to this Letter Book (DMMC, 53.165.223).

3. Francis Hopkinson, *Account of the Grand Federal Procession Philadelphia*, 1788, ed. by Whitfield J. Bell, Jr. (The Old South Association, Boston, Mass.) Old South Leaflets, nos. 230-31.

4. Humphreys was a protégé of Philip Syng, and moved into his house a few doors below the Coffee House in 1772. The Continental Congress commissioned Humphreys in 1774 to make the impressive presentation urn for their first secretary, Charles Thomson. The engraved inscription on it was signed by James Smither who advertised in 1768, "Performs all manner of Engraving in Gold, Silver, Copper, Steel, and all other metals" (review, "Philadelphia Silver Exhibition", *Art Quarterly*, Spring 1957, pp. 45-46); *Philadelphia Silver Exhibition*, 1956, no. 179, illustrated).

5. Joseph and Nathaniel also ordered many other forms from England: punch ladles with whale bone handles, fluted soup ladles, bellied pint mugs, caster sets with spare glasses, teaspoons and tongs in shagreen cases, pocket nutmeg graters, and coral and bells.

6. Because of the difference in weights it is possible that pattern No. 1 was the earlier style of double-bellied, domed base cream pot, while pattern No. 2 was the lighter urn-shaped cream pot with square foot.

7. A coffeepot of this type was lent anonymously to the 1956 Philadelphia Exhibition (no. 423). It is unusual in being single-bellied and having wide flat fluting which hangs down from the top and comes up from the base.

8. In 1788 tankards of this sort were made by Joseph Anthony, Jr., for presentation to Gunning Bedford and Charles Jarvis by John Penn and John Penn, Jr. (*Philadelphia Silver Exhibition*, 1956, nos. 15 & 16, illustrated).

9. English hooped tankards and mugs undoubtedly served as the models for those made by Philadelphia goldsmiths, although Joseph, Jr., and Nathaniel did not record in their letter book orders for these forms from London.

10. *Pennsylvania Packet*, Oct. 23, 1789; Prime, *Arts and Crafts, 1786-1800*, p. 143.

11. Joseph Richardson, Jr., "Account Book," 1796-1801, HSP. All subsequent references to accounts indicate this source.

12. *Pennsylvania Journal*, Oct. 4, 1783; *Pennsylvania Packet*, Jan. 5, 1790.

13. The handles on these objects suggest that they might also be the same form Joseph sometimes referred to as a pannikin for in several instances he spoke of pannikins with black ebony handles. In another instance, Joseph described a pannikin as being hooped and having an engraved cipher and ornament.

14. Joseph Richardson, Jr., "Letter Book", DMMC, 53.165.209. All subsequent references to orders indicate this source.

15. The cream pots ordered were to be urn-shaped with square feet and to weigh about 5 oz. each. Half were to be burnished and half polished inside and out. Miscellaneous objects imported included 12 pairs of patent shoe buckles, 4 dozen silver thimbles with steel tops "not very long", 20 oz. of coral beads "smaller than the last," and 12 polished steel pocket book clasps. This latter item was also ordered in plated silver.

16. His final letter to them was written on May 25, 1793, when he sent a bill of exchange for £50 and a bar of gold. He requested that any "over plus" in his favor be made up by a shipment of as many children's coral and bells as would balance the account.

17. A bill to Samuel Wheeler from Joseph Richardson, Jr. in 1801 has survived and was illustrated along with the sugar bowl and tongs mentioned in it in the catalogue of the 1938 Colonial Dames Exhibition (Phoebe P. Prime, *Three Centuries*, pp. 161–162). The bill totalled $214.90.

18. On the last pages of Joseph's ledger is a long list of numbered tea set pieces of silver which he had on hand, with a notation "these numbers are in the large trunk." This gives the weight, cost per ounce, and total value of each piece.

19. Milo M. Naeve in a letter to the author, March 15, 1960, suggested that Daniel Trotter may have done this since he recorded in his account book charges for carving handles for various Philadelphia goldsmiths, including a person identified as "R." The Trotter accounts are for 1793 so this assumption cannot be verified by Joseph Richardson, Jr.'s only extant account book of 1796–1801.

20. Whether Joseph made fluted pieces before this time is not known, but the style probably postdates his partnership with his brother at least since no examples of it have been found bearing their joint mark.

21. Between 1798 and 1799, John Ashley was charged 15 shillings per ounce for the making of two baking dishes weighing almost 60 ounces altogether, and shortly thereafter for one weighing about 21 ounces, and another weighing only 17 1/2 ounces.

22. *Pennsylvania Journal*, Dec. 15, 1763. Cited by Phillips, *American Silver*, p. 92.

23. Miss Clarissa T. Chase lent doll's teaspoons and bow sugar tongs made by Joseph Richardson, Jr. to the Colonial Dames exhibition in 1938, no. 80 in the catalogue. These once belonged to Margaret (Hill) Morris.

24. Register of the Medal Dies of the United States, HSP.

APPENDIX B. *Settlement of the Hulbeart Estate*

1. DMMC, Prime Cards.
2. *Pa. Gaz.*, May 24, 1759, in DMMC, Prime Cards.
3. DMMC, Prime Cards.
4. *Ibid.*
5. *Ibid.*

6. *Pa. Gaz.*, April 7, 1763.
7. DMMC, Prime Cards.
8. Prime, *Arts & Crafts, 1721-1785*, pp. 52-53.
9. Author's italics.
10. DMMC, 53.165.95, p. 45.

APPENDIX C. *Scales and Weights Sold by Joseph Richardson*

1. Correspondence about scales and weights, unless otherwise specified, refers to the Letter Book, DMMC, 53.165.95.

APPENDIX D. *Letter Book of Joseph Richardson*

1. Prime, *The Arts & Crafts, 1721-1785*, pp. 41-102. Edmund Milne may have bought these items from one of the sources used by Joseph Richardson, since the latter makes reference to Milne's also having an account with the firm of How & Masterman, London goldsmiths (Joseph Richardson, *Letter Book*, (DMMC, 53.165.95, p. 26).
2. R. W. Symonds, "The English Export Trade in Furniture to Colonial America," *Antiques*, XXVIII (October 1935), 156.
3. A summary of information about Wagstaffe can be found in Martha G. Fales, "Thomas Wagstaffe, London Quaker Clockmaker," *Connoisseur*, CLI (November 1962), 193-201.
4. Joseph Downs, *American Furniture: Queen Anne & Chippendale Periods* (New York, 1952), p. 207.
5. Eckhardt, *Pennsylvania Clocks*, (New York 1955), p. 136.
6. In 1763, Captain Charles Ridgely of Maryland bought goods from Wagstaffe while in London, "chiefly plate," amounting to £64/18/6. The story of Wagstaffe's attempt to collect payment from Ridgely over the next six years is told by W. D. Hoyt, in "A London Shopkeeper's Struggle to Recover a Colonial Debt," *Maryland Historical Magazine*, XLV (June 1950), 126-33.
7. John Hayward, Victoria and Albert Museum, to the author, July 11, 1956. On an undated page in Richardson's Commonplace Book is a note preceding a 1744 entry: "George Ritherdon at Mr. Winnes Goldsmith without Aldgate, London."
8. *London Goldsmiths*, p. 271.
9. Charles C. Oman to the author, August 31, 1953.
10. Britten, p. 462.
11. Sir Ambrose Heal, the outstanding authority on English trade cards, to the author, July 4, 1956.
12. For example, on December 4, 1766, Richard Wistar of New Jersey, upon the recommendation of his brother-in-law Isaac Greenleafe, wrote to Mildred and Roberts ordering a long list of fabrics to supply his country store. (See indexed references to Daniel Mildred in *Pa. Mag.*; Richard Wistar, "Letter Book," 1759-72, microfilm, DMMC, M-220. Original owned by Miss Elizabeth M. Wistar).
13. An effort was made to locate one of their shop bills. Sir Ambrose Heal, had no ex-

ample in his collection of How & Masterman or of George Ritherdon (Sir Ambrose to the author, July 3, 1959). A photograph of a trade card for George Ritherdon is now in the Heal Collection of Trade Cards at the British Museum, but there is no notation as to where the actual card is (Charles C. Oman to the author, May 29, 1964).

14. How & Masterman are listed by Heal as goldsmiths at 1 White Hart Court, Gracechurch Street, the same street on which Wagstaffe's shop was located (*London Goldsmiths*, p. 178). Masterman is listed at the same address, between 1769–73, and How & Masterman are listed there between 1750 and 1760 (Britten, pp. 406, 434).

15. John Hayward to the author, July 11, 1956. This omission is probably explained by C. C. Oman's addition to the 1959 edition of his *English Domestic Silver* (London), p. 19: "It is a great pity that Sir Charles Jackson did not warn his readers that the register of marks of large plate workers covering the years 1738–58 are missing from the series at Goldsmith's Hall."

16. Charles C. Oman to the author, August 31, 1953.

17. Tolles, *Meeting House*, p. 90.

18. DMMC, 53.165.148.

19. DMMC, 53.165.223.

20. Much later, in 1794, Charles Gilchrist advertised in Philadelphia "gold and silversmith's sweeps purchased by assay, which will enable him to give the true value." (Alfred Coxe Prime, *The Arts & Crafts in Philadelphia, Maryland, and South Carolina 1786–1800*, Series 2 [The Walpole Society; Topsfield, Mass. 1932], p. 117).

21. *Exhibition of Old American and English Silver*, (Pennsylvania Museum, May 1917), No. 397.

22. DMMC, 53.165.298a.

23. Francis Hill Bigelow, *Historic Silver of the Colonies* (New York, 1917), p. 410, illus. No. 303.

24. William D. Winter, *Marine Insurance, Its Principles & Practice* (3rd ed: New York, 1952). Marine insurance is one of the oldest forms of indemnity, dating back to the twelfth century. In the article on insurance in the 1761 London edition of Rolt's *A New Dictionary of Trade and Commerce*, the custom for insuring about the time of Richardson's loss on the *Julian* is described: "It is said that very few insure the whole ship, but subscriptions are usually for sums certain, as 100 l. 500 l. or 1000 l. at the rate or premium current (sometimes 30 or 40 *per cent* in times of war), which, when the adventure is borne, the insurers receive; but if a loss happen the premium is deducted, together with the usual abatement, and then the insured receive about 80 *per cent* in common cases."

Bibliography

Books

Abbey, Staton, *Goldsmith and Silversmith's Handbook*, New York, 1952.

Abbott, George Maurice, *A Short History of the Library Company of Philadelphia*, Philadelphia, 1913.

Avery, C. Louise, *Early American Silver*, New York, 1930, 1968.

Bentley, William, *The Diary of William Bentley, D.D.*, II, Salem, Mass., The Essex Institute, 1907.

Bigelow, Francis Hill, *Historic Silver of the Colonies*, New York, 1917.

Bridenbaugh, Carl, *Cities in the Wilderness*, New York, 1938.

─────, *Rebels and Gentlemen*, New York, 1942

Brix, Maurice, *List of Philadelphia Silversmiths and Allied Artificers from 1682 to 1850*, Philadelphia, 1920.

[Budworth, William], *A Touch-Stone for Gold and Silver Wares*, London, 1677.

Burton, E. Milby, *South Carolina Silversmiths*, Charleston, S.C., 1942.

Britten's Old Clocks and Watches and Their Makers, 7th ed. New York, 1956.

Buhler, Kathryn C., *Colonial Silversmiths, Masters and Apprentices*, Boston, 1956.

─────, *Mount Vernon Silver*, Mount Vernon, Va., 1957.

─────, *American Silver 1655-1825 in the Museum of Fine Arts Boston*, Boston, 1972, 2 vols.

─────, and Graham Hood, *American Silver Garvan and Other Collections in the Yale University Art Gallery*, New Haven, 1970, 2 vols.

Catalogue of the Library Company of Philadelphia 1741, Philadelphia, 1956.

Catalogue of the Reifsnyder Collection, American Art Association, Inc., New York, 1929.

Clayton, Michael, *The Collector's Dictionary of the Silver and Gold of Great Britain and North America*, New York and Cleveland, 1971.

Cramer, *Elements of the Art of Assaying Metals*, London, 1741

Currier, Ernest M., *Marks of Early American Silversmiths*, Portland, Maine, 1938.

Davidson, Marshall, *Life in America*, I, Boston, 1951.

Bibliography

Dawson, Nelson, *The Goldsmith's and Silversmith's Work*, New York, 1907.

Diderot, Denis, *Encyclopédie, VIII*, Paris, 1776.

Dow, George Francis, *The Arts and Crafts in New England, 1704-1775*, Topsfield, Massachusetts, 1927.

Downs, Joseph, *American Furniture: Queen Anne & Chippendale Periods*, New York, 1952.

Drepperd, Carl W., *American Clocks & Clockmakers*, Garden City, 1947.

Dunlap, William, *A History of the Rise and Progress of the Arts of Design in the United States, I*, Boston, 1918.

Eckhardt, George H., *Pennsylvania Clocks and Clockmakers*, New York, 1955.

Engle, William, ed., *Pennsylvania Archives, 11, 12*, Series 3, Harrisburg, 1897.

Ensko, Stephen G. C., *American Silversmiths and Their Marks III*, New York, 1948.

_____, *American Silversmiths and Their Marks*, New York, 1927.

Exhibition of Old American and English Silver, Pennsylvania Museum, May, 1917.

Fales, Martha G., *American Silver in the Henry Francis du Pont Winterthur Museum*, Winterthur, 1958.

_____, *Early American Silver*, New York, 1970, 1973.

The Folger Coffee Company Collection of Antique English Silver Coffee Pots, Milwaukee, 1964.

Freeman, Samuel T. & Co., *Catalogue*, Philadelphia, January 26-30, 1959.

French, Hollis, *List of Early American Silversmiths & Their Marks*, New York, 1917.

Gillingham, Harrold E., *Indian Ornaments Made by Philadelphia Silversmiths*, New York, 1936.

Gottesman, Rita Susswein, *The Arts and Crafts in New York 1726-1776*, New York, 1938.

Gottesman, Rita Susswein, *The Arts and Crafts in New York 1777-1799*, New York, 1954.

Hardie, James, *Philadelphia Dictionary*, Philadelphia, 1793.

Hazard, Samuel, ed., *Pennsylvania Archives, 4*, Series 1, Philadelphia, 1853.

Heal, Sir Ambrose, *The London Furniture Makers, 1660 to 1840*, London, 1953.

_____, *The London Goldsmiths, 1200-1800*, Cambridge, 1935.

Heffner, William Clinton, *History of Poor Relief Legislation in Pennsylvania*, Cleona, 1913.

Hoban, Charles F., ed., *Votes of the Assembly, Pennsylvania Archives*, Series 8, VIII, Philadelphia, 1935.

Honeyman, A. Van Doran, and Nelson, William, *Documents Relating to the Colonial History of the State of New Jersey, XXIX*, Series 1, Paterson, 1917.

Hoopes, Penrose R., *Shop Records of Daniel Burnap Clockmaker*, Hartford, 1958.
Hornor, William M., *Blue Book. Philadelphia Furniture, William Penn to George Washington*, 1935.
Illustrated History of the United States Mint, Philadelphia, 1888.
Jackson, Sir Charles J., *English Goldsmiths & Their Marks*, London, 1921.
Johnson, Samuel, *A Dictionary of the English Language*, I, Philadelphia, 1819.
———, *The Rambler*, II, London, 1793.
Jones, E. Alfred, *The Old Silver of American Churches*, Letchworth, England, 1913.
Jordan, John W., *Colonial Families of Philadelphia*, 2 vols., New York, 1911.
Kellock, Katherine Amend, "Joseph Richardson," *Dictionary of American Biography*, ed. by Dumas Malone, XV, New York 1948.
Kettell, Russell Howes, ed., *Early American Rooms*, New York, 1967.
Matthews, Mitford M., ed., *A Dictionary of Americanisms*, Chicago, 1956.
Miller, V. Isabelle, *Silver by New York Makers*, New York 1937.
Minutes of the Common Council of the City of Philadelphia 1704 to 1776, Philadelphia, 1847.
Montgomery, Thomas Lynch, ed., *Pennsylvania Archives*, Series 6, I, Harrisburg, 1906; Series 6, III, Harrisburg, 1907; Series 5, V, Harrisburg, 1906.
Moreau de St. Méry's American Journey 1793-1798, trans. by Kenneth and Anna M. Roberts, Garden City, N.Y., 1947.
Myers, Albert Cook, *Hannah Logan's Courtship*, Philadelphia, 1904.
———, ed., *Narratives of Early Pennsylvania, New Jersey, and Delaware*, "Original Narrative Series," New York, 1911.
Nelson, William, and Ricord, Frederick W., eds., *Documents Relating to the Colonial History of the State of New Jersey*, X, Newark, 1886.
Nettels, Curtis P., *Roots of American Civilization*, New York, 1938.
Oman, Charles, *English Domestic Silver*, London, 1959.
The Oxford English Dictionary.
The Oxford Universal Dictionary.
Padelford, Philip, ed., *Colonial Panorama 1775*, The Huntington Library, San Marino, California, 1939.
Pennsylvania Marriages Prior to 1790, Baltimore, 1968.
Phillips, John Marshall, *American Silver*, New York, 1949.
———, "Faked American Silver," in *Antiques Fakes and Reproductions* by Ruth Webb Lee, Framingham Centre, Mass., 1938.
Pleasants, J. H. and Sill, H., *Maryland Silversmiths 1715-1830*, Baltimore, 1930.
Pollen, John Hungerford, *Gold and Silversmith's Work*, London, n. d.
Pope, Alexander, *The Rape of the Lock*, Canto V., lines 87-96.
Prime, Alfred Coxe, *The Arts and Crafts in Philadelphia, Maryland and South Carolina*, First Series, 1721-1785, Topsfield, Mass., 1929; Second series, 1786-1800, Topsfield, Mass., 1932.
Prime, Mrs. Alfred Coxe, *Three Centuries of American Silver*, Philadelphia, 1938.

Ricord, Frederick W., ed., *Documents Relating to the Colonial History of the State of New Jersey, XVIII*, Trenton, 1893.

Rolt, *A New Dictionary of Trade and Commerce*, London, 1761.

Roth, Rodris, *Tea Drinking in Eighteenth-Century America: Its Etiquette and Equipage*, Washington, D. C., 1961.

Rules of Discipline of the Yearly Meeting of Friends Held in Philadelphia, Philadelphia, 1843.

Schoepf, Johann David, *Travels in the Confederation*, trans. and ed. by Alfred J. Morrison, Philadelphia, 1911.

Scott, Kenneth, *Counterfeiting in Colonial America*, New York, 1957.

Seaman, Mary T., *Thomas Richardson of South Shields and His Descendants*, New York, 1929.

Sewall, Samuel, *Diary of Samuel Sewall*, Collections of the Massachusetts Historical Society, V, Series 5, Book 1, Boston, 1878.

Sheffield, John Lord, *Observations on the Commerce of the American States*, London, 1784.

Sherrill, Charles H., *French Memories of Eighteenth-Century America*, New York, 1915.

Smith, William Roy, "Edward Shippen," *Dictionary of American Biography*, ed. by Dumas Malone, *XVII*, 116.

State of Pennsylvania, *Minutes of the Supreme Executive Council of Pennsylvania*, Harrisburg, 1852.

⸺, *Minutes of the Provincial Council of Pennsylvania*, Harrisburg, 1852.

Thomas, Gabriel, *An Historical and Geographical Account of the Province of Pensilvania and of West-New-Jersey in America*, London, 1698.

Tolles, Frederick B., *George Logan of Philadelphia*, New York, 1953.

⸺, *Meeting House and Counting House*, Chapel Hill, N.C. 1948.

van Laer, A. F. F., ed. & trans., *Correspondence of Maria van Rennselaer*, Albany, 1935.

Wainwright, Nicholas B., *A Philadelphia Story*, Philadelphia, 1952.

Watson, John F., *Annals of Philadelphia and Pennsylvania, in the Olden Time*, 2 vols., Philadelphia, 1868.

Wertenbaker, Thomas Jefferson, *The Founding of American Civilization, The Middle Colonies*, New York, 1938.

Weslager, C. A., *The Richardsons of Delaware*, Wilmington, Delaware, 1957.

White, Francis, *Philadelphia Directory*, Philadelphia, 1793.

Williams, Carl M., *Silversmiths of New Jersey 1700–1825*, Philadelphia, 1949.

Winter, William D., *Marine Insurance, Its Principles & Practice*, 3rd ed., New York, 1952.

Wright, Louis B., *The Atlantic Frontier*, New York, 1951.

Wood, Juliana R., *Family Sketches*, Philadelphia, 1870.

Periodicals

"Abstracts of Wills," *New-York Historical Society Collections*, XXV (1893), 391–393

Allison, P., and Penrose, Boies, eds., "Early Government of Pennsylvania," *Pa. Mag.*, X (1886).

Balch, Thomas, "Dr. William Shippen, the Elder," *Pa. Mag.*, I (1877), 212–13.

Bigelow, Bruce M., "The Walter Newbury Shipping Book," *Rhode Island Historical Society Collections*, XXIV (1931), 75.

Catalogue, *Silver Exhibition*, Pennsylvania Museum, 1917.

Colonial Dames, *Silver Exhibition*, Philadelphia, 1929.

Dennis, Jessie McNab, "London Silver in a Colonial Household," *The Metropolitan Museum of Art Bulletin*, XXVI (December 1967), 174–179.

deLancey, Edward F., "The Burgher Right of New Amsterdam," *New-York Historical Society Collections*, XVIII (1885), 53.

Eckhardt, George H., "Edward Duffield, Benjamin Franklin's Clockmaker," *Antiques*, LXXVII (March 1960), 286.

Fales, Martha G., "English Design Sources of American Silver," *Antiques*, LXXXIII (January, 1963), 82–85.

————, "Some Forged Richardson Silver," *Antiques*, LXXIX (May 1961), 466–69.

————, "Thomas Wagstaffe, London Quaker Clockmaker," *Connoisseur*, CLI (November, 1962), 193–201.

Frontispiece, *Antiques*, LIX (January 1951), 34.

Gillingham, Harrold E., "Cesar Ghiselin, Philadelphia's First Gold and Silversmith 1693–1735," *Pa. Mag.*, LVII (July 1933), 244–59.

————, "Early American Indian Medals," *Antiques*, VI (December 1924) 312–15.

————, "A Philadelphia Silver Porringer," *Pa. Mag.*, LV (1931).

————, "The Cost of Old Silver," *Pa. Mag.*, LIV (1930).

————, "Pens and Pencils," *Antiques*, IX (January 1926), 33–34.

————, "Fountain Pens and Pepys," *Antiques* IX (June 1926), 384.

Hornor, William M., Jr., "The Richardson Family, Silversmiths of Philadelphia," *Antiquarian*, XIV (May 1930), 42.

Hough, Oliver, "Atkinson Family of Bucks County, Pennsylvania," *Pa. Mag.*, XXXI, (1907), 433.

Hoyt, W. D., "A London Shopkeeper's Struggle to Collect a Colonial Debt," *Maryland Historical Magazine*, XLV (June 1950), 126–33

Leach, Josiah Granville, "Colonial Mayors of Philadelphia," *Pa. Mag.*, XVIII (1894), 420.

Miller, V. Isabelle, "American Silver Spout Cups," *Antiques*, XLIV (August 1943), 73–75.

Morris, Anna Wharton, "Journal of Samuel Rowland Fisher, 1779–1781," *Pa. Mag.*, XLI (1917), 274–333.

Norman-Wilcox, Gregor, "Some Unpublished American Silver," *Antiques*, XXXI (March 1937), 126–129.

"Notes," *Pa. Mag.*, *XIX* (1895), 531; *XXVIII* (1904), 105; *XXXV* (1911), 388–89.
Pennsylvania Museum Bulletin, No. 68, Philadelphia, 1921.
Pennypacker, Samuel W., "The Settlement of Germantown," *Pa. Mag.*, *IV* (1880), 21.
Philadelphia Silver Exhibition, Philadelphia, 1956.
Phillips, John Marshall, "Johannis Nys," *Bulletin of the Associates in Fine Arts at Yale University*, *VI*, New Haven, 1933.
———, "Marked American Gold in the Garvan Collection," *Bulletin of the Associates in Fine Arts at Yale University*, *VII*, New Haven, 1937.
———, *Masterpieces in American Silver*, The Antiques Magazine, New York, 1949.
Richardson, Edgar P., "Remnants, Precious to Antiquaries...," *Antiques*, *LXXIII* (March 1958), 264.
Rhode Island Historical Society Collections, *XXIV* (1931), 75.
"Shop Talk," *Antiques*, *LIV* (September 1948), 152.
Seabury, P. G., "Early Marriages in Newport, Rhode Island, from Friends' Record," *New England Historical and Genealogical Register*, *XVIII* Albany (1864), 241.
Stockwell, David H., "A 1757 Inventory of Silver," *Antiques*, *LXIX* (January 1956), 58–59.
Stone, Frederick D., "A Vindication of William Penn," *Pa. Mag.*, *VI* (1882), 175.
Symonds, R. W., "The English Export Trade in Furniture to Colonial America," *Antiques*, *XXVIII* (October 1935), 156.
Williams, Carl M., "An Unrecorded Goldsmith," *Antiques*, *LI* (January 1947), 40–42.
Winterthur Newsletter, *1–10*.
Woodhouse, Samuel W., Jr. "American Craftsmanship in Gold," *Antiques*, *XX* (July 1931).
———, "Colonial Craftsmen of Philadelphia," *Art and Archaeology*, April, 1926, 182–86.
———, "John DeNys, Philadelphia Silversmith," *Antiques*, *XXI* (May 1932), 218.

Manuscripts

JOSEPH DOWNS MANUSCRIPT AND MICROFILM COLLECTION
HENRY FRANCIS DU PONT WINTERTHUR MUSEUM

Prime Cards, Excerpts from 18th Century Newspapers.
Richardson Family Papers, including Account Book of Francis Richardson, Letter Books of Joseph Richardson, Sr., and Joseph, Jr., and Nathaniel Richardson, and Many Miscellaneous Items.
Microfilm copy of Richardson account books. Original at Historical Society of Pennsylvania.
Latimer, Dr. Henry, inventory of estate, 1820.
Webb, Joseph, Account Book, 1744–1750.

HISTORICAL SOCIETY OF PENNSYLVANIA

Autograph Collection
Collection of the Genealogical Society of Pennsylvania, "Records of Christ Church Philadelphia Baptisms 1709–1768," *I*.
Gratz Papers, Case 17, Box 17.
Henderson, Robert, Receipt Book, Am. 9118.
Logan Papers, *II, XIII, XIV, XIX, XX, XXII*.
Map of Philadelphia and parts adjacent, Heap and Scull, 1750.
Monthly Meeting of Friends of Philadelphia, 1766–1774, Miscellaneous Papers, Box 3.
Non-Importation Act.
Norris Papers, Family Accounts, *III*
Pemberton Papers, *II, XII, XIII, XVIII, XXI, XXIX, XXXIX*.
Philadelphia Monthly Meeting Records.
Register of the Medal Dies of the United States, Am. 8896.
Richardson, Rebecca, "Letter Book and Some Accounts," 1681, 1588–89, Josephine R. Howell Collection, No. 571.
Richardson, Joseph, Account Books, 1733–1740, 1745–1748.
Richardson, Joseph, Jr., and Richardson, Nathaniel, Account Book, 1777–1790.
Richardson, Joseph, Jr., and Nathaniel, Receipt Book, 1780–1800.
Richardson, Joseph, Jr., Account Book, 1796–1801, M89; Ledger, 1796–1831, M208, M89.
Charles Norton Smith Papers, *I*.
Staufer Collection, *XXVII*.
Three Lower Counties 1655–1805.
Wilson Papers, *VII*.

ARCH STREET MEETING, LIBRARY, PHILADELPHIA

Minutes of the Monthly Meeting, *E-1–E-10*.
Permits of Interment in Friends Burial Ground.
Records of Marriages, *E-26*.

PHILADELPHIA COUNTY COURT HOUSE

Wills — Nathaniel Allen, L-28.
      Hannah Growden, S-443.
      Joseph Growden, F-82.
      Lydia Peel, S-418.
      Oswald Peel, N-274.
      Francis Richardson, No. 127.
      Joseph Richardson, Sr., No. 344, and Codicil, Q-345.
      Joseph Richardson, Jr., 68, 42.

Mary Richardson, U–33.
John Stamper, S–151.

Deeds — F–6, 269; H–8, 178; H–9, 445; H–19, 536; I–1, 415; I–11, 127; I–12, 196; O, 482; S, 196; S, 338; S, 340.

CHESTER COUNTY COURT HOUSE

Wills — David Lloyd, No. 395.
Grace Lloyd, No. 1850.

Deeds — S–338; S–340; S–196; C_2 112; C_2 110.

Orphan's Court Records.

PHILADELPHIA CONTRIBUTIONSHIP

Minute Book, 1752–85.
Journal, 1752–18.
Numerical Book, 1752–85.
Ledger, 1752–85.
Surveys: 662, 76, 2002, 2003.

LIBRARY COMPANY

Minutes
Record Book A.
Catalogue of Library Company, 1770.
Smith, Mss., VI

PENNSYLVANIA HOSPITAL

Minutes, I, II.

AMERICAN PHILOSOPHICAL SOCIETY

Penn, William, Cash Book.

NEW YORK PUBLIC LIBRARY

Henderson, Robert, Day Book and Journal, 1779–91.

PRIVATELY OWNED

Ball, William, Account Book, owned by William Ball, West Chester, Pennsylvania.
Richardson, Francis, Marriage Certificate, copy owned by the late Mrs. Alfred Coxe Prime, Paoli, Pennsylvania.
Notes and clippings concerning early American silversmiths compiled by the late Mrs. Alfred Coxe Prime.

NEWSPAPERS

Boston Chronicle, August 1–8, 1768.
Pennsylvania Gazette, 1737–1788.
Philadelphia Inquirer, October 22, 1947.
Evening Public Ledger, Philadelphia, June 22, 1940.

Index

References to illustrations are italicized.

Abbot, Samuel, *45*
Abraham (button maker), 272
Addison, Joseph, on coral and bells, 296
Advertising, 68, 210; by Frank Richardson, *22-23*, 28; by Joseph Richardson, 68, 203, 208, 247-48; by Joseph Richardson, Jr., 184
Albany Conference (1754), 38
Alford, Samuel, 202-03
Alford, Thomas, 202-03
All, Capt., 259-60
Allen, Hannah, 35, 46, 205, 216-17, 277
Allen, James (silversmith), 8, 270, 272
Allen, Joseph, 245-46, 249-50
Allen, Mary, 35-36. *See also* Richardson, Mary (Allen)
Allen, Nathaniel (father of Mary Allen), 35, 37-38, *278*
Allen, Nathaniel (brother of Mary Allen), 44
Alms plate, *268*
American Bullion and Refining Office, 183
Anderson, Bart, i, 271
Anderson, Edward, 143

Anderson, William (silversmith), 289
Andrew, John (silversmith), 295
Annealing, 54, 57
Anthony, Joseph, and Son, 305
Anthony, Joseph, Jr. (silversmith), 159, 184, 290, 305, 308
Antimony, 281
Anvil, 55, 272, 280, 282
Apprentices, 199, 271
  runaway, 23, 288
Apprenticeship, 5, 8, 11, 18, 33, 44-45, 62-66, 112, 157, 159, 165, 203, 205, 209, 211, 213, 226, 271, 276, 286-89, 305
Arch Street Historical Society, 209
Arch Street Meeting House, *ii*
Argol, 8, 269, 272, 274
Argyles, 184
Arm bands, 38, 140, 159, 298, 307, *133*; made by Joseph Richardson, 38; made by Joseph Richardson, Jr., *159*
Armitt, John, 132
Armitt, Mary, 294, 297
Armitt, Stephen, 77, 293

Arms. *See* Coat of Arms
Armstrong, Col. John, *124*
Ashley, John, 309
Ask, Gilbert, *6*, *11-12*, *20-23*, *26*, *29-30*, *54-55*, *60*, *72*, *84*, *100*, *115*, *120*, *127*, *132-34*, *162*, *167*, *178-81*
Aspdin, Mathias, 284
Assaying, 55, 72, 162, 215-16, 224, 228-30, 238, 243-44, 254, 259-60, 282-83, 291, 308, 311, *25-26*
Assay office, 72, 291
Atwater Kent Museum, 209
Axford, Samuel (turner), 283

Bailey, Emmor, 304
Ball, William (silversmith), 40, 165, 205, 210, 288
Bancker, Adrian (silversmith), 288
Bands. *See* Arm bands; Wrist bands
Bank of North America, 162
Bank of Pennsylvania, 162
Bank of the United States, 183
Barbados, 7, 202. *See also* West Indies
Barter system, 17, 30, 34, 62,

Barter system (*cont.*)
    184, 270, 274, 277, 285, 305
Bartram, William (silversmith), 290
Baskets, cake or bread, 184, 186; made by Joseph Richardson, Jr., 197
    sugar, made by Joseph Richardson, Jr., 197
Bauduy, Helen Cruon, 156
Bayley, John (silversmith), 204, 278, 288, 290
Beading, 166–67, 172, 175, 184, 186–89
Beads, 14, 203, 213, 223, 264, 291, 299, 302–03, 309; made by Joseph Richardson, 144; made by Joseph Richardson, Jr., 196
    Coral, 14, 155, 223, 227, 231, 239, 253, 255, 257–58
    jet, 204
Beake irons, 282
Beakers, 111, 268
Bedford, Gunning, 308
Beekerdike, Esther, 285
Beer, 273–74
Belknap, Helen M., i
Bell, Capt. William, 67, *69*
Bell, John (hosier), 17, 274
Bellows, 54, 57
Bells, 249
Bermuda, 67, 105, *69*
Besley, Thauvet (silversmith), 294
Best, James, 260
Betts, Elinor M., i
Bickly, Abraham, 111
Biddle, Owen, 291
Biggs, Thomas (mathematical instrument maker), 205
Bills of exchange, 22–23, 76, 206, 218–19, 221–23, 225–26, 228–30, 232–40, 242–43, 247–49, 251, 300–01, 303–04, 309, *182*
    protested, 219, 243, 251
Bills, shop, 213, 220, 225–26, 310. *See also* Trade cards
Binding wire, 204, 270, 272
Bingham, James, 295
Birmingham, goods imported from, 164, 301

Bissell, Mr. and Mrs. Alfred, *162*
Blain, Mrs. Daniel, 7, *80, 85,* 88
Bland, Elias (merchant), 219, 233; letters to, 220, 234
Blow-pipe, 57, 204, 206
Blunston, Samuel, 78, 124, 292, 294–95
Bobs, 201; made by Joseph Richardson, 38, 146
Bodkin, 16, 196, 262, 297; made by Joseph Richardson, 139, *122*
Boiler, 184, 186. *See also* Saucepans
Boiling silver, 17, 57–58, 300
Bolitho, Capt., 221, 227, 231–32, 304
Bollman, Erick, 184
Bond, Williamina, 304
Boozes, 65
Borax, 204, 272, 281
Bortman-Larus American Collection, *109*
Bosses, 136
Boston, trip to, made by Francis Richardson, 5–6
Boston, Museum of Fine Arts, ii, 58, 122, 271, 288, 293, 295, 297, *97, 144*
Boston silversmiths, 9, 58, 284, 291
Bottle, 17
    bosom, 16–17, 274
    smelling, 16, 204
    tickets, 186
    tops, 16
Bowditch, J., 307
Bowdle and Needles, 305. *See also* Needles, William
Bowls, 65, 95–98, 103, 172, 216–17, 292, 294, 300; made by Joseph Richardson, 95–96, *59–63*
    breakfast, made by Joseph Richardson, 77, 292, 294
    punch, made by Joseph Richardson, Jr., 197
    slop, 96, 172, 187, 203, 214, 233, 255–75, 261, 285, 287, 292–93, 305; made by Joseph Richardson, 77, 95, 55, *166*; made by

Joseph and Nathaniel Richardson, 172, *136, 147*; made by Joseph Richardson, Jr., 187, 305, 307; *166, 169*
    sugar. *See* Sugar dish
Boxes, 11, 204, 288–89; made by Francis Richardson, 9; made by Joseph Richardson 132–35
    patch, 204, 271; made by Francis Richardson, 13, *3,* 8
    pepper, 16, 18, 53, 61, 261, 285, 288, 302; made by Francis Richardson, 9. *See also* Casters
    shell, 133–34, 196
    snuff, 16, 53–54, 184, 200, 204, 213, 223, 229, 231, 262, 264, 287–89, 291, 300; made by Joseph Richardson, 67, 132–35, *116–18*; made by Joseph Richardson, Jr., 196
Boyles, William, 277
Bracelet, made by Joseph Richardson, Jr., 196
Bradford, William, 203
Brandy, 302
Branson, William, 271, 7
Brass wire, 272
Bread basket. *See* Basket, cake or bread
Brewster, Capt. William, 302
Breyer, Henry W., Jr., 2, 4, *99*
Brig & Snow, Sign of the, 290–91
Bright, Anthony (silversmith), 66, 132, 281, 288
Bright, Jane, 66
Bringhurst, John, *107*
Brinton, Jane Hill, *168*
Brion, W., 274
British Museum, 311
Broadgate, Thomas, 18
Brooches, 53, 203–04, 262, 298, 307; made by Joseph Richardson, 38
Brothers, Michael (silversmith), 202–03
Brown, Preserve (brewer), 36
Bruff, Charles Oliver (silversmith), 61, 285

Index

Buckles, 16, 18, 28, 51, 53–54, 61, 63, 65, 67, 165, 183, 196, 199–201, 203–06, 210, 213, 216, 222–25, 231, 240, 253, 261, 269–73, 287–88, 292, 299–300, 302; made by Francis Richardson, 9, 13, *1, 9*; made by Frank Richardson, 24; made by Joseph Richardson, 33, 147–48, *129–30*; made by Joseph Richardson, Jr., 196
  belt, 200
  for horse, 136
  girdle, 200
  knee, 149, 200, 203, 213, 221, 224, 229–31, 235–37, 242, 255, 258, 263, 285, 299
  rims, 30
  shirt, 300
  shoe, 5, 30, 132, 142, 148–49, 200, 203–04, 213, 219–21, 223–26, 229–31, 235–37, 242, 255, 258, 263, 272, 285, 289, 300, 302, 309
  sleeve, 201
  stock, 33, 199–201, 203–04, 224, 229–31, 253, 255, 258, 260, 288, 292
  stone, 203, 224
  waist, 204
Bu(d)den, Capt. 205, 218, 227, 234–37, 240–46, 250
Buhler, Mrs. Yves H. (Kathryn C.), ii, 289, 295
Bullit, Mr. and Mrs. Orville H., *154*
Bunting, Philip S., 155
Burbin, Thomas, 273
Burden, Ruth, 91
Burlington, N. J., Joseph Richardson, Jr.'s house in, 156–57, 162
Burn, James, 300
Burnap, Daniel, (silversmith), 298–99
Burnishing, 58, 129, 186, 228, 244, 258, 300, 309
Buttons, 16, 18, 28, 35, 51, 53–54, 61, 63, 65, 142, 147, 165, 183, 196, 199–201, 203–04, 206, 213, 234, 240, 244, 262, 272, 274, 276, 282–84, 287, 291, 300; made by Francis Richardson, 9; made by Frank Richardson, 24; made by Joseph Richardson, 33, 67, 146; made by Joseph Richardson, Jr., 196
  children's, 146, 222, 229, 239, 245, 258, 260
  coat, 18, 299–300
  crystal, 146, 220, 222–23, 229, 231, 239, 245, 253, 255, 258, 260
  enameled, 204
  jacket, 203, 291, 300
  sleeve, 203, 262, 299
  stamps for, 240, 244, 283

Cabeen, Edmund H., *177*
Cable, Robert. *See* Keeble (Keable), Robert
Caddy shell, made by Joseph Richardson, Jr., 197
Caddy, tea. *See* Tea caddies
Cadman, John, 17
Cadwalader family, 293
Cadwalader, John, 274
Cadwalader, Martha, 297
Cake Basket. *See* Basket, cake or bread
Calbert, Mary, 295
Caldwell, J. E., Co., 216
Calendar, Julian and Gregorian, 265–266
Calendar, William, 297
Calipers, 55
Calvert, Mary, *84*
Can(n), 28, 30, 63, 76, 118, 166, 210, 214, 234, 255, 261, 271, 283, 285, 287, 289, 294–95, 300, 306; made by Francis Richardson, 13, *6*; made by Frank Richardson, 24, *18*; made by Joseph Richardson, 60, 111–14, 177, 277, 290, *82–86*; made by Joseph and Nathaniel Richardson, 177, *157*; made by Joseph Richardson, Jr., 306
Canbe, Benjamin, 273
Canbey, John, 273
Candlesticks, 76, 139, 156, 182–84, 186, 204, 206, 263; attributed to Joseph and Nathaniel Richardson, 182, *144*
  enameled, 204, *206*
  French plate, 204
  tea, 206
Cane ferrules. *See* Ferrules
Cane head. *See* Heads for canes and whips
Canisters. *See* Tea caddies
Carbin, Theodore (jeweler), 205
Carlisle, Abraham (silversmith), 155, 303
Carnan, John (silversmith), 281
Carolines. *See* Coins, carolines
Carroll, Patrick, 304
Carson, Mrs. Joseph, 94
Cases, 136, 214, 263, 291, 294, 297, *120*
  fishskin, 137, 214, 239, 297
  fountain pen, 135
  instrument, 137, 213, 223, 231, 239, 297
  ivory memorandum, 137, 230, 239
  japanned, 301
  needle, 136, 291, *120*
  pencil, 137, 213, 230, 291
  pocket, 300
  shagreen, 68, 103, 207–08, 214, 223, 227, 230, 253–55, 257, 260, 263, 301–02, 305, 308
  spectacle, 137, 285
  toothpick, 16, 18, 137, 204, 291, 297
  tweezer, 203, 291
  watch, 16, 273, 287, 297, 300; made by Joseph Richardson, 137
Casters, 64–65, 166, 184, 186, 203–04, 206, 213–14, 221, 223, 226, 229, 234–35, 239, 241, 253, 255, 283, 285, 287, 292, 295; made by Frank Richardson, 24; made by Joseph Richardson, 122–25, *105–08*
  frames for, 124, 214, 229, 306

Casters (*cont.*)
glass linings for, 122, 186, 226, 234–35, 239, 241, 255, 263
sets of, 292, 308
Casting, 57, 64, 111
Catherell, Edward, 119
Chafing dishes, 149, 299–300
Chains, 16, 18, 53–54, 64, 137, 139–40, 195–96, 200, 204, 210, 213, 221–22, 227, 230, 236, 240–41, 261–62, 270, 273, 289; made by Francis Richardson, 9; made by Frank Richardson, 24; made by Joseph Richardson, 67, 140–41, 144–46; made by Joseph Richardson, Jr., 195
scissor, 196, 204, 222, 227, 262
See also Watch chains
Chalkley, Martha, 82
Chalkley, Thomas, 82
Chamber's *Dictionary*, used by Joseph Richardson, 35, 281
on goldsmith's work, 282
Chapes and tongues, 13, 16, 149, 202, 204, 206, 213, 216, 219–24, 228, 230–31, 235, 237, 240, 242, 253, 255, 258, 269, 275, 299, 300, 302
Charges for silversmithing, 5, 7, 18, 24, 33, 38, 59–61, 64, 77–78, 86, 89, 91–92, 95–96, 99, 105, 112, 114, 119, 124, 126, 128, 132, 135, 137, 139–40, 143, 147, 149, 187–89, 191, 197, 213, 225–27, 232, 234, 240, 244, 256–57, 269–70, 272, 284–85, 289, 292–300, 303, 305–307, 309–10, *10, 28, 45, 52, 60, 70–71, 93–94, 98, 175*
Charleston Museum, 289
Chase, Clarissa T., 309
Chasing, 65, 78–79, 82, 84, 92–93, 98, 106, 122, 124, 133, 137, 203–04, 219–21, 223–27, 229–30, 233–36, 247, 255, 258, 292, 307

Chatelaine hook, 144; made by Joseph Richardson, 136, *161*; made by Joseph Richardson, Jr., 181, *161*
Cheeseman, Catherine, 286
Cherokee Indians, 307
Chester County Historical Society, i, *39, 68, 76*
Chocolate pots, made by Joseph Richardson, Jr., 189
Christ Church (Devonshire, Bermuda), *69*
Christian, crucibles delivered to, 205
Church silver, 75
Ciphers, 54, 59, 79, 92–93, 98, 106, 126, 132, 146, 159, 172, 179, 186, 191, 196–97, 203, 222, 229, 231, 239, 255, 260, 280, 284, 305–06, 309, *24, 35, 40, 43, 47, 57, 61, 109, 116*
Clark Art Institute, Sterling and Francine, *175*
Clark, Benjamin, 284
Clasps, 54, 65, 147, 199–200, 214, 287, 291, 306, 309; made by Frank Richardson, 24; made by Joseph Richardson, 143–44; made by Joseph Richardson, Jr., 196
book, 291
pocket book, 214, 240–41, 262
shoe, 200, 262
stock, 30, 144, 199–200
Clement, John, 293
Clifton, John, 119
Clock and watch business, 23, 28, 30, 63, 272–73, 276 287
Clockmakers, 28, 59, 137, 140, 205, 272–73, 275, 288–89, 291, 297–98, *19, 27, 124*
Clocks, 23, 30, 51, 59, 63, 155, 210–11, 219, 266, 273, 275–77, 300, 302, *131*; made by Frank Richardson, 28, *19*
cases for, 274, 279, *27*
hands for, 272–73

movements for, 30
Clymer, Dr. George, 97, 144
Coates, Beulah, 272
Coates, Elizabeth Gardner, *81*
Coates, Mary, *116*
Coates, Samuel, *81*
Coates, Sarah, *90*
Coat of arms, iv, v, 58, 60, 87, 98, 113, 117, 126, 165, 284, 290, *32, 44, 62, 85–86, 90, 92, 110, 139, 143, 149, 173–74*
Cocks, silver wine, 65, 135, 184, 261, 296
Coffee, James, 39
Coffeepots, 53, 63, 65, 92, 105–06, 166, 184, 210, 213, 216, 226, 231, 233, 236–37, 241, 255, 260, 285, 287, 293, 302, 305, 308; made by Joseph Richardson, 78–79, 82–83, 87, 168, *32–33, 35–37*; made by Joseph and Nathaniel Richardson, 168, *139–41*; made by Joseph Richardson, Jr., 187, 306, *166, 169*
Coffeepot, Sign of the, 290
Coins, iv, 7, 17, 54, 60–62, 68, 183–84, 208–09, 216, 238, 241–46, 251–52, 259, 268, 271–72, 285, 300–02, *69*
carolines, 209, 285
crown, French, 294
dollars, 7, 241, 244
doubloons, 216, 243, 257, 285, 300
guineas, 208, 274, 285
johannes, 209, 285; half johannes, 209
Louis d'or, 285
moidores, 208, 285, *69*
pieces of eight, 62, 209, 238, 245–46, 285, 301
pistoles, 209, 285, 300, *69*
real of eight, 285
Coin silver, 291
Coliston, Elizabeth, 273
Collins, Thomas, 304
Colman, Harry, 274
Colonial Williamsburg, *65–66*
Combs, Capt., 274
Commonplace book, kept by Joseph Richardson, 64–65,

Index

Commonplace Book (*cont.*) 68, 199-201, 286-87, 290, 29
Condy, Capt. Benjamin, 205, 238
Connell, William (clockmaker), 211
Continental Congress, 306, 308
Convoy, American, ships traveling in, 218, 225, 232-33, 235-36, 239, 241
Conway, James (schoolmaster), 18, 274
Conyers, Richard (silversmith), 281
Cook, Bently, 271
Cooper, Joseph, 295
Coral, 16-17, 135, 144, 196, 200, 203, 213, 223, 244, 247, 253, 255, 262, 264, 270, 273-75, 288, 296, 302-03, 309
 and bells, 16, 54, 64, 186, 200, 203, 213, 219-21, 223-24, 226-27, 239, 244-45, 247, 255, 258, 262, 287, 291, 296, 308-09; made by Francis Richardson, 9; made by Joseph Richardson, 135, *119, 121*; made by Joseph Richardson, Jr., 195
 See also Beads, coral
Cornelians, 204
Couch, cane, owned by Francis Richardson, 6, 53, 266, 275
Coultas, Elizabeth, *127*
Counterfeiting, 60, 268, 284
Courtenay, Hercules (carver), 87, 133, 296
Court House (York, Pa.), bell ordered by Joseph Richardson for, 249
Cousins, Leonard, 30
Coventry, Mr., 135
Cowan, Mr. (watchmaker), 296
Cowrie shells, 133, 196
Cox, John, 67, 294
Cox, William, 137
Cramer's, *Elements of the Art of Assaying Metals*, 25-26
Cranes, 76, 291, 296; made by Joseph Richardson, 135

Crawford, James, 197
Cream pots, 53, 65, 89-91, 166, 184, 186, 204, 206, 217, 221, 230-31, 234, 237, 241, 253, 255, 260-61, 263, 293, 302, 309; made by Joseph Richardson, 64, 78; made by Joseph and Nathaniel Richardson, 167-68, *136-38*; made by Joseph Richardson, Jr., 187-89, 305, *166-69, 171-73*. *See also* Ewers; Milk pots; Urns, cream
Crison, James, 135
Crittenham (Cheltenham?), Pennsylvania, 4, 266
Crosbey, Joshua, 59, 62
Crosses, for Indians, made by Joseph Richardson, 38, 298
Crosses, table, 184
Crown. *See* Coins, crown, French
Crown and Pearl, Sign of the, 290
Crucibles, 30, 55, 204-05, 208, 214, 253, 255, 260, 270, 272, 274, 281
Cruets, 214, 229
 stands for, 124, 263
Crystals, 30, 137, 143, 146-47, 203-04, 253, 273, 300
Cuff links. *See* Links of buttons
Cundy, Capt. Benjamin, 205, 238
Cup and Crown, Sign of the Golden, 290
Cups, 53, 63-64, 75, 111, 118-19, 162, 269, 287-88, 295, 300; made by Francis Richardson, 8; made by Joseph Richardson, 118-19
 butter, 63, 295
 cordial, 119, 287
 egg, 156, 263
 spout, made by Joseph Richardson, 119, 295, *92*
Cup, Sight of the Golden, 290
Curtin, Mrs. Thomas J., ii, *131*

Dalmas, Mark (baker), 274
Darley (or Darby), William, 304

Dates, method of citing, 266
Davey, John (silversmith), 203
David, John (silversmith), 68, 124, 155, 203, 210, 293, 303
David, Peter (silversmith), 67
Dawson, Jonathan (clockmaker), 275
Deerfield, Historic, Inc., 209
Deer's foot, tipped by Joseph Richardson, 300
Delaware Indians, 37-38, *124*
de Matteo, William, ii
dePeyster, Abraham, 266
Depuy, Daniel (silversmith), 40, 204, 210, 303
Derbory, Daniel, 18, 272
Desk, owned by Joseph Richardson, 23
Devonshire Parish (Bermuda), 67, 105, *69*
Devon tribe, 69
Dial, Mrs. N. Victor, *148*
Dial plates, 244
Diamonds, 196, 203
Dickinson family, 43
Dies, 60, 72, 74, 140, 211, 234, 240, 244, 282-83, 298
Dinsmore, Silas, 307
Dinwiddie, Gov. (of Virginia), 132, *116*
Dishes, made by Joseph Richardson, Jr., 191, 309, *174-75*
 baking, 191, 309, *175*
 celery, 191
 chafing, 149, 299-300
 strawberry, 191
 vegetable, 191
Dollars. *See* Coins, dollars
Doubloons. *See* Coins, doubloons
Dowig, George (silversmith), 281, 283, 288
Doz, Andrew, 282
Dragon (vessel), 243
Drason, Capt., 274
Drawback, 218, 221, 241, 303
Drawing bench, 57, 280, 282
 plates, 282
 tongs, 282
Drewry, George, 202
Drinker, Henry, 189
Drinking tubes, 196

Duché; Anthony, 34, 37
Duché, Catherine, 34
Duché, Jacob, 282
Duché, John, 37
Duffield, Edward (clockmaker), 140, 291, 298, *124*
Dummer, Jeremiah (silversmith), 9
Duncan, Capt., 227–28
du Pont, Mrs. S. Hallock, *152, 165*
Dupuy, Daniel (silversmith), 40, 204, 210, 303
Dupuy, Daniel, Jr., 287
Durham Iron Works, 34
Dutch Minister, 132
Dutens, Charles (jeweler), 65, 287, 290
Duty, 43–44, 155, 218, 221, 253–54, 303

Earbobs, 140; made by Joseph Richardson, 38, 298; made by Joseph Richardson, Jr., 307
Earle, Mrs. Richard B., Jr., *75*
Earrings, 16, 196, 203–04, 206, 262; made by Joseph Richardson, 146
  stone, 204
Ear wires, 203
Edwards (silversmiths), 291
Edwards, Ann, 297
Edwards, Elizabeth, 128
Egdon, Capt., 247
Elfreth, Jeremiah, Jr. (silversmith), 64, 276
Elfreth, Jeremiah, Sr. (blacksmith), 33, 64, 276
Emerson, Lambert, 145
Emlen, George, 60, 77, 105, 140, 292, 294, 296, 300, *70*
Emlen, George, Jr., 140
Emlen, Hannah, *32, 71–72, 75*
Emlen, Joseph, 292
Emlen, Mary, 105
Emlen, Mary (Heath), *70*
Emlen, Samuel, 91, *52*
Emson, Hannah, 18
England, objects imported from, 137, 144, 207, 253, 273–75, 281, 301, 304
  silver imported from, iv, 16–17, 22, 42–44, 65, 68, 75–79, 86, 91–93, 95, 98–100, 103, 106, 112, 122, 124, 126–29, 133, 135–37, 139, 143, 146, 148, 153–57, 164–65, 181, 184, 186, 203–05, 210–60, 273–74, 287, 294, 297, 299, 303, 308–09
  silver and gold sent to, 55, 183, 207, 215–16, 224, 228–31, 238, 241–47, 250–51, 253–54, 256–60, 281, 301, 303, 309
  tools imported from 5, 55, 186, 282–83
England, Daniel, 268
England, Joseph, 268
England, Mary, 268
England, William, 8, 268
English silver, influence on American silver, v, 13, 76–77, 79, 89, 133, 166, 183, 308
Engraving, iv–v, 13, 17, 28, 54, 58–60, 69, 79, 84, 86, 92–93, 98, 106, 113, 117, 119, 126, 129, 133, 135–36, 139, 143–44, 147, 155, 159, 161–62, 168, 172, 175, 177, 179, 181, 186, 188–89, 191, 195, 197, 225, 230, 235, 237, 240–41, 244, 253, 255, 280, 283–84, 291, 296, 305–06, 308–09, *24, 27*
Ensko, Stephen G. C., 217
Étui cases, 53, 137, 297, 300, *85*
Eversley (partner of Frank Richardson), 23
Ewers, 224, 227, 230, 283
  milk, 89, 211, 219–20
Eye, 136

Fabrics. *See* Textiles
Fakes, 60, 74, 307
Falconer, Capt. Nathaniel, 230–32, 234–36, 243, 254, 256, 259
Fales, Dean A., Jr., ii
Faris, William (silversmith), 288
Faulkner. *See* Falconer
Federal Procession. *See* Grand Federal Procession
Ferrules, 16, 184, 188, 269; made by Joseph Richardson, 137, *121*; made by Joseph Richardson, Jr., 196, 306
Files, 8, 30, 57, 186, 204, 269, 272–73, 282
Filings, 64, 281. *See also* Sweepings, shop
Finch, Henry, 246, 250, 252
  letter to, 252
Finglass, Capt., 239, 243
Fireplace equipment, 18, 48, 51, 266, 275
Fire scale, 57
Fisher, Esther, 119
Fisher, Jeremiah and Elizabeth, *62*
Fisher, John, 86, 295
Fisher, Joshua, 119
Fisher, Lydia, 119
Fisher, Miers, 195, 209
Fisher, S. L., *75*
Fisher, Thomas, 119
Fish knives. *See* Knives, fish
Fishskin cases. *See* Cases, fishskin; Cases, shagreen
Fish trowels, 184
Fitch, John (silversmith), 283
Fitzwater, Elizabeth, 294
Fitzwater, Mary, 23
Flasks, 57
Flat irons, 30
Flatting mill, 179, 183, 211, 232, 234, 239, 268, 282–83
Flatware, 210
Flower, Rebecca, 287
Fluting, 189, 191
Ford (counterfeiter), 284
Ford, Mrs. Edsel, *10, 101*
Ford Museum, The Henry, *63*
Forge, 18, 37, 54, 57, 272, 281
Forging, 55, 57, 111, 306
Forks, 65, 269; made by Joseph Richardson, Jr., 196
  sucket, 269
Fountain pen, 65, 76, 135, 287, 296
  case, 135
Fowls, Isaac (turner), 283, 293
Foxe, John, *The Third Volume of the Ecclesiastical Historie*, owned by Joseph Richardson, 54
Frames, spectacle, made by Francis Richardson, 9;

Index

Frames, spectacle (*cont.*)
  made by Joseph Richardson, 137
  miniature, made by Joseph Richardson, Jr., 196
Frampton, Elisabeth, 266
Frampton, William, 266
Francis and Relfe, 233
Francis, John, 288
Francis, Tench, 251, 306–07
Franklin, Benjamin, 35, 278, 284–85
Franklin, Mrs. Walter S., 276, *15, 17, 59, 102*
Franks, David and Margaret (Evans), 89
French crown. *See* Coins, crown, French
Friend, Capt., 228–29, 233, 238, 241, 243, 247, 250–51
Friendly Association of Regaining and Preserving Peace with the Indians by Pacific Measures, 38, 157, *124–25*
Friends. *See* Society of Friends; Quakers
Friends Central School Association, 162
Friends School, 44, 66
Front St. (Phila., Pa.), Joseph Richardson's home and shop on, 33–34, 48, 154, 159; home of Francis Richardson on, 7
Fruit plates. *See* Plates, fruit
Fry, William, 145, 297
Fueter, Daniel Christian (silversmith), 291
Furkel, Jennifer, ii
Furniture, 34; owned by Richardsons, 6, 17, 34, 48–54, 266, 274–75, 279, 305, *23, 131*
Furniture design, relationship to Phila. silver, 91, 93, 106, 132, 172

Gadrooning, 83–83, 91, 95, 98, 106, 122, 167, 175, 239, 255
Galloway, John, 304
Garnet, 203

Gaskin, Benjamin, 155, 302
Gebelein, J. Herbert, 79
Gee, Joseph (silversmith), 165
Germantown, Pa., summer home of Joseph Richardson, 36
Germon, John (silversmith), 165
Gethen, John (silversmith), 290
Ghiselin, Cesar (silversmith), 5, 8–9, 268, 282, *1*
Gibbon, Capt., 233
Gilbert, John, 291
Gilchrist, Charles, 283, 311
Glass cruets. *See* Cruets
Glasses for caster sets, 308
  for clocks, 273
  for spectacles, 137, 239
Glassgow, Patrick, 143
Glass linings,
  for casters, 186, 234, 241
  for mustard casters, 122, 226, 235, 239, 255, 263
  for salts, 122, 166, 184, 186, 221, 224–25, 229, 231, 239, 253, 255, 258, 261, 264
Glass show case, 54, 103, 132, 139, 146, 199–201, 266, 281, 297
Goblets, 184, 263
Godhard, Hagan & Co., 251
Gold, Joseph Richardson sends to England, 215–16, 230–31, 309;
  objects made of, 9, 14, 16, 18, 28, 30, 35, 53, 59–60, 62–63, 65, 67, 133, 135, 139, 143–48, 195–96, 199–201, 203–04, 206, 223, 228, 231, 243, 253, 255, 261, 268, 272, 274, 276, 283–85, 291, 296–300, 306, *11, 126–30, 179*
  old, 183, 202
  N. C., assayed by Joseph Richardson, Jr., 308
  refining of, 281
Golding, Abigail, 268
Goldsmiths. *See* Silversmiths
Goldsmiths' Company, London, iii, 290
Goldsmiths' Hall, 5, 69, 214, 216

Goodson, Jobe, 272
Gorgets, 60, 298, 307; made by Joseph Richardson, 38, 141, *125*; made by Joseph Richardson, Jr., 159
Grafton, Mary, *73*
Graham, Henry, 285
Grand Federal Procession, 165
Grater, 18; made by Joseph Richardson, Jr., 196
Graver, 58
Greenleafe, Isaac, 310
Gregorian calendar. *See* Calendar, Julian and Gregorian
Griffitts, Nathaniel, 300
Grime, Thomas, 300
Griscom, Samuel, 297, 299
Growden, Elizabeth, 79
Growden family, 79, 216, *34*
Growden, Hannah, 46, 205
Growden, Joseph, 6
Growden, Lawrence, 6, 33–34, 68, 285
Gaudeloupe, Joseph Richardson's shipping venture to, 40, 65
Guest, John, 306
Guillim, John, *Display of Heraldry*, 284
Guinea. *See* Coin, guineas

Haines, Caspar Wistar, *61*
Haines, Reuben, *61*
Hair
  bobs, made by Joseph Richardson, 38, 298
  device, 196
  pipes, 306
  plates, made by Joseph Richardson, 38, 298
  rings, 143
Hall, David, 203
Hallmarks, 69, 72, 291. *See also* Silversmiths, marks of
Halsted, Benjamin (silversmith), 288
Hamilton, Andrew, 300
Hamitt, Capt., 224, 233, 236–37 243
Hammer, 55, 57–58
Hammerslough, Philip H., 67, *91, 105, 122, 123, 147, 173*

Hand and Earring, Sign of the, 290
Hand-in-Hand Company, 36
Handles for coffee and tea pots, 86–87, 187–88, 309
Harbeson, Benjamin, 40
Hardware, 17–18, 23, 204, 206, 266, 271–72, 275, 277
Harper, David (silversmith), 40, 42, 64–65, 78, 96, 112, 119, 122, 136–37, 139, 142, 147, 287, 294–96, 298, 300
Harrison, Samuel, 9
Hartley, Charles, 298
Hartley, James, 306
Hartshorn, Robert, 95
Hasell, Brother, 18
Hastings, Elizabeth, *45*
Hathaway, Calvin, i
Haverstick, William (silversmith), 296
Hayward, John, 311
Hayward (Haward), Mary, 18
Haward, Rebecca, 3, 265. *See also* Richardson, Rebecca (Haward)
Heads for canes and whips, 137, 203
Heal, Sir Ambrose, 211, 310
Hearts, 262; made by Francis Richardson, 9; made by Frank Richardson, 24; made by Joseph Richardson, 136
Heath, Mary, *70*
Henry Ford Museum. *See* Ford Museum, The Henry
Henry Francis duPont Winterthur, Museum. *See* Winterthur Museum
Herford (Herreford), 18, 20, 46, 66, 279
Hessian crucibles, 55. *See also* Crucibles
Heurtin, William (silversmith), 23
Hiam, Thomas (linen draper), 274
Hibberd, Benjamin, 271, *6*
Hibberd, Josiah (brother of Philip), 13, 271, *6*
Hibberd, Josiah (son of Philip), 271
Hibberd, Philip, 18

Higby, Joseph, 191, 197, *175*
Hill, Mary, 272, *10*
Hill, Richard, 297
Hill, Richard, Jr., 284, *28*
Hinderson, William (silversmith), 288–89
Historical Society of Pennsylvania, i–ii, 13, *1, 9, 28, 32, 41, 49, 51, 54–55, 72, 84, 100, 110, 124–25, 131*
Holcomb, Hannah, 39
Hollingshead, William (silversmith), 281
Holmes, Joseph (linen draper), 274
Holton, Elizabeth, 297
Hooks, 16, 262, 270, *120*; made by Francis Richardson, 9; made by Joseph Richardson, 147; made by Joseph Richardson, Jr., 181, *161*
and eyes, 262
chatelaine, 144; made by Joseph Richardson, 136, *161*; made by Joseph Richardson, Jr., 181; *161*
stay, 132, 147, 204, 287–88
Hooten, Benjamin (hatter), 203
Hopkins, Robert, 296
Hopkinson, Sarah, *77*
Hopkinson, Thomas, 35, 299
Horse bosses, 76
Horton, Capt., 302
Hoskins, Jane, 231
Hoskins, Joseph, 154, 297
Hoskins, Ruth, 46, 154, *161*. *See also* Richardson, Ruth (Hoskins)
House, Capt., 217, 230–32
House, George, 18
Household goods, 3
House, Joseph, 300
How, Thomas, 214
How, Thomas, and Masterman, John, 76, 78, 91, 100, 103, 112, 122, 124, 127, 129, 133, 137, 148, 213–14, 242, 297, 310–11. *See also* Masterman, John
letters to, 225–26, 228–30, 233, 236, 238–42
How, Masterman and Archer, 214, 216, 290
letters to, 243–45

Howell, James (silversmith), 159, 305
Howell, Josephine R., 265
Howell, Rebecca, 248, 250–53
letters to, 246, 249, 251–52
Hoyd, Robert (hatter), 289
Hudson, William and Hannah, *16*
Hudson, William, Jr., 144
Hughes, Bezaliel, *120*
Hulbeart, Philip (silversmith), 67, 202–06, 210, 309–10, *180*
Hulbeart, Philip (uncle of silversmith), 205–06
Hulbeart, William, 205–06, 245–47, 250
letter to, 251
Hull, John (silversmith), 9
Hummel, Charles F., i
Humphreys, Richard (silversmith), 165, 290, 305–06, 308
Hunt, Edward (silversmith), 8, 268
Hunt, George, 248
Hunt, John (cooper), 247–48, 268
Hunt, Margaret, 248
Hunt, Samuel, 248
Hunt, William, 248
Hurd, Jacob (silversmith), 293, 297
Hurd, Nathaniel (silversmith), 58, 284
Hurds (silversmith), 291
Hussey, Stephen (silversmith), 305
Hutton, Ann (Vanlear), 286
Hutton, Catherine (Cheeseman), 286
Hutton, John S. (silversmith), 62–63, 78, 112, 119, 122, 125, 132, 285–87, 295

Imports, 17, 22, 30, 42–43, 55, 68, 91, 93, 98, 99–100, 137, 144, 186, 207, 253, 273–75, 281–83, 287, 301, 304
silver, 16, 65, 75–79, 86, 92, 95, 103, 106, 112, 122, 124, 126–29, 133, 135–37, 139, 143, 146, 148, 153–57, 164–66, 181, 184, 186, 203–05,

Index

Imports (cont.)
210–60, 273–74, 294, 297, 299, 303, 308–09
Indians, 37–38, 159, 307, 124–125, 132–34. See also Delaware Indians; Cherokee Indians
Indian silver, 297–98, 306–07
jewelry, 38, 60, 140–41, 146 159, 161
medals, 161, 197; made by Joseph Richardson, 124; made by Joseph Richardson, Jr., 134
Indian Trader (vessel), 236
Ingersoll, C. Jared, 140
Ingersoll, Jared, 154
Ingersoll, Jared and Elizabeth (Pettit), 140
Ingliss, John, 294
Ingot mold, 55
Ingots, 272
Instrument cases. See Cases, instrument
Insurance, 36–37, 48, 54, 217–18, 221, 223–24, 226–32, 235–45, 252–53, 256, 258–59, 275, 311
Ivory memorandum books. See Memorandum books

Jackson, Elizabeth, 272
Jackson, Sir Charles, 311
Jackson, Thomas (potter), 281
James, Philip, 6
Japanned wares, 186, 301
Jarvis, Charles, 308
Jefferson, Thomas, on fountain pens, 296
Jeffords, Mrs. Walter M., 3, 40, 52, 56, 70, 77, 89, 96, 106, 108, 160
Jeffords, Walter M., 130
Jet beads. See Beads, jet
Jeweler, iii, 142, 202, 205, 288, 290
Jewelry, iv, 9, 16–17, 72, 164, 203–04, 210, 297, 306; made by Joseph Richardson, 142–49; made by Joseph Richardson, Jr., 159, 196, 307. See individual items

Jewels, 292
Johannes. See Coins, johannes
Johnson, Benjamin (silversmith), 203
Johnson, Samuel, on coral and bells, 296; on save-alls, 184
Jones, Abraham, 280
Jones, Amos, 290
Jones, I., 95
Jones, John, 267–68
Jones, John, Jr., 267
Jones, Margaret, 18
Jones, Owen, 250
Judkins, Matthew (silversmith), 274
Julian calendar. See Calendar, Julian and Gregorian
Julian(na) (vessel), taken by French privateers, 217–18, 231, 242, 311

Keeble (Keable), Robert, 8, 18, 270, 273, 12
Keeble, Thomas (pewterer), 271
Keith, George, 4
Kendall, Benjamin, 246, 250–52
Keys, 136–37
Kinsey, John, 300
Kirkbride (widow), 100
Kitanning medal (1756), 140, 124
Knitting needles. See Needles, knitting
Knitting reel. See Reel, knitting
Knitting sheaths. See Sheaths, knitting
Knives, 65
fish, 184
pen, 16
Knowland, Mary, 297
Knowles, John, 119
Knurling, 239

Label, silver, 186, 263; made by Joseph Richardson, Jr., 196
Lace
burnt, 273
gold, 243

Ladd, Hannah, 91
Ladles, 182, 262, 292, 296; made by Joseph Richardson, 126–28; made by Joseph and Nathaniel Richardson, 181, 162; made by Joseph Richardson, Jr., 187, 191, 195, 306, 176–77
punch, 187, 200, 203, 211, 232, 287, 295–96, 308
salt, 225, 229, 261–62
sauce, 263
soup, 127, 181, 187, 191, 195, 254–55, 257, 260–61, 295, 303, 308
Lamerie, Paul (silversmith), 89
Lamps, 184
Lashner, Jacob, 3
Latimer, Dr. Henry, 276, 17–18, 59
Latimer, John R., 24, 276
Lawrence, Thomas, 299
Leach, Thomas, 89, 300
Leacock, John (silversmith), 40, 204, 210, 278, 290
Lead, 281
Leddell, Joseph, 284
Letitia Court (Phila., Pa.), house and shop of Francis Richardson in, 7; shop of Frank Richardson in, 23
Letter Book of Joseph Richardson, 75, 86, 210–60, 310–11
Letters, silver, made by Joseph Richardson, Jr., 196
Levy, Nathan, 128
Lewis, Giles, 66, 288
Lewis, Harvey (silversmith), 159
Lewis, Howell and Smith (silversmiths), 305
Lewis, Sarah, 66
Lewis, Thomas, 66
Library Company of Phila., ii, 30, 35, 45, 54, 276
Frank Richardson founder of, 30
Lighthouse at Cape Henlopen, 45
Lin, Joseph, 300
Links of buttons, 16, 199–200, 299–300; made by Joseph

Links of buttons (cont.)
  Richardson, 146, *120*. See
    also Buttons
Lisle, Maurice, 155, 157, 302
Littell, *111*
Little, Mrs. Bertram K., 281
Lloyd, Grace (Growden), 34,
  39-40, 300, *20*, *121*
Lloyd, Hannah, 205
Lloyd, Thomas, 127
Lockerman, Gov., 3
Lockets, 9, 14, 28, 30, 59, 143-
  44, 195-96, 199-201, 203-
  04, 206, 262, 272, 291;
  made by Francis Richard-
  son, 9, *11*; made by Joseph
  Richardson, 144, *126-28*;
  made by Joseph Richard-
  son, Jr., 195-96, *179*
Logan family, 32, 43, *85*
Logan, Hannah, 67
Logan, James, 35, 267, 269,
  294-95
Logan, James and Sarah (Read),
  271
Logan, Maria Dickinson, *72*
Logan, Robert R., 43, *71*, *83*
Logan, Sarah, *86*, *110*
Logan, William, 300, *71*
London
  trip of Francis Richardson to,
    5-6, 17
  trip of Frank Richardson to,
    22-23
  silversmiths of, 5, 8. See also
    individual names
Looking glasses, 17, 48, 53,
  266, 269, 273-75
Looking Glass, Sign of the,
  274
Lord, James, 147
Louis d'or. See Coins, Louis
  d'or
Lownes, Edward (silversmith),
  293
Lownes, Joseph (silversmith),
  290, 293
Lowry, Robert, 217

McClelland, Capt., 217, 238
McCoole, John, 117
McDugal, Capt. Henry, 235
McFarland, David M., *168*
McIlhenny, Henry P., i

McIlwain (Mickelwain),
  James, 299
McIlwain (Muckelvane), 299
McNeil, Mr. and Mrs. Henry S.,
  137
McNeil, Robert L., Jr., ii
Macca (McKay?), James, 293-
  95
Machon, Austin, 290
Mackland, James, 9
Madiera, Louis C., i
Marceloe, Isaac, 23
Market St. (Phila., Pa.), house
  of Joseph Richardson, Jr.
  on, 157, 159
Marks, Joseph, 294
Marks, silversmith's. See Sil-
  versmiths, marks of
Marrow scoops, 139, 156, 195,
  297
Marsey, Samuel, 274
Marshall, Capt., 248
Marshall, Christopher, 188
Mason, Grace, 297
Masterman, John (silversmith),
  44, 46, 91, 139, 154, 166,
  186, 207-08, 214, 281, 300
  letters to, 253-58, 268
Masterman and Archer, 42,
  206, 214, 251-52
  letters to, 245-50
  See also How and Masterman
Masterman & Son, 303, *131*
Mather, James, 295
Mather, John and Mary, *96*
Mather, Mary, 285
Maunsell, Robert, silversmith,
  271
Medals, 297-98, 307; made by
  Joseph Richardson, 140-
  41, *124*, *134*; made by
  Joseph Richardson, Jr.,
  161, *134*
Meed, William (paver), 18
Melson, Eleanor, ii
Melting pot, 55, 204, 272. See
  also Crucibles
Memorandum books, 137, 213,
  230, 239
Meredith, Charles, 218, *182*
Meredith, Reese, 300
Merrett, Isaac, 274
Merriday, Jon, 271
Merrill, Richard, *137*

Metropolitan Museum of Art,
  289, *32*, *38*, *110*, *126*
Mickelwain (McIlwain?),
  James, 299
Microscope, owned by Joseph
  Richardson, 53
Mildred and Roberts, 213, 217,
  243, 310
  letters to, 237, 240, 242
Mildred, Daniel, 37, 76, 103,
  106, 133, 135, 139, 207,
  211, 213-14, 216-18, 237,
  242, 275, 299, *80*, *182*. See
  also Mildred and Roberts
  letters to, 220, 222, 225-29,
  231, 234
Mildred, J., 23
Milk ewer. See Ewers, milk
Milk pots, 63, 77, 89, 91, 146,
  224, 227, 239, 285, 287,
  292-93, *66*; made by Frank
  Richardson, 24; made by
  Joseph Richardson, 77,
  89-91, *45-49*. See also
  Cream pots
Mills, Edmund (silversmith),
  203
Milne, Edmund (silversmith),
  40, 65, 68, 203, 210, 238,
  290, 310
Miniature frame. See Frames,
  miniature
Mint, United States, 308
Mirrors. See Looking glasses
Mode, William, 59
Moidores. See Coins, moidores
Molds, 55, 58
Molding trough, 30
Montgomery, Charles F., i
Moons (Indian jewelry), made
  by Joseph Richardson, 38,
  298
Moor, Abraham, 35
Morgan, Evan, *98*
Morris, Anthony, 129, 292
Morris, Anthony, Jr., 297
Morris, Benjamin W., 195
Morris, Deborah, *39*
Morris, James. See St. Morris,
  James
Morris, Joseph, 144
Morris, Margaret (Hill), 309
Morris, Sally, 77
Morris, Samuel, 61, 275, 285

Index

Morris, Sarah, *81*
Mors, William, 272
Mote spoon. *See* Spoons, strainer
Moulton, Mary, 291
Moyamensing Road (Phila., Pa.), Joseph Richardson's property on, 34, 37
Muckelvane, (McIlvain), William, 122
Mugs, 13, 162, 263, 308; made by Francis Richardson, 9 child's, 195
  See also Cans
Munn, Charles Allen, *110*
Murdock, Neighbor, 291
Murray, Rebecca (Richardson), 267. *See also* Richardson, Rebecca (1685–?), and Young, Rebecca
Murray, Thomas, 267–68
Museum of Fine Arts, Boston. See Boston, Museum of Fine Arts
Museum of the City of New York, 286, 294
Mustard pot, 285. *See also* Casters
Mustard tankard, 197, 263
Myers, John (silversmith), 159, 304–05

Naeve, Milo M., i, 309
Nameplates, 59
Nealing tongs, 57. *See also* Annealing
Neat, Capt., 231–32
Necklaces, 14, 54, 142–43, 204, 206, 272–74, 291, *11, 126–28*; made by Joseph Richardson, 144; made by Joseph Richardson, Jr., 196
Needles, 159
  knitting, 136, 297
  See also Cases, needle
Needles, William (silversmith), 157, 305
Negroes, 3, 18, 20, 46, 66, 266, 288
Neptune (vessel), 240–41
Newberry, Walter, 4
Newberry, Walter, Jr., 6, 274
Newbold family, *100*
Newport, R. I., description by Joseph Richardson, Jr., of, 157
New York, home of Francis and Rebecca Richardson in, 3–4
New York silversmiths, v, 23, 61, 65, 270, 291
  See also individual names
Nickelson, Capt., 222, 227, 229
Nicklin, Phillip, 188
Nipples, 30, 136
Nixon, Thomas, 147
Noble, Anthony, 140
Non-Importation Agreement, 42, 44, 210, 254
Norris, Charles, 299
Norris family, 43
Norris, Isaac, 148, 269, 271
Norris, Mary (Lloyd), 271
Norton, Thomas, 196
Nowland, Mary, 297
Nutmeg graters, 65, 135, 196, 262, 287, 291, 308
Nys, Johannis (silversmith), 5, 8–9, 267, 269–70, 272

Offley, Daniel, 281
Oil stones, 272–73
Old gold, 183, 202
  Joseph Richardson buys, 61
  plate, 62
  and silver, 18, 54, 57, 61–62, 155, 183–84, 204, 271–72, 285, 300, 302–04, *149*
Old Swedes Church tankard, possibly by Joseph Richardson, 117
Oman, Charles C., ii, 267, 271, 311
Onslow, 191
Osage warrior, painting of, by Saint-Memin, *133*

Paintings,
  Osage warrior, *133*
  portrait of John S. Hutton, 286
  portrait of Joseph Richardson, Jr., *131*
  tea drinking, *66*
Pannikins, 63, 76, 309; made by Joseph Richardson, 125–26
Pans, silver, 305
Pap boats, made by Joseph Richardson, 125–26, 295
Parham, William (silversmith), 155, 303
Parker, Isaac (silversmith), 209
Parry, T., 209
Paschall, Elizabeth, 9
Paschall, Elizabeth Coates, 272, *1, 9*
Paschall, Joseph, 119
Paschall, Joseph and Elizabeth, 93
Paschall, William (silversmith), 8, 268
Patch boxes, 13, 204, 271
Patten, Capt., 222
Patterns, 57–58, 87, 132, 146, 148, 166, 216, 222–24, 232, 234, 236–37, 240–41, 244, 280, 283–84, 293, 299, 308
Paxton, Isaac, 155
Pearse, John (silversmith), 268
Pearse, Nicholas, 268
Peel, Grace, 98, *64*
Peel, Lydia, 98, *50–51, 64*
Peel, Oswald, 91, 95, 98, 119, 293, *50–51, 64*
Pemberton family, 92, 110, 149, 151
Pemberton, Henry R., *110*
Pemberton, Israel, 278
Pemberton, Israel, Jr., 62, 124, 126, 129, 135, 285, 295
Pemberton, James and Phoebe (Lewis) Morton, *149*
Pemberton, John, 250
Pemberton, Mary, 151
Pencils, sliding, 291
Pendants, 137
Penington, Edward, 79, *35, 54*
Pennefather (silversmith), 281
Penn, John, 308
Penn, John, Jr., 308
Penn, Letitia, 5
Penn, Memorial Museum, William, *121*
Pennsylvania
  Assembly, 6, 33, 38, 43–44, 247; failure of, to set up assay office, 72
  Hospital, ii, 35, 37, 45, 60, 211, 284; proprietors of, 37–38
Penn, William, 3–5, 37, 54, 265, 267–68, *125*

Penrose, Boies, 90
Penrose, James, 90
Penrose, Sarah, 11, *3*
Penrose, Thomas, 90
Pepper box. *See* Boxes, pepper
Pepys, Samuel, on fountain pens, 135
Perkins, 275
Perry, Marsden, 217
Peterson, Henry (silversmith), 117, *87*
Pewter, 17, 53, 59, 216, 223-24, 266, 275
Philadelphia
　almshouse, 44
　attempts to establish assay office in, 72, 291
　Contributionship, ii, 36, 60, 284
　County Court House, ii, 13-14
　Museum of Art, i, 24, 103, 209, 268-69, *8, 18-19, 27, 31, 42-43, 45, 62, 71-72, 82-83, 86, 93, 95, 116, 135-36, 145, 149, 153, 156-57, 161, 163-64, 169, 171-72, 174, 176*
　silver, characteristics of, 13, 129, 172, 179, 191, 271; *7, 160*; relationship of furniture design to, 91, 93, 106, 132, 172
　silversmiths, iv, 5, 7-9, 30, 40, 63-67, 72, 155, 159, 191, 202-04, 210, 268, 278, 284, 286, 288-91, 293, 303, 305, 308-09; *1-2, 87*; in Federal Procession, 165
　yellow fever epidemic in, 156, 304
Phillips, John Marshall, i, 74, 269-70, 296
Phips, Hannah, 35
Phoenix (vessel), iii
Pickering, Timothy, on yellow fever in Philadelphia, 304
Pieces of eight. *See* Coins, pieces of eight
Piercing, 24, 28, 122, 124, 149, 166, 175, 181, 186-87, 191, 203-04, 213, 225, 230, 241, 244, 300
Pinchon, William, 281
Pincushion hoops, 16, 196, 200, 213, 222, 261, 297; made by Francis Richardson, 9; made by Joseph Richardson, 139, 145
Pins, made by Joseph Richardson, Jr., 196
Pipe lighters, 291
Pistole. *See* Coins, pistoles
Pitch, 58
Pitts, John (silversmith), 289
Pitts, Mary, 289
Pitts, Richard (silversmith), 67, 289
Pitts, Richard, Jr., 289
Pitts, William Welshman, 289
Planishing, 58
Plate, old, 62
Plates, fruit, 149, 299
Plated silver, 133, 137, 156, 162, 164, 183-84, 204, 206, 214, 263, 304, 306, 308-09
Pleasants, Samuel, 306
Pliers, 8, 269, 272-73
Plumley, George (brazier), 272
Plumsted, Clement, 34, 87, 89, 277
　widow of, 293
Plumsted, Elizabeth, *44*
Plumsted, Mary, *44*
Plumsted, Thomas (ironmonger), 17, 273
Plumsted, William, 295
Pocketbook, 300
Polishing, 57-58, 112, 124, 129, 166, 175, 186, 214, 226, 228, 235, 258, 276, 283, 294, 309
Poolgreen, James, 78
Pope, Alexander, on coral and bells, 135
Porringers, 11, 18, 53, 61, 63, 76, 111, 177, 269-71, 275-76, 287, 289, 292, 295, 300, 302; made by Francis Richardson, 8-9, 13, *2, 4-5*; made by Frank Richardson, 24, *15-17*; made by Joseph Richardson, 58, 64, 119, 290, *93-100, 112*
　anvil for making, 282
Poseys, 9, 59, 143, 268, 291, 298
Pots. *See* Crucibles; Milk pots
Potter, Mr. and Mrs. William H., 50

Potts, N., *128*
Powel, Elizabeth, 306, *143*
Powel, Samuel, 54, 61, 268, 277, 284-85, *24, 143, 174*
Powel, Samuel, Jr., 285
Pratt, Henry (silversmith), 9, 30, 290, *2*
Pratt, Matthew, 290
Price, Grace, 287
Prime, Mrs. Alfred Coxe, ii, 267
Pryor, M., 306
Pulos, Arthur J., ii
Pumice, 206, 273
Punches, 203-04, 211, 234, 240, 244, 269, 283, 298
　center, 55
　cutting, 8, 269
Punch ladles. *See* Ladles, punch

Quakers,
　customs of, 17, 34-36, 39, 42-44, 46, 214, 265
　persecution of, 4
　tastes of, 13, 35, 54, 67, 93, 217
　tenets of, 23, 35-40, 43, 45-47, 60, 67
　See also Society of Friends

Radley, Daniel, 273
Raising, 112
Rakestraw, William, 18
Raley, Robert L., 279
Ralph, John, 224. *See also* Relfe, John
Randolph, Capt. Edward Fitz, 279
Randolph, Edward, 305
Randolph, Edward, Jr., 159
Rattles. *See* Coral, and bells
Rawle, Francis, 79
Rawle, Margaret, *141*
Rawle, Rebecca, 79
Read, George, 152
Real of eight. *See* Coins, real of eight
Reeding, 191
Reel, knitting, 262
Reeves, Stephen, 204
Refiners, iii
Refining, 55, 183, 199, 215, 281-82

Index

Relfe, John, 233. *See also* Ralph, John
Repair work, 16-17, 28, 135, 139, 149, 184, 186, 272-73, 298-300
Repoussé, 57, 79, 82, 84, 91, 93, 122, 132
Revere, Paul (silversmith), 58, 86, 276, 297
Richards, Philip, 266
Richards, Samuel (silversmith), 159, 305
Richardson & Co., 159
Richardson & Eversley, 23
Richardson, Benjamin (1714-14), 7
Richardson, Capt. Joseph (counterfeiter), 60, 284
Richardson, Elizabeth (Betsy; 1742-1804; daughter of Joseph and Hannah), 34-35, 53, 277
Richardson, Elizabeth (1788-?; daughter of Joseph Jr. and Ruth), 155
Richardson, Elizabeth (Growden; ?-1714; wife of Francis Richardson), 6-7, 34
Richardson, Elliot, Jr., 118
Richardson family Bible, 35, 265-66, 274
Richardson, Frances, ii, 131
Richardson, Francis (?-1688; merchant), iv, 3, 265-66
  arrival in America, 265
  estate of, 266
  marriage of, 265
Richardson, Francis (1681-1729; silversmith), iv, 3-21, 57, 67, 137, 153, 265-76, 287, 16
  account book of, 12
  apprentices of, 8, 11, 18, 33
  death of, 18
  education of, 5, 267
  furniture of, 17, 274-75
  home of, 7, 18, 20, 275
  imports of, 17
  inventory of, 271-72, 274, 281, 4, 13-14
  marks of, 9, 11, 28, 1-2
  marriages of, 6-7, 267-68
  moves to Philadelphia, 266
  and Nys, 269-70
  property owned by, 4, 7, 20
  repair work of, 16
  ships to England, 17
  shop of, 7, 18
  silver, made by, 8-9, 11, 13-14, 16, 18, 24, 28, 271-72, 3-12; owned by, 11, 271, 275
  tools and equipment of, 281-82; bequeathed to Joseph, 13-14
  trips of, to Boston, 5-6; to London, 5-6, 17, 273-74
  will of, 20
Richardson, Francis (Frank; 1706-82; silversmith and merchant), iv, 7, 11, 18, 20-30, 33, 38, 40, 59, 62-63, 68, 112-13, 124, 213, 221, 228, 268, 271, 275-76, 282, 287, 289, 293-95, 297, 299, 144
  advertisements of, 22-23, 28
  clock business of, 23, 28, 30, 63, 273, 19
  dry goods business of, 22-23
  education of, 18, 274
  education of, 18, 274
  home of, in Chester, 23
  imports of, 22-23
  marks of, 11, 24, 28, 15
  marriage of, 23
  partner of, 23
  and Pennsylvania Hospital, 30, 37
  property owned by, 22-23
  silver made by, 24-28, 124, 271, 293, 15-18
  trip to London of, 22-23
Richardson, Francis (b. 1746; son of Frank and Mary), 23, 43, 276, 278
Richardson, Grace (1743-44), 34
Richardson, Hannah (Worrill; 1716-47; wife of Joseph Richardson), 34-35
Richardson, Hannah (1748-1817), 35-36, 302
Richardson, Hannah (1791-1866), 155
Richardson, John, 292
Richardson, John (1688-88; son of Francis and Rebecca), 4
Richardson, John (1708-9; son of Francis and Elizabeth), 7
Richardson, John (1729-30; son of Francis and Letitia), 7
Richardson, John (b. 1753; son of Frank and Mary), 23
Richardson, John (1786-86; son of Joseph, Jr., and Ruth), 154
Richardson, John (1790-1866; son of Joseph, Jr., and Ruth), 155, 162
Richardson, John and Ann, 24, 96, 276, 15, 17-18, 59
Richardson, Joseph (1711-84; silversmith), iv, 7, 18, 20, 22-23, 28, 30, 33-149, 153, 268, 275-76, 281, 298
  account book of, 180
  advertisements of, 68, 203, 208, 247-48
  apprentices of, 40, 42, 44-45, 62-66, 96, 112, 119, 122, 125, 132, 136-37, 139, 142, 147, 153, 199, 211, 226, 287-88, 294-96, 299
  bill for silver of, 28
  books owned by, 51, 54, 24
  buys old silver from Samuel Morris, 61
  character of, 46-47
  commonplace book of, 35, 54, 64-65, 68, 199-201, 287, 29
  contributions to worthy causes by, 35-37, 43, 45, 47
  death of, 46, 154
  death of wife Hannah, 35
  education of, 18, 274
  encouragement of domestic manufacturers by, 43
  as an engraver, 28, 58-60
  engraves nameplates, 19, 27
  executor of estates, 42, 66-67, 202-06
  as a Friend, 36, 38-39, 42-43, 46-48, 93, 140-41
  furniture owned by, 34, 48-54, 279, 23
  houses of, 22, 36, 48-54, 154, 280, 293

Richardson, Joseph (*cont.*)
  imports and sells scales and weights; 68, 307-09, 310, *30-31*
  silver, 42-44, 75-79, 86, 91-93, 95, 98-100, 103, 106, 112, 122, 124, 126-29, 133, 135, 137, 139, 143-44, 146, 148, 166, 210-60, 297, 299
  income of, 33, 38, 43, 60-62, 277
  insurance on property of, 36-37
  inventory of estate of, *21-22*
  letter book of, v, 75, 86, 210-60
  letter from Aunt Grace Lloyd to, 40, *20*
  and Library Company, 35, 45, 54
  life of, 33-47, 276-79
  labeled weights and scales of, *30-31*
  marks of, 69-74, 91, 294, 296, *32*
  marriage of, to Hannah Worrill, 34; to Mary Allen, 35
  member of local organizations, 35-38, 45, 54, 60
  orders bell for York Court House, 68, 249, 290
  and the Pennsylvania Hospital, 35, 37, 45, 60
  property owned by, 20-21, 33-34, 36, 38, 40, 43-44, 47, 277, 279
  repairs to house and shop of, 36, 45
  repairs silver, 28, 135, 139, 149
  settlement of his estate, 155
  shipping ventures of, 30
    Guadeloupe, 40
    sends cans to Carolina, 30, 67, 289
    sends cranberries to England, 243
  ships gold and silver to England, 55, 183, 207, 215-16, 224, 228-31, 238, 241-47, 250-51, 253-54, 256-60, 281
  shop of, 36-37, 48-54, 68, 280
  showcase of, 103, 139, 146, 199-201, 297
  signs the Stamp Act, 42
  silver made by, 28, 33, 38, 58, 60, 64, 67, 75-149, 168, 177, 277, 284-85, 290, 292-300, *33-65, 67-130, 161*. See also individual forms
  silver owned by, 53, 293, 297; *33, 56*
  tools of, 281-83
Richardson, Joseph, (1784-93; son of Joseph, Jr., and Ruth), 154, 156
Richardson, Joseph (merchant), 24, 37, 42, 63, 222, 277-78
Richardson, Joseph, Jr. (1752-1831; silversmith), iv, 37, 44-45, 66, 153-97, 214
  advertisement of, 184
  appearance of, 157, 308
  apprentices of, 157, 159, 305
  assayer of U. S. Mint, 162
  assays specimen of N. C. gold, 308
  business affairs, 156-57, 162
  character of, 157
  death of, 162
  description of Newport, R. I., by, 157
  education of, 44
  furniture owned by, 305
  home of
    on Front St., 154
    in Burlington, N. J., 156-57, 162
    on Market St., 157, 159
  inheritance of, 301
  on importance of early American silver, 197, 298
  imports scales from England, 304
    silver, 156-57, 184, 186, 203-04, 309
    tools from England, 186
  income of, 305
  lends money to Howell, Lewis & Smith, 159
  marks of, 183, *163*
  marriage to Ruth Hoskins, 46, 154-56
  melts gold dust, 159, 305
  portrait of, 308, *131*
  property owned by, 154, 156-57, 159, 162, 301
  repair work of, 184
  sells japanned wares, 186
  shipping ventures, 157
  ships gold to England, 309
  silver made by, 159, 161, 167-97, 305-07, 309, *132, 134, 164-179*. See also Richardson, Joseph and Nathaniel, silver made by
  silver owned by, 301-02, *34*
  supplies scales to Bank of the United States, 305
    to Bank of Rhode Island, 305
  tools bequeathed to son John, 162
  trip to Boston, 157, 305
  George Washington, patron of, 161
Richardson, Joseph and Nathaniel (w. 1777-90; silversmiths), 46, 53, 139, 153-97, 214, 303
  begin business, 45, 153-54, 300
  as Friends, 153, 155
  import goods from England, 300-03
    scales from England, 301
    silver, 153-55, 165-66, 181, 300, 308
  inventory of the shop of, 261-64
  lives of, 300-08
  living quarters of, 45, 53, 154
  lives of, 300-08
  mark of, 167, *135*
  order clocks, *131*
  partnership terminated, 156
  settle Syng estate, 155
  shipping venture to West Indies, 155
  ship silver and gold to England, 301, 303
  shop of, 154
    inventory of, 156
  silver made by, 167-68, 172, 175, 177, 179, 181-82, 308-09, *123, 136-62*
Richardson, Letitia (Swift; ?-c. 1734; wife of Francis Richardson), 7, 11, 20, 33, 64, 268, 275, *2, 4*

Richardson, Mary (1749-1835; daughter of Joseph and Mary), 37, 46, 216, 279, 302. *See also* Taylor, Mary
Richardson, Mary (1781-1837; daughter of Joseph, Jr., and Ruth), 154
Richardson, Mary (Allen; 1716-87; wife of Joseph Richardson), 35-36, 38, 44, 46, 51, 53, 79, 154-55, 214, 217, 278, 301-02, *33, 56, 126, 137, 161*
Richardson, Mary (Fitzwater; ?-1771; wife of Frank Richardson), 23
Richardson, Nathaniel (1754-1827; silversmith and ironmonger), iv, 37, 44-45, 66, 153-57, 162-83, 301-02
   becomes ironmonger, 155
   clock owned by, *131*
   character of, 156
   death of, 156
   home of, 45, 53, 154
   property owned by, 301
   silver made by, 168, 172, 175, 177, 179, 181-82, *136-60, 162*
   owned by, 302
   woodworking hobby of, 155
Richardson, Nathaniel (1793-1872; son of Joseph, Jr., and Ruth), 155-57, *131*
Richardson, Rebecca (Haward; ?-1705; wife of Francis), iv, 4-6, 39, 266, 274
Richardson, Rebecca (1684-84; daughter of Francis and Rebecca), *3*
Richardson, Rebecca (1685-?; daughter of Francis and Rebecca), 3-4, 7, 267. *See also* Murray, Rebecca (Richardson); Young, Rebecca
Richardson, Rebecca (1785-1826; daughter of Joseph and Mary), 39, 302, *56, 120*
Richardson, Robert, 24
Richardson, Ruth (Hoskins; 1756-1829; wife of Joseph Richardson, Jr.), 154, 181

Richardson, Samuel, 278
Richardson, Sarah, 63, 154
Richardson, Thomas, 7
Ridgely, Capt. Charles, 310
Rigg, Richard (linen draper), 274
Ring and Dove, Sign of the, 290
Rings, 28, 54, 59, 61, 65, 72, 140, 142, 196, 199, 201, 203-04, 262, 268-69, 273-74, 284, 291, 298-300; made by Francis Richardson, 9; made by Joseph Richardson, 38, 143
   crystal set, 143
   finger, 306
   hair, 143
   hollow, 299
   motto, 298
   mourning, 72, 143, 299
   seal, 143
   stone, 143
Ritherdon, George (silversmith), 76, 103, 124, 127, 129, 139, 211, 213-19, 281, 294, 310-11
   letters to, 220, 224, 230-31, 234-36, 238, 241
Rittenhouse, David, 260
Robart, R. (haberdasher), 274
Robb, Mr. and Mrs. David B., 5, *16*, 36
Robb, Elizabeth Woolman, *16*
Robens, Joseph (cutler), 274
Roberts, Edward, 274, *112*
Roberts, Elizabeth, 135
Roberts, Hugh, *84*
Roberts, Samuel, 203
Robertson, Alexander, 67, 289
Robeson, Andrew and Magdalen, 295
Robeson, Capt., 232, 236, 283
Robinson, Ebenezer, 18
Roffe, Will (hatter), 274
Rollers for flatting mill, 232, 234, 239, 283
Rolt, *A New Dictionary of Trade and Commerce,*
   on duties and drawbacks, 218
   on hallmarking, 291
   on insurance, 311
   on protests, 219
Ross, Capt., 246
Rotten stone, 204

Rum, 3, 155, 271, 274
Rummers, 306
Rush, Dr. Benjamin, and yellow fever epidemic, 304
Russell, John (silversmith), 209
Rutter, John, 272
Rutter, Ruth A., 196

Saint-Memin, painting of Osage warrior by, *133*
St. Méry, Moreau de, on the display of silver in Philadelphia, 307
   on yellow fever epidemic, 304
St. Morris, (St. Maurice), James (silversmith), 63-64, 287, 299
Saltpeter, 204, 272, 281
Salts, 63, 65, 122, 166, 175, 177, 184, 186, 203, 213, 221, 224-25, 229, 231, 239, 241, 253, 255, 258, 261, 283, 285, 287, 290; made by Joseph Richardson, 122-25, 290, *101-04*; made by Joseph and Nathaniel Richardson, 175, 177, *152-53*; made by Joseph Richardson, Jr., 197
   cellar, 197
   glass linings for, 122, 166, 184, 186, 221, 224-25, 229, 231, 239, 253, 255, 258, 261, 264
Salvers, 9, 24, 53, 63-64, 76, 100, 103, 105-06, 166, 175, 197, 221, 225-26, 230-31, 233, 235, 237, 253, 255, 261, 263, 287-88, 290, 294, 300, 302, 304; made by Francis Richardson, 9; made by Frank Richardson, 24; made by Joseph Richardson, 64, 100, 105-06, 290, *32, 69-81*; made by Joseph and Nathaniel Richardson, 175, *150-51*; made by Joseph Richardson, Jr., 197
Sand casting. *See* Casting
Sand cushion, 58
Sandiver, 204, 272, 281
Sandwith, Mary, 42

Sansom, William, 188
Sansum, Samuel, 223
Sarrazin (silversmith), 289
Satterthwaite, James, 40
Sauceboats, 60, 126, 166, 177, 210, 263, 292, 295, 300; made by Joseph Richardson, 60, 126–38, *109–10*; made by Joseph and Nathaniel Richardson, 177, *154–55*
Saucepans, 177, 184, 295; made by Joseph and Nathaniel Richardson, 177, *156*; made by Joseph Richardson, Jr., 184, *164–65*
Sauer, Christopher, 44
Save-all, 184
Savery, Mrs. Addison, *27*
Savery, William (cabinetmaker), 46
Scales and weights, 48, 55, 68, 154, 156, 159, 162, 204, 207–09, 211, 214, 227, 253–59, 263, 272, 301, 304–05, 310, *26, 30–31*
Scattergood, Thomas, 305
Schoepf, David, on Philadelphia trade to West Indies, 302
Schooling, 5, 18, 35, 44, 62, 66, 274, 286
Schuylkill Navigation Company, 162
Scissors, 144–45
  chains for, 196, 204, 222, 227, 262
Sconces, 16, 139
Scoops, made by Francis Richardson, 9; made by Joseph Richardson, 139; made by Joseph Richardson, Jr., 195. *See* Marrow scoops
Scorpers, 204–05
Scratch brush, 58
Seal, 54, 60, 64, 139–40, 196, 200, 203, 205, 273, 284, 291, 306; made by Joseph Richardson, 140–41; made by Joseph Richardson, Jr., 306
  block, 204
  cutting, 306
  ring, 143

Setze, Josephine, ii
Sewall, Samuel, 4
Sewing equipment, 17, 139
Shagreen. *See* Cases, shagreen
Sharples, Phebe, 13, 271, *6*
Shears, 55, 270, 272
Sheffield, 164. *See also* Plated silver
Sheffield, Lord, report on silver made in America, 164
Shells, 204, 264. *See also* Boxes, shell
Sheraton, Thomas, on decline of rococo style, 183
Sherlock, Samuel, 67, 105, *69*
Shields, Mrs. James H., ii
Shields, Thomas (silversmith), 290
Ship, Sign of the, 213, 274
Ship and Crown, Sign of the, 220
Shippen, Edward, iv, 4, 6–7, 266–68, 274
Shippen, Edward (cousin of Frank and Joseph Richardson), 22, 267
Shippen, Edward and Rebecca, 267
Shippen, Elizabeth (1691–92), 267
Shippen, Esther James, 6
Shippen, Joseph, 272
Shippen, Rebecca Richardson, iv. *See also* Richardson, Rebecca (Haward)
Shipping, iv, 3, 17, 22, 30, 40, 42–45, 65, 67, 75–77, 91, 153, 155, 157, 164, 186, 207, 210–60, 273–75, 282–83, 289, 291, 299, 301–02, 308–09. *See also* England, silver imported from
Ships. *See* Vessels
Shirlock, Capt., 240–41
Shoemaker, Jacob, 46
Shoemaker, Sarah, 79, *32, 35, 48, 54*
Shop bills, 213, 220, 225–26, 310. *See also* Trade cards
Shop signs, 68, 213, 274, 290–91
Showcases, 54, 103, 132, 139, 146, 199–201, 266, 281, 297
Shuttlesworth, Mrs. William, *34*

Sibthorpe, Christopher (cabinetmaker), 274
Silver,
  cleaning of, 17, 28
  coin, 291
  cost of, 302
  filings, 204
  imported, iv, 16, 65, 86, 91–93, 95, 99–100, 103, 106, 122, 126–28, 135–37, 139, 143, 146, 148, 153–57, 164–66, 181, 184, 210–60, 273–74, 287, 294, 297, 299, 303, 308–09
  lace, 136, 204
  old, 18, 54, 57, 61–62, 155, 183–84, 204, 271–72, 285, 300, 302–04, *149*
  plated, 133, 137, 156, 162, 164, 183–84, 204, 206, 214, 263, 304, 306, 308–09
  pre-rolled, 183
  refining of, 281. *See also* Refining
  sterling, 291
  stolen, iv, 68, 199, 281, 296
  turners, 283
  value of, 61, 154, 186, 213, 240, 259, 303, 311
Silversmithing, developing of craft of, iii, 5
  methods of, 5, 54–58, 179, 183, 272, 282, 299, *127*
  repair work, 149
  See also Charges for silversmithing
Silversmiths, *see* individual names
Silversmiths, business of, 153, 156–57, 163, 184, 197, 210, 245, 247, 282, 303
  first American, iii, 8
  income of, 7, 17, 24, 33, 38, 60–63, 65–67, 77–78, 112, 114, 119, 124, 126, 128, 132, 135, 137, 139–40, 143, 147, 149, 184, 187–89, 191, 197
  marks of, iv–v, 5, 9, 11, 24, 28, 61, 63, 66, 68–69, 72–74, 117, 203, 216, 271, 286, 289–94, 296, 305, 311, *1–2, 15, 32, 87, 135, 163*
  shops of, 7–8, 18, 33, 36–37, 45, 48–54, 57, 154, 280–81;

Index

Silversmiths (cont.)
  Joseph Richardson's shop, 48-54
  tools of, 33, 179, 181, 203-04, 210-11, 214, 269-70, 272-73, 280-83, 299; imported from England, 17, 186. See also specific tools
Simmins and Alexander (silversmiths), 290
Simmins, Capt., 274
Sims, Joseph, 125
Sims, William, 290
Sinkler, Caroline, 293
Sinkler, Wharton, *141*
Sirl, Elizabeth, 293
Skewer, made by Joseph Richardson, 139, *123*; made by Joseph and Nathaniel Richardson, *123*
Skillet, 55
Skiner, Mathew (watchmaker), 290
Skinner, Abraham, 103
Skyrin, Mary Sandwith, 42
Slaves, 46. See also Negroes
Smither, James, 155, 284, 306, 308
Smither, James, Jr., 159, 306
Smith, John (merchant), 35-36, 67, 105, 277, 296
Smith, John and Hannah (Logan), 286, 290, *110*
Smith, Joseph D. (silversmith), 159
Smith, Martha, *82*
Smith, Robert, 196
Smith, William, 196
Snarling iron, 57-58
Snuff boxes. See Boxes, snuff
Snuffers, *184*
Snuff mill, 135
Society of Friends, iv, 3-4, 6-7, 17, 23, 34-40, 42, 44-47, 60, 67, 140-41, 153, 155, 157, 159, 214, 217, 267-68, 273, 290, 308
  dates used by, 265-66
  and the Indians, 297-98
  See also Quakers
Socket and bells. See Coral, and bells
Solder, 57, 64-65, 67, 204, 283, 288
Soldering, 58, 179, 272, 300

Sommers & Son, 154, 156, 301, 305
Soup ladle. See Spoons, soup; Ladles, soup
South Shields (England), ancestral home of Richardson family, iv
Spahr, Mrs. Boyd Lee, 57
Sparks, Capt. James, 242-43, 251, 256-58
Spectacles, 9, 16, 48, 54, 65, 137, 196, 204, 214, 239, 241, 287, 297. See also Frames, spectacle; Cases, spectacle
Spoon boat or tray, 76-77, 100, 292, 294, *66*; made by Joseph Richardson, 77, 100
Spoons, 7-9, 13, 16-18, 24, 51, 54, 58, 65, 67, 75-76, 99-100, 122, 129-30, 159, 181-82, 184, 195, 199, 200, 204, 213, 225, 261, 268-70, 272, 275, 285-87, 289-92, 296, 300, 305-06, 309, *66*; made by Francis Richardson, 8-9, 13, 16, *10*; made by Frank Richardson, 24; made by Joseph Richardson, 58, 99, 122-30, 290, *65-66*, *113-15*; made by Joseph and Nathaniel Richardson, 182, *162*; made by Joseph Richardson, Jr., 159, 184, 187, 195, 305-06
  cases for, 204
  children's, 195
  chocolate, 129
  custard, 129, 290, 296
  dessert, 187, 195, 306
  doll's, 309
  folding, 268
  gravy, 195
  marrow, 139, 156, 195, 262, 297
  mote, 103
  mustard, 122, 262
  pap, 66, 129, 285
  pocket, 200
  salt, 122, 187, 224, 229, 231, 239, 255, 300
  sauce, 191
  serving, 289, 295
  soup, 126-28, 230, 295-96, *111-12*. See also Ladles, soup
  strainer, 103
  See also, Tablespoons; Teaspoons
Spreagele, Cristion, 274
Spring, John, 279, 282
Springs, 30
Spurs, 64-65, 137, 204, 206, 214, 229, 255, 261, 288, 300; made by Joseph Richardson, 137
Stakes, 57, 282
Stamp, 8, 244, 269, 282-83
Stamp Act, 42, 210, 247
Stamper, John, 135
Stanbury, Nathan, 267
Stands, 78, 221, 225-26, 230-31, 233, 235, 237, 253, 255, 263. See also Salvers
Stanton, D., 36
Starr, S. L. W., 7, *80, 85, 88*
Stedman, Charles, 241
Stevenson, Stiles, 22
Stewardson, Margaret H., 61
Stocker, William, 293
Stockwell, David, 288
Stone, 143, 146-47, 292
  earrings, 204
  ring, 291
Story, Thomas, The Journal of the Life of, owned by Joseph Richardson, 54
Strainers, 8, 16, 24, 28, 53-54, 99, 103, 145, 200, 203, 213-14, 223, 230, 287, 294, 300-01; made by Francis Richardson, 8, 16; made by Frank Richardson, 24; made by Joseph Richardson, 103; made by Joseph Richardson, Jr., 187, 306
  lemon, 232, 294
  punch, 53, 103, 187, 200, 261, 294, 302, 306
  tea, 103
Stretch, Peter (clockmaker), 267, 272
Stuart, Robert S., 267, 279, *112, 114*
Studs, 9, 28, 53-54, 67, 146-47, 199-201, 262, 271; made by Francis Richardson, 9; made by Joseph Richardson, 146

Sugar dish, 53, 63, 65, 77, 91–95, 166, 172, 186–87, 197, 203, 217, 225, 230, 233, 253, 255, 261, 287, 292–94, 300, 302, 305–06 309, *66*; made by Joseph Richardson, 77, 91–93, 95, *32, 50–58*; made by Joseph and Nathaniel Richardson, 172, *136, 145–46*; made by Joseph Richardson, Jr., 187, 305–06, *166, 169–71*
Sulphur, 55, 281
Sun dial, 64, 305
Supply (sloop), 3
Surnam, Henry (lapidary), 288
Sussel, Arthur, *126*
Swage, 182, 291
Swain, Mrs. Richard, 293
Sweeney, John A. H., i
Sweepings, shop, 215, 238, 281, 311
  washing, 64
Swift, John (silversmith), 7, 216, *34*
Sword hilts, 67, 141–42, 210, 287, 289, 298, 300
Swords, 142, 298
Sympson, *A New Book of Cyphers*, 280, 284, *35*
Syng, Mary, 291
Syng, Philip (1676–1739; silversmith), 8–9, 272; *1–2*
Syng, Philip, Jr. (1703–89; silversmith), 9, 30, 66–67, 72, 132, 155, 202–03, 206, 278, 284, 289, 291, 298, 308

Table crosses, 184
Tablespoons, 53, 129, 186–87, 195, 204, 206, 226, 228, 230, 232, 255, 258, 261, 289, 296, 302, 305; made by Francis Richardson, *10*; made by Joseph Richardson, *113–15*; made by Joseph and Nathaniel Richardson, *162*
Tambour shuttles, 184
Tankards, 7–9, 13, 24, 28, 33, 54–55, 57, 61, 63, 65, 68, 75–76, 111, 114, 117–18, 179, 184, 196, 261, 271, 278, 283–84, 287–88, 295–96, 300, 308; made by Francis Richardson, 8–9, 13, *7*; made by Frank Richardson, 24; made by Joseph Richardson, 33, 114–18, *87–91*; made by Joseph and Nathaniel Richardson, 179, *158–60*; made by Joseph Richardson, Jr., 196–97
  mustard, 197, 263
Tantum, Joseph (looking-glass maker), 17, 275
Taylor, Abraham, 295, 300
Taylor, Capt., 222
Taylor, Mary, 159
Taylor, Mrs. R. Stewardson, *53, 61*
Taylor, Samuel, 46
Tea and coffee sets, 76–106, 159, 189, 213, 305–06, *66*; made by Joseph and Nathaniel Richardson, *136*; made by Joseph Richardson, Jr., 159, 187, 189, 305–06, 309, *166, 169*
Tea boards, 17
Tea caddies, 98, 172, 175, 186, 261, 294, *66*; made by Joseph Richardson, 98–99, *64*; made by Joseph and Nathaniel Richardson, 172, 175, *148–49*
Teakettle-on-stand, *frontispiece*, 76, 87–89, 293; made by Joseph Richardson, 87–89, *44*
Teapots, 16, 18, 24, 53, 63, 65, 77–78, 83–84, 86–87, 89, 91–92, 105, 145, 166, 168, 186–88, 210, 221, 225, 230, 233, 235, 237, 241, 253, 255, 261, 276, 286–87, 292–93, 301–02, 304–05, 307, *66*; made by Frank Richardson, 24; made by Joseph Richardson, 77–78, 83–84, 86–87, 93, *38–43*; made by Joseph and Nathaniel Richardson, 168, *136, 142–44*; made by Joseph Richardson, Jr., 187–88, 305–07, *166–67, 169*
Teapot, Sign of the, 290
Teaspoons, 16, 53, 63, 99–100, 103, 129, 186–87, 195, 199–200, 203–04, 214, 219–21, 223–26, 230–31, 234–35, 244, 253, 255, 260–61, 270–71, 276, 281, 285, 291, 294, 301–02, 305–06, 308, *66*; made by Joseph Richardson, 65
Teasts, 282
Tea tables, 17
Tea urns, 165, 184, 186
Terdiman, Mrs. Susan, ii
Textiles, 6, 17–18, 22, 34, 43, 53, 63, 270–71, 273–75, 277, 285, 288, 310
  sold by Francis Richardson, 266
Thimbles, 9, 16, 54, 62, 139, 165, 196, 200, 203–04, 206, 213, 219–20, 222, 224, 230–31, 245, 247, 253, 255, 258, 262, 270–71, 288, 291, 297, 309; made by Francis Richardson, 9; made by Joseph Richardson, 139; made by Joseph Richardson, Jr., 196
Thomas, Gabriel, on Shippen house and garden, 5
  on silversmith's fees, 7, 60–61
Thompson, James (silversmith), 273
Thompson, Jonah, 82
Thompson, Lydia, 82, *93*
Thompson, Rebecca, 82
Thomson, Charles, 306, 308
Thomson, Rachel, 295
Tiers, Mr. and Mrs. Paul, *74*
Tiffany and Company, *158*
Tilghman, Joseph, 188
Tillit, Capt., 233, 251–52
Tillona, Francesca, ii
Toast racks, 156, 263
Tolles, Frederick B., 35, 214
Tongs, 100, 103, 186, 195, 223, 230, 253, 255, 291, 294, 300, 306, 308–09, *66*; made by Francis Richardson, 8,

Index

Tongs (*cont.*)
    16; made by Frank Richardson, 24; made by Joseph Richardson, 77, 100, 103, *67–68*; made by Joseph Richardson, Jr., 187, 195, 306, 309, *178*
    annealing, 57
    sliding, 204
    sugar, 187, 261
    tea, 8, 16, 24, 53–54, 63, 65, 77, 99, 103, 165–66, 195, 199–200, 204, 206, 214, 219–21, 227, 231, 234–35, 239, 244, 253, 255, 260, 276, 287, 292, 301
Tongues, 253, 255, 258, 300. *See also* Chapes and tongues
Tools and equipment, 6, 8, 17, 20, 30, 33, 54–55, 57–58, 72, 162, 186, 203–04, 210–11, 214, 269–70, 272–73, 280–83, 288, 299, *13–14, 25–26*. *See also* specific tools
Tortoise shell, 204
Touchet, Samuel, Esq., & Company, 233
Touchstone, 55, 204, *26*
Townshend Acts (1767), 43
Toys, made by Joseph Richardson, Jr., 195
Trade cards, 68, 281, 290. *See also* Shop bills
Trays. *See* Salvers
Trenchard, James, 155, 304
Tresse, Margaret, 268
Trimble, Joseph and Jane, *168*
Trotter, Daniel (cabinetmaker), 293, 309
Trotter, Joseph, 299
Trotter, William, 195
Tubes, drinking, 196
Tumblers, 53, 63, 118–19, 197, 263, 286, 302, 306; made by Joseph Richardson, 118–19; made by Joseph Richardson, Jr., 197, 306
Turner, James (silversmith), 284
Tweezers and cases, 203, 291, 297

Ullman, Mrs. Harry M., *48, 103, 107*
Umbrella, 136
United States Government, 306
    Mint, Joseph Richardson, Jr., assayer of, 162
Urns, 165, 184, 186, 306, 308
    cream, 91, 165–66, 258
    sugar, *146, 166, 169, 170–71*
    tea, 165, 184, 186
Useful Miscellanies, owned by Joseph Richardson, 54

Vanderspiegle, Mrs. Elizabeth (Robinson), 117, 295
Vanderspiegle, William, 295
Vanlear, Ann, 286
Vessels
    Dragon, 243
    Indian Trader, 236
    Julian(na), 217–18, 231, 242, 311
    Neptune, 240–41
    Phoenix, iii
    Supply, 3
Vilant, William, 9, *1*
Vinaigrettes, 132
Virginia Museum of Fine Arts, 289
Vises, 57, 272, 282
Voltaire, on Penn's treaty with the Indians, 37

Wagoner, Vincent, 272
Wagstaffe, Thomas (clockmaker), 76, 128, 137, 139, 207–08, 211, 214, 220, 233, 249, 283, 294, 310–11
    letters to, 219, 222, 226, 228, 232, 234, 239, 244, 248, 250–51, 256–59
Waid, Capt., 258
Waide, Bartholomew, 296, *32, 113*
Wainwright, Nicholas B., ii, 279
Wainwright, Samuel, 271
Waite, Joseph, 18
Waiters (weighters), 77, 105, 162, 186, 210, 225–26, 231, 241, 287, 292, 294, 306; made by Joseph Richardson, 77; made by Joseph Richardson, Jr., 306. *See also* Salvers
Ward, James (clock and watchmaker), 272–73
Warder, John, 191
Warner, Edward, 274
Warner, James, 39
Warnts, Leonard, 251
Washington, George, patron of Joseph Richardson, Jr., 161–62, 307
    appoints Joseph Richardson, Jr., assayer of U.S. Mint, 162
Waste bowls. *See* Bowls, slop
Watches, 28, 53, 63, 145, 204–05, 210–11, 213, 219, 223, 226, 228, 232, 234, 236, 238, 240–41, 244, 249–52, 257, 270, 272–73, 276, 290, 297
    cases for, 16, 137, 273, 287, 297, 300
    chains for, 53, 64, 67, 140, 146, 200, 204, 221–22, 227, 230, 236, 240–41, 261, 270, 273, 289
    glasses for, 204
    keys for, 136–37
    pendants for, 213, 223
    straps for, 137. *See also* Clock and watch business
Water St. (Phila., Pa.), lot owned by Joseph Richardson on, 38
Watson, Mrs. Charles G., ii
Watson, John, on Washington silver, 162
    on John S. Hutton, 286
Wayne, John, 304
Weights and scales. *See* Scales and weights
Wesfeld, Will (camblet seller), 274
West, Elizabeth, 197
West Indies, 7, 40, 65, 72, 155, 157, 202, 217, 232, 291, 302, *82*
Wetherill, Samuel, 106, *74*
Wharton, Isaac, *141*
Wharton, Joseph, 303
Wheeler, Israel, 306
Wheeler, Samuel, 309
Whip, 16, 274, 300
    ferrules, 139, 276
    heads, 139

Whistle, 18, 135, 203; made by Francis Richardson, 18; made by Joseph Richardson, 135. See also Coral, and bells
Wickes, George (silversmith), 293
Widet, Capt., 239
Wilcocks, Richard H., 189, 305
Wilcox, Barnabus, 7
Wilcox, John, 300
Wilcox, Sarah, 7
Wilkbank, Abram, 299
Willard, Thomas, 60
Williams, Hezekiah, 302
Williams, Richard N., II, i
Willin, Charles, 299
Willis, Jonathan, 157
Wiltberger, Christian (silversmith), 155, 303
Wincoop, Abraham, 101
Wine, canary, 6
Wine cocks. See Cocks, silver wine
Winne, William (silversmith), 211, 310
Winterthur Museum, i, 13, 54, 63, 147, 199, 202, 209, 211, 218, 279, 289, 296, 308, 6, 11–12, 20–25, 29–30, 35, 60, 119–20, 127, 132–34, 162–63, 166, 178–82
Wireman, Mrs. Henry B., ii
Wistar family, 60
Wistar, Caspar (brassfounder), 119, 272, 294, 305
Wistar, Caspar and Catherine (Jansen), 94
Wistar, Elizabeth M., 310, 32, 113
Wistar, Margaret, 53, 61
Wistar, Richard, 46, 310
Wistar, Sarah, 77
Wistar, Thomas, 298
Witchell, Nicholas (glover), 17
Wolfe, Beatrice B., i
Woliston, Thomas, 285
Wood, Elizabeth Ingerman, i
Wood, John (clockmaker), 59, 137, 205, 272, 297, 27
Wood, John, Jr., 304
Wood, Juliana R., 46, 217, 34
Woodhouse, Dr. Samuel W., 294
Woolman, Caroline Elizabeth, 16
Woolman, John, 39, 67, 214, 247
Woolman, Uriah, 247
Workbench, 57, 282
Working block, 55
Workshop. See Silversmiths, shops of
Worner, Iwon, (Ivan Warner?), 18
Worril(l), Hannah, 34. See also Richardson, Hannah (Worrill)
Worril(l), Richard, 34
Wright (silversmith), 289
Wright, Benjamin, 6
Wright, Capt., 275
Wright, James, 293

Wrist bands, 38, 140, 159, 298, 307; made by Joseph Richardson, Jr., 159, 132, 163. See also Indian silver, jewelry
Wyatt, A. J., 31, 71, 86, 153, 156–157, 169, 171, 176

Yale University Art Gallery, frontispiece, ii, 297, 37, 44, 46–47, 58, 73, 78, 87, 98, 104, 111, 117, 128–30, 139, 143
Yarnal(l), Mordecai, 35
Yarnall, Sarah, 106, 74
Yellow fever, 156, 304
Yetton, James, 288
Yetton, Jane, 288
Yetton, Randall (silversmith), 66, 288
York County Court House, bell ordered for, by Joseph Richardson, 68, 290
You, Daniel (silversmith), 282
Young, John, 297
Young, Rebecca, 268, 287
Young, Rebecca (Flower), 287
Young, William (silversmith), 65, 204, 226, 287–88
Young, William and Rebecca, 287

Zachary, Lloyd, 296
Zane, Isaac, 63

26   Bro: Francis is Dr

1735
     To Silver for Sundry things 274:9:6
     to Cash Due to me for pd &c — £18:1:
August 25   to Silver for a Quart Tankard. 28: 0 —
    28   to Do by James — — — — — — 4: 0
     to Do pr button — — — — — 0:8:18
     to Silver for Quart Tankard — 26:19 —
     to Silver by James — — — — — 4: 0
     to Repairing a pr Large wrought Buckels — 0: 2:
     to a Gold Ring mending & a pr Chape tongs 0: 5:
     to Silver — — — — — — — 6: 0 —
     to Cash — to pay to Traselt — — 1:15
     to Silver for a Tankard — — 17: 6
     to Silver for Do — — — — 6: 0 —
     to 6 tea Spoons wt a dwt 2:3 — — 1: 6:
     to Silver towards ye tankard above 6:14 6
     to Silver for a Quart Tankard — 81:11:6
     to Graving a pr Gold Buttons & Studs — 0: 2:
     to Perceing 2 Straners & Graving Locket 0: 3
October 24   to Cash — — — — — — 5: 0 —
     to Silver — — — for Cans 16: 0
     to Do — — — — — 3-17
Novemr 26   to Cash — — — — — — 3: 5:
     ~~to Silver for a half pint &c~~
     to Silver for a half pint Cans 12 oz
     to Do for Milk pott — — — 2-8-12
     to a pr of Buckels wt — — — 1: 7 —
     to fashin — — — — — — 0: 9: